Safeguarding Adults and the Law

by the same author

Care Act 2014
An A–Z of Law and Practice
ISBN 978 1 84905 559 8
eISBN 978 0 85700 991 3

How We Treat the Sick
Neglect and Abuse in Our Health Services
ISBN 978 1 84905 160 6
eISBN 978 0 85700 355 3

Quick Guide to Community Care Practice and the Law
ISBN 978 1 84905 083 8
eISBN 978 0 85700 373 7

Community Care Practice and the Law
Fourth Edition
ISBN 978 1 84310 691 3
eISBN 978 1 84642 859 3

Betraying the NHS
Health Abandoned
ISBN 978 1 84310 482 7
eISBN 978 1 84642 569 1

Safeguarding Adults and the Law
Third Edition

An A–Z of Law and Practice

Michael Mandelstam

Jessica Kingsley *Publishers*
London and Philadelphia

First published in 2008
This edition published in 2019
by Jessica Kingsley Publishers
73 Collier Street
London N1 9BE, UK
and
400 Market Street, Suite 400
Philadelphia, PA 19106, USA

www.jkp.com

Library of Congress Cataloging in Publication Data
Names: Mandelstam, Michael, 1956- author.
Title: Safeguarding adults : an A-Z of law and practice / Michael Mandelstam.
Other titles: Safeguarding adults and the law
Description: Third edition. | London ; Philadelphia : Jessica Kingsley   Publishers, 2019. | Includes bibliographical references and index.
Identifiers: LCCN 2018045014 | ISBN 9781785922251
Subjects: LCSH: People with disabilities--Legal status, laws, etc.--Great
   Britain. | People with disabilities--Abuse of--Great Britain--Prevention..
   | Community health services--Law and legislation--Great Britain. |
   National health services--Great Britain. | Social service--Great Britain.
Classification: LCC KD737 .M35 2019 | DDC 362.941--dc23 LC
record available at https://lccn.loc.gov/2018045014

British Library Cataloguing in Publication Data
A CIP catalogue record for this book is available from the British Library

ISBN 978 1 78592 225 1
eISBN 978 1 78450 499 1

Printed and bound in Great Britain

Author's note

Jessica Kingsley has supported me to write books for 30 years. This book is the last one of that era, due to her recent retirement. I don't have the words to express what that support has meant, in enabling me to articulate and write about things that both she and I have considered important. Also many thanks to Victoria Peters, at Jessica Kingsley Publishers, for all her help in getting this book into shape – and to her colleagues behind the scenes. And thanks to the staff at the public library in Sudbury, Suffolk, who continue to help me so much.

Disclaimer

In a book of this nature and complexity, there will almost inevitably be mistakes. These are down to the author. In addition, the law (both legislation and legal case law) is constantly evolving. The book is up to date to the beginning of December 2018.

Contents

Introduction

Issues and challenges for safeguarding in the social and health care context

This book is about adult safeguarding, a term used to refer to the protection from abuse or neglect of vulnerable adults. At one extreme, abuse and neglect may be associated with reckless, sadistic, bullying, dishonest and opportunistic individuals, who may be known to the victim or sometimes strangers who deliberately pick on vulnerable adults. There is also more systemic neglect perpetrated or tolerated by institutions and organisations, including NHS hospitals and independent care providers. Equally, neglect might result when a family member, faced with the difficult task of caring, might become so worn down and overwhelmed that the informal care being provided becomes neglectful, albeit unintentionally.

The book limits itself to abuse and neglect suffered by adults who in a sense are 'vulnerable'. This is a term eschewed by the Department of Health and is consequently absent from the Care Act 2014, the central legal pillar of adult safeguarding. Yet, paradoxically, the word 'vulnerable' remains important in adult safeguarding because it occurs in other relevant legislation and is used frequently by the courts in various, and important, legal judgments. The Care Act refers instead to adults with care and support needs who experience, or are at risk of, abuse or neglect. Which category of person, in all but name, covers those people who are vulnerable.

Aim of the book

The book aims to assist not just professionals and practitioners in statutory services, including local authorities, the National Health Service, police, voluntary bodies, professional bodies and independent providers, but also others, such as family members, who sometimes feel compelled to undertake their own safeguarding activities in order to try to prevent abuse or neglect, put a stop to it if it is already occurring, or try to hold somebody accountable after the event. And who unexpectedly find themselves dealing with legislation they had not known existed, and sometimes grappling with both complex legal rules and evasive organisations seeking to avoid that accountability.

Scope of the book

The focus is on England. It would be impractical, in a book of this nature and detail, to cover all four countries within the United Kingdom. Even within England, the amount of law is significant and inevitably the book is selective to a degree. Nonetheless, there is some legislation that is common across the United Kingdom, such as the Human Rights Act 1998; other legislation has differences but also many similarities – for example, the Care Act 2014 applying to England and the Social Services and Well-being (Wales) Act 2014.

Content of the book

The book covers an extensive amount of legislation and other law relevant to adult safeguarding. However, such law comes to life only when seen in action. Therefore, the book makes reference to, and provides summaries of, many legal cases to give substance to legal rules and their application to everyday practice.

The cases could be viewed as painting an unremittingly gloomy and depressing picture, but if adult safeguarding is to make headway, it needs to know what it is up against. Furthermore, the awful circumstances of abuse or neglect do need to be spelt out. For example, it was only the graphic descriptions of neglect, set out in the independent inquiry into events at Stafford Hospital, that blew away irrevocably the web of denial, evasion and euphemistic explanation of the hospital's management, the strategic health authority and the Department of Health.[1]

Background to adult safeguarding

In the early 1980s, adult safeguarding – or adult protection as it was and is sometimes still called – was recognised, explicitly in its own right, neither in policy nor in law. By the early 1990s, it had raised its head hesitantly in two publications by the Social Services Inspectorate, then part of the Department of Health in England: *Confronting elder abuse* and *No longer afraid*.[2] During the 1980s and 1990s, child protection would dominate, just as, generally speaking, it continues to do.

The Department of Health had missed the boat in 1990, when it failed to refer to adult safeguarding in the NHS and Community Care Act of that year. By 2000, finally, it felt moved to act but appeared too nervous and uncertain about putting anything in law. Instead, it produced statutory guidance called *No secrets*.[3]

The strength of this guidance lay in its formal recognition of adult protection and the increased focus in practice on safeguarding activity that followed its publication. Its weakness was that it did not constitute law and did little to explain how it related to the community care legislation existing at that time. Consequently, for the following 15 years, the legal foundation of adult safeguarding remained muddy and – despite all the valuable and well-intentioned work of local authorities – subject to uncertainties.

During this time, the Scottish Parliament stole a march and passed the Adult Support and Protection (Scotland) Act 2007, with explicit definitions and legally enforceable powers of entry and intervention. Lagging behind, the Care Act 2014 finally placed adult safeguarding in England on a statutory

---

1   Francis, R. (Chair). *Independent Inquiry into care provided by Mid Staffordshire NHS Foundation Trust January 2005–March 2009*. London: The Stationery Office, 2010.

2   Social Services Inspectorate. *Confronting elder abuse*. London: Department of Health, 1992. Also: Social Services Inspectorate. *No longer afraid: the safeguard of older people in domestic settings*. London: Department of Health, 1993.

3   Department of Health. *No secrets: guidance on developing and implementing multi-agency policies and procedures to protect vulnerable adults from abuse*. London: DH, 2000.

footing, although with less clarity and conviction and with fewer legal powers than in Scotland. The Social Services and Well-being (Wales) Act 2014 also contains adult safeguarding provisions, with Welsh local authorities being given more legal power (in particular, a power of entry to a dwelling) than their English, but less than their Scottish, counterparts.

Therefore, a remaining question about adult safeguarding in England is whether further legislation is needed, giving local authorities some sort of last-resort coercive power of entry and intervention, in relation to vulnerable adults generally, with or without mental capacity.

Salient and troubling aspects of adult safeguarding

The book depicts generally an unflattering side of human behaviour underlying both the perpetration of and sometimes – more concerningly – the response to the abuse and neglect of vulnerable adults, whether that perpetration and response are individual or organisational in character. Over and above this, and during the researching and writing of the book, a number of issues have stood out which are distinctly troubling. They pertain not just to adult safeguarding narrowly viewed but more widely to the system of social and health care. The paragraphs below seek to encapsulate these issues.

SOCIAL SERVICES: ITS UNCERTAIN AND DIVERGENT ROLE. Local authority social services sit at the centre of adult safeguarding, with the Care Act 2014 the legal foundation stone. However, the role of social services is by no means straightforward and is characterised by legal complexity, uncertainty and sometimes misunderstanding.

First, protecting people from abuse or neglect applies under the Care Act 2014 to adults with care and support needs, and their informal carers, only. And since the meaning of 'care and support' has been held legally to be of broad application, there is some uncertainty as to how to define the categories of adult covered by the Act.

Furthermore, the Care Act 2014 is not a coercive piece of legislation, meaning that social services cannot force anybody – victim, perpetrator or another organisation – to do anything. Under the Act, social services makes enquiries into abuse or neglect, can request cooperation from other bodies and – more generally – can offer information, advice, care and support services, but cannot directly do much else in a wider sense.

This means, therefore, that other organisations acting under other legislation are crucial to adult safeguarding – for example, the police under criminal law, the NHS under the NHS Act 2006, the Care Quality Commission or Disclosure and Barring Service under regulatory legislation, the Court of Protection under the Mental Capacity Act 2005 and so on. In other words, there is sometimes a misunderstanding, both within and outside of social services, as to its remit and the extent of its legal powers. There is a sense in which social services is the well-meaning emperor lacking the meaningful clothes which they are presumed, wrongly, by many to have.

Yet those other organisations follow their own legislation, rules, policies and priorities, which do not mirror those of social services, and around which they sit therefore in a rather loose and erratic orbit.

Second, and following on from the first point, social services plays divergent roles. On the one hand, it is provider of social care in the form of care and support. On the other, its safeguarding role means that it acts almost as an unofficial 'police' force in terms of enquiring into, and making judgements about, neglect or abuse.

This divergence can create genuine difficulty about what to do – a simple example being a woman in a care home who asked for practical help to manage her finances separately from her long-standing partner and to deal with his aggression during the night. Social services failed to provide the practical help (the care and support role) but, against the woman's wishes, instead informed the police (the formal safeguarding role) who visited the home to talk to her and her partner. She consequently became distressed and wouldn't talk to the police, and her partner committed suicide. The ombudsman criticised the local authority for failing to evidence a reasoning process, weighing up the different options (flowing from its care and support and its safeguarding roles), before it informed the police.[1]

---

1   LGO, *London Borough of Hounslow*, 2017 (16 010 076).

Third, a misunderstanding of the legal limits to its safeguarding role can lead to social services acting in coercive, threatening and restrictive ways, which are unlawful and, far from preventing harm, can amount to abuse.[1] For example, intervening disproportionately, breaking up family relationships unnecessarily, depriving people of their liberty unlawfully and breaching their human rights.[2]

Fourth, as the lead agency in safeguarding, social services has a duty under the Care Act 2014 to cooperate with other key organisations, such as the NHS, in the delivery of social care, and with other organisations such as the police in safeguarding. There is a risk of it sometimes being hamstrung, hesitating to call the NHS to account for what are obviously safeguarding matters, in the cause of good relations between the local authority and NHS body at both practitioner and management level.

Fifth, social services is the commissioner on a large scale of social care services – for example, care agencies and care homes – which are not necessarily of good quality and may sometimes result in the neglect or abuse of service users. This can place social services in the peculiar position of making many safeguarding enquiries into care, which it has itself commissioned, and give rise to conflicts of interest.

Sixth, in similar vein, social services is effectively the lead member of local safeguarding adults boards, along with the NHS and police. A question arises as to how far social services will be motivated to drive a board's activity in the direction of exposing and publishing failings (sometimes large-scale) in the commissioning and provision of social care and health care by itself and its key partner, the NHS.

NHS NEGLECT: ELEPHANT IN THE ADULT SAFEGUARDING ROOM. The – or at least the largest – elephant in the adult safeguarding room is arguably neglect (wilful or otherwise) in the National Health Service, particularly when it comes to older hospital patients with complex and multiple needs. Both its existence and its persistence remain something of an enigma. Yet

---

1   *A Local Authority v A and B* [2010] EWHC 978 (Fam).

2   Department of Health. *Care and support statutory guidance.* London: DH, 2016, para 14.98.

one is driven against one's instinct to conclude that exist it does, and that adult safeguarding remains somewhat peripheral to it. The argument that the NHS provides a lot of excellent care, and therefore that reports of poor care and neglect must be exaggerated, suffers from an intense lack of logic. In hospitals, as in the world at large, the good can cohabit all too easily with the bad.[1]

Like true elephants in the room, neglect is sometimes not seen even though in plain sight, if seen, not acknowledged, or, if acknowledged, little or nothing is done about it either at all or timeously and effectively. Particularly striking are the scale of neglect that can occur, tolerance of it, the fact that the greater the scale of neglect so the less the response may be, deep-seated conflicts of interest, concealment and the logical link between some health policies and poor care and neglect.

No aspect is more disturbing than the treatment of those staff who raise concerns – whistleblowers – within the NHS, no matter how well founded and justified those concerns. They are sometimes suppressed by NHS management with a degree of ruthlessness that – one supposes – could only be fuelled by a cocktail, shaken in different combinations depending on the circumstances, of fear, insecurity, weakness and ambition on the part of those who do the suppressing. The phenomenon of 'retaliatory referrals' is one reaction by NHS employers. These involve an NHS employer going to huge and persistent lengths (and sometimes great expense) to try to destroy the career of a practitioner, by referring them to a professional regulatory body, such as the General Medical Council, and accusing them, typically, of incompetence or mental illness – with no foundation for such accusations. See *Whistleblowing*.

Closely linked, a partner in arms with whistleblowing is the extent to which problems of poor care and neglect are sometimes concealed, systemically and variously, by NHS bodies, NHS England and the Department of Health: see *Concealment*. Indicators of the extent of poor care and neglect within the NHS, and therefore of the challenge posed to adult safeguarding as an activity, include the following.

---

1 Francis, R. (Chair). *Independent Inquiry into care provided by Mid Staffordshire NHS Foundation Trust January 2005–March 2009.* London: The Stationery Office, 2010, p.180.

- **Evidence.** First, the evidence of a significant and consistent vein of poor care and neglect within the NHS is overwhelming: see *National Health Service*.

- **Inverse and perverse law of inaction.** Second, an inverse and perverse law sometimes operates: the larger the scale of neglect within the NHS, the less likely it is that anything will be done, either at all or without determined effort by either family members or committed and courageous whistleblowers.

- **Older people with complex needs at risk of neglect.** Third, a class of hospital patients – elderly with multiple needs and often admitted unplanned and as an emergency – appears to be at particular risk of poor care and neglect owing to their numbers, the complexity and nature of their needs, and hospitals being unable or unwilling to provide appropriate treatment and care. Not least because the model of health care offered in hospitals is to a significant degree inimical to the needs of such patients.[1] See *Older people in hospital*.

- **Corrosion of culture of good practice.** Fourth, the consequence is that poor care can all too easily flourish and act as the seedbed of neglect, sometimes on a large scale. The corrosion of a culture of good-quality care on a ward or in a unit can lead to staff genuinely not recognising neglect even though it is before their eyes. In which case, the possibility of raising a concern or safeguarding alert would be stillborn. This can lead ultimately to dehumanisation of patients, inhumane care and even a disregard for human life. See *Culture of care*.

- **Suppression of those who raise concerns.** Fifth, once poor care and neglect are well rooted, formidable obstacles can prevent remedial action. For example, health and care workers may fear, or be indifferent to, raising concerns – or simply believe that it would be pointless to do so. Their ruthless treatment by the NHS suggests that such fear can be well founded. See *Whistleblowing*.

- **Conflicts of interest impeding adult safeguarding.** Sixth, significant conflicts of interest may come into play, since the NHS is a key safeguarding agency under the Care Act and member of local safeguarding adults boards, but at the same time might be the provider or commissioner of the poor or neglectful care. Constructive cooperation can in some circumstances lapse into cosiness, with local statutory services – for example, the police – excessively trusting another and accepting their reassurance and guidance.

---

1   Francis, R. (Chair). *Independent Inquiry into care provided by Mid Staffordshire NHS Foundation Trust January 2005–March 2009.* London: The Stationery Office, 2010, p.400.

At a higher level, the Department of Health and government ministers are themselves subject to political sensitivities, which can sometimes cause or perpetuate (or even do both) the neglect of patients. See **Conflicts of interest within adult safeguarding**.

- **Concealment of poor care and neglect.** Seventh, concealment by NHS organisations of sometimes very serious neglect can come in the form of, for instance, flat denial, oleaginous euphemism, suppression or manipulation of information, doublespeak and straightforward irrationality. See **Concealment**. Thus, major neglect or abuse – involving hundreds of deaths – may become known only fortuitously and haphazardly; for example, events at Stafford Hospital and Gosport War Memorial Hospital came to light only because of determined relatives. Which means that such poor care and neglect may well be ongoing today – but we would not necessarily know about them.

- **What to do with the elderly.** Eighth, and last, there is a risk, not new, that the old, with their complex and multiple needs, somehow don't count and are not meaningful[1] within both health care, especially hospital care, but also care more generally. Which, in turn, could undermine the effectiveness of adult safeguarding. See **Older people, care and safeguarding**.

In summary, there would appear to be a fundamental problem concerning elderly patients with complex needs, how they are perceived, treated and cared for – in (or indeed out of) hospital. Basically, what is to be done with them? Fortunately, however, adult safeguarding, practically and legally, does not have to answer that overarching, social conundrum. Its role is simply to protect people from and respond to abuse or neglect. It is no accident that, when outlining the role of local safeguarding adults boards, Department of Health guidance states that, in their strategic role, boards should be focusing on the 'safety of patients in its local health services'.[2]

A consequence of a blind eye and inaction, in relation to poor care and neglect in the NHS, risks a particular irony. Namely, that adult safeguarding, collectively speaking, might, for instance, go to some lengths to protect an elderly woman from a degree of financial exploitation by a neighbour or relative, for example, but then effectively stand by whilst the same woman is

---

1   Stewart, Dr M. *My brother's keeper?* London: Health Horizon, 1968.

2   Department of Health. *Care and support statutory guidance*. London: DH, 2016, para 14.134.

admitted to hospital, is not cared for properly, is neglected and suffers. See *Scale of neglect or abuse*.

INFORMAL CARERS: SAINTS OR SINNERS? Local authorities and the NHS are increasingly, and sometimes desperately, looking to family carers to relieve them of the burden of meeting people's longer-term health and care needs. A Secretary of State for Health, in 2015, stated no less, lamenting the fact that we live in England with merely 16 per cent of inter-generational households, compared with Italy which has 39 per cent.[1] The implication is that informal care of relatives is less easy in England.

There is no legal obligation on informal carers to care for an adult; for that one must hark back to now obsolete legislation containing the so-called liable relatives rule, found in section 42 of the National Assistance Act 1948 and, immediately before that, the Poor Law Act 1930. Nevertheless, many relatives wish to do the caring, or sometimes feel forced to do so because of the lack of or limited help from statutory services. Yet the pressure of intensive, unremitting informal care of a person with complex needs should not be underestimated[2] and can sometimes lead to neglect on the part of a carer, albeit unintentional and borne of exhaustion, sleep deprivation, depression, etc.

For whatever reason (good or bad), it occurs, neglect by informal carers, typically family members, may be just as much a reality as neglect by anybody else. Inter-generational households, hankered after by Secretaries of State for Health, do not necessarily mean good care of the elderly and the return to a golden age. For example, a district nurse in rural Suffolk, talking of the 1920s (with the liable relative rule in force), noted that 'the old people were not taken care of'.

This is another thing which people like to think now, that grandfathers and grandmothers had an honoured place in the cottage. In fact, when they got old they were just neglected, pushed away into corners. I even found them

---

1   Wright, O. 'Jeremy Hunt calls for national debate about caring for the elderly.' *The Independent*, 1 July 2015.

2   Marriott, H. *The selfish pig's guide to caring*. Clifton-upon-Teme: Polperro Heritage Press, 2003.

in cupboards. Even in fairly clean respectable houses you often found an old man or woman shoved out of sight in a dark niche.[1]

In any event, in the eyes of statutory services informal carers sometimes come to occupy, closely in time, the role of both saint and sinner. Social services, in its care and support role (see above), may be only too pleased that a family member is doing all the caring. Yet the same social services, in its adult safeguarding role, might then too readily treat the same carer in relation to lapses in the standard of care as abusive or neglectful and trigger punitive legal action. This might include the criminal – for example, conviction for manslaughter – or separation under the Mental Capacity Act of long-standing partners or spouses, even though Department of Health guidance warns against premature action taken against carers and reminds social services that they have duties to support carers in their caring role.[2] Despite this, some evidence suggests that carers are not being supported as both the legislation and guidance states they should be.[3]

It is something of an irony that hundreds of people may be neglected and die at the hands of the State in NHS hospitals – for example, Stafford Hospital or Gosport War Memorial Hospital – with little action taken against anybody, whereas an elderly man is convicted of the manslaughter of his wife with multiple needs including dementia, challenging behaviour and diabetes, having undertaken a daunting caring task and finally snapping – even though he himself was exhausted, sleep-deprived, depressed and developing dementia.[4]

FINANCIAL ABUSE: SHEER OPPORTUNISM. The sheer opportunism and diversity, in terms of financial abuse of vulnerable adults (typically theft or fraud), is breathtaking. It can involve an assortment of people in a position of responsibility, more or less formal, including paid carers, care managers,

---

1   Blythe, R. *Akenfield, portrait of an English village*. London: Allen Lane, 1969, p.199.

2   Department of Health. *Care and support statutory guidance*. London: DH, 2016, paras 14.40–14.46.

3   Bennett, B. *Care Act for carers one year on: lessons learned, next steps*. London: Carers Trust, 2016.

4   *R v Beaver* (2015) unreported, Court of Appeal.

professionals (health, social care, legal, financial), legally appointed financial attorneys or deputies, neighbours, acquaintances, relatives, church ministers. It is opportunism associated generally with desperation or greed but above all fuelled by the promise that money brings.

The financial abuse, sometimes amounting to a criminal offence, seems often to be committed by a person with no history of dishonesty, including close family members (e.g. with a power of attorney), at best totally misunderstanding their legal duty, at worst lured on by temptation. In contrast, there are (sometimes relatively sophisticated) rogue traders targeting vulnerable people systematically, or, for example, individuals with drug problems, cannily befriending and then stealing, also systematically, from strangers in the form of vulnerable individuals. See *Fraud*; *Theft*; *Lasting power of attorney*.

RELATIVES IN ADULT SAFEGUARDING. The failure sometimes of key statutory services to prevent, investigate and act in relation to neglect or abuse – and instead actively, or by omission, conceal what is occurring or did occur – means that relatives themselves may have a key role, albeit unofficial, to play in adult safeguarding. In other words, they cannot necessarily rely on statutory services to act and to ride to the rescue, so to speak, as might be expected. Yet it can be difficult, emotionally and practically, for many people to challenge those in authority. It is worth quoting at length the Gosport War Memorial Hospital Inquiry's perceptive encapsulation of this:

> **Loneliness, upset, anger, reluctance and difficulty in challenging those in authority.**
>
> It is a lonely place, seeking answers to questions that others wish you were not asking. That loneliness is heightened when you're made to feel even by those close to you that it's time to get over it and to move on. But it is impossible to move on if you feel that you have let down someone you love, and that you might have done more to protect them from the way they died.
>
> Many of the families to whom the Panel has listened feel a measure of guilt, albeit misplaced. The anger is also fuelled by a sense of betrayal. Handing over a loved one to a hospital, to doctors

and nurses, is an act of trust and you take for granted that they will always do that which is best for the one you love. It represents a major crisis when you begin to doubt that the treatment they are being given is in their best interests. It further shatters your confidence when you summon up the courage to complain and then sense that you are being treated as some sort of 'troublemaker'.

Many of the family members from Gosport have a background in the services. They were brought up to believe that those in authority are there to serve and to protect the community. The relatives did not find it easy to question those in senior positions. It says something about the scale of the problem that, in the end, in spite of the culture of respecting authority, the families, as it were, broke ranks and challenged what they were being told about how their loved ones were treated and how they died.[1]

It is notable that without persistent relatives, we would simply not know, for instance, about the standards of care and many avoidable deaths at Stafford Hospital,[2] nor about the hundreds of deaths at Gosport War Memorial Hospital. This, despite being dismissed as irrelevant lobbyists by senior NHS management, as in the case of Stafford Hospital,[3] and as deluded troublemakers by the police in relation to Gosport War Memorial Hospital.[4]

Relatives might also sometimes seek to use the Freedom of Information Act, whether in a specific instance, or relating to systemic neglect or abuse. The Act, however, is not always so easy to use. It applies to public bodies only and, with more health and social care now provided by the independent sector, information may be more difficult to come by. In addition, the Act contains a number of exemptions to the duty to provide the information

---

1   Jones, Reverend J. (Chairman). *Gosport War Memorial Hospital: the report of the Gosport Independent Panel*. London: The Stationery Office, 2018, p.vii.

2   Leigh Day & Co. 'Judicial reviews and the Mid Staffordshire inquiries.' *News*, 12 May 2010. Accessed on 14 July 2017 at: www.leighday.co.uk/Human-rights-and-public-law/Health-social-care/Human-rights-in-healthcare/Mid-Staffordshire-Inquiry/Judicial-reviews-and-the-Mid-Staffordshire-inquiri.

3   Smith, R. 'Mid Staffs: David Nicholson apologises for scandal as "a human being and as CEO".' *Daily Telegraph*, 31 January 2013.

4   Jones, Reverend J. (Chairman). *Gosport War Memorial Hospital: the report of the Gosport Independent Panel*. London: The Stationery Office, 2018, para 12.58.

sought. These exemptions are perfectly understandable and, on their face, reasonable, but would seem to be premised on the notion of public bodies acting in good faith which, in adult safeguarding, cannot always be relied on. See *Freedom of Information Act 2000*. For instance, the Department of Health used the Act to deny, for ten years, the publication of a 2003 report into events at Gosport War Memorial Hospital.[1]

CRIMINAL RECORD CERTIFICATES AND BARRED LIST. A notable legal battleground has, over many years, developed around the regulation of individuals working with vulnerable adults, namely the system of criminal record certificates and, separately, the system of barring people from working with vulnerable adults.

Both systems have been designed, clearly, to protect vulnerable adults, but both have been exposed, at times, as potentially too blunt and drastic in their application. Through a series of legal cases focusing on article 8 of the European Convention on Human Rights, the courts have forced on central government changes to what information is included in criminal record certificates. This is so that a better and more proportionate balance is struck, and workers are not semi-criminalised disproportionately for the rest of their life (e.g. for stealing two bicycles when they were 11 years old).[2] At the time of writing, tensions remain, and the courts continue to expose some of the injustices to which central government appears to remain, even now, so doggedly attached. See *Criminal record certificates; Barred list*.

WILFUL NEGLECT AND ILL-TREATMENT: CRIMINAL OFFENCES. The criminal offences of wilful neglect and ill-treatment in health and social care are of central importance to adult safeguarding. They have potential application to a wide range of omissions or commissions by care staff and managers in hospitals, care homes and care agencies (and sometimes by

---

1   Jones, Reverend J. (Chairman). *Gosport War Memorial Hospital: the report of the Gosport Independent Panel*. London: The Stationery Office, 2018, paras 4.91, 4.93.

2   *R (T) v Secretary of State for the Home Department* [2014] UKSC 35, paras 41, 50, 59.

informal carers). A glance at convictions reveals a grim, dispiriting and diverse catalogue of neglect and abuse.

However, these two criminal offences lie within three different pieces of legislation: Mental Capacity Act 2005, Mental Health Act 1983, and the Criminal Justice and Courts Act 2015. Therefore, there are different circumstances in which the offences can apply, depending on which Act is used. Furthermore, even those elements of the offences which are common across all three Acts are slightly confusing and sometimes subject to misunderstanding.

More generally, the offences would seem to be unevenly prosecuted and, in particular, to have been little used in the NHS context when compared with the context of care homes. This is not for want of serious cases of neglect in hospitals, sometimes on a large scale. See ***Wilful neglect or ill-treatment***.

PROTECTION OF VULNERABLE ADULTS WITH MENTAL CAPACITY TO MAKE UNWISE DECISIONS. A conundrum in adult safeguarding is about how to protect vulnerable adults who nonetheless cannot be shown to lack the mental capacity to take certain decisions for themselves, even if those decisions lead to significant detriment – for instance, through exploitation or self-neglect.

The conundrum comes about, partly, because of the 'watershed' nature of mental capacity assessments. Lacking capacity, a person can be protected in their best interests; with capacity, they cannot unless they are able and willing to consent and to cooperate. For those near the 'border', the line between being deemed capacitous or not may be fine and depend even on who has done the assessment and when. Given that, legally, lack of mental capacity must be established only on the balance of probability, this fine line is nonetheless also a hard line. A person is either on one side of the border or the other; and on the capacitous side of the line, best interests protection is legally not possible and is an irrelevance – but that doesn't mean that some sort of help and protection is not still needed and would not be of significant benefit.

For the capacitous, help can, of course, be offered under the Care Act. But there are other legal channels as well, although these are not always easy to delineate clearly or to use. They include coercive legal power to enter a dwelling (under legislation other than the Care Act) and also application to the High Court for it to exercise its inherent jurisdiction to protect a vulnerable adult from neglect or abuse, usually with a view to some sort of order or injunction being made against the third party responsible for the neglect or abuse. Criminal law may come into play in some circumstances, even when a vulnerable adult has in law consented (that is, with mental capacity) to what has happened – for example, to giving money or property away but only under the undue influence, amounting to dishonesty, of another person (Theft Act 1968); or to sexual activity, involving a mentally disordered person, who has been subject to inducement, threat or deception (Sexual Offences Act 2003). See *Vulnerability*.

Adult safeguarding: the future?

This is not a book that advocates what adult safeguarding policy should look like, nor is it about crystal-ball gazing; it is primarily a law book. However, a few general thoughts on the past and the present and what these might mean for the future are as follows.

REGULATING BEHAVIOUR BETWEEN PRIVATE INDIVIDUALS. There is no magic wand with which to wave away most abuse or neglect of vulnerable adults, especially abuse or neglect perpetrated by private individuals against private individuals. Certainly, the State can pass new legislation, such as the Care Act 2014, but also other statutes containing new criminal offences. Recent examples include the offences of modern slavery, controlling and coercive behaviour, forced marriage, as well as extensions to the offences of wilful neglect and ill-treatment, encompassing corporate offences, in 2015.

Even so, there is only so much the State can do and it might anyway not be entirely straightforward. For instance, giving a family member a lasting power of attorney – to manage a relative's affairs when that relative loses capacity – can be done relatively easily. And once executed and registered, there is no default system of checking and monitoring what the family member is doing. One reason for this is so that the system is not unduly difficult and burdensome for families; otherwise, few might use it. However, a significant number of powers of attorney are abused, and for every one case that comes to light there may be many that don't. Leading to one Court of Protection judge to state that, with so few safeguards, he would never himself make a power of attorney.[1] Therefore, it could be argued that the answer to the dilemma – of a more or less burdensome system, with more or fewer safeguards – is not always intuitively obvious.

THE STATE'S PERPETRATION OF NEGLECT AND ABUSE: HOW FAR HAVE WE MOVED ON FROM THE PAST? It might be thought, in the 21st century, that at least the State could control what *it* does and would not itself be perpetrating neglect or abuse. After all, society and governments pride themselves on how we have advanced, compared with past times. Certainly, we would like to think so when casting back, for example, to a ground-breaking book published in the 1960s called *Sans everything*, which described the plight of older people warehoused in long-stay geriatric wards,[2] and further back, to the Poor Law and the workhouse. Surely, we have moved on?

Yet, it is not certain how far we have done so. For example, as recently as 2008, the Mental Health Act Commission, in its biennial report about mental health services, made comparisons with the *Parliamentary Inquiry into madhouses of 1815/16*. The latter Inquiry had identified a number of 'basic evils'; the Commission had found these alive and well in the 21st century, nearly 200 years later, undermining people's dignity, privacy and safety.[3]

In similar vein, the Department of Health has in the recent past deployed, absurdly, the mantra 'world class commissioning' of health care, meant to represent just how advanced we were.[4] This at the very time when the NHS was enmired in a series of scandals involving large-scale neglect of mainly older people. One of these was Stafford Hospital, the events at which the

---

1   Walters, M. 'I would never sign a power of attorney – retired judge.' *Daily Telegraph*, 15 August 2017.

2   Robb, B. *Sans everything*. London: Nelson, 1967.

3   Mental Health Act Commission. *Risk, rights, recovery: twelfth biennial report, 2005–2007*. London: MHAC, 2008, pp.10–11, 17–29.

4   Department of Health. *World class commissioning: an introduction*. London: DH, 2009, p.2.

Department, initially at least, attempted to gloss over. The vacuous use of such grandiose language – a smokescreen masking the reality beneath, preventing discussion and therefore obstructing solutions – is harmful in itself for obvious reasons.

Indeed, the plight of older people with complex needs in our hospitals recalls another element of the past. As already noted above, the current system of hospital care is not set up to meet the needs of such patients, even though they occupy the majority of hospital beds. Consequently, logically but detrimentally, the system sometimes works to avoid admitting to hospital patients who clinically need to be there, to fail to diagnose and treat them properly while there, to provide poor care and even to neglect them, and then to discharge them prematurely.

This is suggestive of an element of the Poor Law of the 19th century, a principle known as 'less eligibility'.[1] In short, conditions in the workhouse were to be made so bad that only absolute desperation would drive somebody to it. The irony is that the Poor Law held the elderly and infirm in the workhouse in higher esteem than the 'able-bodied' but destitute.[2] The position in hospital is now reversed in that patients with simpler, easier needs – relatively the more able-bodied – are favoured, whilst the elderly and infirm are now effectively the unwanted. Unwanted by NHS Trust management because such patients, often emergency admissions, threaten the achievement of financial, political and elective treatment targets.

CURRENT TRENDS IN HEALTH AND SOCIAL CARE. With an ageing population and significant numbers of older people with multiple and complex needs, it is arguable that certain current trends in health and social care might lead to the need for more safeguarding. For instance, both social services and the NHS talk increasingly of prevention and of increasing

---

1   Commissioners for Inquiring into the Administration and Practical Operation of the Poor Laws. *Report from His Majesty's Commissioners for inquiring into the administration and practical operation of the poor laws.* London: House of Commons, 1834, Part 2, Section 1, para CXV.

2   See e.g. National Trust. *The Workhouse, Southwell.* Swindon: NT, 2002, pp.14–15.

people's own resilience to look after themselves. Both worthy and justifiable approaches, up to a point.

But what about those people who already have significant needs, who are not 'resilient' (whatever that means) for good reason and who may be vulnerable to neglect or abuse – but who are effectively discarded? Such as the 83-year-old pensioner suffering from dementia, sent home by ambulance from hospital in the middle of the night, family not informed, no hospital record of the treatment she had received, hospital knowing that she lived alone – found dead the next day, clutching a bible, at home.[1] Or the elderly woman visited at home by social services, assessed as managing her own personal care, and then having her case closed to assistance – even though it was recorded that she was unkempt, her knickers were around her knees, there was evidence of faeces on the floor and she was not taking her medication.[2]

Social services are now assisting ever fewer people, excluding them on the grounds of legal 'non-eligibility'. In 2015, it was reported that those accessing local authority care services had fallen by half a million since 2008/9 (a drop of 30%), despite the population continuing to age, with the number of over-80s having risen by 800,000 in the last decade.[3] And for those social services do help, in care homes or own homes, the commissioning of services has been cut to the bone – with the increased risk therefore of shortcuts being taken by care homes and care agencies. It is certainly arguable, for example, that the fine and dedicated care provided by often poorly trained, poorly supervised and poorly paid care workers is in spite of the system, not because of it.

At the same time, the NHS has reduced by tens of thousands the number of hospital beds, and consequently hospitals are over-occupied, which puts patients at risk. For instance, between 1997 and 2007, 32,000 beds were lost despite the NHS Plan in 2000 stating that 7000 new beds were needed

---

1   Tozer, J. 'Why was my mum sent home from hospital to die alone?' *Daily Mail*, 9 February 2007.

2   Henwood, M. and Hudson, B. *Lost to the system? The impact of Fair Access to Care.* London: Commission for Social Care Inspection, 2008, pp.8–12.

3   Franklin, B. *The end of formal adult social care.* London: Centre for Later Life Funding, 2015, p.3.

by 2010.[1] Between 2010 and 2016, a further 52,000 were lost.[2] In particular, the priorities and care pathways to which the NHS operates are not geared to emergency admissions of older people with complex and multiple needs. All this, in both health and social care, would seem to increase the risks of abuse or neglect, and therefore the need for adult safeguarding to play in the future an ever greater, firefighting role.

---

1 Donnelly, L. 'NHS hospitals lose 32,000 beds in a decade.' *Daily Telegraph*, 24 May 2008. Also: Department of Health. *Implementing the NHS Plan: developing services following the National Beds Inquiry*. Health Service Circular 2001/03. London: DH, 2001, para 7.

2 British Medical Association. *State of the health system: beds in the NHS: England*. London: BMA, 2017, including p.8.

Legal framework of adult safeguarding

The legal framework relevant to adult safeguarding is extensive, as can be seen immediately below. There are overall three points to make about it. First, the Care Act 2014 sits at the hub but is not a coercive piece of legislation. Under it, social services make enquiries into abuse or neglect, can request cooperation from other bodies and can offer information, advice, care and support services, but cannot directly do much else in a wider sense.

Second, therefore, other bodies under other legislation might be required for adult safeguarding to be effective – for example, the police under criminal law, the Care Quality Commission or Disclosure and Barring Service under regulatory legislation, the Court of Protection under the Mental Capacity Act 2005 and so on.

Third, if one piece of legislation is not relevant or appropriate, another might be. For example, a vulnerable adult might have capacity to handle their money under the Mental Capacity Act, and to consent to giving it away – but an exploitative perpetrator could in some circumstances still be convicted of dishonesty under the Theft Act 1968.

Fourth, a single case can involve a great deal of law. For instance, the following example based on an actual case resulting in criminal conviction:

Neglect of care home resident: multiple legal ramifications. A care home resident is found badly neglected (left to crawl around the floor, demented, with rashes and sores, naked, malnourished). She might have been placed by a local authority in the first place to meet her needs (Care Act). Enquiries would be triggered by reports of her neglect (Care Act). Her human rights would have been breached (arguably article 3 of the European Convention on Human Rights, inhuman or degrading treatment), and she would scarcely have been cared for in her best interests (Mental Capacity Act).

The nurse manager of the home might be prosecuted and convicted of the criminal offence of wilful neglect (Mental Capacity Act), placed on the barred list (Safeguarding Vulnerable Groups Act) and referred to her professional body (Nursing and Midwifery Order 2001). The care home might be inspected, warned or worse by the Care Quality Commission (Health and Social Care Act 2008).[1]

- **Welfare**

    » *Care Act 2014*: local authority duties to protect from abuse and neglect, to make enquiries – also safeguarding adults boards

    » *National Health Service Act 2006*: NHS duty to provide treatment and care

    » *Mental Health Act 1983*: mental health, including offences of wilful neglect and ill-treatment

    » *Mental Capacity Act 2005*: key principles relating to capacity, and offences of wilful neglect and ill-treatment

    » *Inherent jurisdiction*: High Court's residual power to intervene outside of legislation – sometimes used to protect vulnerable adults

- **General rights**

    » *Human Rights Act 1998*: integrates the European Convention into United Kingdom law

    » *European Convention on Human Rights*: key rights relating to inhuman and degrading treatment, deprivation of liberty, private life, etc.

    » *Equality Act 2010*: protection against discrimination

---

1   Based on Bunyan, N. 'BUPA put profit first at filthy and understaffed care home, says judge.' *Daily Telegraph*, 17 March 2012; Stewart, G. 'Merseyside care home manager struck off.' *Liverpool Echo*, 31 May 2013.

- **Regulation of health and care providers** (including the NHS)

  » *Health and Social Care Act 2008*: regulatory framework for health and care providers, enforced by the Care Quality Commission

  » *Health and Social Care Act (Regulated Activities) Regulations 2014*: specific duty to protect service users from abuse and neglect

- **Regulation of health and safety**

  » *Health and Safety at Work Act 1974*

- **Regulation of individuals**

  » *Police Act 1997*: criminal record certificates

  » *Rehabilitation of Offenders Act 1974*: criminal record certificates

  » *Rehabilitation of Offenders Act 1974 (Exceptions) Order 1975*: criminal record certificates

  » *Safeguarding Vulnerable Groups Act 2006*: barred list preventing person working in regulated activity

- **Regulation of professionals**

  » *Medical Act 1983*: regulation of medical doctors by the General Medical Council

  » *Nursing and Midwifery Order 2001*: regulation of nurses, health visitors and midwives by the Nursing and Midwifery Council

  » *Health and Social Work Professions Order 2002*: regulation of range of other health professionals and social workers by the Health and Care Professions Council

- **Regulation of information**

  » *Freedom of Information Act 2000*: rights of access to non-personal information

  » *Data Protection Act 2018 and General Data Protection Regulation (GDPR)*: rights of access, and of disclosure, relating to personal information

  » *Common law of confidentiality*: the court's approach, in common law, to questions of confidentiality and disclosure

  » *Employment Rights Act 1996*: protection for whistleblowers

- **Law relating to will and gifts** (including law of equity)

  » *Undue influence*: express, or presumed, including on vulnerable adult

  » *Fraudulent calumny*: poisoning the mind of the testator against a beneficiary

  » *Unconscionable bargain*: inequality of bargaining power

  » *Proprietary estoppel*: assurance given about transfer (gift) of property

- **Law relating to rights of entry to a dwelling**

  » *Police and Criminal Evidence Act 1984 (section 17)*: power of police to enter a dwelling to save life and limb

  » *Public Health Act 1936, Environmental Protection Act 1990*: power of environmental health officers to enter dwelling for public health purposes

  » *Mental Health Act 1983, section 135*

  » *Mental Capacity Act 2005*: Court of Protection order

  » *Inherent jurisdiction*: High Court order

  » *Animal Welfare Act 2006*

  » *Gas Act 1986, Electricity Act 1989, Water Industry Act 1991*

  » *Fire and Rescue Services Act 2004*

- **Criminal offences against the person**

  » *Criminal Justice and Courts Act 2015*: wilful neglect or ill-treatment (see also Mental Health Act 1983 and Mental Capacity Act 2005 for same offences)

  » *Suicide Act 1961*: aiding or abetting suicide

  » *Corporate Manslaughter and Corporate Homicide Act 2007*

  » *Common law manslaughter*

  » *Murder*

  » *Domestic Violence, Crime and Victims Act 2004*: causing or allowing death of a vulnerable person in a domestic setting

  » *Assault or battery, common law* (Criminal Justice Act 1988, section 39 for sentencing)

- » *False imprisonment, common law*

- » *Offences Against the Person Act 1861, section 47*: actual bodily harm

- » *Offences Against the Person Act 1861, sections 18–20*: grievous bodily harm/ with intent

- » *Offences Against the Person Act 1861, section 16*: threat to kill

- » *Offences Against the Person Act 1861, section 21*: choking

- » *Offences Against the Person Act 1861, section 22*: application of stupefying or overpowering drugs

- » *Offences Against the Person Act 1861, sections 23–24*: poisoning with intent to injure, aggrieve or annoy

- » *Medicines Act 1968, section 58*: unlawfully administering medication

- » *Modern Slavery Act 2015*: slavery, human trafficking, forced labour and domestic servitude

- **Civil torts**

  - » *Common law of negligence* (duty of care, causation of harm)

  - » *Trespass to the person* (assault, battery, false imprisonment)

- **Sexual offences, forced marriage, circumcision**

  - » *Sexual Offences Act 2003*: general sexual offences, additional offences when the victim has a mental disorder

  - » *Social Behaviour, Crime and Policing Act 2014, section 121*: forced marriage offence

  - » *Female Genital Mutilation Act 2003, Prohibition of Female Circumcision Act 1985*

- **Financial and property crime**

  - » *Theft Act 1968*: theft, robbery, blackmail, burglary

  - » *Fraud Act 2006*: fraud, including by abuse of position

  - » *Forgery and Counterfeiting Act 1981*: forgery and counterfeiting

- **Domestic violence, injunctions, etc.**

  » *Family Law Act 1996*: non-molestation orders, occupation orders, forced marriage protection orders

  » *Crime and Security Act 2010*: domestic violence protection notices and orders

  » *Serious Crime Act 2015, section 76*: offence of controlling or coercive behaviour in an intimate or family relationship

- **Anti-social behaviour, harassment, fear of violence, etc.**

  » *Anti-Social Behaviour, Crime and Policing Act 2014*

  » *Public Order Act 1986, section 4*: fear of violence

  » *Public Order Act 1986, section 4A*: intentional harassment or alarm or distress

  » *Public Order Act 1986, section 5*: harassment or alarm or distress

  » *Protection from Harassment Act 1997, sections 1, 4*: course of conduct amounting to harassment/causing another to fear

  » *Criminal Justice and Police Act 2001, section 42A*: harassment of a person in his home

A–Z list

Note on terminology used in references

COP stands for Court of Protection.

EWCA stands for England and Wales Court of Appeal.

EWHC stands for England and Wales High Court.

HL stands for House of Lords, which has since become the Supreme Court.

LGO stands for Local Government Ombudsman. In June 2017, the office of the ombudsman became known as Local Government and Social Care Ombudsman. However, since a majority of ombudsman investigations cited come before that date, the abbreviation LGO has been retained for convenience.

SC stands for Supreme Court.

A

Abuse

Abuse is a term recurring in the Care Act 2014, which is civil law. The term appears also in the Health and Social Care (Regulated Activities) Regulations 2014, which the Care Quality Commission use to regulate and inspect health and social care providers. These regulations effectively contain elements of civil and criminal law.

The term should be distinguished from its criminal law equivalent – 'ill-treatment' – a criminal offence occurring in at least three other pieces of legislation.[1]

ABUSE: CARE ACT 2014. Abuse is something against which local authorities have a duty to protect people with care and support needs.[2] The Care Act does not define the term, merely states only, and selectively, that abuse includes financial abuse. And that financial abuse in turn includes:

- having money or other property stolen

- being defrauded

- being put under pressure in relation to money or other property, and

- having money or other property misused.

Statutory guidance is more forthcoming, urging local authorities not to limit their view of abuse, and giving examples:

---

1   Mental Health Act 1983, s.127; Mental Capacity Act 2005, s.44; Criminal Justice and Courts Act 2015, ss.20–25.

2   Care Act 2014, s.1.

- **Abuse: examples in Care Act guidance.** Examples include physical abuse, domestic violence, sexual abuse, psychological abuse, financial or material abuse, modern slavery (encompassing slavery, human trafficking, forced labour and domestic servitude), discriminatory abuse (including forms of harassment, slurs or similar treatment because of race, gender and gender identity, age, disability, sexual orientation or religion), organisational abuse.[1]

Since the term is undefined and the Act and guidance merely give examples, the dictionary meaning of the term is also relevant. For example: 'use to bad effect or for a bad purpose, or maltreat, or practise corruptly'.[2] (Neglect, a term also occurring in the Care Act, is dealt with separately in the Care Act guidance: see *Neglect*.)

ABUSE: HEALTH AND SOCIAL CARE (REGULATED ACTIVITIES) REGULATIONS 2014. The term 'abuse' occurs in regulatory legislation applying to health and social care providers in England. These have a duty to safeguard service users from 'abuse' and 'improper treatment'. The relevant regulations define abuse as follows (and include both ill-treatment and neglect within the definition – in contrast to the Care Act 2014 which distinguishes abuse from neglect):

- **Abuse: regulatory legislation.** Abuse means (a) behaviour that is an offence under the Sexual Offences Act 2003, (b) ill-treatment (whether of a physical or psychological nature) of a service user, (c) theft, misuse or misappropriation of money or property belonging to a service user, or (d) neglect of a service user.[3]

The regulations distinguish ill-treatment, part of the definition of abuse, from improper treatment – from which service users must also and separately be safeguarded. It is slightly unhelpful that the regulations and the Care Act do not contain the same terminology. The term 'ill-treatment' also appears separately in criminal law: see *Wilful neglect or ill-treatment*.

---

1   Department of Health. *Care and support statutory guidance*. London: DH, 2016, para 14.17.

2   Allen, R.E. (ed.). *Concise Oxford Dictionary*. Oxford: Oxford University Press, 8th edition, 1990.

3   SI 2014/2936. Health and Social Care Act (Regulated Activities) Regulations 2014, r.13.

Acts of care or treatment (mental capacity), see *Mental capacity*

Adult protection

In contrast perhaps to the term 'child protection', the term 'adult protection' is little used in practice by local social services authorities, the NHS, the police and other agencies. Most use the term 'safeguarding adults'. Nevertheless, the Care Act 2014, governing adult social care, refers mostly to 'protection' of people from abuse and neglect and not to 'safeguarding':

- **Well-being.** The definition of well-being includes nine elements, one of which is protection from abuse and neglect. Whatever a local authority does under the Care Act in relation to an individual, it must promote a person's well-being.

- **Overarching principle.** Whatever a local authority does under the Care Act in relation to an individual, it must have regard to the need to protect them from abuse and neglect.

- **Assessment.** Assessment of adults or carers under the Care Act 2014 leads to an 'eligibility' decision, about whether a person is legally entitled to have their care and support needs met. Eligibility in turn is determined by the answer to three questions, the third of which is whether there is a significant impact on the person's well-being. Part of the definition of the latter is protection from abuse and neglect, and thus every eligibility decision must consider the question of abuse and neglect.

- **Cooperation.** Local authorities have a duty to cooperate with defined statutory bodies (including the NHS, police, prison and probation services, and other bodies – e.g. care providers or primary medical providers such as general practitioners). One of the listed purposes of cooperation is protecting adults with needs for care and support who are experiencing, or are at risk of, abuse or neglect.

- **Enquiries.** A local authority's duty to make enquiries into abuse or neglect is dependent, amongst other things, on whether or not the adult is able to protect themselves from the abuse or neglect.

- **Safeguarding adults boards.** The objective of a safeguarding adults board is to help and protect adults in the area from abuse and neglect.[1]

Advance decisions

Advance decisions are provided for under sections 24–26 of the Mental Capacity Act 2005. They are about advance refusal of medical treatment, anticipating the future when the person has lost capacity to make that decision. In such circumstances, an advance decision is binding (on treating health care staff) if the decision is legally valid and applicable. If it is about life-sustaining treatment, it must be in writing, signed and witnessed.

Advance decisions are not intrinsically anything to do with safeguarding. Nevertheless, they might become so, for example, if the person did not have the capacity to make the decision in the first place or did have capacity but had been coerced or threatened into making the decision. Conversely, blatant disregard of an obviously valid advance decision, and the consequent subjection of a person to invasive, hopeless and undignified treatment, could be regarded as abusive – and legally found a compensation payment.

> **Subjecting a woman to what she considered degradation, contrary to her advance decision.** The family of an 81-year-old woman received a £45,000 payout from the NHS after she was kept alive against her will. She had made an advance decision, fearing degradation and indignity more than death. It precluded life-prolonging treatment, including food, although did not preclude pain relief to treat distressing symptoms. The decision was to have effect once she was no longer of sound mind or suffered from a list of medical ailments. She then suffered a catastrophic stroke that left her unable to walk, talk or swallow. However, the George Eliot Hospital, in Nuneaton, Warwickshire, misplaced the advance decision. Instead, she was fed artificially for 22 months, first in hospital, then in a care home, where she became agitated and tried to pull out the tubes in her arm – only for staff to put mittens on her hands.[2]

---

1   Care Act 2014, ss.1, 6, 9, 10, 13, 42, 43.

2   Paduano, M. 'Pay-out after woman was kept alive against her will.' *BBC News*, 6 December 2017. Accessed on 12 June 2018 at: www.bbc.co.uk/news/uk-england-coventry-warwickshire-42240148.

Advance decisions should be distinguished from 'do not resuscitate notices', which may give rise to adult protection issues if improperly used: see ***Do not resuscitate orders*** (more fully: do not attempt cardio-pulmonary resuscitation notice: DNACPR).

Advocacy

Health and social care legislation provides for the appointment of statutory advocates in certain circumstances.[1] The first two of these make specific reference to adult protection. This is under the Care Act 2014, Mental Capacity Act 2005 and Mental Health Act.

ADVOCACY: CARE ACT ADVOCATES. The Care Act places a duty on local authorities to appoint independent advocates, if certain conditions are met. The two conditions are that the person would struggle to understand things like assessment, care planning, review and safeguarding, and does not have an appropriate family member or friend to represent and support them. In relation to safeguarding, conflict of interest – or current or previous safeguarding issues – involving that family member or friend could make him or her inappropriate. The purpose of an independent advocate, overall, is to facilitate the individual's involvement in the relevant process, through representation and support.

Section 67 of the Care Act covers assessment of care and support needs and other related issues. Section 68, more specifically, covers safeguarding enquiries taking place under section 42 of the Act – or safeguarding adults reviews, conducted by safeguarding adults boards, under section 44 of the Act.

- **Advocacy: first condition, substantial difficulty in understanding.** The local authority must consider that, were an independent advocate not available, the person would experience substantial difficulty in doing any one of the following: understanding the relevant information; retaining that information; using or weighing that information as part of the process of

---

1   Mental Health Act 1983, ss.130A–130D. And: SI 2008/3166. Mental Health Act 1983 (Independent Mental Health Advocates) (England) Regulations 2008.

being involved; communicating the individual's views, wishes or feelings (whether by talking, using sign language or any other means).[1]

These four abilities are based on section 3 of the Mental Capacity Act 2005. However, that Act is concerned with an *inability* to do any of these, whereas the Care Act refers instead to *substantial difficulty*, therefore encompassing lack of mental capacity but extending more widely – namely to those with mental capacity but nonetheless experiencing substantial difficulty, for whatever reason.

Guidance gives examples of why substantial difficulty might arise: dementia, learning disabilities, brain injury, mental ill health, somebody with Asperger's syndrome, a confused older person, a person who is nearing the end of their life and disengaged from the process.[2]

- **Advocacy: second condition, family member or friend available.** The duty to appoint an independent advocate does not arise if the local authority is satisfied that there is instead somebody else appropriate to represent and support the person, so as to facilitate the latter's involvement. The appropriate person cannot be anybody who is providing care and support for the person, either professionally or for payment.[3] Therefore, the appropriate person would typically need to be a family member or friend.

- **Advocacy: consent.** A family member or friend cannot in any event be appropriate to represent and support the person, unless the latter consents, or, if the person lacks capacity to take this decision, the local authority believes it is in their best interests that the family member fulfil that role.[4]

In contrast, the appointment of an independent advocate does not rely on the person's consent. However, were such consent withheld, and non-engagement or non-cooperation were to result, the advocate's effectiveness would be compromised.

---

1   Care Act 2014, ss.67, 68.

2   Department of Health. *Care and support statutory guidance: issued under the Care Act 2014.* London: DH, 2016, para 7.16.

3   Care Act 2014, ss.67, 68.

4   Care Act 2014, ss.67, 68.

ADVOCACY: INAPPROPRIATENESS OF FAMILY MEMBER OR FRIEND.
The local authority might sometimes not be satisfied about the appropriateness of a family member or friend – for instance, if the family member or friend is opposed to, or impervious to, what the person wants, or because there is evidence of some other clear conflict of interest.[1]

- **Advocacy: strength of duty.** An early legal judgment under the Care Act held that a failure to appoint an advocate when the triggering conditions were met – simply because the local authority had not commissioned sufficient numbers of advocates locally – was unlawful. Nor was it acceptable for the local authority to argue that the appointment of an advocate would have made no difference to the final decision. Because how could the local authority possibly know this, if the person was unable to participate in the process?[2]

ADVOCACY: INDEPENDENT MENTAL CAPACITY ADVOCATES. The Mental Capacity Act 2005 provides for independent mental capacity advocates (IMCAs) to be appointed by local authorities in certain circumstances.[3] This is a duty in relation to serious medical treatment, care home stays of more than eight weeks, and hospital stays of more than four weeks – assuming there is not an appropriate friend or relative to support the person. In addition is a power, rather than a duty, to appoint an IMCA in relation to adult protection.

- **Role of independent mental capacity advocate.** The core role of an IMCA is to provide support, obtain and evaluate relevant information, ascertain what the person's wishes, feelings, beliefs and values might be (if the person had capacity), ascertain alternative courses of action, and prepare a report for the authorised person who instructed him or her. The advocate subsequently

---

1   Department of Health. *Care and support statutory guidance*. London: DH, 2016, para 7.36. For instance, this sort of point was made in a different context, under the Mental Capacity Act 2005. The judge pointed out that the role of a person's relevant representative was to maintain contact with, support and represent the person lacking capacity, under para 140 of schedule A1 of the 2005 Act. The representative, a family member, could not do this if his view of the person's best interests was contrary to the wishes and feelings of the person lacking capacity. She didn't want to be deprived of her liberty in the care home, yet he thought it was in her best interests: *AJ v A Local Authority* [2015] EWCOP 5, para 84.

2   *R (SG) v Haringey LBC* [2015] EWHC 2579 (Admin), paras 53–56.

3   Mental Capacity Act 2005, ss.35–39.

has the same rights to challenge the decision as if he or she were any other person engaged in caring for the person or interested in his or her welfare.[1]

- **Power to instruct IMCA in case of abuse or neglect.** A power (rather than a duty) arises to appoint an IMCA if adult protection measures are being or are going to be taken – whether or not there are family or friends appropriate to consult. The power arises if an NHS body or local authority proposes to take or has taken protective measures, for a person lacking capacity (a) following receipt of allegation of abuse or neglect (by another person); or (b) in accordance with arrangements made under adult protection guidance issued under section 78 of the Care Act 2014. Protective measures are defined to include measures to minimise the risk that any abuse or neglect of the person, or abuse by the person, will continue.[2]

Separate rules govern the appointment of IMCAs, specifically in relation to authorisation of a deprivation of liberty by a local authority.[3]

Alarm, see *Harassment, alarm or distress*

Anti-social behaviour

The Anti-Social Behaviour, Crime and Policing Act 2014 provides for anti-social behaviour injunctions. In summary:

- **10 years and over.** They can apply to people aged 10 or above.

- **Engaging in anti-social behaviour:** (i) The court must be satisfied on the balance of probabilities that the person has engaged or threatens to engage in anti-social behaviour; and (ii) the court considers it just and convenient to grant the injunction to prevent the person engaging in anti-social behaviour.

---

1 Mental Capacity Act 2005, s.36. And: SI 2006/1832. The Mental Capacity Act 2005 (Independent Mental Capacity Advocates) (General) Regulations 2006. And see Local Authority Social Services Act 1970, s.7 as amended.

2 Mental Capacity Act 2005, ss.36–39. And: SI 2006/2883. The Mental Capacity Act 2005 (Independent Mental Capacity Advocates) (Expansion of Role) Regulations 2006.

3 Mental Capacity Act 2005, ss.39A–39D.

- **Applications.** Injunctions can be applied for by a range of agencies including local authorities, housing providers, the police, Transport for London, Environment Agency, an NHS security body.

- **Length of time.** The length of time of the injunction must be specified (in case of a person aged under 18, it must be no more than 12 months).

- **Purpose of injunction.** An injunction may prohibit the person from doing anything, or require the person to do anything, described in the injunction.

- **Anti-social behaviour: definition.** The definition of this behaviour is:

  a. conduct that has caused, or is likely to cause, harassment, alarm or distress to any person

  b. conduct capable of causing nuisance or annoyance to a person in relation to that person's occupation of residential premises, or

  c. conduct capable of causing housing-related nuisance or annoyance to any person.

- **Power of arrest.** The court may attach a power of arrest (in case of breach of the injunction) if it thinks that (i) the anti-social behaviour consists of or includes the use or threatened use of violence against other persons, or (ii) there is a significant risk of harm to other people. Otherwise, a warrant for the person's arrest can be applied for, in case of breach of the injunction.

- **Breach of a civil order.** This is punishable as a contempt of court.

- **Exclusion from dwelling.** An injunction can be made excluding a person aged 18 or over from the dwelling in which they live, if the court thinks that (i) the anti-social behaviour consists of or includes the use or threatened use of violence against other persons, or (ii) there is a significant risk of harm to other people.[1]

Such injunctions can be used to protect vulnerable adults – as well as anybody else, even without a pre-existing vulnerability.

---

1   Anti-Social Behaviour, Crime and Policing Act 2014, ss.1–13.

Vulnerable people harassed by 83-year-old man. An 83-year-old man who terrorised two vulnerable people by repeatedly demanding money and cigarettes was given a three-month custodial sentence, suspended for a year, after breaching an injunction a total of 20 times. His relentless campaign had left the victims living in fear in their own homes. The injunction banned him from visiting two separate areas of Worksop and causing nuisance or annoyance to two people in particular. The injunction also banned him from shouting, swearing, violence or threats of violence.[1]

Injunction against person selling drugs to vulnerable people. Oxford City Council was granted a two-year injunction against an Oxford resident. The injunction banned him from engaging in behaviour likely to cause harassment, alarm, annoyance or distress to any person in Oxford, from entering the city centre unless for certain approved appointments and from contacting victims in the case. He had been involved in a range of anti-social behaviour, including supplying drugs to vulnerable people. The prosecution was brought, in partnership, by Oxford City Council's Anti-Social Behaviour Team and Thames Valley Police.[2]

Injunction against woman from entering independent living scheme for elderly people. A woman was sentenced to eight weeks in prison for breaching her anti-social behaviour injunction three times. She had continued to enter an independent living scheme that she was banned from, following allegations of theft and financial abuse towards elderly residents. CCTV showed her entering the premises.[3]

Breach of injunction by son, in relation to his vulnerable father. An anti-social behaviour injunction (under previous legislation, section 53 of the Housing Act 1996) was made against a man, who had assaulted his father, a vulnerable adult. Despite understanding the injunction, the son visited

1   Peck, J. '"You'll go to jail if you don't behave" – 83-year-old menace warned after breaching Anti-Social Behaviour Injunction 20 times.' *Lincolnshire Live*, 25 April 2018. Accessed on 12 June 2018 at: www.lincolnshirelive.co.uk/news/local-news/youll-go-jail-you-dont-1498964.

2   Oxford City Council. 'Oxford City Council granted injunction following anti-social behaviour.' 29 June 2017. Accessed on 12 June 2018 at: www.oxford.gov.uk/news/article/471/oxford_city_council_granted_injunction_following_anti-social_behaviour.

3   'Woman jailed after breaking ASB injunction.' *Mix96* (Aylesbury), 13 March 2017. Accessed on 7 February 2018 at: www.mix96.co.uk/news/local/2245062/woman-jailed-after-breaking-asb-injunction.

his father and drank heavily with him. The police attended and arrested the son, who was subsequently sentenced to eight weeks in prison for contempt.[1]

Gang targeting vulnerable adult's home. A member of a gang who bullied a vulnerable man in his home was sentenced to six weeks in prison for breaching an injunction (made under previous legislation) aimed at protecting the man. Housing officials had voiced fears that the 29-year-old victim's life could be at risk because of the activities of the gang. Twelve local people were each given an anti-social behaviour injunction, barring them from going into his flat or entering the area around the property. The gang had been involved in incidents of serious criminal and anti-social behaviour at the flat on numerous occasions since late 2010. Their actions included drug taking, stealing their victim's belongings and shopping, arson, threats to neighbours and noise nuisance well into the early hours.[2]

Anti-social behaviour, hate crime, possession proceedings: failure to consider injunction, suicide and death. A woman killed herself and her disabled adult daughter – by setting fire to the car they were in. She had been in despair at the persistent harassment, suffered over a period of ten years, at the hands of a group of local youths. However, when asked, she had chosen not to support criminal prosecution.

A serious case review concluded that the local authority and the police should have looked much harder at how to classify what was going on and what they could do about it. At least three alternatives identified were anti-social behaviour (leading to voluntary good behaviour contracts or court injunctions), disability hate crime (prosecution), or possession proceedings taken against the perpetrators.[3]

1   *ISOS Housing v Lawson* [2014] EW Misc B42 (CC).

2   Black, D. 'Northumberland MP's praise as bully is jailed.' *The Journal* (Northumberland), 11 June 2011. Accessed on 7 February 2018 at: www.thejournal.co.uk/news/north-east-news/northumberland-mps-praise-bully-jailed-4429586.

3   Leicester, Leicestershire and Rutland Safeguarding Adults Board. *Executive Summary of Serious Case Review in relation to A and B*, 2008.

ANTI-SOCIAL BEHAVIOUR: CRIME AND POLICING ACT 2014: CRIMINAL BEHAVIOUR ORDERS. A court can make a criminal behaviour order if:

- **Harassment, alarm, distress.** The court is satisfied, beyond reasonable doubt, that the offender has engaged in behaviour that caused or was likely to cause harassment, alarm or distress to any person.

- **Prevention of behaviour.** The court considers that making the order will help in preventing the offender from engaging in such behaviour.

- **Purpose.** The order has the purpose of preventing the offender from engaging in such behaviour by containing prohibitions or requirements – and it is made in addition to a sentence being imposed or a conditional discharge.

- **Length of time.** Between one and three years for somebody aged under 18; not less than two years up to an indefinite period of time otherwise.

- **Offence.** It is an offence to breach a criminal behaviour order.[1]

Indefinite criminal behaviour order to prevent man from targeting vulnerable victims, including those suffering from dementia. A 42-year-old man had a history of targeting elderly victims for cash. He was given a criminal behaviour order, for an indefinite period, after a successful application by Northamptonshire Police and partner agencies. He had previously been subject to a community protection notice which he had breached on a number of occasions by targeting very vulnerable victims and attempting to dishonestly obtain money from them. This had resulted in multiple safeguarding referrals made in relation to concerns about vulnerable victims, some of whom suffered from dementia. The order barred him from entering a particular address, from contacting a number of named witnesses and from causing nuisance or harassment by approaching any member of the public in Northamptonshire with a view to begging, cheating or otherwise dishonestly seeking to gain money or property.[2]

---

1   Anti-Social Behaviour, Crime and Policing Act 2014, ss.22–33.

2   Northamptonshire Police. 'Criminal Behaviour Order imposed on man with a history of targeting elderly victims in Kettering.' Undated. Accessed on 12 June 2018 at: http://northants.police. uk/press-release/criminal-behaviour-order-imposed-on-man-history-targeting-elderly-victims-kettering.

Five-year criminal behaviour order for drug user defrauding elderly women with sob story. A 30-year-old drug user targeted two elderly women just weeks after release from prison, having been sentenced previously for similar offences. She would knock on doors, ask to use the telephone, make up a story about a broken-down car or her sick children, take money for a taxi and never return it. She now pleaded guilty to two charges of fraud by false representation and two of breaching a previous criminal behaviour order, imposed in 2015. She was sentenced to two years' imprisonment – and given a further five-year criminal behaviour order.[1]

Criminal behaviour order to exclude certain individuals from the dwelling of two vulnerable adults. A man was issued with a two-year criminal behaviour order prohibiting him from entering an address or loitering outside it. The application was made by the police, supported by a borough council. It followed two other related CBOs and a partial property closure. Two vulnerable adults had been exploited by a number of individuals who were visiting their homes, normally when their benefits were due, and helping themselves to their belongings, medication and food. They would typically stay until the money ran out. The police and other agencies had carried out joint door-to-door enquiries to ascertain the extent of the anti-social behaviour and its impact on neighbours. The victims' homes were also visited by the police crime reduction adviser to help make them more secure, and healthcare professionals were involved to ensure the safety of the residents concerned.[2]

Appropriate adult

Vulnerable adults are sometimes *suspects*, rightfully or wrongfully accused of a criminal offence. They are therefore not covered by criminal law provisions in place to assist vulnerable or intimidated *witnesses*. They are entitled to have an appropriate adult present when interviewed by police, under the Police and Criminal Evidence Act 1984. The details are beyond the scope of this book.

1   Wright, S. 'Sob story fraudster jailed for "dreadful offending" against vulnerable elderly people.' *Bradford Telegraph and Argus*, 23 June 2017.

2   Surrey Police. 'Criminal Behaviour Order issued to protect vulnerable victims in Guildford.' 11 July 2016. Accessed on 28 February 2018 at: www.surrey.police.uk/news/criminal-behaviour-order-issued-to-protect-vulnerable-victims-in-guildford.

Assault

The word 'assault' is used commonly to refer to physical attacks. However, technically, common assault occurs when a person intentionally or recklessly causes somebody else to apprehend or anticipate any immediate and unlawful violence or touching.[1]

Battery occurs when a person intentionally or recklessly applies unlawful force to somebody else – that is, intentional touching of another person without the consent of that person and without lawful excuse. It need not necessarily be hostile, rude or aggressive.[2] So, if there has been a battery, the charge should be 'assault by beating'.[3]

Assault and battery are (probably) still to be regarded as common law offences.[4] However, sentences arising on conviction are governed by legislation: section 39 of the Criminal Justice Act 1988, with a maximum six months' imprisonment. This should be contrasted, for example, with the maximum of five years' imprisonment for the offence of ill-treatment (which could include what would otherwise be assault and battery).

In the context of vulnerable adults, the following examples illustrate a wide range of abuse that could lead to prosecution and conviction for assault or battery.

Care worker convicted for bumping person with learning disabilities down stairs. A carer pulled a care home resident down stairs by her ankles when she refused to have a bath. The 57-year-old resident, who suffered from severe epilepsy, was not injured. She had fallen asleep on the sofa, was assisted to get to bed but needed a bath at 5 am. She went to the stairs but sat down and would not move. Having tried to persuade her to move, the care worker then dragged her to the bathroom. She was convicted

---

1   *R v Savage and Parmenter* [1991] AC 699 (House of Lords).

2   *Faulkner v Talbot* [1981] 3 All ER 468 (Court of Appeal).

3   *DPP v Little* [1992] 1 QB 645.

4   *DPP v Little* [1992] 1 QB 645 suggested that assault and battery were statutory offences, but this may not be correct: *Haystead v Chief Constable of Derbyshire* [2000] 3 All ER 890.

of common assault, sentenced to 150 hours of community service and ordered to pay £200 in compensation and £300 court costs.[1]

Daughter, a retired nurse, spitting at her mother. A former nurse was convicted of common assault on her 91-year-old mother, after she was caught on a hidden camera, placed by her brother in their mother's kitchen. She ripped her mother's clothes and was spitting, screaming and elbowing. She was given a 12-month community sentence of 100 hours' unpaid work and ordered to attend five sessions on stress management. Her defence was that she had been ground down by stress and criticism, she was highly regarded in the community and the offence was out of character. A restraining order was imposed, prohibiting her from visiting her mother without other family members present. The judge said: 'It is a very sad case and I think everybody can relate to it in some way.'[2]

Barber shaving the word 'fool' into the hair of a person with learning disabilities. A barber was convicted of assault, after shaving the word fool into the hair of a person with learning disabilities. Before starting work at the hair salon, he had been a support worker in a care home. He was sentenced to an 18-month community order and a three-month curfew. He had to pay £775 costs and £300 compensation to the victim.[3]

Care assistant bending thumbs back. When a care assistant bent back the thumbs of residents as part of the way she handled them, she was found guilty of six offences of assault.[4]

Nurse forcing deodorant into a person's mouth. A nurse at a care home was jailed for 15 months on various charges, including assault, for stuffing a deodorant can into the mouth of a 95-year-old man to stop him shouting.[5]

---

1   McKeown, R. 'Carer, 56, found guilty of common assault at £2,200 per week Woodlands Care Home in Hampshire.' *Southern Daily Echo*, 28 July 2014.

2   Cooper, R. 'Son who feared his 91-year-old mother was being abused left shocked when hidden camera reveals his own SISTER spitting in her face.' *Daily Mail*, 6 July 2012.

3   'Barber who shaved word "fool" into hair of customer with learning difficulties is spared jail.' *Daily Mail*, 4 November 2011.

4   *Mwaura v Secretary of State for Health* [2006] 687 PVA/688 PC (Care Standards Tribunal hearing: conviction mentioned in report of hearing).

5   Davidson, C. 'Nurse jailed for abuse of care home patients.' *The Scotsman*, 18 May 2007.

Nurse: tirade of abuse and slapping. A nurse, acting as matron, screamed a tirade of abuse at a mental health patient in a nursing home, before slapping her twice across the face. The assault was witnessed by an inspector from the local NHS primary care trust. The nurse was sent to prison for three months for common assault.[1]

Deputy care home manager: painful use of massage. The deputy manager of a care home was jailed for three months for assault because of the manual method of massage which she used to relieve constipation of a resident. She and other staff had all been on a training course which had taught that this method was 'outlawed'. The resident, with dementia, had struggled and was screaming in pain; when staff members had asked the deputy manager to call a doctor, she had refused, saying it would look bad for the home.[2]

Punching, slapping, mishandling residents. Two care workers were sentenced for assault, on evidence that they had punched, slapped and mishandled residents, whom they had been described as treating like animals on a cattle farm. The home had previously been heavily criticised by the Commission for Social Care Inspection for employing staff who had not been properly checked.[3]

Throwing a cup of tea at a resident. A care worker at a care home in Portsmouth was sent to prison for assaulting residents. She had thrown a cup of tea at a woman in her eighties who wouldn't get up from her chair; she had claimed to be following the example of a more senior colleague who used casual violence to get the residents to comply with a strict routine.[4]

Penalty kicking a resident with dementia. A psychiatric nurse was sentenced to four months in prison for kicking a 55-year-old woman with dementia. He kicked her as she lay on her back on the floor of her room in a care home run by Care Unlimited. She developed a massive bruise, and the kick was described as having the force of a penalty kick. The nurse had

---

1   'Nurse who slapped patient is struck off.' *Bury Times*, 2 November 2006.

2   Gould, M. and Revill, J. 'Adult care ban on 700 staff.' *The Guardian*, 24 July 2005.

3   'Improved staff checks came too late to prevent abuse.' *Community Care*, 30 August 2007.

4   'Care homes.' *File on 4*, BBC Radio 4, 18 September 2007.

> worked at the care home for seven years, had an unblemished work record
> and had been in nursing for 40 years.[1]

There must, however, be evidence of intention (or at least recklessness) for the offence to be committed.

> **Care workers pouring talcum powder into mouth: insufficient evidence of intention or recklessness.** When three carers were accused of assault, by pouring talcum powder into the mouth of an 87-year-old care home resident, they were acquitted. Whilst the district judge noted that the care had been below standard, and two of the carers admitted using unnecessary force when washing and handling the woman, nonetheless he could not be sure beyond reasonable doubt of intention or recklessness.[2]

Assessment (Care Act), see *Care Act 2014*

Assisted suicide

Suicide was decriminalised in 1961. However, assisted suicide continues to be a criminal offence. In terms of safeguarding, there might sometimes be issues of abuse concerning mental capacity, undue influence, pressure, duress, etc., and a local authority's duty to make enquiries under the Care Act 2014 would therefore be triggered.[3] Under the Suicide Act 1961, in summary:

- **Encouragement or assistance.** It is an offence to do something that is capable of encouraging or assisting the suicide or attempted suicide of another person – and is intended to encourage or assist suicide or an attempt at suicide.

- **Offence even if not suicide or attempt.** The offence can be committed even if the act does not result in suicide or attempted suicide.

---

1   'Nurse jailed for assaulting patient at Sutton care home.' *Your Local Guardian*, 12 September 2011.

2   Dayani, A. 'Ban them for life.' *Birmingham Evening Mail*, 4 February 2004.

3   *Re Z* [2004] EWHC 2817 (Fam).

- **Arranging for somebody else to commit the act.** In addition, if a person arranges for a second person to commit such an act, then the first person as well as the second will be liable.

- **Intent not effectiveness.** There is encouragement or assistance, even when the act could never have constituted *effective* encouragement or assistance. (An illustration would be giving a person a supposedly lethal drug which was in fact a vitamin pill.)

ASSISTED SUICIDE: HUMAN RIGHTS. The offence itself was initially considered to be consistent with human rights. This was established in a case involving a woman with motor neurone disease, who wanted an assurance that her husband would not be prosecuted if he assisted her to commit suicide. It was held that the existence of the criminal offence did not contravene article 2 (right to life), article 3 (inhuman or degrading treatment) or article 8 (right to respect for private life).[1]

In 2009, however, a further case was brought, which held that under human rights law, a reasonable amount of guidance was required, to give some clarity as to when a prosecution might be likely.

Prosecution for assisting a person to travel to a clinic abroad for assisted suicide. The question was whether a woman's husband would be prosecuted for helping his wife (who had multiple sclerosis) travel to a country (Switzerland) where assisted suicide was legal. The destination would be a clinic which assists people to commit suicide. It was argued that the Code for Prosecutors used by the Crown Prosecution Service was inadequate to deal with such cases – and that article 8 of the European Convention demanded accessibility and foreseeability in relation to how decisions to prosecute would be taken. The House of Lords agreed with this argument and found a breach of article 8 of the Convention.[2]

---

1   *Pretty v United Kingdom* [2002] 2 FCR 97, European Court of Human Rights.

2   *R (Purdy) v Director of Public Prosecutions* [2009] UKHL 45.

ASSISTED SUICIDE: PROSECUTION GUIDELINES. Following this legal case, the Director of Public Prosecutions produced guidelines to make clearer the effect of the law. They set out two lists of factors, one which would tend to result in prosecution and the other which would not. Factors that would make prosecution more likely are as follows, in summary:

- **Age:** the victim was under 18 years of age.

- **Mental capacity:** the victim lacked mental capacity.

- **No clear decision:** the victim had not reached a voluntary, clear, settled and informed decision to commit suicide.

- **No clear communication:** the victim had not clearly communicated the decision to commit suicide.

- **Victim did not ask for help:** the victim did not seek the encouragement or assistance of the suspect personally or on his or her own initiative.

- **Motives other than compassion:** the suspect was not wholly motivated by compassion – for example, he or she was motivated by the prospect of gain from the person's death.

- **Pressure:** the suspect pressured the victim to commit suicide.

- **No reasonable steps by suspect:** the suspect did not take reasonable steps to ensure that any other person had not pressured the victim to commit suicide.

- **Suspect's history:** the suspect had a history of violence or abuse against the victim.

- **Victim's capability:** the victim was physically able to undertake the act that constituted the assistance him or herself.

- **Suspect unknown to victim:** the suspect was unknown to the victim and encouraged or assisted the victim to commit or attempt to commit suicide by providing specific information via, for example, a website or publication.

- **Activities of suspect:** the suspect gave encouragement or assistance to more than one victim who were not known to each other.

- **Payment:** the suspect was paid by the victim or those close to the victim for his or her encouragement or assistance.

- **Professional involvement:** the suspect was acting in his or her capacity as a medical doctor, nurse, other healthcare professional, a professional carer (whether for payment or not), or as a person in authority, such as a prison officer, and the victim was in his or her care.

- **Public place:** the suspect was aware that the victim intended to commit suicide in a public place where it was reasonable to think that members of the public may be present.

- **Organisation or group involvement:** the suspect was involved in an organisation or group, a purpose of which is to provide a physical environment (whether for payment or not) in which to allow another to commit suicide.[1]

Conversely, a prosecution would be less likely, in summary, as follows:

- **Clear decision:** the victim had reached a voluntary, clear, settled and informed decision to commit suicide.

- **Compassion:** the suspect was wholly motivated by compassion.

- **Minor assistance:** the actions of the suspect, although sufficient to come within the definition of the offence, were of only minor encouragement or assistance.

- **Dissuasion:** the suspect had sought to dissuade the victim from taking the course of action which resulted in his or her suicide.

- **Reluctance:** the actions of the suspect may be characterised as reluctant encouragement or assistance in the face of a determined wish on the part of the victim to commit suicide.

- **Reporting to police:** the suspect reported the victim's suicide to the police and fully assisted them in their enquiries into the circumstances of the suicide or the attempt and his or her part in providing encouragement or assistance.[2]

ASSISTED SUICIDE: FEW PROSECUTIONS. The courts have continued to find the legislation, supported by these guidelines, consistent with human

---

1   Director of Public Prosecutions. *Policy for Prosecutors in Respect of Cases of Encouraging or Assisting Suicide*, 2010.

2   Director of Public Prosecutions. *Policy for Prosecutors in Respect of Cases of Encouraging or Assisting Suicide*, 2010.

rights, stating that any change in the law would be for Parliament rather than the courts. And they have noted that, in any case, there are few prosecutions.[1] It was reported that between 2009 and 2018 there were 138 cases referred to the Crown Prosecution Service by the police and recorded as assisted suicide, but only three prosecutions.[2]

> **Nurse taking her 93-year-old father to Dignitas not prosecuted.** A 66-year-old former nurse took her 93-year-old father to Dignitas in order for him to die. Seven months later, the Crown Prosecution Service confirmed she would not be prosecuted. She spent £15,000 on arranging this. The police had been very supportive, as had the local community and social media. The father was a veteran of the South Wales Borderers and served in the Parachute Regiment of the British Army. During World War Two he fought in Italy, Algeria, Tunisia, France, Greece, Palestine and Egypt. His health had declined following the death of his wife in 2011.[3]

Even a successful prosecution may not result in a heavy sentence, depending on the case.

> **Helping wife with multiple sclerosis commit suicide.** A man helped his wife commit suicide. She had already tried to commit suicide twice before. One day he came home from work. She had left a note saying she had taken 175 valium tablets. She was still alive but had a plastic bag over her face. He tightened the bag, rather than see another failed suicide attempt – she had blamed him for the previous failures. He was sentenced to nine months in prison suspended for a year and had to do 50 hours of unpaid work. He was otherwise entirely of good character and no risk to the community.[4]

---

1   *R (Conway) v Secretary of State for Justice, and Crown Prosecution Service* [2017] EWHC 640 (Admin).

2   Crisp, W. 'Daughter who took her father to Dignitas speaks of relief as CPS finally announces she will not face charges.' *Daily Telegraph*, 15 June 2018.

3   Crisp, W. 'Daughter who took her father to Dignitas speaks of relief as CPS finally announces she will not face charges.' *Daily Telegraph*, 15 June 2018.

4   Cumming, J. 'Man aided his ailing wife's suicide.' *The Scotsman*, 15 September 2006.

B

Barred list

Under the Safeguarding and Vulnerable Groups Act 2006, the Disclosure and Barring Service (DBS) – formerly the Independent Safeguarding Authority (ISA) – maintains two barred lists: one in respect of working with adults in regulated activity, the other in respect of working with children.[1] If a person is placed on either barred list (or on both), then he or she is unable, lawfully, to work in regulated activity with adults or children (or both). The rules and issues are dealt with below under the following headings:

- Barred list: proportionality of rules and background

- Barred list: for adults, key points

- Barred list: placing people on the list

- Barred list: length of bar and review

- Barred list: appeals against inclusion

- Barred list: appeals and error of fact or law

- Barred list: pattern of referrals

- Barred list: misuse of the barring system by employers

- Barred list: balancing the duty to suspend, dismiss and refer – with the principle of good faith in employment contracts.

---

1   These lists replaced two previous lists: the POVA (Protection of Vulnerable Adults) and POCA (Protection of Children Act) lists, held by the Secretary of State.

BARRED LIST: PROPORTIONALITY OF RULES AND BACKGROUND.

Central government has struggled to formulate legal criteria for barring that strike the right balance between protecting vulnerable adults (and children) and treating workers fairly. Workers are placed on what is called a barred list by the Disclosure and Barring Service (DBS), on various grounds, ultimately on the ground that they would pose a risk to vulnerable adults.

Under the forerunner of this scheme (operated by the Independent Safeguarding Authority), many Tribunal cases were heard on appeal, in which the Tribunal considered fact, evidence, law, reasoning and ultimately a fair 'merits'-based outcome for the worker. There are now fewer such appeals, because central government changed the law, reducing the grounds on which appeals can be made to mistakes of fact or law only, but not to fairness or the merits of a barring decision.

Overall, this could be regarded as a retrospect step since poor decision-making by the DBS is now more difficult to challenge. And, in a system of health and social care, which is underfunded, with significant numbers of poorly paid and non-professional trained staff caring for people with complex needs, those staff need a degree of protection when the apparent neglect or abuse of which they are accused is sometimes more closely linked to systemic failures within organisations than to individual failings.

The importance of protecting vulnerable adults is counter-balanced, therefore, by the seriousness of draconian and excessive barring practice, not only in terms of loss of employment but also in terms of stigma:

- **Effect of being barred.** The scope of the ban is very wide. The ban is also likely to have an effect in practice going beyond its effect in law. Even though the lists are not made public, the fact is likely to get about and the stigma will be considerable. The scheme must therefore be devised in such a way as to prevent possible breaches of the article 8 rights (respect for private life).[1]

BARRED LIST: FOR ADULTS, KEY POINTS. In summary, key points about the barred list for adults are as follows:

---

1   *R (on the application of Wright and others) v Secretary of State for Health and another* [2009] UKHL 3.

- **Barred list for adults.** The barred list is underpinned by the Safeguarding Vulnerable Groups Act 2006 (SVGA) and associated regulations. Inclusion on the list means that a person is prohibited from working with vulnerable adults. The 2006 Act applies to England and Wales and, by extension, to Northern Ireland. It does not apply to Scotland. However, it contains a provision, in section 54, to give effect to the corresponding Scottish legislation, the Protection of Vulnerable Groups (Scotland) Act 2007. The latter has an equivalent provision, in section 87, to give effect in Scotland to the 2006 Act.

- **Information about a person held on the barred list.** Regulations prescribe the information about a person which is to be held on the barred list. The information includes, for example, any alternative names and aliases, address, information submitted by the individual in any monitoring application, information relevant to the barring decision, information from relevant registers (kept by a professional body) or supervisory authorities (regulatory body such as the Care Quality Commission), relevant police information provided to the DBS, reasons for barring, information (including representations from the individual) relevant to any subsequent appeal or review, the outcome of any such appeal or review.[1]

- **Offence of working if on the barred list.** It is an offence for a barred person to seek to, to offer to or actually to engage in regulated activity. The offence carries a maximum sentence of five years in prison. There are two main defences: the person could not reasonably have known that he or she was on the barred list or the person thought it was necessary to engage in that activity to prevent harm to a vulnerable adult.[2]

- **Duty of providers to check.** Regulated activity providers have a duty to check whether a person is barred, before they permit a person to engage in regulated activity. Likewise, personnel suppliers. The duty to check is discharged if the provider has (a) obtained information as to whether the person is barred from the DBS, or (b) obtained an enhanced criminal record certificate (under the Police Act 1997, which will indicate whether a person is

---

1   SI 2008/16. The Safeguarding Vulnerable Groups Act 2006 (Barred List Prescribed Information) Regulations 2008.

2   Safeguarding Vulnerable Groups Act 2006, s.7.

barred), or (c) checked such a certificate and received up-to-date information about it under section 116A of the Police Act.[1]

It is an offence for a person to allow an individual barred from regulated activity to engage in that activity, if the person knows or has reason to believe the individual is barred – and if the individual engages in the activity. The maximum penalty is five years in prison. There are defences based on lack of knowledge or on necessity to prevent harm.[2]

- **Duty of providers to refer to DBS.** Regulated activity providers have a duty to provide information to the DBS. The duty is triggered if the provider or person has withdrawn permission for the individual to engage in regulated activity or would have done so if the individual had not already ceased to engage in that activity. This must have been because the provider (a) thinks the person falls into the category of person where placing on the barring list is automatic, or (b) the person has engaged in 'relevant conduct'.

Alternatively, the reason could be that the 'harm test' is satisfied in relation to the individual. The harm test is that the individual may harm a child or vulnerable adult, cause a child or vulnerable adult to be harmed, put a child or vulnerable adult at risk of harm, attempt to harm a child or vulnerable adult, or incite another to harm a child or vulnerable adult.

A comparable duty applies to personnel suppliers.[3]

- **Definition of vulnerable adult.** A vulnerable adult is defined as being 18 years or more and means any person 'to whom an activity which is a regulated activity relating to vulnerable adults…is provided'.[4]

- **Family or personal relationships.** The Act does not apply to activity carried out in the course of a family or personal relationship.[5]

- **Regulated activity provider.** A regulated activity provider is defined as a person responsible for the management or control of a regulated activity. An organisation running an adult placement scheme counts as a regulated

---

1 Safeguarding Vulnerable Groups Act 2006, s.34ZA.

2 Safeguarding Vulnerable Groups Act 2006, s.9.

3 Safeguarding Vulnerable Groups Act 2006, ss.35–36.

4 Safeguarding Vulnerable Groups Act 2006, s.60.

5 Safeguarding Vulnerable Groups Act 2006, s.58.

activity provider, if there is a requirement to register under section 10 of the Health and Social Care Act 2008.

However, a person is not defined as a regulated activity provider if he or she is an individual and the arrangements made are private arrangements. The arrangements are private if the regulated activity is for the person himself or herself; likewise, if they are for a vulnerable adult who is a member of the person's family or a friend of the person.[1]

The recipient of a direct payment, under the Care Act 2014, is not a regulated activity provider for the purposes of the Act. However, if that recipient receives a direct payment on behalf of a person lacking capacity, and the recipient is not a close relative or friend of the person, then that person does count as regulated activity provider.[2]

- **Definition of regulated activity.** Includes provision of health care, personal care, social work, assistance with household matters needed because of age, illness or disability (managing cash, bills, shopping), relevant assistance in the conduct of an adult's own affairs (in relation to various functions under the Mental Capacity Act 2005), conveyance (travel) as prescribed where need is due to age, illness or disability.[3]

- **Sharing information between organisations.** A detailed set of provisions governs information disclosure, obliging or permitting various bodies and the ISA to share information. These include, broadly, the DBS obtaining information from, and providing information for, the police; regulated activity providers providing information to the DBS (and committing an offence if they fail to do so without reasonable excuse); local authorities referring individuals to the DBS, and the latter obtaining information from local authorities; various professional bodies providing information for the DBS, and vice versa, and likewise the Care Quality Commission.[4]

- **Liability for mistakes.** No claims for damages are possible in respect of an individual being included, or not included, on a barred list, or in respect of

1   Safeguarding Vulnerable Groups Act 2006, s.6.

2   Department of Health. *Guidance on direct payments for community care, services for carers and children's services, England 2009.* London: DH, 2009, para 154 (guidance prior to the Care Act, but which presumably still applies, on this point).

3   Safeguarding Vulnerable Groups Act 2006, s.5, schedule 4(7).

4   Safeguarding Vulnerable Groups Act 2006, ss.39–50A.

the provision of information – unless the provider knew the information was untrue. However, this does not affect the power of the courts to award damages under the Human Rights Act 1998 against a public authority.[1]

BARRED LIST: PLACING PEOPLE ON THE LIST. The DBS places an individual on the barred list in four main ways. Apart from the first category outlined below, the individual has the right to make representations – a right included in the legislation because of previous legal case law.[2]

- **Automatic barring with no representations allowed.** First, if certain prescribed criteria – relating to particular criminal offences – apply to the individual, barring by the DBS is automatic, without the right to make representations.[3] Regulations stipulate that the offences in this category are those sexual offences contained in sections 30–41 of the Sexual Offences Act 2003, involving victims with a mental disorder.[4]

- **Automatic barring: but representations allowed before person is placed on list.** Second, if certain other prescribed criteria apply, the person will be in line for barring. But only if the criteria apply for barring under this section, namely, certain convictions or cautions – and if the person has been or might in future be engaged in regulated activity with vulnerable adults. The DBS must then give the person the opportunity to make representations within a prescribed time.

  If representations are not received within a set period of time, then the person will be added to the list. If representations are received in time, then the DBS must place the person on the barred list but only if: (a) it is satisfied that the criteria (certain convictions or cautions) apply; (b) it has reason to believe that the person is or has been or might in future be engaged in regulated activity

---

1   Safeguarding Vulnerable Groups Act 2006, s.57.

2   See e.g. *R (Wright) v Secretary of State for Health* [2006] EWHC 2886 (Admin) (High Court); [2007] EWCA 999 Civ (Court of Appeal), involving a psychiatric nurse who had previously won awards for excellence and innovation in dementia care. Also: *R (Royal College of Nursing) v Secretary of State for the Home Department and the Independent Safeguarding Authority* [2010] EWHC 2761 (Admin).

3   Safeguarding Vulnerable Groups Act 2006, schedule 3, para 7.

4   SI 2009/37. The Safeguarding Vulnerable Groups Act 2006 (Prescribed Criteria and Miscellaneous Provisions) Regulations 2009.

relating to vulnerable adults; and (c) it is satisfied that it is appropriate to include the person in the adults' barred list.[1]

Regulations state that a person comes under this category where a person is the subject of a risk of sexual harm order under the Sexual Offences Act 2003 or the Protection of Children and Prevention of Sexual Offences (Scotland) Act 2005 – or has been convicted of, or cautioned in relation to, a specified offence.

Specified offences include, for example, murder, kidnapping, false imprisonment, infanticide, rape, a range of other sexual offences, offences against the person, ill-treatment or wilful neglect, causing or allowing the death of a vulnerable adult.[2]

- **Barring, relevant conduct and representations.** Third, if it appears to the DBS that the person has engaged in 'relevant conduct' and it proposes to include the individual on the list, it must give the person the opportunity to make representations as to why he or she should not be included.

  If the DBS is satisfied that the person has engaged in the relevant conduct, and it appears to the DBS that it is appropriate to include him or her on the list, then it must do so. But only if, in addition, it has reason to believe that the person is or has been, or might in future be, engaged in regulated activity relating to vulnerable adults.

  Relevant conduct is conduct, in summary: (a) conduct which endangers a vulnerable adult or is likely to endanger a vulnerable adult; (b) conduct which, if repeated against or in relation to a vulnerable adult, would endanger that adult or would be likely to endanger him; (c) conduct involving sexual material relating to children (including possession of such material); (d) conduct involving sexually explicit images depicting violence against human beings (including possession of such images), if it appears to the DBS that the conduct is inappropriate; (e) conduct of a sexual nature involving a vulnerable adult, if it appears to the DBS that the conduct is inappropriate.

---

1   Safeguarding Vulnerable Groups Act 2006, schedule 3, para 8, as amended by s.67 of the Protection of Freedoms Act 2012.

2   SI 2009/37. The Safeguarding Vulnerable Groups Act 2006 (Prescribed Criteria and Miscellaneous Provisions) Regulations 2009.

Endangering a vulnerable adult occurs when the worker harms, causes to be harmed, puts at risk of harm, attempts to harm, or incites somebody else to harm a vulnerable adult.[1]

Relevant conduct. A nurse was placed on the barred list for (a) pinching the nipples of patients and (b) being stern and authoritarian. The Upper Tribunal held that, as a matter of law, the latter would not normally amount to 'relevant conduct' – but could do. The question was whether his behaviour intimidated patients or put them in fear. In this case, there was sufficient evidence that it did intimidate and fell within 'relevant conduct'.[2]

- **Barring, risk of doing harm and representations.** Fourth, and last, is the 'risk of harm' test. If it appears to the DBS that a person may harm a vulnerable adult, cause a vulnerable adult to be harmed, put a vulnerable adult at risk of harm, attempt to harm a vulnerable adult or incite another person to harm a vulnerable adult, then the DBS must give the person an opportunity to make representations as to why he or she should not be barred. If it appears appropriate to include the person on the barred list, the DBS must do so. But only if it has reason to believe that the person is or has been, or might in future be, engaged in regulated activity relating to vulnerable adults.[3]

BARRED LIST: LENGTH OF BAR AND REVIEW. Regulations set out minimum periods of barring to be applied to people on the barred list. The minimum barring period is one year for a person under 18, five years for a person aged between 18 and 25, and ten years for those 25 or over. The regulations also govern how much time must elapse before the person can seek a review. Generally, the period is one year for people under 18, five years for people aged between 18 and 25, and ten years in any other case.[4]

In addition, the DBS can exercise a discretion at any time to review. However, it must be satisfied that it is not appropriate for the person to be

---

1   Safeguarding Vulnerable Groups Act 2006, schedule 3, para 10.

2   *KS v Information Safeguarding Authority* [2011] UKUT 426 (AAC).

3   Safeguarding Vulnerable Groups Act 2006, schedule 3, para 11.

4   SI 2008/474. The Safeguarding Vulnerable Groups Act 2006 (Barring Procedure) Regulations 2008.

included in the list, in the light of (a) information which it did not have at the time of the person's inclusion in the list, (b) any change of circumstances relating to the person concerned or (c) any error by the DBS.[1]

BARRED LIST: APPEALS AGAINST INCLUSION. Appeals lie to the Upper Tribunal against the decision of the DBS to include a person on the list or not to remove him or her from the list.

Appeals to the Tribunal can be made only on the ground that a mistake has been made on a point of law or on a finding of fact. However, the decision made by the DBS as to whether it is 'appropriate' to bar a person is a question of neither law nor fact, and so cannot in principle be appealed to the Tribunal. If the Tribunal finds no mistake of fact or law, then it must confirm the DBS decision. Appeals can only be made with permission of the Tribunal.

Beyond the Tribunal, an appeal to the Court of Appeal on a point of law may be made, with that Court's permission.[2] These grounds of appeal are narrower than used to be the case, under previous comparable legislation in the form of the Care Standards Act 2000. Nonetheless, unreasonableness, irrationality or disproportionality can sometimes be regarded as a matter of law – thereby giving the Tribunal some room for challenging the judgement of the DBS. The following represent key points about what the Tribunal can or can't consider:

- **Mistake on point of law or finding of fact only.** An appeal can only be made to the Tribunal on a point of law or fact.[3]

- **No appeal on whether it is appropriate to bar.** The DBS decision overall is whether it is appropriate that a person be barred: this is not a point of law or fact. A direct challenge to the appropriateness of the barring decision is therefore not possible.[4]

---

1   Safeguarding Vulnerable Groups Act 2006, s.18A, as amended by s.71 of the Protection of Freedoms Act 2012.

2   Safeguarding Vulnerable Groups Act 2006, s.4.

3   Safeguarding Vulnerable Groups Act 2006, s.4.

4   *R (Royal College of Nursing) v Secretary of State for the Home Department and the Independent Safeguarding Authority* [2010] EWHC 2761 (Admin).

- **Tribunal cannot decide on appropriateness even after successful appeal on law or fact.** The Court of Appeal has held that even if an appeal is successful on a point of law or fact, the Tribunal cannot go on to decide the question of whether it is appropriate that the person be barred or not. This remains for the DBS to decide.[1]

- **Unreasonableness, irrationality and disproportionality.** These are concepts that are part of public law in terms of traditional judicial review and human rights. The question of whether it is appropriate to bar somebody on the facts could involve consideration of whether a proportionate response to those facts should be barring. The courts have therefore held that an appeal would not be precluded on such grounds.[2]

- **Irrationality, perversity.** The Tribunal can interfere with DBS decisions on these grounds, where an overwhelming case is made out that the Tribunal reached a decision which no reasonable tribunal, on a proper appreciation of the evidence and the law, would have reached.[3]

- **Weighing of facts and proportionality.** Once proportionality comes into the picture, then the Tribunal is able, as a matter of law, to question the weight which the DBS has given to certain facts about the case, even if there is no dispute about the bare facts themselves.

  However, the Tribunal will not consider whether it would have reached the same decision as the DBS – only whether the evidence available to the decision-maker, the DBS, could justify the decision it took. If not, the decision would be disproportionate and therefore be an error of law.[4]

- **Oral hearings.** The legislation does not demand that the DBS grant oral hearings to those it is minded to bar; equally, this is not prohibited. However, the Tribunal has also noted the High Court's view that a failure or refusal to conduct an oral hearing in circumstances which would allow of an argument that the failure or refusal was unreasonable or irrational would itself raise the

---

1   *SB v Independent Safeguarding Authority* [2012] EWCA Civ 977, appearing to contradict an earlier Tribunal decision: *VT v Information Safeguarding Authority* [2011] UKUT 427 (AAC).

2   *R (Royal College of Nursing) v Secretary of State for the Home Department and the Independent Safeguarding Authority* [2010] EWHC 2761 (Admin).

3   *XY v Independent Safeguarding Authority* [2011] UKUT 289 (AAC).

4   *SB v Independent Safeguarding Authority* [2011] UKUT 404 (AAC).

prospect of an appeal to the Upper Tribunal on a point of law.[1] Thus, whilst the Tribunal has accepted that there is no automatic right to an oral hearing, it encourages the DBS to consider the circumstances in which it would be appropriate to hold an oral hearing. There may well be circumstances in which the common law duty of procedural fairness may point to the need for an oral hearing.[2] (The Tribunal noted in 2011 that so far the ISA had granted no oral hearings at all, in a single case.[3] The Court of Appeal, in 2012, noted that the ISA seemed to have a policy of granting no oral hearings at all, but made no comment on legal soundness of the policy.[4])

- **Standard of proof.** Proceedings before the DBS and the Upper Tribunal are civil in nature. The standard of proof is therefore not the high (beyond reasonable doubt) level applied in criminal proceedings. The Tribunal has pointed out that the DBS is an independent public body that accepts referrals from employers and other bodies which 'think' that an individual has engaged in 'relevant conduct', or poses a risk of harm, and which then makes factual findings in the context of an overall assessment as to future risk. In that context, formal legal notions such as the 'burden of proof' may not be apposite.[5] Therefore: 'a criminal prosecution may not succeed, for any number of reasons, but there may still be sufficient evidence to conclude on the balance of probabilities that the alleged abuser has engaged in "relevant conduct" with children and should be prevented from working with children'.[6]

BARRED LIST: APPEALS AND ERROR OF FACT OR LAW. The following are summaries of a number of cases in which the Tribunal considered whether to interfere with a decision of the DBS (or its predecessor, the Independent Safeguarding Authority) on a question of law or fact.

---

1   *R (Royal College of Nursing) v Secretary of State for the Home Department and the Independent Safeguarding Authority* [2010] EWHC 2761 (Admin).

2   *XY v Independent Safeguarding Authority* [2011] UKUT 289 (AAC).

3   *SB v Independent Safeguarding Authority* [2011] UKUT 404 (AAC).

4   *SB v Independent Safeguarding Authority* [2012] EWCA Civ 977.

5   *XY v Independent Safeguarding Authority* [2011] UKUT 289 (AAC).

6   *XY v Independent Safeguarding Authority* [2011] UKUT 289 (AAC).

Misconstruing a doctor's report: proportionality and error of law. The matter of proportionality arose as a matter of law, in a case involving a school teacher who, under some stress, had assaulted a pupil in the classroom – an obviously excessive response to abuse, misbehaviour and rank disobedience. He was convicted in the Crown Court and given a community service order, having already spent eight months on remand. He was placed on the children's barred list but also on the adults' barred list. It was the latter against which he appealed.

The Upper Tribunal found in his favour on the grounds of disproportionality. The ISA had misconstrued a doctor's report that had referred to certain safeguards which would mean the risks posed by the teacher would be low. The ISA had nonetheless barred him absolutely. This was disproportionate and therefore an error of law.[1]

Decision letter from the DBS – and error of law. If the DBS writes a decision letter, which appears to indicate an error of law, the Tribunal will look at the substance of the decision lying behind the letter – before deciding whether the letter represents a true error of law.

For example, when a music teacher was sent a barring letter, it stated that the ISA did not find 'that the evidence provided by you in your representations is sufficient to disprove the allegations made against you'. Had this been a true reflection of the ISA's decision-making, it would have been an error of law, because it would have been a reversal of the burden of proof.[2]

In the same vein, unhelpfully brief decision letters might fail to reflect the more complex decision that has taken place, and so be criticised by the Tribunal; but nonetheless it remains the substance of the decision which must be examined.[3]

Considering relevant information (probation report): point of law. A failure to obtain and to consider relevant information can amount to an error of law. In one case the ISA failed to make efforts to get hold of an up-to-date Probation Service report. The ISA claimed that it was not 'charged with an investigative function'. The Tribunal disagreed, quoting from the ISA's

---

1   *PH v Independent Safeguarding Authority* [2012] UKUT 91 (AAC).

2   *XY v Independent Safeguarding Authority* [2011] UKUT 289 (AAC).

3   *VW v Independent Safeguarding Authority* [2011] UKUT 435 (AAC).

own guidance for its staff: 'The second stage is information gathering. The ISA considers all the facts it has on the case and may seek additional material from a range of other sources to ensure it has all known relevant information.' The Tribunal went on to say the guidance was 'unsurprising and accurate as a statement of law'.[1]

Furthermore, the failure to obtain the Probation Service report meant that a conflict of evidence was not solved, and irrational weight was given to a police report which, far from containing facts, in substantial measure comprised non-factual material.[2]

Reaching conclusion not supported by the evidence (testimonials): error of fact and law. The DBS might make material errors of fact and law in one and the same breath. For instance, in considering testimonials put forward on a person's behalf in one case, the ISA had given them little weight. This was partly on the basis that of seven testimonial writers, the ISA concluded that only two were aware of the person's criminal conviction. In fact, at least three had stated explicitly their awareness, and awareness could be inferred in the other four. The Tribunal noted that the ISA had made a mistake as to the facts – but also an error of law, since it had adopted a position open to no reasonable decision-maker on the evidence before it.[3]

Not putting information to the person: error of law. Failing to put certain material to the person, resulting in a mistaken view of the facts, might also be a material error of law. For instance, information relied on by the ISA stated the person was seeking a job involving contact with children. This point was not put to the person. In fact, the sports organisation involved provided a letter (to the Tribunal) stating that the work would have involved largely adults and that in any case no trainees were allowed to work unsupervised.[4]

DBS not following its own guidance: error of law. In one case, the ISA had barred a person without following the procedures about taking certain cases to line management and the ISA Board, in its own structured judgement procedure (SJP) to be used by staff. The guidance was that normally a

1   *VW v Independent Safeguarding Authority* [2011] UKUT 435 (AAC).

2   *VW v Independent Safeguarding Authority* [2011] UKUT 435 (AAC).

3   *VW v Independent Safeguarding Authority* [2011] UKUT 435 (AAC).

4   *VW v Independent Safeguarding Authority* [2011] UKUT 435 (AAC).

decision to bar would require definite concerns across at least two areas of the SJP. In the absence of such a profile, the decision to bar could be maintained but only if the case was taken to line management and then to the Board for a final decision. In the particular case, the case was not escalated to the Board as required and no adequate explanation was given for that departure from published guidance. This amounted to a clear error of law on the part of ISA.[1]

Public confidence but not giving in to the baying of the mob. The Tribunal has acknowledged the relevance, albeit limited, of public confidence to decisions to bar. In one case, given that the Tribunal found that the person did not represent a risk of harm to children, the only possible reason for maintaining his inclusion on the list was public confidence. The Tribunal stated that public confidence could play a supportive role in marginal barring decisions but rarely and highly exceptionally would be the main factor.[2] The Court of Appeal has held, however, that whilst public confidence is not an inevitable trump card, nonetheless it must be placed in the scales, without giving in to the 'baying of the mob', when consideration is being given to the personal characteristics and interests of an appellant.[3] It approved the approach outlined in a previous case, which recognised the vital importance of public confidence, without giving in to the baying of the mob.[4]

BARRED LIST: PATTERN OF REFERRALS. Under a previous system of barring, involving a Protection of Vulnerable Adults (POVA) list, a significant number of people appealed to the Care Standards Tribunal against their inclusion on the list.

The important distinction to bear in mind is that – as outlined above – the Upper Tribunal's remit now is more circumscribed than that of the former Care Standards Tribunal. This means that the following examples are not a precise guide to the bringing, or success, of appeals under the current

---

1   *VT v Information Safeguarding Authority* [2011] UKUT 427 (AAC).

2   *VT v Information Safeguarding Authority* [2011] UKUT 427 (AAC).

3   *SB v Independent Safeguarding Authority* [2012] EWCA Civ 977.

4   *Secretary of State for Children v BP* [2009] EWHC 866 (Admin).

scheme. Nonetheless, some of these cases remain a useful guide as to the sort of matter that is likely to come before the DBS under the new system of barring. In the following cases, for example, the appeals failed.

> **Stealing money from 88-year-old resident in flat:** care worker admitting this, 'put her hands up' to it, walked out on her job, paid the lady back, did some community service and hung her head in shame for years.[1]
>
> **Care worker with mental health problems:** stealing money, returning it, expressing deep regret, but might do it again.[2]
>
> **Care worker fraudulently obtaining cheque from service user:** claiming her spectacles had been lost and money needed to buy new ones.[3]
>
> **Former doctor, photographs:** taking of objectively obscene photographs of elderly residents by a care worker, apparently formerly a medical doctor – compounded by disingenuousness and the fact that he was an intelligent man with professional medical training.[4]
>
> **Leaving resident heavily soiled and wet:** senior care worker failing to check during the night according to the care plan for double incontinence.[5]
>
> **Bending back the thumbs of residents:** premeditated actions against elderly, mentally ill residents.[6]
>
> **Force-feeding by senior care worker:** trying to force food into residents' mouths.[7]
>
> **Care worker, catalogue of mistreatment of people with learning disabilities:** sleeping on duty, taunting residents, flicking water at them, distressing residents.[8]

---

1   *DG v Secretary of State* [2006] 824 PVA.

2   *SM v Secretary of State* [2007] 1006 PVA.

3   *Nkala v Secretary of State for Health* [2007] 1015 PVA.

4   *Kalchev v Secretary of State for Education and Skills* [2005] 589 PVA/590 PC.

5   *Kostadinov v Secretary of State for Health* [2008] 1418 PVA.

6   *Mwaura v Secretary of State for Health* [2006] 687 PVA/688 PC.

7   *Jackson v Secretary of State for Health* [2005] 623 PVA/624 PC.

8   *Close v Secretary of State for Health* [2006] 852 PVA.

Care worker, striking after being spat at: a domiciliary support worker had, in his own words, 'lost it' when a man with challenging behaviour struck out and spat at the worker in the shower.[1]

Dragging 20-stone resident across the floor: a senior care worker in a care home had manoeuvred across a fallen resident, weighing 20 stone, by holding and pulling his underpants.[2]

Controlled drugs: poor management and incorrect administration by a registered mental health nurse.[3]

Domiciliary care worker crossing the line between paid carer and friend: risk of financial harm, but not barred, because was caring person and had little training, no supervision and no management.[4]

Multiple failings in care: involving a registered mental health nurse acting as care home manager – including (a) lack of staff supervision, monitoring and training; (b) failure to check staff references; (c) failure to keep service user files up to date with relevant information; (d) failure to provide adequate wound care and pressure sore care; (e) failure to monitor the weight of residents; and (f) failure to provide adequate care and neglecting residents.[5]

BARRED LIST: MISUSE OF THE BARRING SYSTEM BY EMPLOYERS.

An employer might make a referral to the DBS for all the wrong reasons, in order to victimise a member of staff who has whistleblown to the regulator about poor practice.

Employer victimising worker by making unwarranted referral. A Somerset care worker was employed at the Moorlands care home in 2008. The employer sacked the care worker. She went to an Employment Tribunal and won; the employer then referred her to the Independent Safeguarding

---

1   *SP v Secretary of State* [2006] 725 PVA/726 PC.

2   *Del Mundo v Secretary of State for Health* [2005] 557 PVA/558 PC.

3   *EK v Secretary of State* [2006] 0716 PVA/0717 PC.

4   *Mrs P v Secretary of State for Education and Skills* [2005] 562 PVA/563 PC.

5   *JF v Secretary of State* [2005] 591 PVA/592 PC.

Authority (ISA) to try to get her banned from working in the care sector. A further Tribunal found that 'the giving of the anonymous information and then the formal referral were malicious and an attempt to get back at the claimant with the respondent believing that it would never come to light that it was him because of data protection'. The care worker succeeded in gaining further damages for this ill-founded disclosure to the ISA.[1]

BARRED LIST: BALANCING THE DUTY TO SUSPEND, DISMISS AND REFER – WITH THE PRINCIPLE OF GOOD FAITH IN EMPLOYMENT CONTRACTS. More generally, when suspending and dismissing employees (and then coming under a duty to refer to the DBS), employers should bear in mind the implied duty and principle of good faith in employment contracts.

Court of Appeal warning management against kneejerk reactions in case of two nurses accused of restraint. In 2012, the Court of Appeal heard a case in which it found that an NHS Trust had overreacted to a restraint issue, in respect of two nurses with long, unblemished work records, whom it had suspended and then dismissed. It referred to the duty of trust and confidence an employer has towards an employee, and noted that kneejerk reactions by management, through over-eager suspension and dismissal, breach this duty.[2]

The Court of Appeal had referred to an older case, which had analysed the potential human and legal consequences of what the court characterised as an overreaction – leading to breach of the principle of good faith in employment contracts and to financial compensation payable for psychiatric personal injury to the member of staff concerned who had effectively been wrongly accused of abuse.

Premature suspension of social worker, employer thereby breaching employment contract. A residential social worker was suspended following potential allegations made by a child with learning and communication

---

1   'Somerset care home worker wins further damages.' *BBC News*, 30 May 2012. Accessed on 13 August 2012 at: www.bbc.co.uk/news/uk-england-somerset-18264272.

2   *Crawford v Suffolk Mental Health Partnership NHS Trust* [2012] EWCA Civ 138.

difficulties. Following a 'strategy meeting', a decision was taken to hold an investigation under section 47 of the Children Act 1989.

The investigation concluded that the child had never disclosed any abuse in relation to any member of staff, and while in therapy had never said anything that could be construed as an allegation of abuse. The social worker was immediately reinstated; but by then she was ill and had by and large not worked since the suspension. She claimed loss of earnings and damages for personal injury caused by breach of contract; she now suffered from clinical depression caused by the suspension.

Suspension of member of staff must be reasonable and proper. The court held that it was quite proper for the local authority to investigate and make inquiries; but it did not necessarily follow that a member of staff, who may have been implicated in the risk to the vulnerable person, had to be suspended. The question should be whether, in the individual circumstances, it was reasonable and proper to do so. The court thought not. The strategy meeting had itself recognised that the information was 'difficult to evaluate', and to describe it as an allegation of abuse was putting it 'far too high'.

Kneejerk reaction damaging relationship of trust and confidence with employee. The court also asked whether there were no other alternatives, such as a short period of leave or a transfer to other useful work. It noted that employers owe duties to their long-serving staff, and defensive management responses which focus solely on their own interests do them little credit. Instead, there had been a 'kneejerk' reaction. The local authority had seriously damaged the relationship of trust and confidence between employee and employer – a relationship implied into contracts of employment. The claimant was entitled to damages.[1]

Best evidence, see *Witnesses*

Best interests, see *Mental capacity*

---

1   *Gogay v Hertfordshire County Council* (2001) 1 FLR 280 (Court of Appeal).

Brexit

The United Kingdom leaving the European Union will not *directly* affect the application of the European Convention on Human Rights to domestic law.[1]

Burglary

The offence of burglary comes under section 9 of the Theft Act 1968 and involves (a) a person entering a building as a trespasser with the intention of stealing or inflicting grievous bodily harm or doing unlawful damage; and (b) having entered a building, the person steals or attempts to steal something or inflicts or attempts to inflict grievous bodily harm.

Burglars sometimes specifically target vulnerable people, as the following examples illustrate.

> **Gaining trust of elderly person: then combining burglary, theft and fraud.** A woman was sentenced to 28 months in prison for burglary, theft and fraud by false representation. First, she stole the purse of an 84-year-old woman at a bingo hall. Then she returned the purse, after using the victim's bank card. She subsequently gained the trust of the elderly woman. On one occasion she stole the house keys, using them to enter the house and steal the replacement bank card. She later attempted to withdraw cash from the victim's account by claiming to be a co-signatory. She stole a total of £800 from the victim. She had presented herself as a Good Samaritan but was in fact manipulating the victim.[2]
>
> **Burgling 600 homes of elderly people, particularly the blind, deaf and partially sighted.** One burglar raided 600 homes within 18 months and travelled hundreds of miles in order to steal £267,000 by deceiving vulnerable elderly people, some in their nineties. He posed as a police officer and targeted, in particular, blind, deaf and partially sighted people. Sometimes he would persuade people to give him their valuables to take

---

1   See e.g. Joint Committee on Human Rights. *The human rights implications of Brexit.* London: House of Commons, House of Lords, 2017.

2   Merseyside Police, 'Sentencing of Kayleigh Teare for fraud, burglary and theft.' 26 May 2017. Accessed on 9 February 2018 at: https://merseyside.police.uk/news/latest-news/2017/05/sentencing-of-kayleigh-teare-for-fraud-burglary-and-theft.

to the police station for safekeeping; at other times, he would simply rifle under beds for cash or other valuables. After being caught and admitting burglary by deception, he asked for 587 similar offences to be taken into account. He was jailed for seven years.[1]

Burglars offering to cut hedge of 91-year-old man. Two brothers called at the home of a 91-year-old man, offered to cut his hedge, entered the house, restrained the man, stole his wallet with money, newspaper cuttings of funerals (of his wife, older brother and stepson), documentation for his pacemaker and bank cards – 'exactly the sort of offence which is likely to cause extreme distress to an elderly man'. They were convicted of burglary and sentenced to seven and eight years in prison, given that they had been convicted previously for similar offences of targeting the elderly.[2]

Impersonation of police officer: 93-year-old man the victim. A 22-year-old man impersonated a police officer and entered the home of a 93-year-old man, whom he proceeded to lock in the kitchen. He then stole £140 in cash. The judge was in no doubt that he was targeting elderly people; when the perpetrator stated that he thought the victim was in his sixties rather than his nineties, the judge noted that he was not convinced that 'had he shown you his birth certificate that you would have immediately backed away rather than thinking that you had a sort target in front of you'. The perpetrator had a father involved in crime as a way of life, had been physically abused as a child, left home to live rough with travellers, and had shown remorse. The judge had sentenced him to five years in prison; this was reduced to three and a half years on appeal.[3]

Distraction burglary: 'water board' official. A man claiming to be from the water board gained entry to a house where an elderly woman was living. Claiming to be checking the water, he went upstairs. He stole a watch from her bedroom, and a mobile phone and £200 from her son's room. The offender had been sent to prison previously for the same type of offence. The court stated that burglary of this type 'casts a shadow on the lives

---

1   Bird, S. 'Conman jailed for 600 raids in just 18 months.' *The Times*, 8 February 2003.

2   *R v Cawley* [2007] EWCA Crim 2030.

3   *R v McInerney* [2002] EWCA Crim 3003.

of elderly people: they begin to dread the unexpected knock on the front door'. On appeal, the defendant was sentenced to eight years in prison.[1]

Former care agency carer committing burglary. A home help working for a care agency admitted four charges of burglary. For example, he went to the home of one 75-year-old woman to help her with the cleaning and took £75 from a fruit bowl. He was suspended, he then resigned, but returned to another client unofficially, again to help with cleaning, but took £120 from her purse, and £400 savings in an envelope also went missing.[2]

Burglar masquerading as carer in sheltered housing. A 77-year-old retired lady was watching television in her sheltered accommodation flat. The burglar entered her flat through the unlocked door. She said that the warden had let her in and that she was her care worker. The victim said her daughter was her care worker. The burglar took the victim's bag. The victim tried to take it back. She was struck on the back of the head with a kettle containing hot water. She screamed for help. Her neighbours heard, and the burglar was stopped outside by a group of people.

The perpetrator was sentenced to prison for some nine years. Her appeal failed. The effect on the victim was serious – not just physical hurt but fear, flashbacks, panic attacks. Previously, in 2004, for six almost identical burglaries of vulnerable people in their own homes, she was sentenced to 66 months' imprisonment. Straight away, whilst on licence, she did the same again – five more burglaries of vulnerable people in their own homes. She was sentenced to six years' imprisonment. She had been let out on four days' temporary release on licence when she committed the current offence, which, in contrast to the others, was accompanied by violence.[3]

1   *R v O'Brien* [2002] EWCA Crim 787.

2   Hudson, C. 'Carer stole from patients.' *Macclesfield Express*, 22 November 2006.

3   *R v Collins* [2012] EWCA Crim 1161.

C

Care Act 2014

It is beyond the scope of this book to set out the Care Act in detail. The Act is about adult social care in general, distinguished from health care under the NHS Act 2006. However, it is specifically relevant to adult safeguarding in several ways, through its focus on protecting people from abuse or neglect. In summary:

- **Well-being.** When functioning under the Care Act in respect of an individual, there is a general duty under section 1 to promote the well-being of that individual. The definition of well-being includes protection from abuse and neglect. See *Well-being*.

- **General principles.** In carrying out functions under the Care Act in respect of an individual, a local authority has a duty, also under section 1, to have regard to a number of issues, including the need to protect people from abuse and neglect.

- **Cooperation.** There is a duty, under sections 6 and 7, on defined, statutory services to cooperate with each other, including protecting people with care and support needs from abuse and neglect. See *Cooperation*.

- **Assessment and eligibility.** When assessing the needs of a person (an adult in need or an informal carer) under sections 9 and 10 of the Care Act, a local authority must conclude the assessment with a decision about a person's eligibility for help in meeting their needs. One of the eligibility questions is whether there is a significant impact on the person's well-being, of which one of the elements is defined as protection from abuse or neglect. See *Eligibility*.

- **Refusal of assessment.** Under section 11, if an adult refuses an assessment, the local authority is not required to assess, and the section 9 duty to assess falls away. However, the duty persists in certain circumstances. One of these is if the person lacks mental capacity to take that decision about assessment and the local authority is satisfied the assessment would be in the person's best interests.

Another is if the person – with or without mental capacity – is experiencing, or is at risk of, abuse or neglect. The wording of the section suggests knowledge by the local authority of the abuse or neglect issue – rather than merely reasonable cause to suspect them (as is the case under section 42, in relation to the duty to make safeguarding enquiries).

- **Making enquiries.** If certain conditions are met, a local authority has a duty to make enquiries into abuse or neglect and then to decide what should be done – all under section 42. See *Enquiries*.

- **Safeguarding adults boards.** Local authorities have a duty to set up a local, multi-agency, safeguarding adults board (SAB). A SAB has a duty generally to help and protect adults at risk of abuse or neglect, and a more specific duty, if certain conditions are met, to conduct a safeguarding adults review, when something has ostensibly gone wrong. This is under sections 43 and 44. See *Safeguarding adults boards*.

- **Prisons.** The section 42 duty to make safeguarding enquiries, and the holding of safeguarding adults reviews, are expressly disapplied in the case of prisons under section 76. See *Prisons*.

- **Delegation.** A local authority is precluded, under section 79, from delegating its safeguarding decision-making functions – in relation to the responsibility for making enquiries (or having them made by somebody else) and deciding what should be done as a result of those enquiries – in relation to safeguarding adults boards. However, it appears that this exclusion does not apply in the case of the NHS, to whom these functions could be delegated.[1]

Care and health providers

Health and care providers in England – including NHS hospitals and community health services, care homes and care agencies – are subject to

---

1   SI 2000/617. NHS Bodies and Local Authorities Partnership Arrangements Regulations 2000. Also, Department of Health. *Care and support statutory guidance*. London: DH, 2016, para 18.5.

regulation by the Care Quality Commission (CQC). The CQC applies a test of fundamental standards contained within the Health and Social Care Act (Regulated Activities) Regulations 2014. These include a duty to safeguard service users from abuse, neglect and improper treatment – as well as a range of other duties relating to essential aspects of care and therefore relevant to neglect or abuse. The primary duty of such providers to safeguard service users lies within these regulations, and not the Care Act 2014. For more detail, see *Care Quality Commission*.

Although it is the care provider that is directly accountable under the 2014 regulations, a local authority (or NHS body) should nonetheless avoid an 'out of sight, out of mind' approach. For instance, if a local authority places a person in a care home or with a care agency, and the care provider breaches these regulations, the local ombudsman tends to find fault with the local authority as a matter of course. This is because the ombudsman can investigate what the provider has done (or not done) on behalf of the local authority and thus link the fault of the provider with the local authority[1] – on the straightforward ground, as the ombudsman might typically put it, that the local authority 'remained responsible for Mrs H's care while it funded her placement and…for some poor standards of care and treatment Mrs H received in the home'.[2]

Local authority held responsible for litany of failure by a care home in basic, essential standards of care. The local ombudsman found fault with a local authority, which had placed a woman in a care home, in relation to a range of failings by the home under the Health and Social Care Act (Regulated Activities) Regulations 2014. These included record-keeping (in respect of the risk of falls and of bowel movements), reviewing and reassessing the person's care plan, getting outside help in relation to management of health needs, delay in providing a suitable hospital bed, manual handling equipment and procedures, adequate nutrition and hydration, personal hygiene (hand care, nail care, shaving), communication with the family,

---

1   Local Government Act 1974, s.25(7).

2   LGO, *Nottinghamshire County Council*, 2016 (15 019 148), para 37.

> administration of medication (including pain relief), inappropriate giving of notice to resident to leave care home.[1]

Care Quality Commission

The Care Quality Commission (CQC) is an independent body, whose role under the Health and Social Care Act 2008 is to register, review and investigate health (and social) care providers. Overall, it is about ensuring minimum standards in health and social care and thus is directly relevant to the prevention of abuse or neglect, or to action to be taken when it occurs.

It has the power to issue statutory warning notices, impose, vary or remove registration conditions, issue financial penalty notices, suspend or cancel registration, prosecute specified offences and issue simple cautions. Urgent cancellation orders can be sought from a justice of the peace if there is a serious risk to a person's life, health or well-being. The Commission must carry out periodic reviews of NHS bodies and local authorities. It can conduct special reviews and investigations.[2] It must recommend special measures to the Secretary of State in the case of failing local authorities.[3]

The Commission has powers of entry and inspection and the power to require information, documents and records it considers are necessary or expedient for any of its regulatory functions.[4] The Act places restrictions on the disclosure of personal information which the Commission has obtained, but then provides an extensive list of permitted disclosures.[5]

CARE QUALITY COMMISSION: FUNDAMENTAL STANDARDS, INCLUDING SAFEGUARDING. The CQC regulates providers using a set of regulations setting out minimum or fundamental standards for providers, including hospitals, care homes and care agencies. These are the Health and Social

---

1   LGO, *Kent County Council*, 2016 (15 012 483).

2   Health and Social Care Act 2008, s.46.

3   Health and Social Care Act 2008, s.50.

4   Health and Social Care Act 2008, ss.60–64.

5   Health and Social Care Act 2008, ss.76–80.

Care Act (Regulated Activities) Regulations 2014. Generally relevant to safeguarding are a number of requirements, including the following:

- **Fit and proper person test, individuals or partnerships:** providers (individual or partners of a partnership) must be fit and proper (including good character, health, appropriate criminal record certificate); otherwise the provider must not carry on regulated activity (regulation 4).

- **Fit and proper person test, directors:** a service provider (not applying to partnerships) must not appoint a director unless the director is fit and proper, including that 'the individual has not been responsible for, been privy to, contributed to or facilitated any serious misconduct or mismanagement (whether unlawful or not) in the course of carrying on a regulated activity or providing a service elsewhere which, if provided in England, would be a regulated activity' (regulation 5).

- **Appointments, directors, managers, secretaries:** a service provider (not applying to partnerships) must give the CQC details of anybody they employ as a director, manager or secretary who is responsible for supervising the management of regulated activity, and must take all reasonable steps to ensure that the person is of good character, has the necessary qualifications (and competence, skills, experience), is of sufficient health to do the job, etc. (regulation 6).

- **Fit and proper person test, registered managers:** a person must not manage regulated activity unless they are fit and proper (regulation 7).

- **Person-centred care:** the care and treatment of service users must (a) be appropriate, (b) meet their needs and (c) reflect their preferences (regulation 9).

- **Dignity and respect:** service users must be treated with dignity and respect – including privacy and supporting autonomy, independence and involvement in the community (regulation 10).

- **Consent:** care and treatment of service users must only be provided with the consent of the relevant person – subject to mental capacity considerations and rules under the Mental Capacity Act 2005 (regulation 11).

- **Safe treatment:** care and treatment must be provided in a safe way (regulation 12).

- **Safeguarding:** service users must be safeguarded from abuse and improper treatment (regulation 13).

- **Nutrition and hydration:** people's nutritional and hydration needs must be met (regulation 14).

- **Premises and equipment:** premises and equipment used by the service provider must be (a) clean (including relevant standards of hygiene), (b) secure, (c) suitable for the purpose for which they are being used, (d) properly used, (e) properly maintained and (f) appropriately located for the purpose for which they are being used (regulation 15).

- **Complaints procedure** (regulation 16).

- **Record-keeping:** should be accurate, complete and contemporaneous (regulation 17).

- **Staffing:** there must be sufficient numbers of suitably qualified, competent, skilled and experienced staff (regulation 18).

- **Fit and proper test, staff:** includes that the staff be of good character, have relevant qualifications (and competence, skills, experience), be able – by way of health – to perform required tasks, have a criminal record certificate, etc. (regulation 19).

- **Duty of candour:** the provider must act in an open and transparent way in relation to care and treatment provided to service users in carrying on a regulated activity. As soon as reasonably practicable after becoming aware that a notifiable safety incident has occurred the provider must notify the service user (or person acting lawfully on their behalf) that the incident has occurred and provide reasonable support (regulation 20).

- **Duty of candour, notifiable safety incident (NHS):** this is an unintended or unexpected incident that occurred in respect of a service user during the provision of a regulated activity that, in the reasonable opinion of a health care professional, could result in or appears to have resulted in:

  a. the death of the service user, where the death relates directly to the incident rather than to the natural course of the service user's illness or underlying condition, or

b. severe harm, moderate harm or prolonged psychological harm to the service user. (regulation 20)

- **Duty of candour, notifiable safety incident (other provider):** this is an unintended or unexpected incident that occurred in respect of a service user during the provision of a regulated activity that, in the reasonable opinion of a health care professional:

a. appears to have resulted in:

  » the death of the service user, where the death relates directly to the incident rather than to the natural course of the service user's illness or underlying condition

  » an impairment of the sensory, motor or intellectual functions of the service user which has lasted, or is likely to last, for a continuous period of at least 28 days

  » changes to the structure of the service user's body

  » the service user experiencing prolonged pain or prolonged psychological harm, or

  » the shortening of the life expectancy of the service user; or

b. requires treatment by a health care professional in order to prevent:

  » the death of the service user, or

  » any injury to the service user which, if left untreated, would lead to one or more of the outcomes in paragraph (a) above. (regulation 20)

Coroner raises concerns about failure in duty of candour. A coroner's regulation 28 report concerned a woman who was admitted to the Pilgrim Hospital in Lincolnshire after a stroke but staff failed to properly observe her and raise the alarm when she deteriorated. She was transferred by ambulance to another hospital in a deep coma, without protection of her airway, without escort and without clinical review, after her deterioration. The United Lincolnshire NHS Trust did not conduct an internal investigation. It gave no evidence of either an awareness of the issues arising from this inquest or any steps to reduce the risk for similar patients in future. It did not speak with the woman's family, as the duty of candour required it to do. The Care Quality Commission was reportedly considering whether to take against the Trust.[1]

CARE QUALITY COMMISSION: ABUSE AND IMPROPER TREATMENT.

The above stipulations under the regulations, concerning fundamental standards of care, clearly relate to safeguarding generally – for example, maintaining a person's nutrition and hydration. However, the regulations, in addition, include the following specific regulation, concerning safeguarding, breach of which could lead to prosecution:

- **Protection from abuse and improper treatment:** service users must be protected from abuse and improper treatment.

- **Systems, prevention:** systems and processes must be established and operated effectively to prevent abuse of service users.

- **Systems, investigation:** systems and processes must be established and operated effectively to investigate, immediately upon becoming aware of, any allegation or evidence of such abuse.

- **Discrimination, restraint, degrading, disregarding needs:** care or treatment for service users must not be provided in a way that:

    a. discriminates under the Equality Act 2010,

    b. includes acts intended to control or restrain a service user that are not necessary to prevent, or not a proportionate response to, a risk of harm posed to the service user or another individual if the service user was not subject to control or restraint,

    c. is degrading for the service user, or

    d. significantly disregards the needs of the service user for care or treatment.

- **Deprivation of liberty:** a service user must not be deprived of their liberty for the purpose of receiving care or treatment without lawful authority.

---

1   *Regulation 28 report to prevent future deaths: Elaine Bradbrook*, issued by H.J. Connor, Assistant Coroner for Nottinghamshire, 14 February 2018. Accessed on 17 August 2018 at: www.hsj. co.uk/download?ac=3038435. And: Lintern, S. 'CQC investigates Trust over "duty of candour" breach.' *Health Service Journal*, 17 August 2018.

- **Abuse:** includes:

    a. any behaviour towards a service user that is an offence under the Sexual Offences Act 2003

    b. ill-treatment (whether of a physical or psychological nature) of a service user

    c. theft, misuse or misappropriation of money or property belonging to a service user, or

    d. neglect of a service user.

- **Restraint or control:** a person controls or restrains a service user if that person (a) uses, or threatens to use, force to secure the doing of an act which the service user resists or (b) restricts the service user's liberty of movement, whether or not the service user resists, including by use of physical, mechanical or chemical means (regulation 13).

Guidance supporting the regulations includes further detail about what is required in relation to safeguarding.[1] The CQC is legally obliged to take account of the guidance.[2]

CARE QUALITY COMMISSION: DUTY TO REPORT INCIDENTS TO.

Regulations state that the registered person must inform the Care Quality Commission of certain types of harm suffered by a service user – including abuse or allegations of abuse.[3] NHS bodies need not report to the Commission if they have instead reported the incident to the National Health Service Commissioning Board (NHS England).[4]

- **Death of a service user:** must be reported, together with the circumstances, if it occurred whilst services were being provided or as a result of their being provided.

---

1   Care Quality Commission. *Guidance for providers on meeting the regulations: Health and Social Care Act 2008 (Regulated Activities) Regulations 2014 (Part 3) (as amended); Care Quality Commission (Registration) Regulations 2009 (Part 4) (as amended).* London: CQC, 2015, pp.45–50.

2   Health and Social Care Act 2008, s.25.

3   SI 2009/3112. Care Quality Commission (Registration) Regulations 2009.

4   SI 2009/3112. Care Quality Commission (Registration) Regulations 2009, r.16.

In the case of an NHS body, a local authority exercising public health functions (within the meaning of the National Health Service Act 2006) or a provider of primary medical services, the registered person must notify the Commission without delay of the death of a service user where the death:

a. either occurred whilst services were being provided in the carrying on of a regulated activity, has, or may have, resulted from the provision of services by a health service body, or local authority exercising public health functions (within the meaning of the National Health Service Act 2006), in the course of carrying on a regulated activity, or has, or may have, resulted from the provision of primary medical services in the course of carrying on a regulated activity and those services were provided within the period of two weeks prior to the death of the service user; and

b. cannot, in the reasonable opinion of the registered person, be attributed to the course which that service user's illness or medical condition would naturally have taken if that service user was receiving appropriate care and treatment.[1]

- **Death or unauthorised absence of person under the Mental Health Act 1983.** The death or unauthorised absence of a service user detained (or liable to be detained) under the Mental Health Act 1983 must be notified without undue delay.[2]

- **Reporting injury, abuse, deprivation of liberty, police involvement.** In addition, a range of other incidents must be reported without delay. These include injury, deprivation of liberty, abuse, police involvement, safety of service including adequacy of staff. In summary:

  » **injury** to the service user which a health professional reasonably believes has resulted in (i) an impairment of the sensory, motor or intellectual functions of the service user which is not likely to be temporary, (ii) changes to the structure of a service user's body, (iii) the service user experiencing prolonged pain or prolonged psychological harm, or (iv) the shortening of the life expectancy of the service user

---

1 SI 2009/3112. Care Quality Commission (Registration) Regulations 2009, r.16.

2 SI 2009/3112. Care Quality Commission (Registration) Regulations 2009, r.17.

» **injury** to a service user which a health professional reasonably believes requires treatment to prevent death and injury which, if left untreated, would lead to one or more of the outcomes outlined immediately above

» **deprivation of liberty:** request to a local authority for a standard authorisation to deprive a person lacking capacity of his or her liberty – or application to a court for the same purpose

» **abuse:** any abuse or allegation of abuse in relation to a service user

» **police:** any incident which is reported to, or investigated by, the police (this does not apply to an NHS body)

» **safety:** anything that may prevent the safe provision of services or adherence to registration requirements including insufficient number of qualified, skilled and experienced staff – and other issues affecting the provision of services.[1]

Carers (Care Act)

Protection from abuse or neglect of informal carers of adults with care and support needs comes under the Care Act. That is, local authorities should be protecting informal carers from abuse or neglect, although the specific duty to make safeguarding enquiries – under section 42 in relation to adults in need – does not extend to carers. See *Enquiries*.

- **Well-being:** local authorities have a general duty to promote the well-being of informal carers, including protecting them from abuse or neglect: see *Well-being*.

- **General principles:** local authorities have a duty to have regard to a number of principles, including the need to protect people from abuse or neglect (including carers).

- **Assessment and eligibility:** local authorities have a duty to assess carers who appear to be in need of support. An eligibility decision must consider the well-being of the carer, including protection of the carer from abuse or neglect. A carer is eligible for support if:

---

1   SI 2009/3112. Care Quality Commission (Registration) Regulations 2009, r.18.

» **necessary care:** the carer's needs arise as a consequence of providing necessary care

» **health or outcomes:** the effect of the needs is that the carer's physical or mental health is at risk or the carer is unable to achieve at least one outcome, and

» **well-being:** whether, as a consequence, there is or is likely to be a significant impact on the carer's well-being.[1]

• **Safeguarding enquiries:** the specific duty to make safeguarding enquiries, under section 42 of the Care Act, does not apply to carers but only to adults with possible care and support needs.

CARERS: ELIGIBILITY FOR SUPPORT. If informal carers are assessed to be eligible, then they are entitled to support from the local authority under section 20 of the Care Act 2014. The carer's needs can be met either by support provided directly to the carer or by providing care and support directly to the adult (such as a respite service, thus giving the carer a break).

Given the pressures that can be placed upon family and other informal carers, the provision of such support may be crucial in the context of safeguarding. The support may alleviate pressures, thereby diminishing the risk of care of the adult in need becoming neglectful or abusive (albeit unintentionally). Conversely, if it is the carer herself or himself suffering abuse or neglect, eligibility would mean the local authority would be obliged to support and help protect the carer. A failure to ask the required legal questions can foreseeably result not only in a carer breaking down, but also in them harming the adult being cared for – as occurred when a man, struggling significantly to care for his mother with mental health needs, first lost his job and then ended up assaulting his mother – after several, obviously legally inadequate, carer assessments.[2] Three questions determine eligibility of the carer:

• **necessary care:** whether the carer's needs arise as a consequence of providing necessary care

---

1   Care Act 2014, s.1. And: SI 2015/313. Care and Support (Eligibility Criteria) Regulations 2015.

2   LGO, *Essex County Council* 2018 (17 018 510).

- **health or outcomes:** whether the effect of the needs is that the carer's physical or mental health is at risk or the carer is unable to achieve at least one outcome, and

- **well-being:** whether, as a consequence, there is or is likely to be a significant impact on the carer's well-being.[1]

The questions need to be asked in order. Eligibility depends on the answer 'yes' to all three questions. The responsible local authority is the authority in whose area the cared for adult (but maybe not the carer) is ordinarily resident.

- **Eligibility of carers: necessary care.** The carer's needs must arise as a consequence of providing necessary care for an adult. Guidance states that if the adult could perform the task themselves, then the carer might be doing something that is not necessary.[2]

- **Eligibility of carers: impact on health or unable to achieve outcomes.** The second question is whether the effect of the needs is such that 'any' of the specified circumstances applies to the carer. Both circumstances are therefore not required, only one. The first circumstance is that the carer's physical or mental health is, or is at risk of, deteriorating. The second, alternative, circumstance is that the carer is unable to achieve at least any one of the outcomes listed:

  » carrying out any caring responsibilities the carer has for a child

  » providing care to other persons for whom the carer provides care

  » maintaining a habitable home environment in the carer's home (whether or not this is also the home of the adult needing care)

  » managing and maintaining nutrition

  » developing and maintaining family or other personal relationships

  » engaging in work, training, education or volunteering

  » making use of necessary facilities or services in the local community including recreational facilities or services, and

---

1   SI 2015/313. Care and Support (Eligibility Criteria) Regulations 2015.

2   Department of Health. *Care and support statutory guidance: issued under the Care Act 2014.* London: DH, 2016, para 6.116.

» engaging in recreational activities.

- **Inability to achieve an outcome.** A carer's inability to achieve an outcome is defined legally – as opposed to actually – if one of the following applies. Namely, that the carer:

  » is unable to achieve it without assistance

  » is able to achieve it without assistance but doing so causes the carer significant pain, distress or anxiety, or

  » is able to achieve it without assistance but doing so endangers or is likely to endanger the health or safety of the carer, or of others.

- **Significant impact on well-being.** The third question is whether there is a significant impact on the carer's well-being, requiring scrutiny of the definition of well-being in section 1 of the Care Act. See **Well-being**. The impact could be a likelihood only, but must be significant.

  The definitional elements of well-being are (emphasis added): personal dignity; physical and mental health and emotional well-being; *protection from abuse and neglect*; control by the individual over day-to-day life (including over the care and support provided to the adult and the way in which it is provided); participation in work, education, training or recreation; social and economic well-being; domestic, family and personal relationships; suitability of living accommodation; the adult's contribution to society.

CARERS: RESPONSIBLE FOR ABUSE OR NEGLECT. The pressure of intensive, unremitting informal care of a person with complex needs should not be underestimated.[1] It can lead to care becoming unintentionally neglectful or even abusive. In turn, safeguarding concerns may arise, accompanied by accusations and referrals being made to the police, Court of Protection legal cases and local ombudsman investigations. Thus, in the eyes of statutory services, informal carers can occupy, closely in time, the role of saint and sinner. Too readily, adult safeguarding, including legal action of one sort or another (including criminal, or separation under the Mental Capacity Act of

---

1   Marriott, H. *The selfish pig's guide to caring*. Clifton-upon-Teme: Polperro Heritage Press, 2003.

long-standing partners or spouses), can sometimes take aim at these carers disproportionately and punitively.

Care Act guidance warns against over-hasty vilification of carers in safeguarding. It points out that:

- **Informal carer: unintentional neglect or abuse.** 'The circumstances surrounding any actual or suspected case of abuse or neglect will inform the response. For example, it is important to recognise that abuse or neglect may be unintentional and may arise because a carer is struggling to care for another person. This makes the need to take action no less important, but in such circumstances, an appropriate response could be a support package for the carer and monitoring. However, the primary focus must still be how to safeguard the adult.'[1]

- **Support for carer.** 'Assessment of both the carer and the adult they care for must include consideration of the wellbeing of both people. Section 1 of the Care Act includes protection from abuse and neglect as part of the definition of wellbeing. As such, a needs or carer's assessment is an important opportunity to explore the individuals' circumstances and consider whether it would be possible to provide information, or support that prevents abuse or neglect from occurring, for example, by providing training to the carer about the condition that the adult they care for has or to support them to care more safely. Where that is necessary the local authority should make arrangements for providing it.'[2]

- **Carers and pressure sores.** Additional guidance urges sensitivity and a constructive approach when it comes to pressure care: 'Where unintentional neglect may be due to an unpaid carer struggling to provide care an appropriate response would be to revise the package of care and ensure that the carer has the support and equipment to care safely. In these circumstances it can be highly distressing to talk to carers about abuse and neglect, particularly where they have been dedicated in providing care but have not been given advice and support to prevent pressure ulcers.'[3]

---

1   Department of Health. *Care and support statutory guidance*. London: DH, 2016, para 14.40.

2   Department of Health. *Care and support statutory guidance*. London: DH, 2016, para 14.46.

3   Department of Health and Social Care. *Safeguarding adults protocol: pressure ulcers and the interface with a safeguarding enquiry*. London: DHSC, 2018, p.12.

Equally, a carer might themselves be subject to abuse or neglect, as pointed out in Department of Health guidance. If a carer experiences intentional or unintentional harm from the adult they are supporting, consideration should be given to:

- **Provision of support:** 'whether, as part of the assessment and support planning process for the carer and, or, the adult they care for, support can be provided that removes or mitigates the risk of abuse. For example, the provision of training or information or other support that minimises the stress experienced by the carer. In some circumstances, the carer may need to have independent representation or advocacy; in others, a carer may benefit from having such support if they are under great stress.'

- **Involving other organisations:** 'whether other agencies should be involved; in some circumstances where a criminal offence is suspected this will include alerting the police, or in others the primary healthcare services may need to be involved in monitoring'.[1]

The following ombudsman case illustrates the sensitive issue of whether to label the care provided by an informal carer as neglectful and trigger safeguarding enquiries.

> **Unintentional neglect and safeguarding?** A couple lived together at home. She had dementia. He cared for her. She had been found wandering in the streets several times. The local authority visited. The husband said that he sometimes left his wife alone and locked the front door. He had no memory of her leaving the house and he didn't want an increase in outside care arranged by the local authority. A community mental health doctor then raised a safeguarding concern, on the basis that the wife was deteriorating and was underweight, the husband looked tired and withdrawn, and the son was concerned about his mother's wandering and that his father was worn out.
>
> The local authority triggered a safeguarding investigation, and a multi-disciplinary meeting noted that: the investigation had established neglect; the son disagreed with the use of the word 'neglect'; the GP agreed the husband was not neglecting his wife; the husband wanted his wife home (she was temporarily in a care home) and the son suggested a sitter; a

---

1   Department of Health. *Care and support statutory guidance*. London: DH, 2016, para 14.48.

request for a permanent care home placement nearer the husband had been made; and the safeguarding investigation would be closed because the risk had been reduced.

The ombudsman did not find fault in the decision to carry out a safeguarding investigation, since 'neglect' could be unintentional. However, the actual investigation was poor since the investigation was too slow and poorly written, the invitation to the case conference was vague, the investigation report was not issued in good time before the meeting and record-keeping of the discussion was poor or absent.[1]

CARERS: PRESSURE EXPERIENCED BY AND SAFEGUARDING. As outlined immediately above, the Care Act has increased the rights of informal carers to both assessment and to support (following a finding of eligibility).[2] Such elevation of legal entitlement suggests that, in the future, increased reliance will be placed on informal carers to meet the needs of relatives with care and support needs. It was no accident that in 2015 the Secretary of State for Health stated that families need to care for each other more and lamented the fact that we live in England with merely 16 per cent of inter-generational households, compared with Italy which has 39 per cent.[3]

There is not, currently in English law, the equivalent of the old 'liable relatives' rule under section 42 of the original National Assistance Act 1948 and, before that, in section 14 of the Poor Law Act 1930. This was a rule that placed a legal duty on close family members to care for each other. But as social care support from the State diminishes, particularly for the elderly population, greater pressure will *de facto* be placed on family members and other informal carers.

Legal cases, of one type or another, illustrate the pressures on informal carers – and likewise sometimes on local authorities, both in terms of finding the resources to support carers, as well as judging the proportionality of any safeguarding interventions.

---

1   LGO, *London Borough of Bromley*, 2016 (15 013 228).

2   Care Act 2014, ss.10, 20. And: Care and Support (Eligibility Criteria) Regulations 2015.

3   Wright, O. 'Jeremy Hunt calls for national debate about caring for the elderly.' *The Independent*, 1 July 2015.

Lack of support for husband leading to safeguarding and perverse use of financial resources. A local authority was seeking to prevent the return home of a woman, lacking mental capacity, from hospital to her husband. It sought a deprivation of liberty order from the Court of Protection. The authority had convened a safeguarding meeting, such were the concerns about the husband's care. One of the issues was that her husband had been struggling to care for her because of a lack of respite for him. But this lack was due to the outcome of the rigid policy of the local authority itself, which stipulated a maximum per week of three hours' respite to carers, irrespective of need. The husband had become worn down and frustrated, under strain and disengaged from services, which had not helped his wife's best interests.

The judge found the local authority's position perverse, given how it was significantly contributing to the crisis. He also noted that, financially, the legal case it was pursuing would outweigh the cost of providing more respite care.[1]

The fine line between good care, safeguarding concerns and even criminality was evident in the following two cases of long-standing spouses caring and then killing.

Conviction for manslaughter of spouse of 60 years: main carer, had dementia, a urinary infection, was exhausted, was sleep-deprived and was depressed. A man was the main carer of his wife of 60 years. She had dementia, needed daily insulin injections and was aggressive towards him. Medical professionals said he cared for her well but was struggling. On one occasion he forgot to give his wife her insulin injection which resulted in her being hospitalised for a short time. Some months later he stabbed his wife several times in the chest with a kitchen knife and she died. He was convicted of manslaughter (rather than murder) because of diminished responsibility. Sentenced to three years in prison, he appealed against the sentence, which was reduced – to 24 months' suspended sentence, together with a 12-month residency requirement (with his daughter) and 12-month mental health requirement.

---

1   *A London Local Authority v JH* [2011] EWHC 2420 (COP), p.46.

Following the incident, he was interviewed by four medical experts who noted that he had at times become cross with his wife and wanted to hit her – but did not tell anyone about the difficulties he faced. He had lost a significant amount of weight over the previous year whilst caring for his wife and had a urinary tract infection. He himself was in the early stages of dementia and had a lack of self-control because of it. In addition, he was suffering from physical exhaustion, lack of sleep and a depressive condition.[1]

78-year-old wife stabbing 79-year-old husband: strain and depression. A judge recognised the strains of caring when he imposed a two-year community sentence, rather than a prison sentence, on a 78-year-old woman who had entered the court on a Zimmer frame. She had 'flipped' with the stress of caring for her 79-year-old husband who had Alzheimer's disease. She stabbed him 17 times, in their bungalow, with a carving knife. When police arrived, she would not let go of the knife and they used a taser gun to subdue her. He survived the attack. She pleaded guilty to wounding with intent to cause grievous bodily harm.

The judge stated:

[T]hey had been happily married for 40 years and were devoted to each other. In 2003 [he] began to experience signs of memory loss. He eventually contracted dementia and it got progressively worse. She was his sole carer... Caring for anyone with dementia should not be underestimated. She found herself under a great strain and contracted a depressive illness. Plainly at the time of this incident the balance of her mind was disturbed against a background of great domestic upheaval. There are very exceptional cases when justice should be tempered with mercy. This is one of them. In almost every case of wounding with intent any defendant who either pleads or is found guilty can expect to receive a sentence measuring in years. For reasons I hope are obvious I am satisfied it would be contrary to the interests of justice to follow the guidelines in this case.[2]

---

1   *R v Beaver* (Unreported), Court of Appeal, 24 March 2015.

2   Bentley, P. 'Wife, 78, tasered twice after she stabbed her Alzheimer's suffering husband 17 times when she cracked under the pressure of caring for him.' *Daily Mail*, 21 May 2012.

It is of note that sentencing guidelines on manslaughter refer to factors reducing the seriousness of the offence or in personal mitigation, including the offender being 'sole or primary carer for dependent relatives'.[1]

Choking

It is an offence to attempt to choke, suffocate or strangle any other person – or by any means calculated to choke, suffocate or strangle, attempt to render any other person insensible, unconscious or incapable of resistance. The attempt behind the act must be to commit an indictable offence, in which case it is classed as a felon and subject to life imprisonment. This is a felony and subject to life imprisonment.[2]

Civil law

Civil law is distinguished from criminal law. Different remedies and standards of proof are involved. See *Remedies*.

Civil orders and injunctions

Civil orders made by a court can have the effect of protecting somebody from a range of behaviours perpetrated by others. Within adult safeguarding, such orders may help protect a vulnerable adult and be an alternative (or an addition) to the criminal justice system. Use of such an alternative is sometimes connected to the victim's unwillingness to participate in criminal proceedings, a lack of evidence sufficient for such proceedings, a failed prosecution – or simply that the behaviour in question does not constitute a criminal offence.

Civil orders relevant to safeguarding relate, for example, to protection from harassment, non-molestation, occupation, forced marriage, anti-social behaviour and domestic violence notices and orders (see separate headings

---

1   Sentencing Council. *Manslaughter: definitive guideline*. London: SC, 2018.

2   Offences Against the Person Act 1861, s.21.

in this book). In addition are common law injunctions, sometimes called assault and trespass injunctions, designed to prevent intrusion on property or assault (these cannot have a power of arrest attached in case of breach, although breach will still be a contempt of court).

Although these orders are primarily civil in nature, there is a crossover with criminal law. For example, the Protection from Harassment Act 1997 contains criminal offences as well, whilst breach of a civil injunction under the Act can be a criminal offence; so, too, breach of a non-molestation order under the Family Law Act 1996. Penal notices and powers of arrest can be attached to occupation orders. Breach of a civil order without good reason anyway risks contempt of court and a possible prison sentence.

Coercive behaviour, see *Controlling or coercive behaviour*

Cold-calling, see *Rogue trading*

Commissioning of services

Department of Health guidance states that the activity of safeguarding adults is not a substitute for care providers' responsibilities to provide safe and high-quality care and support, or for commissioners regularly assuring themselves of the safety and effectiveness of commissioned services.[1] Put another way, this is pointing out that commissioning and providing poor-quality care is likely to lead directly to safeguarding issues. This has been egregiously demonstrated in the case of hospitals (see *National Health Service*). The following illustrative cases centre largely on local authority commissioning and provision and are given in some detail as a reminder of the practicalities of commissioning and caring for highly vulnerable people, with more or less complex needs.

---

1   Department of Health. *Care and support statutory guidance*. London: DH, 2016, para 14.9.

Safeguarding issues resulting from inadequate, cheaper care home placement by local authority, contrary to a social work assessment. A man had vascular dementia, diabetes, epilepsy and a history of stroke and cardiovascular accidents. He had limited mobility needing help from two carers to mobilise, was doubly incontinent and needed support with all medication, food and fluid intake. His dementia limited his ability to communicate and he displayed challenging behaviour at times, including shouting and banging on the table. He became agitated in noisy environments.

The NHS placed him in a care home which met his needs well, at £800 per week. But the NHS subsequently withdrew funding, handing over his care to the local authority which had an upper cost limit of £495 per week. It assessed him and identified that moving him would be detrimental, but moved him all the same, relying on the new care home's assertion that it could meet his needs and not properly checking its suitability.

His health declined. Apparent failings in care included difficulty in managing his behaviour, a pressure sore, inadequate documentation, being left in discomfort, being inappropriately clothed and dehydration. In addition, the local authority failed to regard the son's comments as a complaint, failed to monitor the care provider's response to concerns raised, delayed in holding a strategy meeting, closed the safeguarding investigation without adequate explanation and failed to review continuation of placements at the home. Furthermore, the decision to close the safeguarding investigation was not based on any report by the local authority, was not recorded and was contrary to its own policy. This was all fault.[1]

Winterbourne View: NHS commissioning abusive care at huge cost, without monitoring or review. Systemic abuse of people with severe learning disabilities at Winterbourne View Hospital, run by Castlebeck Ltd, resulted in a number of staff being convicted of wilful neglect. Patients were placed by the NHS, most detained under the Mental Health Act 1983, at an average weekly cost of £3500. The subsequent serious case review

---

1   LGO, *Worcestershire County Council*, 2014 (12 004 137). See also, for example, in relation to domiciliary care and an inadequate personal budget, care plan and care provided all putting a woman at risk of neglect: LGO, *London Borough of Bexley*, 2016 (15 020 770).

found, amongst other things, poor commissioning practices, in terms of checking, monitoring, reviewing and the raising of safeguarding concerns.[1]

Woman's death, following council's apparent indifference to the fate of elderly people. The complainant's elderly parents were both in their nineties when they began to receive services provided by care agencies on behalf of the council. Even before his father died, he had been complaining to the council that agency staff frequently missed calls or arrived late – in which case, many elderly people like his mother tried to get up to make their own meals, putting their health in danger. On one occasion, his mother fell in the bedroom at 12.30 pm. She was unable to get up, but expected a lunchtime visit, so lay on the floor waiting for the carer. After an hour, she realised nobody was coming. She then used her alarm. A few days later there was no breakfast-time call; she managed to get herself up, but she went without breakfast or medication.

Carer arriving with no torch: woman startled and falls and dies. Finally, a home help made a tea-time call in January. She did not have a torch, which she was meant to have, to illuminate the door entry key pad. So she banged on the living room window. The woman was startled. As she tried to hurry into the kitchen to switch on the light, she fell on to the corner of a table. The home help let herself in, got the woman off the floor, made her a cup of tea and a sandwich, wrote up the daily log without mentioning the fall, and left. Two days later, the woman's son arrived to find his mother slumped in her chair unable to move. A doctor was called. She had suffered eight broken ribs as a result of the fall. The doctor made an incorrect diagnosis; appropriate treatment was delayed. She died two weeks later after the onset of pneumonia. The carer was dismissed for failing to report the incident.

Failure of council to respond to reports of missed or late calls: routine contract compliance checks not enough. The ombudsman was scathing. She stated that:

> councils must respond to reports of missed or late calls by agency staff and follow up complaints by or on behalf of vulnerable service users as a matter of urgency. It cannot be left to routine contract compliance checks to find out whether planned services are really

---

1   Flynn, M. *Winterbourne View Hospital: a serious case review.* Bristol: South Gloucestershire Safeguarding Adults Board, 2015, pp.95–104.

being delivered. It can never be acceptable for elderly people whose care is the responsibility of the Council to wait long periods of time for the next meal or for their medication to be given.

Maladministration: failure to act on previous complaints and make alternative arrangements. The council's failure to take up promptly complaints of missed calls was maladministration; likewise, its failure to consider whether to make alternative arrangements. When an agency is failing, the council 'must simultaneously look and act in two directions at the same time – to the contractor to improve performance and to the client to assess and respond to the risk posed to them by the contractor's failures'.

Furthermore, the way in which the complaint was then handled – including a failure to coordinate papers for the review panel stage – contributed to the complainant's impression that the council was merely going through the motions and that it 'did not care what was happening to its elderly and vulnerable clients'.[1]

Council fails to do anything about an inadequate care agency: elderly woman lies on the floor all day and dies. The woman, 79 years old, used a wheelchair, having had both legs amputated. She had generalised arthritis, diabetes controlled by diet and a hearing impairment. She was highly dependent and required daily contact.

Stroke, heart attack, hypothermia. On one particular day in March 2003, the care agency contracted to provide care failed to visit in the morning. The carer, who had decided not to work that day, had not informed the agency. The early-evening visit did not take place either. Later that evening, she was found on the floor and admitted to hospital. During the period she lay on the floor, she had suffered a stroke, a heart attack and hypothermia. She died eight days later. The time she spent on the floor before she was helped was some 13 hours after the time set for the morning visit. She was without food or water. The cause of the accident was probably the failure of the carers to visit her. 'She was badly let down by the Council and its provider.'

Known inadequacies of care agency. However, the inadequacies of the care agency on that particular day were not uncharacteristic. They were already well known to the council and included inappropriate and untrained staff, a failure to log in and out or report to the office, failure of the back-

---

1   LGO, *Sheffield City Council*, 2007 (05/C/06420).

up telephone system, and failure to ensure all carers had access to a care plan explaining entry and emergency arrangements. In addition, a significant number of complaints had been made in the past about missed or late visits. These problems had existed for nine months, from the start of a block contract the council had with the care agency, yet the council's interventions had failed to protect service users.

Given the background of complaints during 2002 about the care agency involved, the council 'failed to understand that it was dealing with a provider that was acting dangerously towards some service users. It failed to understand the random nature of the problem. The Council failed to monitor the reports of missed visits.'

Previous survey revealing serious shortcomings in agency. By January 2003, an audit of the care agency had revealed that, of a survey of 20 service users, 75 per cent did not have care plans, 60 per cent lacked a written assessment by the provider, and 60 per cent had received no risk assessment. Of 20 staff files reviewed, there was no evidence that the company employed as many people as it claimed to, and staff were averaging considerably more than 48 hours per week of work. There was no evidence of induction training; no training schedule was in place. Complaints made by service users were not recorded on their files. For 25 of 43 visits surveyed, carers provided less than 25 per cent of the time they had been commissioned to spend.

Inadequate investigation of incident. In addition, the council's investigation of the incident involving the death of the woman was inadequate. It lacked a sense of urgency, and the responsible officer was content to leave matters largely with the company and to correspond with it over several months. The information the council did obtain showed that, in the week before the incident, the woman had experienced the same failings experienced by other service users including a lack of continuity in care because of the involvement of different carers, truncated visits, possible missed visits, and use of inappropriate staff. The inappropriate staff comprised one who had been banned from working with service users, and another who, in January (so the agency had informed the council), had been sacked for misconduct. Overall, the council failed to consider what measures to take to safeguard service users. All this was maladministration.[1]

---

1   LGO, *Blackpool Borough Council*, 2006 (03/C/17141).

Woman wrongly kept in hospital for ten years, during which time she was abused by other patients. At the age of 18 years, a woman with severe learning difficulties was received into guardianship by the local authority; she resided at a care home. Following concerns about her behaviour, she was admitted in March 1990 to hospital under section 3 of the Mental Health Act 1983; this compulsory detention replaced the guardianship order. Six months later, in September 1990, the consultant psychiatrist wrote to the local authority, stating that a further stay in hospital was not warranted; the section 3 detention ceased.

Local authority not wanting to pay for a placement. However, the local authority failed to put in place any plan for discharge because it was concerned about the cost of any such placement, and also argued with the NHS about who should be responsible for the funding.

The woman finally left hospital in 2001, having spent over ten years as an informal, compliant but incapacitated patient. Consequently, aftercare duties under section 117 of the 1983 Act were never triggered and the local authority was never tested on its potential duties under section 117. The ombudsman concluded that if it had been, the authority would have 'fallen far short' of its responsibilities.

Abuse of woman by other patients neither investigated nor prevented. The evidence suggested that the woman did not need to be a long-stay patient. A consequence of this unnecessary stay in hospital was that the local authority had neither investigated nor prevented the abuse the woman suffered at the hands of other patients during her inappropriate hospital stay. For example, as early as 1991, a local authority mental health management officer wrote to the director of social services about the woman's deteriorating welfare, bites on her legs inflicted by another patient, and her shoddy clothing.

The ombudsman found that the local authority had failed in its duties, notwithstanding legal uncertainties during some of the period about NHS 'continuing care' responsibilities, and recommended £20,000 compensation.[1]

Importance of reviewing and reassessing placements of vulnerable adults. A local authority had for six years failed to assess and review a woman with learning disabilities in a foster placement (first as a child,

---

1   LGO, *Wakefield Metropolitan District Council*, 2003 (01/C/15652).

then as an adult). The foster carers had not been registered as they should have been. The foster family obstructed her in contacting the previous foster family. She was not allowed to use sign language (her preferred means of communication), deprived of hearing-aid batteries, treated like a child, forced to share a bedroom, prevented from having a relationship with somebody at work and instead encouraged to have an inappropriate relationship with an older family acquaintance. The first assessment after all this time came when an adult protection investigation was launched.[1]

Thus, poor commissioning can lead to a local authority or NHS body being held responsible, as well as the provider:

- **Delegation and maladministration.** Section 25 of the Local Government Act 1974, which governs the local ombudsman's work, states that the local authority remains responsible for what is done on its behalf, as demonstrated in the first of the cases, immediately above.[2]

- **Delegation and negligence.** The courts have ruled that in negligence cases (in common law) local authorities remain legally liable in some circumstances, even when they have taken all reasonable care in contracting out a service, particularly in the case of vulnerable people. For example, in the case of children at school (and maybe elderly people in a care home), the courts have held that certain core functions, and therefore legal liability, is ultimately not delegable in the sense of avoiding liability.[3]

- **Delegation of core functions.** Beyond the commissioning of services, a local authority retains legal responsibility, under section 79 of the Care Act, for core functions carried out, on behalf of a local authority, by another body (although not in relation to criminal proceedings, or to contractual issues between the local authority and the other organisation).

For example, when a local authority delegated its core social care assessment and eligibility functions for people with Asperger's syndrome to an NHS

---

1   LGO, *Birmingham City Council*, 2008 (05/C/18474).

2   LGO, *Worcestershire County Council*, 2014 (12 004 137), paras 2, 45. And LGO, *London Borough of Ealing*, 2013 (12 012 697), para 42.

3   *Woodland v Essex County Council* [2013] UKSC 66, para 23.

Trust, the complaint and finding of maladministration lay against the local authority.[1]

Concealment

The degree to which organisations, notably those charged with caring for and safeguarding people, will seek to conceal serious neglect or abuse can be extreme and magnify the original wrong tenfold. Concealment takes the form of blanket denial, withholding information, manipulation of information, euphemism, ruthless suppression of whistleblowers, government departments blocking the holding of independent inquiries, etc.

When apparent concealment involves more than one agency, it can appear – for example, to relatives trying to find out what has happened – to be the consequence of a conspiracy. The Gosport War Memorial Hospital Inquiry, which found multi-agency failure and cover-up, considered this point of view, understood it but rejected it as an explanation. Instead, it considered carefully that a coincidence of interests could lead to identical, dismissive responses to concerns raised, without necessarily indicating a conspiracy. It is worth quoting at some length.

Gosport: coincidence of interests and dismissive approach by various organisations but no conspiracy.

First, each organisation may have acted in its own interests and those of its leaders, motivated by reputation management, career self-preservation and taking the path of least resistance. This coincidence of interests would itself lead to identical responses across organisations, without there being a conspiracy between the organisations.

The second possibility is that there was collusion – a conspiracy between organisations to ensure that the views of the families were consistently frustrated. It is not clear what the underlying motivation would be for such a course, but it is understandable that the almost uniform consistency with which all concerns were

---

1   LGO, *Somerset County Council*, 2015 (13 019 566), paras 3, 35.

> dismissed and families were rebuffed might lead to suspicions of collusion or conspiracy between organisations.
>
> The documents the Panel has reviewed do not contain evidence in support of such collusion or conspiracy. They show that the underlying explanation is the tendency of individuals in organisations, when faced with serious allegations, to handle them in a way that limits the impact on the organisation and its perceived reputation. This does not diminish the importance or the impact of organisations acting similarly and prioritising compliance with their own processes. Too readily opting for what is convenient within an organisational setting is the enemy of recognising the real significance of concerns and allegations.
>
> The Panel is able to say in this case that there was a coincidence of interests across organisations; and that this may well have been sufficient to explain their conduct, including at times their dismissive treatment of the families.[1]

The NHS has been responsible for significant concealment, to the extent that an offence of providing false or misleading information was created, particularly with the NHS in mind, following events at Stafford Hospital.[2] The following are examples of various forms of concealment emanating from the NHS.

> **Central government toning down the healthcare regulator for political reasons.** Sir Ian Kennedy, Chairman of the Healthcare Commission (predecessor to the Care Quality Commission), noted that it was no accident that a former healthcare regulator, the Commission for Health Improvement, was abolished because it was acting too independently of central government. Its successor, the Healthcare Commission, had criteria for inspection imposed upon it by central government. The Secretary of State for Health requested that the categories and criteria used be revisited, because too many hospitals had been graded as weak or fair, and

---

1 Jones, Reverend J. (Chairman). *Gosport War Memorial Hospital: the report of the Gosport Independent Panel*. London: The Stationery Office, 2018, paras 12.49–12.52.

2 Care Act 2014, ss.92–94. And SI 2015/988. False or Misleading Information (Specified Care Providers and Specified Information) Regulations 2015.

the message had to be made more politically acceptable. The Department of Health viewed events at Stafford Hospital as an awful story, rather than indicating the need to change the NHS, and had a tendency to shoot the messenger.[1]

Euphemism and management-speak from the healthcare regulator. Even in 2018, with more pressure on the Care Quality Commission (CQC) following so many scandals, it is notable that its reports – even its critical reports – tend not to spell out in everyday language the implications for patients, in terms of describing poor care, neglect and suffering of elderly people in hospital. They tend instead to use dry, euphemistic language, somewhat abstract and uninformative.

A simple example would be a highly critical report into the East of England ambulance service, which referred to poor response rates, effectiveness and safety.[2] It didn't refer to the practical implications for individual people, such as a person suffering a stroke waiting 18 hours for an ambulance and subsequently dying – as revealed only by whistleblowers.[3] Nor that the local NHS organisations had played down the problem during the previous winter and had only agreed to a February 'risk summit' after whistleblowers – again – had revealed the implications for patients.[4]

The CQC's predecessor, the Healthcare Commission, could be a lot more explicit, as it was, for example, in its report about Stafford Hospital.[5] Likewise, in its reports on Maidstone and Tunbridge Wells NHS Trust (complete with colour photographs of conditions on the wards) and

1   'Deaths figure "removed from Stafford Hospital report".' *BBC News*, 4 May 2001. Accessed on 12 May 2011 at: www.bbc.co.uk/news/uk-england-stoke-staffordshire-13288896. For further details, see Francis, R. (Chairman). *Report of the Mid Staffordshire NHS Foundation Trust Public Inquiry. Volume 2: analysis of evidence and lessons learned.* London: The Stationery Office, Chapter 9.

2   Care Quality Commission. *East of England Ambulance NHS Trust: inspection report.* London: CQC, 2018.

3   Illman, J. 'Ambulance delays review "doesn't tally with frontline experience", say whistleblowers.' *Health Service Journal*, 29 May 2018.

4   Grimmer, D. '"Risk summit" ordered after whistleblower raises concerns about East of England Ambulance Service patient deaths.' *East Anglian Daily Times*, 23 January 2018.

5   Healthcare Commission. *Investigation into Mid Staffordshire NHS Foundation Trust, March 2009.* London: HC, 2009.

Stoke Mandeville Hospital.[1] Even so, it was only the independent inquiry into events at Stafford Hospital which really spelt out – without being sensationalist but in graphic descriptions and terms that everybody could understand – the enormity of the neglectful care that had been provided for patients,[2] through the simple expedient of talking to the relatives who had witnessed it and conveying their observations and experiences into print.

Lack of transparency and candour into investigation of deaths in the NHS. The Care Quality Commission reported on the haphazard way in which deaths in NHS settings are investigated, particularly in relation to people with learning disabilities and elderly people with mental health problems – and on the lack of kindness, respect and honesty afforded to bereaved relatives.[3]

Concealment of infection and death at Stoke Mandeville. At Stoke Mandeville Hospital, the Healthcare Commission found that, despite the two very serious outbreaks of *Clostridium difficile*, the NHS Trust board had consistently resisted the recommendations of its infection control team and had not publicly owned up to what was going on. The Commission found that the Trust changed its approach only when the Department of Health found out and, more particularly, following a leak to the Press.[4]

Incomplete, misleading information given by an NHS Trust and its chief executive in Kent: infection, poor care and many deaths. At Maidstone and Tunbridge Wells NHS Trust, the Healthcare Commission uncovered a catalogue of incomplete, misleading and belated information given by the Trust and, in particular, the chief executive – to the public, the press and to the Commission itself. This was while poor care practices and *Clostridium difficile* were running unchecked and killing scores of patients

---

1   Healthcare Commission. *Investigation into outbreaks of* Clostridium difficile *at Stoke Mandeville Hospital, Buckinghamshire Hospitals NHS Trust, July 2006.* London: HC, 2006. Healthcare Commission. *Investigation into outbreaks of* Clostridium difficile *at Maidstone and Tunbridge Wells NHS Trust, October 2007.* London: HC, 2007.

2   Francis, R. (Chair). *Independent Inquiry into care provided by Mid Staffordshire NHS Foundation Trust January 2005–March 2009.* London: The Stationery Office, 2010.

3   Care Quality Commission. *Learning, candour and accountability: a review of the way NHS trusts review and investigate the deaths of patients in England.* London: CQC, 2016, p.6.

4   Healthcare Commission. *Investigation into outbreaks of* Clostridium difficile *at Stoke Mandeville Hospital, Buckinghamshire Hospitals NHS Trust, July 2006.* London: HC, 2006, pp.7, 63.

at the Trust. The chief executive deprived even her own trust board of relevant information. The Commission also found that while the board was making statements about how patient safety was a priority, the Trust's actual practice was almost diametrically opposed to this. The statement was meaningless. Managers referred to the 'positive spin' employed by the chief executive.[1]

Pure fabrication about the standard of care. At Maidstone and Tunbridge Wells NHS Trust – in the midst of scores of avoidable deaths, chaos, overcrowding, filth, infection and lack of basic care and dignity – a nursing report was submitted to the Trust board. The report assured the board that every patient had received 'the best care in the best place on the ward', a claim dismissed as pure 'fabrication' by the Healthcare Commission.[2]

Good care reported amidst poor care and neglect. Whilst hundreds of patients were subjected to highly neglectful and degrading care, and hundreds of 'excess' deaths occurred, at Stafford Hospital, the chief executive and board reported to the regulatory body, Monitor, that the hospital was providing good care. On that basis, the Trust was awarded foundation status by Monitor, and members of the board responded by awarding themselves pay rises.[3]

Irrationality of denying the bad with reference to the good. There is an intense lack of logic when poor care and neglect in a particular hospital are denied on the basis that the same hospital provides good care. This was noted by the independent inquiry into events at Stafford Hospital. The latter was indeed providing some good care, but consequently some senior staff and managers were unable to grasp that in hospitals, as in the world at large, the good can cohabit with the bad.[4]

---

1   Healthcare Commission. *Investigation into outbreaks of* Clostridium difficile *at Maidstone and Tunbridge Wells NHS Trust, October 2007.* London: HC, 2007, p.94.

2   Healthcare Commission. *Investigation into outbreaks of* Clostridium difficile *at Maidstone and Tunbridge Wells NHS Trust, October 2007.* London: HC, 2007, p.94.

3   Evans, M. 'Failed hospital bosses given pay rises while crisis unfolded: senior managers who oversaw one of the worst scandals in the history of the NHS awarded themselves bumper pay increases at the same time as hundreds of patients were needlessly dying, it can be disclosed.' *Daily Telegraph*, 26 February 2010.

4   Francis, R. (Chair). *Independent Inquiry into care provided by Mid Staffordshire NHS Foundation Trust January 2005–March 2009.* London: The Stationery Office, 2010, p.180.

Morecambe Bay: suppression of critical report. In 2010, it emerged that University Hospitals of Morecambe Bay NHS Foundation Trust had concealed, for a year, a highly critical report (the Fielding report), which it had commissioned about the safety of its maternity services. The regulator, the Care Quality Commission, had, during this time, not seen the report and failed to take decisive action against the Trust. Instead, the Commission had relied on assurances given by the Trust.[1] By 2012, the Commission belatedly launched a full-scale investigation which uncovered serious concerns relating not just to maternity services but also to emergency services.[2]

Department of Health's attempt to play down events at Stafford Hospital. When patients and relatives demanded a public inquiry into events at Stafford Hospital, the government refused; it only acceded, in the end, to an independent inquiry, when threatened with judicial review by Cure the NHS, a group of relatives of dead patients.[3]

Department of Health's attempt to play down events at Gosport War Memorial Hospital. In 2003, Professor Richard Baker submitted a report to the Department of Health about deaths at the hospital. The Department then resisted publication for ten years, using the Freedom of Information Act 2000 rules concerning exemption from publication. Following its eventual publication in 2013, civil servants advised a Health Minister, Norman Lamb MP, that there should be no public inquiry. He has since stated that he found this 'horrific and there has been a real systemic failure here, a closing of ranks in my view and a sense that ordinary people just weren't being listened to at all, and an unwillingness by the NHS to face up to some really serious allegations about what happened in that hospital'. He overruled the civil servants and appointed an independent inquiry, which

1   Smith, R. 'Morecambe Bay hospitals: regulator should have acted sooner.' *Daily Telegraph*, 14 July 2012.

2   Care Quality Commission. *University Hospitals of Morecambe Bay NHS Foundation Trust and Royal Lancaster Infirmary Furness General Hospital: investigation report.* London: CQC, 2012.

3   Leigh Day & Co. 'Judicial reviews and the Mid Staffordshire inquiries.' *News*, 12 May 2010. Accessed on 14 July 2017 at: www.leighday.co.uk/Human-rights-and-public-law/Health-social-care/Human-rights-in-healthcare/Mid-Staffordshire-Inquiry/Judicial-reviews-and-the-Mid-Staffordshire-inquiri.

reported in 2018, 30 years after the misuse of life-shortening opiates had begun, resulting in the deaths of at least 450 patients.[1]

NHS chief executive's claim that cutting staff and hospital beds would be exciting and good for patients. When large hospital staff and bed reductions were announced for Southampton General Hospital in June 2006, following similar cuts the year before, the chief executive stated that not only was it all about improving services for patients but that it would be 'exciting' for staff.[2] By 2010, it was reported that transfers, not clinically justified, of patients from ward to ward in the hospital were high, with the clear potential for clinical detriment (whether infection or other matters). Between July 2008 and July 2010, an average of 5922 patients were admitted monthly, and of these, 703 would be transferred for non-clinical reasons, that is, 12 per cent of admitted patients.[3]

For example, one patient in Southampton General Hospital was admitted following a fall. She recovered from the fall with no injuries within 24 hours but was kept in the hospital because of a urine infection. She was moved to four different wards for no obvious reason. She then developed pressure sores which became infected with MRSA. This was not diagnosed by the hospital while she was in their care. After eight weeks in hospital she was declared medically fit and released to a care home where she died six weeks later. The principal cause of death on her death certificate was MRSA.[4]

NHS chief executive's boast of clinical sustainability whilst cutting beds. In 2008 a war veteran died a painful death from pressure sores at the Queen's Hospital, Romford. In 2009, the coroner held that neglect had contributed to his death. The pressure sores were due to two separate 12-hour waits on trolleys in the hospital because of a shortage of beds.[5] In 2006, the chief executive of the newly built hospital had announced the

1 Watt, M. 'Gosport hospital deaths: NHS closed ranks, says Norman Lamb.' *BBC News*, 19 June 2018. Accessed on 20 June 2018 at: www.bbc.co.uk/news/uk-politics-44542622.

2 Makin, J. (2006) 'Job cuts will lead to a better service.' *Southern Daily Echo*, 28 June 2006.

3 West, D. (2010) 'Hospital bed transfers put thousands of patients at risk of infection.' *Nursing Times*, 5 October 2010.

4 Patient Opinion. Accessed on 20 October 2010 at: www.patientopinion.org.uk/opinions/14654.

5 Schlesinger, F. 'Coroner's fury as great-grandfather, 86, dies after being dumped on A&E trolley for 19 hours TWICE.' *Daily Mail*, 22 May 2009.

closure of 190 beds and the cutting of 650 staff. But, he noted, patient care would not suffer because these reductions were 'clinically sustainable'.[1]

Confidentiality

Information disclosure is governed by various law, including the Data Protection Act 2018 and General Data Protection Regulation (GDPR), the Human Rights Act 1998, and the common law of confidentiality. See also *Information disclosure*; *Data protection*; *Human rights*.

Common law means it is not in legislation but has been developed by the courts through legal case law. In summary, confidential information disclosure – generally and in the context of adult safeguarding – is about balancing the private and public interests of confidentiality against the private and public interests of disclosure, with a starting general presumption against disclosure. In terms of adult safeguarding:

Breaching confidentiality of mental health patient: risk of harm to others. A consultant psychiatrist prepared a report for a patient prior to a mental health review tribunal hearing. The report was unfavourable, and the patient withdrew his application. However, the consultant was so concerned about the potential danger that the man represented that he sent the report to both the Home Office and the hospital where the man was detained. The court held that the breach of confidentiality was justified in the public interest.[2]

Disclosure of mental health patient's information to mother: common law and human right used to determine issue, since Data Protection Act was too general. A mother was the nearest relative under the Mental Health Act 1983 to her adult son who was under the guardianship of the local authority. He lacked the capacity to take the relevant decisions for himself. She wished to gain access to her son's council files and to his medical records. The council was prepared to allow experts appointed by the mother

---

1   '£24 million debt NHS trust cuts 650 jobs: Up to 650 jobs are to be cut and 190 beds closed by an NHS trust that is trying to tackle debts.' *BBC News*, 28 April 2006. Accessed on 20 July 2010 at: http://news.bbc.co.uk/1/hi/england/london/4954818.stm.

2   *W v Edgell* [1990] 1 All ER 835 (Court of Appeal).

to have access, and for them to communicate information as they thought fit to the mother and her solicitors. The mother challenged this.

Human rights and common law demanding balance. The court accepted that the Data Protection Act 1998 helped little; its generality meant that it did not prevent disclosure to the mother, but nor did it require the local authority positively to disclose. The judge turned to the common law of confidentiality and to human rights. Both required a balance to be struck between the 'public and private interests in maintaining the confidentiality of this information and the public and private interests in permitting, indeed requiring, its disclosure for certain purposes'.

The interests to be balanced consisted of the confidentiality of the information, the proper administration of justice and the mother's right of access to legal advice (relating to the guardianship, the mother's exercise of the nearest relative function, and her possible displacement as nearest relative by the local authority); the rights of the mother and son to respect for their family life and adequate involvement in decision-making processes; the son's right to respect for his private life; and the protection of the son's health and welfare. The court held that the balance came down in favour of disclosure to the mother and her solicitors as well as the experts.[1]

Disclosure by local authority of personal details of social work student to university. A woman was known to social services, because of concerns and difficulties about the bringing up of her child. The woman subsequently wished to study to become a social worker. The local authority had concerns about her fitness for such a job; it disclosed its concerns to the university.

The court held that in this instance the local authority's disclosure was lawful, even though it had not maintained confidentiality. The matter was one of public interest. Good practice would have involved the council informing the woman first, so that she could seek an injunction to prevent disclosure; however, breach of good practice did not equate to a breach of the duty of confidence. Likewise, the claim failed under article 8 of the European Convention (right to respect for privacy); the means were proportionate, and the purpose was to protect others from unsuitable social workers.[2]

1   *R v Plymouth City Council, ex p Stevens* [2002] EWCA Civ 388.

2   *Maddock v Devon County Council* (2003) unreported, case Ex190052, Exeter District Registry, High Court (QBD).

Nursing home death and disclosure by police to the regulatory body.
The matron of a nursing home was interviewed following the death of a
resident alleged to have followed an overdose of diamorphine. The police
concluded there was insufficient evidence to bring charges. The United
Kingdom Central Council for Nursing, Midwifery and Health Visiting began
an investigation. The police sought the matron's permission to disclose, to
the Council, the statements she had made at police interview. The Royal
College of Nursing, on behalf of the matron, refused that permission.

The court ruled in this case that the police could in such circumstances
pass on such confidential information in the interests of public health
or safety. Nevertheless, generally, a balance had to be struck between
competing public interests in such circumstances; the individual should be
notified about the proposed disclosure; and in case of refusal, the court
could be applied to.[1]

CONFIDENTIALITY: AND PRESSING NEED TEST. In common law there
is a presumption, which can be displaced, of non-disclosure of personal
information. The courts have typically looked for a 'pressing need' test,
before any disclosure is made, even in a case in which disclosure would seem
the obvious option.

Disclosure to caravan site owner of risk to children. A married couple
was released from prison, where they served sentences for serious sexual
offences against children. They went to live on a caravan site in the North of
England. The local police asked them to move from the site before Easter,
when many children would be visiting. The couple refused. The police
disclosed their background to the caravan site owner. He asked them to
leave. The couple claimed they had been treated unfairly and should have
been shown the allegations.

The court held that they should have been informed of the gist of the
information held by the police, but that this would not have affected the
conclusion. The police needed to apply a 'pressing need' test as to whether

---

1   *Woolgar v Chief Constable of Sussex Police* [2000] 1 WLR 25 (Court of Appeal).

to disclose, based on as much information as possible. The disclosure was lawful.[1]

Failure to apply pressing need test to the facts of the case: unlawful police disclosure to education department of a local authority. An uncorroborated allegation was made that a man had abused a child at a hostel for vulnerable children. A few years later a further allegation that he had abused his daughter was made by his wife during acrimonious divorce proceedings. No action was taken, but the family was placed on the child protection register. He then set up his own bus company with a contract to run school bus services. The police and social services disclosed his background to the education department of the local authority. The latter terminated the contract.

The court held that the disclosure by the police and by social services was unlawful because (a) disclosure should be the exception and not the rule and (b) there was no evidence that either agency had applied the pressing need test in terms of considering the facts of the particular case.[2]

NHS alert letter: justification by way of proportionality of disclosure and pressing need for it. An alert letter was issued, containing details of allegations made about a medical doctor in relation to indecent assaults on female patients.[3] Even after a decision had been taken that he would not be prosecuted, and the General Medical Council did not pursue the matter, the alert letter remained.

The Court of Appeal did not find this unlawful, noting that a balance had to be struck between the interests of the doctor and that of patients. The 'nature and strength of the allegations and the vulnerability of the class of persons to be protected are likely to be at the centre of the decision-maker's consideration'. In terms of human rights, under article 8 of the European Convention, the court accepted that the alert letter constituted an interference with respect for private life. However, such interference could be justified if it was proportionate ('necessary in a democratic society') with a legitimate aim in mind (protection of patients). The question was

1   *R v Chief Constable of North Wales, ex p AB* [1998] 3 WLR 57 (Court of Appeal).

2   *R v A local authority in the Midlands, ex p LM* (2000) 1 FLR 612.

3   HSC 2002/011. Department of Health. *Issue of Alert Letters for health professionals in England.* London: DH, 2002.

effectively the same as that posed by the common law, namely whether there was a pressing need.

However, the court did emphasise that such alert letters needed to be reviewed at short intervals, with substantive consideration to be given to whether they should remain in circulation. This was because, in this particular case, a number of errors had been made, contrary to the Department of Health's guidance.[1]

The following case involved a local authority wishing to disclose information about a woman working in a care home in the area of a different local authority. The judge did approve disclosure but was meticulous in weighing up the relevant and competing factors before reaching a decision, and insisting on the safeguards that would be required.

Disclosure of safeguarding concerns by local authority to a care home about an employee: meticulous balancing exercise required. A mother had assaulted her eight-year-old daughter, who was subsequently removed from the mother after the local authority had applied for and obtained a care order. The mother still worked at a care home for older people in the area of a second local authority. The first local authority wished to inform both the second local authority and the woman's employer about the background to the care proceedings. The judge referred to the Department of Health guidance and to its exhortation for inter-agency arrangements, as well as to the Protection of Vulnerable Adults list kept by the Secretary of State, and the statutory duty of care providers to refer care workers in case of misconduct causing harm (or risk of harm) to a vulnerable adult.

The first local authority believed that, whatever the Secretary of State decided, nonetheless the employer (and second local authority) needed to be able to discharge their statutory duties under the Care Standards Act 2000. They could only do that if the first local authority disclosed the information to them. The judge then set out the competing considerations.

Considerations against disclosure. Potentially militating against disclosure were (a) the impact of disclosure on the child (there would be no benefit for the child in disclosure); (b) the consequences for the family (the woman might lose her job, she might not find easily other employment, the

---

1   *R (D) v Secretary of State for Health* [2006] EWCA 989.

child might be upset if she became aware of the effect on her mother); (c) risk of publicity with potentially serious consequences for the child; and (d) importance of encouraging frankness in children's cases (fear of publicity may deter people revealing what is happening to children).

Considerations for disclosure. In favour of disclosure were: (a) the gravity of the conduct and risk to the public if there were no disclosure (serious assault on child meant that there was a real and potent risk to vulnerable adults); (b) evidence of a pressing need for disclosure (there was both a right and a duty to disclose); (c) interest of other bodies in receiving the information (significant obligations on second local authority and employer to carry out statutory duties); and (d) public interest in disclosure (strong and potent – with the need for public safety outweighing the mother's right to respect for her privacy, under article 8 of the European Convention on Human Rights).

Balance in favour of disclosure but with safeguards. The judge was quite clear that disclosure was the proper course but needed first to be satisfied that confidential discussions between the two local authorities and the employer could adequately address the question of avoiding publicity.[1]

In the following case, the pressing need test surfaced in relation to disclosure of safeguarding concerns, relating to a disabled man and the risk he might pose to children.

Scattergun and unjustified disclosure by local authority of information about a direct payment recipient's criminal conviction for a sexual offence committed against a child. A local authority had discovered, belatedly, that one of its direct payment recipients had been convicted some years ago, of a sexual offence against a child.

First, it contacted nine organisations for whom the man provided services, to inform them about the conviction, effectively demanded that he step down from all the bodies and committees he was involved with – and would make disclosure to all his known contacts. However, it did not establish that the work he provided for these organisations had anything to do with children: it did not. There was no pressing need demonstrated, since the pressing need, if any, was to protect children.

---

1   *Brent LBC v SK* [2007] EWHC 1250 (Fam).

The second issue was that the local authority had noted that the contract the man and his partner had with their carers (employed through direct payments money provided by the council) had recently been amended, to the effect that children were not to come to the house. The man had said he would abide by this condition. However, the local authority did not trust him, given a previous conviction for dishonesty. The local authority now wanted the man and his partner to provide each employee with a letter, setting out the view of the local authority that children should stay away. The local authority's insistence on this, and its discounting of his assurance – along with the grave suspicions which the carers would have (two out of three didn't have children anyway) – was not justified.

Third, the local authority insisted that the direct payments should be paid through a managed account over which the local authority would have oversight and therefore be aware of each individual employee – with a view, therefore, of each of those employees receiving the letter about keeping children away. Just as with issue 2, the Court of Appeal found that this was not justified. It also found that the direct payments legislation anyway did not allow this.

The court relied both on article 8 of the European Convention (right to respect for private life) and the common law in reaching its conclusions in this case.[1]

CONFIDENTIALITY: GENERAL MEDICAL COUNCIL. An example of guidance about the balance to be struck between maintaining confidentiality and disclosure is that issued for doctors by the General Medical Council. Generally, doctors have a duty to preserve confidentiality even if the patient will be put at risk of serious harm or death:

- **Patient with capacity: confidentiality even if risk of serious harm or death.** 'If an adult patient who has capacity to make the decision refuses to consent to information being disclosed that you consider necessary for their protection, you should explore their reasons for this. It may be appropriate to encourage the patient to consent to the disclosure and to warn them of the risks of refusing to consent... You should, however, usually abide by the

---

1   *H and L v A City Council* [2011] EWCA Civ 403 (Court of Appeal). And: *H and L v A City Council* [2010] EWHC 466 (Admin).

patient's refusal to consent to disclosure, even if their decision leaves them (but no one else) at risk of death or serious harm. You should do your best to give the patient the information and support they need to make decisions in their own interests – for example, by arranging contact with agencies to support people who experience domestic violence. Adults who initially refuse offers of assistance may change their decision over time.'[1]

However, the public interest might require disclosure in case of risks to other people or serious crime:

- **Serious risk to other people, serious crime: disclosure justifiable.** 'If it is not practicable to seek consent, and in exceptional cases where a patient has refused consent, disclosing personal information may be justified in the public interest if failure to do so may expose others to a risk of death or serious harm. The benefits to an individual or to society of the disclosure must outweigh both the patient's and the public interest in keeping the information confidential... Such a situation might arise, for example, if a disclosure would be likely to be necessary for the prevention, detection or prosecution of serious crime, especially crimes against the person. When victims of violence refuse police assistance, disclosure may still be justified if others remain at risk, for example from someone who is prepared to use weapons, or from domestic violence when children or others may be at risk... Other examples of situations in which failure to disclose information may expose others to a risk of death or serious harm include when a patient is not fit to drive, or has been diagnosed with a serious communicable disease, or poses a serious risk to others through being unfit for work.'[2]

The guidance goes on to consider neglect and abuse in the context of people lacking capacity to consent to disclosure:

- **Patients lacking capacity, abuse and neglect: importance of reasoning and justification whether or not to disclose.** 'Even if there is no [other] legal requirement to do so, you must give information promptly to an appropriate responsible person or authority if you believe a patient who lacks capacity to consent is experiencing, or at risk of, neglect or physical, sexual or emotional

---

1   General Medical Council. *Confidentiality: good practice in handling patient information*. London: GMC, 2009, paras 57–59.

2   General Medical Council. *Confidentiality: good practice in handling patient information*. London: GMC, 2009, paras 63–66.

abuse, or any other kind of serious harm, unless it is not of overall benefit to the patient to do so… If you believe it is not of overall benefit to the patient to disclose their personal information (and it is not required by law), you should discuss the issues with an experienced colleague. If you decide not to disclose information, you must document in the patient's records your discussions and the reasons for deciding not to disclose. You must be able to justify your decision.'[1]

Conflicts of interest within adult safeguarding

Certain fundamental conflicts of interest sit at the heart of adult safeguarding. For example, evidence suggests significant levels of poor care and neglect within health and social care services. Yet many of these services are provided or commissioned by NHS bodies or local authorities, the very bodies charged with safeguarding adults. As the Gosport War Memorial Hospital Inquiry pointed out, there is a tendency for 'individuals in organisations, when faced with serious allegations, to handle them in a way that limits the impact on the organisation and its perceived reputation'.[2] Furthermore, financial, management and political targets may all get in the way of preventing, acknowledging or responding to neglect or abuse – as illustrated so clearly by events at, for instance, Stoke Mandeville, Maidstone and Tunbridge Wells and Stafford Hospitals.[3]

In addition, safeguarding adults boards, responsible for local safeguarding strategy and for conducting safeguarding adults reviews, have as two (of three) of their key members local authorities and the NHS. Even the third key agency in safeguarding, and member of safeguarding adults boards, the

---

1   General Medical Council. *Confidentiality: good practice in handling patient information*. London: GMC, 2009, paras 63–66.

2   Jones, Reverend J. (Chairman). *Gosport War Memorial Hospital: the report of the Gosport Independent Panel*. London: The Stationery Office, 2018, para 12.51.

3   Healthcare Commission. *Investigation into outbreaks of* Clostridium difficile *at Stoke Mandeville Hospital, Buckinghamshire Hospitals NHS Trust, July 2006*. London: HC, 2006, pp.7, 63. Healthcare Commission. *Investigation into outbreaks of* Clostridium difficile *at Maidstone and Tunbridge Wells NHS Trust, October 2007*. London: HC, 2007. Francis, R. (Chair). *Independent Inquiry into care provided by Mid Staffordshire NHS Foundation Trust January 2005–March 2009*. London: The Stationery Office, 2010.

police, may be tempted to seek reassurance and guidance from their partner safeguarding agencies – for example, the NHS – even when those are the very same agencies responsible for, and sometimes keen to play down, the neglect in question. The Gosport War Memorial Hospital Inquiry noted:

Police seeing guidance and reassurance from the hospital and viewing relatives as troublemakers.

From the start, the mindset was one of seeing the family members who complained as stirring up trouble, and seeing the hospital, by contrast, as the natural place to go for guidance and assurance. As such, the police did not attempt to conduct enquiries in the same way as they would have done in a different setting; that is, one not involving medical decisions and treatment given in a hospital. The documents show that the police viewed the allegations as matters for the Trust and the regulatory bodies.[1]

All of this is why guidance on safeguarding adults boards (SABs) states that it is 'important that SAB partners feel able to challenge each other and other organisations where it believes that their actions or inactions are increasing the risk of abuse or neglect. This will include commissioners, as well as providers of services.'[2]

Safeguarding adults boards do not have a duty to publish safeguarding adults reviews, merely a power. Some tend to publish more, some less. It is argued by some that non-publication means that those contributing to the review will speak more freely; equally, the fear is that non-publication could become a way for the members of boards to safeguard their own reputations at the expense of transparency.

In similar vein, a draft Health Safety Investigations Bill published in 2017 proposed an independent Health Service Safety Investigations Board. This was to be based on the approach to investigation of air and marine accidents – that is, learning lessons and not blaming or attributing fault. The Board

---

1   Jones, Reverend J. (Chairman). *Gosport War Memorial Hospital: the report of the Gosport Independent Panel.* London: The Stationery Office, 2018, para 12.58.

2   Department of Health. *Care and support statutory guidance.* London: DH, 2016, para 14.134.

would be prohibited from disclosing information obtained in connection with an investigation. Thus, a 'safe space' would be created, in which people would speak more freely. The Bill also made similar provision for accredited NHS Trusts to conduct investigations on the same principle, involving other NHS Trusts and also themselves. A Parliamentary Committee opposed the notion of such safe space investigations being undertaken by NHS Trusts (as opposed to the Board), since the conflicts of interest would be too great.[1]

Contact with people lacking capacity

Safeguarding grounds are sometimes used to implement restrictions on contact between a person lacking capacity and relatives or friends. This takes place typically in care homes but may occur elsewhere.

The Care Quality Commission has published guidance about visiting in care homes and makes the point about how important it is for the welfare of residents and the right to respect for private and family life under article 8 of the European Convention on Human Rights. It notes, however, that rights under article 8 are not absolute and need to be balanced against other rights and the rights of other people. So, 'there may be a small number of very specific circumstances where care providers can restrict, or even refuse, visitors'. Clearly, a demonstrable risk to other residents could justify a restriction – whether or not the resident has capacity to request the visit.[2]

CONTACT WITH PEOPLE LACKING CAPACITY: EXAMPLES. A restriction to safeguard a person lacking capacity would have to be justified in terms of being in a person's best interests, be a less restrictive option and be proportionate. Arguably major contact restrictions – and disputes about them – can only be resolved ultimately and legally in the Court of Protection, even if there is a deprivation of liberty authorisation, granted by the local

---

1   House of Commons Joint Committee on the Draft Health Service Safety Investigations Bill. *Draft Health Service Safety Investigations Bill: a new capability for investigating patient safety incidents.* London: The Stationery Office, 2018, paras 144–150.

2   Care Quality Commission. *Information on visiting rights in care homes.* London: CQC, 2016, para 12.

authority, already in place. Examples, of which there are many, of barring or restriction of contact being approved by the Court of Protection, include:

- restricting contact between a mother and her son (in a care home setting)[1]

- restricting the contacts of a woman with learning disabilities, with mental capacity to engage in sexual relations, because she lacked the capacity to understand the risks she was placing herself at in those relationships[2]

- barring a father and grandmother from contact with a young woman for four years (other than supervised telephone contact) because of the extreme distress and disturbance caused when contact took place[3]

- barring a man from visiting his elderly wife with Alzheimer's disease in hospital, on the grounds that before she lost capacity she had decided she wanted to end the relationship, not to see him and not have him involved in her care.[4]

In any event, a decision to bar a visitor to a care home on grounds of risk (whether or not the resident has capacity) would have to be justified at the very least in terms of a sound decision-making process.

Daughter banned from care home after complaining about her mother's care. A care home banned a woman from visiting her mother in a BUPA-run care home after she had made complaints about care standards. She was banned without warning, without reasons, without any duration for the ban, and without conditions for its lifting. The staff at the home also prevented the daughter and medical doctor from visiting without good reason. The ombudsman had seen no evidence for the claim that Ms X or her partner acted in a way – as had been alleged – that led to police being called. The ombudsman concluded that staff at the care home banned the daughter because she had made valid complaints. This meant regulation 16 of the Health and Social Care (Regulated Activities) Regulations 2014 was breached: complainants must not be discriminated against or victimised. In particular, people's care and treatment must not be affected if they

---

1   *Dorset County Council v PL* [2015] EWCOP 44.

2   *Derbyshire County Council v AC* [2014] EWCOP 38.

3   *A Local Authority v B, F and G* [2014] EWCOP B18.

4   *RGB v Cwm Taf Health Board* [2013] EWHC B23 (COP).

make a complaint, or if somebody complains on their behalf. The care home was acting on behalf of the local authority, so the ombudsman held the latter to be at fault.[1]

Lack of justification for two-year ban on man from visiting his partner in a care home: on grounds of risk but without risk assessment. A woman was admitted to a care home. Her partner was subsequently banned for two years from visiting on grounds of threatening behaviour.

Lack of structured decision-making process and review. The ombudsman found several failures attaching to the decision. There was no structured decision-making process. Any restriction on visiting should have been on the basis of the woman's own wishes, a best interests decision and a risk assessment. Yet the local authority failed to consult the woman but at the same time advised the care home to call the police if necessary. The request not to visit was not reviewed – but such a restriction should have been regularly reviewed. The care home should not have threatened the woman with eviction if she wanted her partner to visit her. Somehow, the local authority concluded that it had not banned the partner, even though it quite clearly had. It claimed there was a risk assessment in place but there was no evidence of this.

Lack of records and inadequate risk assessment. The care provider had no records of the alleged threats made by the partner, or of the particular incident it claimed to have referred to the police (but it had no incident number). It should have kept such records and reported incidents to the local authority. When the local authority decided to lift the ban, it failed to tell the care home. The care home said he posed a risk both to staff and other residents, but there was no evidence that he posed a threat to other residents. The care home finally did a risk assessment over two years after he had been banned, but it was not robust: it did not substantiate the allegations. There were no current evidenced risks to the woman. And the care home had reinforced its ban, in response to the partner complaining to the Care Quality Commission. The care provider also made a number of inaccurate statements.

---

1   LGO, *Liverpool City Council*, 2018 (16 010 110).

All of the above was fault, some of it by the local authority, some by the care home (but the local authority was anyway accountable for the care home's faults).[1]

Man banned from visiting his sister in care home: lack of risk assessment and proportionality. A care home banned a man from visiting his sister, who had learning disabilities. The man had raised concerns about his sister's care. The local authority supported the ban as proportionate and necessary. The ombudsman found fault on the part of the local authority on several grounds. There was no evidence of a risk assessment or of consideration of any less restrictive way of managing any risk. The sister might have had capacity to express her views, but it was not clear whether this had been considered. Any restriction should have been for a specific period and reviewed; the local authority had no plans to review. The local authority failed to appoint an independent mental capacity advocate, after removing the brother as the 'relevant person's representative' (RPR) under the rules of the Mental Capacity Act 2005 – even though this meant there was then nobody to support the sister. The new RPR, the social worker and the deprivation of liberty team appeared to have had little contact with the sister, despite stating that they would review the ban.[2]

More particularly, the following cases demonstrate the pitfalls to avoid when safeguarding concerns are blown out of proportion and a local authority's actions become – arguably, if unintentionally – abusive.

Banning a man from visiting his partner and childhood friend on unspecified and uninvestigated grounds: breach of human rights. An elderly man and elderly woman, after long separate marriages, had both lost their spouses. They now rekindled a childhood acquaintance. He moved in with her and a personal, intimate relationship developed. She then had to move into a care home. Concerns were then expressed about the way in which he spoke to her, other residents at the home and to her daughters. A meeting was held, and local authority staff looked into the matter.

Wrongly barring the man on the say-so of the woman's daughters. The social workers acknowledged that it had to be ascertained whether the woman

---

1   LGO, *Nottinghamshire County Council*, 2017 (16 009 251), paras 35–47.

2   LGO, *Norfolk County Council*, 2017 (16 013 714), para 57.

had capacity to make a decision about the visits, but that in the meantime a decision was taken that the man and his family should be forbidden from visiting. The basis for this was that the woman's daughters, as next of kin, were entitled to take the decision. This was despite the fact that, more than once, the woman had said she wanted visits from both her daughters and the man. There was no evidence that the social workers had conducted a best interests decision. The local authority argued, however, that the care home had anyway taken a decision to prohibit him from visiting, so the local authority couldn't have done anything about it anyway. The man was very unhappy and ended up not seeing the woman for nearly two years.

Unacceptable delay in mental capacity assessment. The local authority sought to obtain a medical assessment of the woman's capacity; but it took ten months for this to happen. This was unacceptable delay.

Consideration of less restrictive option. In any case, even had the local authority taken the view from the outset that she lacked capacity, it should have considered her best interests, not just gone along with the daughters. And this would have involved considering not just whether the ban was justifiable but also whether some less drastic arrangement was possible – for example, supervised visits.

Extent of alleged harm. The alleged harm in question had only ever been words, not physical harm; but there was not even a record of this. The only recorded note was that, on one visit, when he left she had been distressed – but no record of why. It was this note that prompted the daughters to attend a meeting and ask for the ban. When her capacity was finally ascertained, and the Court of Protection became involved, it was decided that she should see him (albeit observed), and it went very well; she smiled and they got on very well.

Breach of article 8. In the event, the judge held that the man's human rights had been breached – namely, right to respect for private life under article 8 of the European Convention.[1]

Preventing a daughter from visiting her dying mother: arbitrary injustice without legal (or evidential) justification. The local government ombudsman found maladministration when a local authority prevented a woman, for a period of about six weeks, from visiting her mother in a care home, between 19 December and 2 February. By the time she was finally permitted to visit,

---

1   *City of Sunderland v MM* (2011) 1 FLR 712.

her mother had suffered a stroke, did not recognise her daughter and died the next day. The decision was made by the local authority and care home, not by the woman, whose mental capacity had not been assessed (although it transpired she did have capacity, but by then it was too late). The local authority had ignored the rules in the Mental Capacity Act of assuming a person has capacity unless it is established that they don't.

> Ms B [the daughter] was told unexpectedly – and without there being any evidence – that she was regarded as a threat to her own mother, denied access to her, made to hand over a Christmas gift outside the home and made to wait for over a month for the Council's processes before finally being told that she could see her mother. By then her mother was unable to recognise or communicate with her daughter.
>
> Two days before Christmas, officers of the Joint Service knew that Ms B's brother had withdrawn his allegation that she was a risk to their mother. From then there were no grounds for preventing mother and daughter from seeing each other.
>
> Knowing that Mrs B was dying, officers of the Joint Service arranged a specialist assessment of whether she had the capacity to decide whether she wanted to see her daughter. During the month that it took for this assessment to be done, Mrs and Ms B were prevented from seeing each other – although there was no legal power to stop Ms B from visiting her mother. The Investigating Officer was wrong to say that the effect of requesting the assessment was to 'freeze any further decision-making'… The maladministration deprived Ms B of the opportunity to speak with her mother before they were separated forever by death. The nature and scale of this injustice is difficult to express or quantify.[1]

Equally, if a resident has the mental capacity to decide that they wish – or do not wish – to see a relative, this is their decision, even if the consequence is to their own detriment. The local ombudsman has made a number of findings to this effect, when safeguarding concerns were raised by another family member.

---

1   LGO, *Leeds City Council*, 2011 (10 012 561).

Contact with daughter: mother's capacity to decide. An elderly woman lived with her son. The daughter complained that she was being denied sufficient access to her mother, and that the local authority should have intervened. The local authority made enquiries, concluding that the case was one primarily of intra-family conflict, and that the mother could make her own decisions about maintaining contact with the daughter, the frequency of that contact, where the visits should take place and whether visits should be supervised. The local authority could not hold a best interests meeting, since the mother did not lack the relevant mental capacity. There was fault in the local authority's decision.[1]

Contact with daughter. A woman received a compensation award and gave the partner of one of her daughters control over her finances. The other daughter believed the partner was abusing his position and raised a safeguarding alert. The mother then complained about this sister's visits, but the local authority found both that the woman had capacity to manage her money and to decide about visits. When she subsequently lost capacity, it became apparent that the partner had indeed been financially abusing the mother; the local authority also decided that it was in the best interests of the mother to be visited by this daughter. The ombudsman found no fault.[2]

Controlling or coercive behaviour

The Serious Crime Act 2015 contains a criminal offence of coercive or controlling behaviour. In summary, the key ingredients are:

- **behaviour:** person A repeatedly or continuously engages in behaviour towards another person B that is controlling or coercive

- **personal connection:** A and B are, at the time of the behaviour, personally connected

- **serious effect:** the behaviour has a serious effect on B, and

---

1   LGO, *Wakefield City Council*, 2017 (16 015 137). Also: LGO, *London Borough of Barnet*, 2017 (16 016 672).

2   LGO, *North Lincolnshire Council*, 2016 (15 015 381).

- **knowledge:** A knows or ought to know that the behaviour will have a serious effect on B.

In addition:

- **Personal connection:** means (a) A is in an intimate personal relationship with B or (b) A and B live together and (i) they are members of the same family, or (ii) they have previously been in an intimate personal relationship with each other.

- **Children:** the offence doesn't apply to parents of children under 16.

- **Serious effect (fear, alarm, distress):** means (a) it causes B to fear, on at least two occasions, that violence will be used against B, or (b) it causes B serious alarm or distress which has a substantial adverse effect on B's usual day-to-day activities.

- **Defence:** it is a defence for A to show that (a) in engaging in the behaviour in question, A believed that he or she was acting in B's best interests, and (b) the behaviour was in all the circumstances reasonable. But this is not a defence in relation to fear of violence.

- **Penalty:** five years' maximum prison sentence.

Statutory guidance states that:

- **Controlling behaviour:** is a range of acts designed to make a person subordinate and/or dependent by isolating them from sources of support, exploiting their resources and capabilities for personal gain, depriving of them the means needed for independence, resistance and escape, and regulating their everyday behaviour.

- **Coercive behaviour:** is a continuing act or pattern of acts of assaults, threats, humiliation and intimidation or other abuse that is used to harm, punish or frighten their victim.

The guidance also makes clear the relevance of this criminal offence to vulnerable adults who may face additional risks related to their impairment.[1] The following examples of convictions illustrate that other offences may be involved.

---

1   Home Office. *Controlling or coercive behaviour in an intimate or family relationship: statutory guidance framework*. London: The Stationery Office, 2015, pp.3, 7.

Woman convicted for controlling and coercing a vulnerable adult. A 22-year-old woman was convicted of controlling and coercive behaviour towards her partner, who suffered from hydrocephalus (build-up of fluid inside the skull) that made him vulnerable. She used blunt objects to strike him, wounded him with a knife and didn't help him get to hospital. He was not permitted to sleep in the same bed as her. He was seen on occasions with black eyes and to be limping and with his arm in a sling. A neighbour had seen her 'armed' with a screwdriver or hammer; another had heard him shouting, 'Get off me. Get off my head. Don't keep doing that to my head.' When paramedics were called, they noted injuries to his hand and burns to arms and legs, which were being self-treated with cling film: 5 per cent of his total body surface was scalded. She inflicted these injuries with boiling or hot water.

She was jailed for seven and a half years and given a restraining order banning her from contacting the victim. Seven years of the sentence was for the offence of grievous bodily harm, the remaining six months for the offence of coercive and controlling behaviour. She was a high performer at school, a trained gymnast, had a degree in fine arts, had raised money for children in Africa, and been a volunteer for an animal charity.[1]

Man convicted for controlling or coercive behaviour. A man was convicted in the following circumstances. He rarely allowed the victim to go out alone, but when she did, he would keep track of where she had gone, including making her keep parking receipts. He continuously belittled her and made her believe she needed only him, pushing her family and friends away. He checked her social media accounts and phone messages and controlled her appearance by telling her what to wear and changing her hairstyle. After one argument, he assaulted her, but she escaped and called the police.

The sentence given for the controlling or coercive behaviour was 18 weeks' imprisonment, suspended for 18 months, with a community order for 18 months. In addition, he was convicted of assault (18 weeks' imprisonment concurrent, suspended for 18 months) and of two counts of criminal damage to property valued under £5000. He was also ordered to pay costs.[2]

1   Ward, V. 'Controlling girlfriend "first woman convicted" of new domestic abuse offence.' *Daily Telegraph*, 16 April 2018.

2   'Man sentenced for controlling or coercive behaviour.' Crown Prosecution Service, 27 April 2016. Accessed on 28 February 2018 at: http://blog.cps.gov.uk/2016/04/man-sentenced-for-controlling-or-coercive-behaviour.html.

Cooperation (Care Act)

The Care Act contains three key duties, relevant to safeguarding, for organisations to cooperate with each other.

The first and second can be characterised as more general duties – not to be dismissed, but normally less easy to enforce in any one individual case. The third is more specific and therefore, in principle at least, more amenable to enforcement. Overall, the cooperation must relate to, or be relevant to, adults in need and carers. The purposes of cooperation include, but are not limited to, the following:

- promoting the well-being of adults and carers in the area

- improving the quality of care and support for adults, or support for carers, in the area

- 'smoothing' the transition process for children when they become adults (age 18) for the purposes of the Care Act, and

- identifying lessons for the future from cases of adults who have experienced serious abuse or neglect.

Although the last is clearly the most relevant to adult safeguarding, the first is also, since the definition of well-being includes protection of the individual from abuse and neglect. So, too, the second, since poor-quality care commissioned by local authorities and the NHS increases the risk of neglect or abuse.

COOPERATION: GENERAL DUTY ON STATUTORY PARTNERS. Section 6 of the Care Act states that statutory partners must cooperate with one another. Statutory partners are defined as local social services authorities, housing authorities, NHS bodies, police, probation service, prison service, Department of Work and Pensions.

Section 6 is more of a general duty, compared with section 7 (see below) which applies specifically to the case of each individual person. The courts tend anyway not to be enthusiastic about legal cases being brought by one statutory agency against another – something they have made clear in the past when considering a similar duty of cooperation under section 27 of the

Children Act 1989.[1] Furthermore, in the following case, in which reference to the Care Act duty of cooperation was made, the court found that the cooperation duty could in principle anyway only go so far.

Failing to agree how to meet the care and support needs of an elderly prisoner, on his release. The duty of cooperation might require good faith discussions between partners but not extend to forcing a partner to do something it believes it has no statutory duty to do. This became clear when the probation service and a local authority failed to agree about their respective legal duties and responsibilities to meet the needs of a disabled prisoner being discharged to a hostel, which meant he could not be released, an impasse the judge felt unable to remedy.[2]

COOPERATION: BETWEEN A LOCAL AUTHORITY'S SEPARATE DEPARTMENTS. In addition, a local authority must make arrangements for ensuring cooperation between its social services, housing, children's services and public health departments.

COOPERATION: GENERAL DUTY TO COOPERATE WITH OTHER ORGANISATIONS. Section 6 of the Care Act states, separately, that local authorities must cooperate with other bodies it considers appropriate – whose activities relate to adults with care and support needs or to carers. Examples of those with whom the local authority 'may' consider it appropriate to consult are:

- providers of care and support, or support services, in relation to prevention, delay or reduction of need under section 2 of the Care Act

- providers of primary medical, dental, ophthalmic and pharmaceutical services (i.e. general practitioners, dentists, opticians and pharmacists)

---

1   *R v Northavon District Council Ex p. Smith* [1994] 2 AC 402. And: *R (C1 and C2) (by their mother and litigation friend) v London Borough of Hackney* [2014] EWHC 3670 (Admin).

2   *R (John Taylor) v Secretary of State for Justice, National Probation Service North West Division v Wakefield Council, The Parole Board* [2015] EWHC 3245 (Admin).

- independent hospitals

- private registered providers of housing (e.g. housing associations).

There is, however, no reciprocal duty on these other bodies to cooperate with the local authority.

COOPERATION: SPECIFIC DUTY. Section 7 of the Care Act places a more specific cooperation duty on statutory partners when a request is made in relation to a particular adult in need of care and support, a carer, a child's carer or a young carer. (The duty also relates to a request made to any other local authority not defined as a statutory partner.)

The requested party must comply with the request unless it gives written reasons as to why it considers that compliance (a) would be incompatible with its own duties or (b) would otherwise have an adverse effect on the exercise of its functions.

The reference to incompatibility of function means that partners cannot, for instance, force each other to do something that they are not legally empowered to do. Nor, if the request is about functions that are compatible, can the requester dictate what the organisation requested should do.

> **Incompatibility and adverse effect on functions.** In a dispute about tracheostomy care for a child, the court noted that the provision of such specialist health care could not, as a matter of law, come under the Children Act 1989 – and so the local authority could not provide it. Such provision would be incompatible with their functions.
>
> Conversely, the NHS was providing a certain level of tracheostomy care but refused to provide more. The cooperation duty did not mean that the NHS was bound by the local authority assessment of the amount of care required (and therefore be under a duty to provide it). Otherwise, there could be prejudice to (i.e. adverse effect on) the discharge of other NHS functions.[1]

---

1   *R (T) v London Borough of Haringey* [2005] EWHC 2235 (Admin), paras 95–101.

Nonetheless, despite these provisos, the cooperation duty is there to be used, and a failure by a local authority to make reasonable efforts to utilise it might lead to the local ombudsman finding maladministration.

Using the Care Act cooperation duty in making safeguarding enquiries. A vulnerable man, possibly with autism and learning disabilities, but so far undiagnosed, was the focus of both assessment and safeguarding duties (after he had been assaulted) on the part of the local authority. One of the difficulties in reaching a conclusion about his needs and what to do about them was a continuing absence of assessment by the Autism Spectrum Team (ASC), an NHS-based team.

In relation to both the assessment and the safeguarding investigation, the ombudsman referred to the duties of cooperation in sections 6 and 7 of the Care Act. It was maladministration that the local authority had not made greater efforts to get the NHS ASC team involved: after two years, the assessment was still pending.[1]

Likewise, if a partner refuses to comply with a request, without clear reasons being given, then the courts may find the duty has not been complied with. In the following case, a similar duty to that under the Care Act was considered under section 27 of the Children Act 1989.

Refusal to comply with request: but no evidence of undue prejudice on the discharge of functions. A social worker made a recommendation to a housing department that a family be rehoused, in relation to the management of risk for a six-year-old autistic child. The housing authority refused. It simply looked at the family's situation again and assessed that they should remain where they were. This was unlawful. What the local authority should have done was to take a decision based upon the safety, risk and overcrowding issues the social worker had identified. If it was going to argue that compliance with the request would unduly prejudice the discharge of its housing duties by giving greater priority to the family, then it had to evidence this. However, it had put forward no evidence that a decision

---

1   LGO, *Kent County Council*, 2016 (15 018 466), para 28.

to rehouse would have this effect, especially since there was discretionary power – meaning flexibility – contained within the allocation policy.[1]

Coroners

Abuse or neglect of a vulnerable adult, associated with a death, may trigger the involvement of a coroner, who in turn might then shed light on the circumstances of the death – for example, contributory neglect. The relevant rules are contained in the Coroners and Justice Act 2009 and include:

- **Deaths in general.** Deaths in general must be reported to the local Registrar of deaths. Normally, a medical doctor provides the cause of death on a signed medical certificate, on receipt of which the death can be registered by the Registrar.

- **Suspicious deaths, unknown cause, state detention.** However, a senior coroner must conduct an investigation if he or she has reason to suspect that (a) the deceased died a violent or unnatural death, (b) the cause of death is unknown, or (c) the deceased died while in custody or otherwise in state detention.[2]

- **Discontinuation of investigation.** The coroner must discontinue an investigation if an examination reveals the cause of death and the coroner thinks it is not necessary to continue the investigation. However, this rule does not apply if the coroner has reason to suspect that the deceased (a) died a violent or unnatural death or (b) died while in custody or otherwise in state detention. If requested to do so by an interested person, the coroner must provide a written explanation of a decision to discontinue the investigation.[3]

- **Inquest with or without jury.** An inquest must be held without a jury, unless the coroner has reason to suspect any of the following:

  » the deceased died in custody or otherwise in state detention – and that (i) the death was a violent or unnatural one, or (ii) the cause of death is unknown

---

1   *R (KS) v Haringey London Borough Council* [2018] EWHC 587 (Admin), para 66.

2   Coroners and Justice Act 2009, s.1.

3   Coroners and Justice Act 2009, s.4.

» the death resulted from an act or omission of (i) a police officer, or (ii) a member of a service police force – in purported execution of the officer's or member's duty

» the death was caused by a notifiable accident, poisoning or disease.

Alternatively, the coroner has a power, rather than duty, to hold an inquest with a jury, if the coroner thinks that there is sufficient reason for doing so.[1]

- **Inquest not deciding civil or criminal liability.** An inquest hears evidence from witnesses but is not a trial. The findings of the coroner must not be framed in such a way as to apparently determine any question of civil or criminal liability.[2]

- **Inquest verdicts.** Inquest verdicts generally include, for example, natural causes (including fatal medical conditions), accident or misadventure, alcohol- or drug-related death, lawful killing, unlawful killing, suicide, open verdict (in the absence of sufficient evidence for any other verdict). Neglect causing death could be the verdict, but more often neglect will be deemed to have contributed to, rather than caused, death.

- **Inquests and state involvement.** If a person has died and the State or its agents have failed to protect the person against human or other risk, then an 'enhanced' inquest is held, as demanded by Article 2 of the European Convention on Human Rights.

- **Inquests and neglect.** An inquest might include questions of neglect. Neglect has been defined by the courts in this context as 'a gross failure to provide adequate sustenance, medical attention or shelter for a person in a position of dependency, whether by reason of a physical or mental condition'.[3]

- **Coroner reports expressing wider concerns.** If a coroner believes that anything revealed by an investigation gives rise to concerns about the risk of future deaths, the coroner must report this to a person who may have

---

1   Coroners and Justice Act 2009, s.7.

2   Coroners and Justice Act 2009, s.10.

3   *R v North Humberside Coroner, ex parte Jamieson* [1995] QB 1.

the power to take relevant action. Such reports are known as regulation 28 reports.[1]

CORONERS: AND ADULT SAFEGUARDING. The findings of coroners can cast light on neglect or abuse of vulnerable adults, sometimes by registered health and care providers, sometimes at the hands of private individuals. Such findings may also prompt subsequent police involvement and prosecution.

Death of epileptic patient by drowning: contributed to by neglect. In the much-publicised case of Colin Sparrowhawk, who suffered from epilepsy, a coroner's inquest concluded that serious failings in bathing arrangements amounted to neglect which contributed to his death.[2] (Subsequently, a health and safety at work prosecution took place against Southern Health NHS Foundation Trust, and the learning disability unit was closed.)

Five patients dying from falls in four months in frailty unit of hospital. A coroner heavily criticised East Kent Hospitals University Foundation Trust after five patients died within four months in the same frailty unit in the hospital. Overall, risk assessments were inadequate, incomplete, not reviewed or not enforced.[3]

Coroner putting pressure on NHS England to report on fatal attacks on hospital ward. The Leeds coroner put pressure on NHS England to complete an investigation into a fatal attack on a ward at St James's Hospital, in which one patient – whose anti-psychotic medication had been stopped – killed two other patients. This was 15 months after the NHS England investigation had been initiated. A report by the Trust itself had found that staff on the ward where the attack took place had experienced 46 separate violent incidents during a 12-month period but had little or no training of mental healthcare. Prior to the coroner's intervention, the incident had never previously been made public and the families of all three men

---

1   Coroners and Justice Act 2009, schedule 5, para 7. And: Coroners (Investigations) Regulations 2013, rr.28–29.

2   Morris, S. 'Neglect contributed to teenager's death at NHS unit, inquest finds.' *The Guardian*, 16 October 2015.

3   Moore, A. 'Trust criticised after five falls deaths in frailty unit.' *Health Service Journal*, 28 February 2018.

had accused the NHS of trying to cover up the incident and of avoiding addressing their concerns.[1]

Gross failures of statutory services and providers in the care of a man who choked on his own faeces. A coroner found 'gross failures' by various agencies in the care of a man with learning disabilities that led to him choking on his own faeces and dying in Ipswich Hospital after surgery had removed 22lb of faeces. He was born with moderate learning disabilities and bowel problems, and family members said they provided daily laxatives and a high-fibre diet to alleviate his constipation. He was moved to a care home in Lowestoft in 1999, which was turned into a supported living complex in 2009. This resulted in changes to his diet and a reduction in monitoring his bowel movements, leading to his constipation worsening. This had been the start of a chain of events that led to his death; without them, his 'death would not have occurred'.[2]

Prison sentence for wilful neglect of care home resident, following coroner involvement. In one case, it was following the involvement of a coroner that a care home owner was charged and sent to prison for six months for wilful neglect. The resident concerned had died of septicaemia and pneumonia, having been found previously by his family in soiled clothing, sweating and unconscious. He had been dehydrated and lost two stones in weight in the period prior to his death.[3]

Neglect of 93-year-old man by woman who lived with him. A 93-year-old man died, malnourished with multiple bed sores on arms, back, hips, buttocks, groin, legs and feet, and stuck in the foetal position unable to uncurl. A 54-year-old woman had been living with him and had told police that she loved him and looked after him. The coroner found that the man's death had occurred 'aggravated by neglect', and that he would be writing to several agencies.[4]

---

1   Lintern, S. 'NHS England given deadline for fatal hospital attack inquiry.' *Health Service Journal*, 15 March 2018.

2   Handley, R. '"Gross failures" in constipation death.' *East Anglian Daily Times*, 8 February 2018.

3   Narain, J. 'Care home boss jailed after wilful neglect killed Alzheimer's patient.' *Daily Mail*, 21 May 2008.

4   'Inquest results in neglect verdict.' *Westmoreland Gazette*, 21 December 2001.

Care and neglect of patients in hospital. A coroner in 2006 threw light on standards of care at Tameside Hospital, when investigating the deaths of several patients;[1] and, similarly, at the Queen's Hospital, Romford, in relation to the suffering, neglect and death from pressure sores of an 89-year-old war veteran.[2]

Admission to hospital of care home resident. In 2012, a coroner stated that she found it

> very alarming that such a vulnerable person who relied on professionals for her care and support was presented to hospital in the way she was. The vulnerable in our society must be properly cared for on all levels and their dignity protected. I think that [the woman] was not afforded the care and dignity she deserved on this occasion.

The 94-year-old woman concerned had been admitted to hospital, five weeks after going into a care home in reasonable health. On admission to hospital, she had a chest infection, pneumonia, pressure sores, septicaemia and ear and urinary infections. She died about two weeks later.[3]

Coroners might be challenged, for example, by family members, for failing to hold an inquest into the death of a relative.

Death in care home: reason to suspect unnatural death and failure to hold an inquest. Expert evidence suggested that the death of a care home resident in 2002 had been caused or contributed to by excessive doses of an anti-psychotic drug, coupled with the restrictive effect of a bucket chair and a possible failure to give adequate antibiotic treatment for pneumonia. The bucket chair was a low-slung seat from which elderly, and maybe restless, residents would have difficulty getting up unless assisted.

---

1   Fielding, F. (Professor Dame). *Independent review of older people's care at Tameside General Hospital.* Manchester: NHS North West, 2007, p.2.

2   Schlesinger, F. 'Coroner's fury as great-grandfather, 86, dies after being dumped on A&E trolley for 19 hours TWICE.' *Daily Mail,* 22 May 2009.

3   '"She looked like a concentration camp victim": coroner slams care home after emaciated pensioner was admitted to hospital weighing five-and-a-half stone.' *Daily Mail,* 26 April 2012.

This gave reasonable cause to suspect that the death was unnatural under section 8 of the Coroners Act 1988. However, the coroner failed to hold an inquest; a successful judicial review case was brought, challenging this decision. The death had taken place in the Maypole Nursing Home in Birmingham, operated by two general practitioners. Most of the residents were funded by social services and the NHS. A number of residents had died. The National Care Standards Commission had taken steps to close the home compulsorily, although the owner closed it voluntarily. The strategic health authority also investigated and disciplinary action was taken by the General Medical Council against the two general practitioners, who were suspended.[1]

Corporate financial abuse, see *Financial abuse: corporate*

County lines

So-called 'county lines' involve exploitation of vulnerable young people and adults by violent gang members, based in cities, in order to move and sell drugs across the country more widely.[2] See also *Cuckooing*.

- **Vulnerable people and children.** Typically involved are city-based organised crime gangs extending drug dealing activity into new areas, many of which are coastal towns. The gangs recruit vulnerable people, often children, to act as couriers and to sell drugs. A telephone number is established locally, potential buyers use it and local runners are dispatched to make deliveries via a telephone 'relay or exchange' system.

- **Location to store drugs.** Gang members enter into relationships with young women in order to secure a location for drugs to be stored in the new area. In addition, violence is used against drug users to coerce them to become runners, enforce debts and use their accommodation as an operating base.

---

1   *Bicknell v HM Coroner for Birmingham/Solihull* [2007] EWHC 2547 (Admin).

2   Home Office. *Criminal exploitation of children and vulnerable adults: County Lines guidance.* London: HO, 2018.

- **Modern slavery.** The Crown Prosecution Service encourages prosecutors to consider all available charges, including under the Modern Slavery Act 2015, where there has been deliberate targeting, recruitment and significant exploitation of young and vulnerable people.[1]

- **Other criminal law.** A range of criminal law may be relevant, including injunctions under the Police Act 2009 to prevent gang-related violence and activity, Misuse of Drugs Act 1971, Prevention of Crime Act 1953 and the Criminal Justice Act 1988 (offences involving offensive weapons and articles which have a blade or are sharply pointed – used, in the context of county lines, for example, to counter competition), Firearms Act 1968, Offences Against the Person Act 1861, Sexual Offences Act 2003.

- **Prosecution of vulnerable adult.** If adults are selling drugs on behalf of the 'traffickers', there is a defence potentially open to them if they can prove they were compelled to commit the offence and that the compulsion was attributable to slavery or relevant exploitation. Those who were under 18 at the time of the offence do not need to prove compulsion. This defence is under section 45 of the Modern Slavery Act 2015. Exploitation, defined in section 3 of the Act, does not – in the case of a vulnerable adult – require force, threat or deception. In any case, it may not be in the public interest (and unattractive to juries) to prosecute an exploited individual, who has been the subject of multi-agency safeguarding efforts.[2]

An example of a conviction, under the Modern Slavery Act, was as follows:

County lines conviction: vulnerable woman and modern slavery. Two London gang members, running a county line drug operation, were convicted under the Modern Slavery Act 2015, after using a vulnerable 19-year-old woman to transport and sell drugs in Wales. They also admitted conspiracy to supply Class A drugs. The young woman had been reported as missing and was found at an address used by the gang, which had lured the woman into a car, following a brief online conversation, before driving her to Wales. There she met a man who told her she 'belonged to him' and destroyed her

---

1   'Drug offences.' Crown Prosecution Service (undated). Accessed on 28 February 2018 at: www.cps.gov.uk/legal-guidance/drug-offences.

2   Crown Prosecution Service. *'County lines' typology.* London: CPS, 2017.

mobile phone. She was held at an address for five days, during which time she was forced to store Class A drugs against her will.[1]

Court of Protection

The Court of Protection operates under the Mental Capacity Act 2005. Lack of mental capacity generally makes an adult more vulnerable, and therefore interventions by the Court of Protection sometimes involve safeguarding issues – that is, a best interests decision might be required in order to protect a person from harm, which sometimes might be in the form of abuse or neglect.

Conversely, the decision is sometimes to protect a person from an intervention – for example, by a local authority – ostensibly designed to benefit the person, but which might in fact be an intervention that is not only unlawful but sometimes itself abusive.

It is beyond the scope of this book to set out in detail the procedural workings of the Court of Protection. But it may be called on, for example, to decide matters about a person's mental capacity, best interests, deprivation of liberty, lasting power of attorney, deputyship, advance decisions. These – together with relevant Court of Protection case law and decisions – are covered under their own headings in this book.

Courts, see *Remedies*

Covert medication

The giving of medication covertly is not necessarily abusive. However, guidance states that it should not be given to a person with the mental capacity to make the decision about whether or not to take it. If, on the other

---

1   'County Line criminals convicted in landmark Modern Slavery case.' *Policeprofessional. com*, 6 December 2017. Accessed on 3 October 2018 at: www.policeprofessional.com/news/%c2%91county-line%c2%92-criminals-convicted-in-landmark-modern-slavery-case.

hand, a person lacks capacity, covert medication may sometimes be given, but only following a best interests meeting.[1]

> **Covert medication to treat HIV for a woman with serious mental disorder.** A woman suffered from a serious psycho-affective disorder. She was in the grip of powerful delusions. She did not believe that she was HIV-positive, instead believing that she was a participant, with her husband, in a film about HIV. She did not have a husband but believed she did in the form of a celebrity sportsman. She also believed that when blood samples were taken from her by the hospital staff, it was done for the purposes of drinking her blood. She was sure she was not HIV-positive. If she had learnt she was being secretly and clandestinely administered with anti-retroviral treatment, she would have been upset.
>
> The court accepted that it might seem a strong step to take in authorising a course of medication that involved deception, but it was undoubtedly in her best interests as it would save her life.[2]
>
> **Failure to provide covert medication causing harm: fault leading to injustice.** An elderly man with Alzheimer's disease, and lacking capacity, required medication in the form of Risperidone to calm his agitated behaviour and to help him sleep. He entered a care home for respite (he lived otherwise at home with his wife). Failure to put in place a covert medication plan was maladministration. It was clearly called for and the consequence was distress and admission to hospital for 15 weeks. The failure was due to practical events, lack of communication and many avoidable delays.[3]

Crime and Security Act 2010, see *Domestic violence: protection notices and orders*

---

1   National Institute for Clinical Excellence. *Medicines management in care homes: quality standard.* London: NICE, 2015, Quality Statement 6. Nursing and Midwifery Council. *Standards for medicine management.* London: NMC, 2007, p.32.

2   *Re AB* [2016] EWCOP 66, paras 14, 16, 26.

3   LGO, *Staffordshire County Council*, 2017 (17 008 171).

Criminal behaviour orders, see *Anti-social behaviour*

Criminal Justice and Courts Act 2015, see *Wilful neglect or ill-treatment*

Criminal law

Criminal law is distinguished from civil law. Different remedies and standards of proof are involved. Abuse or neglect identified under the Care Act 2014, a piece of civil legislation, may or may not amount also to an offence under criminal law. See *Remedies*; *Standard of proof*.

Criminal record certificates

Enhanced criminal record certificates are provided under the Police Act 1997. The overall purpose of the criminal record certificate scheme is to put a potential employer in possession of both conviction and sometimes non-conviction information about a potential employee – to assist the former in deciding whether to employ the latter to work in regulated activity with adults (or to work with children). Extensive legal case law has explored the balance between protecting those adults, without at the same time disproportionately and unfairly stigmatising and semi-criminalising workers.

The rules and issues are covered below under the following headings:

- Criminal record certificates: background
- Criminal record certificates: application
- Criminal record certificates: levels of disclosure
- Criminal record certificates: mandatory information
- Criminal record certificates: minor offences
- Criminal record certificates: effect of adverse information.

CRIMINAL RECORD CERTIFICATES: BACKGROUND. A notable legal battleground has, over many years, developed over regulation of individuals working with vulnerable adults, namely the system of criminal record certificates and, separately, the system of barring people from working with vulnerable adults. Both systems have been designed, clearly, to protect vulnerable adults, but both have been exposed, at times, as potentially too blunt and drastic in their application.

Through a series of legal cases focusing on article 8 of the European Convention on Human Rights, the courts have forced on central government changes to what information is included in criminal record certificates. This is so that a better and more proportionate balance is struck, and workers are not semi-criminalised disproportionately for the rest of their life (e.g. for stealing two bicycles when they were 11 years old). At the time of writing, tensions remain, and the courts continue to expose some of the injustices to which central government appears to remain so doggedly attached.

CRIMINAL RECORD CERTIFICATES: APPLICATION. An employer must obtain the application form from the Disclosure and Barring Service (DBS); the applicant then completes the form and returns it to the employer. The latter then sends it to the DBS, who sends it back to the applicant – the employer then asks to see it. This means that the worker will have the opportunity to make representations to, or challenge, the DBS about any content – before the employer sees the certificate.[1]

CRIMINAL RECORD CERTIFICATES: LEVELS OF DISCLOSURE. The Police Act 1997 provides for three different levels of disclosure.

- **Basic disclosure.** The first is basic disclosure, which contains details of convictions held in central police records that are not 'spent' under the Rehabilitation of Offenders Act 1974.

- **Standard disclosure.** The second is standard disclosure, containing details of spent and unspent convictions, but also cautions, reprimands and warnings recorded centrally by the police. The disclosure will also indicate whether the

---

1   Police Act 1997, s.113; and see Protection of Freedoms Act 2012, Explanatory Notes, s.79.

person is on the barred list held by the DBS and thus unsuitable to work with vulnerable adults.[1]

Certain convictions do not become spent under the provisions of the 1974 Act – for example, in relation to the provision of care services to vulnerable adults, representation or advocacy services for vulnerable adults (approved by the Secretary of State or under statute), health services.[2] Therefore, such convictions continue to be disclosed for the purpose of standard and enhanced certificates.

- **Enhanced disclosure, including 'soft' information.** The third level is enhanced disclosure, which contains the same information as a standard disclosure, but can also contain additional, 'soft', non-conviction information held in local police records, but not on the Police National Computer. The question concerning this additional information is whether the local chief officer of police reasonably believes it to be relevant and, in his or her opinion, ought to be included in the certificate.[3]

Enhanced disclosure applies to workers who are working with vulnerable adults. Vulnerable adult is defined as under the Safeguarding Vulnerable Groups Act 2006: see *Barred list*.

When enhanced disclosure is made, 'suitability' information must be included. This is (a) whether the applicant is barred from regulated activity, (b) if the applicant is barred, certain details about the circumstances, and (c) whether the DBS is considering whether to include the applicant in the adults' barred list.[4]

Disclosure of soft information: balanced consideration required. The Supreme Court considered a case concerning a woman who was working as a midday assistant at a secondary school, about whom child protection concerns had been disclosed in the form of soft information within her enhanced criminal record certificate. She had lost her job. The court clarified that, in the light of article 8 of the European Convention on

---

1   Police Act 1997, s.113A.

2   SI 1975/1023. Rehabilitation of Offenders Act 1974 (Exceptions) Order 1975, schedule 1, paras 12–13.

3   Police Act 1997, s.113B.

4   Police Act 1997, s.113BB.

Human Rights, a balance had to be struck between protection of children and the right to respect for private life of the worker. This balance meant that a presumption of disclosure (in relation to adults or children) was not the correct legal position. Instead, there should be no precedence and no presumption either way.[1]

Soft information: failed prosecution or no prosecution. The Supreme Court has stated that 'there may be no logical reason to exclude information about serious allegations of criminal conduct, merely because a prosecution has not been pursued or has failed. In principle, even acquittal by a criminal court following a full trial can be said to imply no more than that the charge has not been proved beyond reasonable doubt. In principle, it leaves open the possibility that the allegation was true, and the risks associated with that'.

But it was concerned that whilst, in practice, there is emphasis on an employer not excluding the convicted from consideration for employment, there was not apparently the same emphasis in relation to the acquitted, who would surely deserve greater protection from unfair stigmatisation. Especially as inclusion of acquittal information, even in neutral terms, may be a 'killer blow' to the person's employment prospects if the employer takes the view that inclusion means that the police believe in the person's guilt.[2]

- **Common law disclosure.** In addition, the Police Act 1997 stated previously that the CRB (now the DBS) had to ask the chief police officer to provide any information relevant as to the person's suitability[3] – that is, information that the chief police officer thought ought to be provided, ought not to be included in the certificate in the interests of the prevention or detection of crime, but which could nevertheless still be disclosed to the registered body.

This rule has now been removed; so-called 'brown envelope' information will no longer be provided. However, it would remain open to the police, using their common law powers to prevent crime and protect the public, to pass

---

1   *R (L) v Commissioner of Police for the Metropolis*, Michaelmas Term [2009] UKSC 3.

2   *R(R) v Chief Constable of Greater Manchester* [2018] UKSC 47, para 67.

3   Police Act 1997, s.113B(4).

such information to a potential employer where they considered it 'justified and proportionate'.[1]

- **Dispute process about information included in enhanced certificate.** There is a dispute process in relation to soft, non-conviction information supplied by the police.[2] This allows the person to apply to an independent monitor (appointed under section 119B of the 1997 Act), for the latter to decide whether such information is relevant and should be included in the certificate. The independent monitor has then to ask the police to review whether the information concerned is relevant and ought to be included on the certificate.

  If, following that review, the independent monitor decides that the information either is not relevant or should not be included in the certificate, the independent monitor must inform the DBS, who must issue a new certificate which excludes that information.[3]

  The dispute process was introduced following the importance the courts had attached to representations, as being a component of legal fairness.[4] One such older case was as follows:

Importance of representations. A man applied to be a college lecturer in welding. The Manchester police supplied information about an allegation, never substantiated, about historic sex abuse dating back 15 years. The result of the disclosure was that he found it impossible to get the job. The court was clear that fairness demanded that he should be able to make representations first, not least because there 'did not appear to have been any detailed consideration of what the risk was that [the man], as a welding lecturer in a further education college, would come into contact with a child'. Disclosure had been a breach of his rights under article 8 of the European Convention; it had been disproportionate.[5]

---

1   Protection of Freedoms Act 2012, Explanatory Notes, para 331.

2   Police Act 1997, s.117A.

3   Protection of Freedoms Act 2012, Explanatory Notes, para 341.

4   *R (L) v Commissioner of Police for the Metropolis*, Michaelmas Term [2009] UKSC 3.

5   *R (C) v Secretary of State for the Home Department* [2011] EWCA Civ 175.

CRIMINAL RECORD CERTIFICATES: MANDATORY INFORMATION. For enhanced criminal record certificates, as explained above, there is a discretion and judgement to be applied about 'soft information'. However, no such discretion or judgement exists in relation to information held centrally on the Police National Computer. Such information must, as a matter of law, be disclosed.

- **Police National Computer: convictions, etc.** The Police and Criminal Evidence Act 1984 now states that not just convictions but also cautions, reprimands and warnings should be held on the Police National Computer (PNC).[1] Additional, soft, information is not.

- **Guidelines on retention and stepping down of records.** The police operate to guidelines published by the National Police Chiefs' Council. The guidelines state that records on the PNC will be deleted only when a person reaches 100 years of age – although chief police officers can exercise their discretion, in exceptional circumstances, to delete conviction records, specifically those relating to non-court disposals (e.g. adult simple cautions and conditional cautions), as well as any 'event history' owned by them on the PNC but only where the grounds for so doing have been examined and agreed.[2]

- **Retention of records of minor offences.** The consequence of this rule is that the police hold information on the PNC concerning very minor misdemeanours, which would in principle continue to be disclosed on standard and enhanced criminal record certificates. For example, a 40-year-old man received a £15 fine for theft from Marks and Spencer when he was 15. Similarly, a 19-year-old woman in Stafford had wanted to become a carer; however, a reprimand she had received as a 12-year-old for a minor assault was still coming up on criminal record checks.[3]

CRIMINAL RECORD CERTIFICATES: MINOR OFFENCES. The Supreme Court considered the following case and held that disclosure of the minor offence committed when the man was 11 years old was in line with the legal

---

1   Police and Criminal Evidence Act 1984, s.27.

2   National Police Chiefs' Council. *Deletion of records from national police systems (PNC/NDNAD/IDENT1)*. Fareham: ACRO, 2015, para 1.6.5.

3   *Chief Constable of Humberside Police v Information Commissioner* [2009] EWCA Civ 1079.

requirements of the interlocking legislation: the Police Act 1997 and the Rehabilitation of Offenders Act 1974 (Exceptions) Order 1975. However, these rules were inconsistent with article 8 of the European Convention on Human Rights, because they operated indiscriminately and therefore, in some cases (not all), disproportionately.

> **11-year-old's theft of two bicycles.** The claimant was a 20-year-old student. He was applying for admission to a sports studies degree course and had applied for an enhanced criminal record certificate to facilitate his entry. The certificate was duly issued but contained details of a warning for theft of two bicycles, issued to him in 2002 when he was 11 years old, by the Greater Manchester Police. This warning would continue to appear on his criminal record certificate indefinitely, in line with legislation – but inconsistently with human rights.[1]

As a result, the law was amended, meaning that certain offences – though still recorded on the PNC – will not, after a certain period of time, appear in criminal record certificates.[2]

- **Over-18, minor offence, conviction.** For those 18 or over at the time of the offence, an adult conviction will be removed from a DBS criminal record certificate if 11 years have elapsed since the date of conviction, if it is the person's only offence and if it did not result in a custodial sentence. Even then, it will only be removed if it does not appear on the list of more serious offences.[3] If a person has more than one offence, then details of all their convictions will always be included.

---

1   *R (T) v Secretary of State for the Home Department* [2014] UKSC 35, paras 41, 50, 59.

2   SI 1975/1023. Rehabilitation of Offenders Act 1974 (Exceptions) Order 1975. Amended by SI 2013/1198. Rehabilitation of Offenders Act 1974 (Exceptions) Order 1975 (Amendment) (England and Wales) Order 2013.

3   Disclosure and Barring Service. *List of offences that will never be filtered from a DBS certificate.* London: DBS, 2013. See also: SI 1975/1023. Rehabilitation of Offenders Act 1974 (Exceptions) Order 1975, r.2A, which in turn refers to a range of offences listed or contained in various other legislation, including, for example, those listed in schedule 15 of the Criminal Justice Act 2003, wilful neglect and ill-treatment within the Mental Health Act 1983 and the Mental Capacity Act 2005, etc.

- **Over-18, minor offence, caution.** An adult caution will be removed after six years have elapsed since the date of the caution – and if it does not appear on the list of more serious offences.

- **Under-18, minor offence.** For those under 18 at the time of the offence, the same rules apply as for adult convictions, except that the elapsed time period is 5.5 years. The same rules apply as for adult cautions, except that the elapsed time period is two years.[1]

However, the courts have criticised the amendments to the law as being still inconsistent with human rights in relation to key limitations in the amendments, which do not apply in case of a defined serious offence or in relation to the multiple conviction rule.[2] Consequently, the rules can still operate indiscriminately and disproportionately. For instance, the court considered the following example, the case of a man who had committed a serious offence 31 years ago.

> **Serious offence rule: application to offence committed when person aged 16, over 30 years ago: continued disclosure on certificate.** In November 1982, when 16 years of age, a young man was convicted of aggravated bodily harm, under section 47 of the Offences Against the Person Act 1861. He received a conditional discharge for two years and was bound over to keep the peace for 12 months. It had to be disclosed on any criminal record certificate.
>
> In the 31 years that have passed, he committed no further offence, and made a success of his life. He now wished to obtain a qualification teaching English as a second language and, to that end, in 2013, he began a training course with a view to obtaining a Certificate in English Language Teaching to Adults. He applied through his College to the DBS for a criminal record certificate, which showed his conviction. Because it was a serious offence, as set out in Schedule 15 of the 2003 Act, it had to be disclosed under the current statutory regime for disclosure.

---

1   Disclosure and Barring Service. *Filtering rules for criminal record check certificates*. London: DBS, 2013.

2   Serious offence as defined in schedule 15 of the Criminal Justice Act 2003.

> The court held this to be in breach of human rights, under article 8 of the European Convention on Human Rights.[1]

Similarly, the courts found the automatic multiple conviction rule to be in breach of human rights in the following case, highlighting its potential arbitrariness and unlawfulness.

Multiple conviction rule penalising former vulnerable women, themselves victims. The three women involved had committed soliciting offences, consequent on their vulnerability when first required or persuaded by 'boyfriends' to prostitute themselves. They were subject to violence and abuse at the hands of these men who groomed, trafficked and prostituted them at the ages of 14, 15 and 18, respectively. Since the first two were under the age of consent, they themselves had been victims of crime in relation to the very activity which resulted in their own convictions for soliciting offences. The first woman had committed 50 soliciting offences up to 1998, the second 49 up to 1988, and the third nine offences up to 1992. They had all long since removed themselves from prostitution.

The court held that these cases illustrated that the multiple conviction rule operated in an indiscriminate and arbitrary manner and was not in accordance with human rights law. The rule operated in such a way that any link between the past offending and the assessment of present risk in a particular employment was either non-existent or at best extremely tenuous.

The women were not statutorily barred from working with children or vulnerable adults (it was for the prospective employer to decide), but throughout their lives they would have to disclose their convictions. And they would be at a disadvantage in the recruitment process, and, even if successful in their application, would suffer embarrassment and stigma.[2]

CRIMINAL RECORD CERTIFICATES: EFFECT OF ADVERSE INFORMATION. Inclusion on the barred list held by the DBS legally precludes a person working with vulnerable adults, but this is not the legal effect of information disclosed in connection with a criminal record

---

1   *R (P) v Secretary of State for the Home Department* [2017] EWCA Civ 321, paras 44–45, 96.

2   *R (QSA) v Secretary of State for the Home Department* [2018] EWHC 407 (Admin).

certificate. It is simply for the prospective employer to judge whether any adverse information is relevant to the prospective employee being taken on.

For instance, in the following case, the registered nurse would have a 'formidable hurdle' to overcome, given the content of the criminal record certificate, but this did not mean she should not be given the chance to do so.

> **Enhanced criminal record certificate detailing criminal charges being brought against a nurse.** A registered nurse wanted to appeal to the Care Standards Tribunal against a decision by Welsh Ministers not to register her as a manager of a care home. She was on police bail at the time, having been charged with wilful neglect. This was for allegedly failing to ensure that junior staff knew what was required of them, following the death of a resident with senile dementia. A decision had been made not to register her, partly (there were other reasons) with reference to the contents of an enhanced criminal record certificate, which outlined a police investigation into a number of deaths.
>
> By the time the court considered the issue, the position had moved from a police investigation to actual criminal charges. However, the court stated that she was still entitled to have her case considered by the Tribunal, even though she would have a formidable hurdle to overcome.[1]

Although employers should have a balanced and fair policy about employing ex-offenders,[2] some may in practice simply rule people out without fair consideration. This has been pointed out by the courts; inclusion of adverse information in a certificate can be a 'killer blow', making a fair and proportionate system of disclosure in certificates, consistent with human rights, essential.[3]

> **Acquittal information being included in certificate: employer reaction and possible stigmatisation.** A teacher had been acquitted when, as a taxi driver, he had been charged with sexual assault. The court held that it was

---

1   *Welsh Ministers v Care Standards Tribunal* [2008] EWHC 49 (Admin).

2   Chartered Institute of Personnel and Development (CIPD). *Employing ex-offenders: a practical guide.* London: Criminal Records Bureau (undated).

3   *R (L) v Commissioner of Police for the Metropolis* [2009] UKSC 3; [2010] 1 AC 410, para 75.

proportionate and justifiable that the acquittal be included in his enhanced criminal record certificate but noted its concern about how employers might in practice react to acquittal information being included and the risk of the person being stigmatised.[1]

Blanket policy by employer on 'clean' certificate. Allegations of sexual abuse made against a deputy principal of a college for young autistic adults were disclosed. The court upheld the decision of the police to supply details of the allegations in a criminal record certificate. Consequently, the man had been instantly dismissed because his employer had a blanket policy of insisting on a 'clean certificate'.

 The court was troubled by this, because the law (at that time) imposed a relatively low threshold for disclosure and employers needed to understand this; a properly formed decision by the employer would take account of other information or explanation provided by the employee, additional to what appeared in the certificate. But a blanket policy did not allow for this to happen. The court suggested that the person might therefore have a reasonable prospect of contesting his dismissal in such circumstances before an Employment Tribunal.[2]

An employer's decision might, of course, turn out for better or worse.

Care worker taken on despite caution for assault: regarded as a hard-working and respected employee. Three weeks after having received a police caution for assaulting a vulnerable patient, a 69-year-old patient with dementia, a care worker was employed in another nursing home. His new employer explained that it was fully aware of his history and had carried out the necessary criminal record and POVA checks. It regarded him as a hard-working and respected employee.[3]

Care worker taken on following theft conviction: steals again. A carer with a drugs problem had been convicted previously of stealing his father's cheque book. The care agency with which he had now started work carried

1   *R (R) v Chief Constable of Greater Manchester* [2018] UKSC 47, paras 64–68.

2   *R (Pinnington) v Chief Constable of Thames Valley* [2008] EWHC 1870 (Admin).

3   'Care home employs nurse cautioned for patient attack.' *This is Cornwall*, 2008. Accessed on 23 October 2008 at: www.thisiscornwall.co.uk.

out a criminal record check but decided to employ him even so. Within six weeks of starting his new job as a home carer, he had stolen money from clients in their own homes, was prosecuted and admitted four charges of burglary. The employer said after the case that it would in future 'blacklist' carers known to have a criminal record.[1]

Crown Prosecution Service

The Crown Prosecution Service (CPS) is the principal agency responsible for criminal prosecutions. It must apply the *Code for Crown Prosecutors* when making prosecution decisions.[2] (The Health and Safety Executive can prosecute under health and safety at work legislation, and the Care Quality Commission can do so under the Health and Social Care Act 2008. Likewise, local authority trading standards officers.)

CROWN PROSECUTION SERVICE: TWO-STAGE PROSECUTION TEST.

In deciding whether to prosecute, the CPS applies a two-stage test. The first is the evidential stage.

Prosecutors must be satisfied that there is sufficient evidence to provide a realistic prospect of conviction. They must consider what the defence case may be, and how it is likely to affect the prospects of conviction. A case which does not pass the evidential stage must not proceed, no matter how serious or sensitive it may be. The evidence must be capable of being used in court, and be credible and reliable.

A prosecution will then usually take place unless the prosecutor is satisfied that the second state of the test is not satisfied, because there are public interest factors tending against prosecution which outweigh those tending in favour. Factors to consider in reaching this decision include:

- seriousness of the offence

- culpability of the suspect

---

1   Hudson, C. 'Carer stole from patients.' *Macclesfield Express*, 22 November 2006.

2   Crown Prosecution Service. *The Code for Crown Prosecutors*. London: CPS, 2018.

- circumstances of, and harm caused to, the victim – including vulnerability of victim and whether offence was motivated by discrimination based on the victim's characteristics (e.g. age, disability, ethnic or national origin, religion, gender, etc.)

- adverse effect of prosecution on victim: if there is evidence that prosecution is likely to have an adverse impact on the victim's health, it may make a prosecution less likely, taking into account the victim's views (however, the CPS does not act for victims or their families in the same way as solicitors act for their clients, and prosecutors must form an overall view of the public interest)

- suspect under 18: best interests of welfare of child or young person must be considered

- impact on community

- proportionality of prosecution.[1]

In one case involving a vulnerable adult, the courts found that the Crown Prosecution Service had acted irrationally by failing blatantly to adhere to the Code, consequently also breaching article 3 of the European Convention on Human Rights.

Failure to adhere to the Code in a case involving a mentally disordered victim: irrationality and breach of human rights. The CPS had wrongly jumped to conclusions about the credibility of the victim. He was a man who suffered from a history of psychotic illness, involving paranoid beliefs and auditory and visual hallucinations. On Boxing Day, part of his ear had been bitten off. Based on a doctor's report, to the effect that his mental condition might affect his perception and recollection of events, the CPS decided not to prosecute.

The judge was scathing, since the medical report was clearly insufficient to lead to the conclusion that the victim's identification of the suspect was the result of hallucination and that therefore he was not a credible witness. The CPS decision was 'irrational' in the true sense of the term. It suggested either a misreading of the report or an unfounded stereotyping

---

1   Crown Prosecution Service. *The Code for Crown Prosecutors*. London: CPS, 2013.

of the victim as someone who was not to be regarded as credible on any matter simply because of his history of mental problems.[1]

CROWN PROSECUTION SERVICE: AGGRAVATING FEATURES. Under section 146 of the Criminal Justice Act 2003, it is an aggravating feature of an offence (i.e. makes it more serious) if the offender showed hostility towards the victim based on the latter's disability, or if the offence was motivated by hostility towards people who have a disability (sometimes referred to as disability hate crime). Similarly, under section 143, if the victim has been targeted on account of their vulnerability.

- **Hostility.** The CPS has pointed out that for section 146 to apply there does indeed need to be that hostility. It applies where the offender assumes a person is disabled, even if that assumption is false. There is no statutory definition of a disability-related incident, but the Crown Prosecution Service takes it to mean 'any incident, which is perceived to be based upon prejudice towards or hatred of the victim because of their disability or so perceived by the victim or any other person'. Picking on a disabled person because he or she is an easy target would therefore not in itself trigger section 146.[2]

  However, even in the absence of hostility, knowledge of a person's disability (cerebral palsy), and taking advantage of that known vulnerability, can still amount to an aggravating feature (under section 143 – see immediately below).[3]

- **Culpability and vulnerability.** Alternatively, under section 143 of the Criminal Justice Act 2003, the court must – in considering the seriousness of any offence – assess the offender's culpability in committing the offence and any harm which the offence caused, was intended to cause, or might foreseeably have caused. The Sentencing Guidelines Council notes that culpability will be greater where a vulnerable victim has been targeted

---

1   *R (B) v Director of Public Prosecutions* [2009] EWHC 106 (Admin).

2   Crown Prosecution Service. *Policy for prosecuting cases of disability hate crime.* London: CPS, 2007, paras 2.2 and 2.5.2.

3   *R v Bridge* [2012] EWCA Crim 2270, para 123.

because of age, youth, disability or the job they do. Relevant factors would also include abuse of power and abuse of a position of trust.[1]

Conviction for threatening behaviour: restraining order to prevent further threat. A man with hearing difficulties was given a suspended jail term and a two-year restraining order after threatening to cut his disabled neighbour's remaining arm off during a row over loud music. He had reportedly sworn and used a derogative term for disabled people before saying he would like to 'do' the victim. His behaviour was described in court as a disability hate crime. A two-year restraining order was imposed.[2]

Targeting elderly and vulnerable people: legally aggravating features. A man committed 38 burglaries within the space of a few months. He posed as a policeman. He visited houses asking that people give him their cash and other valuables for safe keeping at the police station. He would even suggest that people speak on the phone to somebody pretending to be his superior. He targeted mainly elderly, or very elderly, people.

Aggravating features were: professional planning, working as a group, targeting elderly and vulnerable people, inducing fear, the special trauma of posing as police and warning victims of the specific risk of burglary, planning entry into their homes when they were present and leaving them fearing that they might be attacked by criminals and, the last feature common to both appellants, the high value to the victims of the property stolen, either cash or jewellery. The two perpetrators (he had an accomplice) were sentenced to seven and 12 years in prison respectively.

Reference was made to section 143 of the Criminal Justice Act 2003, in relation to similar offences having been committed before (before committing these burglaries, the man had just been released on licence, having been previously convicted for similar offences).[3]

CROWN PROSECUTION SERVICE: OLDER PEOPLE. In 2008, the CPS published guidance specifically about prosecuting crimes against older

1   Sentencing Guidelines Council. *Overarching principles: seriousness.* London: SGC, 2007, pp.5–6.

2   Adwent, C. 'Partially-deaf Bury St Edmunds man spared jail after threatening to cut disabled neighbour's remaining arm off.' *East Anglian Daily Times*, 7 June 2017.

3   *R v Casey* [2007] EWCA Crim 2568.

people. It stressed that it regarded crime against older people as serious and that it was therefore likely that a prosecution would be needed in the public interest. It listed various factors that will make a prosecution more likely. In summary:

- the offence is serious

- the defendant was in a position of authority or trust

- there are grounds for believing that the offence is likely to be continued or repeated

- the victim is vulnerable

- the victim is injured

- the defendant was motivated by prejudice or discrimination

- a weapon was used

- the defendant has made threats before or after the attack

- the defendant planned the attack

- there is a continuing threat to the health and safety of the victim or anyone else who is, or may become, involved

- the defendant has a criminal history, particularly involving convictions for offences against older people.[1]

Cuckooing

The term 'cuckooing' refers to criminal gangs targeting isolated and vulnerable individuals living, typically, in housing association and council accommodation by befriending them, then taking over their homes to deal drugs.[2] (See also *County lines*.) Under section 76 of the Anti-Social Behaviour Act 2014, the police or a local authority can issue a closure notice. This can be followed by a closure order made by a magistrates' court under section 80 of

---

1   Crown Prosecution Service. *Crimes against older people: prosecution policy.* London: CPS, 2008, para 4.8.

2   Doward, J. 'Vulnerable tenants targeted by drug gang "cuckoos".' *The Guardian*, 3 October 2010.

the Act, on grounds of disorderly, criminal or offensive behaviour, nuisance or disorder.

In some circumstances, under section 8 of the Misuse of Drugs Act 1971, an occupier of premises may be guilty of an offence if he or she knowingly permits or allows the premises to be used for the production or supply of controlled drugs.

Culture of care

If poor care takes hold – for example, in a hospital or care home – it can form a seedbed for systemic neglect. In other words, systemic neglect does not generate spontaneously, since it requires a culture to feed it. The gradual corrosion of good-quality care on a ward or in a unit can lead to staff becoming increasingly tolerant of poor care and genuinely not recognising the neglect or abuse in plain sight – and, ultimately, lead to indifference and disregard for human suffering and death, as the following examples show.

Normal and terrifying? Lord Robert Winston, a leading fertility expert and an active New Labour supporter, had recently been made a peer by the then Prime Minister, Tony Blair. He then accused the government of overseeing deeply unsatisfactory medical care and of deceiving the voters. His attack was born not just from professional frustration but from the personal, too. He bemoaned the fate of his diabetic 87-year-old mother admitted to hospital a few weeks before: a 13-hour wait in casualty, admission to a mixed-sex ward, medication not given on time, missed meals, found lying on the floor by the morning staff, contracting an infection and developing an ulcer on her leg. He was quoted as saying there was nothing unusual in this; it was 'normal': 'The terrifying thing is that we accept it.'

Panic in government reportedly followed. So much so that Tony Blair announced a few days later, on David Frost's television programme, that health spending would increase significantly. Which it did. But it was not spent on those patients such as Lord Winston's mother; she, with great respect and figuratively, is still lying on the floor 18 years later.[1]

---

1   Mandelstam, M. *How we treat the sick*. London: Jessica Kingsley Publishers, 2011, p.18,

Indifference to suffering. A National Confidential Enquiry into Patient Outcome and Death of older people requiring surgery in hospital found that not only were many not receiving appropriate medical diagnosis and intervention, but they were not receiving pain relief. This, in the Enquiry's view, indicated 'what must sometimes be an organisational failure to respond to suffering'.[1]

Disregard for human life. The Gosport War Memorial Hospital Inquiry, investigating the deaths of hundreds of patients at the hospital, concluded that there was a disregard for human life and a culture of shortening the lives of a large number of patients by prescribing and administering 'dangerous doses' of a hazardous combination of medication not clinically indicated or justified. They show too that whereas a large number of patients and their relatives understood that their admission to the hospital was for either rehabilitation or respite care, they were, in effect, put on a terminal care pathway.[2]

Culture of unprofessional, counter-therapeutic and degrading and cruel practices. Two students raised concerns about the care of elderly people in the North Lakelands NHS Trust, including patients being tied up on commodes, fed while on commodes and denied, deliberately, pullovers and blankets. The Trust's initial response was to refer to 'issues that are open to misunderstanding...departures from accepted practice, but with good intent...issues that require review to ensure that the best approach is being used' – and to put the students' concerns down to their lack of understanding of the relationship between theory and practice. The Commission for Health Improvement concluded that a culture had developed within the Trust that allowed unprofessional, counter-therapeutic and degrading – even cruel – practices to take place. These practices went unchecked and were even condoned or excused when brought to the attention of the Trust.[3]

1   Wilkinson, K. *et al. An age-old problem: a review of the care received by elderly patients undergoing surgery.* London: National Confidential Enquiry into Patient Outcome and Death, 2010, pp.4–7.

2   Jones, Reverend J. (Chairman). *Gosport War Memorial Hospital: the report of the Gosport Independent Panel.* London: The Stationery Office, 2018, p.viii.

3   Commission for Health Improvement. *Investigation into the North Lakeland NHS Trust, November.* London: CHI, pp.1, 9.

The erosion of standards and culture of care – the extent of the departure – can be illustrated by comparing a statement from the NHS Constitution with the description of a patient in Stafford Hospital.

Humanity and kindness. 'We respond with humanity and kindness to each person's pain, distress, anxiety or need. We search for things we can do, however small, to give comfort and relieve suffering... We do not wait to be asked because we care.'[1]

Humanity and kindness?

We got there about 10 o'clock and I could not believe my eyes. The door was wide open. There were people walking past. Mum was in bed with the cot sides up and she hadn't got a stitch of clothing on. I mean, she would have been horrified. She was completely naked and if I said covered in faeces, she was. It was everywhere. It was in her hair, her eyes, her nails, her hands and on all the cot side, so she had obviously been trying to lift herself up or move about, because the bed was covered, and it was literally everywhere and it was dried. It would have been there a long time, it wasn't new.[2]

Cyberbullying

Cyberbullying involves the use of electronic communication to bully a person – for example, by sending messages of an intimidating or threatening nature. It is referred to in Department of Health guidance on the Care Act as a type of abuse, which local authorities have a duty to make enquiries about.[3] It is not, in itself, an explicitly named crime in legislation. However, for example, the following criminal offences may be associated with it:

- **Protection from Harassment Act 1997:** it is a criminal offence to pursue a course of conduct that amounts to the harassment of another, which the

---

1   Department of Health. *The NHS Constitution*. London: DH, 2012, p.14.

2   Quoted in: Francis, R. (Chair). *Independent Inquiry into care provided by Mid Staffordshire NHS Foundation Trust January 2005–March 2009*. London: The Stationery Office, 2010, p.55.

3   Department of Health. *Care and support statutory guidance*. London: DH, 2016, para 14.17.

perpetrator knows or ought to know amounts to harassment. This could include repeat emails, for instance.

- **Communications Act 2003:** section 127 contains a criminal offence of sending a message or other matter that is grossly offensive or of an indecent, obscene or menacing character.

- **Malicious Communications Act 1988:** section 1 contains an offence for a person to send a letter, electronic communication or article of any description, conveying a message which is indecent or grossly offensive or is a threat, or conveying information which is false and known or believed to be false by the sender – and which, in either case, is intended to cause distress or anxiety to the recipient.

- **Public Order Act 1986:** section 5 contains an offence of using threatening, abusive or insulting words, behaviour, writing or any visual representations likely to cause harassment, alarm or distress within the hearing or sight of a person (could be relevant in relation to camera or video functionality of electronic communications). Section 4A contains a similar offence.

- **Computer Misuse Act 1990:** covers, for instance, unauthorised access to a person's computer.

Social media bullying: guilty of harassment. A teenager who posted death threats on Facebook was convicted of harassment and sentenced to three months in a young offender's institution. The victim had been targeted for four years previously, including a physical assault and damage to her home, for both of which the teenager had been convicted. The teenager was also issued with a restraining order, banning her from contacting the victim in the future.[1]

---

1 Carter, H. 'Teenage girl is first to be jailed for bullying on Facebook.' *The Guardian*, 21 August 2009.

D

Data protection

In the context of adult safeguarding, the victim, victim's family, alleged perpetrator (or anybody else) may wish to find out what personal information is being held about them by, for instance, a local authority, NHS body, the police, a safeguarding adults board. It might be about safeguarding enquiries being made, a safeguarding adults review, conclusions being drawn and a decision made. The holding and disclosure of personal information is governed by data protection legislation. The rules and issues are covered below under the following headings:

- Data protection: 2018 Act and General Data Protection Regulation (GDPR)

- Data protection: personal information

- Data protection: general principles

- Data protection: special categories of personal data

- Data protection: consent

- Data protection: vital interests of the person

- Data protection: provision of health or social care under statutory functions

- Data protection: balancing exercise informed by human rights and common law principles

- Data protection: getting hold of information about oneself

- Data protection: third-party information

- Data protection: refusing subject access to parent or where somebody lacks capacity

- Data protection: refusing subject access to health and social care data on grounds of serious harm

- Data protection: law enforcement

- Data protection: dead people.

DATA PROTECTION: 2018 ACT AND GENERAL DATA PROTECTION REGULATION (GDPR). The holding and disclosure of personal information has until recently been governed by the Data Protection Act 1998.

In 2018 – with a two-year transition period – the 1998 Act was replaced by the General Data Protection Regulation (GDPR) (EU 2016/679), a European Union Regulation which is directly effective in the United Kingdom, and by the Data Protection Act 2018. If the GDPR becomes ineffective following Brexit (the UK's departure from the European Union), then it is expected that the Data Protection Act 2018 will function so as to maintain consistency and continuity with the GDPR. The Data Protection Act 2018 itself cross-refers to the GDPR. It is beyond the scope of this book to set out in any depth the provisions. For ease of reference, the abbreviation DPA/GDPR is used in the following paragraphs.

DATA PROTECTION: PERSONAL INFORMATION. If a person is making the request in relation to their own personal information, the request must be made under the DPA/GDPR. If they are requesting somebody else's personal information, the request must be made under the Freedom of Information Act 2000.

The DPA/GDPR contain provisions relevant to the holding, sharing and destruction of information in the context of safeguarding adults – in particular the data protection general principles. In summary:

- **Personal data.** The Act applies to data controllers in respect of personal data. This means any information relating to an identified or identifiable living individual. In turn, this means a living individual who can be identified, directly or indirectly, in particular by reference to (a) an identifier such as a name, an identification number, location data or an online identifier, or (b) one or more factors specific to the physical, physiological, genetic, mental, economic, cultural or social identity of the individual (DPA 2018, section 2).

- **Special categories of personal data.** Special rules apply to certain types of data: revealing racial or ethnic origin, political opinions, religious or philosophical beliefs, or trade union membership, and the processing of genetic data, biometric data for the purpose of uniquely identifying a natural person, data concerning health or data concerning a natural person's sex life or sexual orientation (GDPR, article 9).

- **Processing.** Processing means an operation or set of operations which is performed on personal data, or on sets of personal data, such as: (a) collection, recording, organisation, structuring or storage, (b) adaptation or alteration, (c) retrieval, consultation or use, (d) disclosure by transmission, dissemination or otherwise making available, (e) alignment or combination, or (f) restriction, erasure or destruction (DPA 2018, section 2).

- **Health record.** Consists of data concerning health – and has been made by or on behalf of a health professional in connection with the diagnosis, care or treatment of the individual to whom the data relates (DPA 2018, section 184).

DATA PROTECTION: GENERAL PRINCIPLES. Personal data must be:

- processed lawfully, fairly and in a transparent manner (fairness, lawfulness and transparency)

- collected for specified, explicit and legitimate purposes and not further processed in a manner that is incompatible with those purposes (purpose limitation)

- adequate, relevant and limited to what is necessary in relation to the purposes for which they are processes (data minimisation)

- accurate and, where necessary, kept up to date; every reasonable step must be taken to ensure that personal data that are inaccurate, having regard to the purposes for which they are processed, are erased or rectified without delay (accuracy)

- kept in a form which permits identification of data subjects for no longer than is necessary for the purposes for which the personal data are processed (storage limitation)

- processed in a manner that ensures appropriate security of the personal data, including protection against unauthorised or unlawful processing and against accidental loss, destruction or damage, using appropriate technical or organisational measures (integrity and confidentiality). (GDPR, article 5)

Latitude is given by the Act, so that terms such as adequacy, relevance, excessiveness and length of time can be interpreted – and justified – depending on context and circumstances.

> **Length of time of retention of information: Soham case.** In the Soham murder case, involving the death of two school girls at the hands of a school caretaker, police failed to retain – for any length of time – information concerning successive complaints made in the past about the conduct of the eventual murderer. Had they done so, a picture might have been built up of the risk which he posed. The failure to retain this information appeared to be based on a misunderstanding of the Act – the police not realising that a justification could have been given under the Data Protection Act 1998 for keeping the information, in terms of purpose and length of time.[1]

Thus, information can be retained for a long time.

> **Holding of information on the Police National Computer: £0.99 theft of a packet of meat, etc.** The Court of Appeal considered in 2009 the lawfulness of holding old, minor conviction information on the Police National Computer. The records included the details of the theft in 1984 of a packet of meat valued at £0.99 with a fine of £15; of an offence of attempted theft committed 25 years ago and involving a fine of £25; and of a person under 14 years old who was cautioned for a minor assault, had been told that the information would be deleted when she reached 18, but had now been informed that it would not in fact be deleted until she was 100 years old.[2] The Court of Appeal held that the holding of such

---

1   Bichard, M. *The Bichard inquiry report.* London: The Stationery Office, 2004, pp.86, 127.

2   Information Commissioner's Office. 'Police told to delete old criminal conviction records.' Press release, 1 November 2007.

information was neither excessive for the purpose of police work, nor longer than necessary.[1]

DATA PROTECTION: SPECIAL CATEGORIES OF PERSONAL DATA. In the context of this book, special categories of personal data particularly relevant include those relating to a person's health. (There are also special rules concerning the processing of information relating to criminal convictions or offences.)[2]

There is a general prohibition on the processing of special categories of data under article 9 of the GDPR, which prohibition, however, is subject to various provisos:

- **Prohibition:** processing of personal data revealing racial or ethnic origin, political opinions, religious or philosophical beliefs, or trade union membership, and the processing of genetic data, biometric data for the purpose of uniquely identifying a natural person, data concerning health or data concerning a natural person's sex life or sexual orientation is prohibited. Unless various exceptions apply, including the following:

- **Consent:** the data subject has given explicit consent to the processing of those personal data for one or more specified purposes.

- **Employment, social security, etc.:** processing is necessary for the purposes of carrying out the obligations and exercising specific rights of the controller or of the data subject in the field of employment and social security and social protection law.

- **Vital interests in case of lack of capacity:** processing is necessary to protect the vital interests of the data subject or of another natural person where the data subject is physically or legally incapable of giving consent.

- **Data subject disclosure:** processing relates to personal data which are manifestly made public by the data subject.

- **Legal claims, etc.:** processing is necessary for the establishment, exercise or defence of legal claims or whenever courts are acting in their judicial capacity.

---

1   *Chief Constable of Humberside Police v Information Commissioner* [2009] EWCA Civ 1079.

2   GDPR, EU 2016/679, aa.9–10 and Data Protection Act 2018, schedule 2.

- **Public interest:** processing is necessary for reasons of substantial public interest – proportionate to the aim pursued, respect the essence of the right to data protection and provide for suitable and specific measures to safeguard the fundamental rights and the interests of the data subject.

- **Health or social care:** processing is necessary for the purposes of preventative or occupational medicine, for the assessment of the working capacity of the employee, medical diagnosis, the provision of health or social care or treatment or the management of health or social care systems and services – or pursuant to contract with a health professional.

- **Public health:** processing is necessary for reasons of public interest in the area of public health.

DATA PROTECTION: CONSENT. Consent is subject to the following rules:

- **Demonstrable consent:** where processing is based on consent, the controller must be able to demonstrate that the data subject has consented to processing of his or her personal data.

- **Intelligible and accessible request for consent:** if the data subject's consent is given in the context of a written declaration which also concerns other matters, the request for consent shall be presented in a manner which is clearly distinguishable from the other matters, in an intelligible and easily accessible form, using clear and plain language. Any part of such a declaration which constitutes an infringement of this Regulation shall not be binding.

- **Withdrawal of consent:** the data subject shall have the right to withdraw his or her consent at any time. The withdrawal of consent shall not affect the lawfulness of processing based on consent before its withdrawal. Prior to giving consent, the data subject shall be informed thereof. It shall be as easy to withdraw as to give consent.

- **Extent of consent:** when assessing whether consent is freely given, utmost account shall be taken of whether, *inter alia*, the performance of a contract, including the provision of a service, is conditional on consent to the processing of personal data that is not necessary for the performance of that contract.

- **Special categories of personal data:** consent must be explicit.[1]

---

1   GDPR, EU 2016/679, a.7.

DATA PROTECTION: VITAL INTERESTS OF THE PERSON. It will be noticed that under article 9 of the GDPR, in the case of special categories of personal data, the fact that a person (with capacity) refuses to consent to disclosure of personal information (second point above), such that his or her vital interests would be compromised, is not in itself sufficient to justify disclosure. Thus, Department of Health guidance has in the past noted:

- **Distinguishing between harm to data subject and harm to other people.** It is important to distinguish between serious harm to the individual to whom information relates and serious harm to others. Confidential information can be disclosed without consent to prevent serious harm or death to others. This is likely to be defensible in common law in the public interest.

  Where the patient is an adult lacking capacity, the Mental Capacity Act applies, and the best interests of the patient concerned can be sufficient to justify disclosure – that is, information can be disclosed to prevent a patient who lacks capacity from being harmed.

  However, an individual's best interests are not sufficient to justify disclosure of confidential information where he/she has the capacity to decide for him/herself. There has to be an additional public interest justification, which may or may not be in the patient's best interests.[1]

DATA PROTECTION: PROVISION OF HEALTH OR SOCIAL CARE UNDER STATUTORY FUNCTIONS. Disclosure – even without consent – may be justifiable as part of providing health or social care, as part and parcel of the carrying out of statutory functions (e.g. social services functions, NHS functions). Department of Health guidance has in the past stated:

- **Disclosing information for social services functions.** Local social services authorities may disclose information in a number of circumstances when carrying out their social services functions – even if consent has not been obtained. For instance, information may be shared with line managers, other people caring for a client – such as a voluntary body or foster carers – and

---

1   Department of Health. *Confidentiality: NHS Code of Practice: supplementary guidance: public interest disclosures.* London: DH, 2010, paras 7–9.

other departments or agencies including health, education, child protection, inspection teams, legal advisers, finance staff, police.[1]

DATA PROTECTION: BALANCING EXERCISE INFORMED BY HUMAN RIGHTS AND COMMON LAW PRINCIPLES. The data protection principles, outlined above, are so broadly drawn that, in case of disclosure matters, the courts have in some circumstances held that the Act only gets one so far. It might both justify disclosure and non-disclosure. In which case, the decisive balancing act has to be performed with reference to principles established in other areas of law such as human rights and the common law of confidentiality.[2]

The key point is that disclosure has to be justified; the Act by no means imports carte blanche for the sharing of information, willy-nilly. Equally, it fully supports justified disclosure. It all depends.

DATA PROTECTION: GETTING HOLD OF INFORMATION ABOUT ONESELF. Under the GDPR, people (data subjects) have various rights in relation to their own information – with provisos. In summary, these rights include a right of access, right to rectification, right to erasure, right to restriction of processing, right to data portability. The restrictions are various, including in relation to public security; prevention, investigation, detection or prosecution of criminal offences; and protection of the data subject or the rights and freedoms of others.[3]

DATA PROTECTION: THIRD-PARTY INFORMATION. A controller is not obliged to disclose information to the data subject to the extent that doing so would involve disclosing information relating to another individual who can be identified from the information. However, this rule is subject to

---

1   Department of Health. *Data Protection Act 1998: guidance to social services*. London: DH, 2000, para 6.18.

2   *R v Plymouth City Council, ex p Stevens* [2002] EWCA Civ 388.

3   GDPR, EU 2016/679, aa.13–23.

exceptions, including in the case of health or social care data where the third party is a health or social care professional.[1]

DATA PROTECTION: REFUSING SUBJECT ACCESS TO PARENT OR WHERE SOMEBODY LACKS CAPACITY. On request by the parent of a person under 18 – or where the person is incapable of managing his or her own affairs and the person making the request has been appointed by a court to manage those affairs – rights to access health or social care information do not apply if compliance with the request would mean disclosure of information:

- which was provided by the data subject in the expectation that it would not be disclosed to the person making the request

- which was obtained as a result of any examination or investigation to which the data subject consented in the expectation that the information would not be so disclosed, or

- which the data subject has expressly indicated should not be so disclosed.[2]

DATA PROTECTION: REFUSING SUBJECT ACCESS TO HEALTH AND SOCIAL CARE DATA ON GROUNDS OF SERIOUS HARM. The subject access rules do not apply to health or social care data if the serious harm test is met.

In relation to health data, this exemption is when disclosure would be likely to cause serious harm to the physical or mental health or condition of the data subject or of any other person. If the data controller is not a health professional, then the data controller must seek the opinion of a person who appears to be the appropriate health professional about whether the exemption applies.

In relation to social work data, the exemption applies if disclosure would be likely to prejudice the carrying out of social work, because it would be

---

1   Data Protection Act 2018, schedule 2, para 15.

2   Data Protection Act 2018, schedule 3.

likely to cause serious harm to the physical or mental health of the data subject or another individual.

Social work data relate to data processed by a local authority in connection with its functions under the Local Authority Social Services Act 1970.[1]

DATA PROTECTION: LAW ENFORCEMENT. The DPA 2018 sets out separate provision in relation to law enforcement. Law enforcement means prevention, investigation, detection or prosecution of criminal offences or the execution of criminal penalties, including the safeguarding against and the prevention of threats to public security. The basic data protection principles apply but with some modification:

- **Lawful and fair:** the processing must be lawful and fair. There are added conditions and safeguards if the processing is sensitive, involving data relating to (a) racial or ethnic origin, political opinions, religious or philosophical beliefs or trade union membership; (b) the processing of genetic data, or of biometric data, for the purpose of uniquely identifying an individual; (c) the processing of data concerning health; (d) the processing of data concerning an individual's sex life or sexual orientation.

- **Purpose:** the law enforcement purpose must be specified, explicit and legitimate, and not processed in a manner incompatible with that purpose. The data could be used for other law enforcement purposes, as long as the data controller is legally authorised to process the data for that other purpose and the processing is necessary and proportionate.

- **Adequate, relevant, not excessive:** the data must be adequate, relevant and not excessive in relation to the purpose for which it is processed.

- **Accuracy:** data must be accurate and kept up to date, and every reasonable step must be taken, without delay, to rectify or erase data that are inaccurate.

- **Length of time:** data processed for any of the law enforcement purposes must be kept for no longer than is necessary for the purpose for which it is processed.

- **Security:** data must be processed in a manner that ensures appropriate security of the personal data.[2]

---

1   Data Protection Act 2018, schedule 3.

2   Data Protection Act 2018, ss.33–40.

Subject access rules operate with provisos in the context of law enforcement. The data controller may restrict access, necessarily and proportionately, to (a) avoid obstructing an official or legal inquiry, investigation or procedure; (b) avoid prejudicing the prevention, detection, investigation or prosecution of criminal offences or the execution of criminal penalties; (c) protect public security; (d) protect national security; (e) protect the rights and freedoms of others.[1]

DATA PROTECTION: DEAD PEOPLE. The DPA/GDPR do not apply to information relating to dead people, since they cover personal data relating only to a living person.[2] Thus, a request for information about a deceased person will come under the Freedom of Information Act 2000. In some circumstances, it may come under the Access to Health Records Act 1990.

Deprivation of liberty

Under the Mental Capacity Act 2005, deprivation of liberty (DOL) is a legal term used to describe a particular type of best interests decision in relation to a person who lacks the mental capacity to decide themselves about their care, treatment or living arrangements. The term ultimately derives from, and is defined in relation to, article 5 of the European Convention on Human Rights. For adults, such deprivation must be legally authorised, by a local authority under rules contained in the Mental Capacity Act 2005, or by the Court of Protection.[3]

At the time of writing, the law concerning DOL has become complex, unwieldy and burdensome – even fallen into a degree of disrepute. To the extent that legal concerns about liberty have, in the view of some, disproportionately and sometimes harmfully obscured the need of good-quality care and supervision for highly vulnerable people.[4] Consequently, the

---

1   Data Protection Act 2018, s.43.

2   Data Protection Act 2018, s.3.

3   Mental Capacity Act 2005, ss.4A–4B.

4   E.g. Ashton, G. 'DOLS or quality care?' *International Journal of Mental Health and Capacity Law 22*, 2016, 102–106.

Law Commission is proposing reform.[1] In July 2018, the Mental Capacity (Amendment) Bill was published, with a view to amending some of the procedural rules associated with deprivation of liberty.

It is beyond the scope of this book to set out details of the rules (and proposed amendments) relating to DOL, not least because DOL is not, by definition, explicitly about protecting people from abuse or neglect. Legally, under the Mental Capacity Act 2005, it is about protecting a person from harm.[2] And harm does not necessarily entail abuse or neglect, but may do in some circumstances.

DEPRIVATION OF LIBERTY: KEY POINTS. For the purpose of this book, key points include the following:

- **Human rights.** DOL engages article 5 of the European Convention on Human Rights, which provides that deprivation of liberty is lawful as long as relevant legal, procedural rules are followed.

- **Three conditions leading to DOL.** Deprivation of liberty occurs when the circumstances amount to an objective deprivation of liberty, the person cannot give valid consent (e.g. lacks capacity) and the State is in some way involved.

- **Objective deprivation.** The ingredients required to establish an objective DOL have been defined as a person being subject to continuous supervision and control and not free to leave, in the context of being confined in a particular, restricted space for a non-negligible period of time.[3]

- **Restriction of liberty.** A DOL is, legally, of greater import than mere restriction of liberty, although the distinction is not one of nature or substance but of degree and intensity.[4]

- **Local authority or Court of Protection.** For deprivation of liberty of an adult to be lawful – on grounds of lack of mental capacity – either a local authority must authorise it, using complicated rules contained within the

---

1   Law Commission. *Mental capacity and deprivation of liberty.* London: LC, 2017.

2   Mental Capacity Act 2005, schedule A1, para 15.

3   *Storck v Germany* [2005] 43 EHRR 96; *Stanev v Bulgaria* [2012] 55 EHRR 696.

4   *Stanev v Bulgaria* [2012] 55 EHRR 696.

Mental Capacity Act 2005 and known as deprivation of liberty safeguards (DOLS), or the Court of Protection must authorise it.

- **Limits to local authority authorisation of DOL.** A local authority can only authorise a DOL if the person is aged at least 18 and is in a care home or hospital,[1] and even then only if the DOL is not contentious (e.g. in terms of the person themselves or family members seriously disagreeing).[2] Any other DOL of an adult in other settings, in relation to lack of mental capacity, must be authorised by the Court of Protection.

- **Best interests.** Under the relevant provisions in the Mental Capacity Act 2005, a DOL is in a person's best interests if: (a) the person is, or is going to be, a detained resident; (b) it is in his or her best interests to be a detained resident; (c) in order to prevent the person coming to harm, it is necessary for him or her to be a detained resident; (d) being a detained resident is a proportionate response to the likelihood of him or her suffering harm and to the seriousness of that harm.

- **Deprivation of liberty safeguards (DOLS).** The term 'deprivation of liberty safeguards' (DOLS) refers to the procedural requirements in the Mental Capacity Act 2005 designed to ensure that local authorities do not arbitrarily deprive people of their liberty. The term is not *as a matter of course* anything to do with 'safeguarding', as it is understood under the Care Act 2014, in relation to protecting people from abuse and neglect.

DEPRIVATION OF LIBERTY: SAFEGUARDING. The care required for a person, in their best interests, must be to protect them from harm (and sometimes will, therefore, protect them more specifically from abuse or neglect). There are at least two additional ways in which safeguarding matters may arise in relation to the operation of the deprivation DOL:

- **applying the rules abusively:** failure to follow the rules, in contentious cases, resulting in an abusive or neglectful deprivation of liberty

- **losing the wood for the trees:** focus by local authorities on following the procedural rules, in entirely non-contentious cases, at the expense of focusing

---

1 Mental Capacity Act 2005, schedule A1.

2 See e.g. *London Borough of Hillingdon v Neary* [2011] EWHC 1377 (COP).

on the quality of care actually being provided – such that neglectful or abusive care might be commissioned or at least overlooked. This is because deprivation of liberty is generally about liberty and its curtailment, not the standard of care that is then provided.

Depriving people of their liberty unlawfully can give rise, in principle and depending on the circumstances, to a range of legal implications, including breach of the Human Rights Act 1998, the criminal offence or civil tort of false imprisonment, kidnapping, assault and battery, wilful neglect or ill-treatment, or breach of the Health and Social Care Act (Regulated Activities) Regulations 2014 (enforced by the Care Quality Commission).[1]

The courts have found breach of human rights, or the ombudsman maladministration, in the following cases about DOL, all of which referred to safeguarding matters (actual or purported), one way or another.

Mental capacity. Depriving an elderly man of his liberty for 16 months, from his lifelong family home and his cat, without having established that he lacked the relevant mental capacity – and adopting a grossly disproportionate approach to a potential safeguarding issue.[2]

Best interests and less restriction. Removing an autistic man from his father without following the DOLS procedures generally, and the best interests and less restriction rules in particular.[3]

DOLS rules and best interests. Removing a man with severe learning disabilities from his foster carer without applying the DOLS procedures generally, on the basis of unsubstantiated safeguarding concerns, and without applying the best interests and least restriction rules.[4]

Mental capacity and best interests. Preventing an elderly man, against his wishes and those of his brother (with whom he lived all his life, both former coal miners), from dying in his own home – without a lack of mental

---

1 Law Commission. *Mental capacity and deprivation of liberty: a consultation paper.* London: LC, 2015, paras 15.26–15.32.

2 *Essex County Council v RG* [2015] EWCOP 1.

3 *London Borough of Hillingdon v Neary* [2011] EWHC 1377 (COP).

4 *G v E* [2010] EWHC 621 (Fam), High Court, March 2010.

capacity having been established, and without a best interests process having been undertaken.[1]

Ignoring the DOLS rules. Removing an elderly woman from her son's care without investigating the safeguarding concerns that had been raised, without following the DOLS procedures and without authority from the Court of Protection.[2]

Best interests and less restriction. Removing a young woman with learning disabilities from her family on the basis of wholly inadequate safeguarding enquiries, without following the DOLS procedures and the best interests and less restriction principles in particular.[3]

Deputies

The Court of Protection has a power to appoint a deputy to manage somebody's property and affairs and, sometimes, their health and welfare. The court's powers are outlined in sections 15–20 of the Mental Capacity Act 2005.

Deputyship is not intrinsically anything to do with adult safeguarding but may be relevant in at least two ways: first, if the court appoints a deputy in order to protect a person's finances (or even health and welfare) from abuse or neglect by others (for instance, family members); second, if the appointed deputy themselves acts in an abusive or neglectful manner.

- **Orders preferred to deputies.** A decision of the court is to be preferred to the appointment of a deputy. The powers conferred on a deputy should be as limited in scope and duration as is reasonably practicable.

---

1   Health Service Ombudsman and Local Government Ombudsman. *Investigation of a complaint against Moss Valley Medical Practice, Chesterfield Royal Hospital NHS Foundation Trust, Derbyshire County Primary Care Trust, Derbyshire County Council, Sheffield City Council* (94049/11020887 and 11020888), paras 109–118.

2   *Milton Keynes Council v RR* [2014] EWCOP B19, paras 19–23.

3   *Somerset County Council v MK* [2014] WL 8106551.

- **Scope of welfare decisions.** Personal welfare decisions could include, in particular, where the incapacitated person is to live, with whom he or she should have contact, consent or refusal to health care treatment.

- **Age of deputy, joint or several.** A deputy must be at least 18 years old. Two more deputies may be appointed to act jointly or severally.

- **Restraint.** If a deputy restrains the person, such intervention must be within the scope of the deputy's authority, necessary and proportionate, and the person must lack capacity or the deputy reasonably believes that the person lacks capacity in relation to the matter.

- **Property, wills.** A deputy cannot be given power to settle any of the person's property, to execute the person's will or to exercise any power vested in the person (e.g. trusteeship).

- **Life-sustaining treatment.** A deputy cannot refuse consent to life-sustaining treatment.

- **Limit to authority.** A deputy cannot make a decision inconsistent with the scope of his or her authority or with a decision made by the donee of a lasting power of attorney.

- **Contact and health care.** A deputy cannot be given powers to prohibit a named person from having contact with the person lacking capacity, nor to direct a person responsible for the person's health care to allow somebody else to take over the responsibility.

Receiverships (dealing only with property, business, finance), previously put in place by the former Court of Protection under Part 7 of the Mental Health Act 1983, remain valid but are treated as a deputyship, limited to the scope of the original power.[1]

The court might appoint family members. In their absence, a professional deputy might be appointed, sometimes a local authority, although the court sometimes alludes to a possible conflict of interest in relation to the latter.[2]

---

1   Mental Capacity Act 2005, schedule 5.
2   *GGW v East Sussex County Council* [2015] EWCOP 82, para 39.

DEPUTIES: FINANCIAL ABUSE. Although deputyship is subject to a greater degree of routine scrutiny than lasting power of attorney, financial abuse may nevertheless occur.

> **'Looting' of a woman's finances by two family deputies.** Two women had been appointed deputies for their aunt, who was over 90 years old and in a care home. Her estate was some £500,000 (£300,000 of which was inherited from her daughter) plus an occupational pension and State pension. The care home fees were £495 per week. The deputies were her late husband's great-niece and his niece. They visited her frequently and did various things with her.
>
> They allowed her £314 in personal allowance from 25 August 2010 to 25 August 2011. It was spent on either hairdressing or chiropody. However, they had made gifts to themselves, other family members and charities amounting to £231,000, and incurred expenses of £46,000 (comprising cars and computers). The deputyship order allowed them to make small gifts, which against an estate of that size could have amounted in total to a few thousand pounds each year. Otherwise, greater gifts would have needed the permission of the Court of Protection, so this permission was applied for in retrospect. The judge noted that although they were the 'only visitors that GM receives...this does not give them a licence to loot'. The deputyships were revoked.[1]

Direct payments

Under the Care Act 2014 and NHS Act 2006, local authorities and NHS clinical commissioning groups (CCGs) respectively have a duty and a power, with certain provisos, to give people direct payments – that is, a sum of money, under the person's control, with which they can purchase services or sometimes daily living equipment to meet their assessed, eligible needs. Generally, the person must express a choice to have their needs met in this way, have the mental capacity to make that choice and, in the local authority's view, be able to manage (with or without assistance) the payment.

---

1   *MJ, JM v The Public Guardian* [2013] EWHC 2966 (COP).

Alternatively, if the person cannot consent to the payment, then somebody else – such as somebody with a lasting power of attorney, a deputy or a suitable family member – can receive it instead and apply the money in the person's behalf and in that person's best interests.[1]

DIRECT PAYMENTS: MISUSE AND SAFEGUARDING. Direct payments sometimes can afford the opportunity for abuse to take place.

- **Person lacking capacity: payment made to somebody else.** If a person lacks capacity and payment is made to somebody else, the risk might increase of precisely 'unsuitable' people receiving the money and misusing it. Donees of a lasting power of attorney or deputies appointed by the Court of Protection will be deemed to be suitable, although the local authority or CCG must still decide whether it is appropriate to make the payment. A proportion of people with a lasting power of attorney or with deputyship are more than capable of abusing it.

- **Direct payments and criminal record checks.** In any case, other 'suitable' people can receive the payment when the person in need lacks mental capacity; these may or may not be family members or friends already involved in providing care for the person lacking capacity. A criminal record check is necessary where the proposed suitable person is not a family member or friend providing care.[2]

  This rule aside, adult direct payment recipients do not have a duty to ensure that a criminal record check is carried out on anybody they may be employing. Direct payment recipients cannot request directly enhanced criminal record certificates themselves, because only bodies registered with the Disclosure and Barring Service can do so. Nonetheless, a request could be made by the recipient to an 'umbrella' body – that is, an organisation (such as a local authority or local voluntary body) registered with the DBS to request a check on other people's behalf.

---

1   Care Act 2014, ss.31–32, and SI 2014/2871. Care and Support (Direct Payments) Regulations 2014. And: NHS Act 2006, s.12A , and SI 2013/1617. National Health Service (Direct Payments) Regulations 2013.

2   SI 2014/2871. Care and Support (Direct Payments) Regulations 2014. And: SI 2013/1617. National Health Service (Direct Payments) Regulations 2013.

- **Direct payments and fraud.** In 2011, the Audit Commission produced a report on fraud perpetrated against local authorities; it pinpointed direct payments as a factor in increasing levels of fraud.[1] The City of London Police, too, have alluded to the dangers if direct payments are not well managed, including the risk of systematic exploitation by organised criminals.[2]

A few examples of abuse of direct payments are as follows. The financial detriment might be suffered by the direct payment recipient; alternatively, it might be the recipient themselves acting dishonestly.

Social worker defrauding local authority. In Essex, a social worker defrauded Essex County Council of £25,000. She had claimed for a phantom carer, whom she interviewed but did not employ – but 'stole' her identity. She was given a 15-month prison sentence and struck off the register of social workers.[3]

Fraudulent use of direct payments by both father and son. A serious case review found that a direct payment continued to be paid for many months to a 70-year-old man – even after he had been murdered and buried in the back garden by his son. The father had serious health problems, including ulcerative colitis, heart problems, a problem with his salivary glands, the after-effects of pneumonia and rheumatism. He received nutritional supplements, had a stoma and required continence aids. Between August 2008 and February 2009, the man had no contact with social services or the NHS; despite this, the direct payments continued to be paid, stopping only when a police investigation began.

In addition, it transpired that the father had, in any case, probably been obtaining the direct payments fraudulently – that is, claiming for carers but relying instead on his son for support and not disclosing his financial

1   Audit Commission. *Protecting the public purse 2001: fighting fraud against local government.* London: AC, 2011, paras 41–50.

2   City of London Police; National Fraud Intelligence Bureau. *Assessment: financial crime against vulnerable adults.* London: Social Care Institute for Excellence, 2011, p.41.

3   McGregor, K. 'Jailed social worker struck off after admitting £25,000 fraud.' *Community Care*, 29 September 2009.

affairs fully. After he had been murdered, the son continued to use the direct payments, effectively fraudulently. The money was not recovered.[1]

Woman convicted of fraud, claiming direct payments for her severely disabled daughter. A woman was convicted of fraud involving £17,000 and direct payments to her severely disabled daughter. The woman had set up a trust in the name of her daughter, into which direct payments were paid, made jointly by Gloucestershire NHS Clinical Commissioning Group and Gloucestershire County Council. She had named another daughter, a 42-year-old full-time solicitor, as one of the carers to whom payments were made. However, the payments were made for care, at times when the other daughter was either at work or on holiday.

The woman pleaded guilty to furnishing false information about the other sister's role between 2008 and 2015. It amounted to dishonest accounting. She was given a two-year conditional discharge and ordered to pay compensation of £17,000 within two weeks. The judge, in mitigation, had taken account of the fact that the dishonesty was not for personal enrichment (the trust, not the woman, had benefited from the overpayment) – and of the 'unremitting and exhausting nature of the burden of care' placed on the woman, as her daughter's carer (with a husband in ill health). The NHS Counter Fraud Authority called it a sad case.[2]

£36,000 of false claims set against a direct payment: and remortgaging, through forgery, of service user's house by carer without the disabled person's knowledge. A carer was employed through a direct payment by a mother of four children who had syringomyelia, a muscle-wasting disorder that had slowly robbed her of her mobility. She needed round-the-clock care. The carer put in false time sheets for care her husband allegedly, but not in reality, had provided – amounting to £36,000. In addition, the carer forged the woman's signature and remortgaged her house, without the woman's knowledge. The woman was now facing a £28,000 debt to be paid to the Alliance and Leicester Bank. It was hoped the bank would waive the debt. The carer was sent to prison for 18 months, after being convicted of

1   Flynn, M. *Executive Summary: the Murder of Mr C: a Serious Case Review*. Buckingham: Buckinghamshire Safeguarding Vulnerable Adults Board, 2011, pp.2, 4, 13–15.

2   Hawkins, J. and Gogarty, C. '"A sad case": fraudster mum convicted for £17,000 abuse of benefits after faking time sheets for caring of disabled daughter.' *Cheltenham News*, 14 May 2018.

false accounting, obtaining a money transfer by deception and acquiring, using and possessing criminal property.[1]

Fraudulent receipt of over £100,000 in direct payments. A man was sentenced to 30 months in prison, after fraudulently receiving over £100,000 in direct payments from two local authorities. He had claimed to be severely disabled (but was not), failed to disclose his assets, received payments from two different authorities (Brent and Central Bedfordshire) at the same time and failed to admit that the carer he employed was his wife. Despite claiming to be unable to walk without assistance and visually impaired, he was in fact able to walk unaided and to work, and he drove three separate cars.[2]

Disclosure and Barring Service, see *Criminal record certificates*; *Barred list*

Distress, see *Harassment, alarm or distress*

Do not resuscitate orders

What is often referred to as a 'do not resuscitate order' is effectively an end-of-life medical management plan, described by the General Medical Council as follows:

- **Do not attempt cardio-pulmonary resuscitation orders (DNACPR).** 'If cardiac or respiratory arrest is an expected part of the dying process and CPR will not be successful, making and recording an advance decision not to attempt CPR will help to ensure that the patient dies in a dignified and peaceful manner. It may also help to ensure that the patient's last hours or days

---

1 Cowan, M. 'Acocks Green fraud victim wants bank to wipe "secret mortgage" debt.' *Birmingham Post*, 10 August 2009. Also: Washington, S. '"Cash for care" abuse warning.' *Radio 5 Live*, 18 October 2009. Accessed on 28 August 2012 at: http://news.bbc.co.uk/1/hi/health/8308782.stm.

2 'Man jailed for fraudulently receiving £100,000 in direct payments.' *Community Care*, 28 March 2013.

are spent in their preferred place of care by, for example, avoiding emergency admission from a community setting to hospital. These management plans are called Do Not Attempt CPR (DNACPR) orders, or Do Not Attempt Resuscitation or Allow Natural Death decisions.'[1]

Such a management plan therefore may or may not be based on a formal advance decision that a person has made under the Mental Capacity Act 2005: see **Advance decisions**.

In the case of a person with mental capacity, consultation by the doctors is, normally, legally essential. If lacking capacity, then the person's family must be consulted. It remains for the doctors to make the decision, but they cannot do this lawfully without such consultation; otherwise, they risk breaching article 8 of the European Convention on Human Rights.[2]

Domestic violence

Domestic violence is inflicted on adults with a pre-existing vulnerability, just as on anybody else. Domestic violence is referred to explicitly in some legislation, whilst a range of other legislation is relevant – for example, the criminal offence of battery, of controlling or coercive behaviour, etc. Domestic violence has not been defined in legislation to date, but central government has published a non-statutory, working definition:

- **Non-statutory definition of domestic violence.** Any incident or pattern of incidents of controlling, coercive or threatening behaviour, violence or abuse between those aged 16 or over who are or have been intimate partners or family members regardless of gender or sexuality. This can encompass but is not limited to the following types of abuse: psychological, physical, sexual, financial, emotional.

  Controlling behaviour is a range of acts designed to make a person subordinate and/or dependent by isolating them from sources of support, exploiting their resources and capacities for personal gain, depriving them

---

1   General Medical Council. *Treatment and care towards the end of life: good practice in decision making.* London: GMC, 2010, para 129.

2   *R (Tracey) v Cambridge University Hospitals NHS Foundation Trust* [2014] EWCA Civ 822, para 59.

of the means needed for independence, resistance and escape, and regulating their everyday behaviour.

Coercive behaviour is an act or a pattern of acts of assault, threats, humiliation and intimidation or other abuse that is used to harm, punish, or frighten their victim.[1]

DOMESTIC VIOLENCE: HOMELESSNESS. The Housing Act 1996 states that there are certain circumstances in which it is not reasonable for a person to go on occupying a property, in which case they are deemed unintentionally homeless and therefore eligible for help. For example, it may not be reasonable for a person to continue to occupy accommodation if it is probable that this will lead to domestic or other types of violence against the person.

- **Violence.** Violence means violence from another person – or threats of violence which are likely to be carried out. For the behaviour to constitute domestic violence, there needs to be a (defined) association between the perpetrator and victim. The domestic violence need not be within the dwelling; it can extend to outside the home.[2]

- **Broad interpretation of violence.** Government guidance states that, in this context, domestic violence should not be interpreted restrictively. It should be understood to include threatening behaviour, violence or abuse (psychological, physical, sexual, financial or emotional) between persons who are, or have been, intimate partners, family members or members of the same household, regardless of gender or sexuality.[3]

The courts, in the context of housing legislation about homelessness, have accepted that violence includes physical violence, threatening or intimidating behaviour and any other form of abuse which, directly or indirectly, may give rise to the risk of harm.[4]

---

1 Home Office. 'New definition of domestic violence.' *News*, 18 September 2012. Accessed on 15 October 2012 at: www.homeoffice.gov.uk/media-centre/news/domestic-violence-definition.

2 Housing Act 1996, s.177.

3 Department of Education and Skills. *Homelessness code of guidance for local authorities*, 2006, para 8.21.

4 *Yemshaw v Hounslow London Borough Council* [2011] UKSC 3.

DOMESTIC VIOLENCE: PROTECTION NOTICES AND ORDERS. The Crime and Security Act 2010 allows the police to issue domestic violence protection notices (DVPNs: for up to 48 hours) and to seek, from a magistrates' court, domestic violence protection orders (DVPOs: for up to 28 days). Guidance summarises the overall purpose of these notices and orders:

- **Purpose of notices and orders.** A DVPN is an emergency non-molestation and eviction notice which can be issued by the police, when attending to a domestic abuse incident, to a perpetrator. Because the DVPN is a police-issued notice, it is effective from the time of issue, thereby giving the victim the immediate support which they require in such a situation. Within 48 hours of the DVPN being served on the perpetrator, an application by police to a magistrates' court for a DVPO must be heard. A DVPO can prevent the perpetrator from returning to a residence and from having contact with the victim for up to 28 days. This allows the victim a degree of breathing space to consider their options with the help of a support agency. Both the DVPN and DVPO contain a condition prohibiting the perpetrator from molesting the victim.[1]

In other words, notices and orders are intended to provide immediate protection for a victim of domestic violence, in terms of a physical and mental breathing space so that, with support, options can be considered. Key points are:

- **DVPN: violence or threatened violence.** A DVPN may be issued to a person (P) aged 18 years or over if the police have reasonable grounds for believing that: (a) P has been violent towards, or has threatened violence towards, an associated person, and (b) the issue of the DVPN is necessary to protect that person from violence or a threat of violence by P.

- **DVPN: associated person.** This category includes people who are married or have been married; who are cohabitants or former cohabitants; who live or have lived in the same household, otherwise than merely by reason of one of them being the other's employee, tenant, lodger or boarder; who are relatives; who have agreed to marry one another (whether or not that agreement has

---

1   Home Office. *Domestic Violence Protection Notices (DVPNs) and Domestic Violence Protection Orders (DVPOs) guidance*. London: HO, 2016, para 1.3.

been terminated); in relation to any child, who are either a parent or have parental responsibility for a child.

- **DVPN: molestation.** A DVPN must contain provision prohibiting P from molesting the person for whose protection it is issued, covering both molestation in general, or particular acts of molestation, or both.

- **DVPN: occupation of premises.** If P lives in premises also lived in by a person for whose protection the DVPN is issued, the DVPN may also contain provision:

  » to prohibit P from evicting or excluding from the premises the person for whose protection the DVPN is issued

  » to prohibit P from entering the premises

  » to require P to leave the premises, or

  » to prohibit P from coming within such distance of the premises as may be specified in the DVPN.

- **DVPO: application for.** If a DVPN has been issued, then the police must apply for a DVPO from a magistrates' court within 28 hours.

- **DVPO: conditions for making.** The court may make a DVPO if two conditions are met: first that it is satisfied on the balance of probabilities that P has been violent towards, or has threatened violence towards, an associated person; second, that the court thinks that making the DVPO is necessary to protect the person from violence or a threat of violence by P.

- **DVPN and DVPO: breach of.** In both cases, the person must be held in custody and taken before a magistrates' court.[1]

DOMESTIC VIOLENCE: CAUSING OR ALLOWING THE DEATH OR SERIOUS HARM OF A VULNERABLE ADULT. The Domestic Violence, Crime and Victims Act 2004 contains an offence of causing or allowing the death of – or serious physical harm to – a vulnerable adult (or child). In relation to death, the offence is sometimes referred to as familial homicide. The offence has the effect of overcoming the problem of showing which of two perpetrators committed the act when, for example, each is blaming the other and the evidence is otherwise inconclusive. In outline, it applies when:

---

1   Crime and Security Act 2010, ss.24–31.

- **Death or serious physical harm:** a vulnerable adult dies or suffers serious physical harm, as a result of an unlawful act. Serious harm means grievous bodily harm for the purposes of the Offences against the Person Act 1861.

- **Same household:** the person who committed the act was a member of the same household and had frequent contact with the victim.

- **Risk of harm:** the victim was already at significant risk of serious physical harm by an unlawful act by a member of the household.

- **Causing death or failing to protect:** the person either directly caused the victim's death or serious physical harm, or was or ought to have been aware of the risk, failed to take reasonable steps to protect the victim, and the act occurred in circumstances that the person foresaw or should have foreseen.[1]

Further key points are as follows. They include the point that, in terms of the ingredients of the offence, the victim need not be vulnerable through disability, illness or old age, but instead through, for instance, utter dependency. A related point is that the vulnerability need not be of long standing or permanent, and could arise, for example, from physical attack.

- **Proving the offence.** For the offence to be made out, the prosecution does not have to prove whether the person actually did the act or instead failed to protect the victim.

- **Sentence.** The maximum sentence is 14 years' imprisonment in relation to death and ten years in relation to serious physical harm.

- **Same household: wide definition.** A person could be classed as a member of the same household even if he or she does not live there but visits so often and for such periods of time that it would be reasonable to regard him or her as such a member.

- **Frequent contact.** The perpetrator must have frequent contact with the victim. 'Frequent' and 'contact' are ordinary English words and do not need to be further elucidated.[2]

- **Vulnerable adult: definition.** A vulnerable adult means a person aged 16 or over whose ability to protect himself or herself from violence, abuse or

---

1   Domestic Violence, Crime and Victims Act 2004, s.5.

2   *R v Khan* [2009] EWCA Crim 2, para 29.

neglect is significantly impaired through physical or mental disability or illness, through old age or otherwise.

- **Vulnerable adult: impairment through disability or illness or through old age.** Any illness, physical or mental disability will suffice, provided there is evidence that it caused significant impairment. It does not have to be a recognised medical condition (as, for example, in the Homicide Act 1967). It is for the jury to decide whether the victim was suffering from an illness or disability and, if so, its impact on the adult's ability to protect him or herself. The concept of old age is also not limited. The jury is left to determine what constitutes old age and whether it caused an impairment in the person's ability to protect themselves.[1]

- **Vulnerable adult: meaning of 'or otherwise'.** Vulnerability does not arise from disability, illness or old age only. Whilst these would be 'intrinsic' causes of vulnerability, the 'or otherwise' part of the definition could relate to extrinsic circumstances leading to vulnerability.

- **Utter dependency, sexual abuse, modern slavery.** The causes of vulnerability may be physical, psychological or may arise from the victim's circumstances. This could include 'utter dependency' but is not limited to this. For instance, a victim of sexual or domestic abuse or modern slavery might be in a vulnerable position, having suffered long-term physical and mental abuse – leaving them scared, cowed and with a significantly impaired ability to protect themselves.[2]

- **Vulnerability: arising from violence.** An adult – for example, not old and without physical or mental disability or illness – may nonetheless become a vulnerable adult, under the Act, as a result of a major physical attack.[3]

- **Vulnerability: not necessarily of long standing.** Vulnerability need not be long-standing. It may be short or temporary. A fit adult may become vulnerable as a result of accident, injury or illness. The anticipation of a full recovery may not diminish the individual's temporary vulnerability.[4]

- **Awareness and foresight.** The offence requires awareness of the risk of serious physical harm and foresight of the unlawful act or course of conduct

---

1   *R v Uddin* [2017] EWCA 1072 (Crim).

2   *R v Uddin* [2017] EWCA 1072 (Crim).

3   *R v Khan* [2009] EWCA Crim 2, para 26.

4   *R v Khan* [2009] EWCA Crim 2, para 27.

resulting in death. It applies when the defendant was unaware of the risk, but ought to have been aware of it. And also when he or she did not foresee, but ought to have foreseen, the occurrence of the act. The objective therefore is to include within the ambit of the offence those who chose to close their eyes to a risk of which they ought to have been aware, and which they ought to have foreseen.[1]

- **Foresight of the act or course of conduct.** The act or conduct resulting in death must occur in circumstances of the kind which were foreseen or ought to have been foreseen by the defendants. But the circumstances need not be identical. For example, violence of the same kind but more extreme might be caught, as well as violence taking place in a physically different location than previously.[2]

- **Reasonable steps taken to protect the victim.** Reasonable steps will depend on the individual concerned. For example, in one case involving the death of a woman, murdered by her husband, other family members were convicted under the 2004 Act, including two sisters. However, had either of these themselves been subjected to serious violence, then it might not have been reasonable to expect her to take any protective steps. This illustrated the point that it is the importance of the individual circumstances of the defendant.[3]

Examples of cases include the following.

> **Death of young woman at hands of extended family.** Family members were convicted of causing or allowing the death of a vulnerable adult and conspiracy to pervert the course of justice in the following circumstances. One was convicted of murder.
>
> The dead woman was 19 years old. She lived with extended family. One night she was beaten to death. Before calling the emergency services, the family (i) disposed of her clothes soiled with blood and faeces and her blanket; (ii) moved a bed so that it covered a blood- and vomit-stained rug; (iii) removed the youngest daughter from the house to prevent the police speaking to her; (iv) agreed a false account about where the latter had spent the night; and (v) put the body in the bathroom.

---

1   *R v Khan* [2009] EWCA Crim 2, para 32.

2   *R v Khan* [2009] EWCA Crim 2, para 39.

3   *R v Khan* [2009] EWCA Crim 2, para 33.

Injuries. The dead woman's body had 55 separate areas of injury, including two black eyes, bruising to her head, face and ears both on the left and right, a cut to the head and her lip, with bruising inside her mouth, and injuries to the back of her head, right shoulder, legs and back. She had specific targeted injuries to both breasts, hip, stomach, arms and hands, including defensive injuries. The 'fresh' injuries had been caused by moderate force and within 24 hours of her death. There were older injuries to her arms, legs, face and head.

Lengthy history. There was a lengthy history of isolation and sustained physical and emotional abuse, including beatings on a regular basis and degrading punishments. The other members of the family, including the appellant, were either active or complicit. The regime included physical beatings with objects, being made to eat paper, her own faeces and vomit, force-feeding, deprivation of sleep and water, being made to stand for hours staring into a lavatory bowl, not being allowed to use the lavatory or shower when she needed to, having to use the lavatory or shower under surveillance, being forced to sleep on the floor when she wet the bed and being made to lick the lavatory bowl or seat.

Isolated. She was not allowed a mobile telephone and had no access to social media. She could not socialise with anyone outside the home or speak to anyone about her family in a way that might reveal what was happening to her. When witnesses raised concerns with the school authorities, the deceased was directed to spend break times only with her sister. When the family learnt she had allowed herself to be taken to the school matron for an ear infection, she was punished. Witnesses were so concerned about her being in an emotionally and physically abusive situation that they obtained contact details for a helpline on domestic abuse and for a local charity to give to the deceased. She did not contact either for fear of repercussions at home.

In summary, this was a complex and dysfunctional family. The dead woman had challenged her sister-in-law's strict regime and it was this that brought her into conflict with the family and brought about episodes of punishment beatings.[1]

Vulnerable man living with family killed. In 2010, three members of a family were convicted of the murder of Michael Gilbert, who had lived with them for many years. His headless body was found in a lake. Four other

---

1   *R v Uddin* [2017] EWCA 1072 (Crim).

members of the family were sentenced for 'familial homicide', referring to the offence of causing or allowing death of a vulnerable adult under the 2004 Act.[1]

The victim met one of the family at a children's home when they were in care and 15 years old. He was introduced to the rest of the family and began to live with them. He was a vulnerable adult who had been homeless for part of his life and was estranged from his own family.

He was kept effectively as a slave. He was seriously assaulted and abused for entertainment on a fairly regular basis over a ten-year period. This included being beaten with fists and with weapons, including a baseball bat. He was pulled around by mole grips attached to his testicles. He would be made to stand in water hot enough to blister his feet for weeks. Snooker balls would be dropped on his genitals from a height. His benefit money would be confiscated.

If he managed to get away from the home, he was forcibly brought back. Some of the beatings were recorded on mobile telephones. All the household knew of the situation. Most took part in the abuse. None took any action to prevent the escalating abuse. On occasions, the victim was handcuffed to a bed wearing only night clothes in order to ensure that he did not escape.

After October 2008, the abuse got worse. It included actions such as doing press-ups on a piece of wood placed in his mouth and jumping on his stomach. In January, the victim had become doubly incontinent and his stomach was very badly swollen. He was complaining of stomach pains and asking for medicine. He could hardly walk.

As the month progressed, he was still alive but had suffered beating upon beating and was gravely ill. He was lying on a deflated blow-up bed. He had defecated and urinated where he lay. His stomach looked more swollen than before. He requested and was given medication. He could just about speak. They left him where he lay. He died that evening.[2]

Wife systematically beaten and abused by husband for months: four family members also convicted for doing nothing. A 19-year-old woman was systematically beaten and abused by her husband for three months. When she died, she had 15 broken ribs and bruising over 85 per cent of her body. Her husband was convicted of murder; however, his mother, two

---

1 '"Depraved" family sentenced for killing of man kept as a slave.' *Daily Telegraph*, 26 April 2010.

2 *R v Watt* [2011] EWCA Crim 1325.

sisters and brother-in-law were all found guilty of allowing the death of a vulnerable adult. The Crown Prosecution Service commented that the family had chosen to do nothing and that if 'families or other people with a duty to look after those who need protection deliberately choose not to do so, their neglect will not be ignored by the law enforcement agencies, and prosecution will follow'.[1]

DOMESTIC VIOLENCE: DOMESTIC HOMICIDE REVIEWS. Domestic homicide reviews are held under section 9 of the Domestic Violence, Crime and Victims Act 2004. They focus on the circumstances in which the death of a person aged 16 or over has, or appears to have, resulted from violence, abuse or neglect by (a) a person to whom he was related or with whom he was or had been in an intimate personal relationship, or (b) a member of the same household as himself. Such a review is held with a view to identifying lessons to be learnt from the death.

Duty of candour, see *Care Quality Commission*

---

1   Jenkins, R. 'Women face prison for ignoring a murder under their own roof.' *The Times*, 6 February 2008. See: *R v Khan* [2009] EWCA Crim 2.

Elephant in the adult safeguarding room, see *National Health Service*

Employment Rights Act 1996, see *Whistleblowing*

Endangering life by wilful negligence

Reference to an apparent old common law offence of this description was made in the following case.

> **Excessive fluids forced on care home residents.** Elderly residents in a care home in Clacton were forced to drink vast amounts of liquids by the owner, who was obsessed with avoiding dehydration in residents. Two of them died. It was reported that the owner was given a suspended 15-month prison sentence under a common law offence reportedly not used for 200 years: endangering human life or health by wilful negligence.[1]

Enduring power of attorney, see *Lasting power of attorney*

---

1   Horsnell, M. 'Fluids force fed to elderly in care.' *The Times*, 20 October 2001.

Eligibility (Care Act)

An assessment of 'eligibility' triggers a legal duty, under section 18 of the Care Act 2014, for a local authority to meet an adult's care and support needs. Suspected or actual abuse or neglect is not itself enough to mean that a person is eligible for help. This is in contrast to Wales, where abuse or neglect (or risk of either) alone is sufficient to create a duty to meet an adult's need for care and support.[1]

However, in some cases, the abuse or neglect may anyway, albeit indirectly, give rise to eligibility because of the effect it has on the person's situation. Three questions determine eligibility. They are set out in regulations made under the Care Act:[2]

- **Impairment or illness.** Do the adult's needs arise from, or are they related to, a physical or mental impairment or illness?

- **Outcomes.** Because of those needs, is the adult unable to achieve two or more of the outcomes listed in the regulations?

- **Well-being.** Consequently, is there, or is there likely to be, a significant impact on the adult's well-being?

The questions need to be asked in order. Eligibility depends on the answer 'yes' to all three. (For the eligibility of informal carers, see *Carers*.)

ELIGIBILITY: IMPAIRMENT OR ILLNESS. The first question is about impairment or illness. Guidance states that the local authority should base its judgement 'on the assessment of the adult and a formal diagnosis of the condition should not be required'.[3] (By way of comparison, the equivalent Welsh regulations are more inclusive, referring to physical or mental ill health, age, disability, dependence on alcohol or drugs, or other similar circumstances.)[4]

---

1   Social Services and Well-being (Wales) Act 2014, s.35.

2   SI 2015/313. Care and Support (Eligibility Criteria) Regulations 2015.

3   Department of Health. *Care and support statutory guidance: issued under the Care Act 2014.* London: DH, 2016, para 6.102.

4   SI 2015/1578. Care and Support (Eligibility) (Wales) Regulations 2015, r.3.

ELIGIBILITY: OUTCOMES. The second question relates to outcomes, of which the adult must be unable to achieve at least two or more, because of their needs arising from, or related to, their impairment or illness:

- managing and maintaining nutrition

- maintaining personal hygiene

- managing toilet needs

- being appropriately clothed

- being able to make use of the adult's home safely

- maintaining a habitable home environment

- developing and maintaining family or other personal relationships

- accessing and engaging in work, training, education or volunteering

- making use of necessary facilities or services in the local community, including public transport and recreational facilities or services

- carrying out any caring responsibilities the adult has for a child.[1]

For example, abuse or neglect could undermine the adult's nutrition, hygiene, clothing, personal relationships, getting out into the community, etc.

ELIGIBILITY: LEGALLY NOT ACHIEVING AN OUTCOME. The regulations define legal – as opposed to actual – inability to achieve an outcome. That is, when the adult is:

- unable to achieve it without assistance

- able to achieve it without assistance but doing so causes the adult significant pain, distress or anxiety

- able to achieve it without assistance but doing so endangers or is likely to endanger the health or safety of the adult, or of others, or

---

1   SI 2015/313. Care and Support (Eligibility Criteria) Regulations 2015.

- able to achieve it without assistance but takes significantly longer than would normally be expected.[1]

ELIGIBILITY: SIGNIFICANT IMPACT ON WELL-BEING. The third question is about whether, consequent on the inability to achieve at least two outcomes, there is, or is likely to be, a significant impact on the adult's well-being. This question requires scrutiny of the definition of well-being in section 1 of the Care Act (see *Well-being*). The impact could therefore be a likelihood only, but must be significant.

Guidance states that the local authority 'will have to consider whether the adult's needs and their consequent inability to achieve the relevant outcomes will have an important, consequential effect on their daily lives, their independence and their wellbeing'.[2]

The definitional elements of well-being are: personal dignity; physical and mental health and emotional well-being; *protection from abuse and neglect*; control by the individual over day-to-day life (including the care and support provided to the adult and the way in which it is provided); participation in work, education, training or recreation; social and economic well-being; domestic, family and personal relationships; suitability of living accommodation; the adult's contribution to society.

Clearly abuse or neglect could have the effect of undermining any one, or more, of these elements of the definition of well-being. Protection from abuse or neglect is anyway part of the definition of well-being.

ELIGIBILITY: POWER TO MEET NON-ELIGIBLE NEEDS, OR TO MEET NEEDS IN CASE OF URGENCY. If an adult with care and support needs is assessed as not eligible, the local authority has no duty to provide care and support services but can nevertheless exercise a power (a discretion) to do so. Likewise, if assessment and determination of eligibility have not yet been concluded, the local authority has a power to provide if the person's needs

---

1 SI 2015/313. Care and Support (Eligibility Criteria) Regulations 2015.

2 Department of Health. *Care and support statutory guidance: issued under the Care Act 2014.* London: DH, 2016, para 6.107.

appear to be urgent. These powers both come under section 19 of the Care Act 2014.

Therefore, in the case of abuse or neglect, the local authority would have a power (if not a duty) to meet a person's needs, even if the person wasn't formally eligible.

Enquiries (Care Act)

A duty to make safeguarding enquiries is triggered under section 42 of the Care Act if a local authority has reasonable cause to suspect the following about an adult in its area (whether or not ordinarily resident there):

- **Care and support:** has needs for care and support (whether or not the authority is meeting any of those needs).

- **Abuse or neglect:** is experiencing, or is at risk of, abuse or neglect.

- **Inability to protect self:** as a result of those needs is unable to protect himself or herself against the abuse or neglect or the risk of it.

If there is reasonable cause to suspect these three things, then the local authority must make or arrange enquiries and then decide what should be done:

- **Making or causing enquiries and then deciding:** the local authority must make (or cause to be made) whatever enquiries it thinks necessary to enable it to decide whether any action should be taken in the adult's case (whether under the Care Act or otherwise) and, if so, what and by whom.

Enquiries are meant to be the hub of adult safeguarding. However, section 42 itself confers no coercive power on a local authority: it cannot force anybody to do anything. Nor does it contain any rules even about what help should be offered. So a local authority might decide, on conclusion of the enquiries, that it has a duty or power to protect the person under other parts of the Care Act by providing advice, information, care and support, etc.

In addition, or alternatively, the local authority might refer or apply to other bodies or organisations including, for example, the police, regulatory bodies (e.g. Care Quality Commission), Court of Protection, High Court, etc. And the local authority may request cooperation from various bodies under sections 6 and 7 of the Care Act, particularly from its 'statutory partners' – cooperation, for example, in the making of enquiries as well as in taking action following concluded enquiries. See *Cooperation*.

Section 42 enquiries are considered in some detail below, under the following headings:

- Enquiries: underlying principles

- Enquiries: adult in the area

- Enquiries: reasonable cause to suspect three conditions

- Enquiries: care and support needs (first condition)

- Enquiries: experience or risk of abuse or neglect (second condition)

- Enquiries: inability of adult to protect themselves (third condition)

- Enquiries: health care needs

- Enquiries: informal carers

- Enquiries: present, not past, risk

- Enquiries: consent

- Enquiries: involvement of people and information

- Enquiries: speed

- Enquiries: depth of

- Enquiries: standard of

- Enquiries: factual accuracy

- Enquiries: who makes them

- Enquiries: requesting other organisations to make them

- Enquiries: referral to the police

- Enquiries: general fairness and balance

- Enquiries: following local procedure

- Enquiries: flexible policy and procedure

- Enquiries: deciding what to do

- Enquiries: local authority is decision-maker

- Enquiries: should precede decisions and actions

- Enquiries: rational response to

- Enquiries: and decisions, lack of local authority coercive powers

- Enquiries: protection of adults from third-party violence

- Enquiries: eligibility for ongoing help

- Enquiries: and assessment

- Enquiries: preliminary or 'pre-enquiries'

- Enquiries: 'non-statutory'.

ENQUIRIES: UNDERLYING PRINCIPLES. Guidance states that adult safeguarding should be underpinned by six principles – empowerment, prevention, proportionality, protection, partnership, accountability – and that it is about 'making safeguarding personal'.[1]

Section 1 of the Care Act 2014 itself states more simply that whatever a local authority does under the Act in respect of an individual person – including, therefore, making enquiries – it has a general duty to promote the well-being of that individual. And the definition of well-being includes, for example, protection from abuse and neglect, personal dignity, emotional well-being, control over day-to-day life, keeping restrictions to a minimum, etc.

ENQUIRIES: ADULT IN THE AREA. The duty to make enquiries falls on the local authority where the person is present, not necessarily where they are (legally) ordinarily resident under the slightly confusing 'deeming' rules of the Care Act 2014.

In summary, if a person is living in the community within a local authority area, they would normally be ordinarily resident there. But if they have been placed in that area by a different local authority – in a care home, supported living or shared lives (adult) placement – then the person

---

1   Department of Health. *Care and support statutory guidance*. London: DH, 2016, paras 14.13–14.14.

is deemed to remain ordinarily resident in the area of the placing authority.[1] In which case, the placing local authority would remain responsible overall for meeting the needs of the person under the Care Act – but the duty to make safeguarding enquiries would fall on the local authority, in the area of which the person was physically present in the care home, supported living or shared lives placement.

ENQUIRIES: REASONABLE CAUSE TO SUSPECT THREE CONDITIONS.

The duty to make enquiries is triggered if the local authority has reasonable cause to suspect three conditions. All three conditions must be satisfied for the duty to arise. The first two conditions, relating to care and support needs and to abuse or neglect, appear to cast the net wide. The third condition, about the ability of the person to protect themselves, seems designed to narrow the scope of section 42.

ENQUIRIES: CARE AND SUPPORT NEEDS (FIRST CONDITION). It

is irrelevant whether the person, in fact, has care and support needs. The question is merely whether the local authority has *reasonable cause to suspect* that the person does.

Alternatively, if there are in reality some care and support needs, the person might have relatively low needs and not be eligible for care and support from the local authority – under Care Act eligibility rules.[2] Or he or she might be self-funding, might be looked after by his or her family – or simply not be having his or her needs met at all. The duty to make enquiries would still arise. (If there is no requirement that the person has eligible needs, then it would seem that it is not necessary, under section 42, for a person to have an impairment or illness, the first of the three eligibility conditions under the Care Act generally: see *Eligibility*.)

Care and support is not defined under the Care Act and, as such, is probably capable of broad interpretation. The nearest term in previous legislation – section 21 of the National Assistance Act 1948 – was to a

---

1   Care Act 2014, s.39.

2   Care Act 2014: explanatory notes, para 274.

person's need for 'care and attention'. The courts understood this term, in its natural and ordinary meaning, to be about 'looking after' but to be wider than nursing personal care.[1]

> **Care and attention: wide meaning.** In a case involving a man who was HIV-positive, the courts defined care and attention (of which he was not in need at that point) as follows:
>
> > Looking after means doing something for the person being cared for which he cannot or should not be expected to do for himself: it might be household tasks which an old person can no longer perform or can only perform with great difficulty; it might be protection from risks which a mentally disabled person cannot perceive; it might be personal care, such as feeding, washing or toileting. This is not an exhaustive list. The provision of medical care is expressly excluded.[2]

The courts have likewise already accepted a broad approach, under the Care Act, as to what care and support needs might relate to, beyond personal care or nursing.

> **Care and support needs and range of provision to meet them.** A woman had been the victim of torture, rape, emotional and physical abuse. She suffered from severe mental health problems, including complex post-traumatic stress disorder, insomnia, depression and anxiety. She spoke no English and was said to be illiterate. She had left seven of her eight children and her husband in Afghanistan. Her eighth child had been killed in conflict. She did not know the whereabouts of her remaining children or of her husband. Provision to meet her care and support needs included: improvement of resilience, assistance in learning by rote certain journeys to and from her home, accompaniment to appointments when she did not know the journey, home visits to check home environment, nutritional and shopping advice, assistance from local shopkeeper with using money in the shop, counselling as well as practical advice and other support by Freedom

---

1   *R (M) v Slough Borough Council* [2008] UKHL 52, para 32.

2   *R (M) v Slough Borough Council* [2008] UKHL 52, para 33.

> from Torture, assistance with general matters (including arranging and attending appointments, booking translators, learning English), assistance with domestic and practical tasks in the home, being taken to a day centre by other women in the house.[1]

In short, reasonable cause to suspect that a person has care and support needs suggests a low threshold.

ENQUIRIES: EXPERIENCE OR RISK OF ABUSE OR NEGLECT (SECOND CONDITION).

For this second condition, local authorities must strike a balance between, on the one hand, not acting on totally flimsy or non-existent evidence or indicators, and, on the other, failing to act on reasonable cause for suspicion. Erring too far in either direction could mean either unjustified enquiries or failure to make enquiries that are required. Implications include:

- **Harm need not have been suffered.** There is clearly no requirement in section 42 that there must be reasonable cause to suspect that harm has been suffered by the person. This is for two reasons. First, experience of abuse or neglect does not necessarily mean that harm has yet been suffered: for instance, a hospital patient who, deprived of water, drinks out of a flower pot might be suffering neglect, but not yet harm. Second, in any case, section 42 is not just about experience of abuse or neglect but also risk of it.

- **Abuse or neglect – not harm in itself – is the triggering condition for enquiries.** Reasonable cause to suspect harm, or risk of it, would have much wider implications: many people in need of care and support are at risk of harm of some sort, but relatively little of this harm is anything to do with abuse or neglect. For instance, therefore, not treating a one-off, isolated incident resulting in minor injury as safeguarding – and therefore not triggering enquiries – may be justifiable.[2]

  So this is a distinction with a difference, not least because this condition in section 42 of the Care Act has clearly been deliberately drafted to contrast with a similar phrase in section 47 of the Children Act which triggers a duty

---

1 *R (SG) v Haringey London Borough Council* [2015] EWHC 2579 (Admin).

2 LGO, *Leicestershire County Council*, 2016 (15 014 413).

to make enquiries – but on the basis of reasonable cause to suspect harm to a child.

- **Abuse or neglect need not have occurred.** Reasonable cause to suspect risk of abuse or neglect does not necessarily mean reasonable cause to suspect that abuse or neglect has yet occurred. Meaning that section 42 can be used preventatively.

- **Low threshold.** Section 47 of the Children Act 1989 contains the same phrase – reasonable cause to suspect – in relation to a child suffering, or likely to suffer, significant harm. In that context, the courts have held that reasonable cause to 'suspect' is a lower threshold – more easily triggered – than reasonable cause to 'believe'. The courts have also held, in the Children Act context, that there must be reasonably *objective* grounds for the reasonable suspicion, not just the *subjective* view of the local authority, but the courts would nonetheless be slow to interfere with the local authority's decision about this.[1] The threshold, under the 1989 Act, has been held to be lower even than the balance of probability. In other words, harm does not have to be more likely than not, in order to trigger reasonable cause to suspect it.[2]

In the following court case, therefore, the section 42 enquiries were clearly justified, even though the service users – for whose benefit the enquiries were being conducted – objected.

> **Suspected, unproven, fraud involving direct payments: enquiries justified.**
> A direct payment support provider was suspected of fraud involving service users' money. Not yet proven, there was nevertheless a criminal investigation taking place; on any view, enquiries were justified:
>
> > So far as the local authority is concerned there was clear evidence that the service users including the claimants were at risk of financial abuse. What had been uncovered was a widespread issue and there was an ongoing criminal investigation. As a result of that it was appropriate for the defendant to commence safeguarding enquiries and act in response to those enquiries.[3]

---

1   *Gogay v Hertfordshire County Council* [2001] 1 FCR 455 (Court of Appeal).

2   *R (S) v Swindon Borough Council* [2001] EWHC Admin 334, para 36.

3   *R (Collins) v Nottinghamshire County Council* [2016] EWHC 996 (Admin), para 28.

The following case illustrates a local authority failing to make enquiries (albeit under previous legislation), when there was clearly reasonable cause to suspect experience or risk of abuse or neglect (under what would now be the Care Act).

> **Wrongly not making enquiries despite reasonable cause to suspect.** A man was discharged from hospital to a care home. Concerns became known to the local authority about the role of a woman who had befriended him, his periodic confusion, her living in his home, her control of his finances, care home fees not being paid, the length of time she claimed to have known him, contradictory information provided by her. By this stage, the local authority should have initiated an investigation. Not to do so was maladministration.[1]

Conversely, a challenge to the local authority may be made not about a failure to enquire but the opposite, resulting in unwarranted intrusion. The challenge might be made by the person suspected of abuse or neglect.

> **Reasonable cause to suspect not the same as accepting assertions at face value.** The local authority was justified in making enquiries, under section 42 of the Care Act, in relation to a man's not paying care home fees for his mother in a care home – because of the consequent threat of eviction. However, it was at fault for accepting at face value the hearsay that he was about to remove his mother from the care home, for making a best interests decision – and threatening legal action against the son – without first trying to understand the son's actions (a protest against what he considered poor care: he was trying to arrange alternative care).[2]
>
> **Reasonable cause to suspect: wandering in the street and son's comments about his mother.** A woman with dementia and schizophrenia lived with her son who was her main carer. The police told the local authority that the woman had been found wandering in the street. The emergency services reported that he had said he hoped she would die. He then refused an assessment of either his mother's or his own needs. The local authority

---

1   LGO, *Essex County Council*, 2016 (14 012 127), paras 42–43.

2   LGO, *Durham County Council*, 2016 (15 009 788), paras 31–34.

> made enquiries under section 42 of the Care Act, concluding there was no evidence of neglect. Further enquiries took place shortly after this, along similar lines, including possible misuse of sedative tablets. The enquiries were again closed, but she began to attend a day centre. The son complained, but the ombudsman found the section 42 enquiries justified.[1]

Or the challenge to the making of enquiries might come from the very person whom the local authority is seeking to protect.

> **Man complains about triggering of safeguarding investigation designed to protect him.** A young man lived at home with his family. He had various physical health problems, including Crohn's disease (inflammatory disease of gastrointestinal tract) and arthritis caused by malfunctioning of the body's immune system. When his health deteriorated, safeguarding concerns were raised. He had become sarcopenic (extremely thin), with grey skin, atrophic (muscle wasted) legs with pitting oedema. His breathing was rapid, and he was having difficulty getting his breath. A build-up of fluid on his lungs was developing and his heart was struggling to cope with the extra work.
>
> The man complained, maintaining that the safeguarding investigation should not have been initiated, since the causes of his illness and poor condition had not been explored adequately. The ombudsman noted that it was a complex case, but that the professionals involved in the decision were justified in conducting a safeguarding investigation, in order to find out more.[2]

ENQUIRIES: INABILITY OF ADULT TO PROTECT THEMSELVES (THIRD CONDITION). The inability of a person to protect themselves must be because of their needs for care and support. An example of this is given in guidance which suggests that if a person is neglecting themselves, but can control their own behaviour and decisions, then section 42 enquiries would not be triggered.[3]

---

1   LGO, *Birmingham City Council*, 2016 (16 007 420), paras 7–26.

2   LGO, *Blackpool Borough Council*, 2017 (16 004 644).

3   Department of Health. *Care and support statutory guidance*. London: DH, 2016, para 14.17.

Clearly, an inability to protect oneself would not just be about mental capacity, but could also relate, for instance, to mental health, physical inability or some form of undue influence, coercion or duress.

The issue of self-protection under section 42 has been considered by the courts, although the judge seemed to equate unwillingness to protect oneself with inability to do so. This, as a general proposition at least, does not sound quite right, since inability to do something is not the same as unwillingness.

> **Inability to protect themselves.** When service users objected to the local authority making enquiries into possible fraud by a direct payment support provider – arguing they could perfectly well protect themselves – the judge held that section 42 enquiries were justified. This was on the basis that the service users were vulnerable, and they were either unaware of the fraud or chose not to take any action – either way, this was 'clear evidence' that they could not protect themselves.[1]

ENQUIRIES: HEALTH CARE NEEDS. Care and support needs are legally not the same as health care needs. For instance, meeting care and support needs under the Care Act – by providing services the NHS is required to provide – is generally prohibited; likewise, the provision of registered nursing care. Therefore, in principle at least, if a person were to have health care needs only, but no needs for care and support, then the section 42 duty to make enquiries would seemingly not apply. For example, the following case (not in the safeguarding context) involved the courts identifying health care, but not social care, needs in the case of a man with HIV status.

> **Health care, but not social care, needs.** A man, with HIV-positive status (possibly with AIDS), had needs for a home, subsistence and medication (and a refrigerator for it), but no other daily living needs. He was held by the courts under previous legislation not to be in need of care and attention (a term similar to care and support) for the purposes of adult social care.[2]

---

1   *R (Collins) v Nottinghamshire County Council, Direct Payments Service* [2016] EWHC 996 (Admin), paras 19, 28.

2   *R (M) v Slough Borough Council* [2008] UKHL 52, para 60.

The Law Commission identified this issue, and the uncertainty it could engender, preferring that health care, as well as care and support, needs should have been explicitly referred to in section 42. However, it noted also that whilst 'very many of the people with whom safeguarding and adult protection are generally concerned as a matter of practice do, indeed, have health needs, the overwhelmingly large majority also have at least some social care needs' – in which case, section 42 enquiries would apply to this large majority.[1]

ENQUIRIES: INFORMAL CARERS. The reference to care and support in section 42 means that it clearly does not apply to informal carers. Otherwise, there would be reference to 'support', in addition to 'care and support', as in many other sections of the Care Act that distinguish between them.

However, if a carer is subject to abuse or neglect, other duties under the Care Act apply, including the duty to promote the carer's well-being (which is defined in section 1 of the Act to include protection from abuse and neglect), to provide advice and information, to cooperate with other organisations, to assess and to provide support if a carer is judged to be eligible.[2] Specifically, assessment includes consideration of whether there is a significant impact on the carer's well-being (and therefore the question of protection from abuse and neglect). In any case, the local authority could refer to other agencies – for example, the police – if necessary; section 42 enquiries are not required to do this.[3]

In summary, the exclusion of informal carers from section 42 in no way prevents local authorities from offering suitable assistance to protect those carers from abuse or neglect – whether they are at risk from the person being cared for, or indeed from anybody else.

ENQUIRIES: PRESENT, NOT PAST, RISK. It would seem clear from the wording of section 42 that the duty to make enquiries arises only in relation

---

1   Law Commission. *Adult social care*. London: LC, 2013, para 9.36.

2   Care Act 2014, ss.1, 2, 6–7, 10, 20.

3   Department of Health. *Care and support statutory guidance*. London: DH, 2016, para 14.48.

to current experience or risk of abuse or neglect. If it is in the past, in respect of the individual in question, then the duty does not arise.

> **Safeguarding alert: past risk.** A safeguarding alert was raised on the day a woman was leaving her present care home to go to another. The ombudsman pointed out that the resident was no longer at any potential risk from the previous home, meaning that section 42 enquiries would not be triggered – unless, of course, other residents of the previous home were suspected to be at risk.[1]

On the same basis, if enquiries have begun, they might be curtailed in the absence of any further risk of abuse or neglect – for example, if the resident concerned passed away, the care home involved had closed, and in any case there had been no witnesses to the alleged injury the resident had sustained.[2]

The intent of the legislation seems to be that past abuse or neglect should be considered by safeguarding adults boards (SABs), by way of safeguarding adults reviews under section 44 of the Care Act. See *Safeguarding adults reviews*. Or, less obviously, by a local authority, as part of a safeguarding adults board's functions generally, under section 43 of the Act – less obviously because this power was never added expressly to section 43:

- **Power of local authority to review past cases of abuse or neglect, as part of safeguarding adults board's functions under section 43.** 'It has always been our intention that local authorities (as part of the SAB) can hold reviews into past cases of abuse or neglect under clause 43 [now section 44 of the Act]. We are happy to state this power expressly in clause 43 in order to remove any doubt that the duties of cooperation apply to the performance of relevant safeguarding functions whether they relate to past or present safeguarding concerns. Clause 41 [now section 42 of the Act] relates to immediate action on present risk so changing it would not address the concern raised.'[3]

---

1   LGO, *Durham County Council*, 2016 (15 009 788), paras 47–48.

2   LGO, *Somerset County Council*, 2017 (17 003 737), paras 6, 22.

3   Secretary of State for Health. *Care Bill explained: including a response to consultation and pre-legislative scrutiny on the Draft Care and Support Bill*. London: The Stationery Office, 2013, p.67, para 48.

ENQUIRIES: CONSENT. There is no requirement for the adult to consent to enquiries, although consent should be obtained where practicable.[1] However, with or without consent, the duty persists in principle.

At the same time, the local authority has no legal power to force the adult to engage in the enquiries or indeed to enter the adult's home. Any coercive entry to the adult's home would have, if appropriate, to take place under other legislation and therefore not (directly at least) for Care Act purposes (see ***Power to enter***).

That said, the guidance states that a person's wishes must be taken account of, 'making sure that the adult's well-being is promoted including, where appropriate, having regard to their views, wishes, feelings and beliefs in deciding on any action. This must recognise that adults sometimes have complex interpersonal relationships…'[2]

Closure of financial abuse enquiries in accordance with person's wishes. A woman raised concerns that her father, in a care home, was being financially abused by his partner, in relation to a joint account they held. The local authority initiated enquiries but decided to discontinue them on the basis that the father had the mental capacity to decide how his finances were managed. The ombudsman did not criticise the local authority for discontinuing the enquiries at the time, having taken account of the father's wishes. Nonetheless, ten months later, concerns were raised again, the father was assessed as now lacking capacity and the daughter was made appointee for her father by the Department of Work and Pensions.[3]

ENQUIRIES: INVOLVEMENT OF PEOPLE AND INFORMATION. One of the six principles set out in guidance is empowerment. Thus, keeping people involved and informed is important and is something the local ombudsman has regularly picked up on.

---

1   Department of Health. *Care and support statutory guidance*. London: DH, 2016, para 14.95.

2   Department of Health. *Care and support statutory guidance*. London: DH, 2016, para 14.7.

3   LGO, *Knowsley Metropolitan Borough Council*, 2017 (16 016 208).

Adequate enquiries but lack of communication. A man raised concerns about the care of his father in a care home. The local authority was held to have made enquiries adequately but had failed to explain to the son the nature of its safeguarding investigation, did not set out clearly what it was doing, did not communicate with the family – leading to them feeling excluded – and did not inform the son of the findings of the enquiries in a timely manner. All this was fault.[1]

Failure to involve woman with learning disabilities and her mother in enquiries. An allegation was made that a care worker assaulted a young woman with learning disabilities. The case was complicated by the fact that the alleged perpetrator worked for the same care provider as the woman's mother.

Amongst other things in its enquiries, the local authority assumed the woman lacked mental capacity, didn't talk to her, didn't involve her in the investigation, didn't talk to the mother (assuming a conflict of interest without actually exploring whether this was so), assumed and told the police she had a fear of people in uniforms (so the police didn't talk to her either and she was unable to give her version of events – as the mother put it, her daughter's 'voice was not heard'). The local authority admitted these faults.[2]

Failure to ensure advocate could attend safeguarding meetings. A young man lived at home with his family. He had various physical health problems, including Crohn's disease (inflammatory disease of gastrointestinal tract) and arthritis caused by malfunctioning of the body's immune system. When his health deteriorated, safeguarding concerns were raised. The local authority recognised the need for an advocate but failed to invite the advocate to the safeguarding meeting. This was fault.[3]

Lack of communication with family during investigation. A man broke his wrist in a care home. His daughter raised a safeguarding concern. An investigation (in any case not adequate) took place, but there was insufficient communication with the man's family. They were not consulted or updated on progress or outcomes of the investigation, in accordance

---

1   LGO, *Durham County Council*, 2016 (15 014 024), paras 33–45.

2   LGO, *Sheffield City Council*, 2017 (16 013 737).

3   LGO, *Blackpool Borough Council*, 2017 (16 004 644).

with local guidelines. The family was told in June they would receive a copy of the report of the investigation, but two months later neither this nor any updates had been received. The daughter was not only the person who had raised the safeguarding alert, but she was also responsible for ensuring Mr F was involved and represented as part of the safeguarding investigation. This lack of communication by the local authority was fault.[1]

Distress caused by not communicating with the family. A woman raised safeguarding concerns about her father-in-law in a care home. Her concerns, subsequently generally substantiated, included him being unkempt, unshaven, feet blue with cold, difficulty finding staff to share their concerns with, a member of staff wearing a bobble hat, smells of urine, delay in treating a sore groin, bathing once a week only, failure to inform the family of a hospital admission.

The local authority did investigate adequately and did substantiate the allegations. However, it failed to communicate with the daughter-in-law properly about this. This led to her subsequently complaining. The failure of the local authority to ensure proper communication caused additional stress and anxiety to the daughter-in-law at a time when there had been a bereavement in the family, a change of care home for her father-in-law and she was also handling the complexities of the application for a deferred payment agreement for him. This was fault.[2]

ENQUIRIES: SPEED. Neither the Care Act nor the statutory guidance sets out timescales for the conducting of enquiries. In their absence, the general legal principle is that a specific duty – such as making enquiries under section 42 of the Care Act – should be performed without undue delay – that is, within a reasonable period of time. And identifying that reasonable time will depend upon all the circumstances of the case.[3] So that what is undue delay for one person might not be for another. In addition, the local ombudsman will take account of whether any local policy on timescales has been adhered to.

---

1   LGO, *Essex County Council*, 2017 (15 017 662).

2   LGO, *Milton Keynes Council*, 2017 (17 000 475).

3   *R (D) v London Borough of Brent* [2015] EWHC 3224 (Admin), para 19.

Adequate enquiries but 11 months too long. A local authority adequately investigated a hip fracture that an elderly woman had sustained in a care home but took 11 months to do so. The delay was largely due to the absence from work of the investigating officer. Even so, the delay was too long and was fault.[1]

Four-month delay in holding strategy meeting, despite local five-day time frame. Safeguarding referrals were received by the local authority in April 2015, but no strategy meeting held until July, three months later. The local policy set a five-day time frame. This was fault. The concerns were raised by a charity on behalf of the daughter of a woman with dementia in a care home – about the use of furniture to stop her mother getting up from her chair and walking around, and about being left in pools of urine for long periods of time. However, the local authority had, in any case, immediately ensured one-to-one support for the woman, to ensure her safety.[2]

Eight-month period for concluding enquiries too long, despite lack of statutory timescales. A woman raised concerns about her mother's care in a care home, relating to alleged neglect, emotional abuse, not involving the family in reviews, leaving the call bell out of reach, improper moving and handling, a bedtime regime not in line with the mother's wishes, lack of staff to take the mother to the toilet, seizure management, threats of eviction. The emotional abuse allegation was substantiated: it involved the manager coming into the bathroom when the mother was naked on the toilet, poking her on the nose and saying, 'What have you been saying about staff?'

The local authority was slow to act when concerns were raised. It did not record them as safeguarding concerns for two days and did not hold a strategy discussion for five days. There were problems with the enquiries in terms of communication, timescales and a failure to meet best practice guidelines. Holding a mediation session within the context of the safeguarding enquiries, although well intentioned, resulted in blurred boundaries. The initial enquiries took eight months to complete. While there were no statutory timescales for completing such enquiries, the

---

1   LGO, *Kent County Council*, 2016 (15 019 793).

2   LGO, *London Borough of Croydon*, 2016 (15 020 940).

expectation was for enquiries to be completed in a timely fashion. There was no good reason for such a length of time.[1]

ENQUIRIES: DEPTH OF. Guidance states that enquiries could range from an informal 'conversation' to the more formal, involving a multi-agency approach.[2] It is for the local authority to decide therefore how the enquiries should be carried out and to what depth. In the following examples, the local ombudsman concluded that the local authority had carried out adequate enquiries.

Asking NHS to enquire. The local authority conducted adequate enquiries by requesting the NHS to investigate the care of a care home resident, and then deciding that no further, formal safeguarding action was required once the care home had agreed to certain recommendations about its practices.[3]

Unannounced visit to care home. The local authority made an unannounced visit with a senior social worker and contracts compliance officer, inspected records of the woman suspected to be at risk and of several other residents potentially so, talked to the NHS body which had placed the woman in the care home – and concluded that there was no evidence of neglect or abuse. The ombudsman found no fault.[4]

Asking range of professionals. A local authority considered information provided by a care home resident's sister, the care home, the GP, the NHS Safeguarding Nurse and the manager of the integrated care team. The local authority reported care standards concerns to the Care Quality Commission. It could have scrutinised the deputy manager in relation to medication practices, and its minute taking could have been better. But, overall, there was no fault.[5]

1   LGO, *Rochdale Metropolitan Borough Council*, 2017 (17 006 466), paras 6, 37–38.

2   Department of Health. *Care and support statutory guidance*. London: DH, 2016, para 14.77.

3   LGO, *Durham County Council*, 2016 (15 014 024), paras 30–31.

4   LGO, *Thurrock Council*, 2016 (16 001 733), para 17.

5   LGO, *North Somerset Council*, 2016 (16 000 240), paras 23–24.

Limitations to enquiries. A woman wanted the local authority to investigate her mother's bank accounts; she suspected (correctly, as it turned out) that her mother was being financially abused by her brother-in-law. The local authority established that the mother had capacity to decide who should help her with her finances and declined to act on the daughter's suggestion. The ombudsman found that it would have been beyond the local authority's role and legal powers to do more: there was no maladministration.[1]

Telephone enquiries and decision about what to do. An allegation had been made that an unspecified family member was stalking a woman with learning disabilities. The local authority conducted what it considered to be a proportionate investigation. This involved a planning discussion, a judgement that the risk was low and a telephone conversation with the woman. The conclusion was the woman had the mental capacity to decide whom she wanted to see and that she could decide whether or not to involve the police.

The ombudsman did not find fault in the failure of the local authority to visit the woman. It was a judgement call; there was no information that telephone contact was inappropriate – in fact, it was the woman who phoned the local authority for advice.[2]

Appropriate enquiries in relation to alleged weight loss in care home. A local authority responded to an anonymous complaint it received about the care of a resident of a care home. It took the concerns seriously and investigated, followed its safeguarding procedures, sent its contract monitoring team to the care home and to examine records. In addition, an investigator visited the home, spoke with the resident's case worker, talked to the hospital (to which the resident had been admitted) and interviewed the resident himself (who was satisfied with the care he had received).

On discharge from hospital, he had wanted to return to the care home and he had the mental capacity to take this decision. The local authority found no evidence to support the allegations of malnourishment. The ombudsman concluded that the local authority had responded appropriately.[3]

---

1   LGO, *North Lincolnshire Council*, 2016 (15 015 381), para 51.

2   LGO, *Staffordshire County Council*, 2018 (17 009 452).

3   LGO, *Lincolnshire County Council*, 2016 (15 011 754), paras 29–32.

Adequate enquiries in response to concerns about a care agency. Various concerns arose in early August about a care agency, including a carer not staying for the allotted time, not appropriately providing meals to the service user and not covering a plug socket so that the service user could not access it. The care agency was asked to investigate, which took until September, and a strategy meeting was held in October.

The ombudsman found no fault, stating that there was not unreasonable delay, since the timescale was largely outside the control of social care staff; the enquiry was sufficiently thorough – when the care agency did not initially address the safeguarding concerns properly, social services required it to do so; the complainant had sufficient opportunity to provide evidence and to state her concerns; the findings from the strategy meeting were not biased in favour of the care agency – in fact, the team manager largely upheld the concerns; the care agency had been entitled to respond to what the complainant said in the strategy meeting; the team manager was correct in her view that the strategy meeting should be concerned only with the safeguarding issues, and not with the care agency's business operations – and it was appropriate for the minutes to reflect this.[1]

Hip fracture investigation: all relevant evidence considered. A local authority investigated a fractured hip sustained by a care home resident. The investigation took too long (11 months) but otherwise considered the relevant evidence. It spoke to the woman, sought advice from her GP and the surgeon who treated her in hospital, inspected records from the care home, requested statements from the care home staff, viewed the family's video of the woman explaining her injury in which she said, 'two Indian girls fighting, pushed me', and referred the matter to the police (who viewed the video and decided not to begin a criminal investigation). The local authority concluded that the cause of injury could not be ascertained; the ombudsman found no fault with this conclusion.[2]

Relying on safeguarding nurse in enquiries sufficient. A woman with epilepsy lived in a care home. Her sister became concerned in December about her care, diet and medication; the local authority began safeguarding enquiries, concluding them in February following a best interest meeting. During April, the woman had a urinary tract infection (lack of fluids), had

---

1   LGO, *Essex County Council*, 2017 (16 016 334).

2   LGO, *Kent County Council*, 2016 (15 019 793).

suffered three seizures, had not taken all her anti-seizure medication and was admitted to hospital where she died on 24 April.

Her sister raised a safeguarding concern on 20 April. In October, the local authority concluded its enquiries, upholding a range of concerns about the care home. It passed these findings on to the Care Quality Commission and to its own contracts team. It relied on a hospital safeguarding nurse to examine the resident's notes, rather than a doctor. The ombudsman found no fault in any of this and concluded there was nothing more the local authority could have done. The woman was now dead and there was no further risk to protect her from.[1]

ENQUIRIES: STANDARD OF. Section 42 states that a local authority must itself make, or ask somebody else to make, whatever enquiries it thinks necessary to enable it to decide whether any action should be taken and, if so, what and by whom. For the local authority to be able to take this decision, the enquiries clearly need to be of a certain standard. Sometimes the local authority might have to challenge the organisation or person that it has asked to make the enquiries – or take steps to corroborate those enquiries.[2] A relatively simple example was as follows, involving a fracture in a care home.

Inadequately investigating injury in a care home. A local authority's safeguarding investigation did not adequately address whether a care home's approach to the injury to Ms Y was appropriate given that the injury she had sustained was not further investigated or diagnosed for more than 24 hours. For example, the investigation did not query the lack of follow-up action and the failure to complete an incident form. The apparent failure of staff at the care home to proactively follow up the following day or night after they were first alerted to the resident's painful arm meant that there was a delay in seeking medical treatment. The ombudsman recommended that the local authority satisfy itself that the care home had a procedure for adequately recognising and dealing with such injuries promptly in future.[3]

1   LGO, *Somerset County Council*, 2016 (16 000 240).

2   Department of Health. *Care and support statutory guidance*. London: DH, 2016, para 14.100.

3   LGO, *Oldham Metropolitan Borough Council*, 2018 (16 015 846).

Grossly flawed enquiries by a local authority can lead to draconian, wrong and unlawful decisions being taken.

> **Local authority's incompetent enquiries followed by draconian decision to remove daughter from family.** A 19-year-old woman with learning disabilities came back from a school trip with bruising on her chest. The local authority failed to conduct a competent investigation by omitting to do the obvious: talking to other people on the trip who had witnessed her injuring herself. Instead, the local authority jumped to the conclusion that the mother was responsible. It unlawfully removed the woman from her family for a year, by depriving of her liberty and breaching many of the rules under the Mental Capacity Act 2005, and therefore breaching also the Human Rights Act.[1]
>
> **Unsubstantiated concerns followed by removal of young man from foster carer/adult placement.** Four concerns were raised about a person's foster carer.
>
> First, he had reportedly said that he was put in a wardrobe sometimes. However, a visit to the house disclosed no wardrobe.
>
> Second, it was alleged that when his carer picked him up from school, she wagged her finger at him, behaved aggressively and said that when he misbehaved, he should be put to the wall. The judge commented: 'Whilst I think it likely that F was cross with E and that she probably admonished him, I do not find that she was aggressive, or that this incident is indicative of a pattern of ill-treatment.'
>
> Third, she had asked social workers for help with self-defence training, to help manage him when he became difficult and aggressive.
>
> Fourth, the local authority argued a serious lack of cooperation on the carer's part, yet the judge came to a different conclusion and saw the carer's efforts in a different light – namely a carer who genuinely cared for him and was prepared to fight his corner.
>
> Nonetheless, despite lack of substantiation of the safeguarding concerns, the local authority removed him to a care home. The courts ultimately ruled that this was not in his best interests – but, in any case, the local authority had breached the legal procedures for such a deprivation of

---

1   *Somerset County Council v MK* [2014] WL 8106551.

liberty under the Mental Capacity Act, and thus breached also the Human Rights Act.[1]

Safeguarding investigation: multiple failings. The ombudsman found maladministration, having considered the following points about the investigation carried out. It related to the care provided by a man to his wife with dementia, and her having been found wandering in the streets. The management of the safeguarding investigation was inadequate; investigation was not completed quickly enough (six months); the investigation report was poorly written; invitation to the case conference did not advise what was the purpose of the meeting or who was attending; the investigation report was not issued in good time before the meeting; recording of discussion at meetings was poor or absent.[2]

Adequate knowledge of investigator. The safeguarding investigator was experienced in social work but did not pick up on important discrepancies in recording in the nursing home, or that the resident had been inappropriately physically moved after his fall. The ombudsman found that someone with a knowledge of care standards should have been part of the investigation – or that investigating staff should have been provided with tools to ensure they considered the relevant information. This did not happen and was maladministration.[3]

Inadequate consideration of all the circumstances undermining decision about what safeguarding action to take: death of young, severely disabled woman. A severely physically disabled woman, 26 years old, lived with her parents. She suffered from spinal muscular atrophy, had severe curvature of the spine and was unable to use her legs. She was of very low body weight. Her mother (and father) had always been her main carer. She had specialist equipment and adaptations including a special ripple mattress, a customised electric wheelchair, a special alarm system, a wheelchair-accessible bathroom, a bath cushion, and an adapted toilet seat. She was liable to chest infections, and care had to be taken with her posture both during the day in the wheelchair and during the night; sometimes

---

1   *G v E* [2010] EWHC 621 (Fam), High Court, March 2010.

2   LGO, *London Borough of Bromley*, 2016 (15 013 228), para 28.

3   LGO, *Lancashire County Council*, 2016 (14 001 973), para 32.

her mother adjusted her position (but did not turn her over) in bed several times a night.

Alleged taking of money and slap. The woman attended a day centre run by a voluntary body on behalf of social services. On this particular day she was upset and explained to the manager of the centre that her mother had taken money from her bank account without her permission; and that when she had found out, she had an argument with her mother who had slapped her legs.

Emergency placement organised. The centre manager contacted a social worker who knew the woman. The woman was adamant that she did not want to return home. The mother arrived to collect her daughter but was told that the latter did not want to return home, but not about the allegations. The mother went away and subsequently refused to return to the centre. The social worker talked to his manager and decided to arrange an emergency residential placement. A care home was identified that provided for people with severe physical disabilities.

Transport arrangements. The centre arranged transport to the home, although there was not an escort in the van; the social worker drove behind most of the way. On the way, they collected various belongings from the woman's home; the mother said she was not asked about any equipment her daughter might need or about her care needs. The journey lasted much longer than expected (some two hours) because of traffic jams on the M25.

First night in care home, sickness and death three days later. The woman spent her first night in the care home. She did not have a ripple mattress; a baby alarm was fixed up for her because she could not operate the emergency buzzer system. The notes stated that she needed turning several times a night. In the morning, she felt uncomfortable, felt sick, frail and unwell and wanted to go home. Her parents arrived to collect her. She died of bronchial pneumonia three days later.

Making enquiries before the placement. The local ombudsman pointed out that the mother had given unstinting care and love to her daughter all her life; that the daughter had been upset and that the local authority staff had been right to take her distress seriously. However, it was maladministration not to make proper enquiries before the placement and before deciding that the woman should travel without an escort. In particular, the woman's general practitioner and occupational therapist should have been consulted. This might have resulted in the placement going ahead, an alternative placement or her going back home. In any event the ombudsman was not satisfied that she might still not have contracted the chest infection; thus, he could not blame the council for her death.

Considering a complicated case at a 'deep level'. The ombudsman also agreed with the view expressed by the local authority manager who had led the investigation into the events, that the staff involved had failed to recognise at a 'deep level' that the woman's case was 'problematic'. They should have realised that only her parents had ever looked after her, and that despite her being articulate and intellectually able, they should have talked to the GP and occupational therapist. They had also taken the woman's statements as 'absolute', without attempting to verify what had been said. The care home should have been checked for appropriate equipment and for its ability to assess the woman's needs, given that the local authority staff involved on the day knew little about her needs. Staff should have sensed that the case was 'more complicated than most'. Furthermore, he felt that the woman should have been accompanied in the vehicle during the trip to the care home.[1]

ENQUIRIES: FACTUAL ACCURACY. Reasonable attempts to establish factual accuracy will be fundamental to the adequacy of enquiries.

Hearsay evidence and lack of factual evidence. A local authority made enquiries into alleged verbal abuse, emotional abuse and control and neglect – perpetrated by a daughter against her mother. The safeguarding report substantiated these allegations but only based on hearsay, assumptions, lack of factual evidence and inflammatory language. This was fault.[2]

The following court case is worth digesting in some detail, as an illustration of serious lapses in factual accuracy, relating to the evidence put forward by a local authority – and of the sort of pitfalls that need to be avoided.

'Without notice' application to court lacking evidence and fact: preventing a man returning to the care of his daughter and granddaughter. A local

---

1   LGO, *Kent County Council*, 1999 (98/A/1612).

2   LGO, *Lancashire County Council*, 2016 (15 017 811), para 48.

authority sought a 'without notice' order to transfer a man away from the care of his relatives (daughter and granddaughter) into a care home.

It did so on the basis that (a) the relatives had obstructed a full 'mini-mental state examination'; (b) his previous care home placement had been terminated by the care home because of the verbally abusive and threatening behaviour of the two relatives; (c) he had been assessed during a hospital stay as requiring 24-hour care in a nursing home; (d) the two relatives had removed him from hospital; (e) the relatives lived in a one-bedroom flat in which it would clearly be unsuitable for him to stay; (f) he had complex care needs; (g) his problematic diabetes required careful control but the relatives gave him unsuitable food; and (h) he would be at serious risk of harm in the care of the relatives.

Allegations by the local authority badly flawed. The judge found that virtually all of these grounds had not been made out. The evidence did not support the claim about the mini-mental state examination. The evidence about the behaviour in the care home might have been established but it was highly regrettable that the local authority did not obtain first-hand evidence about the family's behaviour.

Lack of assessment. The assessment, concerning the need for 24-hour nursing home care, was found by the judge to have fallen short of a 'genuine and reasonable attempt to carry out a full assessment of the capacity of the family to meet the relative's needs in the community'. The authority had not in fact carried out such an assessment. When a thorough assessment was finally carried out, it concluded that he could in fact be cared for in the community by his relatives.

Family had not removed man from hospital. It also transpired that the relatives had not in fact removed him from hospital. He had instead been discharged by the hospital itself, and this had followed the non-attendance by a social worker at a case conference. The social worker had instead opted for court action.

Flat had two bedrooms, not one. The flat turned out not to have one bedroom; in fact, it had two. The man clearly did have complex needs, but these did not necessarily rule out care in the community.

Diabetes more stable in the care of his family. On the question of diet, the local authority had claimed that he was regularly fed inappropriately by the relatives. In fact, no evidence was produced to the court about this. The relatives had received training and, by the time of the court case, when he was in the care of his relatives, his diabetes was more stable than it had been in the care home.

'Without notice' application not justified. The judge concluded that given the standoff with the family at the relevant time, a period in the care home might have been justified had the application been made by means of an 'on notice' order. However, a 'without notice' process was not justified. The judge also noted that although a 'without notice' order gives 'liberty to apply' to the other party, for relatives this may mean little. It should be spelt out to the other party that they can challenge the order.

Local authority's belated change of view about the man's best interests. Finally, the judge pointed out that the final allegation, that he would be at serious risk of harm in the care of his relatives, was nonsense – given that by the time of the second court hearing, all were agreed (even the local authority) that his best interests would be served by living with his relatives.

The judge pinpointed the core issue as being lack of communication on the part of the local authority, and the failure by the relatives to make themselves physically and emotionally available to receive any communication.[1]

Similarly, in the following case, a catalogue of allegations was discounted by the judge, as unsupported by the evidence.

Eleven allegations of assault by father on his daughter discounted. Eleven allegations of assault were made against the father of a 30-year-old woman with learning disabilities. Of these, ten had the legal status of hearsay – that is, they were based on what the woman herself had told various professionals. The eleventh allegation was in the form of eyewitness (more precisely, 'ear witness') evidence from two carers. In addition to the specific allegations, the local authority also sought to rely on observations of bruising as evidence of further abuse in addition to the 11 core allegations.

Self-injury and hearsay. The court was extremely wary. First, it was clear from the evidence that the woman was physically vigorous and liable to bruise herself, which she did with some regularity. Second, whilst the court was prepared to admit hearsay as relevant evidence, the court was unconvinced by it. This was largely based on the unreliability of the woman's

---

1   *LLBC v TG* [2007] EWHC Fam 2640.

statements to these professionals. Third, the witnesses were insufficiently reliable, and, on the balance of probability, the judge felt unable to conclude that – on the particular occasion in question – the father had slapped his daughter, causing a cut on her lip.

Unreliability of hearsay accounts. Amongst the judge's reasons were that her level of intellectual functioning, which rendered her incapable of being a witness, compromised the ability of the court to rely upon hearsay accounts. The local authority records were peppered with other allegations made by the woman against professionals which were accepted by the local authority as not being reliable reports. She was at times physically vigorous wherever she was, at home or in professional care. She sustained bruises and other injuries as a result. The local authority accepted that they could not attribute any particular bruise to any particular incident. Since the proceedings began, the very good foster carers had to withdraw from caring for the woman because they considered that she was putting herself at risk of harm (and was being harmed) by physical behaviour in their home.

No basis for singling out parents as responsible for injuries. The judge found it impossible to single the parents out in this regard and make negative findings about the woman's safety in their home, which had been her home for some 30 years, when she is at much the same risk wherever she is because of her challenging behaviour.[1]

ENQUIRIES: WHO MAKES THEM. Section 42 states that either the local authority must itself make enquiries or it must 'cause' them to be made by somebody else. This could be, for example, the police, a hospital or a care home.

The word 'cause' is slightly misleading, since the local authority cannot legally force anybody else to make the enquiries. However, in case of a defined statutory partner under sections 6 and 7 of the Act – about cooperation – the local authority could at least bring a degree of legal pressure to bear. See *Cooperation*.

---

1   *London Borough of Enfield v SA* [2010] 196 (COP).

ENQUIRIES: REQUESTING OTHER ORGANISATIONS TO MAKE THEM.

Section 42 states that local authorities can 'cause' enquiries to be made – that is, ask another body or organisation to make the enquiries – before it, the local authority, decides what should be done. The local authority should consider both the appropriateness of whom it asks, the adequacy of responses it receives and what cross-checking it will undertake – not least, because there might be conflicts of interest.

Winterbourne View: plausible and reassuring (but false) explanations given by provider. When safeguarding concerns were raised at Winterbourne View Hospital, setting for systemic abuse of people with learning disabilities, the hospital would give plausible and reassuring explanations. There were at least five occasions when hospital managers were asked to investigate allegations. However, they failed to produce the required reports and there was no effective system in South Gloucestershire to chase progress. Furthermore, there was an overreliance on telephone discussions, albeit multi-agency ones, rather than meetings followed by the timely distribution of minutes. When meetings were convened, which did not occur as often as they should, representatives from placing authorities and clinicians from outside the hospital were not always present.[1]

Concerns about care of woman with autism in a care home: no explanation of decision to ask provider to investigate. The parents of a woman with autism raised a variety of concerns about her care, including alleged emotional abuse. The care home manager raised an alert. The local authority decided no action should be taken under safeguarding procedures but that the provider should investigate. No explanation of this decision was recorded.

The provider produced a report which, however, set out the questions raised but not its findings. When the local authority finally held a safeguarding meeting, it failed to make a clear decision about whether there had been abuse. This was fault. The local authority should clearly have documented the reasons for decisions it took. If it passed responsibility for an investigation to another organisation, it needed to explain why it considered that appropriate and what factors had been considered, and,

---

1   Flynn, M. *Winterbourne View Hospital: a serious case review.* Bristol: South Gloucestershire Safeguarding Adults Board, 2015, pp.96, 107.

indeed, whether the care provider's staff were sufficiently independent – or seen to be – to consider the issues raised.[1]

Allowing delay and relying on unsatisfactory enquiries by the NHS about hospital care. A local authority requested that a hospital investigate how an elderly patient was being cared for. The local authority waited five months before chasing up the hospital. (The woman had died during this time.) The hospital provided nothing in writing, claimed there was nothing untoward and that it had spoken to the woman's daughter (which it hadn't). The local authority decided to do nothing more; this was maladministration.[2]

Relying on unsatisfactory care home enquiries, without cross-checking. A local authority asked a care home to provide information about the care of a resident who had suffered an accident (and subsequently died). The care home manager reported back that the accident could not have been foreseen or prevented. The local authority accepted the findings without checking the care records, which showed 11 previous incidents similar to the final accident. This was maladministration.[3]

Not making further enquiries after police enquiries were terminated. The ombudsman found fault when a local authority failed to make its own enquiries – into potentially serious abuse of a man with learning disabilities in a care home – once the police investigation had ended because of a lack of forensic evidence.[4]

Conversely, once a referral to the police has been made, it may be reasonable for a local authority to defer its own safeguarding investigation, not least so it has all relevant information.[5]

Asking others to carry out enquiries: appropriateness. A local authority asked a care provider to investigate safeguarding concerns against staff, raised by parents about their autistic son living in supported residential accommodation. The ombudsman found fault with the local authority

1   LGO, *North Yorkshire County Council*, 2016 (14 003 742), paras 34–40.

2   Local Government Ombudsman. *Review of adult social care complaints 2014/15*. London: LGO, 2015, p.12.

3   Local Government Ombudsman. *Adult social care matters: safeguarding vulnerable adults*. London: LGO, 2014, p.5.

4   LGO, *Essex County Council*, 2013 (11 001 206), paras 33, 45.

5   LGO, *London Borough of Bromley*, 2017 (17 008 561).

because there was no evidence that the local authority had considered whether the care home staff were sufficiently independent to consider the issues raised.[1]

ENQUIRIES: REFERRAL TO THE POLICE. Guidance refers to the need for consideration of police involvement:

- **Involvement of the police.** 'Where the safeguarding concerns arise from abuse or neglect, then it would not only be necessary to immediately consider what steps are needed to protect the adult but also whether to refer the matter to the police to consider whether a criminal investigation would be required or is appropriate… In any case where you encounter abuse and you are uncertain about your next steps, you should contact the police for advice… If a professional has concerns about the adult's welfare and believes they are suffering or likely to suffer abuse or neglect, then they should share the information with the local authority and, or, the police if they believe or suspect that a crime has been committed… Although the local authority has the lead role in making enquiries, where criminal activity is suspected, then the early involvement of the police is likely to have benefits in many cases.'[2]

Nonetheless, the guidance does not go so far as to say a formal referral to the police by the local authority must take place in every case when criminal activity is suspected. (A middle way, in some cases, is for local authorities to seek advice from the police at a preliminary stage and in principle, without at that point disclosing personal details.) In the following legal case, referral was not made, because it would not have been in the person's best interests.

Reasons, in the elderly person's best interests, for the Court of Protection not referring two deputies to the police for 'looting' her estate. The Court of Protection ruled that – despite having 'looted' their 94-year-old aunt's (GM) estate, to the tune of some quarter of a million pounds – two deputies should not be referred to the police, even though, in the judge's view, they

---

1   LGO, *North Yorkshire County Council*, 2016 (14 003 742), para 34.

2   Department of Health. *Care and support statutory guidance*. London: DH, 2016, paras 14.41, 14.43, 14.83.

had behaved dishonestly. They were, and had been for many years, her only visitors.

Some of the reasoning was as follows:

> In my judgment, it would not be in GM's best interests for this to be done. Were the police to be alerted to this, I have no doubt that they would wish to contact the deputy, and that further costs would be incurred by him which would have to be defrayed out of GM's estate. I am also concerned that any police investigation would raise a serious risk that [the deputies] would be advised to cease any continuing contact with GM whilst the police investigation, and any subsequent prosecution, were continuing and pending. I am also concerned that a police investigation might result in an approach, or approaches, whether directly by the police themselves, or indirectly through Social Services or some other body, to GM and again that would not be in her best interests.

(However, the court did remove the nieces as deputies, appointed a replacement, professional deputy and ordered an insurance security bond to be triggered, thus ensuring the estate was restored to its previous financial state.)[1]

In the case below the local government ombudsman found no justification for referral to the police, but instead imposition of a blanket policy, which led to misfortune.

Blanket policy of referral to the police, followed by distress of adult in need and suicide of her partner. A long-standing couple moved into a care home; she needed to be there, he didn't. They shared a bank account. They also shared a room in the care home. She reported twice that he had physically abused her in the night – given her 'a good hiding'. Safeguarding enquiries were initiated, but then discontinued when it was agreed that he would have a separate room. A visiting neighbour then reported that, as part of plans for him to move out, he might be using her money to refurbish a flat. A social worker visited and spoke to the woman. She asked for help in altering the arrangements for managing her money but was adamant that

---

1   *In the Matter of GM* [2014] EWCOP 1, paras 57, 96, 98.

she did not want the police involved. However, she did agree to the matter being referred to safeguarding.

Blanket policy. Social services said they were duty-bound to report the allegations of physical abuse to the police, with or without the woman's consent. The police visited to talk to her. She became distressed as a result, and in any case denied that her partner had hit her. The police also spoke to her partner and told him to keep his distance. The next day he left the home and committed suicide. (The council also investigated the alleged financial abuse but did not act on the woman's request to help change the way in which her finances were managed.)

Ombudsman: not aware of any legislation imposing blanket duty to report to police. The local ombudsman was

> not aware of any legislation that makes Councils 'duty-bound' to report these matters to the police. The legislation is clear that it has to obtain permission from the alleged victim (if they have capacity) and that, only when certain strict conditions are met, the Council can share information against a person's wishes. These circumstances need to be very carefully considered and only apply in certain cases (of serious crime, life threatening situations, etc).

Absence of decision-making process in the individual case. The ombudsman had not seen evidence or a record that showed if and how the local authority considered whether it should still involve the police, even though the woman did not want this. This was fault. Once the authority had decided to involve the police, it failed to tell the woman about this, before contact was made. This, too, was fault.[1]

Judging whether to make a referral to the police is not necessarily straightforward and should be given careful consideration, which the Court of Appeal found absent when an NHS Trust referred two of its nurses.

Patient tied to a table by two nurses: defied belief that NHS Trust referred to police. Two nurses, on the evening shift of a mental health ward – understaffed and with some very difficult patients – had tied one patient's chair to a table with sheets around the chair legs. This was clearly

---

1   LGO, *London Borough of Hounslow*, 2017 (16 010 076).

an unconventional method but was designed to keep both him and other patients safe. During the day he had been agitated, aggressive, hitting things, spitting, swearing, throwing drinks, kicking and punching, and generally requiring particularly close attention. The 'safe' and approved handling technique used by staff had caused skin tears on his arms to be opened. Medication had to be administered forcibly because he was refusing both food and medicine. When the evening restraint method became known outside of the ward, the nurses were suspended (and eventually dismissed) and a formal referral was made to the police.

Court of Appeal found it astonishing that a referral to the police was made. The Court of Appeal was highly critical of the decision to make a referral to the police (who took no action). It was

> little short of astonishing that it could ever have been thought appropriate to refer this matter to the police. In my view it almost defies belief that anyone who gave proper consideration to all the circumstances of this case could have thought that they were under any obligation to take that step... [I]t is important that hospitals in this situation must be seen to be acting transparently and not concealing wrongdoing; but they also owe duties to their long serving staff, and defensive management responses which focus solely on their own interests do them little credit.

Not least since nobody had suggested that the nurses were trying to act otherwise than in the patient's best interests.[1]

Dispute with parents about how they lifted their son: referral to police by local authority beggared belief. Local authority occupational therapists offered a portable hoist to the parents of a 21-year-old man; they were manually lifting him each morning out of the sofa bed in which he slept. They were also carrying him sometimes up the stairs. He could not walk, talk, stand or care for himself. The therapists insisted, on safety grounds, that the hoist be used with a hospital bed. The parents refused on grounds of lack of space.

Dispute with parents over hoist and bed. The therapists refused to provide the hoist without the hospital bed. The parents suggested that, instead,

---

1   *Crawford v Suffolk Mental Health Partnership NHS Trust* [2012] EWCA Civ 138.

the local authority should make a direct payment to them for the hoist, so that they could purchase it themselves and take more responsibility for the situation. This request was refused.

Safeguarding referral made to the police. Concerned about the risk to the son (he appeared to lack the capacity to consent to it), the therapists made a safeguarding referral that was passed on to the police. The parents were informed this had happened only belatedly. The ombudsman referred to the local authority's lack of flexibility in what services it was prepared to offer, the absence of a social worker, the lack of a person-centred approach and the fact that the police themselves had deemed the referral inappropriate. It was a service provision issue, rather than a full-blown safeguarding issue.

Maladministration: overreaction of local authority. The ombudsman found maladministration in respect of the adult protection referral, finding that it 'beggared belief'. He referred to the devotion of the family to their son's care, the local authority's procedural shortcomings (including poor record-keeping), the family not being informed and their understandable distress and outrage when they found out about the referral.[1]

ENQUIRIES: GENERAL FAIRNESS AND BALANCE. The courts and local ombudsmen may find fault if enquiries are not conducted in a generally fair and balanced manner.

Scraping the barrel for old and unsubstantiated allegations about the father's abuse of his daughter. A local authority submitted evidence of alleged abuse by a father of his daughter with learning disabilities. The court largely discounted this evidence, finding most of it not made out. However, the order sought by the local authority (to accommodate the daughter elsewhere) was given – albeit on general welfare, rather than on abuse, grounds. The local authority would have been better off arguing the basic welfare case only, without trying to gild the lily with dubious evidence about abuse.

The father's case was that many of the local authority's allegations were old and unfounded, and many related to the stressful time when his wife died from cancer. At the time, the local authority had not acted on any

---

1   LGO, *Luton Borough Council*, 2008 (07/B/07665).

of these concerns. Furthermore, some of his complaints about the local authority's conduct had been upheld.

An incident going back to 1991, related by a support worker, when he allegedly threatened to beat his daughter with a belt, the judge discounted for lack of evidence on the file. A 1992 incident, reported by a nurse, that he had hit his daughter four times with his fist about the head and face, the judge also discounted on the evidence. The older allegations of drinking to excess, the judge also discounted, insofar as they came from his two other children, since they were so hostile to their father. A more recent allegation was also found to be unreliable; the judge took account of the fact that the witness, as a Muslim, did not drink alcohol; and a senior local authority community worker pointed out that the father's explanation was that he relieved pain in his neck and shoulder by rubbing them with Bay Rum, a preparation which can be used for medicinal purposes.[1]

Slanting the evidence in breach of duties of full disclosure and of fairness.
A local authority sought a court order preventing a woman interfering with her husband's removal to hospital in his best interests. It sought to bolster its case with unsubstantiated allegations that she abused him. It also withheld information from the court about the positive aspects of the wife's caring. The court criticised the local authority for acting 'in breach of its duties of full disclosure and fairness'. It had failed to particularise the allegations, to support them with evidence and to give a more balanced account.

Explanation was lacking about how the incidents were raised with the wife or why they were not raised with her – and about why, if they had occurred, her husband had continued to be cared for at home. In addition, reference was not made to the good aspects of her care of, and relationship with, her husband. Particularly in the light of this unbalanced approach by the local authority, the court cautioned that 'without notice' orders – that is, not giving the other side a chance to dispute or respond at the time the order is made – should be exceptional. The court gave the order but on general welfare grounds, rather than on the allegations of abuse.[2]

---

1   *Newham London Borough Council v BS* [2003] EWHC Fam 1909.

2   *B Borough Council v Mrs S* [2006] EWHC 2584 (Fam).

A fair hearing is therefore something both the courts and ombudsmen will look for.

> **Deplorable treatment of a care home owner by a local authority.** Investigating alleged failings in care at a family-run care home, a local authority subjected the elderly care home owner (not the care home manager) to a meeting of eight hours, gave her no proper opportunity to prepare for the meeting, refused to consider her solicitor's letter, had ten people on their side as against the manager, abused the informality of a lunch break – and then drew conclusions about her credibility and fitness to run the home. The court described her treatment as deplorable.[1]
>
> **Mother and stepfather, alleged perpetrators, denied opportunity to respond.** A woman with mental health needs lived at home with her mother and stepfather. She was alleged to have caused physical harm to the stepfather, was arrested and placed in temporary accommodation. She then provided information to a care coordinator which led the care coordinator to make a safeguarding referral, in which she was identified as the vulnerable adult and the mother and stepfather as alleged perpetrators.
>
> The ombudsman accepted that the local authority and NHS Trust involved had a duty to act on the safeguarding concern. However, despite the need for an independent advocate being identified, none was ever appointed. Additionally, not only were the mother and stepfather not given an opportunity to respond to the allegations, but the evidence failed to show that the authority and Trust had even considered the appropriateness and fairness of this, despite the local policy stating that the right to challenge and natural justice must be considered. This failure caused added distress and upset to the mother and stepfather and was fault.[2]
>
> **Deciding prematurely before hearing from both sides of the family: unfair and biased safeguarding meeting.** Mr W helped another family member, Mr X, with his finances and had a power of attorney, although it had never been registered. The latter had learning difficulties, was bipolar and received some care from the local authority. He was vulnerable to financial

---

1   *Davis v West Sussex County Council* [2012] EWHC 2152 (QB), paras 45–47.

2   LGO, *London Borough of Enfield*, 2017 (16 016 072).

exploitation. Both were members of a large family, with complex dynamics involving considerable and long-lasting animosity between siblings.

In early 2017, Mr X stopped eating and drinking and took to his bed. He was not seen by family members for three weeks. When he failed to attend church one Sunday, family members in the town became concerned and went to his house. They say they found him in bed in a weak and dirty condition, with no food or money in the house. On the same day, Mr W visited Mr X and said that Mr X was fit, well and had food and money in the house. He took him shopping and to the Council to pay a bill. More widely, Mr W said that he had invested Mr X's money honestly for years, increasing its value dramatically and ensuring that Mr X had the wherewithal to live independently and defending him from family members who wanted to exploit his vulnerability. Two other family members said that Mr W had abused Mr X over the years, taken steps to isolate him, embezzled his money and enriched himself.

Diametrically opposed versions of events. The ombudsman pointed out that this was a case where there were two diametrically opposed versions of events which could not both be true. Whichever version was true, the other was most probably created for the purpose of deception.

Unfair and biased safeguarding meeting. The safeguarding meeting was divided into two halves. Mr X and other family members attended the first half, Mr W the second. During the first half, allegations were made against Mr W, and the lead safeguarding officer said to Mr X that he should listen to his family because Mr W might not have his best interests at heart. The officer's mind was clearly already made up. When Mr W entered, she immediately told him that she was removing his control over the man's finances. The allegations made against Mr W had been accepted uncritically. The local authority had failed to investigate to establish which of two competing, mutually exclusive versions of events – with a vulnerable individual in the middle – was true. This was fault.

Failure meant that possible danger to vulnerable adult was not properly considered. This failure to use the best evidence, to take decisions fairly and on merit without discrimination or bias, meant that the danger to Mr X was never considered. They failed Mr X and Mr W (and Mrs W, his wife). This was fault and it caused injustice. They all felt as if they were 'on trial' and that their integrity had been brought into question.[1]

---

1   LGO, *Durham County Council*, 2018 (17 000 746).

Lack of fair hearing for allegedly abusive daughter. Abuse allegations were investigated, in relation to a daughter and her mother. It was understandable that the daughter was not invited to the safeguarding meetings since she was the alleged abusive person. However, the allegations were not put to her, depriving her of any opportunity to respond, either then or when the final report – substantiating the allegations – was produced. This was maladministration.[1]

Son accused of assault: not able to give evidence, unsubstantiated allegation. A man in his nineties with dementia lived with his son. An allegation of assault against the son was made. Justifiably, the local authority commenced safeguarding enquiries. However, it then made several errors which caused injustice.

The police understandably became involved, but the local authority did not clarify with the police if or when it was appropriate for the authority to talk to the son. Nor did it talk to the police about whether there were grounds to prevent the son visiting the father (now in a care home). The local authority at no point told the son about the enquiries, leaving him in the dark. The enquiries were closed without considering whether the son might have an alternative version of events. Despite this, the local authority referred to the assault as being substantiated without having considered the evidence – even though neither it, nor the police, had yet conducted a proper investigation, particularly since the son had not been spoken to about the relevant events. The local authority then failed to tell the son where his father was and told him that, in any case, he would not be allowed to visit without police consent and the father's consent. The local authority also informed a third party that the son had assaulted the father: at most it should have referred to an allegation only.[2]

General practitioner, as alleged perpetrator, not asked for her views. A man complained that a GP failed to visit his mother in the care home. The GP was not asked for information or her views about what had happened. This delayed the investigation process and was not in the interests of natural justice. The local authority stated that it was up to the NHS clinical commissioning group (CCG) to decide how to involve the doctor, but the

---

1   LGO, *Lancashire County Council*, 2016 (15 017 811), paras 42, 48.

2   LGO, *Leicester City Council*, 2017 (17 005 924).

> ombudsman found fault with the local authority since it had ultimate responsibility for coordinating the safeguarding investigation.[1]

Of course, fairness in listening to an alleged perpetrator is one thing, but that does or need not mean inviting them to the very same meeting that the alleged victim is attending – not least because that might affect the latter's responses.[2] Initially at least, holding a strategy meeting without input from the alleged perpetrators of a degree of neglect – for example, an elderly woman's son and daughter – could be justified.[3]

ENQUIRIES: FOLLOWING LOCAL PROCEDURE. Whilst local policies and procedures occasionally may need to be departed from in unusual circumstances, they will normally be a means of ensuring that enquiries are carried out fairly, systematically and accountably.

> **Harassment by local authority warden: not investigated properly because it was a local authority service.** Serious complaints, supported by cogent evidence, were made by two residents about persistent bullying and harassment by the warden. The council's response was inadequate. The complainants ultimately had to resort to the local government ombudsman. She found that the council had failed to follow its own adult protection procedures and did not launch a full investigation into the allegations against the warden. This was maladministration.
>
> One of the local authority officers, providing information to the ombudsman, explained that he had pressed for a comprehensive investigation at the first adult protection strategy meeting about the case, but had been refused permission. He stated that in any other case there would have been a full adult protection investigation, but an exception had been made in this case because it was a scheme owned and run by the council itself.[4]

---

1   LGO, *Southend-on-Sea Borough Council*, 2017 (16 005 174).

2   LGO, *Essex County Council*, 2017 (16 013 496).

3   LGO, *North Tyneside Metropolitan Borough Council*, 2017 (17 003 913).

4   LGO, *South Tyneside Metropolitan Borough Council*, 2008 (06/C/18619 and 07/C/01489).

Injuries suffered at a local authority-run respite care facility: failure to investigate. A 30-year-old woman, with severe brain damage, had recently been injured on two occasions at a respite facility run by the local authority. For the first injury, the local authority did not even consider whether to investigate. For the second, it did investigate but failed to identify the perpetrator; however, it was clear that the injuries were inflicted deliberately. The ombudsman found poor record-keeping and communication, together with failure to implement a revised care plan. All this was maladministration. The parents withdrew their daughter from the centre. The local authority should promptly have considered alternative care for her, even if this meant spending scarce resources, since it had a duty to meet her needs. Failure to do this was also fault.[1]

Need to follow local safeguarding procedures about allegations that woman with learning disabilities was assaulted by her parents. A woman with learning disabilities was increasingly arguing with her parents, with whom she lived. The local authority had failed to draw up a care plan that might have identified a constructive way forward. She now alleged that her parents had hit her, locked her in her room and prevented her from seeing her friends. There was a clear written policy and also a procedure to follow in the case of such allegations. They stipulated immediate action to determine the risk and assess everybody's needs. The policy and procedure were not followed. The woman left her home precipitately and unplanned, ending up in an unsuitable adult placement, with a person who lacked the skills to meet her needs. This was maladministration.[2]

Failure to report assaults on woman with severe learning disabilities. A local authority placed a woman in a care home. Weighing only six stone, she was blind, of partial hearing, had virtually no speech and had severe learning difficulties. In an 18-month period, she suffered a catalogue of injuries including a fractured skull, broken fingers, cuts and bruises – and was assaulted by two members of staff.

The local ombudsman found that the care provided was inadequate. The father was only belatedly informed about the fractured skull. Neither the father nor the police were informed about the assaults. And the local

1   LGO, *Bedfordshire County Council*, 2003 (02/B/16654).

2   LGO, *Cumbria County Council*, 2000 (98/C/0002).

authority had amended the investigator's report without telling her. The local ombudsman found maladministration.[1]

Failure, by local authority staff with appropriate knowledge and training, to follow safeguarding procedures. There was an incident in a council-run day centre, involving a vulnerable service user with learning disabilities and yanking, pulling and slapping by a member of staff. Other staff were worried about adverse consequences to them if they reported the incident. One eventually did so but only after a delay; the report was not well received, and procedures were not followed in investigating it. One result of this was that the police were not informed promptly – this could have made a difference to a successful police investigation and to justice being served.

After the incident, the same member of staff continued to abuse and mock service users, display outbursts of temper and deny food to service users. Some other staff simply didn't recognise this as abuse which should have triggered safeguarding procedures. A year later, there was another hitting incident by another member of staff. Again, there was a delay in reporting the second incident, because the same staff member (who had reported the first one) was aware of the previous reaction.

The ombudsman also found delays in investigation of the alleged incidents, failure to maintain records, failure to distinguish fact from hearsay or opinion, endemic poor practice and poor management. In addition, staff charged with investigating the incidents themselves lacked appropriate knowledge, experience and expertise.

The ombudsman found serious maladministration by the local authority, with service users being left at risk of harm and the staff member who reported the abuse also suffering injustice (in the form of stress, fear and anxiety).[2]

ENQUIRIES: FLEXIBLE POLICY AND PROCEDURE. Most local authorities now have detailed written safeguarding policies and procedures, to which staff work. However, a degree of flexibility is sometimes required.

For instance, local authorities often have a policy which prohibits staff from talking to alleged perpetrators. The reason is typically to avoid

---

1   LGO, *Southwark London Borough Council*, 2001 (99/A/4226).

2   Public Services Ombudsman for Wales. *Report on an investigation into complaint no. 1999/200600720 against Carmarthenshire County Council*, 2009.

jeopardising or contaminating any police investigation – or, alternatively, to avoid putting the victim at greater risk. But taken to an extreme, without proviso, such a policy can become counter-productive.

Not talking to husband of a woman with learning disabilities. A local authority had pulled back from talking to the husband of a woman with learning disabilities about contraception (there was a question over his wife's capacity to decide about whether to use it or not). The more he was cut out of the picture, the more obstructive he became. The reason the local authority gave for not talking to him was that there were also abuse concerns, including allegations that he was physically rough with her, threatened her – and caused bruising on her arms.

The judge noted, however, that what needed talking about was not the alleged abuse but the contraception. The local authority's 'safeguarding protocols' did not encompass anyone talking to him, since he was the alleged perpetrator. The rationale of this protocol (to avoid putting the potential victim at increased risk) was one thing if domestic violence was the only issue. But, here, the question of contraception was also, and separately, in issue. The result was that the husband felt increasingly sidelined, and this in turn fuelled his lack of cooperation, meaning that he had not been helped to understand his wife's difficulties. This, in turn, made things even more problematic for her.[1]

Equally, there will in some cases be good reasons for not talking to the alleged perpetrator, for fear not just of undermining the police's gathering of evidence, but of the safety of the victim. For instance, in the case of a young woman murdered by her parents because of her westernised behaviour, it was suggested that the school and police had made things worse by talking to the parents at the wrong time.[2]

ENQUIRIES: DECIDING WHAT TO DO. Section 42 of the Care Act states that once enquiries have been made, the local authority must decide whether anything should be done – and, if so, what and by whom. The language

---

1   *A Local Authority v Mrs A* [2010] EWHC 1549 (Fam).

2   Jenkins, R. 'Catastrophic mistakes by school and police "led to honour killing of girl, 17".' *The Times*, 4 August 2012.

is slightly misleading, because the local authority cannot directly force anybody else to do anything. It can, at best, seek cooperation from statutory partners under sections 6 and 7 of the Care Act. The courts have in the past considered what sort of enquiries should be undertaken and what actions then considered. For example (in a case preceding the Care Act):

Enquiries into proposed assisted suicide and decision about what to do.
The court set out the enquiries the local authority should make in case of a proposed assisted suicide and a trip to Switzerland:

- **intention:** investigate the position of the vulnerable adult to consider her true position and intention

- **legal capacity:** consider whether she was legally competent to make and carry out her decision and intention

- **influence:** consider whether (or what) influence may have been operating on her position and intention and to ensure that she had all the relevant information and knew all available options

- **court application:** to consider whether to invoke the courts to decide about the issue of her competence

- **assistance if mentally incapacitated:** if she was not competent, to provide assistance in her best interests

- **assistance if mentally capacitated:** if she was competent, to allow her in any lawful way to give effect to her decision, although this should not preclude advice or assistance being given about what are perceived to be her best interests

- **informing the police:** to inform the police if there were reasonable grounds for suspecting that a criminal offence would be involved

- **court injunction:** in very exceptional circumstances only, seek an injunction from the courts (using section 222 of the Local Government Act 1972).[1]

---

1   *Re Z* [2004] EWHC 2817 (Fam).

In the following ombudsman case, the actions the local authority took, following enquiries, were 'commendable'.

> **Commendable: local authority enquiries and actions in relation to safeguarding at a care home, despite continuing poor practice at the home.** Concerns were raised about the care of a resident in a care home, including staffing levels, medication administration, not contacting the GP when she was ill and not allowing her to remain in her room when she was ill, poor fluid intake, inaccurate recording, bruising (from manual handling), carers allowing her to urinate in a waste paper basket which was then left in her room, increasing use of agency staff.
>
> The ombudsman found the depth and quality of the local authority's enquiries 'commendable'. The record-keeping was of a high standard; it monitored the care, made numerous unannounced visits, responded to evidence of poor care, gave clear evidence about what needed to improve, kept the enquiries ongoing to ensure that the care home was complying. Despite the best efforts of the local authority, some poor practice persisted, even with the continued involvement of the local authority, including advice and training. The local authority could have communicated better with the daughter of the resident. The ombudsman sent a copy of the investigation to the Care Quality Commission, given the continuing problems at the care home.[1]

Equally, having decided what to do, in terms of a protection plan, the local authority should follow it through.

> **Failure to follow through emergency protection plan following safeguarding enquiries.** A woman raised concerns with a care home about the care of her husband. These included allegations about medication not being taken at the correct time, being left with soiled sheets or no sheets at all, snacks and food not being removed from his room for two days, leaving him without a remote control for the television for four days. She received no reply. The local authority started a safeguarding investigation and notified the Care Quality Commission (CQC). It put in place an interim, emergency protection plan.

---

1   LGO, *North Tyneside Metropolitan Borough Council*, 2017 (15 014 776).

However, during the first month, following the concerns raised, the husband was left in an unsatisfactory situation. The home failed to implement the protection plan, because it did not append it to the husband's main care plan. There was delay in the local authority discovering this and it should have monitored the situation more closely. Failure to check that the plan was being implemented was fault.

Furthermore, once the local authority received an email from the director of the home, querying the existence of the plan, the authority should have visited to check what was going on. This was particularly needed in the light of the negative report from the CQC and the wider safeguarding investigation around alleged organisational abuse. Three months was a long time – too long – to wait to review the case, given all these negative indicators. Overall, the husband received inadequate care for six months, resulting in a hospital admission; this was injustice.[1]

ENQUIRIES: LOCAL AUTHORITY IS DECISION-MAKER. The local authority is, under section 42, the legal decision-maker in terms of what it believes should be done, following enquiries. It should not therefore be unduly swayed by pressure from another organisation, such as the regulator, as occurred in an older case, prior to the Care Act, but nonetheless illustrating the point.

Local authorities, under the thumb of the regulator, abnegating responsibilities and not acting in the best interests of service users. In order to be seen to be doing the right thing in principle, by responding drastically to concerns that had arisen, the local authorities concerned in this case appeared to achieve the opposite. The result was that the rights and welfare of the residents of the care home were not given sufficient attention, and they ended up being removed from the home without due procedure and against their best interests.

The case illustrated the fine line between protection and overreaction and also the sometimes-unsatisfactory interaction between local authorities and regulators. The Tribunal clearly took the view that the local authorities concerned, frightened of the regulator, had behaved in an

---

1   LGO, *Northamptonshire County Council*, 2018 (16 014 260).

unthinking and indiscriminate manner. This was particularly unfortunate since the Commission for Social Care Inspection (CSCI: a forerunner of the Care Quality Commission) had been proceeding on the basis of factual inaccuracies and on an apparently obsessive, excessive and unjustified determination to close the home.

The risks, actual or imagined, to the residents in the care home had not been balanced – by either the CSCI or the local authorities – against the detriment of sudden and compulsory removal of those residents to other care homes. The best interests of the residents suffered as a result.[1]

ENQUIRIES: SHOULD PRECEDE DECISIONS AND ACTIONS. The wording of section 42 is clear in that enquiries of some sort must precede the local authority's decision about what to do. The other way around can lead to unlawfulness, or maladministration and injustice.

Salad and chips and safeguarding: lack of enquiries but woman effectively barred from visiting her sister in a care home. A woman used to visit her sister in a care home. In September 2010, two safeguarding concerns were raised, about the visiting sister taking money out of the sister's account and changing her sister's menu choice from salad to chips.

Informal investigations in March 2011 and December 2011 made no findings of abuse. However, by now the woman had been told not to visit her sister and felt unable to, being made to feel like a 'criminal'. By the time the complaint reached the ombudsmen (local and health), the woman had in effect been unable, or felt unable, to visit for three years. The two ombudsmen concluded that this was maladministration, not least because the allegations had never been investigated, substantiated and followed up.[2]

Unsubstantiated allegations: local authority acting on uninvestigated allegations about a relative, leading to defamation proceedings. The sister and brother-in-law of a woman with learning disabilities complained that she had suffered abuse at two care homes. During a long and protracted dispute,

---

1   *Onyerindu v Commission for Social Care Inspection* [2007] 1041.EA, [2008] 1268.EA.

2   LGO and HSO, *Essex County Council, Suffolk County Council, North Essex Partnership NHS Foundation Trust and Norfolk and Suffolk NHS Foundation Trust*, 2014 (12 004 807 and 12 013 660), paras 79–80.

the owner of one of the care homes made unsubstantiated allegations about the behaviour of the brother-in-law, involving drunkenness, sexual misconduct and racist behaviour. A report by the council's registration and inspection unit repeated the allegations; the report came into the hands of members of another part of the family, which promptly ostracised the brother-in-law. The council wrote to the brother-in-law, repeating the allegations as if they were fact; he regarded the letter as defamatory.

The allegations were finally investigated and found to be without substance; subsequent legal action for defamation was settled by payment of a considerable sum of money and agreement by the council to purge its records and to pay legal costs. In the end, the ombudsman found that abuse had not in fact been suffered by the sister, but he was appalled at the 'almost complete lack of planning' behind one placement and the lack of reasonable social care work that went into it. It was more by luck than judgement that no harm befell her.[1]

ENQUIRIES: RATIONAL RESPONSE TO. When a local authority concludes enquiries and decides what it thinks should be done, the courts or ombudsmen might look at the rationality of the response, if it clearly flies in the face of the evidence, or if the response to the evidence is not explained.

Poor records being deemed 'very good' by local authority: lack of rigour of enquiries. Investigating care of a resident in a care home, various inadequacies in record-keeping were apparent, relating to: gaps in the attendance, input and output charts; nursing care progress/evaluations; medication administration records; energy drink intake; pressure care; care plan (changing diet from normal to soft to liquid). Despite this, the local authority's enquiries concluded that the care home's records were 'very good'. This indicated a lack of rigour in the enquiries, since the records did not support that claim. It was a sweeping statement which did not address the specific concerns raised. This was fault.[2]

Not explaining a finding of lack of neglect. It was maladministration when an investigation concluded, without explaining why, that there was no

1   LGO, *Bromley London Borough Council*, 2003 (01/B/17272).

2   LGO, *Suffolk County Council*, 2017 (16 007 936), paras 46–53.

neglect in a care home, despite inconsistencies in the care home's records – and why it had failed to address all the concerns that had been raised.[1]

Taking no action about dehydration of care home resident, despite evidence of neglect and seriously conflicting information. A woman stayed a few days in a care home, became dehydrated, suffered kidney damage and died a few days later. The care home took months to report back and denied any poor care practices.

The local authority decided to take no action, despite incomplete paperwork and fluid charts which contradicted the care home's report, other seriously conflicting information and the concerns of the woman's GP. Confusingly, it made no finding of neglect, yet reported partial neglect. It did not inform its own contracts department or the Care Quality Commission. All this – and more – was maladministration.[2]

Justifiable conclusion of safeguarding enquiries but still failure to follow up. Under section 42 of the Care Act, the local authority made enquiries into concerns about a home care agency. The local authority concluded by stating that there was little tangible evidence; it was largely the family's word against that of the carers; there was no evidence that the carers were responsible for damage, given that it was a family home with other people around; and the issue of falsified care records was for the contracts team, rather than safeguarding. The ombudsman held that this decision was justifiable.

The local authority asked the care agency to consider the family's concerns as a complaint, and said that it, the local authority, would ask the care agency for the complaint outcome and check that any appropriate action was taken. The authority failed to do this and this was maladministration.[3]

ENQUIRIES: AND DECISIONS, LACK OF LOCAL AUTHORITY COERCIVE POWERS. As already noted, the Care Act does not give local authorities coercive powers (a) to enter a person's home to make enquiries, (b) to force

---

1   LGO, *Nottinghamshire County Council*, 2016 (15 010 488), paras 17–18.

2   LGO, *Oxfordshire County Council and Caring Homes Healthcare Group Ltd*, 2016 (15 007 968 and 15 006 620).

3   LGO, *London Borough of Havering*, 2016 (16 002 895), para 25.

anybody else to make the enquiries, or (c) to force anybody else to take whatever action the local authority believes is appropriate.

In a case involving parents who were locking their adult daughter in her bedroom each night (in her best interests), the courts warned local authorities against exceeding their legal powers in this regard.

Coercing and compelling: local authorities exceeding their legal powers. Welfare legislation does not confer on a local authority 'any power to regulate, control, compel, restrain, confine or coerce...[it is] concerned with the provision of services and support'.[1]

Monitoring and safeguarding, not complete and effective control. The court refuted the idea that the local authority had

> complete and effective control...through its assessment and care plan... A local authority does not exercise 'control', it lacks the legal power to exercise control, over people in the situation of [the daughter or her parents]... [W]hile the local authority performs important monitoring and safeguarding roles, its major function in relation to [the daughter] and others like her is to assess needs and provide services.[2]

Local authorities must work together with people rather than threaten them.

> This [mistaken] attitude is perhaps best exemplified by the proposition that 'in the event that the parents were to disagree with the *decisions* of the local authority (which will always be based upon the opinion of relevant professionals) it would seek to enforce its decisions through appropriate proceedings if necessary'. This approach, which to repeat is not the approach of the local authority in this case, though reflecting what I have come across elsewhere, reflects an attitude of mind which is not merely unsound in law but hardly best calculated to encourage proper effect being given

1   *A Local Authority v A and B* [2010] EWHC 978 (Fam).

2   *A Local Authority v A and B* [2010] EWHC 978 (Fam).

> to a local authority's procedural obligations under Article 8 of the Convention...[1]
>
> Moreover, it is likely to be nothing but counter-productive when it comes to a local authority 'working together', as it must, with family carers. 'Working together' involves something more – much more – than merely requiring carers to agree with a local authority's 'decision' even if, let alone just because, it may be backed by professional opinion... [U]se of the word 'enforce' may belie an overstated understanding of the degree of control which the local authority has in situations such as this.[2]

Thus, when a local authority makes enquiries and then decides what should be done, its ongoing role if any (as opposed to the role of other organisations, such as the police) therefore remains primarily one of care and support. This has been underlined strongly by the courts. For example, in a case in which a local authority had, blatantly unlawfully, removed a young man with autism from his father, the court resorted to ancient freedoms, enshrined in law.

Investigating and providing support.

The ordinary powers of a local authority are limited to investigating, providing support services, and where appropriate referring the matter to the court. If a local authority seeks to regulate, control, compel, restrain, confine or coerce it must, except in an emergency, point to specific statutory authority for what it is doing or else obtain the appropriate sanction of the court... The origin of this basic legal principle is to be found in an era long before the invention of local authorities as we know them. Chapter 29 of Magna Carta 1297 provides that: 'No freeman shall be taken or imprisoned, or disseised of his freehold, or liberties, or free customs, or outlawed, or exiled, or any otherwise destroyed; nor will we not pass upon him, nor condemn him, but by lawful judgment of his peers, or by the law of the land.'[3]

1   *A Local Authority v A and B* [2010] EWHC 978 (Fam).

2   *A Local Authority v A and B* [2010] EWHC 978 (Fam).

3   *London Borough of Hillingdon v Neary* [2011] EWHC 1377 (COP), paras 22–23.

ENQUIRIES: PROTECTION OF ADULTS FROM THIRD-PARTY VIOLENCE.

Legally, it is not the local authority's primary role to protect vulnerable adults from violence inflicted by third parties; that is the responsibility of the police. Department of Health guidance notes that local authority safeguarding activity is not a substitute for the core duties of the police to prevent and detect crime and protect life and property.[1]

Protecting man with Asperger's syndrome from violence: primarily a police responsibility, not social services. A young man with Asperger's syndrome, known to social services, was found dead in a car park; an acquaintance was convicted of manslaughter. A judicial review case was taken against the coroner, the police and the local authority. It was argued, amongst other things, that the local authority had a duty under article 2 of the European Convention on Human Rights 'to have in place appropriate systems to protect the lives of those with Asperger's syndrome from the risk from third parties'. The case failed.

The judge set out at some length what he considered to be the extent of the local authority's duty in relation to article 2 of the European Convention (right to life). He was clear that 'The Council's obligation...was primarily one of support. The primary duty to protect him from a possibly fatal assault fell upon the Police Force.'[2]

Local authority: not liable in negligence for harm suffered by couple with learning disabilities. A local authority was sued in negligence by two people with learning disabilities. They alleged that the local authority had taken inadequate steps to protect them from acquaintances who had physically tortured them one weekend. The Court of Appeal stated that not only had the local authority staff in fact taken adequate steps, but that even had they not done so, the authority would not have been liable. This was, essentially, because, other than in special circumstances, it would not be in the public interest to hold local authorities liable in negligence for harm perpetrated by third parties.[3]

---

1   Department of Health. *Care and support statutory guidance*. London: DH, 2016, para 14.64.

2   *R (AP) v HM Coroner for the County of Worcestershire, Worcestershire County Council, Chief Constable of West Mercia Police* [2011] EWHC 1453 (Admin).

3   *X & Y v Hounslow London Borough Council* [2009] EWCA Civ 286.

ENQUIRIES: ELIGIBILITY FOR ONGOING HELP. Following enquiries, the local authority would only have an ongoing *duty* to provide help for the person if they were assessed to have eligible needs. See ***Eligibility***.

However, it would have the *power* – that is, a discretion – to help in the case of (a) non-eligible need, (b) urgency (before assessment and an eligibility decision), or (c) preventing, reducing or delaying care and support needs.[1]

ENQUIRIES: AND ASSESSMENT. Making enquiries and assessment of care and support needs are separate and distinct functions under the Care Act but might in practice be intertwined and sometimes run in parallel.[2]

For instance, an assessment of an adult or carer under sections 9 and 10 of the Care Act might reveal suspected abuse or neglect – in which case the duty to make enquiries would be triggered as well. Conversely, enquiries being made under section 42 in relation to somebody previously unknown might trigger the duty to assess. Or, in the case of somebody known, to review and to reassess care and support needs, in the light of changed circumstances.

Either way, there is no requirement that an assessment be carried out prior to conducting section 42 enquiries.

ENQUIRIES: PRELIMINARY OR 'PRE-ENQUIRIES'. Uncertain of whether the conditions of a section 42 enquiry are satisfied, some local authorities carry out what they call preliminary or 'pre-section 42 enquiries'. At least two issues arise from this practice. First, as pointed out above, the threshold – 'reasonable cause to suspect' – for section 42 is low, and therefore relatively easily triggered. So, what are called 'pre-enquiries' might sometimes be better referred to as section 42 enquiries.

Second, if such preliminary enquiries are deemed by the local authority as not within section 42, then for clarity it is probably desirable to characterise what they are. Under other provisions of the Care Act, there are various possibilities – for example, an assessment under section 9, a review of a person's situation under section 27, or maybe even just a conversation or information

---

1   Care Act 2014, ss.19, 2.

2   Department of Health. *Care and support statutory guidance*. London: DH, 2016, para 6.57.

exchange under section 2 of the Act covering prevention, reduction or delay of need.

ENQUIRIES: 'NON-STATUTORY'. Many local authorities appear to have adopted the notion of conducting what they call 'non-statutory' enquiries.[1] By this, they mean enquiries that do not meet – for one reason or another – the legal conditions set out in section 42. Guidance states that in this circumstance a local authority can choose to undertake enquiries nonetheless, if it believes this would be proportionate, would enable the local authority to promote the person's well-being and would support a preventative agenda.[2] However, the guidance does not specify under which section of the Act such enquiries would take place.

- **Duty to enquire.** First, there are other parts of the Care Act that distinguish explicitly between a duty and a power: for example, a duty to meet eligible need, and a power to meet non-eligible need (sections 18 and 19). There is no such duty/power distinction option in section 42; there is simply a duty only. So it would seem arguable that any such additional enquiries would not be made under section 42, because they could not be.

- **Other functions under the Care Act and clarity.** Second, 'non-statutory enquiries' would be surely better described – at least in the first instance – as a function under other parts of the Care Act – as the guidance suggests, when it refers to promotion of well-being and the preventative agenda – of which a number can relate to protection from abuse or neglect. For example, conducting assessments of adults in need and carers under sections 9 and 10. Or in relation to section 2 of the Care Act and the provision of preventative services.

A similar point has been made in relation to enquiries made under section 47 of the Children Act 1989, in relation to reasonable cause to suspect a child suffering significant harm (or the likelihood of this). The courts have pointed out that if the section 47 threshold is not crossed, then enquiries

---

1   See discussion of this: Social Care Institute for Excellence. *Adult safeguarding practice questions*. London: SCIE, 2015, p.17. And: Spencer-Lane, T. *Care Act Manual*, 2nd edition. London: Sweet & Maxwell, 2015, p.310.

2   Department of Health. *Care and support statutory guidance*. London: DH, 2016, para 14.44.

could be made under other sections of the Children Act 1989 (or, in some circumstances, under a common law duty of care to take care of looked-after children).[1]

- **Meaning of non-statutory.** Third, 'non-statutory' refers, literally, to something outside of legislation (and therefore to a common law function), which means that any such enquiries would be outside of the Care Act altogether. Yet local authorities and other organisations have long called for adult safeguarding to be put on a statutory footing. The Care Act has now done this and delineated, quite widely, the safeguarding role of local authorities. It would therefore seem odd to adopt, unnecessarily, the notion of 'non-statutory'. If common law is to be cited, surely it should be a last resort, and only after close examination of statutory options already within the Care Act.

Equality Act 2010

The Equality Act 2010 concerns discrimination against people who have 'protected characteristics'. These include age, disability, gender reassignment, marriage or civil partnership, race, religion or belief, sex, sexual orientation. The Act covers both direct and indirect discrimination against people with these characteristics.

- **Disability.** In relation to disability, for example, discrimination is unfavourable treatment arising in consequence of a person's disability, which is not a proportionate way of achieving a legitimate aim. There is also a duty to make reasonable adjustments for disabled people relating to provision of services, criteria, practices, a physical feature or an auxiliary aid.

- **Provision covered by Act.** Activity covered by the Act includes the provision of services to the public, disposal and management of premises including reasonable adjustments, employment, schools, further and higher education.

- **Public sector equality duty.** In addition is what is sometimes called a public sector equality duty. It means that public bodies must have due regard to the need to (a) eliminate discrimination, harassment, victimisation and any other conduct that is prohibited by or under this Act; (b) advance equality

---

1   *Gogay v Hertfordshire County Council* [2001] 1 FCR 455.

of opportunity between persons who share a relevant protected characteristic and persons who do not share it; (c) foster good relations between persons who share a relevant protected characteristic and persons who do not share it.

Thus, for example, failure to make reasonable adjustments in the care of a certain group with a protected characteristic (e.g. a learning disability) might engage the Equality Act.[1]

Estoppel, relying on assurances or promises, see *Proprietary estoppel*

1   Norah Fry Centre for Disability Studies. *The Learning Disabilities Mortality Review (LeDeR) Programme*. Bristol: University of Bristol, NHS England, 2018, p.6.

F

False accounting

An offence of false accounting, in summary, requires dishonesty, with a view to gain or to cause loss to somebody else. It is about destruction, defacing, concealing or falsifying accounts, records or documents – or making use of these, when the person knows they may be misleading, false or deceptive. The maximum penalty is imprisonment for seven years.[1] Examples relevant to safeguarding vulnerable adults include:

Bank manager stealing over £250,000 from elderly people by false accounting and theft. A bank manager, in Richmond, North Yorkshire, admitted six charges of false accounting and nine of theft. She had stolen more than £267,000 and was sent to prison for three years. She took money from the accounts of five customers, some of whom were deceased, with probate pending. She took advantage of situations as they arose between 2008 and 2014, by moving customers' money. She stole £120,000 from one victim, an elderly man, who had since died. Another alleged victim was a 54-year-old man who lost £75,000, in three stages. An elderly woman lost £24,000 and a female pensioner £9,500. The money was stolen in a total of 28 transactions. The bank manager had pleaded depression in mitigation, but the judge said that this, and other stresses at home, did not justify the plundering of people's bank accounts.[2]

Befriending vulnerable adult and obtaining loans by false accounting. The perpetrator befriended a man who had been involved in a serious road traffic

---

1   Theft Act 1968, s.17.

2   'Richmond bank manager Lesley Austin jailed for stealing £250,000 from customer accounts.' *Northern Echo*, 2 December 2015.

accident, leading to amputation of a leg and to permanent brain damage. He suffered from schizophrenia and was an exceptionally vulnerable individual. Since these events he has died. The appellant befriended him in 2012. The friendship came about because the perpetrator was aware that the man had received a very large sum of money in compensation. He persuaded the man to go into business. In order to obtain loans, for which the man would be liable, the perpetrator produced false wage slips in the man's name. On this count of false accounting – there were other offences as well – the perpetrator was sentenced to nine months in prison.[1]

Care home owner stealing money from residents. When a care home owner was convicted of stealing money from residents with learning disabilities, by withdrawing money from their bank accounts, she concealed the theft by false accounting.[2]

False accounting: care home manager taking over £100,000 from severely disabled residents. The manager of a nursing home had obtained well over £100,000 from sick and dying residents to fund an extravagant lifestyle, including six luxury holidays each year. She had access to residents' bank accounts, for example, as a signatory, as well as to residents' cash cards and PIN numbers. She was eventually ordered to pay some £134,000 compensation. The manager appealed her conviction to the Court of Appeal and lost.

The false accounting had involved using the care home's cheque book to obtain items for herself, but falsely writing on the stub that the cheque had been paid to someone doing work for the home. The theft counts typically involved her withdrawing money from residents' accounts, amounts that bore no relationship to the actual expenditure of those residents. Obtaining property by deception involved, for example, using the care home's Barclaycard purportedly for items for the home or for residents, but actually for herself.[3]

---

1   *R v Ashraf* [2015] EWCA Crim 661.

2   'Care home owner guilty of stealing from residents.' *Community Care*, 5 July 2007.

3   *R v Forbes* [2007] EWCA Crim 621. (See also: 'Nursing home matron jailed after stealing £100,000 from dying patients.' *Daily Mail*, 21 August 2006. And: 'Matron ordered to pay compensation.' *Worcester News*, 11 May 2007. Accessed on 2 October 2018 at: www.worcesternews.co.uk/news/1391124.matron-ordered-to-pay-compensation.)

Supported living service: taking people to the bank. Mencap ran a supported living service for people with learning disabilities at a care home in Harborough. One of the staff took residents to the bank, where he withdrew sums for them and entered details in a log book. He falsified the entries, stole a total of £6720 and was convicted of false accounting and theft. He was sentenced to a 12-month community order and 120 hours of unpaid work.[1]

Social services manager: false accounting. When a social services manager took £4000 from elderly women in her care, she was convicted of forgery and of seven counts of false accounting.[2]

Solicitor: 50 offences of false accounting, £1 million stolen from paralysed man. A solicitor was convicted of more than 50 offences of false accounting, having stolen more than £1 million compensation money which had been awarded to his client, who had been paralysed in a road accident. The solicitor was jailed for ten years.[3]

Solicitor abusing role of trustee and attorney. A solicitor was imprisoned for two years, having stolen money in his capacity as trustee of large sums of clients' money or of money belonging to the estates of dead clients, and as holder of power of attorney in relation to clients' affairs. For example, he deprived a Weymouth-based charity, which operated an older persons' care home, of £168,000.[4]

Bank customer adviser transferring money from accounts of elderly and infirm people. A customer adviser at a bank was sent to prison for 15 months, after pleading guilty to 23 offences of false accounting, involving £58,000, over a period of three and a half years. She had transferred money from customer accounts to her own, often via another account first.

---

1   'Carer abused trust by stealing from residents.' *Harborough Mail*, 1 September 2011.

2   'Social services manager stole from elderly.' *Isle of Thanet Gazette News*, 8 February 2002.

3   'Ten year jail sentence for solicitor who stole over £1m compensation from paralysed client.' *Solicitors' Journal*, 15 April 2008.

4   Serious Fraud Office. 'Former solicitor admits to plundering clients' accounts.' Press release, 6 June 2000.

> The four customers were elderly and infirm, including an elderly priest; none had noticed the missing money.[1]

False imprisonment

False imprisonment is a common law criminal offence. It involves 'the unlawful and intentional or reckless restraint of a victim's freedom of movement from a particular place. In other words, it is unlawful detention which stops the victim moving away as he would wish to move.'[2]

Care home residents punished by being falsely imprisoned. Residents at a care home in Devon were routinely punished by being held in empty rooms without food, heating or a toilet, a court heard. Staff imprisoned them in the rooms, often overnight, during 2010 and 2011, as an abusive culture developed. The manager was jailed for 28 months. Twelve other people, including other staff members and the manager's wife, were convicted. The convictions were for the offence of false imprisonment; one of the directors was convicted of breach of the Health and Safety at Work Act 1974.[3]

False imprisonment and death in a shed of vulnerable adult at the hands of those who had befriended him. A vulnerable and epileptic man died after being kept in a shed for a period of four months by three people who had befriended him. He was found dead with extensive bruising and burn marks. The prosecution could not prove that death was not due to his epilepsy; the three defendants were jailed for some ten years each for assault, causing actual bodily harm and false imprisonment.[4] However, a subsequent coroner's hearing concluded that he had been unlawfully killed, almost certainly due to a loss of blood.[5]

---

1   'Mother stole £58,000 from bank to pay school fees.' *Bradford Telegraph and Argus*, 21 August 2008.

2   *R v Rahman* [1985] 81 Cr App R 349.

3   'Thirteen convicted over Devon care home abuse.' *BBC News*, 7 June 2017. Accessed on 12 January 2018 at: www.bbc.co.uk/news/uk-england-devon-40188948.

4   de Bruxelles, S. 'Three tortured shed captive until he died.' *The Times*, 10 July 2007.

5   'Shed captive was unlawfully killed.' *Metro Newspaper*, 28 February 2008.

FALSE IMPRISONMENT: CIVIL LAW. False imprisonment is also a 'tort' in civil law and could underpin a claim for financial compensation. Unlike the criminal offence (see above), it is an offence of strict liability, meaning that a 'state of mind' does not have to be established.[1]

For instance, adults lacking mental capacity are sometimes deprived of their liberty. If the relevant legal rules are not followed, not only will there be a breach of the Mental Capacity Act 2005 and Human Rights Act 1998, but, in principle, the civil tort of false imprisonment could be committed. (However, a deprivation of liberty could occur without false imprisonment necessarily occurring. For example, a person who does not attempt to leave would not in law be falsely imprisoned, whereas if they did try to leave and were stopped they would be.)[2]

> **Unlawful deprivation of liberty: false imprisonment?** When a man lacking capacity was taken to hospital in his best interests, and kept there for care and treatment, the House of Lords (now the Supreme Court) held that 'necessity' justified what would otherwise have been unlawful in terms of the civil tort of false imprisonment. However, the Court of Appeal, which was overruled in the final judgment, had found that the civil tort of false imprisonment had been committed. The European Court of Human Rights subsequently held that the man's human rights had been breached, for want of safeguarding legal procedures, and that the common law of necessity was insufficient for this purpose.[3]

In adult safeguarding, the police are sometimes called – for example, by a care home manager – to prevent family from removing a relative from the home. If the police were given false information – but on that basis nevertheless arrested a person – a civil claim could in principle lie against the person who informed the police. For example, in the following case, just such a claim was made, although it failed in the circumstances of the case.

---

1   Law Commission. *Mental capacity and deprivation of liberty: a consultation paper.* London: LC, 2015, para 15.26.

2   *HL v United Kingdom* [2005] 40 EHRR 32, para 90 (European Court of Human Rights).

3   *R v Bournewood Community and Mental Health NHS Trust, ex parte L* [1999] 1 AC 458.

Civil liability for actively instigating false imprisonment. The parents of a three-year-old child removed the child from hospital, believing that she was not being treated and monitored properly. A member of the hospital security staff rang the police, stating that the child was under a child protection order. On that basis, the police arrested the husband and charged him with kidnapping. When it was established that there was no child protection order, he was de-arrested, then re-arrested on grounds of child neglect, then released 20 hours later without charge. The husband brought a civil claim against the hospital. It failed.

For the hospital to be liable in relation to the actions of the security staff, it was not enough that the latter had merely given information for the police to act on (or not). Instead, he would have to have been the instigator, promoter and active inciter of the arrest. This was not the case: being responsible for giving wrong information to the police was not the same thing as being responsible for the arrest.[1]

False or misleading information

Owing to significant concerns about care providers, particularly NHS providers, an offence of providing false or misleading information was introduced by the Care Act 2014. The concerns had been highlighted particularly in relation to the many deaths at Stafford Hospital.[2] Key points are:

- **NHS.** The offence currently applies to NHS bodies only.

- **Offence.** The offence is that a provider (a) supplies, publishes or otherwise makes available information of a specified description, (b) provision of that information is required by legislation or some other legal obligation, and (c) the information is false or misleading in a material respect.

- **Information.** The information covered by this offence is specified in regulations and concerns various patient information that NHS bodies must supply to the Health and Social Care Information Centre.

---

1 *Ali v Heart of England NHS Foundation Trust* [2018] EWHC 591 (Ch), paras 11, 27.

2 Francis, R. (Chairman). *Report of the Mid Staffordshire NHS Foundation Trust Public Inquiry. Volume 3: present and future, Annexes.* London: The Stationery Office, p.1669.

- **Defence.** It is a defence if the provider can prove that it took all reasonable steps and exercised all due diligence to prevent the provision of the false or misleading information.

- **Penalties.** Include fines, imprisonment, and the making of remedial orders and publicity orders by the court.[1]

Family Law Act 1996

This Act provides for certain civil orders aimed at dealing with forms of domestic abuse or violence. These include non-molestation orders, occupation orders and forced marriage protection orders (see separate headings in this book).

Fear of violence, see *Harassment, alarm or distress*

Female genital mutilation

Female genital mutilation is a criminal offence, perpetrated mainly against female children. However, it could be relevant in the context of this book if performed on an adult (vulnerable or otherwise). Key points are:

- **Legislation.** Female genital mutilation (FGM) has been a criminal offence since 1985, under the Prohibition of Female Circumcision Act 1985. But, under this Act, it was not a criminal offence if the person is taken abroad. However, the Female Genital Mutilation Act 2003 applies to offences committed on or after 3 March 2003. For offences committed before 3 March 2004, the Prohibition of Female Circumcision Act 1985, re-enacted in the Female Genital Mutilation Act 2003, still applies.

- **Scope of offence.** Under the 2003 Act, it is illegal for FGM to be performed, and it is also an offence for UK nationals or permanent UK residents to carry out or aid, abet, counsel or procure the carrying out of FGM abroad on a UK national or permanent UK resident, even in countries where the practice is legal.

---

1   Care Act 2014, ss.92–94. And: SI 2015/988. False or Misleading Information (Specified Care Providers and Specified Information) Regulations 2015.

- **Vulnerable adults.** The 2003 Act refers to an offence against a girl, but girl is defined to include woman. Statutory guidance indicates the relevance of the offence to vulnerable adults, not just girls under the age of 18.[1]

- **Female genital mutilation.** A person is guilty if he or she excises, infibulates or otherwise mutilates the whole or part of a girl's labia majora, labia minora or clitoris.

- **Protection.** It is an offence for a person, who is responsible for a girl under 16, to fail to protect her. Doctors, teachers and healthcare professionals (including social workers) have a duty to notify the police if FGM appears to have been carried out on a girl aged under 18. The 2003 Act also makes provision for FGM protection orders, breach of which, without reasonable excuse, is an offence in itself.[2]

To date there have been no convictions.

Fiduciary duty

A fiduciary duty arises from a legal or ethical relationship of trust, involving the fiduciary (the person with the duty) managing money or other assets of the other person. In the context of this book, for example, people exercising a lasting power of attorney or deputyship owe such a duty to the person lacking mental capacity, on whose behalf they are acting. The Mental Capacity Act Code of Practice notes in relation to deputies (similarly for attorneys):

- **Fiduciary duty.** 'A fiduciary duty means deputies must not take advantage of their position. Nor should they put themselves in a position where their personal interests conflict with their duties. For example, deputies should not buy property that they are selling for the person they have been appointed to represent. They should also not accept a third-party commission in any transactions. Deputies must not allow anything else to influence their duties.

---

1   HM Government. *Multi-agency statutory guidance on female genital mutilation*. London: HMG, 2016.

2   Female Genital Mutilation Act 2003, ss.3A, 5A, 5B, schedule 2.

They cannot use their position for any personal benefit, whether or not it is at the person's expense.'[1]

In the following case, such a duty was breached by a company of professional deputies, who at one time had a contract with a local authority to manage the affairs of a number of adults lacking capacity. The lines between breach of fiduciary duty, financial abuse, fraud and failures in administration were alluded to in the case but not explored or delineated by the judge.

> **Breach of fiduciary duty by professional deputies discharging statutory duties on behalf of a local authority.** The deputyship company admitted that, for the sale of three properties belonging to different protected persons, it instructed a particular estate agency which then charged each of the protected persons 1.5% of the sale price, but also paid to Matrix Deputies Ltd 0.5%. This represented a clear system of financial benefit to Matrix Deputies Ltd at the expense of persons to whom they owed fiduciary duties. Those duties were breached.[2]

Financial abuse

Financial abuse is referred to in section 42 of the Care Act 2014 as including: having money or other property stolen, being defrauded, being put under pressure in relation to money or other property, or having money or other property misused.

In some circumstances, such abuse may equate to a criminal offence, such as theft, false accounting, robbery, burglary, forgery. In others, civil law concepts may apply, such as undue influence, in relation to gifts and wills. And abuse of position by an attorney or deputy under the Mental Capacity Act 2005 might result in the power of attorney or deputyship being revoked by the Court of Protection. (See under the various relevant headings in this book.)

---

1   Department of Constitutional Affairs. *Mental Capacity Act 2005 Code of Practice.* London: HMSO, 2007, paras 8.58 and 7.60 (for attorneys).

2   *Public Guardian v Matrix Deputies Limited, London Borough of Enfield* [2017] EWCOP 14, paras 7, 19, 33.

FINANCIAL ABUSE: CORPORATE. In the wide sense of financial abuse as delineated in the Care Act 2014, financial abuse may occur at the hands of an organisation and be corporate in nature, rather than perpetrated by a rogue individual. For example:

Care home operator pays £2 million in compensation to residents for upfront fees. A care home operator charged every new resident of its care homes a £5000 upfront fee, to cover the cost of maintaining communal facilities and areas – on top of what could be fees of £2000 per week. However, the Competition and Markets Authority pointed out that if a resident died within two years, the upfront fee would be clearly excessive, since the resident would not live to enjoy the fruits of their extra expenditure. The operator, Sunrise Medical, agreed to compensate any resident who stayed no longer than two years up to £3000 each.[1]

Bank fined over £10 million and paying compensation of £29 million for mis-selling care home fee insurance products to vulnerable nursing home residents. HSBC, Britain's largest bank, was fined £10.5 million by the Financial Services Authority for selling unsuitable products to almost 2500 elderly customers. The bank's Nursing Homes Fees Agency (NHFA) subsidiary is also expecting to pay £29.3 million in compensation for the way it advised elderly customers, who had an average age of 83, to buy investment bonds that were used to help them pay for their long-term care. In many cases, the five-year investment period for the bonds was longer than the individual customer's life expectancy.

The offences dated back to 2005–10 when NHFA advised 2485 people to invest in bonds to pay their long-term care costs. The customers were typically in or about to enter long-term care and were recommended to invest for five years – longer than their life expectancy – when products such as higher fixed-interest rate savings accounts or ISAs might have been more suitable.[2]

---

1   'Care homes firm Sunrise to refund "up-front fees" to residents.' *BBC News*, 9 May 2018. Accessed on 9 May 2018 at: www.bbc.co.uk/news/business-44050678.

2   Treanor, J. 'HSBC fined £10.5m for selling five-year bonds to over 80s.' *The Guardian*, 5 December 2011.

Bank forging customer's signature. The Royal Bank of Scotland conceded that a fake signature had been used on an official document, which means a customer was signed up to a financial product she did not want. This admission followed claims by whistleblowers that bank staff had been trained to forge signatures, suggesting widespread malpractice, which the bank denied. However, the bank was forced to apologise after a retired teacher came forward with paperwork that clearly showed her signature was faked on a bank document. She was being charged a fee for payment protection insurance (PPI) – even though she had declined to sign up for it.[1]

Newspaper competition: scam aimed at elderly people. PhonepayPlus, regulator for premium-rate telephone services, imposed a record £800,000 fine against a company, Churchcastle Ltd, whose repeat direct-mail marketing for competitions misled elderly consumers. These competitions were followed up by misleading direct-mail marketing that encouraged consumers, many of whom were elderly, to continue to engage with the premium-rate service, often at considerable expense.

Word search competitions were carried by around 50 publications across the UK, including a number of major national newspapers. Once a consumer had entered the competition and provided contact details, they received a variety of direct-mail marketing that encouraged them to continue to engage with the competition. Some consumers received up to four promotions a week. The marketing was highly personalised and included letters designed to look handwritten. For example, Easter cards gave the impression that the consumer was part of a select group of participants and they were very close to winning. Prizes, such as low-quality jewellery described as 'strictly limited' and 'rare', were also offered. The cost of calling the premium-rate numbers was either unclear or not prominently placed in these direct-mail promotions.[2]

1   Green, J. 'RBS admits forging an elderly customer's signature which left her signed up to a product she didn't want.' *Daily Mail*, 18 February 2018.

2   'Record £800,000 fine for premium phone line.' *BBC News*, 11 October 2012. Accessed on 4 December 2018 at: https://www.bbc.co.uk/news/uk-19906083.

Forced marriage

In forced marriage, one or both spouses do not consent to the marriage but are coerced into it. The duress involved can include physical, psychological, financial, sexual and emotional pressure. In the case of adults lacking the capacity to consent, coercion is not required for a marriage to be forced. Furthermore, adults with support needs are particularly vulnerable to forced marriage, due to reliance on their families for care, communication difficulties and fewer opportunities to talk to anybody outside the family.[1]

- **Criminal offence.** Forced marriage is a criminal offence under the Anti-Social Behaviour, Crime and Policing Act 2014, with a maximum prison sentence of seven years. But it could also involve other criminal offences including fear or provocation of violence, common assault, actual bodily harm, grievous bodily harm, harassment, kidnap, abduction, theft (of passport), threats to kill, false imprisonment and murder.[2]

- **Forced marriage protection orders.** Under the Family Law Act 1996, a court (county court or High Court) can grant civil orders protecting people from being forced into marriage.[3] Such orders might be particularly relevant to adult safeguarding – for instance, where an adult lacking capacity to marry is subject to an 'arranged' marriage; or where a vulnerable adult with capacity, but for some reason unable to give free and informed consent, is being subjected to marriage.

FORCED MARRIAGE: CRIMINAL OFFENCE. It is an offence if a person in England or Wales (a) uses violence, threats or any other form of coercion aimed at causing another person to enter into the marriage, and (b) believes, or ought to reasonably believe, that the conduct may cause the other person to enter into the marriage without free and full consent.

If a person lacks capacity to consent to marriage, then the offence can be committed by any conduct aimed at causing the victim to enter into a

---

1   HM Government. *The right to choose: multi-agency statutory guidance for dealing with forced marriage.* London: Cabinet Office, 2014, pp.1, 18.

2   HM Government. *The right to choose: multi-agency statutory guidance for dealing with forced marriage.* London: Cabinet Office, 2014, p.11.

3   Family Law Act 1996, ss.63A–63S.

marriage – whether or not violence, threats or any other form of coercion are involved.

In addition, it is an offence to practise any form of intention aimed at causing another person to leave the United Kingdom, in order to enter into a marriage which would be an offence in England or Wales. The maximum penalty is seven years' imprisonment.[1]

Conviction of woman for tricking her daughter with learning disabilities into a forced marriage. A woman promised her daughter a holiday in Pakistan. But instead, after taking her there, she told her that on her 18th birthday that she would marry a family relative by whom she had become pregnant on a previous visit in 2012 when she was 13 and he was 29 (following which she had a termination and was placed in a children's home).

Despite her daughter's pleas that she did not want to marry the 34-year-old Pakistani national, the mother planned the wedding day for later that month, on 18 September 2016. She had cried during the wedding and begged her mother not to send her home with the groom after being forced to sign marriage papers. Her mother later abandoned her in Pakistan before lying under oath to a High Court judge in the UK about what had happened. The daughter had learning disabilities, craved the affection of her parents and wanted nothing more than the love and approval of her mother. The woman was given a prison sentence of three and a half years for the forced marriage, and an additional year for perjury.[2]

FORCED MARRIAGE: PROTECTION ORDERS. The key rules within the Family Act 1996, about forced marriage protection orders, are as follows.

- **Definition of forced marriage and considering whether to make an order.** Legislation states that a person is forced into marriage by somebody else if they are not giving free and full consent. Force includes coercion by threats or other psychological means.

---

1   Anti-Social Behaviour, Crime and Policing Act 2014, s.121.

2   Summers, H. 'Birmingham woman jailed for duping daughter into forced marriage.' *The Guardian*, 23 May 2018.

- **Order before or after marriage.** The court can make an order to protect a person from being forced into marriage or to protect a person who has already been forced into one.

- **All the circumstances.** In deciding whether to make such an order, the court must consider all the circumstances – in particular, the need to secure the health, safety and well-being of the person to be protected. Judging a person's well-being requires a consideration of the person's wishes and feelings, appropriate to the person's age and understanding.[1]

- **Prohibitions, restrictions, requirements imposed by an order.** A forced marriage protection order may include prohibitions, restrictions or requirements and other terms as the court considers appropriate. The order may apply to conduct inside or outside England or Wales. It may apply to people who are, or who may in future become, involved in attempts to force a person into marriage.

  It may also apply to other people who are, or who may become, involved in other respects (i.e. other than directly forcing the marriage). Examples of involvement in 'other respects' include aiding, abetting, counselling, procuring, encouraging or assisting another person to force, or to attempt to force, a person to enter into a marriage – or conspiring to force, or to attempt to force, a person to enter into a marriage.[2]

- **Application for an order by the victim or by other people.** Forced marriage protection orders can be applied for by the person who needs protecting or by a specified party. Local authorities are specified as such.[3]

  In addition, if the court gives permission, an application can be made also by others. In deciding whether to give this permission, the court must consider all the circumstances including the applicant's connection with the person to be protected, the applicant's knowledge of the person's circumstances, and the wishes and feelings of the person. It appears that, in the first year of the operation of the legislation, most such applications were being made by the police on behalf of victims.[4]

---

1   Family Law Act 1996, s.63A.

2   Family Law Act 1996, s.63B.

3   SI 2009/2023. The Family Law Act 1996 (Forced Marriage) (Relevant Third Party) Order 2009.

4   McCallum, L. 'A driving force.' *Solicitors' Journal*, 8 December 2009.

- **Victim's wishes.** The victim's wishes are important but not necessarily decisive. The legislation states that the court must have regard to 'the wishes and feelings of the person to be protected so far as they are reasonably ascertainable and so far as the court considers it appropriate, in the light of the person's age and understanding, to have regard to them'.[1]

- **Family proceedings.** There are some circumstances, where family proceedings are already taking place, in which the court can make an order without an application being made.[2]

- **Urgent orders.** In some circumstances, the court can grant an urgent order ('*ex parte*') without first informing the respondent of the proceedings. The court can do this, but must consider all the circumstances including: (a) the risk of significant harm to the person to be protected or somebody else; (b) whether the applicant will be deterred or prevented from applying if an order is not made immediately; (c) whether there is reason to believe that the respondent is deliberately avoiding participation in the proceedings and the person to be protected (or the applicant if not the same person) will be prejudiced by delay.

  If the court does make such an order, it must give the perpetrator an opportunity to make representations at a full court hearing as soon as is just and convenient.[3]

- **Attaching a power of arrest to the forced marriage protection order.** The court can attach a power of arrest to the order and must do so if violence has been used or threatened – unless satisfied that in all the circumstances there will be adequate protection without it.

  However, if the order is made without the perpetrator having been given notice, then a power of arrest can be attached only if, in addition to the (threatened) violence, there is also risk of significant harm – if the power of arrest is not attached immediately.

  If a power of arrest is attached, the police may arrest, without a warrant, a person whom they reasonably suspect of having breached a provision of the order, or who is otherwise in contempt of court.

---

1   Family Law Act 1996, s.63C.

2   Family Law Act 1996, s.63C.

3   Family Law Act 1996, s.63D.

If no power has been attached, but an interested person believes the order has been breached (or that the respondent is otherwise in contempt of court), an arrest warrant can be applied for.[1]

- **Giving an undertaking.** Instead of making an order, the court can accept an undertaking from the respondent – but not if a power of arrest would have been attached, had an order been made. The undertaking is, however, enforceable, to the extent that a breach of it is a contempt of court.[2]

Forgery

Under section 1 of the Forgery and Counterfeiting Act 1981, a person is guilty of forgery if he or she makes a false document, intending that it be used to induce a second person to accept it as genuine and prejudicially to act (or not to act) in respect of that second person or somebody else. A few examples are as follows.

> **Forgery and fraud: nurse and healthcare assistant stealing from vulnerable, reclusive man.** Two women, one a healthcare assistant and the other a nurse, were employed by an 80-year-old, vulnerable, reclusive man. They stole nearly £750,000 from him, £160,000 of which was in forged cheques. Other charges included fraud and conversion of criminal property. The money was spent on, amongst other things, luxury cars and designer handbags. They also started work on an extension to the house, thinking that he had changed his will and made them beneficiaries. A police officer noticed the work and the expensive cars and obtained a production order under the Proceeds of Crime Act 2002, in order to look into the women's financial affairs. One was sentenced to seven years, the other to 27 months.[3]
>
> **Daughter-in-law forging cheques.** When a Suffolk woman obtained more than £13,000 from her husband's vulnerable parents, she was jailed for six months for forgery. She had forged cheques and letters of authority

---

1   Family Law Act 1996, s.63H.

2   Family Law Act 1996, s.63E.

3   'St Albans carers, Celia Brinkley and Kerry Davies, jailed for fleecing elderly man out of £750,000.' *St Albans and Harpenden Review*, 29 October 2013.

to withdraw money from their bank account. She had started taking the money before her husband's father had died and had continued when the latter's wife had gone into a care home.[1]

Forging will of elderly woman in hospital. A woman was convicted of forging an elderly patient's will and sentenced to 14 months in prison. A social worker alerted the police, after the woman had told hospital care staff that she held a lasting power of attorney and that the patient had made a will in her favour. The woman had also tricked neighbours into witnessing the will. The police had traced the victim's son, who was living abroad, and after a lengthy investigation secured a conviction.[2]

Church minister forging powers of attorney and wills. A church minister befriended elderly parishioners, before forging documents with a view to inheriting their property and possessions. He planned to wait until they were close to death before signing their properties over to himself. In one instance, he forged documents giving him power of attorney for a woman. When she moved into a nursing home, he gained control over her house. However, he was caught when one of the women involved made an unexpected recovery from a brain haemorrhage and stroke, after having received the last rites from the minister. She returned home from hospital to find that he had forged her will, which now left the house to him. He was sentenced to 240 hours' community service; one of his victims was appalled that he had not been sent to prison.[3]

Social services manager forging elderly woman's signature. Under pressure from her drug-taking husband, who was physically and mentally abusing her, a social services manager forged the signature of an 84-year-old client, so as to remove money from her savings account. She was convicted of forgery (and false accounting) but given a community sentence rather than prison because of her children.[4]

Carer of woman with multiple sclerosis forging a cheque for £8000. A care assistant employed by a care agency was caring for a woman with

---

1   Hunt, J. 'Elderly couple victims of theft.' *East Anglian Daily Times*, 24 January 2006.

2   Law, A.M. 'Doncaster woman jailed for forging elderly woman's will.' *Doncaster Free Press*, 29 January 2018.

3   Britten, N. 'Trusted minister who fleeced his flock.' *Daily Telegraph*, 9 September 2006.

4   'Social services manager stole from elderly.' *Isle of Thanet Gazette News*, 8 February 2002.

multiple sclerosis who found it difficult to read. The carer would open and read her mail for her. The victim received a statement from her building society concerning an £8000 withdrawal. It transpired that the carer had forged the victim's signature on a letter to the building society, to pay a finance company for a car. The carer was convicted and sentenced to 15 months in prison.[1]

Nurse using pass book of 95-year-old woman. Another carer for a nursing agency acquired the National Savings pass book of a 95-year-old woman in her care. She forged the woman's signature twice, withdrawing a total of £5000. She was sentenced to 15 months in prison on appeal.[2]

Policeman stealing £280,000 from 89-year-old. A policeman extracted some £280,000 from an 89-year-old over a period of three years. He had gained her confidence but was convicted of forgery and using a copy of a false instrument (this included selling her house).[3]

Financial adviser stealing tens of thousands of pounds from vulnerable adults. A financial adviser was convicted of forgery, false accounting, theft and money laundering. This included stealing £185,000 from an elderly woman, an £82,000 legacy bequeathed to a man with learning disabilities, and £31,000 from an 84-year-old man's estate (covered up by forged paperwork suggesting that the dead man had spent the money on foreign trips and double glazing).[4]

Fraud

Financial abuse, in the form of fraud (and theft), is a major issue in adult safeguarding. The following paragraphs deal first with the ingredients of the offence, particularly abuse of a position of trust, and, second, with many examples of convictions for fraud involving vulnerable adults and an extensive range of perpetrators, subject to temptation and exercising opportunism.

---

1   *R v Ross-Goulding* [1997] 2 Cr App R (S) 348.

2   *R v Mangham* [1998] 2 Cr App R (S) 344.

3   'Ex-PC conned victim out of home.' *BBC News*, 5 April 2006. Accessed on 3 October 2018 at: http://news.bbc.co.uk/1/hi/england/essex/4880720.stm.

4   Jenkins, R. 'Financier stole from elderly clients.' *The Times*, 13 September 2006.

FRAUD: INGREDIENTS OF OFFENCE. The offence of fraud is contained in the Fraud Act 2006. The three main offences, found in sections 1–4 of the Act, are fraud by false representation, by failure to disclose information or by abuse of position.

Fraud by abuse of position is made out when a person (a) occupies a position in which he is expected to safeguard, or not to act against, the financial interests of another person, (b) dishonestly abuses that position, and (c) intends, by means of the abuse of that position, to make a gain for himself or another – or to cause loss to another or to expose another to a risk of loss. Abuse can be made out even if the conduct consists of an omission rather than an act.

Previous offences under sections 15, 15A and 16 of the Theft Act 1968, of obtaining property, money transfer or pecuniary advantage by deception, were repealed by the Fraud Act and are, in substance, subsumed now within the 2006 Act. Some of the cases summarised below refer to these previous offences.

FRAUD: EXAMPLES OF FRAUD AGAINST VULNERABLE ADULTS. The following are typical examples of fraud committed against vulnerable adults, with diverse perpetrators: gardeners, bank staff, care workers, care home managers, social workers, social services finance officers, solicitors, parliamentary candidates, estate agents, local authority finance officers, neighbours, people's own relatives, etc.

> **Gardener defrauding elderly woman in her nineties: abuse of position.**
> A gardener was jailed for five years for fraud by abuse of position after befriending a vulnerable, elderly woman in her nineties. He repeatedly stole from her, leaving her without enough money to pay bills. He convinced her to hand over bank details and to write him a cheque for £100,000. The crimes were only discovered when her family began looking into her finances in order to pay for nursing care. He had set up a direct debit from the woman's account to pay for his car insurance, made more than 100 cash withdrawals of £300, pretended to be her grandson to convince an insurance company into cashing out her investment bonds worth £200,000,

and wrote himself a cheque for £100,000, which he got her to sign. She died just before the trial, aged 98.[1]

Massive fraud and changing of a will, by carer from a charity, against 102-year-old woman. A former care worker for Bridlington Friends of the Elderly was jailed for nine years for stealing £289,688 from a 102-year-old woman. She secretly opened a joint bank account with the elderly woman and spent her life savings on two houses. She also wrote herself into the woman's will when the latter's health began to deteriorate after her 101st birthday, despite the woman lacking capacity to change her will. She was convicted of five counts of fraud, two of concealing or converting criminal property, and one of making an article for use in fraud. When the woman died, relatives found that family photographs, fur coats, two Staffordshire pet dogs and £289,688 from her bank account were gone. The carer organised the funeral against the will of the family, reserving no seat for them on the front row, booking too small a church and making little mention of her life in the service.[2]

Fraud about police corruption perpetrated on former civil servant suffering from cancer. The court described this case as the 'worst crime of deception of the elderly ever to be before the courts in Scotland'. A builder was convicted of fraud and sentenced to ten years in prison. He had tricked a retired, 77-year-old civil servant out of his life savings – almost £500,000 in cash – by pretending to lead a secret inquiry into police corruption, for which he required funds. The victim had been a former chief inspector of the pollution inspectorate. He had subsequently been forced to sell his home in order to pay for the care home in which he now lived, suffering from Alzheimer's disease and prostate cancer.[3]

Estate agents: taking money from mentally ill person, fraudulently promising large investment returns. Two Hampstead estate agents

1   'A gardener who fleeced a 97-year-old widow of £170,000 from her life-savings has been jailed.' *Dorset Echo*, 1 August 2017.

2   'Tributes to lovely Edith after "dishonest" carer found guilty.' *Bridlington Free Press*, 29 June 2017. Accessed on 11 October 2018 at: www.bridlingtonfreepress.co.uk/news/tributes-to-lovely-edith-after-dishonest-carer-found-guilty-1-8621739.

3   Harris, G. 'Builder cons man out of £450,000.' *The Times*, 2 March 2002. And: 'Conman jailed for 10 years.' *BBC News*, 22 March 2002. Accessed on 3 October 2018 at: http://news.bbc.co.uk/1/hi/scotland/1887420.stm.

carried out a sophisticated fraud on a rich, vulnerable and mentally ill (schizophrenic), middle-aged man. They were convicted of conspiracy to defraud, two counts of theft and one of obtaining money by deception. The fraud involved persuading the man to give them £200,000 for investment in property, on the promise of a £500 billion return. In addition, they tricked him into giving them gold, jewellery (including his mother's ring), and share certificates worth £600,000. They were sentenced to five years in prison.[1]

Fraudulent 'legal' consultants taking money from elderly people in order to 'protect' them from care home fees. Eight people committed fraud trading under the names Inheritance Protection Services, Inheritance & Probate Solutions Ltd and Goldstar Law Ltd, operating from rented units in Newark while using postal addresses in London. Salesmen with no legal training posed as 'legal consultants' when visiting elderly victims in their own homes. They said they could protect their property and savings from future care home fees by putting them into a 'Trust' document. After telling them scare stories, they pressured them into making upfront payments of about £2000 for what they described as a 'Family Prosperity Trust' or 'Estate Preservation Trust'. But these trusts offered no protection from care home fees and in some situations the trust documents could actually make the financial position worse. Prison sentences were given, up to four and a half years.[2]

Lawyer and parliamentary candidate overcharging two elderly sisters £50,000. A lawyer, parliamentary candidate and former head of administration for a county council grossly abused the trust of two elderly sisters, obtaining some £50,000 from them by overcharging. For instance, he visited one of them in a nursing home, read poetry to her and then charged her hundreds of pounds for the privilege. He was sentenced to three years in prison for obtaining property by deception and theft – and ordered to pay compensation.[3]

---

1   Osley, R. 'Facing prison for £500,000 fraud.' *Camden New Journal*, 10 January 2008. And: Fletcher, H. 'Estate agents "swindled £0.5m out of schizophrenic man".' *The Times*, 9 November 2007.

2   'Newark man was part of gang that conned pensioners.' *Newark Advertiser*, 18 May 2015.

3   'Lawyer stole from elderly sisters.' *BBC News*, 3 October 2003. Accessed on 3 October 2018 at: http://news.bbc.co.uk/1/hi/wales/north_west/3159442.stm.

Solicitor stealing £3 million from estates of dead clients. A solicitor was sentenced to six years in prison for theft and obtaining property by deception. He had stolen money belonging to clients amounting to some £3 million, comprising sums from the estates of recently deceased clients – including £100,000 which was meant to provide income for the deceased client's son who had Down's syndrome.[1]

Directors of a will and probate service, fraud involving £5 million. In general, probate fraud is thought to be an increasing problem, with the Royal National Institute for the Blind estimating in 2004 that it may amount to some £150 million a year, often involving solicitors or legal advisers.[2] In 2005, two directors of a wills and probate service were sentenced, respectively, to three years, nine months (subsequently reduced by 13 months) and to four years, six months in prison for fraudulent trading under (what was then) section 458 of the Companies Act 1985. The client account deficiency stood at nearly £5 million.[3]

Bank finance manager and financial adviser defrauding elderly people. The victims were an 81-year-old gentleman, who had no close relatives and who lived alone, and an 84-year-old lady, who also lived alone. Both had accounts at a bank in Colchester. The perpetrator had been the financial manager there in 1997. In 1998, he was working at a large finance company and renewed contact with the two victims. Both were persuaded by him to invest money in the company. They subsequently paid over cheques in 1999 and 2000. He used the money for his own or his company's purposes, having pretended to them that he was going to invest the money on their behalf. In the first victim's case, this was £10,000; in the second, £52,500.

There was complete recklessness as to the prospect of repayment of money obtained by persistently deceptive behaviour. The perpetrator undoubtedly selected his victims with care and subjected them to a cynical fraud.[4]

Investment adviser obtaining £360,000 from vulnerable people. A so-called investment adviser obtained £360,000 from vulnerable people

---

1   *R v Shaw* [1996] 2 Cr App R (S) 278.

2   'Fraud robs bereaved of £150 million.' *The Times*, 25 July 2004.

3   *R v Furr* [2007] EWCA Crim 191.

4   *R v Hooper* [2003] EWCA Crim 810.

(disabled, dying or bereaved), ostensibly to invest their money, but in fact to put into his own failing business. He was sentenced to four and a half years in prison for obtaining money by deception.[1]

Counter manager at bank taking £167,000 from elderly and sick people. A 59-year-old counter manager at a bank was a respected churchgoer and charity treasurer. She had been employed at the bank for 40 years. Yet she defrauded elderly and sick people of £167,000.

Many of the victims were friends or people she had known for years. They included a man with learning disabilities, retired people and recently widowed people. She also defrauded a hospital league of friends, for which she was treasurer. She massaged figures and transferred money in and out of accounts, making both withdrawals and credits to conceal what was going on. The bank reimbursed the victims in full. The perpetrator was described by many of her victims as apparently generous and thoughtful. She was sent to prison for two and a half years.[2]

A bank customer adviser met with customers face to face to discuss and advise on their financial options, and also to deal with their accounts. The two victims were wealthy, elderly and regular customers. Advised by the adviser, they had each set up an internet banking account with a password of which he was aware. He was thus able to log on to their accounts and fraudulently transfer sums of money from them to his own accounts. He was sentenced to three years in prison for fraud by abuse of position and for theft.[3]

Care home manager forging will and pretending to be daughter of resident. The manager of a care home forged the will of an 82-year-old resident, claiming to be his long-lost daughter, in order to inherit £300,000. She had tampered with her own medical records, inserting the resident's name as that of her father. She also stole tens of thousands of pounds from another, 90-year-old resident. She was convicted on eight counts of fraud and two of theft, receiving a five-year prison sentence.[4]

---

1   Beattie, S. 'Conman jailed for £360,000 fraud.' *Teesside Evening Gazette*, 31 May 2008.

2   Stone, A. 'Bank clerk plundered 167k from friends' accounts.' *Western Mail*, 25 February 2012.

3   *R v Chris* [2018] EWCA Crim 301.

4   'A despicable thief.' *Burton Mail*, 28 March 2012.

Care home manager defrauding residents with dementia of £41,000.
A care home manager defrauded two residents with dementia of over
£41,000. She encouraged them to sign cheques or to use their bank cards
– on 97 occasions. The fraud was detected by other staff who noticed
problems with the accounts of the two residents, aged 82 and 93. Of
previously good character, she was sentenced to 30 months in prison. The
victims would be compensated from her assets: £120 from a bank account
and a television. The £40,000 was apparently missing.[1]

Care home manager stealing £330,000 from employer and residents. A
care home finance manager, who went by the title 'Lady', committed theft,
false accounting and fraud. She was sentenced to 32 months in prison.
She stole £330,000 from her employer, Oakfield Ltd, and from care home
residents at two Northamptonshire care homes, for the finances of which
she was responsible. She had become hooked on buying diamonds on a
television channel, as well as going on cruises and buying champagne. She
had been entrusted with debit cards, petty cash and residents' personal
finances.

The woman had stolen from the company, using its accounts to cover her
personal heating bills and petrol – and to inflate her salary and to pay her
for extra hours which she had not worked (but for which she had forged
spreadsheets). She also charged £17,000 of expenditure directly to the
accounts of residents. In one case, when a resident needed a toothbrush,
the perpetrator told the resident's mother that her daughter had no money
to buy it.[2]

Sheltered housing manager using bank card of 78-year-old man. The
manager of a sheltered housing complex was sent to prison after defrauding
a 78-year-old widower of nearly £4000. She admitted six counts of abusing
her position to commit fraud; this included using the resident's bank card
on shopping sprees in Castleford. She was found not guilty on three other
fraud charges, which related to him changing his will in her favour and

1   'Julie Close stole £41k from residents at Collins Green care home.' *Warrington Guardian*, 18 April
    2012.

2   Dolan, A. '"Lady Glanister" stole £330,000 from the residents of her care homes to buy diamonds,
    cruises and champagne.' *Daily Mail*, 18 April 2012.

fraudulently obtaining cash withdrawals of £10,000 and £2000 from his account.[1]

Fraud: making of elderly woman's will by impostor. The perpetrators, together with another female accomplice, arranged for an 87-year-old woman with very restricted mobility to make a new will. They arranged for her instructions to be transferred from her long-standing solicitors to a new firm with whom she had no previous dealings. The new instructions were given and the will executed. The accomplice posed as the woman, with the two perpetrators present when she signed the will. After the woman had died, they continued to represent that the new will was her true will. They were the main beneficiaries of the residue of the estate, which was valued in the region of £1.8 million, although there was a specific bequest of £10,000 in that will to the female accomplice (who in fact was the mother of one of the perpetrators).[2]

Senior local authority finance officer: taking £600,000 from vulnerable clients. A senior local authority finance officer in Camden, responsible for the finances of vulnerable adults who could not manage their own affairs, was convicted of fraud, having stolen some £600,000 from mentally ill and elderly service users.[3]

Social worker abusing position of deputyship. A local authority social worker, seconded to an NHS Trust, was appointed deputy by the Court of Protection for a mental health service user. She withdrew for herself £21,768.63, partly to fund her use of drugs and alcohol. In 2017 she received a suspended prison sentence after pleading guilty to three charges of fraud by abuse of position and one charge of dishonestly making a false representation. She paid the money back and was in 2018 struck off the social work register by the Health and Care Professions Council.[4]

Carer impersonates dead client. The carer of a woman with multiple sclerosis fraudulently obtained a £5000 loan by pretending to be the dead

1   'Fraud carer jailed.' *Pontefract and Castleford Times*, 17 April 2008.

2   *R v Spillman* [2001] 1 Cr App R (S) 139.

3   Osley, R. 'Jail for £600k Town Hall fraud: "guilty, guilty" says trusted council finance man who bought home in Caribbean with elderly's cash.' *Camden New Journal*, 18 January 2007.

4   Turner, A. 'Social worker struck off after stealing thousands from service.' *Community Care*, 24 April 2018.

woman. She was also convicted of dishonestly obtaining money from the dead woman's estate, by pillaging her bank account after her death.[1]

Care home worker convicted for deceit and breach of trust against elderly people. A woman had obtained a job at a care home for vulnerable elderly people in January 2008 and had free access to the residents' rooms and personal effects. One of these ladies, a 78-year-old, had a bank account and a chequebook which she kept in her handbag. The appellant stole that chequebook and she wrote out a cheque to a loan company for £3100. However, she misspelt the name of the owner of the account and the cheque was dishonoured. The police were informed, and she was arrested. In a search of her home another cheque from the same lady was discovered. That was made out to another company for £641.

As to other counts, another elderly lady of 88 lived over the road from the woman and regarded her as a friend. The woman had a bank card belonging to this lady. The woman would spend time with her, go shopping for her and give her general assistance. In fact, she had used the bank card to make several payments for herself. The woman was convicted for deceit and breach of trust – in the words of the judge, for 'sophisticated and sustained, serious, venal and stupid' crimes against elderly people.[2]

Care worker answering advertisements for carers in *The Lady* magazine. A carer was employed to look after a 90-year-old woman who had been discharged from hospital and required 24-hour care. The carer stole £3300 from a drawer, as well as blank cheques, on which she forged the woman's signature (she was unsuccessful in drawing money on them). She left this employment without notice a day later. She then answered an advertisement in *The Lady* magazine and started work two months later, caring for an 88-year-old, immobile woman. The carer could withdraw £250 cash per week, to cover her wages and housekeeping expenses. On six occasions, the carer exceeded this limit until a total of £3300 had been obtained. The carer pleaded guilty to theft, obtaining pecuniary advantage by deception and obtaining property by deception; she was sentenced to 30 months in prison, reduced on appeal to 18 months.[3]

---

1   'Carer found guilty of fraud on dead woman's estate.' *Wirral Globe*, 1 April 1998.

2   *R v Lawson* [2010] EWCA Crim 193.

3   *R v Donaldson* [2001] EWCA Crim 2854.

Agency care worker using signed, blank cheques. An agency carer cared for an 80-year-old, housebound woman, unable to walk. The carer collected her pension, did a bit of shopping, went to the launderette, cleaned the home and paid bills. At the carer's request, the woman would sign blank cheques, purportedly so the carer could then fill them in to pay the water and electricity bills. In fact, over a two-year period, she wrote out cheques to herself, amounting to £2875. She was convicted of obtaining a money transfer by deception and sentenced to 18 months in prison.[1]

Neighbour opportunistically obtaining and concealing pass book from social worker. A 65-year-old neighbour became friendly with an older woman. As the latter's mental health began to deteriorate, the neighbour began to act as her carer and discovered that she had substantial sums of money in various building society accounts. The neighbour arranged the transfer of one of the accounts into joint names. When she later handed over the woman's documents to a social worker, she retained the pass book, withdrew £44,000 and closed the account. She also obtained a watch, valued between £1200 and £1500, which the woman had left at a jeweller's. She was convicted of theft and obtaining money by deception.[2]

Woman defrauded by her own son. A woman in her eighties was defrauded by her son, who managed to get her house transferred into his name in order to take out an £83,000 loan, before falling behind on the payments. This resulted in bailiffs going to her home and her being at risk of losing her home. Her health deteriorated as she became more and more anxious, and she died aged 89 years. The judge stated that the son had asset-stripped his mother and had perpetrated a confidence trick of a particularly vile sort. He was sentenced to two and a half years in prison.[3]

Former RAF commander defrauding and ruining his two aunts. A former RAF flight commander defrauded three women, including two of his aunts, of over £300,000. He tricked them into investing their savings through him. He had simply used the money for himself, spending it on luxury items. He had obtained enduring power of attorney for one of his aunts who had

1   *R v Roach* [2001] EWCA Crim 992.

2   *R v Starsmeare* [2003] EWCA Crim 577.

3   'Liar son cons OAP mother.' *Eastwood and Kimberley Advertiser*, 19 March 2012.

dementia, and whose money he then used for his own business. She was left £10,000 overdrawn, unable to pay care home fees and financially ruined.

Eventually, social services had approached the Court of Protection, which had removed him as attorney. He was sentenced to two years in prison.[1]

Fraudulent calumny

A person's will (testament) can be challenged, in civil law, on several grounds including undue influence. One form this can take is called fraudulent calumny. It arises if one person poisons the testator's (the person making the will) mind against another person, who would otherwise be a natural beneficiary – by casting dishonest aspersions on the latter's character. The first person must either know that the aspersions are false or not care whether they are true or false.

The burden of proving fraudulent calumny lies on the person who asserts it. It is not enough to prove that the facts are consistent with the hypothesis of undue influence. What must be shown is that the facts are inconsistent with any other hypothesis.[2]

Will overturned: daughter perpetrating fraudulent calumny to poison her mother's mind against her other daughter. A woman changed her will after one of her daughters had convinced her that the other had stolen £500,000 from her bank accounts. The judge analysed the first daughter's behaviour over a period of some months and how this had poisoned her mother's mind. He found that this daughter had perpetrated fraudulent calumny, and that she was 'a thoroughly dishonest and manipulative individual to whom integrity and truth are less important than achieving what she wants, even when she knows she is not entitled to it'.[3]

---

1   Vinter, P. 'Ex-RAF flight commander who swindled his two aunties out of £312,000 is jailed for two years.' *Daily Mail*, 22 May 2012.

2   *Re Edwards dec'd* [2007] WTLR 1387.

3   *Christodoulides v Marcou* [2017] EWHC 2632 (Ch), para 16.

Freedom of Information Act 2000

Relatives, for example, may try, or feel forced, to 'do their own safeguarding'. This might include seeking information under the Freedom of Information Act 2000 to find out what has happened to a family member, what is happening or how it was investigated or dealt with. However, the Act is not always straightforward to understand and to use. It is covered below under the following headings:

- Freedom of information: overview

- Freedom of information: appeals

- Freedom of information: cost exemption and time limits

- Freedom of information: exemptions – absolute, qualified and public interest test

- Freedom of information: summary of exempted information

- Freedom of information: information otherwise reasonably accessible

- Freedom of information: information intended for future publication

- Freedom of information: exemption – investigations and proceedings

- Freedom of information: exemption – prevention or detection of crime, administration of justice, etc.

- Freedom of information: exemption – prejudice to conduct of public affairs

- Freedom of information: exemption – personal information (of applicant)

- Freedom of information: exemption – personal information (of other people)

- Freedom of information: exemption – actionable breach of confidence

- Freedom of information: exemption – legal privilege

- Freedom of information: exemption – prohibition of disclosure under other legislation

- Freedom of information: exemption – vexatious requests.

FREEDOM OF INFORMATION: OVERVIEW. The Act applies only to public bodies and, with more health and social care now provided by the independent sector, information may be more difficult to come by. In addition, the Act anyway contains a number of exemptions to the duty to provide the information sought. These exemptions are perfectly understandable and, on their face, reasonable, but they would seem to be premised on the notion of public bodies acting in good faith which, in adult safeguarding, cannot always be relied on. (See e.g. **Concealment** and **Conflicts of interest within adult safeguarding**.)

Obtaining information from public bodies can be relevant to safeguarding – for example, to uncover details of individual instances of – or of more systemic – abuse or neglect, or to find out how a safeguarding enquiry was pursued, how decisions about what to do were made and – sometimes – whether anything is being concealed.

The Act places a duty on public bodies to provide information, subject to certain rules. Normally, compliance with the request should be within 20 working days, although there are provisos to this. Key points include the following:

- **Freedom of information and safeguarding.** Requests are sometimes made to local authorities or the NHS to access information, which sometimes have a bearing on adult protection and safeguarding issues.

  For example, family members might be doing their own protection or safeguarding work, trying to find out what went, or is going, wrong in the health or social care of a relative. This might involve trying to get hold of investigations, reports, meeting minutes, care plans, evidence of how adult protection or safeguarding procedures were followed, details about staff involved, etc.

  Alternatively, the information requested might be more general. For instance, in cases of systemic, institutional neglect, information about staffing levels and competencies, serious incidents, infection outbreaks, deaths, bed and ward closures (temporary or permanent) and hospital discharge statistics might be all-important for safeguarding purposes.

- **Non-personal information, public bodies.** The Freedom of Information Act 2000 governs requests made to public bodies about information that is non-personal (in relation to the requester). It might be information requested about somebody else (e.g. a dead relative or hospital staff who treated that relative), or it might be non-personal (or at least anonymised) information – for instance, statistics on serious incidents, deaths from infection, pressure sore incidence.

- **Personal information.** In some circumstances, the request will in fact legally come to rest under the Data Protection Act 2018 (DPA) and General Data Protection Regulation (GDPR), even though the person has made the request under the 2000 Act. This might happen if it involves information about the requester. Alternatively, if it does involve somebody else's (such as a relative's) personal information, then the 2000 Act does apply, but reference to DPA/GDPR principles must still be made. On occasion, the request might also come, legally, under other legislation altogether, such as the Access to Health Records Act 1990.

- **Public bodies only.** Independent care providers are not subject to the Freedom of Information Act 2000, because they are not public bodies. Yet ever more health and social care is being contracted out to such providers. Although requests could still be made, under the 2000 Act, to the commissioning NHS body or local authority, these might respond that they do not hold the requested information (because they are no longer running the service) – or that the information is commercially sensitive.

- **Safeguarding adults boards.** Safeguarding adults boards, created under the Care Act 2014, are not listed within the Freedom of Information Act legislation as public bodies. So, the question has arisen as to whether safeguarding adults boards are subject, perhaps indirectly, to FOIA requests: see *Safeguarding adults boards*.

- **Provisos to disclosure.** The Act contains a number of provisos, on the basis of which a public body can refuse to disclose the information sought. These provisos relate, for instance, to law enforcement, an investigation, prejudice in the conduct of public affairs, health and safety, personal information or information originally given in confidence. In addition, requests that would be too expensive to process or vexatious requests also constitute grounds for not making the information available.

- **Striking a balance.** When the Information Commissioner and, beyond the Commissioner, the Information Tribunal hear disputes, they consider these provisos and whether non-disclosure is justified in the particular case. On their face, the provisos are reasonable and attempt to strike a balance between complete openness and legitimate limitations.

- **Balancing exercise presupposes good faith.** The balancing exercise presupposes that public bodies will, by and large, act in good faith. And the approach of the Information Commissioner and of the Information Tribunal seems generally – other than in blatantly obvious instances – to assume that this is indeed the way in which the public bodies act. Unfortunately, this assumption is not always justified.

  Examples, undermining the validity of such an assumption, include the systematic cover-up – uncovered – in relation to the Hillsborough football disaster,[1] the concealment of serious infection and scores of deaths at Maidstone and Tunbridge Wells NHS Trust,[2] central government's attempt to avoid an inquiry into events at Stafford Hospital, maintaining there was nothing more to learn (until threatened with a judicial review legal case),[3] and, most recently, potential cover-up in relation to blood products given to people suffering from haemophilia.[4]

- **Destroying information.** If a request for information has been made, and the applicant would have been entitled to access the information, then an offence is committed if the information is altered, defaced, blocked, erased, destroyed or concealed – with the intention of preventing disclosure. The offence can be committed by the public authority or any person employed by the public authority; if convicted, they would be liable, on summary conviction, to a fine not exceeding level 5 on the standard scale.[5]

---

1   Hillsborough Independent Panel (Chairman: Right Reverend James Jones, Bishop of Liverpool). *Hillsborough: the report of the Hillsborough Independent Panel.* HC 581. London: The Stationery Office, 2012, pp.22–26.

2   Healthcare Commission. *Investigation into outbreaks of* Clostridium difficile *at Maidstone and Tunbridge Wells NHS Trust, October 2007.* London: HC, 2007, p.94.

3   Leigh Day & Co. 'Judicial reviews and the Mid Staffordshire inquiries.' *News*, 12 May 2010. Accessed on 14 July 2017 at: www.leighday.co.uk/Human-rights-and-public-law/Health-social-care/Human-rights-in-healthcare/Mid-Staffordshire-Inquiry/Judicial-reviews-and-the-Mid-Staffordshire-inquiri.

4   Stone, J. and Forster, K. 'Theresa May launches inquiry into contaminated blood scandal.' *The Independent*, 11 July 2017.

5   Freedom of Information Act 2000, s.77.

FREEDOM OF INFORMATION: APPEALS. Under section 50 of the Act, a complainant can apply to the Information Commissioner to decide whether a request for information has been dealt with by a public body in accordance with the Act.

The Commissioner must make a decision unless (a) the complainant has not exhausted any complaints procedure provided by the public body in conformity with the code of practice made under the 2000 Act; (b) there has been undue delay making the application to the Commissioner; (c) the application is frivolous or vexatious; or (d) the application has been withdrawn or abandoned. Appeal lies from the Information Commissioner to the Information Tribunal.[1]

FREEDOM OF INFORMATION: COST EXEMPTION AND TIME LIMITS. Under section 12 of the Freedom of Information Act 2000, a public body does not have to comply with a request to disclose if the cost of complying would exceed the appropriate cost limit, which is set in regulations.[2]

> **Mistreatment, abuse and neglect, request for details of complaints made: exempt.** The information sought was about complaints of mistreatment, neglect and abuse on NHS Trust premises. The request asked for details of complaints made by patients, relatives and staff involving matters such as hydration, nutrition, inappropriate use of diamorphine or potassium chloride, 'do not resuscitate' and 'not for intensive therapy' instructions. The NHS Trust declined to disclose, arguing that to do so would mean exceeding the appropriate limit under section 12 (£450). It explained that complaints records were indexed alphabetically by patient, not by the nature or type of the complaint. The request would involve combing each complaints file for its contents. The Information Commissioner accepted the Trust's argument; there were some 10,000 complaints files.[3]

---

1   Freedom of Information Act 2000, s.57.

2   SI 2004/3244. Freedom of Information and Data Protection (Appropriate Limit and Fees) Regulations 2004.

3   Information Commissioner Decision: *Swansea NHS Trust*, 5 December 2006.

Refusal by Care Quality Commission justified. A refusal, upheld by the Information Commissioner, was that of the Care Quality Commission when it declined, on cost grounds, to supply details of all its enforcement decisions. However, the Commissioner did find that it failed to provide adequate advice and assistance instead, under section 16 of the Act.[1]

FREEDOM OF INFORMATION: EXEMPTIONS – ABSOLUTE, QUALIFIED AND PUBLIC INTEREST TEST. The Freedom of Information Act 2000 effectively creates an expectation that public bodies will confirm or deny that they hold the information sought and will disclose that information.

This twofold duty is, however, subject to specified exemptions. Some of these exemptions are absolute, some are qualified. A qualified exemption means applying a test of whether, in all the circumstances of the case, the public interest in maintaining the exemption outweighs the public interest in disclosure.

The presumption of disclosure in relation to qualified exemptions is the reverse of the test traditionally applied in the common law of confidentiality – namely a presumption of non-disclosure which must be outweighed by a public interest in disclosure.

FREEDOM OF INFORMATION: SUMMARY OF EXEMPTED INFORMATION. The Act sets out provisos to information disclosure by way of a list of exemptions. In summary, some of these are relevant potentially in the context of health and social care:

- information otherwise reasonably accessible to the applicant (section 21)

- information intended for future publication (section 22)

- information held in relation to:

  » security matters (section 23)

  » public authority investigations and proceedings (section 30)

---

1   Information Commissioner Decision: *Care Quality Commission*. Case no. FS50393575, 25 October 2011.

» law enforcement and related matters that would otherwise be prejudiced (section 31)

» court records (section 32)

» audit functions (section 33)

» formulation of government policy (section 35)

» conduct of public affairs that would otherwise be prejudiced (section 36)

» health and safety (section 38)

» personal information (section 40)

» information provided in confidence (section 41)

» legal professional privilege (section 42)

» commercial interests (section 43)

• information, disclosure of which is prohibited by other legislation, is incompatible with any European Community obligation or would be a contempt of court (section 44).

FREEDOM OF INFORMATION: INFORMATION OTHERWISE REASONABLY ACCESSIBLE.

Under section 21 of the 2000 Act, an exemption applies if the information sought is reasonably accessible by other means, and from a public authority (or other body) with a legal obligation to provide it.

Daughter seeking father's medical records. When a daughter sought her late father's medical records under the 2000 Act, the Information Commissioner ascertained that she was entitled to access under the Access to Health Records Act 1990 – in which case it was an exempt disclosure under section 21 of the 2000 Act, because the information was otherwise reasonably accessible and held by a public authority which was obliged to provide it under the 1990 Act.[1]

Man seeking a report about his mother's care in hospital. A man sought a copy of a report by a hospital consultant about the care of his late mother.

---

1   Information Commissioner Decision: *Gloucestershire NHS Primary Care Trust*, 12 November 2007.

The Trust stated it would disclose under the 1990 Act if he provided proof that he was his dead mother's personal representative; it asked to see a copy of his birth certificate as proof. He failed to produce this and gave no reasons for not doing so; he sought the information instead under the 2000 Act. The Information Commissioner held that the Trust was exempt from disclosing under section 21. The request of proof by the Trust, under the 1990 Act, was reasonable.[1]

Information already disclosed about removal of a person's mother from hospital to a care home. A man wanted to obtain the background, details and legal basis for removal of his mother from hospital to a residential home where she subsequently died. The local authority argued that it had already disclosed this information in previous correspondence and in reports produced in response to the man's complaints. Both the Information Commissioner, and then, on appeal, the Information Tribunal, agreed with the local authority and held that section 21 applied.[2]

FREEDOM OF INFORMATION: INFORMATION INTENDED FOR FUTURE PUBLICATION. Under section 22 an exemption to disclosure applies if the information requested is already due for publication at some future date, whether or not that date is determined, and that it is reasonable in the circumstances that the information be withheld. This exemption, amongst others, was used by the Department of Health to block publication of the Black report of 2003, about the deaths of patients at Gosport War Memorial Hospital.[3]

FREEDOM OF INFORMATION: EXEMPTION – INVESTIGATIONS AND PROCEEDINGS. Under section 30, a qualified exemption (i.e. subject to the public interest test) applies to investigations carried out by public bodies (under a duty), which may lead to a person being charged with an offence or

1   Information Commissioner Decision: *Liverpool Women's NHS Foundation Trust*, 19 February 2007.

2   Information Tribunal: *Prior v Information Commissioner* (2006) 27 April 2006.

3   Jones, Reverend J. (Chairman). *Gosport War Memorial Hospital: the report of the Gosport Independent Panel*. London: The Stationery Office, 2018, paras 4.91, 4.93.

to ascertaining whether the person is guilty of an offence already charged, or may lead to the public body instituting criminal proceedings. Likewise, there is a qualified exemption in respect of information obtained from confidential sources during such (and some other) investigations. For instance, section 30 could apply to investigations by the Health and Safety Executive (HSE).

Health and safety investigation: analysis wrongly withheld. The HSE disclosed its factual report about a potentially fatal accident, but not its analysis. The latter did not contain obviously sensitive information, witness statements or information which would assist law breakers. The public interest in exemption was therefore outweighed by that of disclosure.[1]

FREEDOM OF INFORMATION: EXEMPTION – PREVENTION OR DETECTION OF CRIME, ADMINISTRATION OF JUSTICE, ETC. Under section 31, a qualified exemption applies for a variety of reasons – for instance, if disclosure would be likely to prejudice prevention or detection of crime, apprehension or prosecution of offenders, administration of justice, etc. It applies also if another public authority is exercising various functions to determine failure to comply with the law, improper conduct, health and safety, etc.

Refusal to disclose safeguarding activity in relation to three sets of premises. Amongst other grounds, the local authority refused to disclose under section 31 safeguarding referrals, reports and associated actions concerning three sets of premises. It argued that disclosure of any information held, or acknowledgement that information is held or not held, could prejudice any investigation by the Council and other law enforcement agencies into alleged safeguarding concerns, and alert possible perpetrators about current or future safeguarding investigations. This refusal was justified.[2]

Refusal to disclose information by health board, about the death of a person's mother, because of ombudsman investigation. A person requested

---

1   Information Commissioner Decision: *Health and Safety Executive* (2008) 18 February 2007.

2   Information Commissioner Decision: *North Somerset Council*, FS50679642, 7 December 2017.

details of records of a health and social services board investigation relating to the death of his mother. The board resisted disclosure under section 31 because the Northern Ireland ombudsman was investigating in response to a separate complaint made. The Information Commissioner held that disclosure would prejudice the ombudsman's functions, and that the public interest fell on the side of non-disclosure.[1]

FREEDOM OF INFORMATION: EXEMPTION – PREJUDICE TO CONDUCT OF PUBLIC AFFAIRS.

A qualified exemption applies, under section 36 of the Act, if disclosure by a public body would prejudice the effective conduct of public affairs and would be likely to inhibit free and frank provision of advice, or free and frank exchange of views for the purpose of deliberation.

Information about adult protection procedures concerning the death of a person's mother. A person sought information about adult protection procedures in respect of the death of his mother. The local authority put up various arguments, including one under section 36. This was that there was an expectation of confidence between a client and social services, and that clients would fear to provide appropriate information for fear of potential disclosure. This would arguably prejudice the conduct of public affairs. The Information Commissioner gave no view on this particular argument, finding instead that the information sought was anyway exempted from disclosure under sections 40 and 41 relating to personal information provided in confidence.[2]

Medical records of a woman's father. An NHS primary care trust (PCT) argued the section 36 exemption in relation to the medical records of a woman's father. The Information Commissioner was unable to reach a decision on this point because the PCT had destroyed the notes of a panel meeting at which the original non-disclosure decision in relation to section 36 was taken. The Commissioner did not find a breach of section 77 of the 2000 Act – which creates an offence of destroying or otherwise tampering

---

1   Information Commissioner Decision: *Eastern Health and Social Services Board* (2006) 10 July 2006.

2   Information Commissioner Decision: *Trafford Metropolitan Borough Council* (2007) 27 November 2007.

with information with the intention of preventing disclosure – but came close to it. However, there was insufficient evidence of deliberate intent.[1]

Disclosure of child protection serious case review: prejudicial to the conduct of public affairs. The Information Commissioner found that disclosure would inhibit the participation of professionals; this would reduce the effectiveness of the review and in turn have a detrimental impact on child protection. So, whilst there was a high public interest in accountability and scrutiny, there were persuasive arguments for non-disclosure under section 36. Furthermore, the executive summary which was available provided a balanced and coherent overview, without disclosing sensitive information.

In addition, non-disclosure was justified under section 40 because of the personal information inextricably linked to the dead child and surviving members of the family, and the Commissioner could find no condition met in either schedule 2 or 3 of the Data Protection Act that would justify disclosure, in which case the first data protection principle would be breached (fairness and lawfulness). Likewise, the section 41 (duty of confidence) exemption would apply to the information about, or provided by, family members and their associates.[2]

FREEDOM OF INFORMATION: EXEMPTION – PERSONAL INFORMATION (OF APPLICANT). An absolute exemption from disclosure under the 2000 Act applies to personal information on various grounds under section 40. This exemption breaks down into two categories, depending on whether the personal information is that of the applicant themselves – or of other people.

An absolute exemption applies to personal information, of which the applicant is the data subject. Such a request should be dealt with under the Data Protection Act 2018 and General Data Protection Regulation (GDPR). For instance:

---

1   Information Commissioner Decision: *Gloucestershire NHS Primary Care Trust* (2007) 12 November 2007.

2   Information Commissioner Decision: *Plymouth City Council* (2006) 23 August 2006.

> **Family seeking information about complaint made against them.** The parents of a baby asked to see details of a complaint made against them, with a view to identifying the hospital staff who had made the complaint. The Information Commissioner held that the request fell under the Data Protection Act 1998 subject access provisions rather than under the 2000 Act, since it concerned information about the parents themselves.[1]

FREEDOM OF INFORMATION: EXEMPTION – PERSONAL INFORMATION (OF OTHER PEOPLE).

If the request concerns the personal information of other people but not that of the applicant, then an absolute exemption applies under section 40 in two cases: first, if data protection principles would be contravened under the Data Protection Act 2018 and GDPR; second, if any of the exemptions to subject access under that legislation applies.

The Information Tribunal has held that although section 40 represents an absolute exemption, there is actually a balance of competing interests comparable to that applied in the 2000 Act to qualified exemptions[2] – in other words, apparently something of a public interest test by the back door.

> **Daughter seeking information from local authority about her mother's care and investigation: exemption from disclosure under section 40.** In relation to her mother's care, a woman wanted from the local authority copies of notes made by a social worker, written reports, copies of the minutes of a complaints panel meeting, and information about a subsequent complaint about the 'shoddy, superficial and seriously deficient investigation'. The Information Commissioner held that the section 40 exemption applied. The information was personal and release of it without the data subject's (the mother's) consent would breach the data protection principle of fairness and lawfulness. There was no evidence that the mother had given the daughter consent to access the information, or that the daughter had any right to act on her mother's behalf.[3]

---

1   Information Commissioner Investigation: *Southampton University Hospitals NHS Trust* (2007) 2 July 2007.

2   Information Tribunal: *House of Commons v Information Commissioner and Norman Baker, MP* (2007) 16 January 2007.

3   Information Commissioner Decision: *Worcestershire County Council* (2006) 31 May 2006.

Information sought by daughter about adult protection procedures followed by a local authority in relation to care of her now dead mother: exemption from disclosure under section 40 (and section 41). A woman sought information concerning adult protection matters and what the local authority did following notification by a GP of injuries sustained by her now deceased mother whilst in the care of a third party. In particular, she wanted to know how the vulnerable adult protection pathway procedure had been followed, as well as the outcome of the enquiry and documentation concerning the directions given by the GP. The local authority resisted disclosure under section 41 (information given in confidence), section 44 (prohibitions on disclosure because of human rights), section 36 (prejudice to conduct of public affairs) and section 40 (personal information and data protection principles).

Exemption from disclosure under section 40: personal information of primary carer. Under section 40, the information included information about the woman's primary carer who provided virtually 24-hour care, as well as other social services and NHS employees. The information included opinions about the primary carer and references to the carer's personal circumstances, health and financial arrangements.

The Information Commissioner accepted that disclosure of this information would be unfair under the data protection principles because the primary carer would have had a reasonable belief that her interaction with the council was confidential – and access to the information did not outweigh her rights, freedoms and legitimate interests (under schedule 2 of the Data Protection Act 1998).

Likewise, disclosure could be unlawful in terms of breach of confidence of the carer's personal information, some of it 'sensitive' (under the 1998 Act).

Exemption from disclosure under section 41 (duty of confidence). Under section 41, information had derived from the dead woman, the primary carer, the GP and the local health authority. The woman would have had an expectation of confidence, which was important if clients were to share private information with social services. The Information Commissioner held that the duty of confidence towards the deceased survived her death and that a breach would be actionable. Thus, the exemption under section

41 applied. The Commissioner disregarded the section 44 and human rights argument.[1]

Information about critical incident reports: exempt. Information was sought from an NHS Trust about five critical incident reports relating to the murder of a patient. The reports contained personal information about identifiable individuals – including patients or family members – who would not have expected the information they provided to be made public. This was particularly so because the internal review which gave rise to the reports was classed as confidential. Thus, under section 40, the Information Commissioner held it would be unfair, under the first data protection principle, for disclosure to take place.[2]

Information about NHS staff: exempt. A woman wanted the names of several registrars who had worked for a particular hospital consultant; the NHS Trust supplied her with the name of the registrar who had treated her but not others. The Information Commissioner found this justified under section 40, because while registrars might expect their current position to be disclosed, disclosure of past positions would, to a small degree, represent an infringement of privacy.[3] (The Information Commissioner has stated that normally, therefore, releasing the names of staff undertaking professional duties would not breach data protection principles, but would be unfair if the data subject (the staff member) were exposed to a risk of harassment as a result.)[4]

Information about investigation into two departing NHS managers: exempt information. The Information Commissioner held that an NHS Trust could resist disclosure under section 40 of information concerning an internal investigation against two senior executives, which resulted in their departure. The disclosure of the information could have had a harmful effect on the current and future employment prospects of both; they also had a reasonable expectation that the information would not be

---

1   Information Commissioner Decision: *Trafford Metropolitan Borough Council* (2007) 27 November 2007.

2   Information Commissioner Decision: *Mersey Care NHS Trust* (2008) 14 January 2008.

3   Information Commissioner Decision: *St George's Healthcare NHS Trust* (2008) 19 March 2008.

4   *NHS Litigation Authority* (2006) 27 September 2006.

disclosed. Furthermore, the Commissioner was satisfied that the internal investigation had been thorough and independently verified. Thus, the public interest had largely been satisfied.[1]

Similar considerations arose about the departure of a chief executive, following suspension. The NHS Trust and executive had reached a compromise agreement, and not all the allegations were fully investigated. He would not have expected details to be disclosed and to do so would have been unfair.[2]

Exemption from disclosure under section 40: witness statements about untoward incident involving a patient. A woman sought witness statements that had been made about a serious untoward incident involving her late husband. The statements were given during an internal investigation and staff members were informed that their statements would be treated confidentially. The Information Commissioner held that disclosure would breach the first principle of the Data Protection Act – lawfulness and fairness – because of the expectations of the staff about confidentiality.[3]

Information about care and death of mother: an unexplained use of Haloperidol. A man tried to obtain information concerning the death of his mother and her care at Warwick and Heathcote Hospitals. There clearly were some issues, given his mother's active life before she was admitted, unexplained use of Haloperidol and the upholding of his complaint by the Healthcare Commission, which had provided him with a 15-page letter containing the results of its investigation.

The son made a request for further information, including his mother's medical records, the complaints file and the investigator's report. The Trust resisted on section 40 grounds concerning protection of staff. The section 40 argument was not wholly upheld by the Information Tribunal. It held that where staff had already been identified, explicitly or impliedly in the Healthcare Commission report (and letter), then the section 40 exemption

---

1   Information Commissioner Decision: *Nottinghamshire Healthcare Trust* (2007) 13 August 2007.

2   Information Commissioner Decision: *George Eliot Hospital NHS Trust* (2007) 7 June 2007.

3   Information Commissioner Decision: *Central and North West London NHS Foundation Trust* (2008) 17 March 2008.

no longer applied. However, other opinions and views expressed by staff were protected.[1]

Internal report into alleged deficiencies in care on a ward: disclosure denied to whistleblower. A former employee of an NHS Trust requested a copy of an internal report, which had been triggered by allegations originally made by that employee – concerning supervision, management of medical staff and resource levels on a particular ward. The Trust refused disclosure under section 40.

The Information Commissioner upheld this decision; disclosure would have been unfair under the first data protection principle (fairness and lawfulness). This was because staff were likely to have expected confidentiality when interviewed as part of the investigation, and this had in fact been indicated to staff. Furthermore, critical comments made by the Trust about individuals would have caused considerable distress and damaged their employment prospects, if entering the public domain. Undue inferences might be made even about those members of staff who were reluctant or unwilling to provide information during the investigation, if their names were to be disclosed.[2]

Refusal to confirm or deny existence of information: not justified. Section 40 states that there is no requirement even to confirm or deny that the public body holds the relevant information, if to do so would breach data protection principles.

A man and his partner sought the minutes of a meeting alleged to have taken place between the NHS, social services and the police. The NHS Trust refused to confirm or deny that there were any such minutes; this was on the grounds that to do so would provide information about the individuals named in the request and that this would be contrary to the first data protection principle (fairness and lawfulness). The Information Commissioner disagreed, pointing out that he had been provided with no

1   *Johnston v Information Commissioner* (2011). In The First-Tier Tribunal Case No. EA/2011/0055 General Regulatory Chamber Information Rights. (On Appeal from: Information Commissioner's Decision Notice No. FS50297286, 31 January 2011.)

2   Information Commissioner Decision: *University Hospital of North Staffordshire NHS Trust* (2007) 30 August 2007.

evidence that any individual would suffer unwarranted detriment; therefore, the local authority should confirm or deny the existence of the minutes.[1]

Refusal to confirm or deny existence of information held about a nurse, in relation to a patient death: justified. A woman wrote to the Nursing and Midwifery Council. She was seeking disclosure of a statement sent to the Council by a nurse, who worked at Barnet and Chase Farm Hospitals NHS Trust. This was in relation to the death at the hospital of the woman's mother. The Council refused to confirm or deny that it held the information. Its decision was upheld by the Information Tribunal.

This was on the grounds that it would not be fair and lawful to disclose under schedule 1 of the Data Protection Act 1998. This in turn was because of prejudice to the rights and freedoms or legitimate interests of the data subject, as referred to in paragraph 6 of schedule 2 of the 1998 Act. The substantial reason was that confirming or denying would be enough to create prejudice even if the information was held in relation to a trivial or mischievous complaint. And if there was a case to answer, and a hearing held, then it would anyway become a matter of public record.[2]

The reasoning of the Information Commissioner was similar when it upheld an NHS Trust's refusal to confirm or deny whether it was instigating disciplinary proceedings against a particular nurse.[3]

Disclosing existence of gagging clauses: exemption. The question of gagging clauses (termination of employment agreements, in which the departing employee is bound to maintain silence) has arisen in relation to section 40. The Tribunal has held that even confirmation or denial of such a gagging agreement might be exempt under section 40, because of the possible prejudice to the person identified, even by implication. It has also emphasised that the Tribunal has no jurisdiction to decide whether any such gagging agreements contravene the Public Interest Disclosure Act (which could invalidate any agreement requiring confidentiality). This was

---

1   Information Commissioner Decision: *Rotherham NHS Primary Care Trust* (2007) 23 April 2007.

2   *Butters v Information Commissioner* (2009). Information Tribunal Appeal Number EA/2008/0088 (Information Commissioner's Ref: FS50180310).

3   *Central and North West London NHS Foundation Trust* (CNWL). Information Commissioner case: FS50391625, 10 October 2011.

a case in which the information seeker believed that gagging clauses were designed to save higher management from embarrassment.[1]

FREEDOM OF INFORMATION: EXEMPTION – ACTIONABLE BREACH OF CONFIDENCE. An absolute exemption from disclosure applies, under section 41, if the information requested was obtained by the public body from any other person – and if disclosure of that information to the public would constitute a breach of confidence actionable by that person (from whom it was obtained) or by anybody else. This section has been used particularly in relation to people wanting to find out more in relation to the death of a relative – the examples below demonstrate some of the obstacles to disclosure.

Although section 41 is an absolute exemption, the common law involving breach of confidence contains its own public interest test. This means that disclosure will not constitute an actionable breach of confidence if there is a public interest in disclosure outweighing the public interest in confidentiality. Under the common law, there would be a presumption of non-disclosure. This, therefore, is the reverse of the public interest test applied generally under the Freedom of Information Act to qualified exemption from disclosure – which assumes disclosure unless the public interest in confidentiality can be shown to outweigh the public interest in disclosure.[2]

---

1 *Bousfield v Information Commissioner and County Durham and Darlington NHS Foundation Trust, St George's Health Care NHS Trust, Heart of England NHS Foundation Trust, Somerset Partnership NHS Foundation Trust, South Tees Hospitals NHS Trust, University Hospitals of Leicester NHS Trust* (2012). Appeals EA/2011/0212, EA/2011/0213, EA/2011/0247, EA/2011/0250, EA/2011/0251, EA/2011/0252.

2 Information Commissioner Decision: *Hounslow Primary Care Trust* (2008) 19 March 2008.

Information about care of dead relative came ultimately and confidentially from that relative and so attracted confidentiality outweighing public interest in disclosure. A woman wanted to find out about the death of her father in care, by requesting the notes and minutes of a safeguarding meeting. The local authority refused on the grounds that the information had either directly or indirectly, through the professional involved in his care, been obtained from her father. The duty of confidentiality to the deceased outweighed the public interest in breaching it. This was on the basis such a duty of confidentiality survives death.[1]

Information provided by GP in relation to care and death of a man in a nursing home: exempt. A man sought information from an NHS primary care trust about the care of his late father-in-law and issues concerning a nursing home. It included correspondence between the nursing home, a doctor, the police and a coroner. A particular issue arose about the confidentiality of this information provided to the PCT by a GP. The Information Commissioner held that the public interest in the GP discussing issues of performance, with confidentiality assured, outweighed the public interest in disclosure. Likewise, the PCT was justified in withholding – under section 42 (see below) – five pieces of legal advice, on the basis of legal professional privilege.

Information about death of mother: not confidential. When a man sought information about the care and death of his mother – including unexplained use of the drug Haloperidol – the confidentiality of information provided by staff was held not to be covered by the exemption. This was because the Tribunal believed that

> the majority of the disputed information does relate to the normal aspects of the employment of the persons concerned, namely their actions and that of their colleagues and the processes and systems utilized in relation to the case. Whilst there are some elements which amount to a private opinion or judgment, the Tribunal is not satisfied that this is sufficient to impute an expectation of confidence into what was otherwise a non-confidential process.[2]

---

1   Information Commissioner Decision: *Coventry City Council*, FS50658109, 1 August 2017.

2   *Johnston v Information Commissioner* (2011). In The First-Tier Tribunal Case No. EA/2011/0055 General Regulatory Chamber Information Rights. (On Appeal from: Information Commissioner's Decision Notice No. FS50297286, 31 January 2011.)

Confidentiality of the dead: mother seeking information about daughter's death: exempt. A dead woman's mother sought information about her daughter's death. The NHS Trust was not prepared to share the information without the consent of her widower, as next of kin. That consent was not forthcoming. The Trust had, five years previously, admitted liability and reached a settlement with the widower. The Trust argued that the section 41 exemption applied. The Tribunal established that the medical records had been compiled with information from somebody else, namely the dead woman. It then asked in particular a number of key questions.

Would the NHS have a defence to a breach of confidence claim? The first was whether the Trust would have a defence to a breach of confidence claim, were it to disclose the information, because the public interest in disclosure would outweigh the public interest in maintaining confidence. The Tribunal stated that patient confidentiality outweighed by some distance the interests in disclosure.

Another was whether an action for breach of confidence would be defeated because neither the dead woman nor her estate would suffer detriment by disclosure. The Tribunal concluded that it would not necessarily be defeated – since there needed to be no detriment beyond an invasion of privacy, which there would be, given the private information involved.

Did the duty of confidence survive death? A third question was whether the duty of confidence survived the woman's death. The Tribunal was in no doubt that it did. If it did not, doctor and patient trust would be undermined if patients believed that information would be disclosed after death.

Bringing a claim for breach of confidence. Fourth was whether the dead woman's personal representatives would be able to bring a claim for breach of confidence. The answer was yes, and the duty of confidence would last until either the information became public or the public interest in disclosure outweighed that of confidentiality.

Human rights. Fifth, the Trust argued that section 44 of the Act (legal prohibitions), the Human Rights Act 1998 and the European Convention on Human Rights (article 8 concerning the right to respect for privacy) prevented disclosure. The Tribunal did not regard article 8 as a directly enforceable legal prohibition. But, if it was wrong about that, disclosure would not be consistent in this case with article 8, and so would be exempt under section 44.[1]

---

1   Information Tribunal: *Bluck v Information Commissioner and Epsom and St Helier University NHS Trust* (2007) 17 September 2007.

Internal reports about death of patient: exempt from disclosure – section 41. A request was made for internal reports into the circumstances surrounding the death of a patient. The information had come from medical records and interviews with relevant health professionals, from the police and from the coroner. Thus, under section 41, it had been obtained by a public body from somebody else. The Information Commissioner noted that the duty of confidence to the patient survived death, and that there was an obligation of confidence created by the patient/doctor relationship. A breach of confidence action would have been possible if disclosure took place.

The exemption applied under section 41; and no public interest outweighed the duty of confidentiality in terms of (a) the confider consenting, (b) disclosure required by law, or (c) a public interest in disclosure overriding the duty of confidence. Exemption was also justified under section 40, because in the reports there was a small amount of information comprising personal information about the man's family. Because of the sensitivity of the information and the subject, it would have been unfair under the first data protection principle to disclose.[1]

Social services information concerning a dead woman: exempt. When the family of a dead woman wanted to see her social services care records, the local authority cited its duty of confidence to the dead woman. The Commissioner understood the family's wish for disclosure but upheld the authority's stance. It was important that social services' clients had confidence that the professionals caring for them will not disclose to the public sensitive information about them after they have died as this may discourage them from making information available. Otherwise, there would be the potential for prejudice to the effective functioning of social services which is counter to the public interest.[2]

FREEDOM OF INFORMATION: EXEMPTION – LEGAL PRIVILEGE. A qualified exemption applies, under section 42 of the Act, to information that is subject to legal professional privilege. Although this is not absolute,

---

1   *East London and the City Mental Health NHS Trust* (2007) 3 December 2007.

2   Information Commissioner Decision: *East Sussex County Council*. Case No. FS50346570, 21 August 2012.

the Information Tribunal has noted that there is a strong element of public interest built into the privilege and that an equally strong consideration would be required to override it.[1]

> **Barrister's advice to social services: exempt, other than exceptionally.** In a case involving social services and members of his family, the applicant sought disclosure records, transactions and memoranda. Following intervention by the Information Commissioner, these were disclosed, but not the barrister's advice given to the council. The Information Tribunal upheld this non-disclosure under section 42, noting that the powerful arguments in favour of legal privilege can be outweighed exceptionally in the public interest – but not in this case.[2]
>
> **Solicitors' papers about suicide of an NHS patient: varied status.** A woman sought information in relation to the death of her son, after he had jumped from a fourth-floor window, having discharged himself from the care of an NHS Trust earlier in the day. Amongst the information sought were papers lodged with three sets of solicitors. The Trust resisted disclosure on the basis either of legal professional privilege – or that the papers held by the legal firms were not owned by, and held on behalf of, the Trust, but were owned by the solicitors – in which case, they would not come under the Freedom of Information Act at all.
>
> Of the three sets of papers, the Tribunal found that the first did not belong to the Trust, the second were covered by legal professional privilege (the Tribunal emphasised the strength and public importance of this exemption, even though it is qualified rather than absolute), and the third set of papers were not privileged (because they would have been made available to all parties at the inquest, in which case the privilege is waived), did belong to the Trust and so should be disclosed.[3]

1   Information Tribunal: *Bellamy v Information Commissioner* (2006) 27 March 2006.

2   Information Tribunal: *Kitchener v Information Commissioner and Derby City Council* (2006) 20 December 2006.

3   Information Tribunal: *Francis v Information Commissioner* (2008) 21 July 2008.

FREEDOM OF INFORMATION: EXEMPTION – PROHIBITION OF DISCLOSURE UNDER OTHER LEGISLATION. Under section 44 of the 2000 Act, there is an absolute exemption on certain grounds including prohibition by other legislation.

NHS complaint, information sought from health service ombudsman: exempt. In relation to a complaint about an NHS Trust, information was sought from the health service ombudsman who had investigated the complaint, in particular transcripts of certain interviews. However, section 15 of the Health Service Commissioners Act 1993 contains a statutory bar on disclosure by the health service ombudsman of information obtained in an investigation, except in limited situations. Thus, the Information Tribunal held that the information was exempt from disclosure under section 44 of the 2000 Act because of this prohibition in the 1993 Act.[1]

The Information Tribunal has held that this prohibition applies not just to full investigations by the health service ombudsman, but to preliminary enquiries as well.[2]

Information supplied to the health service ombudsman: not necessarily exempt after conclusion of investigation. The Tribunal has held that the exemption does not apply necessarily to the organisations that have supplied information to the ombudsman in the first place. It decided this in a case involving the attempts of a son to find out, from an NHS Trust, about the death of his mother.

> We do not think that our conclusion undermines the conduct of the Ombudsman's investigation. It is required by HSCA section 11(2) to be conducted in private, which will result, directly or indirectly, in the imposition of an obligation on those contributing information or submissions to it to maintain the confidentiality of the process and not, for example, to disclose the lines of enquiry that the Ombudsman may be pursuing or the issues she is putting to those whose actions are being investigated. It does not follow that the basic information, detached from any indication of such

---

1   Information Tribunal: *Parker v Information Commissioner and Health Service Ombudsman* (2007) 15 October 2007.

2   *Thompson v Information Commissioner* (2011). In The First-Tier Tribunal Case No. EA/2011/0164 and 0165. General Regulatory Chamber [Information Rights].

> lines of enquiries or issues, must remain secret, just because it has previously been made available to the Ombudsman as part of her investigation. And, once a report has been issued (or the Ombudsman has decided not to pursue an investigation – as she had done in this case, before the information request had been refused), the privacy of the investigation also falls away.[1]

FREEDOM OF INFORMATION: EXEMPTION – VEXATIOUS REQUESTS.

Under section 14 of the Freedom of Information Act 2000, a public body does not have to comply with a vexatious request. Guidance from the Information Commissioner refers to the key question as being whether the request is likely to cause unjustified distress, disruption or irritation. In addition:

- Could the request fairly be seen as obsessive?

- Is the request harassing the authority or causing distress to staff?

- Would complying with the request impose a significant burden in terms of expense and distraction?

- Is the request designed to cause disruption or annoyance?

- Does the request lack any serious purpose or value?[2]

Some of the examples below illustrate clearly vexatious pursuit of local authorities, NHS or other public bodies. However, on some occasions public bodies are capable of cover-up and obstruction – meaning that now and again the apparently vexatious application for information might be well founded in terms of justifiable persistence.

> **Vexatious request about a social services care plan.** An Age Concern volunteer obsessively pursued information about a woman's care plan drawn up by a local authority and the charges she had paid for that care. The Information Commissioner held that the local authority had correctly

---

1   *Cubells v Information Commissioner* (2012). In The First-Tier Tribunal Case No. EA/2011/0183. General Regulatory Chamber [Information Rights].

2   Information Commissioner's Office. *When can a request be considered vexatious or repeated?* London: ICO, 2012, p.1.

refused on grounds of vexatiousness.[1] The Information Tribunal upheld the decision but gave a few pointers about vexatiousness.

The woman had been overcharged, but this was then rectified. However, the volunteer believed that there were further irregularities. Overall, he went on to write to the local authority 73 letters and 17 postcards and made 20 freedom of information requests. The allegations were investigated by an independent complaints investigator and the Commission for Social Care Inspection; the volunteer did not believe the veracity of these investigations. The police had also advised Age Concern that there was no evidence of dishonesty. At this point, the Tribunal noted, the volunteer should have let the matter drop.

However, the Tribunal did caution against over-simple application of the Information Commissioner's guidance on vexatiousness. For example, the Tribunal could imagine circumstances in which a request creates a significant burden and indeed harasses a public body, but nonetheless could have a serious and proper purpose and so should not be considered vexatious.[2]

Death of wife in hospital: 56 requests for information. A man's wife died at a hospital. He subsequently made 56 requests for information under the Freedom of Information Act. Both the Information Commissioner and the Information Tribunal found in the NHS Trust's favour that the request under consideration was vexatious. The Commissioner stated it was not unreasonable that a member of the family should want to know more about the surrounding circumstances, and, where applicable, to hold an authority to account. However, there must be a limit to such enquiries. Since July 2006, the Trust had fielded 56 separate requests from the appellant.[3]

Seeking correspondence between NHS Trust and coroner: not vexatious. An NHS Trust (which garnered notoriety in 2007 following scores of deaths from infection) wrongly dismissed as vexatious an information request concerning correspondence between the Trust and the coroner, about the death of the man's wife. The man had to make a significant number of requests, partly because the Trust's responses were confusing.

---

1   Information Commissioner Decision: *Norfolk County Council* (2007) 7 November 2007.

2   Information Tribunal: *Coggins v Information Commissioner* (2008) 13 May 2008.

3   *Rigby v Information Commissioner*. In The First-Tier Tribunal Case No. EA/2009/0103. General Regulatory Chamber [Information Rights].

The Information Commissioner held that the requests were not vexatious. However, the particular request for which the Trust had wrongly argued section 14 was in relation to the coroner's report; by virtue of section 32 of the Act (documents held by the public body deriving from a court or inquiry), such disclosure was exempt.[1]

1   Information Commissioner Decision: *Maidstone and Tunbridge Wells NHS Trust* (2007) 19 April 2007.

G

General Medical Council

The General Medical Council (GMC) regulates medical doctors under the Medical Act 1983. The particular relevance to safeguarding is that the GMC's guidance makes two key points: first, that doctors should treat patients with dignity, treat each patient as an individual and support patients; second, that doctors should raise concerns if patients are at risk:

- **Raising concerns.** 'You must promote and encourage a culture that allows all staff to raise concerns openly and safely. You must take prompt action if you think that patient safety, dignity or comfort is or may be seriously compromised:

  » If a patient is not receiving basic care to meet their needs, you must immediately tell someone who is in a position to act straight away.

  » If patients are at risk because of inadequate premises, equipment or other resources, policies or systems, you should put the matter right if that is possible. You must raise your concern in line with our guidance and your workplace policy. You should also make a record of the steps you have taken.

  » If you have concerns that a colleague may not be fit to practise and may be putting patients at risk, you must ask for advice from a colleague, your defence body or us. If you are still concerned you must report this, in line with our guidance and your workplace policy, and make a record of the steps you have taken.'[1]

---

1   General Medical Council. *Good medical practice*. London: GMC, 2006, pp.9, 11.

GENERAL MEDICAL COUNCIL: DOCTORS RAISING CONCERNS. Such is the concern that medical doctors are not speaking out about poor or neglectful care that the General Medical Council issued further guidance in 2012.

It emphasises, bluntly, that doctors have a professional duty to put patients' interests first, even if they are anxious that by speaking out 'nothing will be done or that raising your concern may cause problems for colleagues; have a negative effect on working relationships; have a negative effect on your career; or result in a complaint about you'. The guidance states that the protection of patients overrides personal and professional loyalties, and that the law protects those who raise genuine concerns.[1]

GENERAL MEDICAL COUNCIL: DEALING WITH RETALIATORY REFERRALS. The GMC itself has had a problem in how it identifies and responds to retaliatory referrals to it – by employers who are victimising whistleblowers – with the consequence that the GMC has been at risk of victimising the very doctors it has encouraged, in its guidance, to raise concerns.[2] See *Whistleblowing*.

Gifts

A 'gift' is sometimes at the centre of safeguarding concerns. Made without mental capacity, a gift might be invalid and be 'voidable' and therefore capable of being set aside in civil law.[3] Likewise, a gift made with mental capacity, but subject to undue influence, can be set aside in civil law: see *Undue influence*. In addition, an apparent gift made with mental capacity to make it, if associated with dishonesty, could amount to a criminal offence –

---

1   General Medical Council. *Raising and acting on concerns about patient safety*. London: GMC, 2012, paras 7–10.

2   Hooper, A. *The handling by the General Medical Council of cases involving whistleblowers*. London: GMC, 2015.

3   *Special Trustees of Great Ormond Street Hospital v Rushin* (2000) WL 1151387, para 175.

for example, theft, with the dishonesty made out in terms of blatant, undue influence: see *Theft*.[1]

Grievous bodily harm

Unlawful and malicious wounding, or infliction of any grievous bodily harm, come under section 20 of the Offences Against the Person Act 1861. There is a maximum of five years' imprisonment.

Grievous bodily harm is serious bodily harm including, for example, injury resulting in permanent disability or permanent loss of sensory function, more than minor, permanent, visible disfigurement, broken bones, compound fractures, substantial loss of blood, injuries resulting in lengthy treatment or incapacity, psychiatric injury. Wounding covers more serious cuts or lacerations. Section 18 of the Act contains a similar offence, but there must also be intent to cause wounding or grievous bodily harm.[2]

Targeting of elderly, vulnerable couple: grievous bodily harm. The offender had been smoking crack cocaine at a house near to where the victims, an elderly couple, lived. Later that night, he broke into their house to steal money. He attacked the man, hit him, jumped on him and used his keys as a knuckle duster, pushing him down the stairs. He kicked and punched the wife. He stole £80. The victims were taken to hospital for multiple bruising and abrasions.

The woman was placed in a care home where, several days later, she fell off a commode, hit her head and consequently died. The court wished to make clear that 'those who select elderly or otherwise vulnerable people as victims and then invade their homes in search of gain will receive very severe sentences indeed'. A sentence of 12 years was given.[3]

---

1   *R v Hinks* (2001) 2 AC 241 (House of Lords).

2   Crown Prosecution Service. *Offences against the person, incorporating the charging standard.* London: CPS, undated.

3   *R v Marcus* [2003] EWCA Crim 2005.

Guidance (Care Act)

Statutory guidance has been issued under the Care Act 2014, including a chapter on safeguarding.[1] Local authorities must act under it when performing functions under the Act.[2] This duty applies to local authorities only. However, more specifically, the Care Act states that other members of a safeguarding adults board must, in that capacity, have regard to such guidance as the Secretary of State may issue.[3]

The guidance is called statutory, which means that, although it is not law, it should normally be followed when it is expressed in mandatory terms (i.e. 'must'). If it is departed from, there should be strong reasons.[4]

---

1   Department of Health. *Care and support statutory guidance*. London: DH, 2016, chapter 14.

2   Care Act 2014, s.78.

3   Care Act 2014, schedule 2.

4   *R (Rixon) v Islington London Borough Council* [1997] ELR 66, pp.2–3.

Harassment, alarm or distress

Various law, criminal and civil, applies to the causing of harassment, alarm or distress. The following list is a summary:

- **Harassment (criminal offence): Protection from Harassment Act 1997 (criminal offence).** Under section 2 of this Act, it is a criminal offence for a person to pursue a course of conduct that causes harassment, alarm or distress. Course of conduct means conduct on at least two occasions.

- **Harassment (civil remedy): Protection from Harassment Act 1997 (civil law).** Under section 3 of this Act, damages can be awarded in a civil legal case for (amongst other things) any anxiety caused by the harassment and any financial loss resulting from the harassment. If a court grants an injunction restraining a defendant from pursuing a course of conduct amounting to harassment, the victim can apply for an arrest warrant to be issued if the order has been allegedly breached. If it has been, without reasonable excuse, it is an offence.

- **Stalking: Protection from Harassment Act 1997 (criminal offence).** Under section 2A of this Act, it is a criminal offence if a person pursues a course of conduct amounting to harassment – and the conduct amounts to stalking.

  Examples of stalking given in section 2A are (a) following a person, (b) contacting, or attempting to contact, a person by any means, (c) publishing any statement or other material (i) relating or purporting to relate to a person, or (ii) purporting to originate from a person, (d) monitoring the use by a person of the internet, email or any other form of electronic communication, (e) loitering in any place (whether public or private), (f) interfering with any property in the possession of a person, (g) watching or spying on a person.

Under section 4A of the Act, there is a separate offence if the stalking involves fear of violence or serious alarm or distress.

- **Fear of violence: Protection from Harassment Act 1997 (criminal offence).** Under section 4 of this Act, it is a criminal offence if a person pursues a course of conduct that causes another person to fear – on at least two occasions – that violence will be used against him or her, and if the person knows or ought to know that his or her course of conduct will cause that fear.

- **Restraining orders: Protection from Harassment Act 1997 (restraining order following conviction or prosecution).** Under section 5 of this Act, on a person's conviction, a court can make a restraining order, containing prohibitions, in order to protect a victim from conduct amounting to harassment or which will cause fear of violence. Under section 5A, a restraining order can also be made even on acquittal.

- **Racial or religious motivation: Protection from Harassment Act 1997 (criminal offence).** A separate, and additional, criminal offence applies if a person has committed the offence of harassment, stalking or putting in fear of violence under the 1997 Act which was racially or religiously aggravated. This is under section 32 of the Crime and Disorder Act 1998.

- **Fear or provocation of violence: Public Order Act 1986, section 4 (criminal offence).** Using threatening, abusive or insulting words or behaviour, or displaying or distributing threatening, abusive or insulting writing, signs or other visible representation, intending to cause the victim to fear immediate unlawful violence against them or another, to provoke such violence – or where it is likely that a person will believe that such violence will be used, or where it is likely that such violence will be provoked.

This offence does not apply if the people involved are all in a dwelling, not necessarily the same one. On summary conviction, the maximum sentence is six months in prison or a level 5 fine or both.

- **Intentional harassment, alarm or distress: Public Order Act 1986, section 4A (criminal offence).** Using threatening, abusive or insulting words or behaviour, or displaying or distributing threatening, abusive or insulting writing, signs or other visible representation, with the intention of causing a person harassment, alarm or distress – and actually causing this to that person or another person.

This offence does not apply if the people involved are all in a dwelling, not necessarily the same one. It is a defence if the accused person can prove that he or she had no reason to believe anybody else would hear or see the words, behaviour, etc., and that his or her conduct was reasonable. On summary conviction, the maximum sentence is six months in prison or a level 5 fine or both.

- **Harassment, alarm or distress: Public Order Act 1986, section 5 (criminal offence).** Using threatening, abusive or insulting words or behaviour, or distributing or displaying writing, signs or other visible representations that are threatening, abusive or insulting, within the hearing or sight of a person likely to be caused harassment, alarm or distress by this conduct. This offence does not apply if the people involved are all in a dwelling, not necessarily the same one.

  It is a defence if the accused person can prove that he or she had no reason to believe that anybody else would hear or see the words or behaviour, or that anybody in hearing or sight was likely to be caused harassment, alarm or distress, and that his or her conduct was reasonable. On summary conviction, the maximum sentence is six months in prison or a level 5 fine or both.

- **Sending a message electronically: Communications Act 2003 (criminal offence).** It is a criminal offence to send, or cause to be sent, a message or other matter that is indecent, obscene, of menacing character or grossly offensive. It is also an offence if a person – for the purpose of causing annoyance, inconvenience or needless anxiety – causes a message to be sent or makes persistent use of a public electronic communications network or sends a message which he or she knows to be false.

- **Eliminating harassment against disabled people: Equality Act 2010 (civil law).** Under section 149 of this Act, public bodies have a duty to have due regard to the need to eliminate harassment against disabled people.

Harm, see *Enquiries*

Hate crime, see *Crown Prosecution Service: aggravating features*

Health and Care Professions Council (HCPC)

The Health and Care Professions Council (HCPC) regulates various health professionals including art therapists, biomedical scientists, chiropodists and podiatrists, clinical scientists, dieticians, hearing-aid dispensers, occupational therapists, operating department practitioners, orthoptists, paramedics, physiotherapists, practitioner psychologists, prosthetists and orthotists, radiographers, and speech and language therapists.[1]

From August 2012, it has also regulated social workers. This came about when the General Social Care Council was abolished, and the register of social workers was transferred to the Health Professions Council – which, in turn, changed its name to become the Health and Care Professions Council.[2]

HCPC: RESPECT AND DIGNITY. The standards of conduct state:

- You must treat service users and carers with respect and dignity.

HCPC: RAISING CONCERNS. The standards of conduct state:

- You must report any concerns about the safety or well-being of service users promptly and appropriately.

- You must support and encourage others to report concerns and not prevent anyone from raising concerns.

- You must take appropriate action if you have concerns about the safety or well-being of children or vulnerable adults.

- You must make sure that the safety and well-being of service users always comes before any professional or other loyalties.

- You must follow up concerns you have reported and, if necessary, escalate them.

---

1   SI 2002/254. Health and Social Work Professions Order 2001.

2   SI 2012/1479. The Health and Social Care Act 2012 (Consequential Provision – Social Workers) Order 2012.

- You must acknowledge and act on concerns raised to you, investigating, escalating or dealing with those concerns where it is appropriate for you to do so.

Professionals sometimes face the dilemma of adhering to their professional code by raising concerns, but then experiencing victimisation as a perceived whistleblower: see **Whistleblowing**. A failure to raise a concern could lead to sanctions being imposed by the HCPC:

Social worker's professional obligation to report harm suffered by child. A social worker became aware that a colleague was having a sexual relationship with a 14-year-old girl. He had sufficient opportunity to report the 'inappropriate and illegal' relationship, had failed to do so and had only cooperated in providing information when challenged. He was found guilty of misconduct for failing to report the matter and was suspended from the register for a year.[1]

HCPC: HARMING PATIENTS. If professionals fail to adhere to the code of standards, by harming patients or otherwise acting unprofessionally, the HCPC will apply sanctions. Examples particularly relevant to the safeguarding of adults include:

Sexual activity with a service user: striking off and prison. A social worker engaged in sexual intercourse with a service user suffering from depression. This had created a significant imbalance of power between them. He was removed from the register. His appeal to the Care Standards Tribunal against the order failed.[2] He was also convicted under the Sexual Offences Act 2003 and sent to prison.[3]

---

1   *General Social Care Council v Bester*, GSCC Conduct hearing, January 2010.

2   *Bradford v General Social Care Council* [2006] 792 SW-SUS.

3   Gillen, S. 'DNA evidence convicted social worker of sex with client.' *Community Care*, 18 September 2007.

Health and Safety Executive

In some circumstances, health and safety at work legislation is relevant to safeguarding adults. The Health and Safety Executive (HSE) prosecutes offences committed under the Health and Safety at Work Act 1974. It normally prosecutes organisations but can also prosecute individuals. Various duties are contained within the 1974 Act:

- **Duty to non-employees.** Under section 3, there is a duty on the employer to conduct its undertaking in such a way as to ensure, so far as is reasonably practicable, that non-employees who may be affected are not exposed to risks to their health and safety. In addition, under regulation 3 of the Management of Health and Safety at Work Regulations 1999, there is a duty to carry out a suitable and sufficient assessment of the risks to the health and safety of non-employees arising from, or connected with, the employer's undertaking.

- **Duty of employees towards other people.** Under section 7, individual employees have a duty to take reasonable care of their own health and safety and also that of other people who may be affected by the employee's acts or failure to act.

- **Director or manager: consent, connivance, neglect.** Under section 37 of the 1974 Act, if an offence – such as under section 3 – is committed by the organisation, a director or manager will also be guilty individually if it is proved that the offence was committed with their consent, connivance or neglect.

HEALTH AND SAFETY EXECUTIVE: SAFEGUARDING ADULTS. A failure in a system of work, resulting in neglect or abuse of vulnerable adults, could in principle lead to an HSE prosecution, as in the following case, when section 3 of the Health and Safety at Work Act 1974 was used to prosecute both the company that ran and individual managers of a care home for failing to investigate and prevent a sustained regime of physical abuse.

> **Systemic abuse of people with disabilities in care home: HSE prosecution.**
> People with physical and learning disabilities living in a care home in Hull had been subject to a regime of sustained abuse for three years. This included humiliation, rough behaviour, force-feeding, shouting, slapping,

hair pulling, swearing and dragging residents across the floor. Most of the residents had a mental age of less than two years. Seven carers were sent to prison under section 127 of the Mental Health Act 1983, for ill-treatment and neglect.

In addition, however, under the Health and Safety at Work Act 1974, the company was prosecuted and fined £100,000 together with £25,000 costs. It pleaded guilty to failing to take appropriate action to investigate and prevent the ill-treatment of vulnerable adults.

Separately, five senior managers were also prosecuted for failing to protect residents from this ill-treatment; they had failed to act on reports of abuse. They were fined sums ranging from £4000 down to £360.[1]

Neglect or omission, more generally, may provoke a prosecution under section 3 of the 1974 Act.

Bed rails: death and failure in system of work. A local authority pleaded guilty in relation to the death in a care home of a 23-year-old man, who was quadriplegic and suffered from cerebral palsy. He was asphyxiated as a result of the failure to make sure the bed rails were maintained in effective working order and good repair, and to ensure staff were properly trained in fitting, maintaining and using the bed rails.[2]

Neglect and abuse in care home: HSE prosecution. A couple who ran a private residential home were convicted not only of ill-treatment and wilful neglect (under section 127 of the Mental Health Act 1983) but also of breach of the Health and Safety Work Act 1974.[3] The judge found they had abused their position of trust and created a regime that centred on oppressive conduct and punishment; residents were repeatedly bullied, underfed (one man lost four stone) and given inappropriate medicines.[4]

---

1   Mark, D. 'Care home firm which failed to act on abuse claims is fined £100,000.' *Yorkshire Post*, 28 October 2005.

2   'Council admits safety breaches over man's care home death.' *Walesonline*, 23 November 2007. Accessed on 26 November 2018 at: https://www.walesonline.co.uk/news/wales-news/council-admits-safety-breaches-over-2219954.

3   'Care home pair guilty of neglect.' *BBC News*, 26 April 2004. Accessed on 3 October 2018 at: http://news.bbc.co.uk/1/hi/england/norfolk/3660605.stm.

4   'We just want to clear our names.' *Norwich Evening News*, 26 May 2006.

Yet there have been notable instances of larger-scale failings in the system of work, which the HSE investigated but took no action.

Maidstone and Tunbridge Wells NHS Trust: 90 deaths, no HSE action. Systemic failures in the system of care resulted in 90 avoidable hospital deaths at Maidstone and Tunbridge Wells NHS Trust.[1] A report by the Healthcare Commission revealed gross failings in the system of care and hygiene. The HSE declined to act.[2] Given the strength of the Commission's report, this appeared to be a highly questionable decision.[3]

Stoke Mandeville NHS Trust: widespread infection, and avoidable deaths. A similar scandal at Stoke Mandeville Hospital resulted in nearly 40 avoidable deaths, and the infection of hundreds of others – again due to failures in the system of work, including prioritising targets and finances over patient safety, life and death.[4] Again, a referral was made to the HSE, again no significant action was taken and, again, on doubtful grounds.[5]

Mid Staffordshire NHS Foundation Trust. Widespread poor care and neglect – systemic in nature – was uncovered at Stafford Hospital, primarily through both an independent inquiry and a public inquiry.[6] Many hundreds of people are estimated to have died. The HSE was criticised in the public inquiry for its inaction.[7] It did, eventually, prosecute and secure a

1   Healthcare Commission. *Investigation into outbreaks of* Clostridium difficile *at Maidstone and Tunbridge Wells NHS Trust, October 2007.* London: HC, 2007.

2   Hawkes, N. 'No one to be prosecuted over 90 C *difficile* deaths at Kent hospitals.' *The Times,* 30 July 2008.

3   Moore, A. (2008) 'Trusts warned C diff probe decision sets no precedent.' *Health Service Journal,* 7 August 2008.

4   Healthcare Commission. *Investigation into outbreaks of* Clostridium difficile *at Stoke Mandeville Hospital, Buckinghamshire Hospitals NHS Trust, July 2006.* London: HC, 2006.

5   Health and Safety Executive. *HSE investigation into outbreaks* of Clostridium difficile *at Stoke Mandeville Hospital, Buckinghamshire Hospitals NHS Trust.* London: HSE, 2006.

6   Francis, R. (Chair). *Independent Inquiry into care provided by Mid Staffordshire NHS Foundation Trust January 2005–March 2009.* London: The Stationery Office, 2010.

7   Francis, R. (Chair). *Report of the Mid Staffordshire NHS Foundation Trust Public Inquiry.* Executive Summary and three volumes. HC 898. London: The Stationery Office, 2013.

conviction in the case of one woman who died, in relation to her medication for diabetes.[1]

Such examples appear to contrast starkly with the HSE's greater willingness to prosecute in less serious instances in health and social care – for example, a single hospital patient dying from asphyxiation caught in bed rails, or from a lack of supervision of a person with epilepsy bathing – resulting in his death[2] – or preparedness to prosecute in more serious cases, but outside of health and social care – as when shortcuts taken in the maintenance of an air-conditioning system led to an outbreak of Legionnaire's disease and to five deaths and 172 infected people.[3]

Health and Social Care Act 2008 (Regulated Activities) Regulations 2014, see *Care Quality Commission*

Health and Social Work Professions Order 2001, see *Health and Care Professions Council*

Health providers

Health providers in England must be registered with the Care Quality Commission (CQC), which applies a set of regulations setting out fundamental standards – including a duty to safeguard service users from abuse and improper treatment.[4] See ***Care Quality Commission***.

---

1   'Stafford hospital to be sentenced over poor care of diabetic patient who died.' *The Guardian*, 21 February 2014.

2   Farmer, B. 'Basildon University Hospital trust fined £50,000 over patient's death.' *The Independent*, 8 June 2010. Also: Grubb, S. 'Justice for LB victory as Southern Health NHS Foundation Trust fined over Connor Sparrowhawk's death.' *Oxford Times*, 26 March 2018.

3   Hogg, D. 'Architect fined over deadly outbreak of disease.' *Yorkshire Post*, 1 August 2006.

4   SI 2014/2936. Health and Social Care Act (Regulated Activities) Regulations 2014.

Health Service Ombudsman (HSO)

Under the Health Service Commissioners Act 1993, the Health Service Ombudsman (HSO) investigates complaints against the NHS. Normally, the complainant must first have used the NHS body's own complaints procedure. The ombudsman's remit extends to complaints about NHS-funded healthcare services provided in a private hospital and to complaints about any NHS-funded healthcare services for privately funded patients in an NHS hospital.

HSO: MALADMINISTRATION, FAILURE IN SERVICE. The ombudsman looks for hardship or injustice resulting from maladministration, failure in a service that has been provided or failure to provide a service which it was a function, of the NHS body concerned, to provide. The ombudsman can question clinical judgements. With increased joint working and integration within health and social care, the health service ombudsman can also investigate jointly with the local government ombudsman.[1]

Health Service Ombudsman: lack of care and compassion in hospitals. This report by the ombudsman drew on ten complaints from the many hundreds received annually about elderly care and is unequivocal about the failure of the NHS to provide dignity, compassion and basic care.

The report acknowledged the question of extra resources required in hospitals but stresses the dismissive attitude and indifference of staff. It then describes neglect, including tongues like dried leather, nutrition and hydration ignored, patients squealing with unmanaged pain, pressure sores thriving, call bells out of reach, lack of cleanliness and comfort, multiple unrecorded falls, bathing or showering unavailable, weeping wounds not dressed and an absence of patient monitoring.[2]

Rough handling on hospital ward: safeguarding matter. An elderly woman was admitted to hospital for repair of a fractured hip. She told

---

1   Health Service Commissioners Act 1993, ss.2A, 2B, 3, 18ZA.

2   Parliamentary and Health Service Ombudsman. *Care and compassion? Report of the Health Service Ombudsman on ten investigations into NHS care of older people*. HC 778. London: The Stationery Office, 2011.

her daughter that on Christmas Day a member of the night staff treated her roughly when attending to her because of vomiting and diarrhoea. Now she was frightened. The daughter made an oral complaint. The ward manager investigated and interviewed the staff member but did not tell the daughter of the result of the investigation. The daughter then made a formal complaint; the Trust apologised for not telling the mother and daughter the outcome of the investigation.

The Health Service Ombudsman found that the Trust's complaints procedures and documentation were deficient, and that the Trust had failed to realise that the mother and daughter viewed the incident as an assault. As such, the Trust had not responded sufficiently robustly, and needed to review its complaints policy in the light of the Department of Health's guidance on safeguarding.[1]

No policy or care plan for restraint leading to harm. An elderly man in hospital had chronic obstructive airways disease and peripheral vascular disease, and had suffered a stroke that left him with right-sided weakness. Previously, whilst at home, he had displayed signs of irritability and frustration, and verbal and physical aggression towards his wife. He was admitted to hospital for respite care for social reasons, since he could not cope whilst his wife, his main carer, herself required hospital treatment. He became disturbed during the night, after going to the day room to use his nebuliser. Nursing staff restrained him. When his daughter visited, she found that he had an injured arm, carpet burns on his face and a cut on his hand.

The Health Service Ombudsman found that the NHS Trust had no policy on control and restraint and, in that respect, there was no particular plan for this particular patient. This latter failing was made worse by the fact that there had been a previous incident of restraint a few nights earlier involving the same patient. The ombudsman severely criticised the lack of planning and training which led to a disabled, elderly man being restrained in such a way.[2]

---

1   *Warrington Hospital NHS Trust 2001* (E.1846/99–00 in HSO 2001).

2   *Oldham NHS Trust 1999* (E.1780/97–98). Published in: Health Service Ombudsman. HC 497. *Investigations completed October 1998–March 1999.* London: The Stationery Office, 1999.

Hitting, see *Assault; Ill-treatment*

Honour-based crime

Guidance from the Crown Prosecution Service explains that there is no specific offence of 'honour-based crime', which is an umbrella term to encompass various offences covered by existing legislation. Honour-based violence is a collection of practices used to control behaviour within families or other social groups to protect perceived cultural and religious beliefs and/or honour.[1] Prosecution, therefore, would be for the specific offence such as common assault, grievous bodily harm, harassment, kidnap, rape, threats to kill, murder.[2]

Hospital discharge

Pressures on acute hospitals have, over many years, led sometimes to poor practice in the discharge of vulnerable patients. The pressures show no signs of relenting. There are various factors at play, including an ageing population with increasingly complex needs, closure of tens of thousands of hospital beds from 2000 onward without adequately funded health alternatives in the community, pressures on social care – and so on.

Poor hospital discharge practices are nothing new. Hence, over 20 pieces of guidance about good practice were issued in the ten years up to 2015.[3] The reason for so much guidance is precisely that too many people continue to suffer serious physical, psychological and emotional harm because of poor practice.

Furthermore, it appears that NHS bodies and local authorities are hesitant in regarding poor hospital discharges as anything to do with safeguarding, even though discharge practices would clearly fall under the definition of

---

1   Crown Prosecution Service. *Honour based violence and forced marriage.* London: CPS, undated.

2   Crown Prosecution Service. *Honour based violence and forced marriage: guidance on identifying and flagging cases.* London: CPS, undated.

3   Healthwatch England. *Safely home: what happens when people leave hospital and care settings?* London: HWE, 2015, p.8.

(organisational) neglect provided in Care Act guidance, including ignoring medical, emotional or physical care needs and failure to provide access to appropriate health, care and support services – especially since this same guidance points out that neglect does not have to be intentional.[1] Characteristically, poor discharges may come in the form of:

- being sent home to die without adequate support, causing unnecessary pain and distress

- waiting all day in the discharge lounge to be transported home, becoming distressed and disorientated (e.g. in cases of dementia)

- unplanned discharges in the middle of the night

- absence of communication with families, social care services and care agencies

- absence of care, food, necessary equipment on arrival at home

- being discharged in a dirty, unclothed state

- being discharged malnourished and dehydrated.

The situation shows little sign of alleviation as reports continue to paint a disturbing picture – for example, Healthwatch England,[2] the Health Service Ombudsman[3] and Parliamentary Committees.[4]

> **Hospital discharge report: Health Service Ombudsman.**
>
> This report focuses on nine experiences drawn from recent complaints we have investigated, which best illustrate the problems we are seeing. The people that have come to us have been badly let down by the system. How else do we describe the actions of a hospital sending a vulnerable 85-year-old woman with dementia

---

1   Department of Health. *Care and support statutory guidance*. London: DH, 2016, paras 14.14, 14.40.

2   Healthwatch England. *What happens when people leave hospital and other care settings?* London: HWE, 2015.

3   Health Service Ombudsman. *A report of investigations into unsafe discharge from hospital*. London: HSO, 2016.

4   House of Commons Public Administration and Constitutional Affairs Committee. *Follow-up to PHSO report on unsafe discharge from hospital*. London: The Stationery Office, 2016.

home without telling her family, despite being unable to feed herself or go to the bathroom? How else do we describe the tragic story of a woman in her late 90s who was discharged without a proper examination, to then die in her granddaughter's arms moments after the ambulance dropped her home?

People told us how their loved one's traumatic experience of leaving hospital, including repeated emergency readmissions, added to their pain and grief. One woman captured the sentiment of many, saying she would be 'haunted for the rest of her life' by her mother's avoidable suffering before her death.[1]

Another type of report – perhaps not so helpful to the cause of safeguarding – is that which emphasises financial aspects (and incentives) and therefore, potentially, even quicker and more ruthless discharge of (often older) patients.[2] Or reports which reduce hospital activity, including hospital discharge, to questions of 'operational productivity and performance',[3] inviting parallels with an industrial process of moving inanimate components and goods.

Human rights

The European Convention on Human Rights is integrated with United Kingdom law by the Human Rights Act 1998. Human rights law applies to public bodies and other bodies carrying out functions of a public nature. Key rights for the purpose of this book relate to the right to life, inhuman and degrading treatment, deprivation of liberty and the right to respect for private and family life – articles 2, 3, 5 and 8 respectively.

The overall importance to adult safeguarding of the Human Rights Act 1998 is perhaps threefold in terms of how the Act may be breached: first, if public bodies themselves inflict explicit physical abuse or neglect of people; second, if they intervene in people's lives unlawfully and disproportionately

---

1   Health Service Ombudsman. *A report of investigations into unsafe discharge from hospital.* London: HSO, 2016, p.2.

2   National Audit Office. *Discharging older patients from hospital.* London: NAO, 2016.

3   Lord Carter. *Operational productivity and performance in English NHS acute hospitals: unwarranted variations.* London: Department of Health, 2016.

– for instance, depriving people of their liberty without justification; third, if they fail to intervene to protect people from being abused or neglected by other people – for example, independent care providers or, perhaps, private individuals.

HUMAN RIGHTS: INDEPENDENT CARE PROVIDERS. The courts have held in the past that independent care providers are neither public bodies nor, in the main, bodies carrying out functions of a public nature[1] – meaning they would not have human rights obligations.

For adult social care, section 73 of the Care Act 2014 modifies this. It states that a registered care provider exercises functions of a public nature – but only if a local authority has arranged, or paid for directly or indirectly, the care and support (under sections 2, 18, 19, 20, 38 and 48 of the Care Act). 'Indirectly' means that use of a direct payment made to the service user, for the latter to contract with a provider, is included in this rule.

However, if an individual themselves arranges care, on a self-funding basis, from a care agency or care home, the Human Rights Act would not apply directly to the care provider.

It would seem therefore that, in general, a private hospital or nursing home, treating and caring for NHS patients under contract to the NHS, may not be subject to the Human Rights Act 1998. Of course, the commissioning NHS body would be. (However, a private hospital, treating a detained patient under the Mental Health Act 1983, is carrying out functions of a public nature.)[2]

HUMAN RIGHTS: SAFEGUARDING. The Parliamentary Joint Committee on Human Rights drew attention to a wide range of concerns about the poor treatment of older people in health care, much of it in the context of care and treatment directly provided or commissioned by the NHS. The Committee linked aspects of this poor treatment to particular rights under the European Convention. There appears to be a close correlation between this list and

1   *YL v Birmingham City Council* [2007] UKHL 27, House of Lords.

2   *R v Partnerships in Care Ltd, ex p A* [2002] EWHC Admin 529.

what could constitute abuse or neglect, for the purpose of safeguarding. The list set out by the Committee included:

- malnutrition and dehydration (articles 2, 3, 8)

- abuse and rough treatment (articles 3, 8)

- lack of privacy in mixed-sex wards (article 8)

- lapses in confidentiality (article 8)

- neglect and poor hygiene (articles 3, 8)

- inappropriate medication and physical restraint (article 8)

- inadequate assessment of a person's needs (articles 2, 3, 8)

- over-hasty discharge from hospital (article 8)

- bullying and patronising attitudes (articles 3, 8)

- discrimination on basis of age, disability or race (article 14)

- communication difficulties, particularly for people with dementia (articles 8, 14)

- fear of making complaints (article 8)

- eviction from care homes (article 8).[1]

HUMAN RIGHTS: RIGHT TO LIFE. Article 2 of the European Convention states that everyone's right to life shall be protected by law. It applies sometimes in health and social care, requiring – procedurally – an independent investigation into some deaths, which may involve breach of human rights with the State implicated.[2]

For example, it was only the threat of a legal challenge under article 2, by the relatives' organisation Cure the NHS, that led the government in 2009

---

1   Joint Committee on Human Rights (House of Lords and House of Commons). *The human rights of older people in healthcare.* London: The Stationery Office, 2007.

2   *R (Middleton) v West Somerset Coroner* [2004] UKHL 10.

to appoint an independent inquiry into events at Stafford Hospital, where hundreds of patients had died.[1]

In a 2008 case, the European Court of Human Rights considered the adequacy of legal remedies, both available and used, in a case involving the disappearance of a person with dementia from a nursing home – and emphasised the importance not only of the existence of relevant civil and criminal law, but also of its actually being used.

Disappearance of man's mother from nursing home: human organ gang possibly involved. The European Court stated that there was an obligation by the State to 'make regulations compelling hospitals, whether public or private, to adopt appropriate measures for the protection of their patients' lives and to set up an effective independent judicial system so that the cause of death of patients in the care of the medical profession, whether in the public or private sector, can be determined and those responsible made accountable'.

Following the disappearance and death (presumed, since she was never found) of a woman with Alzheimer's from a nursing home, the European Court interpreted the above requirement broadly and as applicable to the circumstances. Her son suspected abduction by a criminal gang trading in human organs. Although legal remedies – disciplinary, civil and criminal – were in principle available, in practice they had not been used to 'secure an effective possibility to establish the facts surrounding the disappearance'.[2]

HUMAN RIGHTS: INHUMAN AND DEGRADING TREATMENT. Article 3 of the Convention states that no one shall be subjected to torture or to inhuman or degrading treatment or punishment.

The courts have held that ill-treatment must reach a minimum level of severity and involve actual bodily injury or intense physical or mental suffering.

Degrading treatment would occur if it 'humiliates or debases an individual showing a lack of respect for, or diminishing, his or her human

---

1   Leigh Day & Co. 'Judicial reviews and the Mid Staffordshire inquiries.' *News*, 12 May 2010. Accessed on 14 July 2017 at: www.leighday.co.uk/Human-rights-and-public-law/Health-social-care/Human-rights-in-healthcare/Mid-Staffordshire-Inquiry/Judicial-reviews-and-the-Mid-Staffordshire-inquiri.

2   *Dodov v Bulgaria* [2008] European Court of Human Rights, case no. 59548/00.

dignity or arouses feelings of fear, anguish or inferiority capable of breaking an individual's moral and physical resistance'.[1]

A breach of article 3 is primarily about public bodies perpetrating abusive care or treatment – that is, doing something they should not have.

Degrading treatment of severely disabled woman in police cell. A severely physically disabled person had been sent to prison for contempt of court. She had failed to disclose her assets in a debt case. In the police cell she was unable to use the bed and had to sleep in her wheelchair where she became very cold. When she reached the prison hospital, she could not use the toilet herself, the female duty officer could not manage to move her alone, and male prison officers had to assist. The European Court concluded that to detain a severely disabled person – in conditions where she is dangerously cold, risks developing pressure sores because her bed is too hard or unreachable, and is unable to go to the toilet or keep clean without the greatest difficulty – constituted degrading treatment contrary to article 3. Damages of £4500 were awarded.[2]

Group legal cases in respect of Stafford Hospital: article 3 basis for settling. Legal cases were settled out of court with the Mid Staffordshire NHS Foundation Trust, on both article 3 grounds and in negligence.[3] This followed exposure of conditions of care at the hospital following both an independent inquiry and a public inquiry.

Worcestershire hospital: group legal case for appalling and humiliating treatment. In 2012, a group legal action was being taken against the Worcestershire Acute Hospitals NHS Trust, which runs the Alexandra and Kidderminster and Worcester hospitals. The basis of the action was appalling and humiliating treatment, including patients left dehydrated, food left out of their reach, insufficient staff and those present not seeming to care.[4] The action was settled out of court, with an apology

1   *Pretty v United Kingdom* [2002] 2 FCR 97 (European Court of Human Rights).

2   *Price v United Kingdom* [2001] Application 33394/96 (European Court of Human Rights).

3   Leigh Day & Co. 'All Stafford Hospital claims accepted.' *News*, 17 November 2010. Accessed on 12 January 2012 at: www.leighday.co.uk/News/2010/November-2010/All-Stafford-Hospital-claims-accepted.

4   Dayani, A. 'Families to sue over standards of care at Alexandra Hospital, Redditch.' *Birmingham Post*, 10 November 2011.

and compensation – but no admission of liability – in 38 separate cases amounting to a total of £410,000.[1]

Health care examples: article 3. The following examples, identified in the context of the NHS but not taken to court as human rights cases, would suggest probable breach of article 3 rights. For instance, a person with learning disabilities being restrained excessively in a wheelchair for 16 hours a day – or having his arms tied to his wheelchair eight hours daily.[2] Hospital patients being told to relieve their bowels and bladder in bed and then left for hours in wet or soiled bedding.[3] A dying man being nursed in the hospital dining room in front of other patients eating their meals.[4] And hospital patients being tied to commodes for extended periods and given their meals on them.[5]

Article 3 can also apply in 'positive' terms – that is, a public body failing to intervene – even when the abuse is perpetrated by one private individual on another.

Breach of article 3: failure to intervene in safeguarding case. Over several years, a local authority failed to protect four children from the severe neglect of their mother. This was despite overwhelming evidence given to the local authority by many different, reliable sources, about the 'horrific' experiences the children were going through. When a negligence case was brought against the local authority, the courts held there was no common law duty of care owed. However, a breach of article 3 by the local authority in this case was later established in the European Court of Human Rights.[6]

---

1   Donnelly, L. 'Hospital apologises to 38 families for appalling care that saw a patient starve to death.' *Sunday Telegraph*, 22 December 2012.

2   Healthcare Commission and Commission for Social Care Inspection. *Joint investigation into the provision of services for people with learning disabilities at Cornwall Partnership NHS Trust.* London: HC and CSCI, 2006, pp.42, 55.

3   Healthcare Commission. *Investigation into outbreaks of* Clostridium difficile *at Maidstone and Tunbridge Wells NHS Trust.* London: HC, 2007, p.4.

4   Mental Health Act Commission. *Risk, rights, recovery: twelfth biennial report, 2005–2007.* London: MHAC, 2008, p.19.

5   Commission for Health Improvement. *Investigation into the North Lakeland NHS Trust.* London: CHI, 2000, p.29.

6   *Z v United Kingdom* [2001] 2 FCR 246, ECHR, paras 74–75.

> **Failure by Crown Prosecution Service (CPS) to prosecute assault against a man with mental health problems: humiliation and a breach of article 3.** A man suffered from a history of psychotic illness, which involved paranoid beliefs and auditory and visual hallucinations. On Boxing Day, part of his ear had been bitten off. Based on a doctor's report, to the effect that his mental condition might affect his perception and recollection of events, the CPS decided to discontinue the case.
>
> The court found that the CPS had not adhered to Part 5 of the Code for Crown Prosecutors; its decision was irrational. Either it had misread the medical report or it had stereotyped the man as having mental health problems that rendered him a non-credible witness. In addition, the court held that this constituted a breach of article 3 of the Convention. This was because abandonment of the case on the eve of the trial added insult to his injury. It was a humiliation, causing him to feel like a second-class citizen. Far from protecting him against serious assaults, the criminal justice system had in fact increased his sense of vulnerability and of being beyond the protection of the law.[1]

HUMAN RIGHTS: DEPRIVATION OF LIBERTY. Article 5 of the Convention states that 'everyone has the right to liberty and security of person. No one shall be deprived of his liberty save in the following cases and in accordance with a procedure prescribed by law...'

One of the categories of people who can be deprived of their liberty is 'persons of unsound mind'. The procedures prescribed by law are contained within the Mental Capacity Act 2005 and the Mental Health Act 1983. If those procedures are not followed, a breach of article 5 will occur. See *Deprivation of liberty*.

HUMAN RIGHTS: RIGHT TO RESPECT FOR PRIVATE LIFE, FAMILY LIFE AND HOME. Article 8 of the Convention states:

- **Right.** Everyone has the right to respect for his private and family life, his home and his correspondence.

---

1   *R (B) v Director of Public Prosecutions* [2009] EWHC 106 (Admin).

- **Interference with the right.** There shall be no interference by a public authority with the exercise of this right except such as is in accordance with the law and is necessary in a democratic society in the interests of national security, public safety or the economic well-being of the country, for the prevention of disorder or crime, for the protection of health or morals, or for the protection of the rights and freedoms of others.

This means that interference with private life, family life and home is legally permissible but must be justified, within the terms of article 8. Private life has been held to include physical and psychological integrity, and therefore a notion of dignity.[1] In the safeguarding context, interventions inconsistent with the relevant law, consistent with that law but otherwise disproportionate and therefore not 'necessary', or for a purpose other than one of those listed, would mean a breach of article 8. Department of Health guidance on the Care Act alludes to this when it warns local authorities against 'abusive interventions that risk breaching the adult's right to family life if not justified or proportionate'.[2]

Deprivation of liberty and article 8. If a local authority makes an unjustified intervention in the life of a person lacking mental capacity, it might breach also article 8. For example, an unlawful deprivation of liberty under article 5 would generally entail also a breach of article 8.[3]

Privacy and confidentiality. The right to respect for private life also encompasses confidentiality, but interference with confidentiality is permitted if there is sufficient justification on the same basis: in accordance with the law, necessary and for a particular purpose (e.g. protection of health or prevention of crime). It is about balancing the competing interests of confidentiality and disclosure – for example, in a case about whether the local authority could lawfully disclose to a university the background (child protection concerns) of a social work student.[4]

---

1   *Botta v Italy* [1998] 26 EHRR 241.

2   Department of Health. *Care and support statutory guidance.* London: DH, 2016, para 14.98.

3   *London Borough of Hillingdon v Neary* [2011] EWHC 1377 (COP), para 151.

4   *R v Plymouth City Council, ex p Stevens* [2002] EWCA Civ 388.

> The extent of information included in criminal record certificates[1] and the rules about barring people from working with vulnerable adults[2] have also been challenged successfully on the grounds of proportionality.

Article 8 is chiefly about reining in State interference, imposing 'negative' obligations on public bodies. But the courts have held also that article 8 sometimes confers 'positive' obligations to interfere, to protect a person's right to respect for their private life – for example, if a person was being abused or neglected at home.[3]

> **Failure to provide equipment and adaptations or alternative accommodation: 'corporate neglect'.** A local authority failed for nearly two years to meet the assessed community care needs of a seriously disabled woman who had suffered a stroke. This resulted in her and her family living in 'hideous conditions' that breached article 8 of the Convention. She spent the time confined to her living room, unable to access the toilet, wearing incontinence pads, and surrounded by six children, aged between 3 and 20. The judge characterised this as corporate neglect, identified a failure to take positive steps to intervene, and awarded damages of £10,000.[4]

HUMAN RIGHTS: RIGHT TO FREEDOM OF EXPRESSION. This right includes the freedom to hold opinions and to receive and impart information and ideas without inference from the State.

Like article 8, this right is not absolute but subject to a number of provisos. It states that because freedom of expression carries with it duties and responsibilities, it can be subject to formalities, conditions and restrictions. However, these in turn are only justified if they are necessary in a democratic society for a number of specified purposes. These purposes include public safety, the prevention of disorder or crime, the protection of health or morals,

---

1   *R (L) v Commissioner of Police for the Metropolis* [2009] UKSC 3.

2   *R (Royal College of Nursing) v Secretary of State for the Home Department and the Independent Safeguarding Authority* [2010] EWHC 2761 (Admin).

3   *A Local Authority v A and B* [2010] EWHC 978 (Fam).

4   *R (Bernard) v Enfield London Borough Council* [2002] EWHC Admin 2282, paras 29, 33.

the protection of the reputation or rights of others, preventing the disclosure of information received in confidence.

The following case, about safeguarding issues, saw article 10 pitched against article 8 (the privacy of the residents) as a care home sought to prevent a BBC television programme, about poor care practices, being broadcast.

Secret filming in care home: balancing public interest with private life of residents. The media wished to broadcast a programme about standards of care in a care home. The care home sought an injunction to prevent the programme from being broadcast. The BBC argued that it should be allowed to show the programme in line with the freedom of expression and the fact that it was in the public interest to do so. The care home claimed that its objection was based on article 8 – namely, that such filming, even with the identity of individual residents obscured, was still an interference with their private life. The court found in favour of the BBC and refused to grant an injunction to the care home.[1]

---

1   *BKM v British Broadcasting Association* [2009] EWHC 3151 (Ch).

I

Ill-treatment

Ill-treatment is a criminal offence. It is found in three different pieces of legislation alongside the criminal offence of wilful neglect: the Mental Capacity Act 2005, Mental Health Act 1983 and Criminal Justice and Courts Act 2015. For the rules governing both offences, see *Wilful neglect or ill-treatment*.

Independent Mental Capacity Advocates, see *Advocacy*

Independent Safeguarding Authority

This was a former regulatory body that had the power to bar people, thereby preventing them legally from working with children or vulnerable adults. It was superseded by the Disclosure and Barring Service.

Informal carers, see *Carers*

Information disclosure

Effective safeguarding often relies on the disclosure of personal information between different organisations. Serious case reviews regularly identify lack of shared information as a contributory factor in a failure to prevent abuse or neglect.[1]

Equally, however, it does not follow legally that organisations can simply share people's personal information willy-nilly. In other words, a balance is required between sharing information in the cause of safeguarding and preserving people's confidentiality. Within this balance, consent is a fundamental, but not the only, ingredient.[2]

INFORMATION DISCLOSURE: LAW. Three areas of law are, in general, fundamental: the Human Rights Act 1998, the common law of confidence, and the Data Protection Act 2018 and General Data Protection Regulation (GDPR). See *Data protection*; *Human rights*; *Confidentiality*.

INFORMATION DISCLOSURE: OTHER LEGISLATION. In addition, however, a range of other legislation relevant to safeguarding creates duties or powers to disclose information in certain circumstances.

- **Reporting to the Care Quality Commission.** The duty to disclose might be unqualified: for example, a registered care provider must report specifically certain incidents to the Care Quality Commission under the Care Quality Commission (Registration) Regulations 2009 – in which case, unless the legislation itself were to be challenged as inconsistent with human rights, disclosure must be made.

- **Soft information in criminal record certificates.** A duty might be qualified: for example, the duty to consider providing 'soft' information about a person in enhanced criminal record certificates – but only so far as a chief constable reasonably believes it to be relevant and, in his or her opinion, that it ought to be included in the certificate.[3] This question has been answered, in a series of legal cases, with reference to human rights.

---

1 Braye, S. and Preston-Shoot, M. *Learning from SARS: a report for the London Safeguarding Adults Board.* London: LSAB, 2017, para 4.3.2.

2 Department of Health. *Care and support statutory guidance.* London: DH, 2016, para 14.179.

3 Police Act 1997, s.113B.

- **Multi-agency public protection.** There may be a power rather than a duty. For example, under section 325 of the Criminal Justice Act 2003 (multi-agency public protection), a number of organisations have a duty to cooperate which 'may' include information disclosure. In which case, any such sharing in an individual case should be justified in terms of human rights.[1]

- **Power to pass information to certain statutory bodies.** The same considerations – consistency with common law, data protection and human rights – would apply to section 115 of the Crime and Disorder Act 1998 containing a power for any person to pass information to specified bodies, including the police, probation service, local authorities and NHS bodies. The reverse power, for those authorities to give information to any person, is not included.

INFORMATION DISCLOSURE: HARM. The common law principle of confidentiality is a strong one. Absent other specific obligations in legislation to disclose information, there is a strong presumption against disclosing highly personal information without a person's consent, if the only person who would suffer harm is the person themselves – even in the context of safeguarding.

The Data Protection Act 2018 and the General Data Protection Regulation (GDPR) reflect this. For example, disclosure could be made if a person lacks mental capacity (and it is to protect their vital interests), if other people would suffer harm, in order to prevent crime, etc. But harm coming to the person themselves is, alone and without more, not a ground for disclosure.[2]

Thus, General Medical Council guidance for doctors states that 'you should, however, usually abide by the patient's refusal to consent to disclosure, even if their decision leaves them (but no one else) at risk of death or serious harm'.[3] The difficulties this principle can pose for practitioners in the context of health care, social care and safeguarding are exemplified in multi-agency

---

1   Ministry of Justice. *MAPPA guidance 2012 (version 4.1 updated 2016).* London: MoJ, 2012, chapters 9 and 10.

2   Data Protection Act 2018 and General Data Protection Regulation (GDPR) (Regulation (EU) 2016/679), a.9.

3   General Medical Council. *Confidentiality.* London: GMC, 2009, paras 57–59.

guidance on disclosing information about the risk of suicide. It is to the following effect:

- **Strong duty of confidentiality.** It is clear that, where the common law duty of confidentiality applies, practitioners will be under a duty to respect a person's refusal to consent to disclosure of their suicide risk, if the person has capacity and they do not pose a risk to anyone but themselves.

- **Lack of capacity.** A practitioner may need to assess whether the person, at least at that time, lacks the capacity to consent to information about their suicide risk being shared. The Mental Capacity Act makes it clear that a person must be assumed to have capacity unless it is established that they lack capacity, and that a person is not to be treated as unable to make a decision merely because they make an unwise decision.

- **Capacity and imminent risk of suicide.** However, if a person is at imminent risk of suicide, there may well be sufficient doubts about their mental capacity at that time.

- **Lack of capacity: best interests.** If the purpose of the disclosure is to prevent a person who lacks capacity from serious harm, there is an expectation that practitioners will disclose relevant confidential information, if it is considered to be in the person's best interest to do so.

- **Risk to other people, from the potential suicide, justifying disclosure.** Disclosure may also be in the public interest because of the far-reaching impact that a suicide can have on others. For example, the method of suicide could cause potential serious harm to others. The practitioner will need to make a judgement about whether the benefits to an individual or society in disclosing information without consent outweigh both the individual's and the public interest in keeping it confidential. Determining where to draw the line is a matter for professional judgement in each individual case.[1]

---

1   Department of Health, Royal College of Psychiatrists, Royal College of General Practitioners, Royal College of Nursing, British Psychological Society, British Association of Social Workers, College of Social Work, Mental Health Network NHS Confederation, Association of Directors of Adult Social Services. *Information sharing and suicide prevention: consensus statement.* London: Department of Health, 2014.

Equally, there will be circumstances in which disclosure would on the face of it be amply justified, indeed demanded, but it is not made, for whatever reason.

> **Inquest into death of resident: information about his assailant not provided to the care home.** An 86-year-old dementia sufferer, a former police inspector, died in a care home after being kicked by another resident, also with dementia, a 75-year-old miner. The latter was wearing steel toe-capped boots. The man had been placed by Lancashire Care NHS Foundation Trust. At the inquest it transpired that the care home had not been told that the man had previously shown challenging behaviour in previous care home placements, involving aggression and serious injury to other service users. When the home realised the degree of risk he posed two weeks after entering the home, it told the NHS Trust it could not meet his needs and sought help. By October, he was still at the home and, as the coroner put it, support from the Trust was not 'particularly forthcoming'; the jury found that the Trust had failed to provide support in a 'timely and appropriate manner'.[1]

Inherent jurisdiction

The inherent jurisdiction is a residual, common law power of the High Court to hear cases not coming under, or excluded by, legislation – and to intervene. Its relevance to safeguarding adults is that the jurisdiction has sometimes been used to protect or to assist vulnerable adults – and in particular, those with mental capacity.

For example, the Mental Capacity Act 2005 now means that many decisions previously taken under the inherent jurisdiction are now made by the Court of Protection. However, two of the ways in which the inherent jurisdiction might still come into play are as follows.

First, it can apply when a vulnerable person has in principle mental capacity to take a decision, but circumstances mean that he or she is being

---

1   Green, C. 'Dementia sufferer died after suffering injuries in care home row.' *Rossendale Free Press*, 30 June 2016. Accessed on 10 January 2018 at: www.rossendalefreepress.co.uk/news/dementia-sufferer-died-after-suffering-11544911.

prevented from, or hindered in, exercising that capacity. In this type of case, the courts will be slow to make an order against the vulnerable person themselves, but might consider it.[1] Normally, the order will lie against the third party responsible for hindering the exercise of the person's decision-making.[2] An injunction, prohibiting the third party from doing certain things, may be obtained, but the courts have held that a power of arrest cannot be attached – although a breach would risk contempt of court.[3]

Second, when a person effectively lacks mental capacity to take the decision in question but, because of a legal rule (or quirk), the matter cannot be decided under the Mental Capacity Act.

INHERENT JURISDICTION: SAFEGUARDING. Use of the inherent jurisdiction for adults who are vulnerable but with capacity may, on occasion, be a way of trying to protect a vulnerable adult, with capacity, from unwise decisions. However, it is exercised with a degree of caution by the courts – for fear of its becoming coercive and undermining the principle of autonomy and the right of a person with capacity to take unwise decisions. Furthermore, it is not something that a local authority or another public body can exercise directly; an application must be made to court.

Inherent jurisdiction: facilitative rather than dictatorial. The jurisdiction is to help people make decisions freely, rather than trample over their wishes – that is, 'facilitative rather than dictatorial' – and that 'its primary purpose is to create a situation where the person concerned can receive outside help free of coercion, to enable him or her to weigh things up and decide freely what he or she wishes to do'.[4]

Inherent jurisdiction: possibility of restricting vulnerable adult's autonomy. In one case, there was uncertainty about the mental capacity of a clearly vulnerable 18-year-old, who had suffered neglect, together with his younger siblings, at the hands of his mother. The court stated that it 'would

1   *NCC v PB* [2014] EWCOP 14, paras 121–122.

2   *LBL v RYJ* [2010] EWHC 2665 (COP), para 62.

3   *D (Inherent jurisdiction: power of arrest)* [2016] EWHC 2358 (Fam).

4   *A Local Authority v DL* [2012] EWCA Civ 253, paras 7, 67.

be unconscionable and socially undesirable if, due to the weaknesses of an assessment which failed satisfactorily to resolve whether there are reasons to believe that J lacks capacity, he were to find himself beyond the reach of judicial protection. I am clear that he is not. The question that arises is how he can most effectively be protected with the least intrusive and most proportionate curtailment of his autonomy.'[1]

Inherent jurisdiction: vulnerable adults. The inherent jurisdiction 'is not confined to those who are vulnerable adults, however that expression is understood, nor is a vulnerable adult amenable as such to the jurisdiction. The significance in this context of the concept of a vulnerable adult is pragmatic and evidential: it is simply that an adult who is vulnerable is more likely to fall into the category of the incapacitated in relation to whom the inherent jurisdiction is exercisable than an adult who is not vulnerable. So, it is likely to be easier to persuade the court that there is a case calling for investigation where the adult is apparently vulnerable than where the adult is not on the face of it vulnerable.'[2]

Inherent jurisdiction: coercion, undue influence, other factors undermining genuine consent. The jurisdiction can extend to a vulnerable adult who might not be incapacitated by mental disorder or mental illness, but is, or is reasonably believed to be, either (i) under constraint, or (ii) subject to coercion or undue influence, or (iii) for some other reason deprived of the capacity to make the relevant decision, or disabled from making a free choice, or incapacitated or disabled from giving or expressing real or genuine consent.[3]

INHERENT JURISDICTION: VULNERABLE ADULTS WITH MENTAL CAPACITY.

Examples of cases relevant to safeguarding, and involving adults with mental capacity, include the following.

Inherent jurisdiction: protecting elderly, vulnerable parents with mental capacity from their son. An elderly couple, both with the requisite mental

---

1   *London Borough of Wandsworth v AMcC, AJ, CJ, JJ* [2017] EWHC 2435 (Fam), para 82.

2   *Re SA (Vulnerable Adult with Capacity: Marriage)* [2005] EWHC 2942 (Fam).

3   *Re SA (Vulnerable Adult with Capacity: Marriage)* [2005] EWHC 2942 (Fam).

capacity (at the outset of the case), lived with their son. He persistently mistreated them. They continued to be unwilling to take any action against him. The local authority had explored possible legal options but had rejected them all on the basis of the couple's refusal to contemplate them.

The order sought from the court was to try to prohibit the son from behaving in certain ways towards his parents:

1. assaulting or threatening to assault GRL or ML

2. preventing GRL or ML from having contact with friends and family members

3. seeking to persuade or coerce GRL into transferring ownership of the current family home

4. seeking to persuade or coerce ML into moving into a care home or nursing home

5. engaging in behaviour towards GRL or ML that is otherwise degrading or coercive, including (but not limited to): stipulating which rooms in the house GRL or ML can use; preventing GRL or ML from using household appliances, including the washing machine; 'punishing' GRL or ML, for example, by making GRL write 'lines'; shouting or otherwise behaving in an aggressive or intimidating manner towards them

6. giving orders to care staff

7. interfering in the provision of care and support to ML

8. refusing access to health and social care professionals

9. behaving in an aggressive and/or confrontational manner to care staff and care managers.

The court granted the order.[1]

Inherent jurisdiction: communication and marriage of vulnerable adult. A woman was profoundly deaf. She had no speech and no oral communication. She had profound bilateral sensory neural loss and significant visual loss in one eye. She communicated in British Sign Language (BSL), which was

---

1   *A Local Authority v DL* [2011] EWHC 1022 (Fam), upheld on appeal: *A Local Authority v DL* [2012] EWCA Civ 253.

based in English. Her ability to communicate with her parents was very limited because their first language was Punjabi. She had limited capacity to lip-read English. She could not understand, lip-read or sign in either Punjabi or Urdu. Neither of her parents could communicate with her using British Sign Language.

Understanding of marriage. She had been assessed as having a rudimentary but clear and accurate understanding of the concept of marriage, the implications of a marriage contract, of a sexual relationship and its implications. However, the assessing doctor, a chartered forensic psychologist, was concerned that she might marry a person who could not communicate with her, especially outside the UK where she might be surrounded also by people with whom she could not communicate.

Travel to Pakistan for marriage. She had made it clear that although she wished to travel to Pakistan for an arranged marriage, she did not want to live there and wished to return to her home town. If this were not possible, she would rather not marry. However, she did not understand that any such husband might be prevented from returning with her by the immigration authorities. It had now come to the local authority's attention that a trip to Pakistan might be imminent.

Court order to ensure informed consent of vulnerable adult. It was argued that the court should intervene, prohibiting her parents from threatening, intimidating and harassing her, using violence, preventing her from communicating alone with her solicitor, applying for travel documents for her and removing her from England and Wales without express written consent, translated and explained in BSL and duly notarised. They would also be prohibited from making arrangements for her to be married unless they had her express written consent (as above) and notarised consent of the bridegroom, allowed her to return to her home town within four months of the marriage ceremony, allowed her to reside in her home town, allowed a visit by a worker from the British High Commission in Islamabad four months after the ceremony to interview her alone as to whether she wished to return to England and Wales. A power of arrest was also sought, to be attached to any order made.

The court granted the order sought. In summary, the court stated that the person was

> a vulnerable adult who there is every reason to believe may, by
> reason of her disabilities, and even in the absence of any undue

> influence or misinformation, be disabled from making a free choice and incapacitated or disabled from forming or expressing a real and genuine consent.[1]

In the following case, the court appeared to contemplate the possibility of making an order against the vulnerable person herself, if necessary.

Inherent jurisdiction: overbearing by mother of daughter's will: blood transfusion. A young woman, 34 weeks pregnant, had a car accident. She held some Jehovah's Witness beliefs but had never formally been accepted into the faith (of her mother). Before losing consciousness in the hospital, she had spent some time alone with her mother – after which she refused a blood transfusion. The case was referred urgently to the courts.

The Court of Appeal held that, in all the circumstances, she lacked capacity to take the decision that the transfusion could be given. However, if she had been judged to have capacity, the court would have held that her mother had vitiated her ability to make a decision. It was one thing for a person to be persuaded, but another to have their will overborne. In such circumstances, doctors could take the view that the decision was not a true decision and apply to the courts for help.[2]

INHERENT JURISDICTION: UNCERTAINTY ABOUT MENTAL CAPACITY.

Sometimes there is uncertainty about whether a person lacks capacity to make a decision – or has the capacity but is unable to exercise it freely because of undue influence, coercion, duress, etc. One, practical, solution is to take alternative arguments to a court.

Lack of capacity or inherent jurisdiction? The local authority was concerned about the welfare of an elderly, frail, intelligent and capable woman – in particular, in relation to a lodger (introduced through the local church) and her husband, who had moved in to the woman's house in order to provide help at night (in return for free lodgings). Concerns included the woman's personal safety, an issue about changing her will, possible intimidation and

---

1   *Re SA (Vulnerable Adult with Capacity: Marriage)* [2005] EWHC 2942 (Fam).

2   *Re T* [1992] 3 WLR 782.

financial abuse. The local authority made an application to court originally under the inherent jurisdiction, subsequently under the Mental Capacity Act. It was for the court to consider the options in relation to safeguarding the woman.[1]

One reason to keep options open is that in some circumstances, such as undue influence, there remains some legal uncertainty about when to invoke the Mental Capacity Act 2005 and when the inherent jurisdiction.

A person with learning disabilities or dementia might be unable to take a decision, but – apart from impairment or disturbance in mind or brain – also be subject to undue influence by another person. The question then is whether in principle they have mental capacity but are unable to exercise it freely at that time, thus requiring consideration of the inherent jurisdiction, or whether they lack mental capacity.

In short, is mental capacity to be assessed more generally – irrespective of particular circumstances pertaining at the time – or taking into account specific circumstances at the particular time (sometimes referred to as 'situational' lack of capacity)? The answer appears to be that if the impairment or disturbance in mind or brain is a material (but not necessarily the only) cause of the inability to make a decision, then, even if other factors are in play (e.g. undue influence), the person should be regarded as lacking mental capacity under the Mental Capacity Act 2005.[2]

Mental Capacity Act or inherent jurisdiction? The question arose as to whether a woman with learning disabilities could be educated to understand contraception, if her husband allowed professionals access to her. There seemed in hindsight to be a lack of clarity as to which jurisdiction was in play. But, overall, the judgment seems clear that it was primarily the Mental Capacity Act that needed to be considered, not the inherent jurisdiction.[3]

Another case was about whether a 79-year-old woman had the capacity to decide to live with her husband, and how his influence affected her ability

---

1   *London Borough of Redbridge v G* [2014] EWHC 485 (COP).

2   *Re BKR* [2015] SGCA 26 (Singapore Court of Appeal), paras 88–127.

3   *A Local Authority v Mrs A* [2010] EWHC 1549 (Fam). But see comments in: *In re L (Vulnerable Adults: Court's Jurisdiction)* [2013] Fam 1.

to decide. The key question was whether the impairment/disturbance of mind or brain was an effective, material or operative (not necessarily the only) cause of the inability to take a decision – even if other, external, influencing factors were in play. If so, the person would lack mental capacity under the Mental Capacity Act.[1]

INHERENT JURISDICTION: VULNERABLE ADULTS LACKING MENTAL CAPACITY. In some circumstances, an adult might lack capacity to take a decision, but the matter falls outside the Mental Capacity Act 2005. Examples include:

Deprivation of liberty and treatment under the inherent jurisdiction. A patient detained under the Mental Health Act 1983, who needed 'treatment' (in fact, nutrition and hydration) for what the doctors regarded as a physical issue, lacked capacity to consent but was resisting – and therefore needed to be deprived of his liberty in order to administer the treatment. However, this could not be done under either the Mental Health Act (it was not treatment for mental disorder) nor under the Mental Capacity Act (which prohibited deprivation of liberty if a person was already detained under the Mental Health Act). Ultimately, the court authorised the nutrition and hydration under the inherent jurisdiction.[2]

Declaration of invalidity of a marriage. A woman living in England, lacking capacity to marry, had been married in Bangladesh. Her 'husband' then obtained a spouse's visa to enter the United Kingdom, which appears to have been his main motive for marrying. Her parents didn't think they had done anything wrong and couldn't understand the fuss being made. He shared a bedroom and a bed with her in her family home.

Concerns about her welfare reached the local authority. The police obtained a forced marriage protection order. The Court of Protection warned the 'husband' that to have sexual relations with her would be a criminal offence.

---

1   *NCC v PB and TB* [2014] EWCOP 14, para 86. See *Re BKR* [2015] SGCA 26, paras 88–127, for a lengthy discussion of this issue.

2   *An NHS Trust v Doctor A* [2013] EWHC 2442 (COP).

> The Court was able to make declarations and welfare orders under the Mental Capacity Act 2005 but did not believe that the Act allowed it to make a declaration of invalidity of the marriage. Instead, the Court used the inherent jurisdiction to do this.
>
> (The court noted also that it could have made a declaration under the MCA that it was unlawful for the woman to be married in England, but that it could not make a declaration that it was or is unlawful for her to be married in Bangladesh.)[1]

Inhuman or degrading treatment, see *Human rights*

Injunctions, see *Civil orders and injunctions*

---

1   *XCC v AA* [2012] EWHC 2183 (COP).

J

Judicial review

Judicial review is a type of civil legal case that can be brought in the High Court against public bodies only. The purpose of such cases is not to win financial compensation. It is to get the court to overrule the decision of a public body, basically on the grounds that there was something wrong in the decision-making process. The public body may have to retake the decision. Permission is required from the courts to bring a judicial review case.

- **Common law principles.** The courts typically consider whether the public body has behaved irrationally (the public body taking leave of its senses), not taken account of relevant factors, acted illegally (*ultra vires*: doing what the legislation prohibits) or 'fettered of discretion' (rigidly applying a policy without considering exceptions).

- **Human rights and judicial review.** Human rights cases are often (but not necessarily) brought in the form of a judicial review case, a type of case lying against a public body. One or more articles of the European Convention on Human Rights will be argued, in addition to any common law traditional grounds of judicial review. The courts do sometimes award modest financial compensation on human rights grounds.

- **Judicial review in the context of safeguarding adults.** In the context of safeguarding, a judicial review case might be taken, for example, against the Crown Prosecution Service for failing to prosecute in the case of a vulnerable adult,[1] or against a local authority in terms of challenging its decision to make safeguarding enquiries, and then to act, under section 42 of the Care Act 2014.[2]

---

1   *R (B) v DPP* [2009] EWHC 106 (Admin).

2   *R (Collins) v Nottinghamshire County Council* [2016] EWHC 996 (Admin).

K

Kicking, see *Assault; Ill-treatment*

Kidnapping

Kidnapping is a criminal offence. It involves taking or carrying somebody away by force or fraud, without consent and lawful excuse, resulting in an attack on, and infringement of, personal liberty. If somebody lacks capacity, they clearly cannot consent, but for the offence to be committed there has also to be the attack on, and infringement of, personal liberty through force or fraud. And somebody who is compliant, albeit lacking capacity or with other mental health needs, might not be subject to force or fraud at all.[1]

---

1   Law Commission. *Mental capacity and deprivation of liberty: a consultation paper*. London: LC, 2015, para 15.28.

L

Lasting power of attorney

A person (the donee) with a lasting power of attorney is able to take various decisions for another person (the donor) lacking the relevant mental capacity. These decisions can include a range of finance and welfare matters. In itself, such a power of attorney is nothing to do with adult safeguarding. However, some attorneys abuse their power.

A number of conditions must be fulfilled for such a power to be valid. Invalidity of the power may or may not be associated with abuse or neglect. The Court of Protection can revoke the power of attorney, for example, in case of:

- lack of capacity to make the power of attorney in the first place

- fraud or undue pressure

- the attorney not acting in the donor's best interests.

LASTING POWER OF ATTORNEY: KEY POINTS. In short, a person aged 18 years or over, with capacity to do so, can make a lasting power of attorney. This authorises the attorney to deal with property and financial affairs and (or) welfare matters – in the donor's best interests – when the donor loses capacity to take such decisions. Welfare decisions can include matters such as health care, place of residence, contact, etc.

More than one attorney can be appointed. Attorneys can be appointed to act jointly, severally or jointly *and* severally (jointly for some matters, severally for others). Attorneys having to act jointly can be a safeguard against poor (or abusive) decision-making but can also in some circumstances be cumbersome.

There are restrictions on gifts that can be made by attorneys, without express permission being sought from the Court of Protection. The reason for such restrictions is simply the temptation, even for close relatives, that controlling somebody else's money can bring.

The following points are directly relevant to safeguarding – for example, in terms of whether there is in law a power at all, under what conditions it is to be exercised, and whether it is being misused.

- **Capacity and age of donor.** A person, the donor, is able to create a lasting power of attorney, whilst he or she retains the capacity to do so, and must be at least 18 years old.

- **Scope of power.** Such a lasting power can give the attorney authorisation to deal with property and financial affairs, as well as personal welfare matters (including health care decisions) when the donor no longer has capacity.

- **Prescribed form and registered.** The power must be contained in an instrument of a certain form and must be registered with the Public Guardian; otherwise it is not effective.

- **Principles of Act apply.** A lasting power of attorney is subject to the provisions of the Mental Capacity Act 2005, in particular the principles in section 1 of the Act (including best interests), as well as any conditions or restrictions specified in the instrument (section 9).

- **Age of donee.** A donee must be at least 18 years old.

- **Attorneys acting jointly or severally.** Attorneys may be appointed to act jointly, jointly and severally – or jointly in respect of some matters, and jointly and severally in respect of others (section 10).

- **Restraint.** The use of the power to restrain the donor is restricted to where it is necessary and proportionate (to the likelihood of the person suffering harm), and the person lacks capacity, or the attorney reasonably believes that the person lacks capacity in relation to the matter.

- **Welfare powers (useable only on loss of capacity).** The personal welfare powers cannot be used unless the donor lacks capacity or the attorney reasonably believes that the donor lacks capacity.

- **Relation to advance decisions.** The personal welfare power is subject to any advance decision on treatment made by the donor – and does not cover decisions about life-sustaining treatment, unless this has been expressly included by the donor in the lasting power of attorney.

- **Health care treatment.** The personal welfare power can be specified so as to include consent, or refusal of consent, to health care treatment (section 11).

- **Restrictions on gifts.** There are restrictions on gifts, other than on customary gifts or charities to whom the donor might have made gifts, insofar as the value of any such gift is reasonable in respect of the donor's estate.

- **Donor signature.** The donor must sign a statement that they have read the information and want the power to apply when they have lost capacity.

- **Named people to be informed.** The document must name people who should be informed when an application is made to register the power.

- **Attorneys' signature.** The attorneys must sign to say they have read the information and understand their duties, including the duty to act in the person's best interests.

- **Certification by third party of donor's understanding.** The document must include a certificate completed by an independent third party to the effect that, in their view, the donor understands the power being created, no undue pressure or fraud has been used, and there is nothing to stop the power being created (schedule 1).

- **Identity of certifying third party.** The independent third party (not a family member) can be someone who has known the donor personally for two years, or a person chosen by the donor on account of their professional skills and expertise, and whom the donor reasonably considers to be competent to certify the relevant matters.[1]

- **Public Guardian and registration.** The Public Guardian charges registration fees.

---

1   SI 2007/1253. Lasting Powers of Attorney, Enduring Powers of Attorney and Public Guardian Regulations 2007.

- **Separate forms and fees for welfare and finance.** There are separate forms, and fee payable, for a welfare power and a finance power.[1]

- **Registration and use.** Lasting powers of attorney can be registered with the Office of the Public Guardian at any time and cannot be used until registered. A finance, property and business power can be used by the attorney before the donor loses capacity; but a welfare power can be used only when the donor lacks the capacity to take a relevant welfare decision.[2]

LASTING POWER OF ATTORNEY: ENDURING POWER OF ATTORNEY.

Prior to October 2007 and the introduction of lasting powers of attorney were enduring powers of attorney – under the Enduring Powers of Attorney Act 1985.[3] These remain valid if made before that date but can apply to finance and affairs only – not health and welfare matters.

LASTING POWER OF ATTORNEY: ABUSE.

The Court of Protection has pointed out that the scheme of lasting powers of attorney is based on trust. It envisages minimal intervention by public authorities. So the Court is unlikely to use its supervisory powers unless there is particular reason to do so, such as the Office of the Public Guardian raising concerns.[4]

The reason for this is so that the system is not too burdensome, given that arrangements will often be intra-family. However, at the same time, this can lead to a greater risk of abuse occurring. The following represent a sample of cases of financial abuse relating to lasting powers of attorney (or older enduring powers of attorney).

Revocation of a power of attorney (lasting or enduring) by the Court of Protection may or may not be associated also with a separate criminal prosecution of the attorney. The following illustrate all too well the temptation that can overcome trusted family members.

---

1   SI 2007/1253. Lasting Powers of Attorney, Enduring Powers of Attorney and Public Guardian Regulations 2007. And: SI 2007/2051. Public Guardian (Fees, etc) Regulations 2007.

2   Mental Capacity Act 2005, ss.9, 11.

3   See Mental Capacity Act 2005, schedule 4.

4   *Re Harcourt* [2012] WTLR 1779, para 39.

Daughter using power of attorney for mother to steal sister's inheritance.
A tour operator stole her sister's £50,000 inheritance by moving money
from their mother's account. She used a power of attorney to move money
from her mother's accounts into her own. By the time her mother died, she
had taken so much that the sister was left with pennies. She pleaded guilty
to the theft. Sentence was adjourned, pending her swiftly compensating her
brother-in-law (her sister was now dead) by way of showing her remorse.[1]

Son and daughter: immediate abuse of power of attorney. An elderly
grandmother was defrauded of £58,000 by her own son and daughter.
They siphoned off £58,000 of her money into their own pockets just
weeks after they were given legal power of attorney, after their mother
struggled to cope. They spent thousands of pounds on credit card bills,
savings accounts, school fees, Pandora jewellery, furniture, clothing from
Next, White Stuff and Revolve, and purchases from Amazon and Boden.
They defended their actions, claiming their mother had been generous with
them in the past, helping them when they fell into financial difficulty. When
the mother realised what had happened, she stated this was not what she
had intended to happen.

   The judge branded the son's attempt to defend himself by saying he
would have inherited the money anyway as 'disgraceful'. But he did not
sentence them to prison, because of the detrimental impact this would
have on the mother – who had recently suffered a stroke. The daughter was
given a 12-month suspended sentence, ordered to carry out 300 hours of
unpaid work, and obey an 8pm to 7am curfew for four months. The son was
given a ten-month suspended sentence, ordered to carry out 250 hours of
unpaid work, and obey an 8pm to 6am curfew for four months.[2]

Abuse of enduring power of attorney by niece: selling shares. A spinster
in her eighties suffered two strokes and three serious falls. She lost her
hearing and ability to write. She entered a nursing home in 1996. Her
niece, who was the donee of an enduring power of attorney, operated the
power and in March 1997 sold shares worth over £23,000; the next year
she sold more shares worth over £72,000. Both sums were placed in her

1   Rychlikova, M. 'Woman stole her sister's £50,000 inheritance.' *York Press*, 6 November 2015.

2   Mackley, E. 'Siblings Timothy Baumber and Tessa Quelch conned elderly mum out of £58k.'
     Hull Daily Mail, 6 May 2017.

bank account; some of the money was lent to her husband's companies. The courts found that she had abused the power of attorney.[1]

Son with enduring power of attorney: sports car, power boat, selling shares. When the son of an elderly woman had an enduring power of attorney, he used her assets to place a new house in his name, but not his mother's, bought a sports car and power boat, moved large sums of money into a company account owned by his wife, and sold shares and paid the proceeds into another account to be drawn on by his wife. The mother was left with no assets, nothing to pass on to her grandchildren, nothing to use to provide for her own needs at the end of her life. She obtained no benefits from the transfers.

The court noted that the law imposed 'rigorous and inflexible duties on fiduciaries who enter into transactions with the person to whom the duty is owed' – that is, where the mother's assets were flowing directly into the son's possession. This meant justifying the transaction and proving affirmatively that the transaction was fair and entered into on the basis of proper and independent advice. The son and his wife were in clear breach of their fiduciary duty.[2]

Making gifts without the Court of Protection's authorisation: not fatal to continuing as attorney. The donor of an enduring power of attorney was a 90-year-old woman living in a nursing home. There were three siblings between whom there had been a history of hostility. The eldest had been granted the power.

The making of £20,000 of gifts by the donee from the donor's estate, even-handedly to herself and siblings, for estate planning purposes, did not necessarily make the attorney unsuitable – even though she should have sought the Court of Protection's authorisation (because the attorney's power to make gifts was extremely limited). However, at worst, she 'ought to have known the law if she was to take on the responsibility of such an important fiduciary position'. But what had occurred did not portray a picture of greed. Furthermore, the other siblings, who had now brought the case to displace the third sibling, had not complained at the time. It was also possible that, at the time the gifts were made, only shortly after the power had been executed, the donee was acting under the instructions

---

1   *Jennings and Lewis v Cairns* [2003] EWCA Civ 1935.

2   *Hodson v Hodson* [2006] EWHC 2878 (Ch).

of the donor – since the latter might have had capacity to direct that the gifts be made.

In addition, the fact of hostility between the three children did not automatically make the donee unsuitable. In this case, it did not. In other circumstances, it might have done so – for instance, if the donor's estate had been complex and required strategic decision-making requiring consultation and work with the other siblings.[1]

Woman with power of attorney (and beneficiary of will) for husband's uncle: convicted of theft. A 60-year-old woman had an enduring power of attorney on behalf of her former husband's uncle. When his mental health deteriorated, he entered a care home and she then managed his finances. She made cash withdrawals for herself from his building society account, making out cheques to pay off her own overdraft and to buy Christmas presents. He had wanted her to buy a car and had authorised £5000 for this, but she bought one for £4400 and kept the rest. With the money she stole, she funded family holidays as well as her gambling habit, a washing machine and a tumble drier. In total she was charged with, and pleaded guilty to, theft of £17,500. She was sentenced to nine months' imprisonment, as the judge put it, having taken advantage of an elderly and vulnerable victim. The irony, which she was not aware of at the time, was that much of the money she had stolen was from her own inheritance, detailed in the man's will.[2]

Social worker failing to seek Court of Protection order for client, instead obtaining enduring power of attorney for herself and attempting to steal tens of thousands of pounds. A local authority social worker was convicted of theft, having had a 79-year-old woman, with no known relatives, referred to her. The woman had dementia, £25,000 in cash and owned her own home. The social worker helped the woman go into a care home. A consultant psychiatrist recommended that a Court of Protection order be sought because of the woman's lack of capacity to manage her affairs. The social worker took no steps to do this. Instead, she started to steal money and obtained an enduring power of attorney for herself, even though the woman lacked the capacity to make it. The power was not registered with the Court of Protection.

---

1   *Re a power given by Mrs W, a donor* (1999) Chancery (Court of Protection).

2   'Carer jailed for theft from elderly widower.' *Wiltshire Gazette and Herald*, 24 March 2005.

Regular bank withdrawals, selling of house: cheque for £42,000. The social worker then started to make cash withdrawals. She withdrew £8180 from cash machines, followed by other withdrawals at about £250 per week. She eventually sold the woman's house for some £87,000. She then began to write cheques out to herself, including one for £42,000. A further banker's draft for £5000 was made payable to Age Concern – but the social worker's husband was the regional manager of that charity.

Another local authority officer was asked to reassess the woman, now in the care home. This social worker became suspicious when she found out that the social worker was still visiting. It transpired that the social worker had asked the care home to remove the woman's name from the records; and the woman's social services file was missing.

Deliberation, cynicism, most serious breach of trust. The social worker was sentenced to three and a half years in prison, having stolen nearly £65,000. The judge referred to the deliberate plan to take advantage of an old lady who could not look after herself – characterising it as deliberate, cynical, and a gross breach of trust. The social worker knew perfectly well that the victim would not be able to do anything about it. He described it as the most serious breach of trust by a social worker that he had come across in 20 years on the bench. For sentence, the judge took a starting point of five years. After considering the mitigation (guilty plea, good references, high standard of behaviour in prison, low risk of reoffending), he arrived at three and a half years, which sentence was upheld on appeal.[1]

Solicitor defrauding 84-year-old woman who treated him like a son: and had made him beneficiary of her will. A solicitor gained an enduring power of attorney for an 84-year-old woman who treated him like a son. He had known her for 30 years. He was sent to prison for 26 months, for fraud, having stolen £51,000 after she had entered a care home and developed dementia. He withdrew the money from three building society accounts and a Post Office account – before building society staff became suspicious. The irony was that, under the terms of her will (drawn up via another solicitor), he was beneficiary to 50 per cent of the woman's estate.[2]

---

1   *R v Hardwick* [2006] EWCA Crim 969.

2   Blake, M. 'Solicitor jailed for stealing over £50,000 from elderly dementia sufferer who treated him "like a son".' *Daily Mail*, 23 March 2012.

Son stealing £80,000 from his mother. In a further case, a man with power of attorney for his mother was sent to prison for stealing over £80,000, which sum was meant to pay for nursing home fees. Instead, he used it to solve his own financial problems. The judge stated that he had plundered his mother's assets almost to extinction.[1]

Son-in-law stealing £250,000 for luxury lifestyle. After his deaf and blind mother-in-law entered a care home, a man obtained power of attorney. He abused it, stealing nearly £250,000 for a luxury lifestyle. The money should have been used to pay for his mother-in-law's care home fees, but instead went on his business, top-of-the-range cars and expensive holidays. He was sentenced to three years in prison.[2]

Nephew using power of attorney which had never been registered or agreed. A power of attorney, which had never been registered or agreed, was used by a man to steal £75,000 from his elderly aunt with dementia. He drafted it himself and, after his aunt was admitted to a care home, used it to sell her house for £124,000, of which he appropriated £75,000 for himself. He was sent to prison for nine rather than 18 months. In mitigation, he was a hard-working family man, had a mother with mental health problems, had found his father dead aged 14, was close to his aunt and was ashamed of what he had done. A Proceeds of Crime confiscation hearing would be held at a later date.[3]

Son denying his mother slippers and hairdressing. A man was jailed for over five years for stealing more than £260,000 from his elderly mother with dementia. He had lasting power of attorney, began spending her money in local pubs, and then sold her home, buying a property and renting it out for his own benefit. He had also spent money on a pyramid selling scheme, on specialist legal advice following a driving conviction and on loan repayment. His mother was placed at risk of eviction by the care home and relied on the charity of the care home for her hairdressing and to buy slippers. In 2015, his power of attorney was revoked by the Court of Protection.

---

1   'Bankrupt man stole £80,000 from mother.' *Suffolk Free Press*, 20 January 2009.

2   '"Walter Mitty" conman who fleeced his mother-in-law of £250,000 is jailed for three years.' *Daily Mail*, 2 July 2012. (It is not clear from the report what sort of power of attorney it was.)

3   'Bristol man jailed for stealing £75,000 from his elderly aunt.' *Bristol Evening Post*, 28 October 2011.

During the time he had control over his mother's financial affairs he stripped her of her financial assets. At the same time, he met none of the costs of his mother's care, putting her at risk of eviction. He admitted fraud by abuse of position.[1]

Son using mother's money to buy a house and a pick-up vehicle, and to give his daughter rent-free accommodation: revocation of power of attorney. The Office of the Public Guardian applied to the court for an enduring power of attorney, held by a son for his mother, to be revoked. This was on the grounds that he had mixed his own and his mother's monies, bought a new property registered in his name (with the unrealistic claim that his mother could live there even though she needed to be in a care home), had bought a pick-up truck for some £5000 to transfer belongings (although he could have hired one instead much more cheaply), had not paid care home fees (he claimed he would once it was established whether the local authority or the NHS should be responsible for the placement), and did not charge his daughter rent for living in the new property (claiming that his mother would not have wanted him to do so).

The court found against the attorney on all these points. It also departed from the normal rule on costs in such court cases and ordered that the son pay his own costs.[2]

Attorney not paying care home fees for her mother, and other unexplained transactions. A care home owner contacted the local authority, expressing concern that the mother's care home fees were not being paid – and that she was being given very little pocket money by her daughter.

The owner was also concerned because the mother had received a letter from a bank, confirming a loan to her of £5000, and also other correspondence confirming that her credit card applications had been accepted. The daughter also visited only very sporadically, possibly once every two months.

When the Office of the Public Guardian tried to investigate and obtain an explanation from the daughter, the latter persistently failed to cooperate, making a number of excuses. The court found the attorney to have been

---

1   'Harpenden man jailed for defrauding elderly mother.' *Boreham and Elstree Times*, 22 August 2017.

2   *Re Stapleton* [2012] MHLO 72.

deliberately obstructive. It also noted that, as an auditor by profession, a higher standard would be expected from her in terms of managing and presenting her mother's accounts. The power was revoked; a deputy would be appointed instead.[1]

Law courts and legal cases, see *Remedies*

Local Government Ombudsman

Under the Local Government Act 1974, the office of the Local Government Ombudsman independently investigates complaints against local authorities. (In June 2017 it renamed itself the Local Government and Social Care Ombudsman.) Normally, under section 26 of the Act, the complainant must have first gone through the local authority's own complaints process.

The relevance of the ombudsman to adult safeguarding is at least threefold. First, the ombudsman investigates a significant number of safeguarding-related cases – for examples of these, see *Enquiries*. Second, the ombudsman is, in general, more accessible than the law courts. Third, the ombudsman has published specific guidance on safeguarding.[2] Key general points about the ombudsman include:

- **Maladministration and failure in service.** The ombudsman investigates maladministration, failure in a service which it was a local authority's function to provide, or failure to provide such a service. Maladministration is a wide concept, not defined in the Act, but it does not include questioning the merits of professional judgement.[3]

  Findings of maladministration may include reference to unlawfulness, but a finding of maladministration is not a legal ruling as such. And

---

1   *Re Harcourt* [2012] MHLO 74.

2   Local Government Ombudsman. *Casework guidance statement: safeguarding adults boards.* London: LGO, undated.

3   Local Government Act 1974, ss.26, 34(3).

maladministration is a different concept from unlawfulness. There could be maladministration without unlawfulness and vice versa.[1]

- **Timescale.** A complaint should be brought to the ombudsman within 12 months of the complainant knowing of the issue being complained of, although the ombudsman has a discretion to waive this rule.[2]

- **Legal case an alternative remedy.** The ombudsman is prohibited from investigating a case for which a legal remedy could be pursued. However, this rule can be waived if the ombudsman is satisfied that, in the circumstances, it is not reasonable to expect the person to pursue a legal case.[3]

- **Local authority responsible for actions of a provider.** In the case of providers acting on behalf of the local authority, the ombudsman will hold the authority responsible for the actions of the provider.[4]

- **Independent social care providers.** The ombudsman's remit extends to complaints about independent adult social care providers engaging in regulated activity under the Health and Social Care Act 2008, and to investigating alleged injustice.[5]

- **Recommendations.** The local ombudsman makes recommendations by way of remedy. These might relate, for example, to providing a service, changing a policy, paying financial compensation.

The recommendations are not legally binding (although findings of fact are).[6] If local authorities do not comply, the ombudsman can force the authority to make a statement in local newspapers about the case.[7]

As a matter of practice, most ombudsman recommendations are complied with. However, on occasion, they are not. The ombudsman may then publish

---

1 R (*Goldsmith IBS Ltd*) *v Parliamentary & Health Service Ombudsman* [2016] EWHC 1905 (Admin), para 12.

2 Local Government Act 1974, s.26B.

3 Local Government Act 1974, s.26.

4 Local Government Act 1974, s.25.

5 Local Government Act 1974, ss.34A–34T.

6 R (*Gallagher*) *v Basildon District Council* [2010] EWHC 2824 (Admin).

7 Local Government Act 1974, s.31.

a further report calling for compliance.[1] Occasionally, a local authority might remain obdurate. However, a rejection of findings (legally binding) – not just of recommendations (which are not legally binding) – might mean it is acting unlawfully.[2]

---

1   LGO, *Tameside Metropolitan Borough Council*, 2015 (12 019 862). (Further report.)

2   Local Government Ombudsman. *Maladministration causing injustice by Tameside Metropolitan Borough Council: Statement of Non-Compliance with Ombudsman's Recommendations*, 2015, p.2.

M

Making enquiries, see *Enquiries*

Manslaughter

Manslaughter divides into involuntary and voluntary manslaughter. Both may arise in the context of vulnerable adults. These are common law criminal offences, meaning that they are based ultimately on legal case law rather than legislation. However, there is additionally an offence of corporate manslaughter in legislation.

Involuntary manslaughter may be by unlawful act or through gross negligence or recklessness. A charge of murder is reduced to voluntary manslaughter in three instances: diminished responsibility, provocation or acting in pursuance of a suicide pact.[1]

MANSLAUGHTER: INVOLUNTARY, GROSS NEGLIGENCE IN HEALTH AND SOCIAL CARE. Gross negligence resulting in a person's death constitutes the basis of a criminal charge of involuntary manslaughter.

> **Involuntary manslaughter by reason of gross negligence.** When two medical doctors failed to realise the gravity of a patient's condition (toxic shock syndrome), with the consequence that he failed to get the required treatment and died, they were convicted of manslaughter by reason of gross negligence.[2] Likewise, an anaesthetist was convicted in connection

---

1   Homicide Act 1957, ss.2–3.

2   *R v Misra* [2004] EWCA Crim 2375.

with the death of a patient.[1] And another doctor when she gave a fatal injection of adrenaline against the advice of three colleagues.[2]

Death from grossly negligent manual handling in care home. An 86-year-old care home resident with Parkinson's disease, weighing six stone, died from having her neck compressed and two fractured vertebrae. She also had cuts and bruises on her face. A prosecution took place but in the end the accused's plea of manslaughter was accepted, death occurring through grossly negligent 'manhandling' – which she had tried to cover up. The nurse was 62 years old, a devout Christian and mother of five. She was sentenced to 12 months in prison, suspended, because of time already spent in custody and at a bail hostel.[3]

More controversial is when a hitherto promising doctor is convicted of manslaughter (and subsequently struck off), despite significant mitigating factors comprising serious systemic failures within the hospital on the day in question.[4]

Gross negligence contrasts with ordinary negligence, which may precipitate a civil legal case, but not a criminal one.

Death by drowning in a care home: no prosecution for manslaughter, ordinary negligence not enough. A man with profound mental and physical disabilities, who was resident in a local authority care home, died by drowning in five inches of water. The police and Health and Safety Executive both concluded that there was inadequate evidence to prosecute. The Director of Public Prosecutions (DPP) concluded the same.

In the case of one of the care staff, it never crossed her mind that the man might be unsafe in the bath during the four to five minutes that he was left alone, since he had always kept his head out of the water in the past.

---

1   *R v Adomako* [1994] 3 All ER 79 (House of Lords).

2   'Doctor guilty of fatal injection.' *BBC News*, 6 February 2009. Accessed on 1 March 2018 at: http://news.bbc.co.uk/1/hi/england/staffordshire/7874296.stm.

3   Stokes, P. 'Nurse admits manslaughter after Alzheimer's victim dies of broken neck.' *Daily Telegraph*, 26 February 2009.

4   *General Medical Council v Dr. Baba-Garba* [2018] EWHC 76 (Admin). See also: Wollaston, S. 'Letter to the General Medical Council from the House of Commons Health Committee', 5 February 2018.

From an organisational point of view, there was a care plan, but it did not deal with the matter of bathing. The DPP had concluded that a formal policy on leaving a severely disabled person was not required because it was common sense. Furthermore, some risks were managed, some training was provided and staff members were appropriately experienced. The DPP decided that it would be difficult to find a guilty 'directing mind' at organisational level, and that there was an absence of conduct so 'bad' as to be described as gross negligence.

The court held, in reviewing the decision not to prosecute, that even if there had been ordinary common law negligence, criminality or badness still had to be established for a manslaughter case. The presence or absence of subjective recklessness was a relevant issue and the DPP had applied the right legal test.[1]

However, though necessary for the criminal law, gross negligence is not a necessary ingredient to argue a human rights case under article 2 of the European Convention.

Suicide of mental health patient: gross negligence not required for human rights case. When a patient detained under the Mental Health Act committed suicide, it was argued that a failure to take reasonable steps to prevent the risk of suicide constituted a breach of article 2 of the European Convention (a civil, rather than a criminal, offence). The NHS Trust argued that, in order to contemplate a breach of article 2, gross negligence (which would be sufficient to sustain a manslaughter charge) rather than ordinary negligence (which underpins a civil case for damages) was required. The court held that it was not necessary to show gross negligence in order to argue a breach of article 2.[2]

MANSLAUGHTER: GROSS NEGLIGENCE BY INFORMAL CARERS.

Manslaughter prosecutions relating to vulnerable adults arise in relation not just to health and care providers but to family members or friends also. In some cases, the perpetrators are arguably vulnerable themselves. These cases

---

1   *Rowley v Director of Public Prosecutions* [2003] EWHC Admin 693.

2   *Savage v South Essex Partnership NHS Foundation Trust* [2008] UKHL 74.

are particularly relevant, since local authorities, over the last 15 years, have progressively helped fewer people with social care needs – and are increasingly relying on family members to provide care. (They also contrast with the absence of individual or corporate manslaughter charges in cases of systemic, reckless neglect on a large scale, at the hands of health or care providers: see *Manslaughter: corporate* below.)

Woman with Diogenes syndrome, in the care of her daughter, found dead: manslaughter conviction. The daughter was a civilian police worker living in Leeds. She failed to provide adequate food, nourishment and care for her mother. She didn't summon medical help. She finally drove her dead mother to hospital. Her mother had been confined to bed. Death was caused by a combination of malnutrition and infected pressure sores. Police found the property in an uninhabitable state. Rooms were piled high with discarded possessions, soiled clothes, soiled nappies, food waste, bottles filled with urine, human waste and decaying rubbish.

Daughter found guilty of manslaughter despite unusual home circumstances. The daughter argued that she hadn't realised her mother was going to die. Yet the pressure sores were described by the judge as dreadful and shocking. Outside of the home, the daughter was described as professional, diligent, articulate and capable in her work. She was also relatively wealthy. She loved her mother, whilst at the same time neglecting her. The daughter raised the issues of Diogenes syndrome and *folie à deux*. The judge acknowledged her unusual background. He found that mother and daughter were enmeshed and that the mother, but not the daughter, suffered from Diogenes syndrome. But the daughter had become accustomed to that way of life both as a child and adult. She was found guilty of manslaughter.[1]

Informal carers guilty of manslaughter through gross negligence: vulnerable adults both victims and perpetrators. A partially deaf and almost blind man of low intelligence lived with a woman described as his mistress and as ineffectual and inadequate – together with the man's mentally impaired son. The man's sister came to live in the house as a lodger, in one room without ventilation, toilet or washing facilities save for a polythene bucket.

---

1 'Guiseley police worker jailed for letting mum, 82, starve to death.' *Yorkshire Post*, 11 July 2012.

> *Brother and partner did nothing for his helplessly infirm sister in upstairs room.* The sister was morbidly anxious not to put on weight, denied herself proper meals, and spent days at a time in the room. After three years, she had become helplessly infirm. The mistress, who took the sister food, tried to wash the sister with the help of a neighbour, who advised her to contact social services. Also, the licensee of a pub, frequented by the mistress and the man, advised her to get a doctor. The sister refused to give the name of her doctor, whom the man and mistress had attempted to locate. The man tried unsuccessfully to get his own doctor to attend. Neither the man nor the mistress made any further efforts to obtain professional assistance, not even mentioning anything to the social worker who visited the son.
>
> *Sister died of toxaemia from infected bedsores.* Three weeks after the attempt to wash the sister, she died of toxaemia, spreading because of infected bedsores, immobilisation and lack of food. Had she received medical attention during those three weeks, she would probably have survived.
>
> *Reckless disregard by brother and his partner.* The Court of Appeal upheld the conviction (although reduced the sentence) and described gross negligence in the following way:
>
> > The duty which a defendant has undertaken is a duty of caring for the health and welfare of the infirm person. What the prosecution have to prove is a breach of that duty in such circumstances that the jury feel convinced that the defendant's conduct can properly be described as reckless, that is to say a reckless disregard of danger to the health and welfare of the infirm person. Mere inadvertence is not enough. The defendant must be proved to have been indifferent to an obvious risk of injury to health, or actually to have foreseen the risk but to have determined nevertheless to run it.[1]

In the following case, a man had been convicted of the manslaughter of his mother. A further legal case followed as to whether – as a matter of public policy – he should be deprived of what he inherited from her, as a result of his wrongdoing. The court felt not, given his inadequacy to meet the challenges presented by his mother's condition, an inability to recognise that inadequacy and a hesitancy in turning to outside help.

---

1   *R v Stone* [1977] 64 Cr App R 186.

Son convicted of manslaughter of his mother. A woman was described as stubborn, domineering, hugely independent – and as one who shunned any type of 'officialdom', including doctors and home helps. Her son, in his fifties, lived with her. He had limited education, had never had a girlfriend and had worked as a labourer from the age of 15. He rarely went out, except to visit his father's grave; his only friend was his aunt. In January 2004, he called an ambulance. His mother was found suffering from severe bed sores all over her body, with one sore penetrating to her sacrum, large enough to take two fists. She was suffering from breast cancer; her wounds were consistent with lying in urine and faeces for a period of time.

A few months earlier she had suffered a fall. She had refused to go to hospital or have a doctor visit her. At her request, her son provided her with hot drinks, hot meals and whisky. By November he was cleaning her bed sores with antiseptic wipes and dressing them; he did not call the doctor. By December, his mother said it was too much for her to roll over; so he stopped attending to the wound in her back. When asked why he had acted as he did, he said he didn't really know. He accepted he should have called for help. He was prosecuted for manslaughter, pleaded guilty and was sentenced to four years in prison.[1]

In another case, a man pleaded guilty to the manslaughter of his wife, by gross negligence, but the sentence was reduced to reflect a number of mitigating factors.

Neglect of husband for nearly three weeks in not calling for ambulance. The appellant was convicted of manslaughter of his wife by gross negligence. He was her sole carer. She had lost a leg and had osteoporosis which caused brittle bones liable to fracture. In March, she fell, suffering broken bones. The husband did not call an ambulance for nearly three weeks. The wife then died in hospital a few weeks later from pneumonia. The husband was convicted to four years in prison. He appealed.

The sentence was reduced to 30 months. His wife had not wanted to go to hospital. She could have called for assistance herself. Although the

---

1   *Land v Land* [2006] EWHC 2997 (Ch).

neglect lasted nearly three weeks, she did not die during that time; her death was not wholly through the husband's lack of care and gross neglect.[1]

A sentence of two years and eight months' imprisonment was upheld on appeal, against a brother who had stood back and let his sister die.

Sister, in care of brother, found dying in profound squalor. The perpetrator was the brother and carer of his 58-year-old sister who shared a house with him and who is the deceased in this case. She suffered from a mild learning disability and low IQ. She was diabetic, grossly obese and suffered from panic attacks relating to travel, agoraphobia and inability to care for herself. She also suffered from hypertension and poor vision.

One afternoon, he called the emergency services who found the sister lying on the floor in an upstairs bedroom in a state of profound squalor. He told the paramedics that she had been lying there for about two and a half weeks following a fall. During that period the temperatures had been very cold, and the house had limited heating facilities. There was no central heating and no water supply, and although there were two electrical heaters, only one was working and that was downstairs. The bedroom was cold, and she was scantily clad in a nightgown, on wooden floorboards, covered in excrement and urine. She was barely conscious. Her toes and feet were gangrenous and there were pressure sores down her left side. On arrival at hospital, her core temperature was 27 degrees, 10 degrees below normal. She suffered several cardiac arrests in hospital but died in the early hours of the following day, primarily from hypothermia.

The brother was the only person who could have alerted the authorities to her condition. He had been grossly negligent in failing to provide for her basic needs of care, warmth and clothing, and to summon assistance when her condition deteriorated. He must have entered her room every day because he had provided food for her, but the only other care he had given her, until calling for the emergency services when it was too late, was to reposition her television set.

The sentence, while upheld by the Court of Appeal, would have been longer but for the fact that the brother had grown up in a grossly abnormal

---

1   *R v Hood* [2003] EWCA Crim 2772.

family and simply didn't appreciate the extremity of the living conditions in the house. This had impaired his ability to respond to his sister's needs.[1]

In contrast, the next case was about whether a man's partner (a nurse) was potentially guilty of manslaughter for failing to call for medical attention for the man – he had a gangrenous foot and was adamant in not wanting medical help. The coroner thought there was no duty on his partner, and the High Court agreed.

Not calling for a doctor to help man with a gangrenous foot at home: no duty on his partner (a nurse) to call for help. A man died of gangrene resulting from diabetic neuropathy after an injury to his foot. The question was whether the coroner should have returned a finding of unlawful killing on the basis of gross negligence manslaughter – instead of the 'narrative verdict' which he had in fact returned.

The man had very particular beliefs, which included the idea that physical ailments were symptomatic of emotional turmoil. As a result, he was opposed to traditional medical remedies. His GP had previously explained the dangers that could arise from broken skin and his diabetes. He became personally close to a registered nurse, who looked up to him as a spiritual teacher. He injured his foot when he stepped on an electric plug. The condition of the foot slowly deteriorated. As it got worse, he insisted that a doctor not be called; accordingly, the nurse did not call for one.

The coroner decided that, given the man's total opposition to medical help, and his knowledge of the risks he was running, there was not a duty on the nurse such as to return a verdict of unlawful killing (based on manslaughter by gross negligence).

One last question arose. Before he lapsed into unconsciousness for the last two hours of his life, he had not instructed the nurse not to call a doctor. She was therefore no longer bound by what he said when conscious. The coroner decided that, in any event, even if she had acted at that late stage, it would have made no significant difference to his dying. The court therefore upheld the coroner's decision.[2]

---

1   *R v Barrass* [2011] EWCA Crim 2629.

2   *R (Jenkins) v HM Coroner for Portsmouth and South East Hampshire* [2009] EWHC 3229 (Admin).

MANSLAUGHTER: CORPORATE. In the case of gross negligence or recklessness causing death, in health or care (and other organisational) settings, there are two main possibilities. The first is for individual employees, frontline staff or managers to be prosecuted under the common law. The second is for the organisation to be prosecuted under the Corporate Manslaughter and Corporate Homicide Act 2007. In summary, key points from the 2007 Act are as follows:

- **Duty of care, gross breach causing death.** An organisation commits the offence of corporate manslaughter where (a) it owes a duty of care, (b) it grossly breaches that duty because of how its activities are managed or organised, and (c) a person's death results.

- **Management or organisation of activities.** The way an organisation's activities are managed or organised by its senior management must be a substantial element of the breach in the duty of care.

- **Senior management.** This term means the people who play significant roles in (a) the making of decisions about how the whole or a substantial part of the organisation's activities are to be managed or organised, or (b) the actual managing or organising of the whole or a substantial part of those activities.

- **Gross breach of duty.** A breach of the duty of care is gross if it falls far below what can reasonably be expected of the organisation in the circumstances. However, the Act does not apply to a duty of care in relation to matters of public policy, and, in particular, the allocation of public resources or the weighing of competing public interests.

- **Breach of duty in relation to health and safety at work legislation.** If the alleged breach, leading to death, has followed from a failure to comply with health and safety at work legislation, the jury has to consider how serious that failure was and how much of a risk of death it posed. The jury may also (a) consider the extent to which, on the evidence, there were attitudes, policies, systems or accepted practices that were likely to have encouraged any such failure, and (b) have regard to any health and safety guidance that relates to the alleged breach.

- **Conviction: fines, remedial orders, publicity orders.** Conviction can result in an unlimited fine being imposed on the organisation. The Act provides for remedial orders being made by the court, forcing the organisation to remedy the problems that led to the breach; and also for publicity orders forcing the organisation to publish details of the conviction. However, an organisation cannot be committed to prison.

At the time of writing, corporate manslaughter prosecutions and convictions have been few and far between. The following is a rare example from health and social care.

Care home company convicted of corporate manslaughter, owner convicted of manslaughter. A care home owner was sentenced to three years in prison for manslaughter of a woman with dementia, following her admission to the home on discharge from hospital. In addition, his company was fined £300,000 for corporate manslaughter.

A post-mortem report showed neglect had led directly to her death. In 48 days she lost almost half her body weight. She was emaciated, dehydrated and malnourished, and had a severe pressure sore. The basic essentials of human existence were inadequate: food, water, heating, sanitation and cleanliness. In an attempt to cover up the neglect, a meticulous logbook of her care was fabricated, including when she was washed. One of the care workers stated that if a resident was ill and maybe needed hospital admission, the managers told staff to give paracetamol – because the home would not be paid if a resident was in hospital. Sometimes there was a lack of sheets to change the residents' beds, of incontinence pads and even teabags.

A second person was sentenced to one year in prison suspended for two years for breach of the Health and Safety at Work Act 1974.[1]

Corporate manslaughter charges were, in principle, possible to bring in common law prior to the 2007 Act. During the 2000s, in three particular cases – which stand out in a series of scandals – the Healthcare Commission identified large numbers of avoidable deaths – scores in two hospitals, hundreds in a third.

In each of these cases the poor care and deaths flowed from a system of work and management which was grossly flawed, and which could be traced

---

1   'Nottingham care home boss jailed for manslaughter.' *BBC News*, 5 February 2016. Accessed on 12 January 2018 at: www.bbc.co.uk/news/uk-england-nottinghamshire-35499865.

directly to senior management. In the third of these cases, involving Stafford Hospital, the systemic nature of the poor and sometimes appalling standard of care – and the responsibility of senior management – was confirmed by first an independent inquiry and then a public inquiry.

Maidstone and Tunbridge Wells NHS Trust: no corporate manslaughter prosecution. Consideration was reportedly given to corporate manslaughter prosecution at Maidstone and Tunbridge Wells NHS Trust – where up to 90 people died, avoidably, of *Clostridium difficile*, in association with shocking standards of care.[1]

The police stated that 'having reviewed the report and interviewed the author and the experts engaged by the Healthcare Commission, Kent Police has concluded that there is no information to indicate that any grossly negligent act has occurred'.[2] Given just how appalling were the standards reported – and photographed – by the Healthcare Commission, this represents a troubling statement.

The failures in care identified poor prescribing of antibiotics, inadequate monitoring of patients for *Clostridium difficile* and for its associated complications such as dehydration, shortage of nursing staff, extremely poor basic nursing care, serious failures in hygiene and cleaning practices, proximity of beds (some bed heads were no more than 12 inches apart) and over-occupancy of beds.[3]

Stoke Mandeville Hospital: no corporate manslaughter prosecution. Death from infection at Stoke Mandeville Hospital also gave rise to deliberation about manslaughter charges against the Trust Board. Amongst other things, the Trust had persistently ignored the advice of its own infection control team and refused to use side rooms to isolate infected patients. The reason for not doing so related to performance and financial targets, not clinical priorities and patient safety. The crux of the Healthcare Commission's report into events at Stoke Mandeville is that it pointed to the Trust Board's

1   Rose, D. 'Hospital ordered to halt pay off to chief after superbug scandal.' *The Times*, 12 October 2008.

2   Hawkes, N. 'No-one to be prosecuted over 90 C-difficile deaths at Kent hospitals.' *The Times*, 30 July 2008.

3   Healthcare Commission. *Investigation into outbreaks of* Clostridium difficile *at Maidstone and Tunbridge Wells NHS Trust, October 2007*. London: HC, 2007, pp.44–58.

deliberate disregarding of infection control (and associated basic care) in the pursuit of other, essentially political, priorities and targets. This decision, in turn, led to the continuation of a whole range of poor practices associated with between 30 and 40 deaths.[1]

Mid Staffordshire NHS Foundation Trust: no corporate manslaughter prosecution. Many hundreds of people were estimated to have died at Stafford Hospital over a three- to four-year period, due to poor and neglectful care, which in turn could be traced back to a ruthless determination to save money by the Trust Board. The descriptions of the care being provided are harrowing.[2] Yet no manslaughter charges were brought.[3]

When Mrs Gillian Astbury died in 2007 at Stafford Hospital, after she had not been given her insulin, a police investigation was conducted into possible manslaughter (not corporate) charges against three nurses. In the event, in August 2010, the CPS decided there was insufficient evidence. Instead, two nurses were sacked and the third suspended.[4] A month after this decision, an inquest jury would find that Mrs Astbury's death was due to gross defects in care.[5] A prosecution of the Trust, under the Health and Safety at Work Act 1974, was eventually brought, resulting in conviction of a health and safety offence.[6]

In the following case, a corporate manslaughter case was taken (albeit failing) in relation to a shortcut taken with the maintenance of an air-conditioning system. This resulted in an outbreak of Legionnaire's disease, leading to a

---

1   Healthcare Commission. *Investigation into outbreaks of* Clostridium difficile *at Stoke Mandeville Hospital, Buckinghamshire Hospitals NHS Trust, July 2006*. London: HC, 2006, p.2.

2   Healthcare Commission. *Investigation into Mid Staffordshire NHS Foundation Trust, March 2009*. London: HC, 2009. Also: Francis, R. (Chair). *Independent Inquiry into care provided by Mid Staffordshire NHS Foundation Trust January 2005–March 2009*. London: The Stationery Office, 2010.

3   Davani, A. 'Police asked to consider corporate manslaughter charges at Stafford Hospital.' *Birmingham Post*, 9 March 2010.

4   Corser, J. 'Two Stafford Hospital nurses sacked over patient death.' *Express and Star*, 30 August 2010.

5   Grainger, L. '"Appalling" standards in care led to the death of Hednesford grandmother.' *Cannock Chase Post*, 16 September 2010.

6   'Stafford hospital to be sentenced over poor care of diabetic patient who died.' *The Guardian*, 21 February 2014.

number of deaths. Both the council (corporately) and the individual architect involved were prosecuted for manslaughter.

> **Shortcuts on maintenance and inspection contract for air-conditioning system: prosecution.** A council architect and Barrow Council were both prosecuted for manslaughter after a number of people died of Legionnaire's disease at a council arts centre. The architect had cancelled a maintenance and inspection contract for the air-conditioning system. Five people died and another 172 were infected. The manslaughter case failed; both the architect and the Council were subsequently convicted of health and safety at work offences and fined.[1]

In terms of shortcuts being taken with people's welfare and lives, those at Stafford, Stoke Mandeville and Maidstone appear to dwarf those taken in Barrow.

MANSLAUGHTER: INVOLUNTARY, BY UNLAWFUL ACT. Involuntary manslaughter by an unlawful act is distinct from involuntary manslaughter by gross negligence or recklessness. The former must be an act, as opposed to an omission, which a reasonable person would realise would subject the victim to some risk of physical harm, albeit not serious harm – whether or not the perpetrator realised this.[2]

> **Physical abuse of man with learning disabilities by teenagers before death in river.** A man with learning disabilities was subjected to a campaign of physical abuse in his home, by a group of teenagers. Having previously shaved clumps of hair from his head, daubed make-up on his face, urinated in his drinks, smoked cannabis in his flat, scrawled graffiti on his walls and poured bleach on him, they then beat him and threw him into the River Mersey where he died. They were jailed for life for manslaughter. He had learning disabilities, was a heavy drinker and had the capacity to make his

---

1   Hogg, D. 'Architect fined over deadly outbreak of disease.' *Yorkshire Post*, 1 August 2006.

2   Crown Prosecution Service. *Homicide, murder and manslaughter: guidance.* London: CPS, undated.

own decisions – but his vulnerability meant that he 'couldn't say no to the people who came to his door'.[1]

With the bullying or harassment of vulnerable adults in mind, the following convictions are notable, because the actual act causing death was committed by the victims themselves, but the perpetrators of the bullying or harassment were still convicted.

Bullying leading to manslaughter conviction, following suicide of victim. A 19-year-old woman and 15-year-old girl were found guilty of manslaughter, committed two years earlier, of a 19-year-old woman who had thrown herself out of a window. This had followed a number of incidents of escalating violence leading up to the day of the woman's death. On the day of death, the campaign of bullying had included punching, kicking, violent hair pulling, derogatory name calling, grabbing and ripping clothing. The woman had then thrown herself out of a window to escape threats, verbal abuse and physical assault. One of the perpetrators was given a hospital order under sections 37 and 41 of the Mental Health Act 1983. The other was sentenced to eight years in prison.

Controlling and coercive behaviour leading to suicide and manslaughter conviction. A man was sent to prison for ten years for the manslaughter of his ex-girlfriend after she killed herself as a 'direct result' of his controlling behaviour. He had sent her abusive voicemails, texts and Facebook messages and stalked her. He had become very manipulative, controlling and cold, fitted a tracer to her scooter, sent her hundreds of texts and messages when she went out, tracked her on social media and sometimes stopped her from going out. When she tried to leave the house, he would physically throw her to the floor and put his hands around her neck. He had previous convictions for assault and harassment against other partners. He was convicted not just of manslaughter but also controlling and coercive behaviour and of six counts of stalking.[2]

---

1   Carter, H. 'He couldn't say "no".' *The Guardian (Society)*, 15 August 2007.

2   'Man jailed for manslaughter over ex-girlfriend's suicide.' *BBC News*, 28 July 2017. Accessed on 27 June 2018 at: www.bbc.co.uk/news/uk-40758095.

MANSLAUGHTER: VOLUNTARY, THROUGH DIMINISHED RESPONSIBILITY. The charge of murder may in some circumstances be reduced to voluntary manslaughter because of diminished responsibility. This means the person was suffering from such abnormality of mind – whether arising from a condition of arrested or retarded development of mind or any inherent causes or induced by disease or injury – so as substantially to have impaired his or her mental responsibility for his acts or omissions in doing or being a party to the killing.[1]

One such case involved a 72-year-old man who started a relationship with a woman on a low-security, mixed-sex, mental health ward in a care home. He had a history of assaults on women. He stabbed the woman to death, after he had failed to receive a three-weekly injection of anti-psychotic drugs. He was jailed for life.[2] It was similarly manslaughter through diminished responsibility when an 82-year-old care home resident bludgeoned a fellow resident to death with an iron.

> **Care home killing: diminished responsibility through undetected psychopathic illness.** An 82-year-old woman, charged with murder, was convicted of manslaughter on grounds of diminished responsibility. Using an ornamental iron, she had bludgeoned to death a 93-year-old fellow resident in a care home in Newcastle-upon-Tyne. She told police she had not hit the woman enough. She suffered from a psychopathic illness, having previously spent 14 years in secure hospitals and been convicted ten years earlier of grievous bodily harm for attacking a 72-year-old woman with a chair. Her medical records and criminal history had not been passed on to the care home.[3]

A very different type of case might involve family carers who had reached breaking point through stress and themselves were unwell.

---

1   Homicide Act 1957, s.2.

2   Brody, S. 'Council seeks stronger safeguards after killing at Surrey home.' *Community Care*, 12–18 January 2006.

3   Norfolk, A. 'Care home killer, 82, was violent psychopath.' *The Times*, 10 June 2005.

Informal carer himself developing dementia, exhausted, depressed, sleep-deprived: convicted of the manslaughter of his wife with dementia, for whom he was caring. The 82-year-old husband was the main carer for his wife of 60 years. She had dementia and he had to give her daily insulin injections. He had two hours' sleep per night as a result of caring for his wife and she was often aggressive towards him.

He cared for his wife well but was not coping. When arrested, he said that he had stabbed his wife to death. At times he had become cross with his wife and had wanted to hit her, but did not tell anyone about the difficulties he faced, had lost a significant amount of weight over the previous year whilst caring for his wife, had a urinary tract infection, and became weepy after the incident. He himself was in the early stages of dementia and had an adjustment disorder, which meant that he was more likely to lose control. His lack of self-control was due to dementia, physical exhaustion, lack of sleep and depression.

The original conviction of three years' imprisonment, on appeal, was reduced to a 24-month term of imprisonment suspended for 24 months, with a 12-month residential and mental health requirement imposed instead. The offender had been the sole carer of his wife, who had dementia; he was in the early stages of dementia himself; and the strain of caring for his wife and serving part of his sentence had led to a decline in his physical and mental health.

The Court of Appeal stated the case was tragic, but it was not a mercy killing; the husband's responsibility was diminished but not extinguished. It was necessary to balance the sanctity of human life with mercy, given his age and frailty. The prison report painted a sad picture of the husband: the sanctity of human life would not be undermined if the court intervened to reduce the sentence.[1]

Mother killing disabled son, unbearable pressure, diminished responsibility, role of social services. A mother killed her 36-year-old son who had Down's syndrome. She gave him 14 sleeping pills and suffocated him with a plastic bag. She then swallowed some pills herself and attempted to kill herself with a kitchen knife.

The judge acknowledged the exceptional nature of the case and the unbearable pressure she had been under for more than 30 years. She had

---

1   *R v Beaver* [2015] EWCA Crim 653.

pleaded for help from the local authority (social services) and from her GP. Her eldest son gave evidence that her devotion to her disabled son had been saintly. Her son had flourished in early life before developing autism in his twenties and harming himself; he blinded himself in one eye. He had been enrolled in a day centre but was excluded for disruptive behaviour. He did better when assisted by a social integration team, but this was disbanded for lack of funds.

Most recently, social services had not provided a care manager, although it had acknowledged the urgency of her situation. It maintained that it had offered help, but the mother had refused it. She was convicted of manslaughter on the grounds of diminished responsibility and given a suspended two-year prison term.[1]

The following case involved a seemingly vulnerable perpetrator, a vulnerable victim and no outside help – all leading to abnormal stress.

Brutal killing of woman with dementia by 'inadequate' man in situation of abnormal stress. A 20-year-old man pleaded guilty to manslaughter through diminished responsibility. He had killed a 91-year-old woman. She had been living at home with the man and his wife. This had been arranged by the woman's nephew. The wife was the niece of this nephew. The nephew said they could live there if they looked after his aunt. The woman had dementia. She needed assistance 24 hours a day. The couple expected they would have help, either arranged by the nephew or through the local authority. This didn't happen. One evening, after drinking eight bottles of beer, the man snapped. He went up to the woman's room and launched a sustained attack, leaving her with such severe injuries that she died a few days later in hospital.

The man had had a troubled upbringing involving beatings and emotional and sexual abuse. He suffered from long-standing emotional instability and, at the time of the offence, from severe clinical depression. The offence was out of character; there was no continuing risk to anybody else.

The sentencing had to weigh up a brutal killing against the man's youth, inadequacy and mental impairment (mild), and the fact that the

---

1   Laville, S. 'Mother who killed son with Down's syndrome gets suspended sentence.' *The Guardian*, 3 November 2005.

nephew had abdicated his responsibility, leaving everything up to the man and his wife, to cope with a very sick and demanding woman – leading to abnormal stress. On appeal, the sentence was reduced from six to four and a half years.[1]

Father killing daughter: diminished responsibility. When a father suffocated his mentally ill daughter, he was convicted of manslaughter due to diminished responsibility and given a two-year suspended jail sentence. She had repeatedly tried to kill herself, suffered from severe personality disorder and deep depression, and was an alcoholic. She had been asked to leave a specialist NHS unit the day before. The daughter had leaned towards her father for him to cover her head with a plastic bag; when that failed, he suffocated her with a pillow.[2]

Further along the spectrum, such killings may amount to murder, rather than manslaughter through diminished responsibility.

Murder of wife. When a man killed his wife of 33 years (who suffered from an irritable bowel condition), after she had persuaded him to help her die, he was convicted of murder. He had bought her nearly 100 paracetamol tablets, roses and two farewell cards. He placed a plastic bag over her head and smothered her with a pillow.[3]

Mother convicted of murder of her own son. A woman killed her son with an injection of heroin at the nursing home where he was resident. This was following a catastrophic accident when he fell out of an ambulance, could not move, could communicate only by squeezing his hands and had to be tube-fed. She claimed she did it out of love; she was sentenced to life imprisonment with a minimum period of nine years.[4]

1   *R v Slater* [2005] EWCA Crim 898.

2   Smith, L. 'Father who suffocated sick daughter is freed.' *The Times*, 9 June 2001.

3   Batchelor, W. (2007) 'Man guilty of murdering wife in assisted euthanasia.' *The Independent*, 10 May 2007.

4   Bannerman, L. 'Jury heckled over murder verdict for mother who "acted out of love".' *The Times*, 21 January 2010.

MAPPA, see *Multi-Agency Public Protection Arrangements*

Marriage

Marriage tends to become part of safeguarding on the basis of two main concerns: mental capacity and coercion. In terms of the latter, forced marriage is now a criminal offence, and further legislation makes provision for forced marriage protection orders. Arrangements to marry, made for a person who lacks the mental capacity to understand marriage, amount by definition to forced marriage. See *Forced marriage*.

MARRIAGE: MENTAL CAPACITY. As far as mental capacity goes, some of the key points are:

- **Consent to marriage cannot be made on behalf of another person.** Section 27 of the Mental Capacity Act 2005 (MCA) states that nothing in the Act permits a decision about marriage to be made on behalf of somebody else. This means that a best interests decision cannot be made for a person to the effect that they should marry. Therefore, a person lacking capacity cannot in principle marry. (Under section 12c of the Matrimonial Causes Act 1973, a marriage is voidable if 'either party to the marriage did not validly consent to it, whether in consequence of duress, mistake, unsoundness of mind or otherwise'.)

- **Best interests.** Best interests are therefore legally irrelevant when it comes to marriage. Either a person has mental capacity to marry or they don't. For example, in a case about whether a young woman with learning disabilities should marry, the court noted that significant confusion underlay the case. The local authority was asking the court to decide whether it was in the woman's best interests to marry. But, the court had 'no business – in fact…no jurisdiction – to embark upon a determination of that question'.[1]

- **Mental capacity to marry.** The test of capacity for marriage has been set out by the courts: '(1) Does he or she understand the nature of the marriage

---

1   *Sheffield CC v E* [2004] EWHC Fam 2808.

contract? (2) Does he or she understand the duties and responsibilities that normally attach to marriage? The duties and responsibilities that normally attach to marriage are as follows: marriage, whether civil or religious, is a contract, formally entered into. It confers on the parties the status of husband and wife, the essence of the contract being an agreement between a man and a woman to live together, and to love one another as husband and wife, to the exclusion of all others. It creates a relationship of mutual and reciprocal obligations, typically involving the sharing of a common home and a common domestic life and the right to enjoy each other's society, comfort and assistance.'[1]

- **Not setting the bar too high.** The courts have stated that setting the test of capacity for marriage too high could operate as an 'unfair, unnecessary and indeed discriminatory bar against the mentally disabled'.[2]

- **Capacity test is general, not specific to prospective spouse.** The test is whether the person understands the nature of marriage in general; it is not a test that is specific to a particular prospective spouse.[3]

- **Distinguishing capacity for marriage from capacity for sexual activity.** Capacity to understand and consent to marriage automatically embraces sexual activity. The converse is not so; therefore, the test for marriage is higher and more complex. See *Sexual activity*.

As a consequence of these rules concerning marriage, a succession of legal cases has found its way to court in the context of safeguarding. The cases have centred largely, though not wholly, on (younger) adults with learning disabilities. In turn, a subset of these cases has focused on cultural issues.

Not legally a question of wisdom: marriage between a woman with learning disabilities and a convicted sex offender. A 23-year-old woman with learning disabilities wished to marry a 37-year-old man with a history of sexually violent crimes; the court was called on to consider whether or not she had capacity to marry. It made the following point:

---

1   *Sheffield CC v E* [2004] EWHC Fam 2808.

2   *Sheffield CC v E* [2004] EWHC Fam 2808.

3   *Sheffield CC v E* [2004] EWHC Fam 2808.

The question of whether E has capacity to marry is quite distinct from the question of whether E is wise to marry; either wise to marry at all, or wise to marry X rather than Y, or wise to marry S. In relation to her marriage the only question for the court is whether E has capacity to marry. The court has no jurisdiction to consider whether it is in E's best interests to marry or to marry S. It is not concerned with the wisdom of her marriage in general or her marriage to S in particular.[1]

Cultural issues not affecting the validity of a marriage. A man with learning disabilities – who lacked the capacity to understand the nature of marriage – was married, in a Muslim ceremony conducted on the telephone, to a woman in Bangladesh. The intention of the parents was clearly that the matrimonial home was to be in England. Accepting that in this particular case the marriage was contracted in Bangladesh, and was valid in that country, the Court of Appeal was emphatic that it would not be so in England. The court held that the man had to be protected from the abuse that would result, permitted or encouraged by his parents.[2]

Gross interference with autonomy. The courts have stated that to force a marriage on an incapacitous person is a gross interference with his or her autonomy. Its concomitants, sexual relations and, as a foreseeable consequence, pregnancy, constitute not only a breach of autonomy but also bodily integrity, perhaps one of the most severe that can be imagined, and the consequences could be lifelong.[3]

Criminal consequences of abusive and injurious marriage of person lacking capacity. In one case, the courts stated that

the marriage which his parents have arranged for him is potentially highly injurious. He has not the capacity to understand the introduction of NK into his life and that introduction would be likely to destroy his equilibrium or destabilize his emotional state... Were IC's parents to permit or encourage sexual intercourse...NK would be guilty of the crime of rape under the provisions of the

---

1   *Sheffield CC v E* [2004] EWHC Fam 2808.

2   *KC v City of Westminster Social and Community Services Department* [2008] EWCA Civ 198.

3   *XCC v AA* [2012] EWHC 2183 (COP).

> Sexual Offences Act 2003. Physical intimacy which stops short of penetrative sex would constitute the crime of indecent assault... Their engineering of the telephonic marriage is potentially if not actually abusive of IC. It is the duty of the court to protect IC from that potential abuse. The refusal of recognition of the marriage is an essential foundation of that protection.[1]

One ramification of the relatively low threshold required for a person to understand marriage is that a person might, for example, have capacity to remarry but lack the capacity to make a new will – required, since an existing will becomes legally invalid on marriage. This could lead, in some cases, to safeguarding concerns:

> **Woman with dementia remarrying, but unable to make a new will: safeguarding concerns?** An 87-year-old woman with developing dementia remarried, having been befriended by a 63-year-old man. She had the mental capacity to do so but lacked the capacity to make a new will. The woman's daughter had lasting power of attorney – and therefore control of her mother's finances – but did not find out about the marriage until her mother had died. This meant that, in law, the mother died intestate, with her entire estate passing to her new husband. Police spent a year investigating whether the husband could be charged with the criminal offence of forced marriage under the Anti-Social Behaviour Act 2014, but the Crown Prosecution Service brought no prosecution.[2]

Medical Act 1983, see *General Medical Council*

Medication

Misuse of medication, when it is given by one person to another, can give rise to various criminal offences:

---

1   *KC v City of Westminster Social and Community Services Department* [2008] EWCA Civ 198.

2   Ames, J. 'Loophole that lets gold-diggers wed vulnerable elderly.' *The Times*, 21 November 2018.

- **Assault:** common law assault.

- **Imprisonment:** common law false imprisonment.

- **Drugs:** application of stupefying, overpowering drugs with intent to commit an indictable (serious) offence – section 22 of the Offences Against the Person Act 1861 (OAPA).

- **Poison:** poisoning – or administering noxious substance – with intent to injure, aggrieve or annoy – sections 23 and 24 of the Offences Against the Person Act 1861.

- **Administration:** unlawfully administering medication – section 58 of the Medicines Act 1968.

- **Ill-treatment:** section 127 of the Mental Health Act 1983, section 44 of the Mental Capacity Act 2005, sections 20–25 of the Criminal Justice and Courts Act 2015.

- **Regulatory requirements:** failure to comply with regulatory conditions for management and use of medication – Health and Social Care Act (Regulated Activities) Regulations 2014, regulation 12.[1]

Sedating care home residents with unprescribed drugs: conviction under the Offences Against the Person Act 1861. A nurse on night shift at a care home regularly gave six patients unprescribed medication in the form of a fast-acting sleeping pill. The drug used usually works for six hours, is a drug prescribed to patients with depression and panic attacks, has a side effect of drowsiness and is an anti-psychotic drug used to treat restlessness. The patients became unsteady on their feet and were then often taken to bed in a wheelchair, where they slept. This enabled the carer to rest or sleep undisturbed during her shift.

She was observed approaching residents with a glass of orange juice in one hand and putting a small cream-coloured tablet in the residents' mouths. They would all be asleep within five to eight minutes. Suspicions were reported to police and hair samples taken from a total of nine residents – one at a post-mortem; six returned positive for the presence of

---

1   See e.g. Crown Prosecution Service. *Crimes against older people – CPS prosecution policy.* London: CPS, undated. Accessed on 23 December 2016 at: https://www.cps.gov.uk/publication/policy-guidance-prosecution-crimes-against-older-people.

unprescribed drugs.[1] The nurse was convicted under the Offences Against the Person Act 1861 and sentenced to three years' imprisonment.[2]

Mental capacity

A person who is deemed to lack mental capacity to make decisions about significant aspects of their life tends to be more vulnerable to abuse or neglect. Thus, capacity issues form a central, but not the only, plank of safeguarding. The relevant legislation comes in the form of the Mental Capacity Act 2005. The Act operates on two different principles, empowerment and protection, both of which have obvious implications for safeguarding. For the purposes of this book, the Act is covered below under the following headings:

- Mental capacity: empowerment and protection

- Mental capacity: five key principles

- Mental capacity: assumption of capacity

- Mental capacity: assisting people to take decisions for themselves

- Mental capacity: unwise decisions

- Mental capacity: best interests

- Mental capacity: best interests and less restriction

- Mental capacity: best interests and physical risk

- Mental capacity: best interests, available options and resources

- Mental capacity: acts of care or treatment.

MENTAL CAPACITY: EMPOWERMENT AND PROTECTION. The Mental Capacity Act empowers the individual, for example, by insisting that capacity must be assumed until otherwise established, that people should be

---

1   'Carer drugged elderly so she could sleep on duty, jury hears.' *Daily Telegraph*, 21 August 2012.

2   Griffith, J. 'Carer Mirela Aionoaei jailed for drugging dementia patients.' *Getwestlondon*, 26 September 2013. Accessed on 1 March 2018 at: www.getwestlondon.co.uk/news/local-news/carer-mirela-aionoaei-jailed-drugging-5972664.

assisted to make decisions for themselves and that unwise decisions do not necessarily mean incapacity. Even with incapacity established, people should still be involved in decisions as far as possible, and consideration given to achieving their best interests in less restrictive ways. All this is about avoiding the removal, without good reason, of people's fundamental rights.

On the other hand, more traditional protection comes into play when best interests decisions are taken and, in some circumstances, restriction or deprivation of liberty occurs in order to serve those best interests.

This dual function of the Act sometimes results in tension when it comes to safeguarding vulnerable adults – either when an adult with capacity to make certain decisions is making those decisions in such a way as to render himself or herself vulnerable to significant harm, or when an adult lacks capacity and the question arises as to what degree of risk in their daily life is consistent with their best interests.

MENTAL CAPACITY: FIVE KEY PRINCIPLES. It is beyond the scope of this book to consider the Mental Capacity Act 2005 in detail. Instead, it focuses on some aspects particularly relevant to adult safeguarding. The five key principles in the Act are illustrated immediately below, relating to assumption of capacity, assistance to take a decision, unwise decision, best interests and less restriction. Some other aspects are explained in the context of safeguarding under the following headings in this book: *Restraint*; *Deprivation of liberty*; *Lasting power of attorney*; *Deputies*; *Advance decisions*; *Marriage*; *Sexual activity*.

A failure to follow the principles in section 1 of the Act can lead to unlawful and – sometimes – seemingly abusive intervention by a local authority.

MENTAL CAPACITY: ASSUMPTION OF CAPACITY. Section 1 of the Act states that a person must be assumed to have capacity unless it is established that he or she lacks capacity. It is therefore not possible legally to act in a person's best interests unless it is first established that the person lacks the capacity to take the decision in question for him- or herself. The lack of capacity has to be established on the balance of probability (the civil law standard of proof, therefore, and not the criminal law standard of being beyond reasonable doubt).

Nonetheless, in practice, interventions sometimes take place before a lack of capacity is established. Although practitioners involved believe they are acting in good faith and for the best, to protect the person from some form of abuse or neglect, such interventions are not only unlawful but can have serious consequences.

Elderly man, with mental capacity, deprived of liberty unlawfully in secure unit. An elderly man was held in a secure dementia unit of a care home for 16 months, even though for most of this time it had not been established that he lacked capacity to decide where to live – which meant that in law he had mental capacity and had unlawfully, and contrary to human rights, been deprived of his liberty. The trigger for this happening appeared to be a disproportionate response to a safeguarding concern: about possible financial exploitation of the man's generosity by members of the church that the man attended.[1]

Man prevented, unlawfully, from seeing his partner for 22 months. A local authority prevented a man from seeing his partner in a care home for 22 months – ostensibly in the latter's best interests – despite the fact that an assessment of her capacity had taken ten months to obtain, during which period she therefore legally had mental capacity. This was on the basis of unsubstantiated safeguarding grounds. This constituted a breach of human rights.[2]

Daughter banned from seeing her dying mother, despite mother's capacity. A local authority and care home prevented a daughter visiting her mother in a care home for the six weeks it took to assess the mother's capacity to decide about seeing her daughter. The ban was decided upon as being in the mother's best interests, in response to uninvestigated and unsubstantiated safeguarding concerns. The mother, in fact, was finally assessed as having capacity during this time (legally and actually), but by the time the daughter was allowed to visit, the mother had suffered a stroke the day before and did not recognise her daughter; the next day she

---

1   *Essex County Council v RG* [2015] EWCOP 1.

2   *City of Sunderland v MM* (2011) 1 FLR 712.

died. The local authority was criticised severely by the local government ombudsman.[1]

MENTAL CAPACITY: ASSISTING PEOPLE TO TAKE DECISIONS FOR THEMSELVES. Section 1 of the Mental Capacity Act states that a person is not to be treated as unable to make a decision unless all practicable steps to help him to do so have been taken without success.

Examples of practical assistance. In one case, practical assistance would involve working with and educating a woman with learning disabilities to enable her to understand contraception.[2] In another, to assist a man to understand sexual activity (its nature and reasonably foreseeable consequences), so that he could lawfully have sex with his wife. In the latter case, a failure on the part of a local authority to provide such help and education resulted in liability to pay compensation under the Human Rights Act 1998.[3]

MENTAL CAPACITY: UNWISE DECISIONS. Section 1 of the Mental Capacity Act states that a person is not to be treated as unable to make a decision merely because he or she makes an unwise decision. So an unwise decision must not be confused, as a matter of course, with lack of capacity. This rule is one that creates some difficulty in safeguarding, when a local authority wants to protect somebody who is clearly vulnerable but is, in its view, making highly unwise and detrimental decisions, yet cannot be shown to lack capacity. Without establishing lack of capacity, there can be no decision made in the person's best interests.

Unwise decision or lack of capacity: remaining at home instead of a nursing home. A woman wished to remain in her cottage, rather than be deprived of her liberty in a nursing home. The local authority claimed she

---

1   LGO, *Leeds City Council*, 2011 (10 012 561).

2   *A Local Authority v Mrs. A* [2010] EWHC 1549 (Fam).

3   *CH v A Metropolitan Council* [2017] EWCOP 12.

lacked mental capacity and relied on expert evidence to this effect. The woman, however, explained clearly to the judge why she wanted to remain in her own home. In addition, there had been practical care issues in that she had overused a community alarm system, simply because she was lonely, and there were issues about her eating.

However, the judge found that neither of these care issues – loneliness and difficulties with eating – had anything to do with lack of mental capacity. He concluded that the local authority and the experts had fallen into the trap of confusing what they considered an unwise decision with a person's capacity.[1]

On the one hand, therefore, the question is not whether the person is making a rational decision but whether he or she has the capacity to make a rational decision.[2] And 'it is not the task of the courts to prevent those who have the mental capacity to make rational decisions from making decisions which others may regard as rash or irresponsible'. Since many people 'make rash and irresponsible decisions but are of full capacity'.[3]

Thus, in what would be termed safeguarding cases, the courts have refused to intervene and prevent – on the grounds of an unwise decision being made – a 23-year-old woman with learning disabilities marrying a 37-year-old man with a substantial history of sexually violent crimes;[4] likewise, in a case involving a woman with mental health problems whom the local authority wished to prevent from engaging in harmful sexual relationships with men.[5] And similarly:

Capacity to engage in sexual relationship disapproved of by the local authority. A woman suffered from schizophrenia, characterised by prominent visual, auditory and tactile somatic hallucinations, made worse by stress. She had a moderate learning disability and had poor cognitive functioning. She had significantly impaired or non-existent verbal recall

---

1   *CC v KK* [2012] EWHC 2136 (COP), paras 67–73.

2   *Lindsay v Wood* [2006] EWHC 2895 (QB).

3   *Masterman-Lister v Brutton* [2002] EWHC 417 (QB); [2002] EWCA Civ 1889.

4   *Sheffield CC v E* [2004] EWHC 2808 (Fam).

5   *Ealing London Borough Council v KS* [2008] EWHC 636 (Fam).

and was functionally illiterate. She lacked the capacity to litigate, decide where and with whom to live, to determine with whom she should have contact, to manage her own financial arrangements and to marry. But, legally, she had the capacity to consent to sexual relations.

For 15 years, she had conducted a personal, sexual relationship with a man who himself had a psychopathic personality disorder and misused alcohol. He led an unstable and nomadic life; he had been violent towards the woman and was alleged to have used her benefit money to buy alcohol. He had previously encouraged her to follow him, which, according to the local authority, led to deterioration in her mental health. However, equally, it was clear that the relationship was all-important to the woman and that she derived considerable benefit from it in terms of positive emotional feelings. Also, she was more than capable of expressing her wishes and feelings 'as her oral evidence and the manner in which she gave it so vividly demonstrated'.[1]

In a further case:

Assisting a person to understand contraception to decide whether to have a baby. The court contemplated a woman with learning disabilities – if she was shown to have the capacity to decide about contraception – making the decision to have another baby, despite the fact that two babies had previously been removed at birth, on the grounds that she had no concept of what was involved in motherhood. However, it was all a question of whether she had capacity or not, not whether she was making an unwise decision. The judge held that the local authority should make efforts to educate the woman, so that she could take the decision about contraception herself.[2]

The education to be provided in this last case would effectively have been under the second principle in section 1 of the Mental Capacity Act – providing all practicable assistance to enable a person to take the decision for themselves. This raises the question as to whether, in safeguarding, a local authority is *in reality* likely to provide less assistance to somebody about to

---

1   *Local Authority X v MM* [2007] EWHC 2003 (Fam).

2   *A Local Authority v Mrs. A* [2010] EWHC 1549 (Fam).

take a highly unwise decision than to somebody making a 'wise' decision. Clearly, *in principle*, it should make no difference.

The difficulties are self-evident, including for the courts. They have pointed out, for example, that outcomes of a decision can 'cast a flood of light on capacity' and are likely to be important, though not conclusive, indicators.[1] In the following case, the judge appeared to come close to equating wise decisions with capacity and unwise decisions with lack of capacity.

> **Appropriate decisions indicating capacity about diabetic treatment, inappropriate lack of capacity?** A woman in her sixties was diabetic. She had a history of non-compliance with insulin treatment. One day she was found on the floor of her home in rooms covered in faeces and with five dogs in the property. She was very disorientated and unable to stand. She was taken to hospital with a very high blood-sugar level. Since then, there had been similar events. She had multiple health conditions including hypertension and chronic obstructive pulmonary disease. She neglected herself. The judge held that she lacked the capacity to decide about her residence, had capacity to make decisions about her care, but had fluctuating capacity to make decisions about her insulin treatment. She would sometimes accept the insulin, sometimes not, due to her personality disorder and failure to take professional advice. The judge held that when 'making appropriate decisions she has capacity but when making manifestly inappropriate decisions she lacks capacity'.[2]

MENTAL CAPACITY: BEST INTERESTS. Section 1 of the Mental Capacity Act states that an act done, or decision made, under the Act for or on behalf of a person who lacks capacity must be done, or made, in his or her best interests. Section 4 goes on to set out various factors that must be taken account of before a best interests decision can be reached. The best interests decision must be made by the person who is doing the act or making the decision.

- **Best interests, lack of capacity and safeguarding.** Best interests, in relation to an adult, is a term confined to decisions made (or acts done) in relation

---

1   *Masterman-Lister v Brutton* [2002] EWHC 417 (QB); [2002] EWCA Civ 1889.

2   *Royal Borough of Greenwich v CDM* [2018] EWCOP 15, para 52.

to a person lacking the mental capacity to take the decision in question for themselves. It is the fourth key principle set out in section 1 of the Mental Capacity Act 2005. Its relevance to safeguarding is that any decision taken to protect a person from abuse or neglect must be taken in their best interests.

- **Best interests: statutory checklist.** The Mental Capacity Act provides in effect a checklist which must be applied before a person's best interests are determined.

  » **Best interests.** Any act done, or decision taken, for or on behalf of a person lacking capacity, must be in that person's best interests.

  » **Avoiding unjustified assumptions.** In determining best interests, the person making the determination must not make it merely on the basis of the person's age or appearance or a condition or aspect of behaviour, which might lead others to make unjustified assumptions about what might be in his best interests.

  » **Considerations.** The decision-maker must consider all the relevant circumstances and, in particular, the following:

    - **Regaining of capacity.** Consider whether it is likely that the person will at some time have capacity and, if so, when that is likely to be.

    - **Participation of person.** Permit and encourage the person to participate as fully as possible in the decision and any decision affecting him.

    - **Not desiring to bring about death.** Where life-sustaining treatment is in issue, the decision-maker must not be motivated by a desire to bring about the person's death.

    - **Past and present wishes, etc.** If reasonably ascertainable, the person's past and present wishes and feelings (and, in particular, any relevant written statement made by the person when he or she had capacity), beliefs and values, and other factors should be taken into consideration.

    - **Consulting others.** Where consultation is appropriate and practicable, the views of anyone named person by the person, any person caring for the person or interested in the person's welfare, any donee of a lasting power of attorney or any Court of Protection appointed deputy should be taken into account.

- **Reasonable belief.** This section of the Act is complied with if the person doing the act or making the decision reasonably believes that the act or decision is in the best of the interests of the person concerned.[1]

MENTAL CAPACITY: BEST INTERESTS AND LESS RESTRICTION. A failure to consider less restrictive ways of achieving a person's best interests can result in disproportionate and arguably abusive interventions.

For example, when a local authority removed a young man with learning disabilities and autism from his father, and placed him in a care home, it breached the Mental Capacity Act in many respects, including a failure to consider, in subsequent best interests assessment, the less restrictive option of enabling him to return home.[2]

MENTAL CAPACITY: BEST INTERESTS AND PHYSICAL RISK. The courts have been consistent in stating that best interests decisions, in relation to vulnerable adults, should not adopt tunnel vision and focus on physical risk to the person only, but must also weigh up psychological, emotional and quality of life issues. For example:

> **Psychological, emotional, quality of life.** When judging whether a previously very socially active, fiercely independent woman should be effectively forced into a care home where she would be unhappy and distressed – despite the real physical risks to her if she were to be in her own home.[3]
>
> When weighing up whether an elderly woman should go into a nursing home rather than remain with her husband at home.[4]
>
> Or when considering whether a woman should remain in a nursing home where she was very unhappy or return home where a deterioration of her diabetes meant a real possibility that she might die. Keeping her alive

---

1   Mental Capacity Act 2005, s.4.

2   *London Borough of Hillingdon v Neary* [2011] EWHC 1377 (COP).

3   *Westminster City Council v Sykes* [2014] 17 CCL Rep. 139, pp.28–30.

4   *A London Authority v JH* [2011] EWHC 2420 (COP), p.57.

as long as possible, in a setting in which she was miserable, was not in itself an adequate approach to ascertaining her best interests.[1]

Physical safety may be important, but a balance is required between ensuring safety and making a person miserable.[2]

MENTAL CAPACITY: BEST INTERESTS, AVAILABLE OPTIONS AND RESOURCES. Although 'best' is a grammatically superlative word, its application remains rooted in the real world. For example, in terms of what local authorities are obliged to do under the Care Act 2014 in terms of meeting people's care and support needs. This can lead to seemingly harsh best interests decisions, since under the Care Act, the duty is to meet a person's needs in the most cost-effective manner, not necessarily in the 'best' way.

Safeguarding, long-standing elderly couple: woman's best interests to remain in care home because of local authority's lack of resources. A man had been married to his wife for decades. He tried to look after her, became increasingly concerned about her mobility and nutrition, became frustrated and hit her. She was deprived of her liberty in a care home, and he was prosecuted. They were soon reconciled. He wanted her to come home; she too wanted this, albeit lacking capacity. The case went to the Court of Protection for a best interests decision to be made.

The local authority explained that it was not prepared – on grounds of resources – to make a return home possible, because it was cheaper to keep her in the nursing home. The judge held that there was nothing, under the Mental Capacity Act, that he could do, because best interests decisions can only be made based on available options. Any challenge to the options would have to be made, separately, by way of judicial review in relation to the relevant social care legislation (now the Care Act 2014). The Court of Protection, however, could not intervene in this respect. So she would remain, deprived of her liberty in her best interests, in the care home.[3]

---

1   *Re M (Best interests: deprivation of liberty)* [2013] EWHC 3456 (COP), para 38.

2   *Local Authority X v MM* [2007] EWHC 2003 (Fam).

3   *Bedford Borough Council v Mrs. C* [2015] EWCOP 25, paras 25–26.

MENTAL CAPACITY: ACTS OF CARE OR TREATMENT. Section 5 of the Mental Capacity Act provides a general defence to somebody providing care or treatment for a person lacking capacity. This might be in a safeguarding context if, for example, somebody had to act in haste to protect a person and did so reasonably – but hindsight revealed an error about either the person's capacity or their best interests. Equally, a person accused of an abusive action – for example, providing an element of care without a person's consent – might also be protected:

- **Reasonable steps to establish lack of capacity, and reasonable belief in lack of capacity and best interests.** A person is protected from liability if he or she does an act in connection with care or treatment, and he or she took reasonable steps to establish that the person lacked capacity in respect of the matter in question, and reasonably believed that the person lacked that capacity and that it was in his or her own best interests that the act be done.

- **No protection from negligence liability.** However, this does not exclude civil liability for loss or damage, or criminal liability, arising from negligence in doing the act.

- **Not overriding advance decision, or decision by attorney or deputy.** Section 5 does not provide protection to the extent of overriding an advance decision, or a decision made by a person with lasting power of attorney or by a deputy appointed by the Court of Protection.

- **Examples of care.** A Code of Practice gives examples of care that could come under section 5, including help with washing, dressing, personal hygiene, eating, drinking, communication, mobility, and with a person's taking part in education, social or leisure activities. Also: going to a person's house to see if they are all right, doing the shopping with the person's money, arranging household services, providing home help services, undertaking actions related to community care services (e.g. day care, care home accommodation, nursing care) and helping a person move home.

- **Examples of treatment.** Health care and treatment might include diagnostic examinations and tests, medical or dental treatment, medication, taking a person to hospital for assessment or treatment, nursing care, other procedures or therapies (e.g. physiotherapy or chiropody), emergency care.[1]

---

1   Lord Chancellor. *Mental Capacity Act 2005: code of practice.* London: The Stationery Office, 2007, para 6.5.

An example of a person being protected by the provisions of section 5 is as follows, despite the local authority inferring that his care was neglectful of his wife.

> **Elderly man protected by section 5 in caring for his wife in a safeguarding case, despite disagreement with local authority professionals.** An elderly man was caring for his long-standing wife, who had suffered two strokes, had dementia, had vulnerable skin, and was incontinent. He had been in the habit of hoisting her in a certain way and leaving her within her sling, in a chair. The local authority disagreed with this, together with various other aspects of how he cared for his wife. It called an adult protection meeting and decided that she should be deprived of her liberty in a nursing home, one of the grounds being risk of general neglect.
>
> The judge stated as follows:
>
> > As Mrs H's husband, and within the privacy of their own home and relationship, Mr H is not bound to follow professional opinion in every respect, provided that he has good reasons for believing that his wife would prefer him to provide care in a different manner at times, and he uses his long-gained expert understanding of her likes and dislikes, comfort and discomfort, to arrive at a reasonable view as to why it would benefit her to take an advised risk. Such acts would be based on a reasonable belief that the care is in her best interests and covered by section 5. While I must accept that there is a risk to the integrity of the skin, Mr H has learnt that use of the sling enables Mrs H to get out of bed, to participate more, and to be in less pain. Within the privacy of their own home, that appears to be a reasonable position for a married couple to take.[1]

Mental Capacity Act 2005, see *Mental capacity*

---

1 *A London Local Authority v JH* [2011] EWHC 2420 (COP), p.48.

Misleading information, see *False or misleading information*

Modern Slavery Act 2015

Key points from the Modern Slavery Act 2015 include the following:

- **Offence: slavery or servitude.** Holding another person in slavery or servitude – and the circumstances are such that the person knows or ought to know that the other person is held in slavery or servitude.

- **Offence: forced or compulsory labour.** Requiring another person to perform forced or compulsory labour – and the circumstances are such that the person knows or ought to know that the other person is being required to perform forced or compulsory labour.

- **Human rights.** Slavery, servitude and forced or compulsory labour must be construed in line with article 4 of the European Convention on Human Rights.

- **All the circumstances.** In determining whether a person is being held in slavery or servitude or required to perform forced or compulsory labour, regard may be had to all the circumstances.

- **Vulnerability.** For example, regard may be had to any of the person's personal circumstances (such as the person being a child, the person's family relationships, and any mental or physical illness) which may make the person more vulnerable than other persons.

- **Exploitation.** For example, regard may be had to any work or services provided by the person, including work or services provided in circumstances which constitute exploitation.

- **Consent.** A person's consent does not preclude a determination that the person is being held in slavery or servitude or required to perform forced or compulsory labour.[1]

---

1   Modern Slavery Act 2015, s.1.

- **Travel.** It is an offence to arrange or facilitate the travel of another person with a view to them being exploited.

- **Exploitation (including vulnerability).** Exploitation is defined as slavery, servitude, forced or compulsory labour, sexual exploitation, removal of organs; also securing services by force, threats or deception. Also securing services from children or vulnerable persons.[1]

- **Penalties.** Penalties range from life imprisonment to shorter prison sentences up to 12 months and fines.[2]

- **Orders.** The courts can make slavery and trafficking prevention orders and also risk orders.[3]

- **Defences for victims, including for vulnerable adults, who commit an offence attributable to modern slavery or human trafficking.** A person over 18 is not guilty of an offence if they were compelled to do it, the compulsion was attributable to slavery or human trafficking, and a reasonable person in the same situation as the person and having the person's relevant characteristics would have had no realistic alternative. Relevant characteristics mean: age, sex and any physical or mental illness or disability. A similar defence applies for somebody under 18, except that the compulsion element is not required to be shown.[4]

The defence does not implicitly require the defendant to bear the legal or persuasive burden of proof of any element of the defence. The burden on a defendant is evidential. It is for the defendant to raise evidence of each of those elements and for the prosecution to disprove one or more of them to the criminal standard in the usual way.[5]

The following are a few examples of convictions.

Vulnerable men in servitude. Four members of a family, described by the police as 'an organised criminal group', were found guilty of forcing

---

1   Modern Slavery Act 2015, s.2.

2   Modern Slavery Act 2015, s.5.

3   Modern Slavery Act 2015, ss.14, 15, 23.

4   Modern Slavery Act 2015, s.45.

5   *MK v R* [2018] EWCA Crim 667, para 45.

vulnerable men into servitude. This involved controlling, exploiting, verbally abusing and beating the men for financial gain. Vulnerable men – many of them homeless, addicted to alcohol or drugs – were recruited in soup kitchens and outside dole offices and promised cash payments for manual labour. Once in the family's grip, they were forced to work up to 19 hours a day for no pay while being routinely abused, underfed and housed in filthy sheds and horse boxes. The site, a mixture of pristine chalets and smaller caravans sitting on well-kept paved yards, was the scene of abuse and exploitation, according to police. Destitute men were picked up and made to perform manual labour such as Tarmacking and laying paving stones, and menial tasks such as cleaning their bosses' homes. When police found them, they were living in sheds that were 'unfit for human habitation' with no heating. One picture of the sheds in which the men lived showed a sheet covered in human excrement, with discarded budget food wrappers littering the floor.[1]

Conviction, involving vulnerable workers at retail warehouse. Two brothers who targeted vulnerable men in Poland and then trafficked them to work in a Sports Direct warehouse were jailed for six years each, under the Modern Slavery Act.

The brothers deceived and threatened the men, who had their passports confiscated and their wages stolen after they had found work at Sports Direct's Shirebrook warehouse in Derbyshire. The brothers had employed a 'spotter' to identify vulnerable people and send them to the UK on the promise of work and a place to stay. The brothers paid for the men to get to the UK, and when they arrived, they would open up bank accounts for the men on their behalf from which they would withdraw the lion's share of their income. Some victims were left with about £90 a week when they should have received £265. The brothers made an estimated £35,000. The victims were 'totally isolated'.

They were apprehended after one of the victims contacted the police. The brothers pleaded guilty, under the Modern Slavery Act, to conspiracy to arrange travel with a view to exploitation and fraud by false representation.

---

1   'Four found guilty of forcing vulnerable men into servitude.' *The Guardian*, 11 July 2012.

They were also given a two-and-a-half-year sentence for fraud, to run concurrently.[1]

Conviction under Modern Slavery Act: victim storing drugs. There has also been, for example, a conviction of gang members in relation to storing Class A drugs; the victim, used by the gang, had done so (thereby, in principle, committing an offence), but only against her will. The gang that had taken her to Wales, and held her there, was convicted.[2]

Fast-food shops: vulnerable people forced to work for free. The owner of fast-food shops in the north east of England forced victims to work for free and encouraged their addiction to drugs and alcohol. He was sentenced to eight and a half years in prison for modern slavery offences: forcing vulnerable people to work for him in return for accommodation and food scraps. He housed people described as being 'at a low ebb' in properties he owned in central Blyth, Northumberland. He forced them to work at his businesses in Blyth and Sunderland for free, often in poor conditions, and supplied them with alcohol and drugs. He engaged in bullying, threats and violence. The victims were afraid they would lose their housing and be beaten up if they did not comply with his demands. He was paid housing benefit to cover his tenants' rent, but he demanded extra money for gas and electricity. For example, one victim was forced to clear out a sewage pipe without gloves and another had his shoes removed and was made to walk to work barefoot. One man, who had recently been released from prison and had an alcohol problem, moved into the owner's property and was set to work tiling a takeaway, which took all night. The victim had two days off in five months and was paid in alcohol and Valium tablets.[3]

1   Davies, R. 'Brothers jailed for trafficking people from Poland to work at Sports Direct.' *The Guardian*, 23 January 2017.

2   '"County Line" criminals convicted in landmark Modern Slavery case.' *Policeprofessional. com*, 6 December 2017. Accessed on 5 October 2018 at: www.policeprofessional.com/ news/%c2%91county-line%c2%92-criminals-convicted-in-landmark-modern-slavery-case.

3   Perraudin, F. 'Takeaway shop owner in northeast England jailed for slavery offences.' *The Guardian*, 18 June 2018.

Multi-agency approach to safeguarding

Adult safeguarding is envisaged by the Care Act 2014 and its accompanying guidance as essentially multi-agency in nature, based on cooperation, with social services at the hub – and therefore able to utilise a wide range of other agencies and legislation (civil or criminal) in order to tackle issues of abuse or neglect. In other words, the greater the abuse or neglect, so the more resources, expertise and joint working there should be. The reality tends to work otherwise.

Adult safeguarding appears to work better and more comfortably in pursuit of smaller fish, whether it be abusive or neglectful family members, financially abusive neighbours, dishonest care workers or dishonest care home managers, or physically abusive care workers. Conversely, the bigger and more serious the issue, and the more organisational reputations (particularly those of statutory services) at stake, so the more adult safeguarding tends to stutter or to become entirely ineffective – even with multi-agency involvement.

The Gosport War Memorial Hospital Inquiry serves as a very significant case to illustrate how multi-agency involvement can unravel, even when the scale of the safeguarding issue requires precisely that breadth of involvement and expertise, given that it concerned hundreds of deaths over a 12-year period.

Gosport: culture of poor care takes root. Gosport involved development of a culture of poor care which became entrenched, once early doubts expressed by nurses had been discouraged. Nurses subsequently went along for many years with administration of life-shortening opiates, prescribed by the general practitioner at the hospital (overseen in principle by consultants) without clinical justification.

Euphemistic use of language to conceal what is happening. The term 'make comfortable' was shorthand for syringe-driving of opiates, resulting in death within a few days, irrespective of whether pain relief was clinically indicated or needed.

Whistleblowers not listened to. Nurses, in the early 1990s, raised concerns but were effectively discouraged, even intimidated, into dropping them.

Denial. There were numerous instances of denial by the NHS Trust that anything was wrong: denial to families, to the public and the media, and to health service and other organisations.

Relatives had to do the safeguarding. In the absence of anybody else doing anything to safeguard patients in the hospital, relatives began to complain to the hospital and the police.

Safeguarding agencies closing ranks. The police sought guidance and reassurance from the hospital, and accordingly came to view the relatives as troublemakers.

Police and Crown Prosecution Service baulked at the scale of the investigation that would have been required. The eventual police investigations were less than thorough, did not consider all the possible offences that might have been committed and baulked at the scale of what a proper police investigation would have entailed.

Underlying cause of death not queried. The underlying cause of death given in many cases was bronchopneumonia, but this could not be explained on the basis of the clinical information available.

Inquests: not considering all the information. The coroner, holding an inquest into some deaths, excluded relevant information.

Professional regulatory bodies. The General Medical Council and Nursing and Midwifery Council did not act. For example, the former, the GMC, took ten years, following referral, to decide about the actions of the assistant medical officer (a general practitioner) responsible for prescribing the opiates which caused death within a few days. In those ten years, she had left the hospital, worked as a GP and received support from patients. Accordingly, the GMC's disciplinary panel declined to strike her from the medical register. And it declined to consider at all the hospital consultants who, overall, were meant to be responsible for the clinical care of the hospital patients who died.

Consistent multi-agency failures.

The documents that the Panel has found reveal that…during a certain period at Gosport War Memorial Hospital, there was a disregard for human life and a culture of shortening the lives of a large number of patients by prescribing and administering 'dangerous doses' of a hazardous combination of medication not clinically indicated or justified. They show too that, whereas a large number of patients and their relatives understood that their admission to the hospital was for either rehabilitation or respite care, they were, in effect, put on a terminal care pathway. They show that, when relatives complained about the safety of patients and the appropriateness of their care, they were consistently let down by those in authority – both individuals and institutions. These included the senior management of the hospital, healthcare organisations, Hampshire Constabulary, local politicians, the coronial system, the Crown Prosecution Service, the General Medical Council and the Nursing and Midwifery Council. All failed to act in ways that would have better protected patients and relatives, whose interests some subordinated to the reputation of the hospital and the professions involved.[1]

Multi-Agency Public Protection Arrangements (MAPPA)

The Criminal Justice Act 2003 places a duty on 'responsible authorities' to establish arrangements for assessing and managing risks in relation to certain high-risk offenders. They are known as multi-agency public protection arrangements (MAPPA). Apart from the provisions contained within the Act itself, the relevant agencies involved in MAPPA must have regard to guidance issued under section 325 of the Act. The relevance to the safeguarding of vulnerable adults and to this book is that sometimes the offender poses a risk to a vulnerable adult, or the offender themselves has been identified as an adult at risk.[2] In summary:

- **Responsible authorities.** Responsible authorities are defined as the chief of police, probation board and prison service.

- **Categories of offender.** The duty applies to specified categories of violent and sex offenders, as well as to other people who have committed offences and whom a responsible authority considers pose a risk of serious harm to the public.

---

1   Jones, Reverend J. (Chairman). *Gosport War Memorial Hospital: the report of the Gosport Independent Panel*. London: The Stationery Office, 2018.

2   Ministry of Justice. *MAPPA guidance 2012, (version 4.1 updated 2016)*. London: MoJ, 2012, para 13a.19.

- **Three levels of arrangement.** Arrangements function on three levels. The first is single agency (usually the probation service) where there is a lower level of risk. The second involves a higher risk but one not requiring complex management; normally, this will involve more than one agency. At the third level are critical cases involving high risk and/or difficult risk management issues. These require multi-agency public protection panel (MAPPP) meetings.[1]

- **Other organisations with duty to cooperate.** Apart from the three responsible authorities, other named organisations are under a duty to cooperate in MAPPA insofar as such cooperation is compatible with their own statutory functions.[2] They include local social services authorities, clinical commissioning groups, other NHS Trusts, strategic health authorities, Jobcentres Plus, local youth offending teams, registered housing providers that accommodate MAPPA offenders, local housing authorities, local education authorities, electronic monitoring service providers, the Borders Agency.[3]

MAPPA: INFORMATION SHARING. Under a duty to cooperate, agencies 'may' exchange information. Guidance states that therefore the responsible authorities and the 'duty to cooperate' agencies have a statutory power to share information, under section 325 of the Act, in relation to managing the risks posed by the offender.

Disclosure, as opposed to sharing, of information may take place with other agencies, not within the scope of the statutory MAPPA arrangements, for the protection of the public.[4] Generally, both information sharing and information disclosure need to be consistent with the common law of confidence, the Data Protection Act 2018 and the General Data Protection

---

1   Ministry of Justice. *MAPPA guidance 2012, version 4*. London: MoJ, 2012, para 7.1.

2   Criminal Justice Act 2003, ss.325–327.

3   Criminal Justice Act 2003, s.325(6). See: Ministry of Justice. *MAPPA guidance 2012 (version 4.1 updated 2016)*. London: MoJ, 2012, para 3.5.

4   Ministry of Justice. *MAPPA guidance 2012 (version 4.1 updated 2016)*. London: MoJ, 2012, para 10.2.

Regulation (GDPR) – and article 8 of the European Convention on Human Rights.[1]

The following case, heard under previous legislation before registered housing providers were formally under the umbrella of MAPPA, would nowadays be the equivalent of a responsible authority sharing with a non-MAPPA agency – that is, what the guidance calls a third-party disclosure case. The court made clear that information should be disclosed only after careful thought.

Starting point for disclosing information and weighing up competing considerations. A 64-year-old man who had killed his wife was now being released, unconditionally, on licence. A report about his release concluded that the risk of reoffending was unlikely, although it might increase were he to engage in a personal relationship. He was going to live in sheltered accommodation. The probation service disclosed information about the man to the manager of the housing.

The court held that, as a matter of decision-making process, the disclosure was unlawful. This was because the probation service had approached the matter on the presumption that information would be disclosed. Rather, it should have begun with a presumption of non-disclosure and then used the risk assessment to displace that presumption. It should also have explicitly balanced the risk to other people of non-disclosure with harm to the man flowing from disclosure.[2]

MAPPA: REQUESTS FOR INFORMATION: MINUTES OF MAPPA MEETINGS. The guidance also deals with requests for minutes of MAPPA meetings. It points out that requests might come from a variety of sources including offenders, third parties and other organisations (such as the courts, the Crown Prosecution Service, etc.).

The guidance notes that such requests need to be considered in the light of the Human Rights Act 1998, the Data Protection Act 2018 and

---

1   Criminal Justice Act 2003, s.325(6). See: Ministry of Justice. *MAPPA guidance 2012 (version 4.1 updated 2016)*. London: MoJ, 2012, chapters 9 and 10.

2   *R (A) v National Probation Service* [2003] EWHC Admin 2910.

General Data Protection Regulation (for instance, if the offender has made a subject access request) or the Freedom of Information Act 2000 (information requested about other people). And that, under the 2000 Act, a number of rules could apply that would make the requested information, the minutes, exempt from disclosure (in summary):

- information supplied by, or relating to, bodies dealing with security matters (section 23)

- national security (section 24)

- investigations and proceedings by public authorities (section 30)

- law enforcement (section 31)

- health and safety (section 38)

- somebody else's personal information (section 40)

- information provided in confidence (section 41).[1]

Murder

Murder is about a person of sound mind unlawfully killing a human being with intent to kill or cause grievous bodily harm.[2] The following examples make clear the relevance to vulnerable adults.

> **Man with learning disabilities befriended by gang and then murdered.**
> A man with severe learning disabilities was befriended by a 'gang'. He thought they were his best friends. For a year, they exploited and cheated him, taking control of his money, his flat and his life, dragging him around his bedsit on a dog's lead. They then tortured him into confessing falsely that he was a paedophile, sentenced him to death, forced him to swallow 70 painkilling tablets, marched him to the top of a viaduct, forced him over and stamped on his hands as he hung on. He fell 30 metres and died. Three of the gang were convicted of murder, another of manslaughter. During

---

1   Ministry of Justice. *MAPPA guidance 2012, version 4*. London: MoJ, 2012, para 13.39.

2   Crown Prosecution Service. *Homicide, murder and manslaughter: guidance*. London: CPS, undated.

the period in question, social services had been visiting him but stopped before his death, apparently in response to his wishes.[1]

Bet to knock out man with learning disabilities. Two teenagers, both trained boxers, and an older man were involved in a bet made at a bus stop about whether they could knock out a man with learning disabilities. They repeatedly hit him and then chased him across two housing estates, continuing to attack him by punching, stamping, kicking and head-butting. After the murder, they posed for pictures. All three were convicted of murder.[2]

Vulnerable, timid adult strangled on hillside. A vulnerable, timid adult was taken to a remote hillside where he was strangled, hit with a brick, kicked and stamped on, before being set on fire, by two cousins who wrongly believed he was a paedophile. They were given life sentences; the planning, mental and physical suffering of a vulnerable man and the attempt to conceal the body were aggravating features.[3]

Humiliation and drowning of man with learning disabilities. A man with learning disabilities was humiliated, tortured and then thrown into a river to drown by four of his neighbours who suspected he was a paedophile.[4]

Tortured and stabbed: man with learning disabilities. Another man with learning disabilities, wrongly believed by his killers to be a paedophile, was gagged, bound, tortured, stabbed and disembowelled. His two killers were, on appeal, sentenced to 28 years and 22 years in prison.[5]

Hospital matron: poisoning patients. A hospital matron, described as eccentric, bossy, popular and well respected, was charged with poisoning

1   Morris, S. 'Tortured, drugged and killed a month after the care visits were stopped.' *The Guardian*, 4 August 2007.

2   'Boy convicted of "£5 bet" murder.' *BBC News*, 22 January 2008. Accessed on 5 October 2018 at: http://news.bbc.co.uk/1/hi/england/wear/7202351.stm.

3   'Hillside murderers get life terms.' *BBC News*, 4 May 2007. Accessed on 5 October 2018 at: http://news.bbc.co.uk/1/hi/wales/south_east/6624515.stm.

4   Payne, S. 'Four "drowned man they thought was pederast".' *Daily Telegraph*, 22 March 2007.

5   'Murder terms increased by judges.' *BBC News*, 16 February 2006. Accessed on 5 October 2018 at: http://news.bbc.co.uk/1/hi/england/tees/4720642.stm. Also: Vinter, P. 'Killer preyed on "kind Sean".' *Oxford Mail*, 20 April 2007.

three patients, although suspected of having murdered many more. She committed suicide before trial.[1]

Overdose given by nurse to resident with dementia. A nurse drugged an 84-year-old care home resident, who suffered from senile dementia, by giving her an overdose of a sedative (Heminevrin). The judge stated that she had committed murder largely because she didn't want the trouble of caring for the woman, who needed up to half an hour's care and attention from staff every two hours.[2]

Hospital nurse murdering elderly patients. A staff nurse was convicted of murdering four elderly patients and attempting to murder a fifth by means of administering insulin to induce hypoglycaemic coma and death. The judge stated that he was an essentially lazy man who believed that the elderly required too much care. All the victims were frail elderly women admitted to the orthopaedic ward following hip fractures.[3]

1   Jenkins, R. 'Nurse found dead may have killed 23 patients.' *The Times*, 31 August 2005.

2   'Nurse convicted of murder.' *BBC News*, 19 June 2001. Accessed on 5 October 2018 at: http://news.bbc.co.uk/1/hi/health/1396950.stm.

3   Jenkins, R. 'Killer nurse must serve at least 30 years.' *The Times*, 5 March 2008.

N

National Health Service (NHS)

Legally, the NHS has a number of general duties under the NHS Act 2006 to provide medical, nursing, ambulance, aftercare services, etc. These duties are vague and broad in nature but, ultimately, underpin the whole range of health services provided by the NHS.

More specifically, all NHS providers are subject to the Health and Social Care Act (Regulated Activities) Regulations 2014. Amongst other things, these regulations specifically require providers to safeguard service users from abuse, neglect and improper treatment. See *Care Quality Commission*.

In addition, NHS bodies are under a duty to cooperate with local authorities and other statutory partners, as defined in the Care Act 2014. One of the listed purposes of cooperation is the protection of adults, with care and support needs, from abuse and neglect. See *Cooperation*. NHS clinical commissioning groups (CCGs) are a key member of statutory safeguarding adults boards. See *Safeguarding adults boards*.

The NHS, in relation to adult safeguarding, is covered at length below under the following headings:

- NHS: guidance on safeguarding

- NHS: evidence of significant, systemic and enduring poor care and neglect.

NHS: GUIDANCE ON SAFEGUARDING. In 2010, the Department of Health issued guidance to the NHS, entitled *Clinical governance and adult safeguarding: an integrated process*. It states that when NHS Trusts report serious incidents as 'clinical governance' matters, they should be picking out a subset of incidents to be reported also as safeguarding. This would then mean informing the local social services authority (i.e. the local council), which has overall responsibility for coordinating local safeguarding activity.

The guidance revealed the hesitancy in acknowledging neglect or abuse within the NHS if it is systemic, as opposed to perpetrated by a rogue or poor practitioner. It provides an example of pressure sores, stating that because they stemmed from a shortage of beds and associated poor clinical management of the patient, they would not amount to neglect. In other words, the guidance seemed to suggest that neglecting patients was a venial sin, as long as it occurred in the higher cause of finance, performance and patient throughput.

- **Department of Health guidance: shortage of beds and poor care not to be viewed as neglect or as a safeguarding issue.** The guidance gave an example of how a patient was at a high level of risk of developing pressure sores. The patient, however, was moved from ward to ward three times within the first week. A pressure-relieving mattress was identified as part of the care plan but was not applied until the fourth day after admission. The patient had a broken area of skin by then. The mattress had been ordered, but due to the numerous moves and shift changes, inadequate information had been passed on and reviewed. The equipment was therefore delayed in getting to the patient.

  A conclusion was reached in the example that, effectively because of the shortage of beds and associated chaos, there was no intentional harm or neglect. The inference appears to be, according to the guidance, that there would then be no formal safeguarding alert because the example stated also that such an alert would be triggered only by neglect.[1]

Overcrowded hospitals (i.e. running bed occupancy levels too high, generally over 85%) and moving patients rapidly from ward to ward for non-clinical reasons is harmful to patients, but many hospitals in England run close to 100 per cent bed occupancy levels.[2] Yet, too often, senior management in

---

1   Department of Health. *Clinical governance and adult safeguarding: an integrated process*. London: DH, 2010, p.11.

2   British Medical Association. *State of the health system – beds in the NHS: England*. London: BMA, 2017 (including literature review on safe bed levels).

hospitals has reduced bed and staff numbers to meet financial targets, whilst claiming blandly and optimistically that patient care would not suffer.

The implications of the guidance mean that the following patient death from pressure sores, brought about because of a lack of beds in a new hospital (the consequence of deliberate and planned policy), would not be (and was not, apparently) regarded as a safeguarding matter, even though the coroner referred to gross failings and neglect.

War veteran dying of pressure sores brought about by neglect and lack of beds. In 2006, a new hospital was opened, the Queen's Hospital, in Romford. It cost £261 million to build, through the Private Finance Initiative (PFI), and was described by the developers as cleverly combining clinical values with aesthetic qualities.

At the time of opening it was also said to have 'an appearance and an atmosphere...more akin to a hotel than a hospital'. It was to be 'welcoming to patients and visitors alike'.[1] Indeed, it was an award-winning building. A feature emphasised was 'quick access to treatment'. In 2006, the Trust announced the loss of 190 beds and 650 staff because of a financial crisis; the chief executive stated that the reductions were clinically sustainable.[2]

In 2009, a coroner passed a verdict of death by natural causes contributed to by neglect at the Queen's Hospital. The deceased was an 86-year-old man, veteran of the Normandy campaign in the Second World War. He had Parkinson's disease. In early 2008, he died a painful death at the hospital from infected bedsores. These had been caused by his being left on two separate occasions (successive admissions, days apart, to the hospital) on a hospital trolley for 19 hours, after admission with a chest infection. The hospital had insufficient beds.

The result of his being on the trolley the second time was to exacerbate the sores that had developed on the first occasion. One of the sores was classed as grade four, sufficiently deep to expose tendon and bone. The wounds were dressed but a further 12 hours elapsed before he was admitted to a ward where a pressure-relief mattress was finally made available. Too

---

1   Catalyst Lendlease. *Queen's Hospital, Romford, Essex, United Kingdom.* 2010. Accessed on 2 September 2010 at: www.catalystlendlease.com/projects/queens-hospital.pdf.

2   '£24 million debt NHS trust cuts 650 jobs: up to 650 jobs are to be cut and 190 beds closed by an NHS trust that is trying to tackle debts.' *BBC News*, 28 April 2006. Accessed on 5 October 2018 at: http://news.bbc.co.uk/1/hi/england/london/4954818.stm.

> late. Mr Gibson died some days afterwards, of septicaemia resulting from open sores.[1]
>
> The coroner, referring to 'gross failings' and 'neglect', stated:
>
> > It is quite clear from the evidence I've heard that the length of time Mr Gibson waited at A&E [accident and emergency] both the first and second time – the second time added insult to injury to a man already completely dependent – made a significant contribution to his death... He was at very, very high risk of pressure sores and he should have been provided with appropriate protection against worsening of the pressure sores.[2]
>
> (In 2015, the PFI annual interest repayment amount on the hospital stood at a crippling £52 million.)[3]

It is to be hoped that practice in the NHS is changing. Certainly, more recent guidance on pressure sores is clearer. It notes the lack of consensus about when investigating pressure ulcers should involve local authority safeguarding duties as set out in section 42 of the Care Act 2014. It provides guidance and a scoring system, as a way of determining this, and notes that the decision about the making of section 42 enquiries rests with the local authority. It refers to key issues as to whether there has been poor care, neglect or abuse – and, crucially, that neglect may be unintentional, but still be neglect.[4]

NHS: EVIDENCE OF SIGNIFICANT, SYSTEMIC AND ENDURING POOR CARE AND NEGLECT. Department of Health guidance states that neglect might be unintentional, that commissioners of health care and social care should avoid safeguarding issues arising by commissioning good-quality care, and that local safeguarding adults boards must work towards having safe,

1   Schlesinger, F. 'Coroner's fury as great-grandfather, 86, dies after being dumped on A & E trolley for 19 hours TWICE.' *Daily Mail*, 22 May 2009.

2   Schlesinger, F. 'Coroner's fury as great-grandfather, 86, dies after being dumped on A & E trolley for 19 hours TWICE.' *Daily Mail*, 22 May 2009.

3   'PFI loan repayments cost trust running Queen's Hospital £52 million last year.' *Romford Recorder*, 27 August 2015.

4   Romeo, L. *Safeguarding adults protocol: pressure ulcers and the interface with a safeguarding enquiry.* London: Department of Health and Social Care, 2018.

local health services.[1] The examples below are just that: examples from a range of wider sources which – considered fully elsewhere and by 'triangulation' – suggest a significant problem.[2]

It is also arguable that, in terms of adult safeguarding, poor care and neglect constitute the great elephant in the room, the pachyderm that nobody – from government ministers right down to local authorities, NHS bodies and safeguarding adults boards – really wants, or is able, to tackle. Likewise, staff and patients do not believe in poor care and neglect – until, that is, the neglect happens to them or members of their family.

2000: Not because they are old. The Health Advisory Service published *Not because they are old*. It highlighted a string of failings in the hospital care of older people. These comprised deficiencies in the physical fabric of wards, shortage of basic supplies and technical equipment, staff shortages, lack of assistance in helping people to eat and drink, diminution of dignity (related to personal hygiene and dressing) because of the physical environment but also staff attitudes, inadequate communication with patients and relatives because of time pressures on staff – and so on.[3]

2000: North Lakeland NHS Trust: tying people up on commodes. Practices at the North Lakeland NHS Trust, reported on by the Commission for Health Improvement, included the following: a patient being restrained by being tied to a commode, patients being denied ordinary food, patients being fed while sitting on commodes and patients being deliberately deprived of clothing and blankets. An external review had already concluded that the occupational therapy department had made a wooden board and harness for use as a restraint device.[4]

2001: Standing Nursing and Midwifery Advisory Committee: dignity not being preserved. The Department of Health's Standing Nursing and

1 Department of Health. *Care and support statutory guidance*. London: DH, 2016, paras 14.40, 14.9, 14.134.

2 Mandelstam, M. *How we treat the sick*. London: Jessica Kingsley Publishers, 2011, p.46.

3 Health Advisory Service. *Not because they are old: an independent inquiry into the care of older people on acute wards in general hospitals*. London: HAS, 2000, pp.iii–iv.

4 Commission for Health Improvement. *Investigation into the North Lakeland NHS Trust, November*. London: CHI, 2000, p.29.

Midwifery Advisory Committee advised that a 'large critical literature has been amassed which shows that current standards of care often fail to preserve older people's dignity, privacy, autonomy and independence'. The Committee went on to point out that hospital nurses had, in principle, to attend not just to acute symptoms but also to the needs of the whole person, including nutrition, tissue viability and promotion of independent activity. Yet it reported that the nursing care of older people was, in practice, deficient in such very fundamental aspects including the need for food, fluid, rest, activity and elimination, and recognition of people's psychological, mental health and rehabilitation needs.

The Committee identified widespread problems in practice with respect for older people's dignity, promotion of choice and involvement and independence, communication with older people and their carers, individualised care and its management, continence, dementia, mental health, mobility, nutrition and hydration, pain management, palliative care, pressure damage prevention and management.[1]

2002: East Kent Hospitals NHS Trust: overcrowding and poor care. Reporting on East Kent Hospitals NHS Trust, the Commission for Health Improvement found that overcrowding in the hospital's accident and emergency department put patients at clinical risk and staff under unremitting pressure. Patients were simply admitted to any bed, 'causing staff to care for patients they may not have the skills or training to care for and forcing doctors to seek out their patients throughout the hospital'.

The overcrowding and pressure resulted in other compromises in care. Trays regularly came to the ward with dirty cutlery. Food was often cold. There were insufficient toilets and washing facilities for the number of patients, who were sometimes physically examined in open areas. Patients might be left in corridors for days rather than hours. It was difficult for doctors to get to outlying wards; this caused delays in ordering treatments, obtaining drugs and discharging patients; one patient waited more than 14 hours to have a cannula replaced because of difficulty getting in touch with the responsible doctor.[2]

---

1   Standing Nursing and Midwifery Advisory Committee. *Caring for older people: a nursing priority integrating knowledge, practice and values. A report.* London: Department of Health, 2001, pp.17–18, 29.

2   Commission for Health Improvement. *Clinical performance review: East Kent Hospitals NHS Trust.* London: CHI, 2002, pp.5–10.

2002: Gosport War Memorial Hospital: undignified care and reckless administration of palliative care mediation for people who were not dying. The Commission for Health Improvement found inadequate safeguards in Portsmouth for the prescribing of medicines for older people. Concerns had arisen about the deaths of a number of patients. There was no evidence of a policy to ensure appropriate prescription and dose escalation of powerful pain-relieving drugs. Experts commissioned by the police had serious concerns about anticipatory prescribing. There was inappropriate combined subcutaneous administration of diamorphine, midazolam and haloperidol which risked excessive sedation and respiratory depression leading to death. No clear guidelines were available for staff, to guard against their making assumptions that patients had been admitted for palliative rather than rehabilitative care.

Staff failed to recognise potential adverse effects of prescribed medicines. Clinical managers failed routinely to monitor and supervise care on the ward. Wider concerns about care included continence management and claims by relatives that patients were automatically catheterised to save nursing time, patients not being dressed in their own clothes (despite these having been clearly labelled), and physical transfers from one hospital to another involving lengthy waits, inadequate clothing and cover during the journey, and one patient being carried on nothing more than a sheet.[1]

2003: Gosport War Memorial Hospital: Baker report is produced exposing shortening of lives but is not published by the Department of Health for ten years. A report by Professor Richard Baker into deaths at the hospital was commissioned by the Department of Health. It concluded that routine use of opiates before death had been followed in the care of patients of the Department of Medicine for Elderly People at Gosport Hospital, represented in many clinical records by the words 'please make comfortable' – from 1988 onward up to 2000. The practice almost certainly had shortened the lives of some patients, and it could not be ruled out that a small number of these would otherwise have been eventually discharged from hospital alive.[2]

1   Commission for Healthcare Improvement. *Investigation into the Portsmouth Healthcare NHS Trust: Gosport War Memorial Hospital, July 2002*. London: CHI, 2002, pp.12–13, 22–23.

2   Baker, R. *A review of deaths of patients at Gosport War Memorial Hospital*. London: Department of Health, 2013, p.4.

The Department of Health subsequently concealed the content of the report until 2013, using exemptions under the Freedom of Information Act 2000 to resist requests for publication.[1]

2003: Rowan Ward, Manchester: abuse of elderly people with dementia. Concerns arose about Rowan Ward, part of the Manchester Mental Health and Social Care NHS Trust. Initial inquiries suggested that abuse of elderly people with dementia, over a period of several years, included hitting, slapping, stamping on feet, thumb twisting, intimidatory language and emotional abuse in the form of restricting food and playing on known anxieties of patients. The Commission for Health Improvement was called in and confirmed that such practices had been taking place.[2]

2004: National Audit Office: reckless approach to infection control. The National Audit Office issued a report on patient safety and infection. It accurately drew attention to the fact that NHS Trusts had taken their eye off the ball, and in effect anticipated precisely the scandals to come at Stoke Mandeville Hospital and at Maidstone and Tunbridge Wells NHS Trust.[3]

2006: Age Concern England: malnourishment and dehydration in hospitals. The report *Hungry to be heard* highlighted the fact that significant numbers of older people were suffering from malnourishment and dehydration in NHS hospitals.[4]

2006: Healthcare Commission: poor standards of care. The Healthcare Commission, Audit Commission and Commission for Social Care Inspection published a report called *Living well in later life*. Amongst its findings was evidence of ageism towards older people across all services. This included 'patronising and thoughtless treatment from staff', failure to take needs and aspirations of older people seriously, lack of dignity, lack of respect, poor standards of care on general hospital wards, being repeatedly moved

---

1   Jones, Reverend J. (Chairman). *Gosport War Memorial Hospital: the report of the Gosport Independent Panel*. London: The Stationery Office, 2018, p.101.

2   Commission for Health Improvement. *Investigation into matters arising from care on Rowan Ward, Manchester Mental Health and Social Care Trust, September 2003*. London: CHI, 2003, p.8.

3   National Audit Office. *Improving patient care by reducing the risk of hospital acquired infection: a progress report*. London: NAO, 2004.

4   Age Concern England. *Hungry to be heard: the scandal of malnourished older people in hospital*. London: ACE, 2006.

between wards for non-clinical reasons, being cared for in mixed-sex bays or wards, having meals taken away before they could eat them due to a lack of assistance, abuse and neglect. In addition, older people were concerned about access to health in rural areas.[1]

2006: Cornwall Partnership NHS Trust: abuse of people with learning disabilities. The Healthcare Commission, together with the Commission for Social Care Inspection, reported on the Cornwall Partnership NHS Trust. A catalogue of poor and abusive care had come to light, which the NHS Trust itself had belatedly ascertained from members of staff, who reported having witnessed 64 incidents over a five-year period.

They included: staff hitting, pushing, shoving, dragging, kicking, secluding, belittling, mocking and goading people who used the Trust's services, withholding food, giving cold showers, over-zealous or premature use of restraint, poor attitude towards people who used services, poor atmosphere, roughness, care not being provided, a lack of dignity and respect, and no privacy.[2]

2006: Mid Cheshire Hospitals NHS Trust: targets and culture undermining basic standards of care. The Healthcare Commission published its findings on the Mid-Cheshire Hospitals NHS Trust. This included the fact that medication and pain relief were inadequate, and staff shortages affected adversely patient care which was described as generally sloppy. The management of beds focused primarily on the hitting of government-set targets, the system was not working in the interests of patients, and patients were moved to inappropriate wards to their clinical detriment. It was a culture of 'nurses who were rushed, short-staffed, stretched and not delivering basic standards of care'.

Drug rounds might be two hours late because of staff shortage, and medication simply left at patients' bedsides where it was either not taken or taken late. Nutritional drinks were likewise left, becoming warm and undrinkable. Crash trolleys were not properly stocked, and even after the

1   Healthcare Commission, Audit Commission, Commission for Social Care Inspection. *Living well in later life.* London: HC, AC, CSCI, 2006, Summary.

2   Commission for Social Care Inspection, Healthcare Commission. *Joint investigation into the provision of services for people with learning disabilities at Cornwall Partnership NHS Trust, July 2006.* London: CSCI, HC, 2006, p.31.

Healthcare Commission had raised this issue, the problem persisted seven weeks later.

Assistance with eating and drinking was provided only 50 per cent of the time it was needed. Call bells would be out of reach or not answered by staff. Patients could not get to the bathroom, commode or bedpan in time. Only about half of patients were cared for on appropriate wards; those on the wrong wards would be called outliers. Patients were being moved throughout the evening, sometimes after midnight. These movements, for non-clinical reasons, contributed to the spread of infection, in the form of MRSA and *Clostridium difficile*.[1]

2006: Stoke Mandeville; 2007: Maidstone and Tunbridge Wells NHS Trust: pursuit of performance and financial targets, together with concealment of the problems, scores of deaths from infection. In 2006 and 2007, the Healthcare Commission issued two reports concerning outbreaks of the bacterium, *Clostridium difficile*, in Buckinghamshire (Stoke Mandeville Hospital) and in Kent (Maidstone and Tunbridge Wells NHS Trust). In the former, poor infection control was associated with nearly 40 deaths; in the latter with nearly 90 deaths.

What concerned the Healthcare Commission was that in both NHS Trusts it appeared that, at board and chief executive level, the preoccupation was with finance and performance rather than infection control. This led to tardy and ineffective measures to control the infection once it had taken hold – including explicit disregarding of the advice offered by the infection control team.

More generally, this preoccupation with performance and finance led also to infection taking such a hold. Factors included running the hospitals with very high bed occupancy, moving patients from ward to ward for non-clinical reasons in order to meet accident and emergency targets (such moves spread infection and are clinically counter-indicated), reduced staffing levels, an autocratic style of management, staff frightened to speak out, stressed staff and managers, staff shortages, broken cleaning equipment, contaminated bedpans and commodes, lack of time to clean

---

1   Healthcare Commission. *Investigation into Mid Cheshire Hospitals NHS Trust, January 2006.* London: HC, 2006, p.30.

beds and mattresses, not taking patients to the lavatory, and leaving patients in wet and soiled bedding for hours.[1]

2007: Help the Aged: absence of care and dignity for older people. Help the Aged identified a number of factors essential to dignity, including personal hygiene, eating and nutrition, privacy, communication, pain management, autonomy, personal care, end-of-life care, and social inclusion. It pointed out that, ten years before, it had

> uncovered a quiet outrage, of modern hospitals delivering archaic care, of professional care workers acting in an uncaring and inhuman way, of sophisticated health services not even delivering on the basics of toileting, mealtimes and communication... So now, after ten years of initiatives, plans, targets and frameworks, where do we stand...surely, we have moved beyond the basics, the mere minimum entitlement in any decent society. Too often the answer is no...[2]

2007: Healthcare Commission: degrading treatment of patients. The Healthcare Commission highlighted common examples relating to dignity generally, on the basis of complaints received. These included patients not being spoken to in an appropriate manner, not being given proper information, consent not being sought, being left in soiled clothes, being exposed in an embarrassing manner, not being given appropriate food or help with eating and drinking, being placed in mixed-sex accommodation, being left in pain, being in a noisy nocturnal environment causing lack of sleep, using premises that are unclean and noisome (toilets and wards), suffering lack of protection of personal property including personal aids (hearing and visual), being subjected to abuse and violent behaviour.[3]

2007: Tameside Hospital, independent review: failures in most basic care. An independent review of care at Tameside Hospital was published,

---

1   See generally: Healthcare Commission. *Investigation into outbreaks of* Clostridium difficile *at Stoke Mandeville Hospital, Buckinghamshire Hospitals NHS Trust, July 2006*. London: HC, 2006. And also: Healthcare Commission. *Investigation into outbreaks of* Clostridium difficile *at Maidstone and Tunbridge Wells NHS Trust, October 2007*. London: HC, 2007.

2   Levenson, R. *The challenge of dignity in care: upholding the rights of the individual*. London: Help the Aged, 2007, p.4.

3   Healthcare Commission. *Caring for dignity*. London: HC, 2007, p.14.

detailing a long list of failings collated by the Tameside Hospital Action Group. These included basic failures in nutrition, hydration, continence, personal hygiene, care of skin pressure areas, management of infection, nurses' competence, as well as intimidation by staff, dirty wards, alteration of patients' notes by staff, lack of communication from staff, shortage of staff, rudeness of staff, call bells out of reach, patients left to wet their beds and then being left in them – and so on.[1]

2007: Sutton and Merton NHS Primary Care Trust. The Healthcare Commission published its findings into events in the Sutton and Merton NHS Primary Care Trust, concerning services for people with learning disabilities at Orchard Hill Hospital. It found that the way in which people were cared for reflected convenience for the provider rather than the needs of individual service users. This included regimented meal times, unsuitable accommodation and equipment, inappropriate restraint, inappropriate staff behaviour, serious incidents including incidents of assault and sexual offences, inadequate staffing (levels, training, risk management).[2]

2007: MENCAP: treatment of people with learning disabilities in hospitals. A report, *Death by indifference*, highlighted six patients with learning disabilities and the substandard treatment they received in hospital. MENCAP argued that these cases indicate institutional discrimination against people with learning disabilities in the health service.[3]

2008: Mental Health Act Commission: basic evils relating to dignity and safety. The Mental Health Act Commission produced its biennial report of 2008. It felt impelled to make comparisons with the *Parliamentary Inquiry into madhouses of 1815/16*. This had identified a number of 'basic evils' which the Commission had found alive and well and undermining people's dignity, privacy and safety. For instance, restrictions on bathing because of staff shortages, inappropriate restraint, a dying man being nursed in the dining room while other patients were having lunch (again, because of lack of staff), vulnerable women housed with predatory men, blinds to patients'

---

1   Fielding, F. (Professor Dame). *Independent review of older people's care at Tameside General Hospital.* Manchester: NHS North West, 2007, p.5.

2   Healthcare Commission. *Investigation into the service for people with learning disabilities provided by Sutton and Merton Primary Care Trust.* London: HC, 2007.

3   MENCAP. *Death by indifference.* London: MENCAP, 2007, p.2.

rooms being kept open permanently for staff convenience, seclusion rooms with no privacy to use the toilet, new acute wards being run at 135 per cent bed occupancy with patients sleeping in day rooms and staff run off their feet, inappropriate use of closed-circuit television – and a woman in seclusion deprived of sanitary protection whilst menstruating.[1]

2008: Independent inquiry into health care for people with learning disabilities. An independent inquiry set up by the government following MENCAP's report, *Death by indifference*, points to people with learning disabilities receiving less effective health care treatment than others, and to appalling examples of discrimination, abuse and neglect.[2]

2008: Healthcare Commission: more degrading and harmful care. The Healthcare Commission published a report based on the consistent complaints it was receiving about the following matters: patients addressed in an inappropriate manner or being spoken about as if they were not there, patients not given proper information, patients' consent not sought or their wishes considered, patients left in soiled clothes or exposed in an embarrassing manner, patients not given appropriate food or help with eating or drinking, patients placed in mixed-sex accommodation, patients left in pain, a noisy environment at night causing a lack of sleep, wards and toilets unclean and smelly, lack of protection of personal property including hearing or sight aids, patients subjected to abuse and violent behaviour.[3]

2009: Nutrition Action Plan Delivery Board: continuing problems with basic nutrition in hospitals. The Board, a government quango, produced its annual and final report. It advised that there was a significant and continuing problem of malnutrition and help with eating – and that official figures underestimated the prevalence of malnutrition in hospitals and care settings.[4]

1   Mental Health Act Commission. *Risk, rights, recovery: twelfth biennial report, 2005–2007.* London: MHAC, 2008, pp.10–11, 17–29.

2   Michael, J. *Healthcare for all: report of the Independent Inquiry into access to healthcare for people with learning disabilities.* London: Department of Health, 2008, p.7.

3   Healthcare Commission. *State of healthcare 2008.* London: HC, 2008, p.107.

4   Lishman, G. (Chair). *Nutrition Action Plan Delivery Board end of year progress report.* London: Department of Health, 2009, p.5.

2009: House of Commons Health Committee: report on patient safety and care. A House of Commons Health Committee report on patient safety drew attention to what it considered to be widespread defects in the approach to patient safety and welfare in NHS Trusts.[1]

2009: Patients' Association: hospital neglect. The Association published *Patients not numbers, people not statistics*. It contained accounts of neglectful patient care, drawn from the large number of accounts given to them by patients and relatives.

Claire Rayner, then President of the Association, summarised thus:

> For far too long now, the Patients Association has been receiving calls on our Helpline from people wanting to talk about the dreadful, neglectful, demeaning, painful and sometimes downright cruel treatment their elderly relatives had experienced at the hands of NHS nurses. Some found it helped to talk to us, for they had had scant comfort from trying to make complaints or even seek explanations about what had happened to the people they loved, never mind the supportive counselling they should have done... The personal accounts given here are just a few of those brought to us. Some cannot be reported now because the surviving relatives have chosen to go to law, so are *sub judice* and some are frankly too distressing, even worse than those on which we have based our report.[2]

2009: Mid Staffordshire NHS Foundation Trust: shocking care standards and hundreds of deaths. The Healthcare Commission reported multiple failures in care that compromised the dignity of patients. These included *not* doing the following things: answering call bells, assisting people to the toilet or commode, respecting privacy and dignity, giving medication promptly and appropriately and making sure it was taken, helping with food and drink, completing charts accurately, paying attention to skin and avoiding pressure sores.[3] The Commission's draft report originally referred

---

1   House of Commons Health Committee. *Patient safety: sixth report of Session 2008–09. HC 151-I.* London: The Stationery Office, 2009, p.87.

2   Patients' Association. *Patients not numbers, people not statistics.* London: PA, 2009, p.3.

3   Healthcare Commission. *Investigation into Mid Staffordshire NHS Foundation Trust, March 2009.* London: HC, 2009.

to the number of 'excess' deaths being between 400 and 1200; the author of the report was reportedly forced to remove this figure.

2009: Mid Stafford: Thomé and Alberti reports. The Department of Health then published two reports, by Professor Alberti and Dr Thomé, which, given the magnitude of what had occurred, were implausibly anodyne.[1]

2010: Mid Stafford: independent inquiry: horrifying care over three- to four-year period. The subsequent Independent Inquiry into Mid Staffordshire NHS Foundation Trust, which reported in 2010, focused explicitly at the outset on the headings in the Department of Health's document, *Essence of care*, nine years after the latter's original publication date and seven since its revision.

It found deficiencies in continence and bladder and bowel care, safety, personal and oral hygiene, nutrition and hydration, pressure area care, cleanliness and infection control, privacy and dignity, record-keeping, diagnosis and treatment, communication, and the management of discharge from hospital. These were the very types of defect that the Standing Nursing and Midwifery Advisory Committee had stressed nine years before.

Under the heading 'privacy and dignity', in particular, the Inquiry referred to incontinent patients left in degrading conditions; patients left inadequately dressed in full view of passers-by; patients moved and handled in unsympathetic and unskilled ways, causing pain and distress; failure to talk to patients by name, or by their preferred name; and rudeness or hostility. The Inquiry stated that there could be no excuse for such treatment and that respect for dignity should be a priority.

In fact, the priority had been financial and performance targets – so that Foundation Trust status could be achieved. Standards of care had been pared to the bone; this resulted in poor and degrading care, suffering and death.[2]

---

1   Alberti, G. (Professor Sir). *Mid Staffordshire NHS Foundation Trust: a review of the procedures for emergency admissions and treatment, and progress against the recommendation of the March Healthcare Commission report.* London: Department of Health, 2009. Also: Thomé, D.C. (Dr) *Mid Staffordshire NHS Foundation Trust: a review of lessons learnt for commissioners and performance managers following the Healthcare Commission investigation.* London: Department of Health, 2009.

2   Francis, R. (Chair). *Independent Inquiry into care provided by Mid Staffordshire NHS Foundation Trust January 2005–March 2009.* London: The Stationery Office, 2010.

2010: Age UK: continuing malnutrition in hospitals. Age UK followed up Age Concern's 2006 report on malnutrition in hospitals with *Still hungry to be heard*, referring to continuing problems.[1]

2010: National Confidential Enquiry into Patient Outcome and Death: poor care, pressure sores, lack of pain relief for older surgical patients. This was an observational study of 800 elderly patients who had all died within 30 days of surgery. It was entitled *An age old problem*. Its findings included the fact that underlying problems beyond the surgical were not diagnosed or understood, and competent input by hospital consultants with expertise in care of the elderly was often lacking. This meant that recovery from surgery could be jeopardised, always supposing the surgery was performed in a timely manner, which in nearly 30 per cent of cases it was not.

Compared with a typical younger adult, an older person with a fractured hip was more likely to be already dehydrated, have nutritional problems, have thrombotic (blood coagulation) complications, experience slower healing, and be at risk of tissue breakdown (pressure sores).

Only 36 per cent of patients received 'good care', and even this did not mean 'exceptionally brilliant' but merely 'appropriate'. This was particularly troubling because the patients considered in the study were of the type that will become more prevalent as the population of people aged over 85 doubles within the next 25 years.

The study did not even find that, whether or not they were receiving appropriate medical diagnosis and intervention, patients received adequate pain relief. This, in the Enquiry's view, indicated 'what must sometimes be an organisational failure to respond to suffering'.[2]

2010: Patients' Association: patient and relative accounts of continuing neglect in hospitals. The Association issued *Listen to patients, speak up for change*. Like its 2009 predecessor, it drew on case studies to illustrate the type of account given to them by patients and relatives of extremely poor and neglectful care.[3]

---

1   Age UK. *Still hungry to be heard.* London: Age UK, 2010.

2   Wilkinson, K. *et al. An age old problem: a review of the care received by elderly patients undergoing surgery.* London: National Confidential Enquiry into Patient Outcome and Death, 2010, pp.4–7.

3   Patients' Association. *Listen to patients, speak up for change.* London: PA, 2010, p.3.

2011: Health Service Ombudsman report: lack of care and compassion in hospitals. This report drew on ten complaints – representative of the many hundreds received annually about elderly care – about the failure of the NHS to provide dignity, compassion and basic care.

The report acknowledged the question of extra resources required in hospitals but stressed the dismissive attitude and indifference of staff. It described tongues like dried leather, nutrition and hydration ignored, patients squealing with unmanaged pain, pressure sores thriving, call bells out of reach, lack of cleanliness and comfort, multiple unrecorded falls, bathing or showering unavailable, weeping wounds not dressed and an absence of patient monitoring.[1]

2011: Care Quality Commission: 100 dignity and nutrition inspections – widespread breaches of the regulations. The Commission published an overview report of 100 hospital inspections carried out in 2011 – two wards in each hospital – on the theme of nutrition and dignity. It found 20 per cent of hospitals not complying with legal regulations and 50 per cent giving cause for concern. The Commission noted:

> Time and time again, we found cases where patients were treated by staff in a way that stripped them of their dignity and respect. People were spoken over, and not spoken to; people were left without call bells, ignored for hours on end, or not given assistance to do the basics of life – to eat, drink, or go to the toilet.[2]

2011: Action on Elder Abuse: 55 per cent of hospitals non-compliant with dignity and nutrition legal standards. This analysis of the 100 inspection reports from the Care Quality Commission, on dignity and nutrition in hospital, claimed that 55 per cent of hospitals were in fact non-compliant (not the 20 per cent reported by the Commission). This was based on the serious lapses in patient care reported in the individual inspection reports, even of those hospitals *deemed to be compliant* but a cause for concern.[3]

---

1   Parliamentary and Health Service Ombudsman. *Care and compassion? Report of the Health Service Ombudsman on ten investigations into NHS care of older people.* HC 778. London: The Stationery Office, 2011.

2   Care Quality Commission. *Dignity and nutrition inspection programme: national overview.* London: CQC, 2011, p.4.

3   Action on Elder Abuse. *Regulatory activity in hospital settings: a critical analysis of the Care Quality Commission's Dignity and Nutrition Inspection of 100 English hospitals.* London: AEA, 2011, p.79.

2011: Patients' Association: more patient and relative accounts of poor care and neglect. The Association published *We've been listening, have you been learning?* It noted that it felt impelled to produce this further report 'because it needs to be understood that that these stories are not isolated incidents but represent a systemic problem within the National Health Service'.

It concluded:

In the 21st century, in one of the most developed countries and health systems in the world, patients should not be left starving or thirsty, they shouldn't be left in pain and they shouldn't be forced to urinate or defecate in their bed because the nurse designated to them says it's easier for them to change the sheets later than to help them to the toilet now. Yet this is what is happening around the country every day.[1]

2012: patients discharged in middle of night. A Freedom of Information Act request was sent to 170 NHS hospital trusts. Replies came from 100. They revealed that 239,233 patients had been sent home during the night during the previous year. If representative of all Trusts, this would mean 400,000 discharges of this type each year, some 8000 per week. Such discharges could be without warning, be distressing and result in harm to the patient, and be followed by death shortly after.[2]

2012: Care Quality Commission: Leeds General Infirmary. Inspectors from the Care Quality Commission had to help distressed patients during their inspection. Basic failings included patients banging on tables for attention, pleading with staff not to be so rough, waiting for 30 minutes to be taken to the lavatory, not being helped at mealtimes, having requests for help ignored, being laid in undignified or uncomfortable positions. Staffing levels were of concern – for example, one qualified nurse to cover a 30-bed ward at night. The CQC found a lack of safe and effective care.[3]

1   Patients' Association. *We've been listening, have you been learning?* London: PA, 2011, pp.5–7.

2   Bates, C. 'Scandal of NHS patients sent home in the middle of the night to "free up hospital beds".' *Daily Mail*, 12 April 2012.

3   Care Quality Commission. *Review of compliance: Leeds Teaching Hospitals NHS Trust, Leeds General Infirmary.* London: CQC, 2012. And: Ward, V. 'Hospital criticised by watchdog due to staff shortages.' *Daily Telegraph*, 19 April 2012.

2012: University Hospitals of Morecambe Bay NHS Foundation Trust and Royal Lancaster Infirmary Furness General Hospital: belated concerns of the Care Quality Commission result in report, published in July 2012, of serious failings. Failings included a chronic shortage of nurses, doctors and even porters. One in four of accident and emergency staff were agency or casual employees. Security guards were asked to carry out caring duties including helping patients at risk of falling. Those patients at risk of falls were not being assessed or cared for appropriately.

Emergency patients waited in accident and emergency for up to seven hours. Patients were left unattended in corridors and left without pain relief. A suicidal patient was left to wander alone. Staff were reported by patients and relatives as laughing, taunting or being rude. Staff were bullying and aggressive amongst themselves. There was a staff culture of 'shared helplessness'. Seven whistleblowers contacted the CQC, too afraid to report concerns to their own managers.

There were bed shortages and poor community services. Owing to equipment that was old, broken, out of date and not fit for purpose, operations did not take place, blood pressures were not taken, and patients were left to sleep on condemned mattresses.[1]

2012: Royal College of Physicians: inability of hospitals to treat, decently, older people with complex needs. A report in September 2012 identified acute hospitals as being on the edge, in terms of their ability to treat older people with complex needs. It made a direct link with poor care and neglect, such as that uncovered at Stafford Hospital. Amongst its findings was a serious shortage of beds, with a 33 per cent drop in numbers over a decade but a 37 per cent rise in emergency admissions. Nearly 66 per cent of hospital admissions were of elderly patients, increasingly with frailty and/or dementia. To their detriment, older patients were frequently moved up to four or five times during their stay, with no formal handover and often with incomplete notes.

It noted the myth and discriminatory attitude that older people should not be in hospital and are in the 'wrong place'. Instead, it stated that:

---

1 Lakhani, N. 'Damning state of care found at "safe" NHS trust.' *The Independent*, 14 July 2012. And: Care Quality Commission. *University Hospitals of Morecambe Bay NHS Foundation Trust and Royal Lancaster Infirmary Furness General Hospital: investigation report.* London: CQC, 2012.

Older people must have equal access to healthcare services; it is not acceptable to view older people in hospital as being in the 'wrong place'. Hospital services must adapt to ensure that older patients, including those who are frail and have a diagnosis of dementia, have access to safe, high-quality care in settings that meet their needs.[1]

2013: Liverpool Care Pathway report: including financial incentives to place people on a 'conveyor belt to death'. Doubtful use of the Liverpool Care Pathway was exposed in 2013, including financial incentives to place people on what could be viewed as a 'conveyor belt to death', and parched patients desperately sucking wash sponges for moisture. Suspicions had grown that, used inappropriately, the pathway risked causing premature death – especially since some patients might recover. The financial incentives – offered per patient placed on the Pathway – gave rise to concerns about tick-box exercises replacing skilled, clinical judgement, and about hastening death for financial gain to help the financial position of NHS Trusts. The incentives had to stop. As the title of the 2013 report put it, more care, less pathway was required.[2]

2015: Morecambe Bay: independent Kirkup report: systemic failures, lack of honesty and openness. This report on harm and deaths of mothers and babies in maternity services at Morecambe Bay NHS Foundation Trust found a 'series of failures at almost every level – from the maternity unit to those responsible for regulating and monitoring the Trust. The nature of these problems is serious and shocking.' The events represented 'a major failure at almost every level':

There were clinical failures, including failures of knowledge, team-working and approach to risk. There were investigatory failures, so that problems were not recognised and the same mistakes were needlessly repeated. There were failures, by both maternity unit staff and senior Trust staff, to escalate clear concerns that posed a threat to safety. There were repeated failures to be honest and open with patients, relatives and others raising concerns. The Trust was

---

1   Royal College of Physicians. *Hospitals on the edge: the time for action*. London: RCP, 2012, pp.2–3.

2   Neuberger, Baroness J. *More care, less pathway: a review of the Liverpool Care Pathway*. London: Independent Review of the Liverpool Care Pathway, 2013, pp.3, 8, 17, 27, 34.

not honest and open with external bodies or the public. There was significant organisational failure on the part of the CQC, which left it unable to respond effectively to evidence of problems.[1]

2015: Southern Health NHS Foundation Trust: hundreds of unexpected deaths not investigated. An independent report into Southern Health NHS Foundation Trust found that of 722 unexpected deaths – involving people with learning disabilities or mental health needs – only 272 were investigated. The report followed from the preventable death of Colin Sparrowhawk in 2013.[2]

2016: Care Quality Commission: North Middlesex University Hospital. Amongst other things, the Commission found emergency patients waiting too long to be assessed, with a shortage of competent doctors to do the assessment; management experienced by staff as oppressive and overbearing; inaccurate care records and observation charts, incomplete risk assessments; only one commode available for the whole of the emergency department, for up to 100 patients; cardiac machines lacking sets of leads to enable immediate ECG print-outs; lack of wrist-band machines which could mean that, in an emergency, a patient might not be identified; not doing hourly rounds in urgent and emergency services meant that one patient had lain dead for four-and-a-half hours before being discovered; patients' dignity was being compromised by being treated on trolleys in corridors and by being not fully covered up; people routinely waiting longer than four hours to see a doctor; inadequate notes and care plans meaning that patients were at risk of not receiving appropriate care and treatment – and so on.[3]

2017: Sir Robert Francis warns of another major care scandal. Sir Robert Francis, Chairman of the Independent and Public Inquiries into Stafford

1   Kirkup, B. *Report of the Morecambe Bay investigation.* London: The Stationery Office, 2015, paras 3, 25.

2   Mazars. *Independent review of deaths of people with a learning disability or mental health problem in contact with Southern Health NHS Foundation Trust April 2011 to March 2015.* London: Mazars, 2015, p.14.

3   Care Quality Commission. *North Middlesex University Hospital: quality report.* London: CQC, 2016, pp.2–31.

Hospital, warned that another major care scandal was inevitable, given the pressure on the NHS.[1]

2017: British Medical Association warning of continuing over-occupancy of hospital beds and compromise of patient safety. The BMA warned of patient safety continuing to be seriously jeopardised by hospital bed occupancy rates of over 85 per cent, which are deemed to be unsafe.[2] Out of 152 hospitals, 137 hospitals exceeded this rate, a consequence being that, for example, a patient might die after a 13-hour wait on a trolley.[3]

2017: Care Quality Commission: Portsmouth Hospitals NHS Trust, over-occupancy of hospital beds. The Care Quality Commission continued to report on hospitals with inadequate bed capacity, with the consequence, for example, that patients were allocated the next available bed rather than being treated on a ward specifically for their condition, thereby placing them at risk of harm.[4]

2017: Care Quality Commission: mental health services. The Commission identified several areas of concern, including safety concerns (antiquated premises, unsafe staffing levels and poor management of medicines), restrictive practices such as locked wards, staff lacking in skills to de-escalate violence, excessive physical restraint, poor access and lengthy waiting times, poor clinical information systems.[5]

2018: resurgence of use of trolleys in corridors as emergency wards. Long waits on trolleys in corridors were reported around the country in early 2018.[6] Likewise, long waits for ambulances – which, in turn, were

---

1   Lintern, S. 'Francis: top-down pressure on NHS chiefs "depressingly familiar".' *Health Service Journal*, 9 February 2017.

2   British Medical Association. *State of the health system: beds in the NHS: England*. London: BMA, 2017.

3   Triggle, N. 'NHS Health Check: nine in 10 hospitals "overcrowded" this winter.' *BBC News*, 21 February 2017. Accessed on 5 March 2018 at: www.bbc.co.uk/news/health-38853707.

4   Care Quality Commission. *Portsmouth Hospitals NHS Trust quality report*. London: CQC, 2017, p.2.

5   Care Quality Commission. *The state of care in mental health services 2014 to 2017*. London: CQC, 2017, pp.8–9.

6   Illman, J. 'Trolley waits soar to record high.' *Health Service Journal*, 8 February 2018. And: Triggle, N. 'NHS pressure: hospital corridors "the new emergency wards".' *BBC News*, 8 February 2018. Accessed on 5 March 2018 at: www.bbc.co.uk/news/health-42989181.

being delayed by being unable to hand over patients at over-full acute hospitals.[1]

2018: Worcestershire Royal Hospital NHS Trust. A report by Carnall Farrar found hundreds of patients every month waiting more than 12 hours in the emergency department, patients left on trolleys in corridors, patients dying in corridors, so-called 'coding errors' leading to under-reporting of problems, admission of patients (on paper) to 'virtual' wards (i.e. non-existent wards), worsening of ambulance handovers, a normalisation of crisis behaviour.[2]

2018: Kirkup report: Liverpool Community Health NHS Trust: financial focus, poor care, falls, pressure sores, bullying denial. This report found a range of serious failings, with echoes of Mid Staffordshire NHS Foundation Trust. Costs were cut without the risks and consequences being identified. The focus was on finance and becoming a Foundation Trust. Staff reduction and demoralisation occurred, staff sickness increased. Patient harm proliferated including pressure sores and falls. Other serious incidents should have been reported and investigated, reporting was discouraged, incidents were regularly downgraded in importance, and action planning for improvement was absent or invisible. The Trust Board's reaction to the gathering crisis in services was based on denial.[3]

2018: Health Service Ombudsman: mental health services, symptomatic, persistent problems, with shocking and tragic consequences. Based on a sample of 150 complaints, common themes emerging were failure to treat, inadequate assessment (including risk assessment), care plans incomplete or not being followed, poor communication, poor coordination of services.[4]

2018: Care Quality Commission: Dudley Group NHS Foundation Trust, safety and review of deaths. The CQC reported on unsafe services at

---

1 Steward, M. 'Damning dossier from ambulance trust whistleblower claims Christmas and new year deaths were due to delays.' *East Anglian Daily Times*, 20 January 2018.

2 Heather, B. 'Hundreds of patients waiting over 12 hours at strained hospital.' *Health Service Journal*, 21 March 2018.

3 Kirkup, B. *Report of the Liverpool Community Health Independent Review*. Liverpool: Liverpool Community Health NHS Trust, 2018, p.5.

4 Health Service Ombudsman. *Maintaining momentum: driving improvements in mental health care*. London: HMSO, 2018, pp.2–7.

Russells Hall Hospital and imposed a number of urgent conditions to safeguard patients' safety, immediately following the inspection. These conditions related to the management of patients at risk of deterioration and the arrangements for assessing and triaging patients. In response, the Trust launched an independent review into 150 deaths, the implication being that they might have been avoidable. In July 2018, 42 clinicians signed a letter to the Chairman of the Trust, referring to a 'culture of bullying and intimidation where staff are too scared to raise concerns', and indicating the chief nurse and chief executive as culpable.[1]

2018: Gosport War Memorial Hospital Inquiry report: over 450 patients' lives shortened in a culture of disregard for human life, with multi-agency failure to act. An independent inquiry into events at Gosport War Memorial Hospital reported on events that took place at the hospital between 1988 and 2000. It concluded that the lives of over 450 people were shortened as a direct result of the pattern of prescribing and administering opioids that had become the norm at the hospital, and that probably at least another 200 patients were similarly affected.

It stated:

[D]uring a certain period at Gosport War Memorial Hospital, there was a disregard for human life and a culture of shortening the lives of a large number of patients by prescribing and administering 'dangerous doses' of a hazardous combination of medication not clinically indicated or justified. They show too that, whereas a large number of patients and their relatives understood that their admission to the hospital was for either rehabilitation or respite care, they were, in effect, put on a terminal care pathway.

They show that, when relatives complained about the safety of patients and the appropriateness of their care, they were consistently let down by those in authority – both individuals and institutions. These included the senior management of the hospital, healthcare organisations, Hampshire Constabulary, local politicians, the coronial system, the Crown Prosecution Service, the General Medical Council and the Nursing and Midwifery Council. All failed to act in ways that would have better protected patients and

---

1   Harris, R. 'Chief nurse named in whistleblowing letter leaves troubled FT.' *Health Service Journal*, 11 October 2018.

relatives, whose interests some subordinated to the reputation of the hospital and the professions involved.[1]

2018: Care Quality Commission continued to report on unsafe hospitals with bullying culture to deter the raising of concerns. For example: patients waiting in corridors, delays in treatment, delays in admission of patients to beds on the wards, an active policy of placing patients in trolleys on wards to await beds and manipulation of the delays through admitting patients who were approaching the 12-hour target rather than those who had already breached the target – coupled with a bullying culture, one of fear and reprisal amongst staff if they should raise concerns.[2]

2018: Care Quality Commission: Shrewsbury and Telford NHS Trust: patients boarded in corridors and treated like "animals" and "cattle". The CQC warned the Trust that it could be issued with a legal notice and have conditions imposed on it after an unannounced inspection. A leaked letter from CQC sent to the trust chief executive said patients were being treated in "inappropriate areas" that were "not designed for accommodating them." This was known as "boarding", involving patients being treated in corridors or squeezed into extra spaces on wards but without access to piped oxygen or call bells. According to staff, patients with high acuity and dependency needs would often be boarded for five to seven days. The letter said: "Staff across all areas and grades raised concerns with us about this practice and told us they felt it was unsafe, demeaning, undignified, and disgusting. "Two staff members told us they felt patients who were boarded were treated like 'animals' and 'cattle'." The leaked letter was rather more forthcoming than CQC's public report, which was couched in terminology which did not spell out, in ordinary language, the implications for patients.[3]

2018: Care Quality Commission on mental health wards and sexual safety. The CQC reported on sexual safety on mental health wards in hospitals, finding unwanted sexual incidents commonplace, distressing for

1   Jones, Reverend J. (Chairman). *Gosport War Memorial Hospital: the report of the Gosport Independent Panel*. London: The Stationery Office, 2018, Foreword and para 12.10.

2   Care Quality Commission. *Norfolk and Norwich University Hospitals NHS Foundation Trust: inspection report*. London: CQC, 2018, pp.4, 18. See also: Care Quality Commission. *Isle of Wight NHS Trust: inspection report*. London: CQC, 2018.

3   Care Quality Commission. *Shrewsbury and Telford Hospital NHS Trust: quality report*. London: CQC, 2018.

patients, not being prevented and not being acted upon adequately. And, in particular, that safeguarding procedures were not being used appropriately to report on and respond to such incidents.[1]

Neglect

The Care Act repeatedly refers to the protection of adults from abuse and neglect. Guidance refers to neglect as including: ignoring medical, emotional or physical care needs; failure to provide access to appropriate health, care and support or educational services; the withholding of the necessities of life, such as medication, adequate nutrition and heating.[2]

The term also is referred to in the Health and Social Care Act (Regulated Activities) Regulations 2014. Under these regulations, all health and care providers in England have a duty to safeguard their service users from neglect.

The term neglect should be distinguished from the term 'wilful neglect', which constitutes a criminal offence: see *Wilful neglect or ill-treatment*.

Negligence

Civil negligence cases are about seeking financial compensation for harm that has been suffered – usually physical, sometimes psychological or financial – because of breach of a duty of care by somebody who owed that duty. Within health and social care this might typically be in relation to a straightforward accident, in which staff with a clear duty of care have carried out their tasks carelessly – for example, therapists allowing a patient to fall when due care was not taken.[3]

The courts will sometimes protect local authorities and other public bodies from liability in the context of the performance of statutory duties related to safeguarding. This is on the basis that when statutory functions are

---

1   Care Quality Commission. *Sexual safety on mental health wards.* London: CQC, 2018, p.18.

2   Department of Health. *Care and support statutory guidance.* London: DH, 2016, para 14.17.

3   *Stainton v Chorley and South Ribble NHS Trust* (1998), unreported, High Court.

being performed – as opposed to basic (professional) tasks – it is not in the public interest that negligence awards should necessarily follow.

NEGLIGENCE: HARM COMING TO VULNERABLE ADULTS. The following examples indicate examples of liability, arising from neglect of vulnerable adults.

Dehydration and ill-nourishment in hospital, causing death. Following the neglect and death of a man in hospital, a negligence case was settled out of court for some £15,000. A former metal worker, he had been admitted for a broken leg, but within a few days became dehydrated and ill-nourished, eventually dying of renal failure, septicaemia and a chest infection. Fluids and nutrition had not been administered and his poor state of health was only identified when he had been discharged to a rehabilitation unit. He was immediately readmitted to hospital intensive care but died.[1] Despite instructions from doctors to do so, staff had failed to provide a saline drip for 12 days. The hospital stated that it could have done things better but was underfunded.[2]

Care home resident with dementia: huge sore down to the bone. Another case involved an elderly man with senile dementia who went into a care home. Within two months he was in a distressing state, heavily sedated, thin and bony, being shouted at to sit down and often sopping wet. He was admitted to hospital as an emergency, with a huge sore at the base of his spine which had rotted the skin to the bone. The family brought a negligence case against the care home and accepted an out-of-court settlement of £45,000.[3]

Hospital accepting liability for pressure sore and death from septicaemia. In March 2010, the Belfast Health and Social Care Trust admitted liability and made a £40,000 out-of-court settlement in relation to the death of a woman in its care. Her family had claimed she was not treated properly

1   'Settlement over pensioner's death.' *BBC News*, 3 March 2004. Accessed on 5 October 2018 at: http://news.bbc.co.uk/1/hi/england/west_midlands/3530283.stm.

2   Wright, O. and Carson, V. '86-year-old is killed by hospital's cruel neglect.' *The Times*, 8 August 2002.

3   Pannone. 'Pannone wins care home negligence settlement of £45,000.' Press release, 2006.

and died from septicaemia as a result. She was admitted to Royal Victoria Hospital with a suspected broken hip. For about two weeks, staff were undecided about whether it was broken; in the meantime, a pressure sore was allowed to develop on her heel, which turned black and gangrenous.[1]

MRSA infection: hospital accepting liability. When NHS Trusts have taken shortcuts with infection control, and people have suffered or died as a consequence, a negligence case might be possible. For instance, an actress and model was compensated with £5 million for negligence on the part of a hospital which led to her contracting the MRSA infection.[2]

Stafford Hospital: poor care and clinical negligence claims. Following the scandal at the Mid Staffordshire NHS Foundation Trust, where many hundreds of people are thought to have died because of poor care and neglect, the hospital settled claims worth over £1 million on the basis of human rights breaches and clinical negligence claims.[3]

Vicarious liability of employer for employee's acts of abuse. In sexual abuse cases involving children, the courts have held that it is possible to bring a civil case in tort against the employer of the abuser, on the basis of vicarious liability of the employer for the acts of the employee.[4]

NEGLIGENCE: FINANCIAL HARM. Negligence need not always be about physical harm; it can sometimes relate to psychological or financial harm.

Confidence trick on elderly gentleman facilitated by negligent solicitor. An elderly gentleman in Eastbourne, with uncertain understanding and partial memory, had fallen into the hands of a confidence trickster who first cleared out his savings account, then put him up to raising a mortgage

---

1   'Belfast Trust pays damages over pensioner's death.' *BBC News*, 1 March 2010. Accessed on 5 October 2018 at: http://news.bbc.co.uk/1/hi/northern_ireland/8544259.stm.

2   Sanderson, D. 'Leslie Ash gets £5m payout from hospital where she caught MRSA.' *The Times*, 17 January 2008.

3   Leigh Day & Co. 'Mid Staffs cases start to settle.' *News*, 2 March 2010. Accessed on 6 October 2018 at: www.leighday.co.uk/News/2010/March-2010/Mid-Staffs-cases-start-to-settle. And also at: www.leighday.co.uk/News/2011/August-2011/17-more-Stafford-Hospital-families-receive-compens.

4   *Lister v Hesley Hall* [2001] UKHL 22.

on his house, which money was then also taken. However, the court held a solicitor liable for loss of the mortgage money for blatant breach of his duty of care in facilitating the mortgage, even though the money had been appropriated by an unknown third party, for whom the solicitor was, of course, not responsible. The solicitor had failed to check with the man the mortgage proposal that the mortgage lender had sent to the solicitor – precisely to be checked. The man did not want the mortgage, did not need it and could not afford it.

The judge described the facts of this case as quite exceptional and held that the solicitor was liable for the mortgage capital and interest repayments – even though it was the confidence trickster, an unknown third party, who had ultimately walked off with the money.[1]

NEGLIGENCE: PUBLIC BODIES SOMETIMES PROTECTED FROM LIABILITY IN NEGLIGENCE. The courts sometimes protect local public bodies from certain types of negligence case, by holding that the local authority or NHS body did not have a duty of care in the first place. This means that even if there is ostensible carelessness, it is irrelevant because there is effectively no duty to breach.

This can happen when the court perceives that the public body's statutory duties (and sometimes policy or resource issues) are in play. For example, the issue has arisen as to whether it is fair, just or reasonable to impose a duty of care in child protection,[2] aftercare under section 117 of the Mental Health Act 1983[3] and protection of witnesses by the police.[4] The answer in these three cases was that there was no liability in negligence or for breach of statutory duty, precisely because of the complex statutory duties involved.

However, in the first of these cases, involving conspicuous failure of a local authority to act – despite overwhelming evidence from a range of sources that the children in question were being badly neglected – the European Court

---

1   *Finsbury Park Mortgage Funding v Burrows and Pegram Heron* (2002), Brighton County Court, 22 February 2002 and 3 May 2002.

2   *X (Minors) v Bedfordshire County Council* [1995] 2 AC 633. Also: *Barrett v Enfield London Borough Council* [2001] 2 AC 550.

3   *Clunis v Camden and Islington Health Authority* [1998] 3 All ER 180, Court of Appeal.

4   *Chief Constable of Hertfordshire v Van Colle; Smith v Chief Constable of Sussex* [2008] UKHL 50.

of Human Rights held that financial compensation was payable for breach of articles 3 and 8 of the European Convention on Human Rights.[1] Similarly, more recently, the failures of the police to investigate competently a rogue black-taxi driver who assaulted and raped women did not attract a duty of care in negligence – but the courts held that the police could nonetheless be liable to pay damages, via the Human Rights Act 1998, in respect of article 3 of the European Convention.[2]

The courts have struggled to state exactly what the law in negligence is and to maintain a consistent line. All of which makes potentially significant the following case, involving a local authority's failure to safeguard and protect two highly vulnerable adults with learning disabilities from being tortured by a third party.

Failure by local authority to prevent torture of two people with learning disabilities: no negligence liability. Two adults with learning disabilities lived together in a flat, together with the woman's two children, one of whom also had learning disabilities. The family was vulnerable. Two parts of the local authority's social services department had been involved with the family before the relevant weekend.

For a period of time prior to the relevant weekend, the claimants had been befriended and then taken advantage of by a number of youths. This included using the flat as a place at which to live, take drugs, engage in sexual activity, leave stolen goods and generally misbehave. During the relevant weekend the claimants were effectively imprisoned in their own home, and repeatedly assaulted and abused, often in the presence of the two children.

High Court finding of liability. The judge considered in detail the local authority's responses to the deteriorating situation leading up to the weekend. He concluded that before the weekend in question, the council's emergency procedure for moving the couple from their flat should have been triggered. The fact that this did not occur resulted from a lack of cooperation and communication between the social services and housing departments, a failure to appreciate the gravity and urgency of the situation

---

1   *Z v United Kingdom* [2001] 2 FCR 246, ECHR, paras 74–75.

2   *Commissioner of Police of the Metropolis v DSD* [2018] UKSC 11.

indicated by the evidence, and a failure to give the case the priority it warranted. In all the circumstances, it was fair, just and reasonable to impose a duty of care.[1]

Court of Appeal: no liability in principle, even had there otherwise been negligence. The Court of Appeal overruled the High Court's decision. First, uncontroversially, it concluded there had, in any case, been no negligent actions on the part of the social worker involved. Second, more notably, the court held that, because the judgements made by the local authority staff were inextricably linked to its statutory duties under the Housing Act 1996, it would not be fair, just and reasonable to impose liability. Nor under the National Assistance Act. This was so, even had there been negligent or careless actions by local authority officers.

The Court of Appeal confirmed that whilst a judicial review case testing the lawfulness of the local authority actions (a different type of legal case not involving financial compensation) might have been possible, no common law duty of care in negligence automatically attached to that legislation. In some limited circumstances, a separate duty of care might arise in negligence.[2]

Likewise, the following cases:

Local authority not liable for anti-social behaviour resulting in death. A local authority was held as owing no duty of care, for failing to take steps against tenants indulging in anti-social behaviour. A tenant had over a period of years been violent towards another tenant. The allegation was that the local authority had failed to start eviction proceedings sooner, and to inform the victim about a meeting it had held with the perpetrator, threatening him with eviction. Following that meeting, the perpetrator killed the victim. The Supreme Court was clear that it would not be fair, just and reasonable to impose a duty of care on the local authority.[3]

Local authority not liable for failing to move family with severely disabled child. A mother and two children – one of whom had severe physical and learning disabilities – were placed in accommodation close to a family

---

1   *X & Y v Hounslow London Borough Council* [2008] EWHC 1168 (QB).

2   *X & Y v Hounslow London Borough Council* [2009] EWCA Civ 286.

3   *Mitchell v Glasgow City Council* [2009] UKHL 11.

known for its anti-social behaviour, which then harassed and abused the mother and children. The child with severe disabilities attempted suicide. The claim was made against the local authority in negligence. The claim failed. Two key reasons were as follows: the first was that liability in negligence would complicate decision-making in a difficult and sensitive field, and potentially divert the social worker or police officer into defensive decision-making; the second was that, in general, there is no liability for the wrongdoing of a third party, even where that wrongdoing is foreseeable.[1]

Information on criminal record certificate carelessly included: no police liability. A man was initially accused of indecent assault and attempted rape. The police later recorded that he was not responsible for the crime and closed the case. When the man was later applying for a teaching post, a criminal record certificate was required; it contained details of his arrest for the suspected offences. The man then spent nearly a year trying to persuade the police that this information should not have been included. A subsequent certificate omitted the information.

The man complained of psychiatric illness and financial loss and sued in negligence. The High Court refused to strike out the negligence action, meaning the case could at least go to trial, on the basis that the police had 'assumed a responsibility' to act with reasonable care towards an individual, in terms of putting together, on specific request, information to be included in a criminal record certificate.[2]

The Court of Appeal thought otherwise and found in favour of police immunity, stating that a duty of care did not arise under the Police Act 1997 (even had the police behaved negligently). One of the reasons given for this decision was that any such duty of care could conflict with the duty to protect young people.[3]

Death of vulnerable adults: police settling out of court with no admission of liability. A woman killed herself and her disabled daughter after suffering years of anti-social behaviour. The police had failed to identify them as vulnerable, despite numerous referrals and complaints over a ten-year period. The Independent Police Complaints Commission made adverse

---

1 *CN v Poole Borough Council* [2017] EWCA Civ 2185, para 94.

2 *Desmond v Chief Constable of Nottinghamshire Police* [2009] EWHC 2362 (QB).

3 *Desmond v Chief Constable of Nottinghamshire Police* [2011] EWCA Civ 3.

findings in respect of the Leicestershire police. A legal action, brought by the woman's mother, was settled out of court by the police with no liability admitted.[1]

Health care regulator: protection from liability? In a case involving a previous health care regulator (it would now be the Care Quality Commission), the court held that the regulator would not be held liable in negligence in respect of a care home provider, even though the regulator had applied for and obtained an emergency closure order without justification. By the time the care home won a tribunal appeal, irrevocable damage had been done to the business. The tribunal was scathing about the regulator, stating that its original application had included irrelevant and prejudicial information, insinuations of abuse of residents without evidence, and untrue suggestions that the owners had failed to comply with statutory regulations. The court held that the regulator did not owe a duty of care to the care provider and therefore could not be held liable.

However, the court did leave open the possibility that, in principle in such cases,

> it might be fair and reasonable to conclude that the authority did owe a common law duty of care to the residents of a nursing home or a care home if conditions at the home warranting the exercise of the authority's statutory powers had come to the authority's attention, but nothing had been done.

Especially when the consequences were

> to descend upon a home with a number of ambulances and nurses and remove 33 elderly mentally infirm residents to other hospitals and nursing homes without any notice or opportunity to prepare for such a distressing and potentially damaging disruption to their lives.[2]

---

1   'Family of Fiona Pilkington settle claim against police.' *BBC News*, 9 March 2012. Accessed on 5 October 2018 at: www.bbc.co.uk/news/uk-england-leicestershire-17309285.

2   *Trent Strategic Health Authority v Jain* [2009] UKHL 4, paras 20, 44.

Non-molestation orders

Under the Family Law Act 1996, the court can issue civil non-molestation orders, breach of which is a criminal offence. Molestation is not limited to violence or threats of violence. The word is not defined in the Act, but it need not involve violence and could include pestering, annoying, inconvenience, harassing. However, in relation to the adults concerned, there must be an association that in effect is a domestic connection. For a relevant association to apply, the adults must, in summary:

- be, or have been, married

- be, or have been, civil partners

- be cohabitants or former cohabitants, live or have lived in the same household (other than through one of them being the other's employee, tenant, lodger or boarder); this includes same sex cohabitants

- be people who have had an intimate personal relationship of significant duration who have not cohabited

- be relatives

- have agreed to marry (whether or not the agreement has since been terminated)

- in relation to a child, be the parents or have parental responsibility, be party to the same set of family proceedings.[1]

The court has discretion to make an order and must have regard to all the circumstances, including the health, safety and well-being of the applicant, the other party and any relevant child.[2] Breach of an order without reasonable excuse is a criminal offence, with up to five years in prison.[3]

NON-MOLESTATION ORDERS: PROTECTING VULNERABLE ADULTS.
Non-molestation orders are sometimes relevant in the context of safeguarding and protecting vulnerable adults.

---

1   Family Law Act 1996, s.62.

2   Family Law Act 1996, s.42.

3   Family Law Act 1996, s.42A.

Order against son from approaching his mother. A non-molestation order, with a power of arrest, was granted against a man from going within 100 metres of his mother's home, where he had a history of violence and threats of violence against her.[1]

Nursing and Midwifery Council

Under the Nursing and Midwifery Order 2001, the Nursing and Midwifery Council (NMC) regulates nurses, health visitors and midwives. The NMC's code of conduct includes the following:

- Treat people as individuals and uphold their dignity.

- Make sure that people's physical, social and psychological needs are assessed and responded to.

- Act in the best interests of people at all times.

- Respect people's right to privacy and confidentiality.

- Be open and candid with all service users about all aspects of care and treatment, including when any mistakes or harm have taken place.

- Raise concerns immediately if you believe a person is vulnerable or at risk and needs extra support and protection (if necessary, escalate those concerns, and, if you are in a management position, protect anyone you have management responsibility for from any harm, detriment, victimisation or unwarranted treatment after a concern is raised).

- Act without delay if you believe that there is a risk to patient safety or public protection.[2]

Thus, a nurse potentially breaches the Code not just by doing something he or she ought not to, but also by failing to raise concerns.

---

1   *Hutty v Hutty* [2005] EWCA Civ 1026.

2   Nursing and Midwifery Council. *The Code: standards of conduct, performance and ethics for nurses and midwives*. London: NMC, 2015, pp.4–12.

NURSING AND MIDWIFERY COUNCIL: DISCIPLINARY CASES. The following examples are drawn from Nursing and Midwifery Council cases and relate to action taken against nurses in a number of cases relevant to safeguarding – that is, potential abuse or neglect.

Not reporting harm perpetrated by others. A nurse who witnessed a care assistant roughly handling a resident failed to stop it, failed to report it and advised another colleague not to report it. A caution was placed against the nurse's entry in the register. She had a good history, it was an isolated incident, she admitted and regretted it, and had provided good testimonials.[1]

Mocking patients. A nurse put a patient's glass eye in a ward sister's drink, painted a smiley face on a patient's fist-sized hernia, and falsified patient records with a magic pen. She was struck off by the NMC.[2]

Financial abuse of patients. Following conviction in the Crown Court on six counts of theft, five of false accounting and 13 of obtaining property by deception, a nurse was sentenced to 18 months in prison. The Council struck her off from the register, given the gross abuse of trust of the vulnerable people from whom she had dishonestly obtained property.[3]

Physical abuse, unacceptable restraint and violence. A nurse, working in a nursing home, was struck off following a number of allegations including leaving a patient with learning disabilities lying in his own vomit, dragging a patient by his collar, slamming a door in his face, stamping on his foot and calling him a 'thieving bastard'.[4]

Likewise, a nurse was struck off for, amongst other things, rough handling of patients, which represented a failure to treat the patients with dignity and respect.[5]

---

1   Nursing and Midwifery Council: Case 01G2069O, 4 October 2007.

2   Ward, D. 'Nurse who put patient's glass eye in drink is struck off.' *The Guardian*, 17 February 2006.

3   Nursing and Midwifery Council: Case 712H2138E, 28 March 2008.

4   'Nurse who left man lying in own vomit is struck off.' *South Manchester Reporter*, 29 January 2004.

5   Nursing and Midwifery Council: Case 83Y0105W, 6 March 2008.

Striking off followed failures including assaulting a resident (for which she had been convicted in court), rough handling of a resident, slapping the resident's hand and telling the resident that he was a 'naughty boy'.[1]

Striking off followed for a nurse who had spoken inappropriately to a patient by telling him to shut up and had roughly handled him by pinning his arm to the bed and putting his hand around his neck – this was 'wholly unnecessary physical restraint'.[2]

A nurse in a care home was cautioned, having taken hold of a resident's hand, put his arm up his back, marched him to his room and pushed him on to the bed. The Council was concerned at this treatment of a vulnerable elderly resident but took into account that it was not done maliciously, that it was a one-off incident, and that there were no other concerns about the nurse's practice.[3]

A caution followed when a nurse slapped a patient's leg and pulled and yanked it. The nurse nearly suffered removal from the register because physical abuse of an elderly patient with dementia was a very serious matter. But she had a 36-year unblemished work record, it was an isolated incident, and she had impressive references and testimonials. A caution was the proportionate response.[4]

Verbal abuse. Striking off from the register followed findings that a nurse, amongst other things, had said to a patient, 'if you were a dog you would have been put down, instead I'll smack your arse'.[5]

And a nurse was struck off for, amongst other things, slapping a resident, verbal abuse to residents ('get your fucking legs off the lift', 'you can't fucking hear anyway', 'talk to the hand because the face ain't listening') and rough handling of a resident after failing to warn the resident that she was about to move her.[6]

Neglect and emotional harm. A nurse working with people with learning disabilities forced a resident out of a chair, inappropriately requested he

---

1   Nursing and Midwifery Council: Case 02H1244O, 8 January 2008.

2   Nursing and Midwifery Council: Case 87H01616E, 26 July 2007.

3   Nursing and Midwifery Council: Case L71Y1288E, 12 July 2007.

4   Nursing and Midwifery Council: Case 68I0223N, 10 October 2007.

5   Nursing and Midwifery Council: Case 83A0008E, 27 March 2008.

6   Nursing and Midwifery Council: Case 87I1737E, 17 October 2007.

remove his crockery without assistance (this was not part of his routine, it put him at physical risk, added to his mental and emotional distress, and was not part of his formal or informal care plan), saw him fall but failed to provide or allow appropriate assistance to be given, and failed to report the fall. In respect of the latter, he was in a state of shock and disarray; the nurse went on hovering around him. The nurse was struck off.[1]

Inappropriate personal relationships. A nurse was struck off for developing an inappropriate relationship with a patient, who was vulnerable and required care at a time of major crisis in her life; this represented a total abuse of his professional status.[2]

NURSING AND MIDWIFERY COUNCIL: SYSTEMIC CARE FAILINGS. The professional regulatory councils have generally found it a challenge to act against individuals caught up in systemic care failings. There are three main reasons for this.

First, it is more difficult to locate professional and moral responsibility and blame when the matter is institutional. Second, even if responsibility is identified, there might be (understandable) resistance to blaming an individual. Third, the prospect of acting against numbers of professionals within one large workplace, such as a hospital, might be daunting. It would involve considerable work, but also diminish the reputation of the profession as a whole.

Nonetheless, the NMC does sometimes hold individual nurses accountable in the context of systemic failings – whether or not they were responsible for them. However, this seems to tend to occur more in relation to care homes than hospitals – although one notable example of the latter is included below.

Multiple failings in care. The registered manager of a care home was struck off on a host of grounds. These included the finding of a resident sitting in a darkened room with a mattress on the floor and faecal matter

---

1   Nursing and Midwifery Council: Case 79K0365E, 16 July 2007.

2   Nursing and Midwifery Council: Case 89H0066H, 12 September 2007.

on the bedding, and a number of residents with their mattress on the floor. Other failings included missing toilet seats, showers not working, dirty fridges, malodorous rooms, incontinence pads in waste bins in toilets, call bells missing, fluid intake charts not completed, pressure sore wound assessment and management not recorded, etc.[1]

Hospital director of nursing suspended for implementing cuts to care standards. Following the revelations of the independent inquiry into patient care at Stafford Hospital, the Nursing and Midwifery Council imposed an 18-month interim suspension order on the director of nursing, pending further enquiries. The grounds related to allegations about the failure to maintain safe levels of nursing practice, infection control and patient care. The case against her was that they were serious allegations, there was a risk of repetition if she took on a similar senior role elsewhere, and she evinced both denial and lack of insight into the alleged failings. An interim suspension order was justifiable for general protection of the public and of the reputation of the profession and the Council.[2]

Systemic failure in care home in Birmingham. In 2002, a 77-year-old war veteran was admitted to the Maypole Nursing Home. He suffered from Alzheimer's disease and Parkinson's disease, but was otherwise considered to be physically fit. Ten days later he was dead, having been sedated and placed in a bucket chair, which effectively immobilised him and may have restricted his ability to breathe when he contracted a chest infection. The inquest returned a verdict of death from natural causes.

This verdict did not mean that all had been well. By 2003 the home had been closed down because of concerns about the death of 15 other patients as well. As a result, in June 2008, three nurses – including a manager – responsible for the care of patients were struck off the nursing register by the NMC. Their professional misconduct included incorrect medication, inappropriate restraint and failings in both hygiene and personal care. All this led to a lack of dignity for the elderly and vulnerable residents. In addition, two general practitioners (GPs) who owned the home, husband

1   Nursing and Midwifery Council: Case 75U6681E, 27–28 March 2008.

2   Nursing and Midwifery Council. *Interim suspension order decision: Janice Margaret Harry*, PIN 70I1747E, 25 October 2010. London: NMC.

and wife, were struck off the medical register by the General Medical Council.[1]

Pressure sores: nurses held accountable. In 2004, three nurses were struck off for their part in what must have been a systemic breakdown of care for residents, in 2000, at the Wells Spring Nursing Home in Bradford. A fourth nurse received a caution.

A man was admitted to the home just for a week, while his wife underwent cataract surgery. He had long-standing Parkinson's disease but was otherwise described as strong and healthy. By the end of the week, he had developed multiple pressure sores so painful that he cried if they were touched; he was admitted to hospital where he died three months later of bronchopneumonia. His wife had repeatedly asked the home that a pressure-relief mattress be supplied for her husband; it was not. In reaching its decision, the NMC's professional conduct committee stressed personal, professional responsibility: 'Each individual nurse had an obligation to champion the care of this patient and failed.'[2]

Poor pressure sore care practices part of the system of work at the care home. The allegation was that a nurse had been the nurse in charge of three shifts in the working week over a long period of time and had been negligent in her duty towards the residents. During these shifts, she did not care for all the needs of the patients but referred pressure sore issues to the deputy manager. She explained that this was in accordance with an instruction from the management system in the home.

However, the NMC decided that, irrespective of this point, she was responsible for meeting the care needs of the residents; they clearly had such needs, because a number of them had severe pressure sores. The NMC decided to impose interim conditions of practice, rather than to strike her off, particularly because she was now working in an occupational health setting.[3]

---

1   Irwin Mitchell. 'Inquest returns verdict of natural causes in Maypole Nursing Home death.' *News*, 15 March 2010. Accessed on 20 September 2010 at: https://www.irwinmitchell.com/newsandmedia/2010/march/inquest-returns-verdict-of-natural-causes-in-maypole-nursing-home-death.

2   Patty, A. 'Nurses whose lack of care led to pensioner's death struck off.' *The Times*, 30 November 2004.

3   Nursing and Midwifery Council. *Interim order decision: Girlie Franklin*, PIN 73D0633E, 5 October 2010. London: NMC.

Nurse failing to seek assistance but systemic failings at care home. At a care home, in 2006, a nurse failed to seek assistance from a doctor, another nurse or ambulance when a resident's behaviour changed, a bruise appeared on her leg and she screamed in pain. The nurse did not assess properly the manual handling technique to be used after the resident had fallen, and did not, on a subsequent occasion, seek help when the resident fell, sustained bruising and complained of pain. The panel noted that practice in the care home was lax, with little supervision or training; in fact, a former manager described it as horrific. Nonetheless, despite this poor culture, the nurse had to retain responsibility for her own professional conduct within the team. A suspension order was imposed.[1]

NURSING AND MIDWIFERY COUNCIL: RETALIATORY REFERRALS. The NMC faces the same risk as other regulatory bodies of 'retaliatory referrals' made by employers in order to victimise whistleblowers – and the risk of it thereby 'shooting the messenger'. See *Whistleblowing*.

---

1   Nursing and Midwifery Council. *Suspension order: Meundju Hungi*, PIN 03J0092O, 21–23 April 2010. London: NMC.

O

Occupation orders

Under the Family Law Act 1996, the courts have a discretion, and sometimes a duty, to issue occupation orders. These can be on grounds of risk of significant harm to the adult applying for the order (or to a child).

The precise rules vary, depending on the entitlement of the applicant (or the respondent) to occupy the dwelling. There needs to be an association or domestic connection between the applicant and the respondent (see *Non-molestation orders*). The court can include a penal notice and attach a power of arrest to the order.[1]

If the applicant is entitled to occupy the dwelling house, then the order can cover a number of matters that could be relevant to safeguarding vulnerable adults. These are, in summary:

- entitlement to remain in occupation

- requiring the respondent to permit the applicant to enter and remain in the dwelling house or part of it

- regulating the occupation of the dwelling house by both parties

- prohibiting or suspending or restricting the right of the respondent to occupy the dwelling (if he or she is otherwise entitled to do so)

- if the respondent has matrimonial home rights, the restriction or termination of those rights

- requiring the respondent to leave the dwelling or part of it

- excluding the respondent from the specific area within which the dwelling lies.

---

1   Family Law Act 1996, s.33 and following, s.47.

In addition:

- **Relevant factors.** The court must have regard to the respective housing needs and resources of the parties and of any relevant child, the financial resources of the parties, the likely effect of any order or of any court decision not to exercise its powers on the health, safety and well-being of the parties and of any relevant child, and the conduct of parties to each other and otherwise.

- **Significant harm.** The court's power turns into a duty if the applicant or any relevant child is likely to suffer significant harm. However, the order still need not be made if the respondent or relevant child is also likely to suffer significant harm if the order is made and that harm would be as great as, or greater than, the harm attributable to the conduct of the respondent and likely to be suffered by the applicant or child if the order is not made.[1]

- **Applicant without occupation rights.** The court also has a power to make many, but not all, of the orders listed immediately above, in relation to other categories of applicant. These are, namely, (a) former spouse or civil partner with no right to occupy the dwelling, (b) one cohabitant or former cohabitant with no existing right to occupy, (c) neither spouse nor civil partner entitled to occupy, and (d) neither cohabitant nor former cohabitant entitled to occupy.[2]

The following case is an example of the equivalent of an occupation order being obtained from the Court of Protection to protect a vulnerable adult from her family.

Occupation order to exclude exploitative family from woman's home. A woman was in her early eighties, diagnosed with dementia. She gave lasting power of attorney to her son and daughter; her capacity to do so was not in doubt. Her son then unexpectedly moved in with his family and began to make changes, removing photographs of his sister and not allowing her to see or speak to their mother.

Son's family takes over home. He threw things away without asking, including furniture and personal possessions, rearranged the home and changed the lock. The mother became overwhelmed, given she had lived alone for two decades. He made derogatory, untrue and distressing remarks to his mother about his sister. He began spending his mother's money as

---

1   Family Law Act 1996, s.33.

2   Family Law Act 1996, ss.35–38.

if it were his own, making no contributions to utility bills or groceries, and withdrawing cash using her debit card for his own family's benefit.

Son taking control of mother's affairs. The daughter went to solicitors (Martin Searle), who contacted social services. In the meantime, the house was put on the market by the son who had persuaded his mother to revoke the joint powers of attorney and appoint him solely (something she, by now, lacked capacity to do). Requests by the solicitors, acting for the daughter, for information and assistance from the mother's banks and from the Land Registry were ignored because the daughter was no longer an attorney.

Occupation order to exclude family from mother's home. After five months of living with the son, the mother went to a neighbour's house asking for help, asking if she could stay there temporarily. The solicitors made an urgent application to the Court of Protection. The solicitors obtained an occupation order removing the son and his family from the home, with a power of arrest attached – and also an order appointing the daughter as deputy for property and financial affairs.[1]

Older people, care and safeguarding

There is a risk – not new – that older people, with their complex and multiple needs, somehow don't count and are not meaningful,[2] within both health care, especially hospital care, and care more generally – which, in turn, could undermine the effectiveness of adult safeguarding.

The late and eminent geriatrician, Professor John Grimley Evans, wrote of a risk of creating a class, the elderly, 'of *Untermenschen* whose lives and well-being are deemed not worth spending money on'. He maintained that we should not discriminate against older people, but instead base treatment on a person's physiological condition and ability to benefit.[3]

---

1 'Case study: safeguarding & best interests – protecting adults at risk.' Martin Searle Solicitors, undated. Accessed on 2 March 2018 at: www.ms-solicitors.co.uk/community-care-law/safeguarding-vulnerable-adults/case-study-safeguarding-and-best-interests-protecting-vulnerable-adults.

2 Stewart, Dr M. (1968) *My brother's keeper?* London: Health Horizon.

3 Grimley Evans, J. 'Rationing health care by age: the case against.' *British Medical Journal 314*, 1997, 822.

He stated also that older people might need to be wilful, cantankerous and bloody-minded if they are not to be abandoned in terms of health and social care.[1] Baroness Neuberger has asked generally how we, as a society, have come to treat the elderly so badly as to amount to the infliction of 'punishment and neglect for being old'.[2]

> **Baby P, Winterbourne View, Stafford Hospital.** Practitioners in health and social care tend to know something about the death of 'Baby P' in Haringey at the hands of three private individuals, his mother, her boyfriend and lodger (brother of the latter). Similarly, most know about the scandal at Winterbourne View, a small specialist, independent hospital, involving the physical and emotional abuse of relatively small numbers of people with severe learning disabilities at the hands of care workers. And yet few can even begin to recount what happened at Stafford Hospital, which involved systemic poor standards of care and neglect on some wards over a period of four years – and involved many hundreds of avoidable deaths[3] – the poor care and neglect being the key point, the exact number of avoidable or 'excess' deaths, not a straightforward concept, less so.[4]

Of the above three scandals, the last is – or should be viewed as – clearly the most serious, given the numbers of patients involved, the deaths, scale of the neglect and, not least, that it took place at a large NHS hospital run by the State – the most serious morally, professionally, politically and legally. However, the temptation is to point to the 'system', thus somehow absolving individuals of responsibility for their action. Since, if everybody is guilty, then nobody is guilty: *tutti colpevoli, nessuno colpevole*, as the expression goes. The danger of this passive, fatalistic and arguably amoral approach is that neglectful and inhumane care, especially of older people, can come to be regarded as akin to a law of physics such as gravity. Scientific laws,

---

1   Grimley Evans, J. 'Wilful white lions.' *Elderly Care 7*, 1995, 3.

2   Neuberger, J. *Not yet dead: a manifesto for old age.* London: HarperCollins, 2009, pp.269, 272.

3   These statements are based on the many conversations the author has had with a wide range of health and social care practitioners.

4   'Deaths figure "removed from Stafford Hospital report".' *BBC News*, 4 May 2011. Accessed on 5 October 2018 at: www.bbc.co.uk/news/uk-england-stoke-staffordshire-13288896.

of course, are not about human agency and stand outside morality, which concerns judgements about human actions and affairs. For such immutable phenomena, nobody can be held accountable; even worse, nothing can be done about them. Superficially comforting and conscience-salving, such thinking can deeply undermine adult safeguarding.[1]

Perhaps a pervasive mindset relating to elderly patients was illustrated by the following examples, involving two prime ministers.

Apologising for hospital failings but not to the elderly in corridors with complex, emergency needs. In the winter of 2017–2018, hospitals were reportedly overrun with older people stuck for long periods of time, and sometimes dying, on trolleys in hospital corridors because of the shortage of beds,[2] as had been the case the previous year, with a 6000 per cent increase in the number of people waiting on trolleys for more than 12 hours.[3] The consequence of the unplanned, emergency admissions and stays of elderly people meant that elective surgery and treatment were being postponed, often for younger adults or older adults with less complex needs. Yet, when the Prime Minister made an apology, this was – extraordinarily – not aimed at those elderly people languishing and dying in the corridors, but at those who had missed their elective operations.[4]

Bedside televisions and telephones alongside clean wards and good care for the elderly? Another Prime Minister wrote a foreword in a House of Commons Command Paper about the NHS. In an era of 'patient choice', it enthused about bedside pay televisions and telephones in hospitals, in the same paragraph as basic care and clean wards.[5] Expensive (for patients) pay-technology did make its appearance in due course, but not

1   Mandelstam, M. *How we treat the sick*. London: Jessica Kingsley Publishers, 2011, p.362.

2   Campbell, D., Duncan, P. and Marsh, S. 'NHS patients dying in hospital corridors, A&E doctors tell Theresa May.' *The Guardian*, 11 January 2018.

3   Morris, S., Weaver, M. and Siddique, H. 'Three patients die at Worcestershire hospital amid NHS winter crisis.' *The Guardian*, 6 January 2017. Also: Donnelly, L. '6000 per cent rise in number of patients stuck on trolleys for 12 hours.' *Daily Telegraph*, 26 May 2017.

4   Kentish, B. 'Winter crisis: Theresa May apologises to patients for thousands of cancelled operations.' *The Independent*, 4 January 2018.

5   Secretary of State for Health. *The NHS Plan: a plan for investment, a plan for reform*. Cm 4818-I. London: The Stationery Office, 2000, para 1.17.

the clean hospitals and good care for the elderly – since the road was already being beaten to the scandals at Maidstone, Stoke Mandeville and Mid Staffordshire. The government spoke of consumer trappings whilst poor care and lethal infection ran through its hospitals – a case of Nero fiddling while Rome burnt.

Older people in hospital

A class of hospital patients – elderly with multiple needs and often admitted unplanned and as an emergency – appears to be at particular risk of poor care and neglect owing to their numbers, the complexity and nature of their needs, and hospitals being unable or unwilling to provide appropriate treatment and care.[1] They fit ill into the elective treatment, targets, care pathways and financial tariffs, on the basis of which the Department of Health, NHS England and senior NHS management would like hospitals to run.[2] There is a fundamental mismatch between the needs of older people and the health care being provided, made worse by deep-seated negative attitudes towards older people.[3]

OLDER PEOPLE IN HOSPITAL: OVERCROWDING. Older people occupy a significant majority of hospital beds. The number of those beds has decreased in England by tens of thousands since 2000, without community health services taking up the unmet needs, and resulting in over-occupation of hospitals – very significantly over the 85 per cent bed occupancy rate regarded as safe. The consequence for older people can be delayed admission (a trolley on a corridor), admission to an inappropriate ward, lack of basic

---

1   Francis, R. (Chair). *Independent Inquiry into care provided by Mid Staffordshire NHS Foundation Trust January 2005–March 2009.* London: The Stationery Office, 2010, p.400.

2   Cornwell, J. *The care of frail older people with complex needs: time for a revolution. Sir Roger Banister Health Summit, Leeds Castle.* London: King's Fund, 2012, pp.1–3. See also: O'Connor, R. and Neumann, V. 'Payment by results or payment by outcome? The history of measuring medicine.' *Journal of the Royal Society of Medicine 99*, 2006, 226–231.

3   Philp, I. *A new ambition for old age: next steps in implementing the National Service Framework for Older People, a report from Professor Ian Philp, National Director for Older People.* London: Department of Health, 2006, p.4.

care, treatment and rehabilitation, infection, development of other problems (including pressure sores, malnutrition, poor medication management, falls) and premature discharge.[1]

OLDER PEOPLE IN HOSPITAL: DIAGNOSIS AND TREATMENT. Many reports and guidance documents talk about avoiding hospital admission of the elderly and ensuring their swift discharge: see ***Hospital discharge***. They are seen sometimes as bed blockers and frequent flyers, and are referred to as 'crumblies' or, by implication, cabbages when doctors refer to the care of elderly people as akin to 'market gardening', resulting all too easily in 'therapeutic nihilism'.[2] Even the seemingly innocuous term 'elderly' in the clinical context may be used to mask, and avoid the treatment of, a clinical condition.[3]

This approach ignores the fact that elderly people, even with complex needs, can be treated clinically and effectively more often than is commonly supposed and that, far from being dismissed as 'social patients' in the wrong place, they should receive proper diagnosis and treatment, instead of receiving the pseudo-diagnosis of 'acopia' (can't cope).[4] The Department of Health's own older people's 'Tsar', Professor David Oliver, noted that the NHS was systematically failing older people in hospital and that the notion of large reductions in older people attending hospital was 'absolute la la land'.[5]

OLDER PEOPLE IN HOSPITAL: POOR CARE AN INEVITABILITY? Patients with multiple and complex needs are demanding of resources, staffing (numbers and expertise), time, and sufficient hospital beds – all of which are

---

1   See e.g. Appleby, J. *Winter beds pressures*. London: Nuffield Trust, 2016.

2   Oliver, D. '"Acopia" and "social admission" are not diagnoses: why older people deserve better.' *Journal of the Royal Society of Medicine 101*, 4, 2008, 168–174.

3   Falconer, M. 'Out with "the old," elderly, and aged.' *British Medical Journal*, 8 February 2007.

4   Royal College of Physicians. *Hospitals on the edge: the time for action*. London: RCP, 2012, pp.2–3. And: Oliver, D. '"Acopia" and "social admission" are not diagnoses: why older people deserve better.' *Journal of the Royal Society of Medicine 101*, 4, 2008, 168–174.

5   Winnett, R. 'Nursing home health care "worse than in jail".' *Daily Telegraph*, 25 November 2012. And: Calkin, S. 'Plan to keep elderly out of hospital is "la la land".' *Health Service Journal*, 14 March 2013.

in short supply. (This is nothing new: their plight 50 years ago in the long-stay NHS geriatric wards – where they would lose their spectacles, teeth, hearing aids and dignity – was importantly described in the 1960s.)[1]

It is hard to escape the view that some of the worst and larger-scale hospital scandals involving older people have in a sense been less than accidental, since logically the underlying policies and political and financial pressures pointed in that direction[2] – almost an experiment, intentional or otherwise, to see how far elderly care could be cut to the bone before unacceptable consequences flowed, or at least until those consequences would be too difficult to cover up and would become known.

---

1   Robb, B. *Sans everything*. London: Nelson, 1967.

2   Hilton, S. *More human*. London: W.H. Allen, 2015, p.113.

P

Police Act 1997, see *Criminal record certificates*

Power to enter

In relation to suspected abuse or neglect (including self-neglect), the question of gaining entry to a person's dwelling sometimes arises. A vulnerable adult might themselves be denying entry to social services or other agencies, or other adults might be denying access to a vulnerable adult. Power of entry is considered below under the following headings.

- Power to enter: Care Act 2014

- Power to enter: Mental Capacity Act 2005

- Power to enter: inherent jurisdiction of the High Court

- Power to enter: Mental Health Act 1983, section 135 (including suspected ill-treatment, neglect or inability to look after oneself)

- Power to enter: Public Health Act 1936, Environmental Protection Act 1990

- Power to enter: Police and Criminal Evidence Act 1984, section 17

- Power to enter: utility companies

- Power to enter: Animal Welfare Act 2006.

POWER TO ENTER: CARE ACT 2014. The Care Act 2014 gives a local authority no legal power of entry to a person's home, even though the duty to make enquiries into suspected abuse or neglect, under section 42 of the Act, is not dependent on a person's consent.

At one stage, the Care Bill in its passage through Parliament did in fact contain such a power. As a last resort, a local authority would have been able to gain a court order. This would have granted it power of entry to talk to and to assess the person, about whom safeguarding concerns had arisen.[1] However, this part of the Bill was eventually discarded. This means that the position in England now differs from that in both Scotland and Wales, where such a power of entry exists.[2] In England, therefore, a legal power to enter must be sought under other legislation.[3]

POWER TO ENTER: MENTAL CAPACITY ACT 2005. A Court of Protection order could include provision for entry to a person's home – the order being made under section 16 of the Act or, in some circumstances, an interim order being made under section 48.

Monitoring of a vulnerable woman involving entry to the dwelling. Concerns had grown about the welfare of an elderly woman, into whose home a couple (wife and husband) had moved. The judge ruled that the woman lacked the relevant mental capacity and that it was necessary for her welfare to be monitored. There was no evidence whatsoever that the home was other than well maintained and comfortable, and that she had adequate food and nutrition. But there was concern that the couple were not just failing to meet the woman's needs but were abusing her within the home. Monitoring in those circumstances in the interim period was vital. The court therefore ordered that the couple facilitate regular visits by social workers.[4]

Order requiring cooperation of mother and daughter. The mental capacity of a young woman needed to be determined. Both she and her mother denied that she lacked capacity. There were great difficulties in communicating with and obtaining the engagement, assistance and

---

1   Care Bill. Hansard, 10 March 2014, column 47.

2   Social Services and Well-being (Wales) Act 2014, s.127. And: Adult Support and Protection (Scotland) Act 2007, s.37.

3   See e.g. Social Care Institute for Excellence. *Gaining access to an adult suspected to be at risk of neglect or abuse: a guide for social workers and their managers in England.* London: SCIE, pp.8–15.

4   *London Borough of Redbridge v G* [2014] EWHC 959 (COP).

cooperation of both daughter and mother. An interim order was made by the court against both, with a penal notice attached. It was to the effect that the order should contain not merely the appropriate declaration as to the need for the further assessment (confined to the questions of capacity) but also the consequential directions requiring cooperation and facilitation by the daughter and her mother. In addition, the order should contain a liberty to apply as to implementation and enforcement – that is, liberty to apply by the local authority and/or the Official Solicitor in the event of difficulty, that application to be made to the Court of Protection.[1]

POWER TO ENTER: INHERENT JURISDICTION OF THE HIGH COURT. An order made under this jurisdiction could relate to powers to enter – for instance, ensuring that a third party allow access to a vulnerable adult in the dwelling.[2] See *Inherent jurisdiction*.

POWER TO ENTER: MENTAL HEALTH ACT 1983, SECTION 135 (INCLUDING SUSPECTED ILL-TREATMENT, NEGLECT OR INABILITY TO LOOK AFTER ONESELF). A justice of the peace may issue a warrant authorising a constable to enter premises, using force if necessary, in order, if it is thought fit, to remove a person to a place of safety for up to 72 hours. This would be with a view to making an application under the Mental Health Act 1983 or other arrangements for care and treatment.

Such a warrant may be issued if it appears to the justice of the peace, from information received on oath by an approved mental health professional, that there is reasonable cause to suspect that a person believed to be suffering from mental disorder (a) has been, or is being, ill-treated, neglected or not kept under proper control; or (b) is unable to care for himself or herself and is living alone.

POWER TO ENTER: PUBLIC HEALTH ACT 1936, ENVIRONMENTAL PROTECTION ACT 1990. Local authority environmental health departments

---

1   *Re SA; FA v Mr A* (2010) EWCA Civ 1128, para 52.

2   *A Local Authority v DL* [2011] EWHC 1022 (Fam).

have various statutory powers to enter premises to deal with public health problems.

- **Environmental Protection Act 1990 (EPA).** This provides for local authority powers of entry in respect of statutory nuisances. On the production of the requisite authority, an authorised person can enter premises at any reasonable time to ascertain whether a statutory nuisance exists, or to take action or execute work authorised under part 3 of the 1990 Act. In the case of residential property, 24 hours' notice is required, unless it is an emergency such as danger to life or health.[1]

  Statutory nuisance is defined as including premises that are in a state prejudicial to health or nuisance, smoke, fumes or gases emitted from premises so as to be prejudicial to health or a nuisance, any accumulation or deposit prejudicial to health or a nuisance, any animal kept in such a place or manner as to be prejudicial to health or a nuisance, and noise emitted from premises so as to be prejudicial to health or a nuisance.[2] These conditions, which could underpin an intervention, are expressed in quite wide terms. They could clearly be relevant, in some circumstances, to self-neglect.

  A local authority has a duty to serve an abatement notice if such a statutory nuisance exists. If the notice is not complied with, the local authority may itself abate the nuisance and recover expenses reasonably incurred.[3] As a last resort, the council has a power of entry to premises, using force if necessary. An order can be obtained from a magistrates' court.[4]

- **Public Health Act 1936.** Under the Public Health Act 1936, the local authority has powers in respect of certain public health issues referred to in the Act. These include filthy, unwholesome, verminous premises; verminous persons or clothing (including removal of a person); and cleaning or destroying filthy or verminous articles.[5] Also, there is a power to require vacation of premises during fumigation.[6] As a last resort, the council has a

---

1   Environmental Protection Act 1990, schedule 3.

2   Environmental Protection Act 1990, s.79.

3   Environmental Protection Act 1990, ss.81–82.

4   Environmental Protection Act 1990, schedule 3, para 2.

5   Public Health Act 1936, ss.83–85.

6   Public Health Act 1936, s.36.

power of entry to premises, using force if necessary. An order can be obtained from a magistrates' court.[1]

The use of such powers, but also the need to exercise them carefully, was demonstrated in the following local ombudsman case.

Cleaning of premises under the Public Health Act 1936. A man was in poor health with limited ability to care for himself. His home became dirty and cluttered to the point where it required thorough cleaning to prevent a health and safety risk to himself and his care workers. His sister got in touch with the local social services authority which then liaised with the environmental health department. Under section 83 of the Public Health Act 1936, the latter proposed to clean the flat and explained to the sister that it would do the work and recover the cost from her brother. However, the council sent a very much larger bill (over £1100) than the cost (£300) the sister claimed originally to have been advised by the local authority.

The ombudsman concluded that the council had not been clear enough in its explanation; the bill had also been wrongly calculated. It included VAT in error, and an inflated amount for environmental health officer time had been included. He recommended that the bill be corrected and then reduced by £300, that the sister receive £200 in recognition of her time and trouble, that the council review the wording of its letters about such work and charges for it, and that it check that all bills for such work carried out since January 2003 had been correctly calculated.[2]

POWER TO ENTER: POLICE AND CRIMINAL EVIDENCE ACT 1984, SECTION 17. Section 17(1)(e) of the Police and Criminal Evidence Act 1984 (PACE) gives the police a power to enter and search premises without a warrant, in order to save life or limb or prevent serious damage to property.

It is not enough that the police should have a general welfare concern about somebody; this would be too low a test: the concern must be about something serious likely to occur or having occurred.[3]

---

1   Public Health Act 1936, s.287.

2   LGO, *Ealing London Borough Council*, 2004 (03/A/17640).

3   *Syed v Director of Public Prosecutions* [2010] EWHC 81 (Admin), para 12.

Life and limb: not general welfare. A neighbour reported a disturbance to the police; there was probably shouting or screaming, and the man who answered the door to the police was evasive in answering questions. The courts held that this was not enough to invoke section 17(1)(e) and a legal power of entry. There had to be a concern about something more serious – as connoted by the term 'life and limb'.[1]

Serious bodily injury.

> The expression 'saving life or limb' is a colourful, slightly outmoded expression. It is here used in close proximity with the expression 'preventing serious damage to property'. That predicates a degree of apprehended serious bodily injury. Without implicitly limiting or excluding the possible types of serious bodily injury, apprehended knife injuries and gunshot injuries will obviously normally be capable of coming within the subsection.[2]

Immediate threat required to justify entry. A man and wife had an argument. He squirted suntan lotion and threw apples at her. Their children went to a neighbour and the police were called. The man then reportedly took an overdose of tablets. The police arrived and purported to enter under section 17(1)(e) to save life and limb.

The court found no evidence justifying entry. At time of entry, things had calmed down, and the police constable did not consider the overdose, as potential medical emergency (threatening life and limb), to be the primary reason for entering the house. The test was whether the police were entering premises to deal with emergency situations where someone has suffered, or is at risk of suffering, serious injury or loss of life without immediate police intervention, or where serious damage is being done, or is immediately threatened, to the property itself.[3]

Serious domestic violence incident: justification for entry.

> If, for example, a police officer attending a matrimonial home, after the report of a domestic incident, saw upon arrival the wife outside the house suffering from serious injuries inflicted by her husband,

---

1   *Syed v Director of Public Prosecutions* [2010] EWHC 81 (Admin), para 12.

2   *Baker v Crown Prosecution Service* [2009] EWHC 299 (Admin), para 25.

3   *Friswell v Chief Constable of Essex Police* [2004] EWHC 3009 (QB), para 63.

heard the sounds of distressed children and threats to kill his wife, the children or himself, being made by the husband inside, the sound of windows being broken or the like, the powers that he or she has, including the preserved power to enter the premises to deal with an existing or imminent breach of the peace, seem to me to be clear and adequate and, in my view, create no uncertainty as to the lawfulness of appropriate action to tackle such problems.[1]

Saving a child (or a vulnerable adult): justification for entry, even though the caller changed her mind about police involvement. A woman called the police, stating that a drunken man was trying to remove her baby. There was another voice in the background either prompting or interfering. However, by the end of the call, she had changed her mind and said she didn't want the police to come after all. The police went anyway, and attempted to force entry under section17(1)(e).

The police had acted lawfully: an emergency call had been made, in which it was stated that a drunken man was trying to take a woman's child. Although at the end of the report to the police the woman claimed the man had gone without removing the child, and she did not want the police to attend, the original account by her was, on any view, a highly worrying one, and given that there was a voice in the background during the second part of the call interrupting or prompting the woman, the police were fully entitled, as an exercise of their discretion under the section, to enter the premises without a warrant to investigate. This was for the purpose of 'securing (saving) the child'.[2]

There is, however, nothing to stop the police simply making a welfare visit, with consent, rather than forcing entry.

Entry by invitation and with consent.

There can be no doubt that, in the absence of a locked gate or some other notice such as 'Police keep out', police officers, like all other citizens, have an implied licence to enter upon a driveway and

---

1   *Friswell v Chief Constable of Essex Police* [2004] EWHC 3009 (QB), para 73.

2   *Blench v Director of Public Prosecutions* [2004] EWHC 2717 (Admin), para 23.

> to approach the door of a dwelling house if they have, or reasonably think that they have, legitimate business with the occupier.[1]
>
> And if police officers are invited into premises by an occupier, who has been told by them the reason for their visit, then they will enter those premises lawfully, with consent.[2] If, however, an occupier – on such a visit – were to ask the police to leave, by withdrawing permission to enter, the police would have to do so.[3]

In the following case, with safeguarding elements, the judge noted that the grounds for the actions of the police had not been spelt out.

> **Threat to enter and arrest elderly man caring for his wife: unclear grounds for threat.** A man had been denying district nurses access to his wife (who lacked mental capacity), particularly if they came at what he considered the wrong time in relation to his wife's routine, and outside of the times that had been agreed with the nurses.
>
> After a two-week period, during which access had been denied, the police attended, together with district nursing and social services. This followed a request by the district nurses. Initially, the husband again refused access, and the police threatened him with arrest. The husband then allowed access: in fact, his wife's catheter turned out not to be blocked, and her skin to be intact.
>
> The judge noted that the legal basis for entry to the premises and the threat of arrest was unclear:
>
> > The papers do not indicate on what legal basis the police claimed a right to enter the premises without a warrant, nor therefore (if they were seeking to trespass) on what basis they were empowered to arrest Mr H if he refused them entry. The court has not been told that a warrant was obtained under section 135 of the Mental

---

1   *Lambert v Roberts* [1981] 72 Cr App R 223, Donaldson LB. And see: *Snook v Mannion* [1982] RTR 321.

2   *Riley v The Director of Public Prosecutions* [1990] 91 Cr App R 14.

3   *Davis v Lisle* [1936] 2 KB 434, Lord Hewart CJ.

Health Act 1983, or that the 'saving life or limb' provisions in section 17(1)(e) of the Police & Criminal Evidence Act 1984 applied.[1]

POWER TO ENTER: UTILITY COMPANIES. Utility companies have powers to enter under the gas and electricity legislation.[2] These powers are underpinned by sections 1 and 2 of the Rights of Entry (Gas and Electricity Boards) Act 1954. The latter makes clear that entry has to be either with consent or with a warrant obtained from a justice of the peace (a magistrate). See also the Water Industry Act 1991, for rights of entry in relation to water supply.[3]

POWER TO ENTER: ANIMAL WELFARE ACT 2006. This Act contains an offence of causing unnecessary suffering, an animal welfare offence, powers of inspectors or police to alleviate distress of animals, powers of entry (with a warrant) of inspector or constable.[4]

Pressure sores

Pressure sores have long since been a significant issue in adult safeguarding. In some circumstances they are difficult to avoid, but equally they can be caused by poor and neglectful care on the part, in particular, of hospitals and care homes. NHS England has published guidance on how to decide whether the incidence of pressure sores is a safeguarding issue.[5] Pressure sores could, depending on the circumstances, lead to criminal conviction for wilful neglect or gross negligence manslaughter, civil negligence cases for financial compensation and findings by coroners of death having been contributed to by neglect.

---

1   *A London Local Authority v JH* [2011] EWHC 2420 (COP), para 9, p.20.

2   Gas Act 1986 (schedule 2B, paras 23–28), Electricity Act 1989 (schedule 6, paras 7–10).

3   Water Industry Act 1991, schedule 6.

4   Animal Welfare Act 2006, ss.4, 9, 18, 19, 52.

5   Romeo, L. *Safeguarding adults protocol: pressure ulcers and the interface with a safeguarding enquiry.* London: Department of Health and Social Care, 2018.

Prisons (Care Act)

Certain provisions of the Care Act 2014 do not apply to prisons. These are: choice of accommodation, direct payments, continuity of care rules, making safeguarding enquiries under section 42 of the Act, protecting people's property under section 47, safeguarding adults boards' help and protection activities under section 43, and safeguarding adults reviews under section 44.[1]

However, duties that do apply and could legally be relevant to protection from abuse and neglect include, for example, prevention, advice, information, assessment, eligibility, care and support provision, and support provision – not least because under section 1 of the Care Act 2014, local authorities anyway have a general duty to promote the well-being of individuals when performing all these functions. And the definition of well-being includes protection from abuse and neglect.

Guidance points out that there would in any case be nothing to stop safeguarding adults boards and local authorities working, generally, with prisons on safeguarding issues.[2]

Private life, see *Human rights*

Professional regulators

For medical doctors, nurses, midwives, health visitors, social workers, physiotherapists, occupational therapists, speech and language therapists, psychologists, chiropodists, etc., see variously: *General Medical Council*; *Nursing and Midwifery Council*; *Health and Care Professions Council*.

Proof, see *Standard of proof*

---

1   Care Act 2014, s.78.

2   Department of Health. *Care and support statutory guidance*. London: DH, 2016, para 14.6.

Proportionality

Guidance on the Care Act 2014 lists proportionality in safeguarding as one of six key principles and points out that disproportionate intervention by a local authority – for example, to a safeguarding issue within a family – could itself be abusive.[1] Legally, proportionality is fundamental to the application of article 8 of the European Convention on Human Rights in relation to people's right to respect for home, private and family life: see *Human rights*.

Proprietary estoppel (relying on assurances or promises)

A civil, equitable principle known as proprietary estoppel is sometimes applicable to situations which could suggest possible financial abuse, but which can in fact be otherwise explained. For example, sometimes an elderly person decides to leave substantial assets to an informal carer – who may have provided care and services for many years – but does not make this clear in a will. The informal carer might have to apply to court for confirmation of the validity and application of the promise, by claiming proprietary estoppel.

The elements generally required are as follows, in terms of a promise, reliance on that promise and detriment to the person by relying on the promise.

> **Assurance, reliance, detriment required.**
>
> First, a representation made, or assurance given to the claimant; second, reliance by the claimant on the representation or assurance; and, third, some detriment incurred by the claimant as a consequence of that reliance. These elements would...always be necessary but might, in a particular case, not be sufficient. Thus, for example, the representation or assurance would need to have been sufficiently clear and unequivocal; the reliance by the claimant would need to have been reasonable in all the circumstances; and

---

1   Department of Health. *Care and support statutory guidance*. London: DH, 2016, para 14.98.

the detriment would need to have been sufficiently substantial to justify the intervention of equity.[1]

Entitlement on the basis of the promise to gardener/carer: 'this will all be yours one day'. A self-employed bricklayer had begun to provide gardening services to an elderly woman. As she became more incapacitated with arthritis and leg ulcers, he would do more and more for her without payment. This included collecting prescriptions, helping her dress and go to the toilet, making sure she had food and drink, as well as helping in the garden. In the last few months of her life, he did even more. For the last ten years or so, she had stopped paying him. When he queried this, she had said not to worry, to the vague effect that 'this will all be yours one day'.

She died intestate, and the man challenged the extent of his entitlement. Based on proprietary estoppel, the court used its discretion – taking account of a number of factors – and held that his equitable interest amounted to £200,000 out of a house and furniture valued at some £435,000.[2]

Services provided to elderly couple by lodger, promise of home for life: entitlement of the latter. A lodger had increasingly provided services and care to an elderly couple who had told him that whatever happened he would have a home for life. Instead, the house passed first to the man's wife and then, on her death, to her nieces. Far from him having exploited the couple in any way, the court held that he had an equitable interest amounting to £35,000 (out of a house valued at £160,000).[3]

Prosecution, see *Crown Prosecution Service*

Protection from abuse and neglect, see *Care Act 2014*

1   *Thorner v Major* [2009] UKHL 18, [2009] I WLR 776, para 15.

2   *Jennings v Rice* [2002] EWCA Civ 159.

3   *Campbell v Griffin* [2001] EWCA Civ 990.

Public communications systems: improper use, see *Harassment, alarm or distress*

Public Interest Disclosure Act 1998, see *Whistleblowing*

Pushing, see *Assault*; *Ill-treatment*

R

Raising concerns, see *Whistleblowing*

Rehabilitation of Offenders Act 1997, see *Criminal record certificates*

Remedies

Legal remedies for safeguarding-related issues can include the following:

- **decisions and actions of public bodies:** judicial review in the Administrative Court of the Queen's Bench Division of the High Court

- **Mental Capacity Act cases:** Court of Protection

- **vulnerable adults (with mental capacity or otherwise falling outside the Mental Capacity Act):** inherent jurisdiction, Family Division of the High Court

- **disputed wills, gifts, transfer of property:** law of equity (including undue influence and capacity issues), Chancery Division of the High Court

- **negligence:** common law duty of care (and other civil torts, such as trespass to the person), Queen's Bench Division of the High Court

- **civil orders and injunctions:** including non-molestation orders, forced marriage protection orders, anti-social behaviour injunctions, etc., county court, magistrates' court

- **information-related cases (data protection, freedom of information):** Information Commissioner, Lower-tier Tribunal, Upper Tribunal (Administrative Appeals Chamber)

- **whistleblowing cases:** Employment Tribunal, Employment Appeals Tribunal

- **barring cases (Disclosure and Barring Service):** Upper Tribunal

- **criminal offences:** magistrates' court, Crown Court

- **criminal prosecution:** mostly brought by the Crown Prosecution Service (the police can prosecute a small category of cases); also local authority trading standards, Care Quality Commission, Health and Safety Executive

- **private prosecution:** exceptionally, private criminal prosecutions can be taken, by virtue of section 6 of the Prosecution of Offences Act 1985, but these are rare. Private prosecution of some offences requires permission from the Director of Public Prosecutions (e.g. section 127 of the Mental Health Act 1983).

In addition, the Local Government Ombudsman investigates complaints relating to the safeguarding activities of local authorities (and independent care providers), as does the Health Service Ombudsman in relation to alleged abuse or neglect within the NHS. See *Local Government Ombudsman* and *Health Service Ombudsman*. They investigate maladministration and failures in service, but do not make judicial rulings and therefore do not establish legal precedent of any sort.

Restraining orders

Under the Protection from Harassment Act 1997, restraining orders may be made on conviction or acquittal for any criminal offence. A restraining order serves a preventative and protective purpose. Restraining orders are civil behaviour orders and therefore the standard of proof is a civil, rather than criminal.[1]

On conviction, the court can make a restraining order for the purpose of protecting a person (the victim or victims of the offence or any other

---

1   *R v Tara Major* [2010] EWCA Crim 3016.

person mentioned in the order) from conduct which amounts to harassment or which will cause a fear of violence.

On acquittal, the court makes an order if it considers this necessary to protect a person from harassment from the defendant. However, unlike with restraining orders on conviction, there is no power to protect a person from fear of violence that falls short of harassment where the defendant has been acquitted. (Some examples of restraining orders are included in a number of case studies in this book, involving various criminal offences.)

Restraint

Inappropriate restraint of a person could result in various criminal offences being committed: for example, false imprisonment, common assault (both common law offences), actual bodily harm, grievous bodily harm, choking – under sections 47, 18, 20 and 21 of the Offences Against the Person Act 1861; also, the offence of ill-treatment which is contained within the Mental Health Act 1983, Mental Capacity Act 2005 and Criminal Justice and Courts Act 2015.

However, the application of criminal offences presupposes that the restraint is inappropriate. It will not always be so.

- **Proportionate restraint: mental capacity.** Under sections 5 and 6 of the Mental Capacity Act 2005 (MCA), a person lacking capacity can be restrained to protect them from harm, as long as the restraint is proportionate to the risk. Any such restraint would also be subject to the principles in section 1 of the Act, concerning the person's best interests and consideration of less restriction options.

  Restraint under the MCA must be to protect a person lacking capacity from harm. Were it to protect harm to other people or property, it would be taking place under the common law, on grounds of necessity and appropriateness.[1]

---

1   Department for Constitutional Affairs. *Mental Capacity Act 2005: code of practice*. London: The Stationery Office, 2007, para 6.43.

- **Proportionate restraint: mental health.** Likewise, along similar lines of proportionality, restraint is permitted under the Mental Health Act 1983.[1]

- **Health and social care providers.** Registered health and care providers are not permitted to restrain users of services, unless such restraint is necessary to prevent, and is a proportionate response to, a risk of harm posed to the service user or another individual if the service user was not subject to control or restraint.[2]

The following case involved action taken against two nurses following restraint of a patient which the Court of Appeal found unwarranted. Above all, the case highlighted the difficulties of caring for people with significantly challenging behaviour – and of doing this with inadequate staffing levels.

> **Restraint by nurses of a patient at a table at West Suffolk Hospital: excessive safeguarding response by organisation.** One night on a hospital ward, two nurses and two health care workers were the only staff taking care of 17 patients. It was clear from the handover notes from the previous shift that difficulties had been experienced in relation to the handling of the patient. He was 87 and suffered from dementia.
>
> On the day in question, he had been agitated, aggressive, hitting things, spitting, swearing, throwing drinks, kicking and punching, and generally requiring particularly close attention. It was noted that the safe handling technique used by staff on the previous shift had caused skin tears on his arms to be opened. Medication had to be administered forcibly because he was refusing both food and medicine. Because of the spitting, he had also had a mask placed on him. Even during the day, with more staff, the needs of other patients had suffered. All this had been approved by the NHS Trust.
>
> *Tying patient to table.* Now at night-time, with fewer staff than in the day, the nurses placed him in a chair and tied the legs to the table with two sheets, so he could not get up.
>
> *Safeguarding action.* The two nurses were suspended and a referral to the police made. A month later, the police stated they would take no action.

---

1   Department of Health. *Mental Health Act: code of practice.* London: DH, 2015, para 13.34

2   SI 2014/2936. Health and Social Care Act 2008 (Regulated Activities) Regulations 2014, r.13.

The nurses were subject to a disciplinary procedure, accused of assault, negligence and professional misconduct – and then dismissed.

Appeal. The nurses took their case to an Employment Tribunal which they won; the NHS Trust then appealed successfully to an Employment Appeal Tribunal. The nurses then took their case to the Court of Appeal; they won. The court identified two procedural errors made by the Trust.

Perverse approach of the safeguarding response. The court in addition ridiculed the allegation that an assault had taken place and observed that it was not reasonable to dismiss staff with 20 years' service for using restraint on the night shift that was no more detrimental to his dignity than the approved restraint used during the day. Moreover, the evidence showed that during the previous shift the man had been pinned to the chair in virtually the same way, save that instead of achieving this mechanically by tying the chair to the table, it was done by two nurses holding it there. To treat the one as permissible and the other as justifying the dismissal of employees with 20 years' service, simply, it seemed, because it is not an approach permitted by the procedures, was perverse.[1]

Likewise, in the following case, the restraint did not justify the barring of a care worker from working with vulnerable adults.

Tying a person to chair as a temporary measure: not justifying barring of the care worker from working. A care assistant was working the night shift in a care home for people with dementia. Early in the morning, she faced an emergency situation. She was cleaning one resident who had soiled herself. Another resident was in the room hindering her. In order to attend to the first, she tied the second resident to a chair using a sweater or fleece.

Owing to pressure of work and then the need to get off shift for her children, she forgot about the second resident. When the latter was found about half an hour later, the resident was not physically hurt or psychologically affected. The care home alerted the police. The care assistant was dismissed, reported to the Independent Safeguarding Authority and placed on the Protection of Vulnerable Adults (POVA) list, thus barring her from working with vulnerable adults. She appealed.

---

1   *Crawford v Suffolk Mental Health Partnership NHS Trust* [2012] EWCA Civ 138.

> The Tribunal found that barring her was not justified, given that she was working alone that morning, her remorse and her work record.[1]

On the other hand, the following are examples of inappropriate restraint, attracting varied sanctions.

Barricading bedroom door with mop. The Care Standards Tribunal upheld the placing on the POVA list (barring him from working with vulnerable adults and children) of a domiciliary care worker for people with learning disabilities. He had placed a resident at risk of harm by barring his bedroom door with a mop between 11pm and 7am the next morning.[2]

Confused, terrified man with dementia handcuffed and strapped to stretcher. A retired engineer with dementia was in a care home. His mental state was deteriorating, and it had been decided that he should be sectioned under the Mental Health Act. A meeting was called with the daughter but was then brought forward 24 hours, meaning she could not attend. So, without family involvement, he was – in a terrified state – handcuffed and strapped to a stretcher.

The police claimed that it was to protect everybody, including the man himself. They later accepted it had been inappropriate. The man died soon after. Of the police intervention, the coroner stated: 'This is totally ridiculous, officer, it beggars belief. [He] was an elderly, frail and frightened man with little understanding of the world around him and what would happen to him.' The coroner stated that he would be writing to the police about their handling of mental health patients and the use of handcuffs.[3]

Robbery

Under section 8 of the Theft Act 1968, a person is guilty of robbery if he or she steals and immediately before, or at the time of doing so and in order to do so, he or she uses force on any person or puts or seeks to put any person

---

1   *MK v Secretary of State for Health* [2009] UKFTT 150 (HESC).

2   *Johnson v Secretary of State for Health* [2009] 1637 PVA.

3   Narain, J. and Parveen, N. 'Did police have to handcuff dementia patient?' *Daily Mail*, 5 July 2012.

in fear of being subjected to force. The following examples illustrate different patterns of robbery involving vulnerable adults.

Known to be vulnerable: robbery at home of man regularly pestered by children for money. Three men went to the home of the victim whom they knew to be vulnerable. He had learning disabilities and needed help in carrying out basic activities such as washing and shaving. He tended to be pestered by children for money. One of the children to whom he had given money was the stepson of one of the perpetrators. They pushed him into the hallway, demanded money and stole £100, the whole of his savings from benefits. He was punched in the face and suffered fractures to the cheek bone and eye socket. An initial sentence of three years for robbery was increased on appeal to five and a half years.[1]

Known to be vulnerable: woman known to son of carer: he had previously cleaned her windows. An 84-year-old woman lived alone in a flat in Plymouth. The perpetrator's mother was her carer and the perpetrator had previously been to her home to clean the windows. He visited her and stole her pension book and cash. He was arrested that evening, charged and released on bail. Four days later he returned, grabbed her, dragged her into the bedroom, where she ended up on the floor. He stole her purse, pension book and £90 in cash. He gave himself up the following day. He was sentenced to six years in prison.[2]

Plea for medical help, tricking their way into an elderly woman's home, threatening her with a meat cleaver. The perpetrator and her two co-accused went to the home of an 81-year-old woman. They rang the doorbell. The victim got to her front door with the assistance of her Zimmer frame, and when she opened the door, she had taken the precaution of keeping it on the chain. However, one of the perpetrators presented a false story that her mother had collapsed and needed urgent medical help and, reluctantly, the victim opened her front door. The victim was particularly reluctant because she had had a previous unpleasant experience some three weeks before.

Once the chain was taken off the door, the three perpetrators forced their way inside. The victim resisted but was pushed back and ended up on the floor of her front room. They stepped over her and two of them, the

---

1   *R v Randall* [2005] 1 Cr App R (S) 60.

2   *R v Sowden* [2000] Criminal Law Reports 500, Court of Appeal.

females, searched the house while the male stood over the victim holding a meat cleaver, telling her not to move or she would be hit. During the course of the search of the premises, the intruders disabled more than one system by which the victim might have been able to summon help either during the offence or after it had taken place. Jewellery was taken, and a small amount of money together with two purses and other items. The taking of the jewellery included the pulling of a gold chain from the victim's neck in such a way as to break it.

The perpetrator was given an indeterminate sentence, on grounds of public protection under section 225 of the Criminal Justice Act 2003, with a minimum of four years – changed on appeal to a determinate sentence of eight years.[1]

Prior observation: of elderly people near sheltered housing. The perpetrator had been observed earlier that day paying attention to elderly pedestrians near sheltered accommodation. Eventually, he forced his way into the home of a 79-year-old frail man with severe arthritis, who had just returned from a shopping trip. The man was pushed to the floor and had money stolen, before being punched in the face. The perpetrator was sentenced to four years in prison for robbery, a relatively lenient sentence.[2]

Befriending 83-year-old man in post office. An 83-year-old man went to the Post Office to collect his pension and had difficulty getting to his feet. A woman helped him to the bus stop, where she and her son helped him fasten his coat; on getting home he discovered his pension book and £57 were missing. She was convicted of robbery (in relation to the first episode described above) and of theft (for other offences). The offences involved targeting vulnerable people, gaining their trust with a display of false sympathy. She was sentenced to five years for the robbery, with three years for the thefts to run concurrently.[3]

Rogue trading

Rogue trading is typically aimed at older, vulnerable people and can constitute a criminal offence. It may involve cold-calling, but not necessarily.

---

1   *R v Cleary* [2010] EWCA Crim 966.

2   *R v Johnson* [2001] 1 Cr App R (S) 123.

3   *R v Moss* [2005] EWCA Crim 133.

ROGUE TRADING: COLD-CALLING. Relevant legislation includes:

- **Pedlars Act 1871** (requiring licences).

- **Cancellation of Contracts made in a Consumer's Home or Place of Work etc. Regulations 2008.** These stipulate a seven-day cooling-off period. The regulations cover contracts made during both solicited and unsolicited visits for any value over £35. Cancellation must be clearly and prominently displayed in writing, whether or not there is a written contract.

- **Consumer Protection from Unfair Trading Regulations 2008.** These contain several offences relating, for instance, to misleading actions or omissions, aggressive practices and unfair practices.

Abusive cold-calling may involve, for example: intimidation and persistence; false or no names and addresses being given; token work being carried out so that the issue may be regarded as civil and contractual in nature, rather than criminal; taking deposits and never returning them; starting work immediately before people have had a chance to read the small print, then driving people to the bank, there to withdraw large amounts of money, etc.[1]

Identifying abuse and criminal offences may be difficult when traders' names and addresses are rarely known, and cash payments are made on the spot. There is generally slow reporting of doorstep-selling offences, a lack of resources to devote to prevention and detection, reluctance or inability of complainants to give evidence, poor evidence given, and no agreed multi-agency approach. Alleged perpetrators may simply deny everything, and the police may then drop the criminal investigation and say instead that it is just a civil dispute.[2]

ROGUE TRADING: CONVICTIONS. Whether or not involving cold-calling, criminal convictions for rogue trading are sometimes secured, for instance, for the offence of fraud or under the Consumer Protection from Unfair Trading Regulations 2008. Several cases are summarised in detail below, including

---

1   Trading Standards Institute. *Door to door cold calling of property repairs, maintenance and improvements: long overdue for statutory control.* Basildon: Trading Standards Institute, 2003, pp.6–13, 40.

2   Office of Fair Trading. *Doorstep selling.* London: Office of Fair Trading, 2004, pp.93–94.

large-scale fraud, involving very significant sums of money, sometimes perpetrated on a large scale and with varying degrees of sophistication.

Roofer convicted under unfair trading regulations in relation to 97-year-old woman and other victims. A roofer was convicted in relation to dealing with a vulnerable 97-year-old woman from whom he extracted £350 for work that was of no value. This included fraud in that he dishonestly told his victim that he had done work on her porch to the value of £350. There were also convictions under the Consumer Protection from Unfair Trading Regulations 2008, relating to a failure to exercise professional diligence in carrying out his works, engaging in an aggressive commercial practice by pressurising his victim to agree to pay him the £350 for the work he said he had carried out. In addition, in relation to other victims, he failed to disclose cancellation rights to people, and to carry out work properly, in terms of shoddy or valueless work and charging excessively for it after cold-calling his victims. He was sentenced to 32 months' imprisonment.[1]

Unfair trading: five-year criminal behaviour order given to rogue gardener to protect elderly. A rogue gardening trader was given a ten-month suspended prison sentence, 200 hours of unpaid work and ordered to pay £700 compensation to the victim. He was convicted of 'unfair trading' (presumably under the Consumer Protection from Unfair Trading Regulations 2008).

He took advantage of vulnerable homeowners by distributing leaflets and cold-calling to gain gardening contracts. He failed to give the victims their legal right to cancel, carried out the work within the 14-day cooling-off period to a poor standard and charged excessive amounts. In one case he charged £470 for less than an hour's work. He failed to give written contracts detailing the work being undertaken and the price charged and ignored requests by consumers to provide receipts for payment. His failure to keep any business records meant he was unable to justify to Trading Standards the amounts of money taken from vulnerable elderly consumers.[2]

---

1   *R v Jackson* [2017] EWCA Crim 78.

2   Hereford County Council. 'Third conviction for Herefordshire rogue trader.' *News*, 6 October 2017. Accessed on 9 February 2018 at: www.herefordshire.gov.uk/news/article/391/third_conviction_for_herefordshire_rogue_trader.

Stairlift selling: theft and fraud. A man purporting to sell stairlifts was successfully prosecuted by Devon County Council (trading standards). He pleaded guilty to breach of the Theft Act 1968, Consumer Protection Act 1987 and Forgery and Counterfeiting Act 1981. He had posed as a stairlift repairer and installer, and targeted vulnerable elderly and disabled people. He would advise that a stairlift was irreparable, show customers advertisements from two well-known stairlift companies (he had no contract to supply their products or permission to use the trademarks), take their money, take away their existing stairlift – and not deliver the new stairlift. He was an undischarged bankrupt and used a number of false names and addresses.[1]

Roofers sitting on roof drinking tea for a morning. Two 'roofers' called, sat for most of the morning on the roof of the house of an 86-year-old woman with dementia drinking tea, supplied less than £50 of labour and goods, and then charged her £600, escorting her to the bank to withdraw the money. In this case, the offenders were identified by CCTV at the bank and were convicted on the evidence (including that of a neighbour).[2]

Gross overcharging for roof work: fraud. A builder was sentenced to 100 hours' community service under section 2 of the Fraud Act 2006 (false representation of the price of work) after carrying out roofing work for an 81-year-old vulnerable woman. He had called uninvited. The work he had carried out was worth £562 plus VAT; he had in fact charged £4240.[3]

Builder gaining trust of vulnerable person first. A builder used his business to target elderly people by charging a modest price for an initial piece of work, but then following up with subsequent works for which he charged excessive amounts. His customers were duped into parting with substantial sums of money. He was sentenced to five and a half years in prison for theft, and a compensation order and a confiscation order were

1   Devon County Council Trading Standards. 'Devon Trading Standards successfully prosecutes stairlift fraudster.' Press release, 16 April 2007.

2   Trading Standards Institute. *Door to door cold calling of property repairs, maintenance and improvements: long overdue for statutory control.* Basildon: Trading Standards Institute, 2003.

3   Devon County Council Trading Standards. 'Builder sentenced for defrauding elderly resident.' Press release, 16 July 2008.

made against him, each for £141,000. It was not quite a cold-calling case; he distributed leaflets to obtain work.[1]

Rogue trader, building works, fraud followed by further fraud against a 93-year-old woman. The victim was an elderly lady of 93. Some two years before the offence, she had been the victim of a fraud whereby work was carried out to her property over a period of 18 months at highly inflated prices. She paid about £87,500. The matter was not reported to the police, and there is no evidence that the accused was involved in that scheme.

Subsequently, the accused went to her house claiming he was a debt collector. He represented to her that he knew that she had been the subject of what he called a scam by others who, he said, were now in prison. He said that he could get back £39,000 of what she had lost but needed to be paid what he called legal fees. She paid him over £1600. He then tried to persuade her to hand over £14,000 for what he called the debt collector's commission for recovering the debt. When she refused, he got another man to speak to her over the telephone. He claimed to be the perpetrator's boss and persuaded her to hand over more money. She did so.

In total, she had handed over £4600 to the accused over a period of five days. He then tried to get her to pay another £4000 in commission fees, and when she said that she did not have the money, he suggested that she borrow it. Fortunately, when she went to the building society to raise a loan, she was advised to contact the police. The accused was arrested when he called at her home to collect more money. He was given a prison sentence of three and a half years.[2]

Works to drains: tens of thousands of pounds in fraud. The perpetrator and another man called on a house in Dulwich, where the 77-year-old victim lived. They told him that his drains had been investigated with a camera, and they needed repair. That was untrue. Over the coming weeks, they extracted money from him for the repairs they said were needed. He paid them £200 cash, and then gave them a number of cheques. Two were cashed, totalling £10,000. That sum was immediately taken from the account into which it was paid. A further £19,000 worth of cheques was handed over, but fortunately the victim rang his insurers who investigated; the confidence

---

1   *R v Williams* [2001] 1 Cr App R 23.

2   *R v Vinter* [2011] EWCA Crim 3327.

trick was discovered before that further amount was withdrawn from his account.

The fraud had been committed whilst the perpetrator was on licence in respect of a six-year term of imprisonment. That had been imposed for a conspiracy to defraud. In that case, the appellant and others deliberately targeted a vulnerable individual, who was fraudulently advised that building works needed to be undertaken at his property. The cost of this unnecessary work was so high that the victim was persuaded to remortgage his property, put money into an investment scheme (which, he was told, went bust) and then sell his property to cover fictitious losses. As a result, that vulnerable victim lost all that he had, some £300,000.[1]

Fraud: roof tiles, driving victim to bank. The victim of the fraud was an 84-year-old lady who lived in a suburb of Birmingham. The perpetrator and another man had arrived at her home address. The other man had previously done some work at her house. They knocked on the front door. The other man spoke to her and said there were some loose tiles on her roof. He went up a ladder, came down and said they could repair the tiles but would need money upfront.

They took her to a bank in the perpetrator's van. She went in and withdrew £2050 in cash, which was the quotation she had been given for the work. When she got back to the van, there was a female in the front passenger seat. She handed the money to her. They returned to her street. They dropped her on the corner, saying they needed to go and buy the building equipment to make a quick start on the job. The victim went home but never saw the appellant or the other man or the woman again. A neighbour had been concerned about what he had seen at the house.[2]

Fraud: roofs and chimneys, 43 households defrauded, £800,000 obtained. The perpetrator was the leader of a team of rogue builders who defrauded householders in the south-east of England by undertaking repair works to houses, in particular roofs and chimneys, which was unnecessary, dishonestly charging for work which was not carried out, carrying out incompetent and substandard work, and claiming to have carried out work which was not in fact done.

---

1   *R v Cooper* [2012] EWCA Crim 162.

2   *R v Smith* [2012] EWCA Crim 1184.

Over a period from January 2003 until September 2007 about 43 householders were defrauded and about £800,000 was obtained. The perpetrator was involved throughout the conspiracy. The offences followed a very similar pattern. The victims were nearly all either elderly or otherwise vulnerable householders. They would be 'cold-called' and told that work was required, usually to their roof or chimney, and that it required immediate attention. A price would be quoted for the work, but as soon as the work commenced, further, more substantial, problems were 'found', and they were said to require immediate attention. The work carried out would be cosmetic and unnecessary, and the amount charged for the work would be grossly excessive. Any work that was carried out would be to a very poor standard and frequently required rectification by competent contractors.[1]

Fraud: tarmac, initial quote followed by outrageous demand for money and intimidation of series of victim. The perpetrator and his associates would select a suitable victim, and the victims, some ten of them in this case, varied in age from almost 60 to, in one case, 90. They would tell some story to the effect that they had been working in the area for this, that or the other organisation, and they had a quantity of material over, which they could use to tarmac the victims' drives.

Initial reasonable quote. When asked about the price, they would mention a figure of, say, £10. Since that seemed a good bargain, the victims would very often agree to have the work done. There would then be thrust in front of them a piece of paper, some form of contract, the material parts of which were concealed, and they would be invited to sign. They usually did so.

Presentation of enormous bill. In due course, that day or a day or two later, the perpetrator and his friends would come with chippings and tar. They would lay the chippings, usually on a larger area than that contracted for, and then present an enormous bill – £4000, £5000, £6000. When the customer demurred, as of course he always did, the contract would be produced and there it would appear that what the customer was said to have agreed to was not £10 for the whole job but £10 a square yard or a square foot or whatever.

Physical intimidation. In the case of one lady, she was asked to offer a cup of tea to the workers when they came. Shortly afterwards, a lorry

---

1   *R v Baker* [2011] EWCA Crim 150.

arrived and chippings were put on her driveway. At the end of the work she was told that the cost was to be £4000. She was astounded. She said she could not and would not pay that ridiculous amount of money. Then there occurred the feature common to almost all of these cases, which is the particularly unpleasant aspect of this sort of fraud. The three men crowded around her. She became frightened. She pushed them away and returned to her house. But she was told that the money must be produced. It was the appellant who accompanied her to the building society, where she had some savings, who waited with her while she drew out the money and returned with her so that the money could be handed over, which it was. She was defrauded of £4000.

The view of the expert was that the labour was worth about £80, and subsequent inquiries revealed that the load of chippings had been bought for £31. The perpetrator pleaded guilty and was sentenced to four years' imprisonment.[1]

Fraud: repairs, various techniques for extracting further sums of money, 29 vulnerable people defrauded, £140,000 stolen. The perpetrators were all members of the travelling community, largely based in Leicestershire. Between August 2007 and July 2010 at least 29 vulnerable or elderly property owners, or residents, across the country paid a total of £140,528 in cash in consequence of the activities of the offenders and others.

Those sums frequently comprised the life savings of the victims and have not been recovered. In addition, a further £45,090 was sought from owners and occupiers, although not, in the result, obtained.

Property deliberately damaged. The victims were aged between 51 and 97 years. They would be approached at home, or even in the street near their home, and asked if they wanted work undertaken on their property, or they would be confronted with the assertion that repairs were urgently required. Initial quotations were provided. It would then be alleged that further urgent work was required, when in fact it was not. On some occasions the property was deliberately damaged by the offenders to demonstrate that further urgent work was required. Money would be paid, either for no work or for unnecessary work, or for shoddy, incomplete or inadequate work.

Different techniques to extract even more money after the initial fraud. Once contact had been made, a recurring feature was that different techniques

---

1   *R v Richards* [1989] 11 Cr App R (S) 286.

were employed in order to extract further money, including the claim that additional work required special machinery or scaffolding, or that VAT, or some other tax, was due in respect of the payment. Some victims were promised repayment by way of a banker's draft or cheque. They would then be told that the banker's draft or cheque due to them had been completed for a sum greater than the repayment due, and that the problem could only be solved, and the money released, if a further cash payment was made. When the further cash was paid, the banker's draft or cheque would not be forthcoming.

Victims were frequently driven to the bank by the conspirators for the purpose that they be supervised while withdrawing the cash that had been demanded. On other occasions they were followed into the bank. Some of the victims were subjected to threats or pressure, and it was clear that they complied with the demands made upon them by reason of fear or confusion. Casual theft took place from some of the victims' homes. Prison sentences given to the various perpetrators included, for example, six years, four years and eight months, four years, two years – for conspiracy to defraud.[1]

Fraud: selling of useless alarm systems. The perpetrators set up Pentagon Security Systems, of which one perpetrator owned 75 per cent and the co-accused 25 per cent. From May 2007 to June 2008 the company operated a fraud which was directed mainly against elderly people by selling them virtually useless alarm systems for their homes. The alarms were faulty and regularly called the monitoring stations unnecessarily, which led to significant telephone bills of £400 to £500 per month.

Grossly inflated prices. A number of complainants had their phones cut off and struggled to pay the bills. The customers were led to believe that the alarm systems were tailor-made to their needs, but they were not. They were also led to believe that the system had National Security Inspection approval. That was not so. The prices charged were extortionate. In fact, the price fixed usually followed bargaining where grossly inflated prices were suggested and then reduced in order to make it appear as though the customers were receiving a good deal.

Fictitious maintenance, misleading information. The customers were charged for maintenance of the system, although there was none. The

---

1   *R v Newbury* [2011] EWCA Crim 2174.

address given for the company did not exist. In some cases, perfectly good systems were replaced with the dud system. When customers contacted the company about the problems, their complaints received dismissive responses. Potential customers were either telephoned or had their doors knocked. They were given misleading information about the installation. On some occasions they received leaflets about a home safety campaign. One of the perpetrators regularly said that he was calling about the home safety campaign. This was to encourage customers to take on the security system because it was said that it was necessary to keep them safe.

Large numbers of elderly people were deliberately targeted. Sometimes scare tactics were used, where customers were shown clippings from newspapers about attacks on the elderly. The perpetrators' attitude towards the customers was dismissive. Paperwork later recovered revealed that they were described in disparaging and coarse terms.

Serious consequences for victims: facing financial ruin. The judge observed that this was a gross and cynical deception, for the most part targeted at elderly, and often vulnerable, customers, the oldest of whom was 94. Not only had the perpetrators caused them anxiety, but in some cases the customers now refused to open the door and had lost their trust in people. In addition, some of the customers faced ruin because of the economic consequences. The inevitable inference was that the elderly had been deliberately targeted, and they had been treated with disdain and contempt. The two perpetrators were sentenced to 54 months and 30 months in prison respectively.[1]

---

1   *R v Kalian* [2012] EWCA Crim 652.

S

Safeguarding adults

Safeguarding is a general umbrella term used throughout this book for convenience. However, it is not used much in the Care Act 2014, which instead prefers the word 'protection' – that is, protecting adults from abuse or neglect. The word 'safeguarding' is, however, used within the Act in respect of safeguarding adults boards – and it occurs frequently in Care Act guidance.[1]

The word occurs also in the Health and Social Care Act (Regulated Activities) Regulations 2014 which sets out minimum legal standards with which all health and care providers must comply. Likewise, it is used in the title, though not the text, of the Safeguarding Vulnerable Groups Act 2006 (governing the placing of people on barred lists by the Disclosure and Barring Service).

Safeguarding adults boards

Under section 43 of the Care Act 2014, each local authority must establish a safeguarding adults board (SAB). The objective of a board is to 'help and protect adults in its area' – that is, adults about whom the duty to make enquiries arises, under section 42 of the Act.

The SAB 'must seek to achieve its objective by co-ordinating and ensuring the effectiveness of what each of its members does'. It can do anything 'which appears to it to be necessary or desirable for the purpose of achieving its objective'. In particular, it has a duty and power to arrange safeguarding

---

1   Department of Health. *Care and support statutory guidance: issued under the Care Act 2014.* London: DH, 2016.

adults reviews (SARs): see **_Safeguarding adults reviews_**. It must also publish an annual report.[1]

SAFEGUARDING ADULTS BOARDS: MEMBERSHIP. The Care Act stipulates that the three core members of a local board must be the local social services authority, the NHS clinical commissioning group and the police. The membership of a SAB may also include anybody else the local authority considers appropriate, having first consulted the core members.

The chair must be a person whom the local authority considers to have the required skills and experience. There is no requirement that the chair be independent. Statutory guidance states only that the local authority should consider appointing an independent chair.[2]

Members of the board must have regard to guidance issued by the Department of Health.[3]

SAFEGUARDING ADULTS BOARDS: OBTAINING INFORMATION. If a SAB requests information from somebody, the latter must comply with the request – in the following circumstances. The SAB can ask for the information to be supplied to it – the SAB – or to somebody else:

- **Relevant to a SAB's functions.** The purpose of the request must be about enabling or assisting the SAB to exercise its functions.

- **Relevant functions of person requested.** The request must have been made to somebody, 'whose functions or activities' are such that the SAB thinks they are likely to have information that is relevant to the SAB's functions.

- **One of two further conditions must be met.**

  » Either the information that has been requested (a) must relate to the person to whom the request has been made, or to a function or activity of that person, or (b) it must relate to another person, 'in respect of whom' the requested person exercises a function or activity.

---

1   Care Act 2014, schedule 2.

2   Care Act 2014, s.43 and schedule 2. And: Department of Health. _Care and support statutory guidance_. London: DH, 2016, para 14.150.

3   Care Act 2014, schedule 2.

» Or the information is requested from somebody 'to whom information was supplied in compliance with another request under this section', and the information requested is 'the same as, or is derived from, information so supplied'.

- **Use of the information.** Having obtained the information, the SAB – or other person to whom it has been supplied – can use the information only for enabling or assisting the SAB to exercise its functions.[1]

The duty on the requested organisation or person to comply is blunt and, on its face, absolute. However, this duty must presumably be subject to compliance with rules about sensitive personal data under the Data Protection Act 2018 and the General Data Protection Regulation (GDPR), the right to respect for private life under article 8 of the European Convention on Human Rights 1998, and the common law of confidentiality.

SAFEGUARDING ADULTS BOARDS: COMPLAINTS ABOUT. The local ombudsman has expressed the view that local authorities have the key coordinating role and that decisions by a SAB are in effect administrative functions of a local authority,[2] meaning that a complaint about a SAB could be made against the local authority and be investigated by the ombudsman.

SAFEGUARDING ADULTS BOARDS: FREEDOM OF INFORMATION. An Information Tribunal held – *at least in the circumstances of the particular case* – that information relating to a serious case review conducted by the SAB was effectively held by the local authority in its own right (not just on behalf of the SAB). This was important, because the SAB is not listed as a legal body covered by the Freedom of Information Act (FOIA), but the local authority

---

1   Care Act 2014, s.45.

2   Local Government Ombudsman. *Casework guidance statement: safeguarding adults boards.* London: LGO, 2015, pp.3–4.

is. So, the latter was amenable to the FOIA request, which was within the Tribunal's jurisdiction.[1]

On the other hand, in several other cases (some involving children's safeguarding boards) the Information Commissioner (a rung down from the Tribunal) found that the information sought belonged wholly to the safeguarding board, not the local authority – and so was not amenable to disclosure under the FOIA,[2] although communications between the local authority and a safeguarding board would in principle be within the scope of the FOIA.[3] And simply not replying to a request for notes of a safeguarding adults review meeting, within the required timescale, whether not there was an obligation to disclose, is fault.[4]

Safeguarding adults reviews

A safeguarding adults board (SAB) has both a duty and power to arrange a safeguarding adults review (SAR), in certain circumstances, under section 44 of the Care Act. The overall purpose of such a review is to learn lessons and apply them in the future. Each member of the SAB must cooperate in relation to a review and contribute to carrying it out. The focus of a safeguarding adults review could include, for example:

- systemic abuse and criminal ill-treatment of people with severe learning disabilities at a registered hospital[5]

---

1 *McClatchey v Information Commissioner.* First-Tier Tribunal, General Regulatory Chamber (Information Rights), Ea/2014/0252, February 2016, paras 16, 29. And see: McClatchey, T. 'Was action taken over Mental Health Act misuse at Winterbourne View?' *Community Care.* Accessed on 30 September 2016 at: www.communitycare.co.uk/2016/09/19/action-taken-mental-health-act-misuse-winterbourne-view.

2 E.g. Information Commissioner. *Wakefield Metropolitan Borough Council,* FS50628708, 11 October 2016. Also: *Stoke-on-Trent City Council,* FS50566663, 29 September 2015.

3 Information Commissioner. *Kirklees Metropolitan Council,* FS50448670, 12 February 2013.

4 Information Commissioner. *West Sussex County Council,* FS50690732, 19 October 2017.

5 Flynn, M. *Winterbourne View Hospital: a serious case review.* Bristol: South Gloucestershire Safeguarding Adults Board, 2015.

- death of a man with learning disabilities from severe constipation[1]

- death of a man who refused care in a nursing home for his ulcerated, maggot-infested legs[2]

- neglect-related deaths in a care home.[3]

SAFEGUARDING ADULTS REVIEWS: DUTY. The duty to carry out a SAR under section 44 of the Act arises as follows:

- **Adult in area.** It must involve an adult in its area with needs for care and support (whether or not the local authority has been meeting any of those needs).

- **Reasonable cause for concern.** There also must be 'reasonable cause for concern' about how the SAB, members of it or anybody else 'with relevant functions' worked together to safeguard the adult.

- **Death resulting from abuse or neglect.** Either the adult has died and the SAB 'knows or suspects that the death resulted from abuse or neglect'. It is irrelevant whether, before the adult died, the SAB knew about, or suspected, the abuse or neglect.

- **Serious abuse or neglect but not death.** Or the adult is still alive and the SAB 'knows or suspects that the adult has experienced serious abuse or neglect'.[4]

SAFEGUARDING ADULTS REVIEWS: POWER. The SAB has a power, but no duty, to arrange a review in any other case involving an adult in its area with needs for care and support (whether or not the local authority has been meeting any of those needs).[5]

---

1   Flynn, M. and Eley, R. *A serious case review: James.* Ipswich: Suffolk Safeguarding Adults Board, 2015.

2   Braye, S. and Preston-Shoot, M. *Safeguarding adults review: Adult A.* Lewes: East Sussex Safeguarding Adults Board, 2017.

3   West Sussex Safeguarding Adults Board. *Orchid View: serious case review.* Chichester: WSSAB, 2014.

4   Care Act 2014, s.44.

5   Care Act 2014, s.43.

This power could therefore be exercised, for example, in a case involving abuse or neglect which does not fall within the circumstances triggering the duty to arrange a review.

SAFEGUARDING ADULTS REVIEWS: FURTHER RULES. Several requirements attach to reviews:

- **Purpose of review.** Members of the SAB must cooperate in, and contribute to, the review, for the purpose of identifying lessons and applying them in the future.[1]

- **Speed.** Guidance states that reviews should be completed within a reasonable period of time and, in any event, within six months.[2]

- **Annual report.** Schedule 2 of the Act states that a SAB's annual report for the previous year must include the finding of SARs that concluded in that year, ongoing reviews, what it has done to implement the findings of reviews and the reasons for not implementing such findings.

- **Publication.** Guidance states that in the interests of transparency and learning lessons, reports of SARs should be published, within the parameters of confidentiality.[3]

SAFEGUARDING ADULTS REVIEWS: POINTS AND QUESTIONS. Several points, and questions, arise from these rules.

- **Eligibility and ordinary residence not required.** The adult need neither have eligible (under the Care Act) care and support needs nor be ordinarily resident in the local authority's area. Any needs and simply being physically in the area are sufficient.

- **Concern about working together.** Abuse or neglect alone is not enough to trigger the duty. There must also be reasonable cause for concern about how members of the safeguarding adults board – or other relevant organisations – worked together to safeguard the adult. Were they to argue that they had

---

1   Care Act 2014, s.44.

2   Department of Health. *Care and support statutory guidance*. London: DH, 2016, para 14.173.

3   Department of Health. *Care and support statutory guidance*. London: DH, 2016, para 14.179.

worked well together, and that the abuse or neglect was unavoidable, there would be presumably no duty to conduct a review.

(Under similar, though not identical, rules in children's legislation,[1] the courts have ruled that abuse or neglect – failings, in terms of actions or inactions – by a local authority itself would not legally trigger a review, unless the child had been directly in the care of the local authority.[2] Were a similar approach to be adopted in relation to adults, it would mean local authorities would, at least to some extent, be protected from reviews into their own actions or omissions, which arguably might have been abusive or neglectful, unless the SAB decided anyway to exercise its power, rather than duty, to conduct a review: see below.)

- **Death and causation.** In case of death, the abuse or neglect does not have to be 'serious' (although, of course, it could be). However, there must be reasonable cause to suspect that the death resulted from abuse or neglect. If it is clear from the outset that it did not result in death, the duty would not be triggered, no matter how serious the abuse or neglect. This would seem to be something of a loophole. (However, in such a case, the SAB could decide to exercise its power, rather than duty, to conduct a review: see below.)

Refusal to hold a SAR on grounds that neglect did not cause death. A SAB refused to conduct a SAR on the grounds that alleged shortcomings in the care of a man with learning disabilities in a care home did not cause his death, following hospital admission, from pneumonia and an acute kidney injury. This was despite his siblings' concerns that he had required physiotherapy and had an inadequate chair – which meant he lost neck strength, his head sagged on his chest and he developed a serious chest infection.

Instead, the local authority decided to treat the family's request as a complaint and arranged an independent investigation (which was then inadequately conducted). The ombudsman found fault with the investigation – and also stated that the local authority needed to give a fuller explanation about why a SAR was not held.[3]

---

1   SI 2006/90, r.5.

2   *R (Mohammed) v Local Safeguarding Children's Board for Islington (London Borough of Islington)* [2014] EWHC 3966 (Admin), paras 43–46.

3   LGO, *Hertfordshire County Council*, 2018 (17 010 928).

- **Still living.** For an adult still alive, the duty is triggered by 'serious' abuse or neglect only, which thus creates a distinction between serious and 'non-serious' abuse or neglect.

  Guidance states that abuse or neglect is serious if the person 'would have been likely to have died but for an intervention or has suffered permanent harm or has reduced capacity or quality of life (whether because of physical or psychological effects) as a result of the abuse or neglect'.[1]

- **Publication.** Although reference must be made in the SAB's annual report to the findings of SARs in the past year, there is no explicit duty to publish any one report. Guidance states, however, that they 'should' be published. In practice, it appears that some SABs have decided that their default position is not to publish. This appears to be on the ground that individuals and organisations will be more candid and forthcoming if they know that the report will not be published. This approach mirrors a proposed piece of legislation covering the NHS, in which the findings of safety investigations will not be disclosed.[2] The concern is that such non-publication and non-disclosure – whilst well meaning – may result instead in secrecy and be a convenient method of covering up the failings of an organisation – especially if one of those organisations, such as the NHS, is a member of the SAB.

- **Learning lessons.** The local ombudsman may, in response to a complaint, investigate whether relevant agencies – such as the local authority and NHS – have taken steps to learn lessons – as the Care Act states they should – and to implement the recommendations of a safeguarding review.

  For example, as in one case, the ombudsman investigated whether there were clear processes for overseeing implementation, were appointed individuals to oversee agreed actions, were clear time frames for completion – and whether there was a sub-committee of the safeguarding board overseeing this and reporting back to the safeguarding adults board.[3]

Safeguarding Vulnerable Groups Act 2006, see *Barred list*

1   Department of Health. *Care and support statutory guidance.* London: DH, 2016, para 14.163.

2   Department of Health. *Draft Health Service Safety Investigations Bill.* London: DH, 2017.

3   LGO, *Nottinghamshire County Council*, 2016 (16 002 691).

Scale of neglect or abuse

A perverse rule seems sometimes to operate, such that the larger the scale of neglect, suffering or death, the less likely it is that effective and timely safeguarding will take place, in terms of prevention, alleviation or holding people to account. This has been demonstrated, for example, in relation to the scores or hundreds of deaths (variously) at Maidstone and Tunbridge Wells NHS Trust, Stoke Mandeville NHS Trust, Mid Staffordshire NHS Foundation Trust and Gosport War Memorial Hospital.[1] These scandals became known, sooner or later (too late, of course), but in the two most serious cases only with difficulty and, even then, without significant action being taken to hold anybody to account.

Scamming

Scams can include uninvited contact received by email, letter and telephone or in person, involving false promises with a view to trick victims out of money. They include fake lotteries, deceptive prize draws or sweepstakes, clairvoyants, computer scams and romance scams.

Scamming involves deceiving people with flashy, official-looking documents or websites or with convincing telephone sales patter, with the aim of persuading them to send a processing or administration fee, pay postal or insurance costs or make a premium-rate phone call. Doorstep scams are crimes carried out by bogus callers, rogue traders and unscrupulous sales people who call, often uninvited, at people's home under the guise of

---

1   Healthcare Commission. *Investigation into outbreaks of* Clostridium difficile *at Maidstone and Tunbridge Wells NHS Trust.* London: HC, 2007. Healthcare Commission. *Investigation into outbreaks of* Clostridium difficile *at Stoke Mandeville Hospital, Buckinghamshire Hospitals NHS Trust.* London: HC, 2006. Francis, R. (Chair). *Independent Inquiry into care provided by Mid Staffordshire NHS Foundation Trust January 2005–March 2009.* London: The Stationery Office, 2010. Francis, R. (Chair). *Report of the Mid Staffordshire NHS Foundation Trust Public Inquiry.* London: The Stationery Office, 2013. Jones, Reverend J. (Chairman). *Gosport War Memorial Hospital: the report of the Gosport Independent Panel.* London: The Stationery Office, 2018.

legitimate business or trade.[1] Such scamming may amount to the criminal offence of *Fraud*.

A 2016 report into scamming, and how it was evolving into different forms, noted that:

> Every day throughout the country hundreds of people fall victim to criminals who scam them, rip them off or con them. These innocent victims are ruthlessly targeted and exploited by cynical criminals who often focus on the most vulnerable members of our society. The damage they do is huge – victims lose not only their money but frequently their sense of security and dignity is destroyed as well.[2]

Scamming includes doorstep crime, social media crime and scam mail. For example:

Spanish timeshare scam: elderly victims. Tens of elderly victims were tricked out of money on the basis of false promises about returns on investments and of tax and legal fees claims. The cold-calling gang was sentenced to a total of 32 years' imprisonment on offences of conspiracy to defraud and money laundering.

Money lending to vulnerable people. A husband and wife were convicted on seven counts of illegal money lending and each received a 14-month custodial sentence. A total of 50 victims were identified, with many coming from the hospital where the husband worked as a nurse. The total value of their loan book was £540,000. It was a sophisticated, well-planned operation and all the customers could be described as vulnerable. Following conviction, two confiscation orders were made under the Proceeds of Crime Act.

Scam mail. Each year mail scams are estimated to cause between £5 billion and £10 billion worth of detriment to people across the UK. Mail scams often take the form of fake competitions or non-existent lotteries, which victims – particularly people in vulnerable situations – are lured into

1   National Trading Standards Scams Team. 'What are scams?' Accessed on 22 September 2017 at: www.friendsagainstscams.org.uk/article.php?xArt=124.

2   National Trading Standards. *Consumer harm report, 2016*. Basildon: NTA, 2016.

entering. People who are scammed often experience loneliness, shame and social isolation – and many criminals continue to prey on this. More than 220,000 names of victims have been shared between criminals on 'victims lists' and the average age of scam victims is 75. It can be difficult for family members, friends and neighbours to convey some of the problems of scam mail to victims.[1]

Fine wine scam targeting elderly and vulnerable people. Two members of a family of fraudsters who conned elderly investors in a £4.5 million fine wine scam were jailed for a total of ten and a half years. They cold-called victims promising top-end wines as a better investment than stocks and shares, tricking scores of investors into putting thousands of pounds into Australian wine – dubbed the 'best money could buy', with a vow to sell it at massive profits after three years in 'premium storage'. It then wound up the business before investors could retrieve their cash. The money was then in a second company, selling cheap Italian wine at events such as the 2010 World Cup. They obtained an average of £5000 from investors – many of them elderly – and even persuaded some to buy 10,000 bottles of wine a time. In fact, only a fraction of the wine was ever produced. A significant proportion of the victims were elderly and described as vulnerable.[2]

Self-neglect

Care Act guidance states that self-neglect is a form of neglect for the purposes of the Act (which itself refers simply to neglect, without elaboration) and that it may or may not trigger the duty to make enquiries, depending on whether the person is unable to protect themselves because of their care and support needs: see *Enquiries*. The guidance refers to self-neglect as covering a wide range of behaviour, including neglecting to care for one's personal hygiene, health or surroundings and behaviour such as hoarding.[3]

---

1 National Trading Standards. *Consumer harm report, 2016*. Basildon: NTA, 2016.

2 'Fine wine fraudsters jailed for conning elderly investors.' *Daily Telegraph*, 11 September 2013.

3 Department of Health. *Care and support statutory guidance*. London: DH, 2016, para 14.17.

Self-neglect may involve asking several legal questions in exploring whether or not to intervene or how to do so. These might include, for example:

- **Care Act 2014:** whether the person has eligible needs under the Care Act, and therefore whether the local authority has an ongoing duty to work with the person in order to assist them.

- **Mental capacity:** whether or not the person has the mental capacity, under the Mental Capacity Act 2005, to decide about how they are living.

- **Mental health:** whether or not a mental health intervention is required, such as entry with a warrant – to the dwelling under section 135 of the Mental Health Act 1983 – in order to assess the situation.

- **Environmental health:** whether or not a public health risk exists and action, including entry with a warrant, is needed under the Public Health Act 1936 or Environmental Protection Act 1990.

- **Animal welfare:** whether intervention, under the Animal Welfare Act 2006, is required in relation to any associated neglect of animals.

- **Criminal offence:** whether the self-neglect is associated with the criminal offence of wilful neglect by somebody else: see *Wilful neglect or ill-treatment*. Or, in case of death, whether manslaughter by gross negligence might have been committed: see *Manslaughter*.

In the following case, for example, the local authority had properly considered both mental capacity and its duty to try to help somebody.

Hoarding: mental capacity assessment and offer of social care support. A woman had a condition that caused her to hoard objects. A psychologist's report from 2013 stated that she felt overwhelmed and out of control, found it difficult to trust people, and suspected people of having removed things from her property, which she found distressing. In response, the local authority regularly assessed the woman's mental capacity: it repeatedly concluded she had capacity and so it could not act against her wishes. In addition, it made repeated attempts to gain the woman's trust and to persuade her to allow it to de-clutter her property, with mixed success. It was also able to clean to some extent and remove rotting food. The local ombudsman found that the local authority had done what it could, including in relation to its safeguarding policy, and acted without fault.[1]

By contrast:

Failure to provide adequate care to a woman neglecting herself, and to act in line with the Mental Capacity Act. An elderly woman with dementia was unable to look after herself and had a care package organised by the local authority, which had assessed that she became confused at times and forgot both to wash and to eat. She was also unaware of issues concerning cleaning in the house and rotten food. Over the relevant period, despite the visits of carers, she was sometimes left in a dirty house with bed linen and clothing left unwashed, and her personal hygiene, dress and food intake were not adequately monitored.

When she was admitted, by way of a break, temporarily to a care home, so that an assessment could be carried out, the local authority failed to do the assessment. The following month, back at home, in hot weather, she over-dressed, over-exercised and had the radiators on, but the care worker failed to do anything or report what was happening. Her health deteriorated, and she required a prolonged admission to hospital, after which she was unable to return home and moved into residential care.

The local authority was held by the ombudsman to be at fault. Amongst other things, there were clear failings in assessment and care provision, in the care workers failing to report the risks to the woman, in the local authority not communicating to the care workers the identified limits to the woman's mental capacity, and in reviews both of a person's capacity and their care package.[2]

Sexual activity

The issue of sexual relations and activity sometimes arises in the context of safeguarding adults: first, in terms of civil law, whether a person has the

---

1   LGO, *Kingston upon Hull City Council*, 2016 (15 016 533), para 12.

2   LGO, *Worcestershire County Council*, 2011 (09 013 172).

mental capacity to consent to, or to refuse, such activity; second, in terms of criminal offences: see *Sexual offences*.

SEXUAL ACTIVITY: MENTAL CAPACITY. A number of key points are as follows:

- **Mental capacity not partner-specific.** Capacity to engage in sexual activity is not specific to a particular partner: 'a woman either has capacity, for example, to consent to "normal" penetrative vaginal intercourse, or she does not. It is difficult to see how it can sensibly be said that she has capacity to consent to a particular sexual act with Y whilst at the same time lacking capacity to consent to precisely the same sexual act with Z.'[1]

- **Civil and criminal approach to mental capacity.** The House of Lords, in a criminal case about the mentally disordered victim of a sexual offence, averred that capacity issues about marriage and sexual relations were partner- and situation-specific, rather than about a person's more general capacity status.[2]

  It seems that the criminal court was considering a particular situation in which, irrespective of her general capacity to consent to sexual relations, the woman was in fear and panic – and so was deprived either of capacity or at least ability to communicate her wishes *in that situation*. In mental capacity cases involving sexual relations or marriage, the civil court is having to take a more general approach to whether – all other things being equal – a person does or does not have capacity to marry or to engage in sexual activity.

  The best view, therefore, is that the House of Lords failed to outline the difference between a person having capacity generally (all other things being equal) and the exercise of that capacity in a particular situation. Otherwise, a local authority would have to be vetting every potential suitor, or rather sexual partner, to see whether the vulnerable person had mental capacity to have sex with that particular partner.[3]

- **Capacity test: nature of act and reasonably foreseeable consequences.** The test for sexual relations has been held to be as follows and is a much narrower and simpler test than for marriage: 'Does the person have sufficient

---

1   *Local Authority X v MM* [2007] EWHC 2003 (Fam).

2   *R v C* [2009] UKHL 42.

3   *D Borough Council v AB* [2011] EWHC 101 (COP).

knowledge and understanding of the nature and character – the sexual nature and character – of the act of sexual intercourse, and of the reasonably foreseeable consequences of sexual intercourse, to have the capacity to choose whether or not to engage in it, the capacity to decide whether to give or withhold consent to sexual intercourse (and, where relevant, to communicate their choice…)?'[1] This includes, therefore, the person understanding that they can say no.[2] Reasonably foreseeable consequences are limited to pregnancy and health risks.[3]

- **Sexual activity implicit in marriage.** A sexual relationship is implicit in any marriage. Thus, a person who lacked the capacity to consent to sexual relations would necessarily lack the capacity to marry, but the converse would not necessarily be true.[4]

- **Reasonably foreseeable consequences: narrowly interpreted.** A woman's lack of understanding, in relation to the sexual activity, about the intentions of her partners, her own mental health, emotional and social issues, whether any ensuing baby would be taken away from her – and her belief that only marriage and being a mother would make her happy – did not mean that she lacked capacity to understand and consent to sexual activity.[5] Thus, moral and emotional understanding is not required.[6] Likewise, lack of intellectual analysis, and impulsive behaviour, does not mean that a person lacks capacity to engage in sexual activity.[7]

- **Reasonably foreseeable consequences: complications.** The apparently very basic test, concerning the nature of the act and 'reasonably foreseeable consequences', is in fact not quite so straightforward. For instance, in one case, the judge pointed out that with sex between men, the issue of pregnancy did not arise, and in the case of non-penetrative sexual activity, understanding of health issues might not be required either. With some understatement, the

---

1   *X City Council v MB & Ors* [2006] EWHC 168 (Fam).

2   *London Borough of Southwark v KA* [2016] EWHC 661 (Fam), para 53.

3   *D Borough Council v AB* [2011] EWHC 101 (COP).

4   *X City Council v MB & Ors* [2006] EWHC 168 (Fam).

5   *Ealing London Borough Council v KS* [2008] EWHC 636 (Fam).

6   *A Local Authority v H* [2012] EWHC 49 (COP).

7   *A Local Authority v TZ* [2013] EWHC 2322 (COP), para 55.

judge referred to the 'serious management problems' (e.g. for social services) of different kinds of sexual activity practised at different times.[1]

- **Mental capacity: sexual activity distinguished from contact.** A person might have the capacity to engage in sexual activity but lack capacity in relation to understanding the general or wider risk posed by potential partners. In one case, this justified the following management plan: 'if he wants to go off with someone he has just met, the care workers would try to dissuade him, reminding him of the staged approach to new relationships previously discussed and agreed. In the event that he refused to listen to support workers in those circumstances, and where there were concerns regarding the risk of harm, the care worker involved should immediately alert management, who would in turn ensure that legal representatives were informed. A decision would then be taken as to whether the police should be informed, and/or whether an application should be made to the Court of Protection.'[2]

This distinction can lead to difficult decisions being made by statutory services and the Court of Protection. For example, in one case the Court approved a care plan which enabled an autistic woman to have sex – when her husband was out – with a variety of strangers, after she had developed an obsession with men of different ethnic backgrounds. She had been assessed as having the mental capacity to understand sexual relations – but lacking the mental capacity to make decisions as to whether it was safe to have contact with the men, with whom she wanted to have sex. The case was widely reported in the Press, followed rapidly by the Court of Protection reviewing the case.[3]

- **Mental capacity: sexual activity distinguished from contraception.** The courts have considered a separate test as to whether a person understands the question of contraception. The immediate ('proximate') medical issues to be understood and weighed up were: (a) the reason for contraception and what it does (which includes the likelihood of pregnancy if it is not in use during sexual intercourse); (b) the types available and how each is used; (c) the advantages and disadvantages of each type; (d) the possible side effects of

1   *D Borough Council v AB* [2011] EWHC 101 (COP).

2   *A Local Authority v TZ (No. 2)* [2014] EWHC 973 (COP), paras 70–71.

3   *Manchester City Council Legal Services v LC* [2018] EWCOP 30. And see: Norfolk, A. Court brings forward case of "pimped out" autistic woman. *The Times*, 20th October 2018.

each and how they can be dealt with; (e) how easily each type can be changed; and (f) the generally accepted effectiveness of each.

However, understanding what bringing up a child would be like in practice, or whether such a child would be likely to be removed from her care, were not relevant.[1]

Sexual offences

The Sexual Offences Act 2003 contains various criminal offences, including some particularly relevant to adult safeguarding. The Act is covered below under the following headings:

- Sexual offences: general offences

- Sexual offences: children

- Sexual offences: victim with a mental disorder and inability to refuse

- Sexual offences: inability to communicate

- Sexual offences: reasonably knowing that the victim had a mental disorder

- Sexual offences: which offence to prosecute in case of a victim with mental disorder

- Sexual offences: inducement, threat or deception

- Sexual offences: mental disorder and care workers

- Sexual offences: sex offenders register

- Sexual offences: sexual harm prevention orders

- Sexual offences: closure orders.

SEXUAL OFFENCES: GENERAL OFFENCES. General offences include rape. The general offences are of course relevant to vulnerable adults, as to anybody else.

---

1   *A Local Authority v Mrs A* [2010] EWHC 1549 (Fam).

- **Rape:** consists of (a) intentional penetration of vagina, anus or mouth of the victim with the penis; (b) lack of consent; and (c) the perpetrator does not reasonably believe that the victim consents.[1] The question of whether the perpetrator reasonably knows whether the victim is consenting – in the case of alleged rape, for example – may, however, not be straightforward in the case of a vulnerable adult who is the perpetrator.

- **Assault by penetration:** consists of (a) intentional penetration of the vagina or anus with a part of the perpetrator's body or with anything else; (b) the penetration being sexual; (c) lack of consent; and (d) the perpetrator does not reasonably believe that the victim consents.[2]

- **Sexual assault:** consists of (a) intentional touching of another person; (b) the touching being sexual; (c) lack of consent; and (d) the perpetrator does not reasonably believe that the victim consents.[3]

- **Causing sexual activity without consent:** consists of (a) intentional causing of another person to engage in an activity; (b) the activity being sexual; (c) lack of consent; and (d) the perpetrator does not reasonably believe that the victim consents.[4]

SEXUAL OFFENCES: CHILDREN. The Sexual Offences Act 2003 contains criminal offences in relation to children, including offences committed by a person in a position of trust in relation to a person aged under 18 years.[5] These offences are beyond the scope of this book.

SEXUAL OFFENCES: VICTIM WITH A MENTAL DISORDER AND INABILITY TO REFUSE. In addition are offences when the victim has a mental disorder – within the meaning given in section 1 of the Mental Health Act 1983 – namely, any disorder or disability of mind.

---

1   Sexual Offences Act 2003, s.1.

2   Sexual Offences Act 2003, s.2.

3   Sexual Offences Act 2003, s.3.

4   Sexual Offences Act 2003, s.4.

5   Sexual Offences Act 2003, ss.5–29.

Sections 30–33 of the 2003 Act contain offences that are consent-related, because they rely on the victim being unable, because of his or her mental disorder or for a reason related to it, to refuse the sexual activity. The perpetrator must have known or could reasonably be expected to have known that the victim had a mental disorder and that because of it – or for a reason related to it – the victim was likely to have been unable to refuse. Key points are as follows.

- **Various offences.** They are (a) sexual activity with a mentally disordered person; (b) causing or inciting a person with a mental disorder to engage in sexual activity; (c) engaging in sexual activity in the presence of a person with a mental disorder for the purpose of sexual gratification of the perpetrator; and (d) causing a person with a mental disorder to watch a sexual act for the purpose of sexual gratification of the perpetrator.

- **Sexual activity.** For the purposes of sections 30 and 31, the sexual activity constituting an offence is defined as touching involving (a) penetration of the victim's anus or vagina with a part of the perpetrator's body or anything else, (b) penetration of the victim's mouth with the perpetrator's penis, (c) penetration of the perpetrator's anus or vagina with a part of the victim's body, (d) penetration of the perpetrator's mouth with the victim's penis.

- **Inability to refuse or to communicate choice.** The inability to refuse must be because either (a) the victim lacks the capacity to choose whether to agree to the touching (whether because they lack sufficient understanding of the nature or reasonably foreseeable consequences of what is being done, or for any other reason) or (b) are unable to communicate such a choice.

- **Lack of capacity: standard of proof required.** Mental capacity is not defined in the Sexual Offences Act 2003, but the courts have accepted that in effect sections 2 and 3 of the Mental Capacity Act 2005 apply. However, unlike the Mental Capacity Act, which requires only the civil standard of proof (balance of probability) to establish lack of capacity, the Sexual Offences Act requires the criminal standard (beyond reasonable doubt) to establish lack of capacity.[1]

---

1   *R v GA* [2014] EWCA Crim 299, para 29.

- **Enjoyment and capacity.** A defence, or mitigation argued, that the victim said she 'enjoyed' the sexual activity, will be of limited, or no, significance, if the victim was unable to consent.[1]

SEXUAL OFFENCES: INABILITY TO COMMUNICATE. The following cases concerned the issue of inability to refuse or to communicate (see immediately above), despite the victim having in principle the capacity to understand.

Mental capacity to refuse but inability to communicate choice. The victim lived in a public house with her parents. She was 27 years old (but had a much lower developmental age) and had cerebral palsy. A 73-year-old man, of previous good character, allegedly touched her over her clothing in the area of her vagina, whilst exposing himself and placing her hand on his soft penis. The defence accepted that the woman suffered from a mental disorder but argued that she did not lack the capacity to agree to the touching.

The magistrates' court had accepted that she understood the nature of sexual relations but did not have the capacity to understand that she could refuse. The High Court took this reasoning to mean that whilst she might have understood about sexual activity, she was unable to communicate her choice.[2]

Sheltered housing resident sexually assaulting another: sexual activity with mentally disordered resident not able to communicate choice. A man admitted one count of 'sexual activity with a woman with a mental disorder impeding choice'. Both he and she were fellow residents at an Aster Group-owned sheltered housing complex in Wiltshire. She had suffered a series of strokes and had vascular dementia. He had turned off the bedroom alarm system and was carrying out a sex act on his victim when her daughter walked in on him. He was sentenced to a total of 42 months: 32 months for the offence, but also ten months for breaking a previous, suspended sentence for molesting a 12-year-old girl. He was given an indefinite sexual harm prevention order, put on the sex offenders register indefinitely, and

---

1   *R v P* [2015] EWCA Crim 753.

2   *Hulme v Director of Public Prosecutions* [2006] EWHC 1347 (Admin).

told to pay a £170 victim surcharge.[1] When the daughter had entered, it was as if her mother had been frozen to the spot – like a rabbit caught in the headlights of a car. She just sat there, not moving, and her eyes were just staring blankly ahead. She wasn't saying anything.[2]

Inability to communicate because of fear and panic. A woman with serious mental health problems was effectively picked up off the streets and taken advantage of, sexually. The defendant took her to a friend's house, sold her mobile phone and bicycle, gave her crack cocaine, and then asked her to give him a 'blow job'. She gave evidence that she was in a panic and afraid of what else they might do to her; so, she stayed and just went along with it.[3]

The first question was whether a lack of capacity to choose was person- or situation-specific. The answer was yes: once it was accepted that choice is an exercise of free will, and that mental disorder may rob a person of free will in a number of different ways and in a number of different situations, then a mentally disordered person may be quite capable of exercising choice in one situation but not in another.[4]

The second was whether an irrational fear, preventing the exercise of choice, equated to lack of capacity to choose; the answer to this was also yes. The question was whether it did so in the particular situation. The jury had been entitled to decide that it did.[5]

Third was whether the inability to communicate a choice could stem only from a person's *physical* inability related to the mental disorder (and not, for example, from an irrational fear). The answer was no: an irrational fear could rob a person of the ability to choose or to communicate that choice.[6]

1   Corbett, J. 'OAP sex offender jailed for 42 months.' *Wiltshire Gazette and Herald*, 14 November 2017.

2   *File on 4*. 'Sheltered from harm.' BBC Radio 4, broadcast 23 January 2018.

3   *R v C* [2009] UKHL 42.

4   *R v C* [2009] UKHL 42.

5   *R v C* [2009] UKHL 42.

6   *R v C* [2009] UKHL 42.

SEXUAL OFFENCES: REASONABLY KNOWING THAT THE VICTIM HAD A MENTAL DISORDER. The following cases were about whether the perpetrator could reasonably have known that the victim had a mental disorder and so would be unlikely to have been unable to refuse.

Reasonable knowledge: victim, with the communication skills of a young child, had a mental disorder. The 25-year-old victim was unable to refuse because a feature of her extreme autism was that she did whatever she was asked. She had the communication skills of a three-year-old. A 77-year-old retired bus driver saw her at a bus stop and went to her home for sex. She was so distressed at what had happened that she gave up living independently. He was sentenced to nine and a half years in prison. He claimed that he could not reasonably have known about her mental disorder; this claim was rejected.[1]

Reasonable knowledge: taking advantage of a neighbour with severe learning disabilities. A neighbour took advantage, on a number of occasions, of a 20-year-old woman with severe learning disabilities who lived with her parents. This took place first at the neighbour's house, to which the woman had gone invited, and then elsewhere (social club and a lay-by). He was convicted under section 30 of the Sexual Offences Act 2003 and sentenced to four years in prison, increased to five and a half years.[2]

Reasonable knowledge: touching partner's granddaughter with mental age of young child. The 74-year-old defendant lived with the victim's grandmother. The victim was in her twenties, but with a mental age of between four and eight years old. His partner found him with his hand down the front of the victim's trousers. No digital penetration took place. He ultimately pleaded guilty and accepted that he had closed his mind to the reasonable expectation that, by reason of her mental disorder, the victim was likely to be unable to refuse the sexual touching.

He had been cautioned four years before for sexual touching of the same victim. He was now sentenced, under section 30 of the Sexual Offences Act, to three years and nine months in prison (12 months custodial, the rest an extended sentence). On appeal, taking account of his age, medical

---

1   'Sex offender jailed for nine years.' *North Devon Journal*, 10 May 2012.

2   *R v Charles* [2007] EWCA Crim 2266.

condition and all the circumstances of the offence, the court reduced the custodial element from 12 to six months.[1] (Under section 227 of the Criminal Justice Act 2003, an extended sentence consists of a custodial element and a period for which the offender is subject to a licence.)

In the following somewhat unusual case, section 30(1) of the Act provided for a sentencing range of between eight and 13 years. Yet the judge departed from this, arriving at a sentence of only four years. The Court of Appeal subsequently reduced this still further to three years and noted the grey area surrounding the line of criminality which the man had crossed – and the question of reasonable knowledge.

Reasonable knowledge: visiting wife in care home, sexual activity with another resident. The perpetrator's wife suffered from Huntington's disease and was a long-time resident at a care home where he visited her on virtually a daily basis. She could not communicate with him, so he frequently visited other residents at the home and gained a reputation as the 'chocolate man' because he often gave residents chocolate mints.

Victim: pattern of sexual behaviour and other disinhibited behaviour. The 57-year-old victim, BG, had been a resident at the home since 2000. She had suffered a severe stroke in 1999 which had left her with significant cognitive difficulties and unable to care for herself. She had poor vision, little capacity for short-term memory and only patchy long-term memory. She was unable to care for her basic needs without prompting and was generally apathetic, lacking in initiative, and was incapable of even asking for a glass of water.

If she was left alone, she would drift off to sleep and she could not hold full conversations with people but restricted her answers to 'yes' and 'no'. Over her years at the home, BG had displayed both sexual and non-sexual disinhibited behaviour, although there is no evidence that the perpetrator knew of this. Her behaviour had been managed through a behavioural management programme, but she was not someone who was able to decide whether or not to take part in a physical relationship with someone.

On 18 August 2008, the appellant visited his wife at the home. He was seen by two care assistants sitting with BG in the residents' lounge,

---

1   *R v D* [2005] EWCA Crim 1459.

touching BG sexually. The two care assistants noted that both the appellant and BG appeared to be smiling. They reported the matter to the manager, who informed the police and on 20 August 2008 the appellant was arrested.

Perpetrator claims victim was consenting. When he was interviewed under caution, he confirmed the observations of the care assistant. He added that such activity with BG at first occurred a few weeks earlier, on several occasions, when she initiated it, holding his hand and putting it against her breast or vagina. He insisted that she had her own mind and was capable of refusing anything if she wanted to.[1]

Reasonable knowledge. The judge referred to plentiful evidence that the woman lacked capacity to consent and that the perpetrator should reasonably have known this – finding him guilty and a high risk to vulnerable females. He was sentenced to four years in prison.

Appeal: reduction of sentence. On appeal, the sentence was reduced to three years. The Court of Appeal noted that this was a case of ostensible consent, where the defendant's criminality arose out of his lack of judgment in acquiescing to the victim's request. He submitted there was no evidence that the defendant had planned the activity, nor that the victim had suffered mentally or physically as a result of that activity. The care home had in earlier years allowed the victim to behave in this way with others, and the records made it plain that she made sexual demands from time to time of those around her.

The appellant was 62 years old at the time of the offences. He was a man of previous good character. There were many witnesses (18 in all) who wrote of his devotion to his wife and to his two daughters, whose childhood was blighted by their mother's condition, of his exemplary employment record and of his standing in the community.[2]

SEXUAL OFFENCES: WHICH OFFENCE TO PROSECUTE IN CASE OF A VICTIM WITH MENTAL DISORDER. The courts have considered when an offence should be prosecuted as rape rather than as an offence against a victim with mental disorder.

---

1   Bartlett, P. 'Sex, dementia, capacity and care homes.' *Liverpool Law Review 31*, 2010, 137–154.

2   *R v Adcock* [2010] EWCA Crim 700.

Prosecution for rape – or special offence relating to victim with mental disorder. In a House of Lords case, one judge stated that it should be rape if (a) a victim has capacity to choose whether to agree to the sexual activity, (b) she chooses not to consent, (c) is unable to communicate this because of a physical disability, and (d) the perpetrator does not reasonably believe that she consents. On the other hand, if, in such circumstances, the inability to communicate is related to the mental disorder, then the special offences relating to a victim with a mental disorder apply.

Another judge in the same case provided a more detailed response and felt that, in the circumstances, three different charges would have been possible.

Three different charges possible in case of victim with mental disorder. The first charge would be rape which would have required the perpetrator not reasonably believing that the woman was consenting. The second was a charge under section 30 (the actual charge) which required that the perpetrator knew, or could reasonably have been expected to know, that the person had a mental disorder and would be unlikely to be able to refuse. This puts a greater burden of restraint on the perpetrator – because the rape test is about the actual consent of the other person, whereas the section 30 offence is about whether there was an inability to refuse. The third would have been an offence of inducement or threat (see below) which would not have had to rely at all on matters of consent or ability to choose.[1]

SEXUAL OFFENCES: INDUCEMENT, THREAT OR DECEPTION. A further number of offences, under sections 34–37 of the Act, do not require an inability to refuse on the part of the mentally disordered victim. In other words, these offences do not demand that the victim lack capacity to decide and so are not consent-related. However, they do still require the perpetrator to have known, or reasonably be expected to have known, that the victim had a mental disorder.

---

1   *R v C* [2009] UKHL 42.

- **Inducement, threat or deception.** Explanatory notes accompanying the Act state that the purpose of these offences is to criminalise the exploitation of a person with a mental disorder who may have capacity but who is vulnerable to exploitation. For instance, such a person may engage in sexual activity in return for a packet of sweets.[1]

- **Offences.** They are inducement, threat or deception to (a) procure sexual activity with a person with a mental disorder; (b) cause a person with a mental disorder to engage in sexual activity by inducement, threat or deception; (c) engage in sexual activity in the presence, procured by inducement, threat or deception, of a person with a mental disorder; or (d) cause a person with a mental disorder to watch a sexual act by inducement, threat or deception.[2]

The courts have queried an apparent hesitation about prosecuting these offences, but emphasised the value of doing so – or at least considering them in the alternative to other offences.

> **Distinguishing lack of consent, inability to consent – and inducement, threat or deception.** The court queried why, rather than charging section 30 (involving inability to refuse), section 34 (inducement, threat, deception) was not charged in the alternative.
>
> Perhaps the view was taken that the evidence of lack of capacity was more robust than the evidence of any inducement, threat or deception. This is pure speculation. But the alternative charges would have enabled the judge to explain the various concepts by distinguishing them from one another and relating them to the evidence: a lack of consent arising from the lack of either the freedom or the capacity to make that choice; a lack of capacity to make that choice arising from or related to a mental disorder; and a choice procured by threats, inducement or deception of a person with a mental disorder.[3]
>
> **Photographer convicted of sexual offences involving inducement, threat or deception.** A 68-year-old man was found guilty on five counts under the

---

1   Sexual Offences Act 2003, explanatory notes, para 67.

2   Sexual Offences Act 2003, ss.34–37.

3   *R v C* [2009] UKHL 42.

Sexual Offences Act: causing a person with a mental disorder to agree to or engage in sexual activity by inducement, threat or deception; causing a person with a mental disorder to agree to or engage in sexual activity by inducement, threat or deception with penetration; and three counts of sexual activity with a person with a mental disorder whose agreement is obtained by inducement, threat or deception. He had taken explicit pictures of a 'vulnerable' woman having sex, after deceiving her into thinking she could land a role in a future film. The offences were believed to have taken place on and off over a seven-year period.[1]

SEXUAL OFFENCES: MENTAL DISORDER AND CARE WORKERS. A third set of offences, under sections 38–41 of the Sexual Offences Act 2003, applies in the context of care workers and mentally disordered people. The sexual offences do not rely on lack of capacity of the victim to decide. In effect, consent or the absence of it is immaterial:

- **Knowledge:** the perpetrator must have known or reasonably be expected to have known that the victim had a mental disorder.

- **Assumption of knowledge:** if it is proved that the victim has a mental disorder, then it is assumed that the care worker knew or should reasonably have known this, unless sufficient evidence is led to question such an assumption.

- **Offences:** (a) engaging in sexual activity with a person with a mental disorder; (b) causing or inciting sexual activity; (c) engaging in sexual activity in the presence of a person with a mental disorder; or (d) causing a person with a mental disorder to watch a sexual act.

- **Care worker:** means somebody having functions in the course of his or her employment that brings, or is likely to bring, him or her into regular face-to-face contact with the mentally disordered person. Includes (a) in a care home or (b) in the context of the provision of services by the NHS or an independent medical agency or in an independent hospital or clinic. Alternatively, whether or not employed to do so, the perpetrator provides care, assistance or services

---

1   Shepherd, R. 'Milford photographer convicted of taking explicit pictures of vulnerable woman "too ill to return" to country.' *Surreylive*, 9 February 2016. Accessed on 27 June 2018 at: www.getsurrey.co.uk/news/surrey-news/milford-photographer-convicted-taking-explicit-10853308.

to the victim in connection with the victim's mental disorder – and so has, or is likely to have, regular face-to-face contact with the victim.[1]

- **Exceptions, marriage or prior relationship:** the care worker offences do not apply where (a) the mentally disordered person is 16 years old or more, and is lawfully married to the care worker; or (b) a sexual relationship existed between the mentally disordered person and the other person, immediately before the latter became involved in the care of the mentally disordered person.[2] These exceptions would cover, for instance, one partner or spouse now providing care at home for the other who has become mentally disordered during the relationship.

Examples of conviction include:

Social worker's conviction for consensual sexual activity with service user. A senior social worker (approved under the Mental Health Act) was helping a service user suffering from a mental disorder, rooted in post-natal depression. She suffered from low self-esteem. A more intimate relationship developed; she felt sexually attracted to him but could not believe he would be interested in her. They started to touch. She became more and more dependent on him, to the point of obsession. She was still vulnerable, suffering panic attacks and inflicting a degree of self-harm if he did not ring her. He suggested she have a break in a residential home; he visited her there and sexual intercourse took place. She subsequently told the pastoral director at the home. When accused, the social worker denied it, even when forensic examination of a towel showed semen stains.

In passing sentence, the judge characterised the offence as extremely serious. He said that it had devastated the victim, who was an extremely vulnerable woman who had been in the social worker's care. The fact that she was willing was irrelevant to the sentence. Supporting statements in mitigation showed the social worker was a good husband and father, and a good professional. There was a moving letter from his wife (although by the time of the appeal she had withdrawn this support and left the

---

1   Sexual Offences Act 2003, s.42.

2   Sexual Offences Act 2003, ss.43–44.

marital home with the children). The judge sentenced the social worker to 17 months in prison; this sentence was upheld on appeal.[1]

Nurse's conviction for consensual sexual activity with patient. A senior mental health worker for the Cornwall Partnership NHS Foundation Trust had fallen in love with a patient 20 years younger than him and had a sexual relationship with the woman, who had a borderline personality disorder and was mentally unstable. It was a consensual relationship. He was nonetheless convicted under section 38 of the Sexual Offences Act 2003, sentenced to prison for 16 months, received an indefinite sexual offences prevention order and had to sign the sex offenders register for ten years.

The judge explained the seriousness: he was her principal carer. It had been an abuse of his professional position and of the integrity of the mental health service provided in that area. He was a figure of authority and, whether or not he had loved her, he had taken advantage of her to have a relationship. She had suffered the consequences. There was no alternative to immediate custody to show the public abhorrence of what he had done, and the grave breach of trust committed.[2]

Care worker convicted for incident in care home. The victim was a 76-year-old woman with severe dementia, resident in a care home. One evening, contrary to policy and rules, a 22-year-old care worker, with significant learning disabilities, was working on his own. He claimed that he had been left on his own and he took the woman to her bedroom to put her to bed. Shortly after, he activated the emergency alarm – and the woman was taken to hospital for emergency surgery for tears to her perineum. There was grave risk of serious injury or even death. The evidence was that the injuries had been caused by a penis or penis-size object. He was convicted under section 38 of the Sexual Offences Act 2003 and, on appeal, sentenced to seven years' imprisonment.[3]

Sexual assault on care home resident by family man of good character. A sentence of eight years in prison was given to a care worker convicted of sexual assault on an 82-year-old care home resident with dementia – in whose room he was discovered partially clothed. The woman herself was unable, because of her dementia, to give any details of what had happened.

---

1 *R v Bradford* [2006] EWCA Crim 2629.

2 'Married carer "fell in love" with mentally ill woman.' *West Briton*, 5 April 2012.

3 *R v Jones* [2009] EWCA Crim 237.

The man was also put on the sex offenders' register and made subject of a sexual offences prevention order, which barred him taking employment as a care worker. He was a man of hitherto good character, a family man and with a child on the way.[1]

Attempted rape of care home resident by carer with a disabled wife and family. A care home assistant was imprisoned for over five years, after attempting to rape an 84-year-old care home resident. He was supposed to be checking on residents in the early hours of the morning. He climbed on top of her but was unaware that a 'wandering' alarm had recently been installed. He had been a school teacher in Poland, where his disabled wife and family still lived, before coming to work in England. He was ashamed and could not explain the offence, only that he missed his wife. He was placed on the sex offenders' register for life.[2]

SEXUAL OFFENCES: SEX OFFENDERS REGISTER. Conviction for a sexual offence may lead to a person being placed on the sex offenders register under section 80 and schedule 3 of the Sexual Offences Act 2003. This means that the offender becomes subject to notification requirements (a duty to register with the police) under the Act.

Notification periods vary depending on the offence and how it is dealt with by the courts. Indefinite notification, without the possibility of review, has been held by the courts to be incompatible with human rights.[3] Consequently, the Sexual Offences Act 2003 (Remedial) Order 2012 provides for offenders to seek a review after 15 years (or eight years in case of juveniles). Application is first made to the police, then to a magistrate if the police refuse.

SEXUAL OFFENCES: SEXUAL HARM PREVENTION ORDERS. Sexual harm prevention orders replaced sexual offences prevention orders. They can be made by a court if the person has been convicted of any one of a list of specified offences – and if the court is satisfied that it is necessary to make the order to protect (a) the public or any particular members of the public

---

1   'Disgraced Norwich care worker jailed for eight years.' *Eastern Daily Press*, 6 September 2011.

2   'Jail for rape of care home resident.' *Yorkshire Evening Post*, 18 October 2011.

3   *R (F and Thompson) v Secretary of State for the Home Department* [2010] UKSC 17.

from sexual harm from the defendant, or (b) children or vulnerable adults generally, or any particular children or vulnerable adults, from sexual harm from the defendant outside the United Kingdom.

The order can be made either at the time of conviction – or, on application by the police, after conviction – if it is necessary to protect the public from serious sexual harm by the offender. The order can be wide-ranging in terms of prohibitions placed on the person. It must be for a minimum of five years, or at least until a further order.[1]

An order can be wide-ranging and cover various matters – for instance, restrictions on employment or internet use – but it should be specific to the person and proportionate, and other restrictions, not contained within the order, should not be imposed.[2]

SEXUAL OFFENCES: CLOSURE ORDERS. The police have power to issue closure notices in respect of premises used for prostitution, pornography or child sex offences. The notice must state that no one other than a person who regularly resides on, or owns, the premises may enter or remain on them. Within 48 hours of the notice being given, the police must apply to a magistrates' court for a closure order which can remain in effect for up to three months.[3]

Guidance notes:

The closure of premises is a significant step and the persons involved may be children, or other persons who are vulnerable or at risk. It is essential that support interventions are used with enforcement measures, and that the problem is tackled holistically rather than by simply shifting the burden elsewhere. These powers present a real opportunity for multi-agency partners to act swiftly and decisively to tackle sexual exploitation.[4]

---

1 Sexual Offences Act 2003, ss.103A–103K, schedules 3 and 5.

2 *R v Smith and Others* [2011] EWCA Crim 177.

3 Sexual Offences Act 2003, ss.136A–136R.

4 Home Office. *Guidance on closure orders: Part 2a Sexual Offences Act 2003.* London: Home Office, undated, p.4.

Closure order made. A joint initiative between Gloucestershire Constabulary and Gloucester City Council secured a three-month civil closure order, in March 2017, on a residential address. It was believed to have been used in relation to sexual offences. No one was allowed to enter the address until 3 June apart from the homeowner. Any breach would be a criminal offence and could result in an arrest.

A 63-year-old man was also arrested on suspicion of trafficking offences against vulnerable women, of coercive control and of supplying Class A drugs. He was bailed until 3 May in connection with the offences and was also given an interim injunction with strict conditions on his behaviour. Inquiries into the criminal offences continued; meanwhile, any breach of the injunction could result in a custodial sentence.[1]

Slapping, see *Assault*; *Ill-treatment*

Social services

Social services is the term given to what are called 'first-tier' local authorities with statutory responsibilities for social care – including adult social care and adult safeguarding (and likewise for children).[2] Such first-tier local authorities include county councils, city councils, London boroughs, metropolitan borough councils and other unitary councils. These should be distinguished from, for example, local district councils.

There is sometimes uncertainty, perhaps ambiguity, of the safeguarding role and function, legally and practically, of social services. Local authorities are designated the lead safeguarding agency. Primarily, their role under the Care Act 2014 is to assess people's care and support needs and sometimes to meet them. However, they also have a duty to enquire into abuse or neglect, and to liaise with other agencies such as the police, albeit with no powers of coercion attached. Legal misunderstanding sometimes arises, and the

---

1   'Closure order in Abbeydale is "groundbreaking" action.' Gloucestershire Constabulary, 6 March 2017. Accessed on 13 March 2018 at: www.gloucestershire.police.uk/news-room/latest-news/closure-order-in-abbeydale-is-groundbreaking-action.

2   Local Authority Social Services Act 1970, s.1A, schedule 1.

actions of local authorities can become prematurely judgemental, accusatory, threatening and coercive – and yet be ill-evidenced, basically unfair in a legal and administrative sense and without foundation in law. The courts are sometimes severely critical, because of the injustice that can result.[1]

Special measures, see *Witnesses*

Standard of proof

In law there are two standards of proof: civil and criminal.

The civil standard requires proof on the balance of probability – that is, at least a 51 per cent likelihood. This standard is used, for example, by the Disclosure and Barring Service when it considers the evidence as to whether a worker should be placed on a barred list. Which means that a person could be barred even in the absence, or failure, of a criminal prosecution.

The criminal standard is referred to as being sure 'beyond reasonable doubt'. This does not mean absolute certainty in a scientific sense, and thus being certain and being sure amount to much the same thing.[2]

Criminal case failing but civil remedy still available. When three carers were acquitted of assault (feeding talcum powder to an elderly woman), nonetheless two other courses of action followed. First, the local authority terminated its contract with the agency that employed the carers. Second, the woman then brought a civil case against the agency. It was settled out of court, the agency admitting negligence and agreeing to pay over £10,000 in compensation.[3]

Suicide, see *Assisted suicide*

---

1   See e.g. *A Local Authority v A and B* [2010] EWHC 978 (Fam).

2   *R v Stephens* [2002] EWCA Crim 1529.

3   Dayani, A. 'Ban them for life.' *Birmingham Evening Mail*, 4 February 2004. And: Carvel, J. '£10,000 for widow, 89, "fed talcum powder" by carers.' *The Guardian (Society)*, 12 July 2006.

Theft

Under section 1 of the Theft Act 1968, a person is guilty of theft if:

- **Dishonesty:** he or she dishonestly appropriates property belonging to somebody else.

- **Intention:** with the intention of permanently depriving the other person of it.

- **Belief in lawfulness:** such an appropriation is not dishonest if the person believes he or she had a right in law to deprive the other person of it.

- **Belief in consent:** alternatively, it is not dishonest if he or she believed that the other person would consent if the other person knew of the appropriation and the circumstances.

Financial abuse, in the form of theft (and fraud), is a major issue in adult safeguarding. The following paragraphs deal first with the question of adults, with capacity to handle and give away their money, but who are nonetheless particularly vulnerable to exploitation – and whether this can amount to theft; second, with the importance of the word 'dishonesty' in the legal definition of theft; and, third, with many examples of convictions for theft involving vulnerable adults and an extensive range of perpetrators – from family members to professionals in positions of trust, tempted and opportunistic.

THEFT: MENTAL CAPACITY AND EXPLOITATION OF VULNERABLE ADULTS. A vulnerable adult might, with mental capacity (under the Mental Capacity Act 2005), handle the money or property in question, but nonetheless be vulnerable to forms of exploitation. The question is whether a conviction for theft is possible in such circumstances. The answer is sometimes, and the issue may hinge on the 'dishonesty' element of the definition of the offence of theft.

Financial exploitation of vulnerable person: theft conviction even with the person's consent to making a gift. A man of limited intelligence, 53 years old, was assisted and cared for by a 38-year-old woman on a private basis. Over a period from April to November, he made withdrawals almost every day up to the maximum £300 allowed from the building society – to the amount of £60,000 (representing money inherited from his father).

Lack of decisive evidence that victim lacked mental capacity. The money ended up in the carer's bank account. The building society employees stated that the carer did most of the talking and would interrupt the man if he tried to talk. A consultant psychiatrist gave evidence that the man's IQ was between 70 and 80 (as opposed to the average of 90 to 110), that he could lead a normal if undemanding life (he had worked in a dairy as a packer for 30 years) – and that he was naive and trusting and had no idea of the value of his assets or the ability to calculate their value. The consultant accepted, however, that he would be capable of making a gift and understood the concept of ownership – and so would be able to divest himself of money but could probably not take the decision alone.

Jury entitled to find dishonesty, even if man had mental capacity to make a gift of the money. The carer was convicted of theft in the Crown Court; the case went on appeal to the House of Lords, which refused to interfere with the conviction. The court placed great weight on leaving the matter to the jury to decide about whether there had been dishonesty in all the circumstances. It was not crucial whether the man had mental capacity to make a gift of the money. This was because the court was not prepared to read into section 1 of the Theft Act the words 'without the owner's consent'. In other words, consent was not necessarily fatal to the success of a charge of theft (it had been argued that, as a matter of law, it could not be theft if the man did have the capacity to make a gift; and that the Crown Court judge should have directed the jury to that effect).[1]

---

1   *R v Hinks* [2001] 2 AC 241 (House of Lords).

The *Hinks* case, above, effectively overruled a previous Court of Appeal case (*Mazo*), in which a maid, employed by an elderly woman aged 89 years, was prosecuted for allegedly cashing cheques to the value of £37,000 and stealing a brooch and crystal ornament. The appeal against conviction was allowed, on the basis of the failure of the judge's directions to be clear about the relevance of mental capacity (on the assumption that the making of the gift, with capacity – i.e. the owner's consent – could not be theft, unless there was fraud or deception). This meant the jury had felt able to make a moral judgement about the maid, instead of deciding whether there was, in law, theft.[1]

Nevertheless, the *Hinks* case, which takes precedence because it was a House of Lords case, did not follow the *Mazo* approach. Instead, it considered an earlier Court of Appeal case, which had held that consent (and therefore mental capacity) of the owner was not decisive.

Theft of 99-year-old care home resident's assets: conviction still possible even with owner's consent to making a gift. A 99-year-old woman lived in a care home. She was virtually blind. She went to live there in 1991; her daughter died in 1992, and at this point the two owners of the home took control of her affairs, and numbers of cheques were drawn on her account which they argued were gifts. The owners obtained power of attorney and liquidated the woman's gilts and stocks; the proceeds were paid into a bank account held in their names jointly with the woman. Only one signature was required. A series of payments was subsequently made from that account for the benefit of the owners of the home. They were prosecuted for theft.

They appealed against their conviction, arguing that the judge should have directed the jury that there could be no theft if the woman consented to the 'gifts' (and thus had the capacity to give that consent). Furthermore, the judge had failed to indicate the level of mental capacity required in order to make the acts of appropriation dishonest. The appeal failed. The court held that the relevant term in section 1 of the Theft Act 1968

---

1   *R v Mazo* [1997] 2 Cr App R 518. See also: *Director of Public Prosecutions v Gomez* [1993] AC 442.

was 'dishonest appropriation'; this did not necessarily mean 'without the consent of the owner'.[1]

THEFT: TEST OF DISHONESTY. The *Hinks* case, above, indicates the importance of the word 'dishonesty' in defining theft. In that case, involving a gift, the court left it up to the jury to decide whether, in all the circumstances, acceptance of the 'gift' constituted dishonesty. There is both a subjective and objective test for dishonesty.

Dishonesty: objective and subjective tests. The courts had previously given guidance about dishonesty, stating that to establish guilt, there were two tests to apply: the objective and subjective. The objective test, to be applied first, was whether, according to the ordinary standards of reasonable and honest people, the defendant had acted dishonestly. If not, then that was the end of the matter. However, if, according to this objective standard, there was dishonesty, then the subjective test came into play. This was about whether the defendant would have realised that he or she was acting dishonestly by those standards.[2]

In the *Jouman* case, the court stated that the application of the second test did not follow automatically, but only 'if the state of the evidence is such that the offender might have believed that what he or she is alleged to have done was in accordance with the ordinary person's idea of honesty'. However, in that case, there was no such evidence; the defendant's cognitive functioning was within the normal range. She displayed some features of autistic spectrum disorder, but these did not amount to a formal diagnosis to that effect; she was high on the autistic spectrum, but no more. There was no suggestion that she would not have understood dishonesty – she would have known that the money she received from a highly dependent woman was not a genuine gift, given of the woman's free will.[3]

Mental capacity: legal capacity but vulnerable, withdrawal of savings: theft. In the *Jouman* case, the victim lived alone and had no surviving family. Her contacts with the outside world were visits from representatives

---

1   *R v Kendrick* [1997] 2 Cr App R 524.

2   *R v Ghosh* [1982] QB 1053.

3   *R v Jouman* [2012] EWCA Crim 1850.

of Age Concern, from a cleaner – and from a woman who used to work at the Post Office and knew the victim when she paid her rent, and now visited her weekly. The victim was described as having legal capacity, but at risk and vulnerable. She had been left £88,000 by her sister-in-law: she had invested it in July, in an AXA bond. In November, she rang up AXA and then passed the telephone to the woman to ask questions about the bond. In May, the victim made a written request to withdraw the bond, receiving only £60,000 because of punitive withdrawal fees: seven days later, she credited £50,000 to the account of the woman. The latter was found guilty of theft; the victim's dependency on the perpetrator, and breach of trust, were significant factors.[1]

THEFT: PATTERNS AND EXAMPLES INVOLVING VULNERABLE ADULTS.

The following summaries illustrate different types of circumstance involving theft from vulnerable adults.

FAMILY MEMBERS

Man stealing from former partner and her mother. A man was convicted of theft after stealing more than £13,000 from his former partner and from her mother who had dementia. He did this by using their bank cards and PINs, which he had stolen from the kitchen cupboard where they were kept. He also intercepted bank statements so that the theft would not come to light. Much of the money was spent on gambling machines in a betting shop.[2]

NEIGHBOURS

Married couple stealing large sums of money from mentally confused woman. When a social worker and police officer visited an elderly woman, they found her to be frail, dirty and unkempt, and the house to be dirty and smelling of urine. She was apparently happy but mentally confused and forgot who her visitors were after five minutes. It became clear subsequently that two friendly neighbours (a married couple) had over a period from 1995 to 2001 stolen sums of money from the woman amounting to £110,000. The couple unsuccessfully challenged the admissibility of evidence relating

---

1 *R v Jouman* [2012] EWCA Crim 1850.

2 'Gambler avoids jail term.' *Hartlepool Mail*, 31 March 2012.

to the woman's dementia and mental capacity (some of the offences for which they were charged and convicted were also under the Forgery and Counterfeiting Act 1981).[1]

Woman stealing from a terminally ill neighbour. A nurse was found guilty of 55 counts of theft, after stealing thousands of pounds from vulnerable patients at a care home. She stole some £13,000 from the bank accounts of two residents with learning disabilities over a five-year period. She had access to their bank cards. She was also struck off the nursing register by the Nursing and Midwifery Council.[2]

HELP IN THE HOME

Elderly gardener stealing from woman who had suffered a stroke. A woman who had suffered a stroke hired a man to do the gardening. She came to trust him and his partner. He was 77, and his partner, 68 years old. They gained the woman's trust. They then withdrew £2000 from her bank after promising to take care of her bills, tried to change her will and had her £3000 car signed over to them. They were given ten-month jail sentences, suspended for a year. They had to repay the money, were placed under a curfew and fitted with electronic tracking devices.[3]

Neighbourhood watch volunteer stealing life savings of 89-year-old woman. A neighbourhood watch volunteer stole the life savings, £60,000, of an 89-year-old woman, whom he had befriended. He left her with £550. It was used to pay for cocaine, a car and a computer. He had gained her trust because of his position in Home Watch and also as head of a residents' group. He had initially run errands for her. She handed her bank cards to him. He also gained a lasting power of attorney which was registered. In addition, she amended her will, making him executor and sole beneficiary.

However, a social worker became concerned on discovering that he had the keys to the woman's flat and use of her credit cards. He was convicted of both fraud and theft.

1   *R v Bowles (Lewis) and Bowles (Christine)* [2004] EWCA Crim 1608.

2   'Theft shame nurse struck off.' *WalesOnline*, 5 August 2007. Accessed on 8 October 2018 at: www.walesonline.co.uk/news/wales-news/theft-shame-nurse-struck-off-2229884.

3   'UK's oldest tagged couple: pair with a combined age of 145 fleeced vulnerable pensioner who trusted them.' *Daily Mail*, 26 July 2012.

He had previously been well regarded locally and had helped the police tackle the anti-social behaviour of drug addicts. He was sentenced to 28 months in prison.[1]

Housekeeper stealing possessions. The perpetrator stole valuable heirlooms (silver and jewellery) and war memorabilia from elderly and vulnerable clients. She gave them to a dealer who in turn sold them to a pawnbroker. One victim was 86 years old and confined to a wheelchair; another had a degenerative brain condition. She had concealed a previous conviction to secure a housekeeping role with a locum agency. The judge stated that the thefts were cynical, hard-hearted and cruel. She was jailed for 15 months for theft and the dealer for nine (for handling stolen goods and perverting the course of justice).[2]

PEOPLE IN RESPONSIBLE (FINANCIAL) POSITIONS

Head of residents' association stealing £750,000. Over £750,000 was stolen in a theft and conspiracy to steal case involving share certificates, involving the head of a residents' association, a mortgage broker and an unqualified accountant. The victim was an elderly man, in poor health, living near the head of the residents' association. When going into a care home, he entrusted the latter with the keys to his home, who took (on the man's behalf and legitimately) some share certificates to a solicitor (who had power of attorney) for cashing in. However, following that, more shares were sold without the man's knowledge or approval – via a mortgage broker and unqualified accountant. There were also other documents of authority discovered with the man's forged signature. The solicitor discovered the illegal sale of the shares and contacted the police.[3]

Financial adviser stealing millions from vulnerable adults. A financial adviser was convicted of theft, false accounting and forgery. The total amount stolen was some £2 million. His victims included a man with severe learning disabilities, a chronically ill woman and even a member of his own family. He took money he had been given to invest on people's behalf. He

1   Smith, G. 'Neighbourhood Watch volunteer who helped jail drug gang stole £60,000 from pensioner to fund secret cocaine habit.' *Daily Mail*, 25 June 2012.

2   Hills, S. 'Carer jailed for stealing £12,000 of valuable heirlooms and war memorabilia from elderly.' *Daily Mail*, 4 June 2012.

3   *R v Ryan* [2001] EWCA Crim 1956.

also borrowed a client's credit card, before failing to pay back the amount he had 'borrowed'.[1]

Solicitor overcharging amounting to theft. A solicitor (also a coroner) charged 250 per cent more than would have been reasonable from the estates of dead clients. He was found guilty of six counts of theft, amounting to £155,000. Amongst beneficiaries that lost out were the Royal National Lifeboat Institution, the Salvation Army and a cottage hospital in Thirsk.[2]

Bank staff member stealing £2 million from vulnerable customers. A financial adviser working at Lloyd's TSB stole more than £2 million from elderly and vulnerable bank customers, to fund his obsession with exotic birds, including gold macaws at £20,000 a pair and black cockatoos at £20,000 each. He admitted 24 counts of theft and asked for 203 similar offences to be taken into consideration.[3]

Bank manager committing theft. A Barclays Bank manager in Twickenham investigated a £20,000 theft from a customer aged 95, committed by a colleague at the bank. The manager then decided to steal a further £23,000 himself. The manager was convicted of fraud and given a prison sentence of two and a half years.[4]

Bank cashier stealing from 83-year-old customer. A Barclays Bank employee, a cashier, stole £42,000 from an 83-year-old former teacher, now with health problems and confused, by simply transferring money out of his account into other accounts. The theft came to light when a solicitor took charge of the man's affairs, as his mental condition worsened.[5]

HEALTH AND SOCIAL CARE PROFESSIONALS
Social worker stealing from mental health patients. A social worker, in the grip of a loan shark, was convicted of theft, having stolen money from

1   Jenkins, R. 'Financier stole from elderly clients.' *The Times*, 13 September 2006.

2   Norfolk, A. 'Coroner who stole £155,000 from the dead.' *The Times*, 8 February 2003.

3   Barkham, P. 'Fraudster that fluttered inside a suburban banker.' *The Times*, 3 September 2003. Also: McGowan, P. 'Banker stole £2m to buy parrots.' *Evening Standard*, 2 September 2003.

4   'Bank manager investigating colleague's theft from customer aged 95 stole £23,000 himself.' *The Mirror*, 6 September 2011.

5   'Ruthless bank cashier stole thousands from Wood Green pensioner.' *Tottenham & Wood Green Journal*, 7 June 2012.

four mental health patients. She worked in a hospital, obtaining money from patients and pretending to buy things for them. She also stole money from the office lottery scheme. She was sentenced to ten months in prison suspended for two years and ordered to do 150 hours' community service.[1]

Mental health team social worker taking money from patients. A social worker in a mental health team had duties that included looking after the finances of service users. She falsely claimed she bought items for a male patient with £680. She had taken the money on the pretext of buying carpets and a mobile phone for the person. She took money also from a female patient in hospital. The judge referred to her cynical abuse of trust. She would have been sent to prison except for her remorse and her young son.[2] The social worker was also removed from the General Social Care Council's Register.[3]

District nurse stealing from cancer patients. A district nurse in Hereford was convicted of stealing £34,000 from a patient with cancer, whom she was caring for and had befriended. She was sentenced to three years in prison.

Evidence included images on a CCTV camera. This showed her paying money, which she had withdrawn from the victim's account, into her own bank account. She made 119 withdrawals, each consisting of the maximum £300 allowed, amounting to nearly £34,000. This was in addition to a £70,000 gift which the victim had made to her and which she had not declared. She was able to steal the money after obtaining from the victim the code to a safe in which the victim kept her bank card. Police were unable to trace the money; it had been apparently spent.[4]

Nurse using bank cards of care home residents. A nurse was both struck off from the nursing register and sentenced to prison, after she was found guilty of 55 counts of theft. Using the bank cards of a man and woman with learning disabilities, residents at care homes where she worked, she

1   Hunt, K. 'Social worker faces judge after stealing from vulnerable patients.' *Medway Messenger*, 11 July 2008.

2   NHS South Coast Audit's Counter Fraud Investigation Team. *Newsletter*, June 2009.

3   *Buchanan v General Social Care Council*, Conduct Committee, July 2009.

4   Tanner, B. 'Nurse stole £34,000 from cancer patient.' *Worcester News*, 16 March 2012.

stole some £13,000 over a five-year period. She blamed the thefts on the financial pressures following the break-up of a relationship.[1]

Nurse stealing cash card from dying war hero. A nurse (needing to pay her telephone bill) took an 83-year-old, dying patient's cash card from a hospital locker. He had won the Croix de Guerre at the D-Day landings in the Second World War; she was given a suspended three-month jail sentence.[2]

Opportunistic theft by nurse at clinic. A nurse working at a hospital in Leicester stole money from patients while they attended a breast-screening clinic, taking a total of £275 from the handbags of three of them. She was sentenced to 240 hours' community service and also struck off the nursing register.[3]

CARE HOME MANAGERS

Care home manager stealing from people with learning disabilities. A care home manager stole over £14,000 from two residents with learning disabilities, at a care home in Lincolnshire, run by Southern Cross. Instead of using their benefits money to pay for care home fees, she bought goods for herself, including a fridge freezer, clothes, groceries and expensive chocolates.

She was caught out when a colleague checked a bank statement and realised that the listed transactions were nothing to do with the resident. She had also arranged for one resident's benefits to be paid into her account – that resident ended up £3000 in arrears with care home fees. She was convicted of theft and sentenced to one year's imprisonment. She was a trained nurse and previously of good character.[4]

Care home manager stealing from dying woman. A nursing home manager, at Shandon House, Birkdale, stole £2300 from a dying woman, 85 years old with dementia, using the resident's bank card. She spent the money on

1   'Theft shame nurse struck off.' *Icwales*, 5 August 2007. Accessed on 20 August 2007 at: http://icwales.icnetwork.co.uk.

2   'Nurse stole card from dying man.' *The Times*, 3 October 2007.

3   'Patient theft nurse is struck off.' *BBC News*, 17 December 2004. Accessed on 8 October 2018 at: http://news.bbc.co.uk/1/hi/england/leicestershire/4106257.stm.

4   'Care home manager June Anne Walters jailed over "a monstrous breach of trust".' *Stamford Mercury*, 26 August 2011.

lavish meals, cigarettes and clothes. She pleaded guilty on two counts of fraud and was sentenced to nine months in prison.[1]

Cynical disregard for terminally ill residents: raiding of bank account by managing director of care home. A former matron, then the managing director of a care home, admitted 24 specimen counts of theft, false accounting and obtaining property by deception, involving £5515. The total amount of money stolen that might have had to be paid back was in excess of £100,000 – a court order was already in place at the time of conviction freezing an estimated £138,000 of her assets. She had raided the bank accounts of terminally ill residents when she realised that accounting procedures were not as strict as they should have been. The judge referred to her 'cynical disregard' for the families who had relied on her to look after the physical and financial welfare of the residents. She was sentenced to 18 months in prison.[2]

PEOPLE IN PUBLIC POSITIONS

Local councillor, with power of attorney, sentenced for stealing from person with Alzheimer's disease. A 75-year-old councillor was jailed for five years for stealing £154,000 from an elderly Alzheimer's sufferer aged 92, for whom he held power of attorney. He emptied her bank account and spent most of the money on fruit machines and trips to Las Vegas. The judge found gross breach of trust. The theft led to West Berkshire Council losing £76,000 in lost care fees. The perpetrator had been a councillor for 20 years and done work for a number of charities. He had been a friend of the woman but was addicted to gambling.[3]

PAID CARERS

NHS care assistant caught by secret camera in pink teddy bear. A health care assistant attending a 75-year-old leukaemia sufferer stole money in order to go on holiday to Las Vegas. After the family realised that money was going missing, they installed a small surveillance camera, at the suggestion of the woman's granddaughter who was a forensic science graduate. It was placed in the eye of a pink teddy bear in the woman's room and it

---

1   'Birkdale care home boss conned dying patient of savings to dine on steak and wine.' *Liverpool Daily Post*, 6 October 2011.

2   'Jail after theft spree revealed.' *Bromsgrove Advertiser*, 10 August 2006.

3   'Five years for councillor who preyed on dementia sufferer.' *The Oxford Times*, 11 January 2014.

caught on film the care assistant stealing £60. She was convicted and sentenced to six months in prison. The judge referred to the seriousness of the offence, given the age and terminal illness of the victim. The carer worked for Liverpool NHS primary care trust.[1]

Carer stealing from 76-year-old blind woman who treated her 'like a daughter'. A carer (a mother of two children) was treated like a daughter and with absolute trust by a 76-year-old blind woman, for whom she provided care twice a week. In order to obtain bank statements, she had been given the woman's saving account card and PIN – although she had never been asked to withdraw money. The woman regularly paid her late husband's mining pension into the account. In fact, over a 17-month period, about £200 at a time, the carer took over £5000. The thefts came to light when the woman realised she had only £190 left. The carer tried to stop the woman alerting the police. The carer was sentenced to one year's imprisonment.[2]

Ordering bank cards dishonestly. A carer working for a care agency in Winchester took advantage of a 90-year-old client, after the latter had been admitted to hospital. She not only used the woman's bank cards but ordered further bank cards. She stole over £17,000 and was convicted of both theft and fraud and sent to prison, despite being pregnant.

The care company's logged records showed that the carer had been sorting out the woman's finances, something that was of course outside the remit of her responsibilities. The bank paid back the missing money to the woman. The judge commented that such cases were increasing and the elderly had to be protected from 'those like you who succumb to temptation'.[3]

Taping up letter boxes to intercept bank statements. A carer stole £46,000 from a bedridden elderly woman, leaving her only £255. Over a period of two years, she used her debit card to withdraw money from cash machines. She had also taped up the letter box and put a new lock on the outside of the door, so that she could intercept and destroy bank statements. She

1 Hull, L. 'Camera hidden in a teddy bear catches carer stealing £100 from terminally ill pensioner.' *Daily Mail*, 18 August 2008.

2 'Carer is jailed for theft of £5000.' *Northern Echo*, 6 November 2004.

3 Hendy, A. 'Jail for carer who stole £17k from pensioner.' *Daily Echo*, 8 April 2012.

used the money on her wedding, expensive trips and concerts – and to set herself up as a hostess selling lingerie and sex aids. She was sentenced to prison for nine months.[1]

Care home worker using bank card of 92-year-old. A 21-year-old care home worker was jailed for eight months after stealing £6400 from the bank accounts of two care home residents, aged 92 years and 71 years. Her duties had included taking the residents out shopping and she had dishonestly used their bank cards.[2]

Care worker theft precipitates second stroke for care home resident. A 49-year-old care worker at a nursing home was sentenced to four months in prison, after stealing more than £7000 from a 71-year-old resident – who, having suffered a paralysing stroke 30 years before, suffered another on learning of the theft. The carer had stolen the money after the resident had given her cash card and PIN number, so the carer could do the shopping for her.[3]

Carer stealing from bank account of care home resident. A care worker pleaded stress following the break-up of his marriage, after he was convicted of 13 offences of stealing money from a resident with learning disabilities at a care home. The carer had been entrusted with managing the resident's financial affairs and had direct access to his bank account.[4]

Care home assistant taking money from wallets and purses. A nursing assistant at a care home was caught pilfering cash from residents, after a suspicious manager installed a CCTV camera. He would take money from their wallets and purses. A marked note was placed in the wallet of one of the residents to entrap the perpetrator. The amounts taken were relatively small; the total was £120. He was given a suspended prison sentence.[5]

---

1   'Carer steals bedridden gran's £46k life savings to start an Ann Summers business.' *Daily Mirror*, 1 September 2011.

2   'Care home worker jailed for theft.' *Craven Herald*, 20 December 2007.

3   'Law says "sorry" after theft leaves Mary £2000 in debt – and crook gets only 4 months.' *Liverpool Echo*, 18 February 2008.

4   'Carer convicted on theft charges.' *Swindon Advertiser*, 15 June 2001.

5   'Carer caught on CCTV stealing from residents.' *Bristol Evening Post*, 21 December 2011.

Domiciliary carer stealing from wallet. A home carer was caught on CCTV rifling through the wallet of her client, a man with multiple sclerosis whom a team of carers supported in his own home. Suspicions had arisen previously, and police had installed secret cameras. She was sentenced to four months' imprisonment suspended for a year.[1]

Sacked carer returns to known clients to commit theft. A carer had been sacked by a domiciliary care agency, but visited clients nonetheless, pretending she was still working for the agency. She had stolen money from clients' wallets, amounting to several hundred pounds.[2]

Former carer steals from three elderly women. The offences involved theft of £20, £90 and £40 or thereabouts respectively from elderly ladies in their own homes. They were aged 87, 69 and 85. Each had got to know the perpetrator when the latter had been engaged as a carer for them. She gained admission to their homes because she knew them in that capacity. After the first offence she had been arrested; she committed the other two offences while on bail.

The carer appealed against a sentence of nine months' imprisonment, partly on the basis that they were only 'economic crimes' and involved small sums of money. The Court of Appeal rejected the appeal, pointing out that such crimes against the elderly and vulnerable struck at such a person's sense of security, increasing their vulnerability and rendering them more wary of others. Such crimes bore some characteristics of physical offences against the person.[3]

Carer stealing £135,000 from bed-bound woman leaving her with £21.70. A bed-bound elderly woman inherited £180,000 from her husband. This was the cue for her carer to persuade the victim to trust her with her bank account details and bank cards. By writing out cheques and using the cards, she stole some £135,000 to pay for luxuries for her family. The victim was left with £21.70 in her bank accounts. When the police became

1   Alder, A. 'Suspended sentence for money-grabbing carer.' *Bedfordshire on Sunday*, 6 October 2007.

2   'Care worker jailed for theft.' *Dorset Echo*, 12 December 2001.

3   *R v Cutts* [2006] EWCA Crim 2208.

involved, the carer sent highly threatening letters to the victim. A mother of four, she was sentenced to five years in prison for theft and fraud.[1]

Carers targeting and selling goods of elderly people. A carer targeted an elderly couple, stealing not only £7000 using a bank card (£300 a week withdrawn) but also paintings worth £3000 which she sold on eBay. She was sentenced to 18 months in prison. The husband died shortly after; he had trusted her completely, and the family believed the stress contributed to his death.[2]

Live-in carer abuses trust to arrange fake burglary in home of elderly couple. A live-in carer obtained a job to help a retired major-general and war veteran care for his wife. Within nine months, the carer had looked up the value of the antiques in the house and staged a fake burglary. Paintings, objets d'art, jewellery, furniture, silverware and many sentimental items were taken. The wife died two months later, and the husband sold the house. The judge referred to the appalling breach of trust by the carer; she was convicted of conspiracy to steal and conspiracy to obtain property by deception.[3]

Loan of money turning into theft. A woman with multiple sclerosis employed a carer; there was genuine affection between the two women. However, first of all the woman loaned £7500 to the carer; the carer then stole over £3000, which she was able to do because she had access to the woman's money (through credit cards) for doing the shopping. The carer was convicted of theft and sentenced to nine months' imprisonment.[4]

Stealing rings from fingers. A nursing home carer was convicted and imprisoned for stealing four rings from two bed-bound residents, aged 91 and 98, in a care home in Oldham. She sold them to obtain money to send back to her mother in the Philippines who had a kidney infection and also

1   Salkeld, L. 'Thieving carer took £135,000 from widow, 83, blew it on holidays and threatened to burn down her house.' *Daily Mail*, 1 March 2012.

2   Hemsley, A. 'Heartless care worker stole from elderly Winchelsea couple.' *Hastings and St Leonards Observer*, 22 August 2008.

3   'Carer stole antiques from war veteran.' *Daily Telegraph*, 28 November 2007.

4   'Carer jailed for nine months after stealing cash.' *Oxford Mail*, 14 January 2006.

looked after the carer's daughter. Police recovered three of the four rings from pawnbrokers.[1]

BEFRIENDING

Befriending in care home. A woman befriended an elderly lady living in a care home. Twice she forged the lady's signature in letters to the bank, obtaining a total of £11,000. She was sentenced to four months in prison.[2]

Systematic befriending and theft. The befriending and subsequent theft may be systematic, as in the following case involving a heroin addict, who also involved her daughter. The judge referred to the perpetrator as an evil and calculating woman who was a danger to old and infirm people.

Pushing into house and offering sexual services. Sexual assault and burglary: a man aged 58 was at his home address on 20 July 2010 when the defendant rang the doorbell. She pushed past him and entered his flat. Once in the living room, the defendant offered the victim sexual services and sexually assaulted him. The defendant then picked up the victim's wallet and removed £80 before leaving.

Picking up a vulnerable victim at the supermarket. Theft: a man, aged 80, was walking to his local supermarket on 21 August 2010 when he was approached by the defendant and her daughter. They engaged him in conversation. They walked with him to the supermarket and said they would wait outside for him. The victim left by another exit and went home. Whilst in the communal passageway inside the block of flats where he resides, the two women came to the front door and were allowed entry by another resident. The defendant and her daughter then took him by the arms and walked him to his front door, which he opened. They all entered his flat. Whilst the defendant spoke to him in the living room, the daughter took £110 from his coat pocket in the hallway.

Selling mobility scooter and keeping money. Theft: a man, aged 59, had been a friend of the defendant for over a year and had allowed her to stay at his home address from time to time. On one occasion, the defendant had suggested that she could sell a mobility scooter that the victim had inherited from his brother. The victim agreed as he needed the money, but

---

1   'Jailed, carer who stole rings from women aged 91 and 98 from home in Oldham.' *Manchester Evening News*, 6 September 2011.

2   *R v Clarke* [2003] EWCA Crim 1764.

the defendant then sold the scooter and, apart from £5, never gave him any of the proceeds.

Collecting pension and using money of victim. A man, age unknown but who was elderly and with mobility problems, was an acquaintance of the defendant. Knowing that one of his friends was unable to go to the Post Office the next day to collect his pension, she visited him and offered to go instead. He gave her his bank card and PIN, and on returning she told him that she had used the money to pay a debt she owed to a money lender and would pay it back to him the following Friday. No money was ever paid back. £117 was removed from his account.[1]

Controlling and directing an elderly confused man to withdraw money from the building society. An elderly confused man living alone in Birmingham had several building society accounts with significant balances. He came under the control or direction of the perpetrator, who would take him to the building society. Acting ostensibly on the man's behalf, and pretending to be his grandson, the perpetrator would ask for a cheque to be made out to the man and specify the amount and the payee (always one of the perpetrator's associates – one of whom was ordered to pay £27,000 compensation to the victim). He was convicted of theft and sentenced to four years in prison.[2]

Threats to kill

It is a criminal offence to threaten to kill any person, intending that the person to whom the threat is made will fear the threat would be carried out. This is under section 16 of the Offences Against the Person Act 1861.

Transparency, see *Concealment*

---

1   *R v Law* [2012] EWCA Crim 40.

2   *R v Kelly* [1997] Court of Appeal, 14 November 1997.

U

Unconscionable bargains

Unconscionable bargains are part of the civil law of equity. An unconscionable bargain is about setting aside a purchase, made from 'a poor and ignorant man' at a considerable undervalue, unless the purchaser has acted in a manner which is fair, just and reasonable. It is different from undue influence because the parties could be completely unknown to each other, so there need not be some sort of prior relationship. The bargain must be unconscionable in that it involves objectionable terms which have been imposed in a morally reprehensible manner, such that the conscience of the person benefiting is affected.

Put another way, the doctrine applies if the first person suffers from certain kinds of disability or disadvantage; the bargain is oppressive; the other party has acted unconscionably in knowingly taking advantage of the first person. The second person would then have to satisfy a court that the bargain was fair, just and reasonable.[1]

In terms of this book – regarding the protection of vulnerable adults – key points include the following:

- **Protection of the vulnerable:** the doctrines of undue influence and unconscionable bargain share a common root: equity's concern to protect the vulnerable from economic harm.[2]

- **Gifts:** the doctrine would appear to apply to gifts, as well as bargains.

---

1   *Evans v Lloyd* [2013] EWHC 1725 (Ch). Quoting: McGhee, J. *Snell's Equity*. 32nd edition. London: Sweet and Maxwell, 2010, para 8.063.

2   *Lawrence v Poorah* [2008] UKPC 21, para 20.

- **Impaired consent or other vulnerability:** whether there is impaired consent or some other vulnerability, it is the character of the transaction as unconscionable rather than its particular legal characterisation that is important.[1]

Undue influence

Undue influence is a general concept arising in more than one legal context. Significantly for adult safeguarding is that it sometimes provides legal ground for intervention of one sort or another in relation to a vulnerable adult – even if that adult has the mental capacity to make the decision in question which is resulting in, for example, a form of exploitation.

One specific context concerns gifts and wills, for which there are special rules in the law of equity, set out below. Another context, in which the term is more loosely used, relates to the exercise by the High Court of its inherent jurisdiction when, despite a person's possessing mental capacity, the court may in some circumstances, such as undue influence, make an order to protect a vulnerable adult: see *Inherent jurisdiction*. A third can arise indirectly in relation to criminal law. For example, under the Theft Act 1968, one of the required elements, dishonesty, can relate to exploitation of a vulnerable adult, albeit with mental capacity to give away his or her money or property.[2]

UNDUE INFLUENCE: LAW OF EQUITY. Undue influence, specifically in relation to gifts and wills, is part of the law of equity. It developed originally, centuries ago, in the Court of Chancery as a counter-balance to the common law. Like the common law, its rules are not to be found in legislation but have been developed by the courts themselves. It is essentially meant to be about fairness.

The doctrine relies on a person having mental capacity to have made the gift or the will. Otherwise, it is arguable that the person cannot be unduly influenced.[3] A crucial question in undue influence cases is whether the person

---

1   *Evans v Lloyd* [2013] EWHC 1725 (Ch), para 52.

2   *R v Hinks* [2001] 2 AC 241 (House of Lords).

3   *Tchilingirian v Ouzounian* [2003] EWHC 1220 (Ch).

has independently exercised free will after full and informed consideration.[1] There are two types of undue influence, express and presumed: see below.

UNDUE INFLUENCE: SAFEGUARDING. In relation to the safeguarding of adults, the doctrine of undue influence is most commonly used by private individuals – usually but not always family members – to challenge the validity of lifetime gifts or wills.

However, sometimes local authorities take an interest, particularly in the case of lifetime gifts. They are fearful about who will pay the care fees of the person, who has gifted their money elsewhere – as in a legal case involving a woman who had given her house on trust to her son to avoid paying care home fees: the local authority argued the son had unduly influenced his mother.[2] The case was settled out of court. Indeed, the courts have noted a social trend involving transfers of property, sometimes dubious.

> **Brother unduly influenced by his sister.** A vulnerable 70-year-old man – described as physically and mentally disadvantaged all his life – lost his house to the undue influence of his sister. The Court of Appeal referred to a developing social trend of people living longer, the rising value of residential property and inheritors who, waiting longer, become anxious that old age and infirmity will lead to high care costs, as well as inheritance tax on death. Which means that the elderly and infirm are increasingly vulnerable to suggestion and to possible undue influence.[3]

UNDUE INFLUENCE: EXPRESS. Express undue influence applies to wills only, not to gifts. Evidence is required of how exactly the influence was exercised in terms of overt, improper pressure or coercion.[4]

---

1   *Pesticcio v Huet* [2004] EWCA Civ 372.

2   Woolcock, N. 'Widow, 91, sued over nursing home fees.' *Daily Telegraph*, 1 October 2002.

3   *Pesticcio v Huet* [2004] EWCA Civ 372.

4   *Royal Bank of Scotland v Etridge (No. 2)* [2001] UKHL 44.

> **Express undue influence: elderly woman and heavily drinking son.** A woman changed her will and left everything to her heavily drinking son, with whom she lived and of whom she was afraid, whilst disinheriting her other son. The former had taken his mother back to her own home from a nursing home despite medical advice to the contrary; had deterred his brother and wife from visiting, even if there was no formal ban; and had tried to push his brother out of the house on the day that the will was executed. She was frail and vulnerable and frightened of him. The judge found express undue influence and set aside the will.[1]

On the other hand, not all influence is undue, even if there is strong persuasion or family pressure.

> **Express undue influence: influence but not undue.** An elderly woman with early-onset Alzheimer's disease was persuaded by her daughter to change her will largely in favour of the daughter. The daughter had written to her mother about how disappointed she had been over the previous will, and how she had expected her mother would leave the estate to her only surviving child and not split it also with her grandchildren (children of the mother's deceased son). The judge pointed out that not all influence is undue influence, not even influence comprising strong persuasion or heavy family pressure. Furthermore, the judge found no evidence that the daughter had repeatedly pestered or badgered her mother.[2]

UNDUE INFLUENCE: PRESUMED. Presumed undue influence can generally be of wider application, not least because evidence of how any undue influence was exercised is not required, due to the presumption that is applied. The following represents key ingredients of presumed undue influence.

- **Unfair advantage.** One person takes unfair advantage of another where – as a result of a relationship between them – the first person has gained influence or ascendancy over the second, without any overt acts of persuasion.

---

1   *Edwards v Edwards* [2007] EWHC 119 (Chancery).

2   *Scammell v Scammell* [2008] EWHC 1100 (Ch).

- **Trust and confidence assumed.** Some relationships (e.g. parent and child, guardian and ward, trustee and beneficiary, solicitor and client, medical adviser and patient) will give rise to an irrebuttable presumption that a relationship of trust and confidence existed. The reposing of trust and confidence does not have to be proved.

- **Trust and confidence.** Such relationships are infinitely various; a key question is whether the one person has posed sufficient trust and confidence in the other.

- **Reliance, dependence, vulnerability.** It is not just a matter of trust and confidence; reliance, dependence, vulnerability, ascendancy, domination and control are all relevant terms.

- **Transaction calling for an explanation.** Undue influence must be proved by the person alleging it; however, a relationship of trust and confidence, coupled with a transaction that 'calls for an explanation', will normally be enough to discharge this burden of proof.

- **Shift of evidential burden.** The evidential burden then shifts to the other person to counter the inference of undue influence – that is, to rebut the presumption.

- **Degree of disadvantage.** Even within the special class of relationships (assuming trust and confidence), not every gift or transaction will be assumed to have been down to undue influence (otherwise Christmas presents or the payment of reasonable professional fees would be caught); it should be only where the transaction calls for an explanation. The greater the disadvantage to the vulnerable person, the greater the explanation called for.

- **Independent advice.** The receipt of independent advice is a relevant consideration but will not necessarily show that a decision was free from undue influence.[1]

The spectrum of relationships, giving rise to trust and confidence, is therefore wide – in addition to those relationships where the trust and confidence is assumed (e.g. professional and client). For example, aunt and nephew,[2]

---

1   *Bank of Scotland v Etridge (No. 2)* [2001] UKHL 44.

2   *Randall v Randall* [2004] EWHC 2258 (Ch).

elderly man and great-nephew,[1] husband and wife,[2] paid carer and elderly man,[3] elderly man and neighbour,[4] woman in her sixties and alternative group (therapy, art, spiritual).[5]

> **Trust and confidence: depletion of an elderly man's estate by a secretary-companion.** An elderly man's wife died in 1958. Shortly after she died, he employed a woman as secretary-companion. In the last five years before he died in 1964, he made gifts to her of nearly £28,000; his estate had been reduced from £40,000 to £9500. He was elderly, weak, a little vacant, courteous, introspective, depressed at times – a gentle old man. The companion became increasingly entrusted with handling his financial and business affairs. He agreed to sell his house and to move to another house the companion had always wished to reside in, where he was recorded as the 'lodger'. He received no independent legal advice. The judge found a relationship of trust and confidence, and a presumption of undue influence which the companion failed to rebut.[6]

Reprehensible or blameworthy conduct is not required. This is because the courts are looking to see whether a gift was, or was not, made through the independent exercise of free will after full and informed consideration. If not, the transaction may be set aside on public policy grounds, even if there is no evidence of wrongdoing.[7]

> **Taken under the wing of a neighbour, giving his money away: wrongdoing does not need to be proved for undue influence.** A 72-year-old retired teacher and bachelor was living alone. He had become physically dependent on others because of limited mobility. His neighbour, whom he had met at a supermarket when he was holding on to railings and was in distress,

---

1   *Cheese v Thomas* [1994] 1 All ER 35 (Court of Appeal).

2   *Bank of Scotland v Etridge (No. 2)* [2001] UKHL 44.

3   *Re Craig* [1970] 2 All ER 390 (High Court).

4   *Hammond v Osborne* [2002] EWCA Civ 885.

5   *Nel v Kean* [2003] EWHC 190 (QB).

6   *Re Craig* [1970] 2 All ER 390 (High Court).

7   *Pesticcio v Huet* [2004] EWCA Civ 372.

'took him under her wing'. Following a fall, hospital admission and then discharge, he became more dependent.

She 'volunteered to the care authorities' to be responsible for giving him two meals a day. At the suggestion of the care coordinator, he then signed a third-party mandate, authorising her to draw on his current account. After further falls and hospital admission, he said he wanted to make a gift to her of certain investments; these amounted to nearly £300,000, 91 per cent of his liquid assets.

There was a relationship of trust and confidence; the gift was very large. These facts gave rise to a presumption of undue influence. It was for the woman to rebut this. Given that the man had received no advice, independent or otherwise, the presumption was not rebutted, and undue influence was made out.

The court also made the point that this would be so even if the woman's conduct had been 'unimpeachable' and there had been nothing 'sinister' in it. This was because the court would interfere not on the ground that any wrongful act had in fact been committed by the donee but on the ground of public policy. Such public policy required that it be established affirmatively that the donor's trust and confidence had not been betrayed or abused.[1]

Unwise decisions, see *Mental capacity*

---

1   *Hammond v Osborne* [2002] EWCA Civ 885.

V

Visiting bans, see *Contact with people lacking capacity*

Vulnerability

The term 'vulnerable adult' was used previously by the Department of Health in adult protection guidance issued in 2000 for local authorities and other organisations.[1] The Department of Health and the Law Commission subsequently took the questionable view that the term was patronising and disempowering, applied a permanent stigma and suggested that the adult was at fault.[2] Consequently, it is to be found neither in the Care Act 2014 – which put local authorities at the heart of adult protection – or in the accompanying statutory guidance. This is arguably unhelpful, given common use of the term by the courts and its inclusion in other legislation.

VULNERABILITY: USE BY THE COURTS. The courts continue to find the term a useful and essential concept, to frame the exercise of their inherent jurisdiction – an essential tool, sometimes, in adult protection,[3] which local

---

1   Department of Health. *No secrets: guidance on developing and implementing multi-agency policies and procedures to protect vulnerable adults from abuse*. London: DH, 2000.

2   Department of Health. *Safeguarding adults: a consultation on the review of the 'No secrets' guidance*. London: DH, 2008, p.49. And: Law Commission. *Adult social care. Law Com. No. 326*. London: The Stationery Office, 2011, para 9.21.

3   *Amina Al-Jeffery v Mohammed Al-Jeffery (Vulnerable adult; British citizen)* [2016] EWHC 2151 (Fam).

authorities regularly ask the courts to use.[1] This, despite the fact that under the social care statute (the Care Act), the term has now effectively been ostracised.

VULNERABILITY: IN OTHER LEGISLATION. The term 'vulnerable' features in other legislation, including the Housing Act 1996 (housing priorities), Police Act 1997 (criminal record certificates), Safeguarding Vulnerable Groups Act 2006 (Disclosure and Barring Service) and Domestic Violence, Crime and Victims Act 2004 (allowing or causing death or serious harm to vulnerable adult). And 'vulnerable witness' is a term used in the Youth Justice and Criminal Evidence Act 1999.

Consideration by the courts of the term 'vulnerable' in the 2004 Act has proved extremely useful in enabling prosecution for causing or allowing lethal violence in a domestic setting – despite the victim not having any prior disability, illness, impairment or indeed care and support needs.[2]

VULNERABILITY: MENTAL CAPACITY AND PROTECTION. In adult safeguarding, protecting an adult who is vulnerable but who has the mental capacity to make decisions considered to be unwise may not be straightforward – even if the consequence of their decision is highly detrimental to themselves, whether through exploitation or self-neglect, for example. Relevant considerations will include, depending on the circumstances:

- mental capacity and rule about unwise decisions: see *Mental capacity*

- legal powers to enter a dwelling: see *Power to enter*

- use of the High Court's inherent jurisdiction: see *Inherent jurisdiction*

- criminal law offences which do not require a lack of mental capacity to be shown – for example, theft, some sexual offences, wilful neglect or ill-treatment: see variously *Theft*; *Sexual offences*; *Wilful neglect or ill-treatment*.

---

1   *A Local Authority v DL* [2010] EWHC 2675 (Fam).

2   *R v Khan* [2009] EWCA Crim 2. And: *R v Uddin* [2017] EWCA 1072 (Crim).

Vulnerable adults, see *Vulnerability*

Vulnerable witnesses, see *Witnesses*

W

Well-being

Section 1 of the Care Act states that whatever a local authority does under the Care Act, in respect of an individual person, it has a general duty to promote the well-being of that individual. The definition of well-being includes protection from abuse and neglect.

This duty is all encompassing but at the same time vague.[1] Section 1 sits in isolation and by itself has no application or teeth. It takes its hue from other sections of the Act. Whatever a local authority does under other sections of the Act – such as prevention, advice provision, assessment, care and support planning, safeguarding, etc. – only then does the duty to promote well-being gain traction. Furthermore, the word 'general' tends to weaken a duty (e.g. as in section 17 of the Children Act 1989).[2] And the word 'promote' is not, for example, as strong as 'achieve'.

All that said, the definition of well-being has more specific application when eligibility decisions, about people's entitlement to have their needs for care and support met, are made under the Act. This is because the third and final eligibility question is whether there is a significant impact on the person's well-being – including in relation to abuse or neglect.

---

1   *R (SG) v Haringey LBC* [2015] EWHC 2579 (Admin).

2   *R (G) v Barnet London Borough Council* [2003] UKHL 57, House of Lords.

WELL-BEING: DEFINITION. Well-being is defined as follows (emphasis added):

- personal dignity

- physical and mental health and emotional well-being

- *protection from abuse and neglect*

- control by the individual over day-to-day life (including over the care and support provided to the adult and the way in which it is provided)

- participation in work, education, training or recreation

- social and economic well-being

- domestic, family and personal relationships

- suitability of living accommodation

- the adult's contribution to society.

WELL-BEING: WHO IS BEST PLACED TO JUDGE IT IN RELATION TO SAFEGUARDING? Under section 1 of the Care Act, local authorities must have regard to the importance of beginning with the assumption that the person themselves is best placed to judge their own well-being. The rather contorted wording means that local authorities have discretion to take a different view as to a person's well-being in some cases – and to take into account countervailing considerations, especially since section 1 states also that local authorities must have regard to the need to protect people from abuse and neglect.

> **Going against the person's view of their own well-being in a safeguarding case.** A local authority suspected a direct payment support organisation of fraud. It stipulated, therefore, that service users (direct payment recipients) must use a different organisation for support. They did not want to do this and put forward the argument that they were best placed to judge their own well-being. The court took account of this principle but held, overall, that it was outweighed by the need to protect them from abuse or neglect.[1]

---

1   *R (Collins) v Nottinghamshire County Council, Direct Payments Service* [2016] EWHC 996 (Admin).

Whistleblowing

The raising of concerns – popularly called whistleblowing – by employees is a potentially significant way in which abuse or neglect can be countered. It is in effect an informal, irregular, unreliable but potentially all-important form of 'regulation'. It is covered below under the following headings:

- Whistleblowing: overview

- Whistleblowing: legal protection for those who raise concerns

- Whistleblowing: NHS context

- Whistleblowing: employers' strategies of victimisation

- Whistleblowing: retaliatory referrals by employers

- Whistleblowing: Employment Tribunal examples

- Whistleblowing: summary of incentives not to raise concerns

- Whistleblowing: gagging clauses.

WHISTLEBLOWING: OVERVIEW. In health and social care, there are, overall, various legal issues, as well as practical.

- **Professional duty to raise concerns?** Health and social care professionals all have a duty to raise and, if necessary, escalate concerns, under codes of conduct issued by three, key regulatory bodies. See *General Medical Council*; *Nursing and Midwifery Council*; *Health and Care Professions Council*.

- **Non-professionals working in health and social care are not bound by such codes.** However, contracts of employment are likely to state that employees must follow the organisation's safeguarding and whistleblowing policies. In theory at least, a failure to raise concerns could amount therefore to a breach of the employment contract. For instance, NHS standard terms and conditions for employees make it a contractual duty to raise concerns.[1]

- **Regulatory body imposing sanctions for not raising concerns?** If a health or social care professional does not raise concerns, then in principle

---

1   NHS Staff Council. *NHS terms and conditions of service handbook*. London: NHSSC, 2018, para 21.1.

this is a breach of the code of conduct, and the regulatory body could take action against the professional. See *General Medical Council; Nursing and Midwifery Council; Health and Care Professions Council*.

- **Regulatory body penalising professionals for raising concerns?** Employers sometimes make 'retaliatory referrals' to professional bodies if an employee has raised unwelcome concerns. In such cases, the regulatory body is at risk of being duped by the employer and taking action, wrongly, against the employee.[1]

- **Legal protection for whistleblowers.** If employees have serious concerns about matters at work, they are in principle protected if, in certain circumstances, they raise concerns. This protection comes under the Employment Rights Act 1996, as amended by the Public Interest Disclosure Act 1998.

- **Protection in practice for whistleblowers.** There is a significant amount of evidence that those who raise concerns in health and social care are not sufficiently protected. This evidence suggests that the NHS in particular has a tendency to treat some who raise concerns with particular ruthlessness.

WHISTLEBLOWING: LEGAL PROTECTION FOR THOSE WHO RAISE CONCERNS. The Employment Rights Act 1996, amended by the Public Interest Disclosure Act 1998, provides in principle explicit legal protection for workers who raise concerns. In summary, the Act provides for a hierarchy of reasonable actions for the worker to take.

- **Protected disclosure.** For a worker to be protected from detriment, at the hands of an employer retaliating to the disclosure, there needs to be a 'protected disclosure'. A protected disclosure has to (a) be a 'qualifying' disclosure and (b) comply with various requirements relating to whom the disclosure was made.

- **Qualifying disclosure.** A qualifying disclosure means the 'disclosure of information which, in the reasonable belief of the worker making the disclosure', is in the public interest and tends to show one of the following:

---

1   Hooper, A. *The handling by the General Medical Council of cases involving whistleblowers*. London: General Medical Council, 2015.

» a criminal offence has been committed, is being committed or is likely to be committed

» somebody has failed to comply with a legal obligation

» a miscarriage of justice has occurred, is occurring or is likely to occur

» the health or safety of any individual has been, is being or is likely to be endangered

» the environment has been, is being or is likely to be damaged, or

» that information relevant to the above has been, is being or is likely to be deliberately concealed.[1]

- **Good faith.** The disclosure does not necessarily have to be made in good faith if it otherwise meets the requirements. However, if the disclosure is protected but not made in good faith, then a tribunal can reduce a financial award by up to 25 per cent.[2]

- **Public interest.** First, in short, the worker must have a reasonable belief that the disclosure was in the public interest. Second, there may be more than one reasonable view as to whether a particular disclosure was in the public interest.

  Third, the necessary belief is simply that the disclosure is in the public interest; particular reasons why the worker believes this are not of the essence. It might even be that the particular reasons believed by the worker did not reasonably justify that belief, but that it was nonetheless reasonable, for different reasons which he or she had not articulated at the time. All that matters is that the (subjective) belief was (objectively) reasonable.

  Fourth, the genuine (and reasonable) belief, that the disclosure was in the public interest, does not have to be the predominant motive.[3]

- **Disclosure to the employer.** Protection arises if the disclosure is made to the employer, or to somebody else, when the failure relates to the conduct of that other person, or where legal responsibility is held by that other person rather

---

1   Employment Rights Act 1998, s.43B.

2   Employment Rights Act 1998, s.49.

3   *Chesterton Global Ltd v Nurmohamed* [2017] EWCA Civ 979, paras 27–30.

than the employer; likewise, if the disclosure is made to somebody else in accordance with the employer's own procedure.[1]

- **Legal advice.** Disclosures made in the course of seeking legal advice are protected.[2]

- **Disclosure to regulatory body.** Protection is given to a worker who makes a qualifying disclosure (a) in good faith; (b) to a person 'prescribed by the Secretary of State'; and (c) where she or he reasonably believes that the failure is relevant to the prescribed functions of that person – and that the information and allegation are substantially true.[3]

- **Regulatory bodies.** The prescribed organisations, to whom disclosure might be made, include regulatory bodies such as the Healthcare Commission, Care Quality Commission, Health and Safety Executive, local authorities with health and safety enforcement functions, the Information Commissioner.[4]

- **Wider disclosure: basic conditions.** Beyond the employer or a relevant regulatory body comes wider disclosure – for instance, to the press. Protection arises if (a) a qualifying disclosure is made in the reasonable belief that the information disclosed, and any allegation made, are substantially true; (b) the disclosure is not made for personal gain; and (c) in all the circumstances of the case, it is reasonable to make the disclosure.[5]

- **Wider disclosure: further conditions.** In addition, the worker must (a) reasonably believe that he or she would be subjected to detriment if the disclosure were made instead, either to the employer or to the relevant regulatory body; or (b) that, if there is no relevant (regulatory) body, evidence about the failure will be concealed if disclosure is made to the employer; or (c) the worker had previously made a disclosure of substantially the same information to the employer or to a regulatory body.[6]

- **Wider disclosure: reasonableness.** In determining the reasonableness of wider disclosure, the following must be had regard to: (a) to whom the

---

1   Employment Rights Act 1998, s.43C.

2   Employment Rights Act 1998, s.43D.

3   Employment Rights Act 1998, s.43F.

4   SI 1999/1549. Public Interest Disclosure (Prescribed Persons) Order 1999.

5   Employment Rights Act 1998, s.43G.

6   Employment Rights Act 1998, s.43G.

disclosure is made, (b) the seriousness of the issue and whether it is continuing or likely to occur in the future, (c) whether the disclosure breaches a confidentiality duty owed by the employer to somebody else, (d) if disclosure was made previously to the employer or a regulatory body, what action was taken, or might reasonably be expected to have been taken, in disclosing to the employer, (e) whether the worker complied with a relevant procedure of the employer.[1]

- **Disclosure of exceptionally serious failure.** Protection applies to a disclosure in the following circumstances: (a) the worker reasonably believes that the information disclosed, and any allegation contained in it, are substantially true, (b) the disclosure is not for personal gain, (c) the relevant failure is of an exceptionally serious nature, and (d) in all the circumstances of the case, it is reasonable to make the disclosure (in determining this last point, the identity of the person to whom the information was disclosed must be had particular regard to).[2]

WHISTLEBLOWING: NHS CONTEXT. The importance of legal protection for whistleblowers applies across all sectors in health and social care, as do the adverse reactions of employers. However, there is a particular problem within the NHS. In 2015, Sir Robert Francis reported to the Secretary of State for Health as follows, quoted in some detail, given its import for, and perceptions of, the NHS.

Sir Robert Francis: treatment of NHS whistleblowers undermining a humane and patient-centred service.

I would have liked to report to you that there was in fact no problem with the treatment of 'whistleblowers' and their concerns. Unfortunately, this is far from the case. I was not asked to come to judgments about individual cases, but the evidence received by the Review has confirmed to my complete satisfaction that there is a serious issue within the NHS. It requires urgent attention if staff are to play their full part in maintaining a safe and effective service for patients.

---

1   Employment Rights Act 1998, s.43G.

2   Employment Rights Act 1998, s.43H.

In fact, there was near unanimity among staff, managers, regulators and leaders who assisted the Review that action needs to be taken. The number of people who wrote to the Review who reported victimisation or fear of speaking up has no place in a well-run, humane and patient centred service. In our trust survey, over 30% of those who raised a concern felt unsafe afterwards. Of those who had not raised a concern, 18% expressed a lack of trust in the system as a reason, and 15% blamed fear of victimisation. This is unacceptable. Each time someone is deterred from speaking up, an opportunity to improve patient safety is missed.

The effect of the experiences has in some cases been truly shocking. We heard all too frequently of jobs being lost, but also of serious psychological damage, even to the extent of suicidal depression. In some, sad, cases, it is clear that the toll of continual battles has been to consume lives and cause dedicated people to behave out of character. Just as patients whose complaints are ignored can become mistrustful of all, even those trying to help them, staff who have been badly treated can become isolated, and disadvantaged in their ability to obtain appropriate alternative employment. In short, lives can be ruined by poor handling of staff who have raised concerns.

The consistency in the stories told us by students and trainees about the detriments they could face was alarming. These were mainly young people at the start of their careers who genuinely believed they should raise issues for the benefit of patients. Of none of them could it be said that they had axes to grind. Their overwhelming sense was one of bemusement that anyone would want to treat them badly for doing the right thing. Yet we heard far too many stories from them of being bullied, and of their assessments suddenly becoming negative.[1]

Some changes have been made by central government in the last few years. For instance, the NHS is now under a legal obligation of candour to tell patients openly when things have gone wrong.[2] NHS contractual terms and

---

1   Francis, R. *Freedom to Speak Up: an independent review into creating an open and honest reporting culture in the NHS*. London: Department of Health, 2015, pp.4–5.

2   Health and Social Care Act (Regulated Activities) Regulations 2014, r.20.

conditions state that staff have both a right and duty to report concerns.[1] The NHS Constitution refers to the duty staff have to raise genuine concerns.[2] NHS Trusts now appoint Freedom to Speak Up Guardians, supported by the National Guardian's Office, an independent, non-statutory body.[3]

Nonetheless, the intractable nature of the problem identified within the NHS suggests that a cultural change is required, since the obstacles to openness encompass both the personal and the political, as noted by Sir Robert Francis:

Open reporting culture: personal and political obstacles.

The NHS is not alone in facing the challenge of how to encourage an open and honest reporting culture. It is however unique in a number of ways. It has a very high public and political profile. It is immensely complex. It is heavily regulated, and whilst the system consists of many theoretically autonomous decision-making units, the NHS as a whole can in effect act as a monopoly when it comes to excluding staff from employment. Further, the political significance of almost everything the system does means that there is often intense pressure to emphasise the positive achievements of the service, sometimes at the expense of admitting its problems.[4]

Legal protections will not suffice in such a culture and are in any case no guarantee that even a genuine whistleblower will not suffer detriment.[5]

1 NHS Staff Council. *NHS terms and conditions of service handbook.* London: NHSSC, 2018, para 21.1.

2 Department of Health. *NHS Constitution.* London: DH, 2015, p.15.

3 Department of Health. *Learning not blaming: the government response to the Freedom to Speak Up consultation, the Public Administration Select Committee report 'Investigating Clinical Incidents in the NHS', and the Morecambe Bay Investigation.* London: DH, 2015.

4 Francis, R. *Freedom to Speak Up: an independent review into creating an open and honest reporting culture in the NHS.* London: Department of Health, 2015, pp.4–5.

5 For an analysis of legal protections, and their weaknesses, in the NHS context, see: Lewis, J. *et al. Whistleblowing: law and practice.* Oxford: Oxford University Press, 2017, chapter 12.

WHISTLEBLOWING: EMPLOYERS' STRATEGIES OF VICTIMISATION.

Reactions, of some employers in some circumstances, to whistleblowers were analysed in the context of the NHS in an article shortlisted for the Martha Gellhorn Prize for Journalism. The article cited Dr Peter Gooderham who had put his finger on the following:

- **Subtle sanctions:** sanctions, such as reducing secretarial help, cutting teaching budgets, blocking appointments and merit awards, adverse but informal briefing against the whistleblower.

- **Reprisals:** inflict reprisals by searching out misdemeanours, real or imagined.

- **Mental illness:** allege that the whistleblower is mentally ill.

- **Concealment:** refuse to disclose incriminating documents, making use of the Data Protection and Freedom of Information Acts.

- **Threats to other workers:** threaten colleagues who support the whistleblower.

- **Threats to whistleblower:** threaten the whistleblower.

- **Accuse the whistleblower:** accuse the whistleblower of raising concerns belatedly.

- **Deny it is whistleblowing:** claim the matter is an employment one and that public interest disclosure protection does not apply.

- **Gag the whistleblower:** pay off and gag the whistleblower.

- **Retaliatory referral to regulatory, professional body:** concoct complaints about the whistleblower to his or her professional, regulatory body.

- **Prohibitive costs of tribunal case:** saddle the whistleblower with crippling Employment Tribunal costs, even if the whistleblower wins.

- **Sham investigation:** arrange sham, internal investigations.

- **Rigged external investigation:** hold an external investigation, but recruit the panel, control the terms of reference, hold it in secret, and keep much of the final report back from the public.

- **Take refuge in belated, historical public inquiry:** gain succour from public inquiries which come too late and are typically dismissed as dealing only with historical matters.[1]

Examples include:

NHS Trust chairman, raising concerns about patient safety in Lincolnshire: bullied and resigned. Allegations were made by David Bowles, chairman of the United Lincolnshire Hospitals NHS Trust, who resigned in 2009. He cited bullying by the East Midlands Strategic Health Authority (SHA) in relation to the hitting of targets. He was supported by other non-executive members of the Trust's board, in not being prepared to guarantee the hitting of non-urgent targets, at a time when emergency admissions were very high. He wanted to know from the chief executive of the NHS (David Nicholson) 'whether he thinks it is fair and reasonable to ask for that guarantee... I would like to know whether this is a renegade SHA or do ministers agree with unconditional guarantees on non-urgent targets.' His stance was that, were he to offer such a guarantee, this would be at the expense of patient safety.[2]

David Nicholson (later tainted by the scandal at Mid Staffordshire NHS Foundation Trust) then set up an inquiry, chaired by an independent consultant, a former SHA chief executive. The report's findings exonerated the East Midlands SHA of harassment and bullying. However, it did note that: 'Given the increasing pressures on NHS leadership and management that will result from the impact of the economic downturn on public services there is the possibility of firm performance management being interpreted as bullying or harassment.' It refers also to the importance of good relationships and collaborative behaviour.[3]

Whistleblower and member of the Care Quality Commission's board: mental health questioned. After Kay Sheldon had spoken out at the Mid

---

1 Hammond, P. and Bousfield, A. 'Shoot the messenger: how NHS whistleblowers are silenced and sacked.' *Private Eye*, 22 July 2011.

2 Moore, A. 'Resigning trust chair calls for David Nicholson to investigate "SHA pressure".' *Health Service Journal*, 27 July 2009.

3 Department of Health. *Review of allegations of bullying and harassment of the United Lincolnshire Hospitals NHS Trust by the East Midlands Strategic Health Authority: summary of findings, 28th October 2009.* London: DH, 2009.

Staffordshire public inquiry about serious problems at the Commission, relating to patient safety, the chairman of the Commission (Dame Jo Williams) resorted to a typical tactic within the NHS: she questioned the whistleblower's mental health. The chairman asked the Secretary of State to dismiss the whistleblower; the Secretary of State refused. The chairman subsequently apologised to the Health Select Committee and resigned from the Commission.[1]

Heart surgeon, Bristol Royal Infirmary, children's heart surgery: hounded out of medicine in this country. In 1999, by the time Dr (later Professor) Steve Bolsin was giving evidence to the Public Inquiry into children's heart surgery in Bristol, he had been reportedly hounded out of medicine in this country and was working in Australia.[2] He had whistleblown and his concerns were fully vindicated, but the Public Inquiry noted that he had not been heeded and that the 'difficulties he encountered reveal both the territorial loyalties and boundaries within the culture of medicine and of the NHS, and also the realities of power and influence'.[3]

Intelligent and committed paediatrician predicting child protection failure at Great Ormond Street Hospital: vilified and excluded. Dr Kim Holt, together with three other consultants, raised concerns in 2006 with her NHS Trust employer, about cuts to paediatric services at St Anne's Hospital in Haringey and about the implications for child protection. Unfortunately, her concerns were later vindicated; by the time 'Baby P' died in 2007, and a locum paediatrician at the hospital, inexperienced in child protection, had missed life-threatening injuries, there were no experienced consultant paediatricians working there.

After she had taken leave in 2006, partly related to excessive workload, the Great Ormond Street Hospital for Children NHS Trust apparently obstructed her return to work, deeming her unfit. Between 2007 and 2010,

1   Cassidy, S. 'Former chief "sorry" for attack on whistleblower: Dame Jo Williams tells MPs she was wrong to cast doubt on board member's mental health.' *The Independent*, 12 September 2012.

2   'Bolsin: the Bristol whistle blower.' *BBC News*, 22 November 1999. Accessed on 20 September 2010 at: http://news.bbc.co.uk/1/hi/health/532006.stm.

3   Kennedy, I. (Chair). *Learning from Bristol: the report of the Public Inquiry into children's heart surgery at the Bristol Royal Infirmary 1984–1995*. Cm 5207(1). London: The Stationery Office, 2001, p.161.

it seems that though she was fit to return to work, she was not supported to return to her post and remained on authorised, paid leave.[1]

One view is that Dr Holt was 'subjected to the rage of a managerial machine that tolerates no dissent'.[2]

Another was that of a report commissioned by NHS London, which stated that nobody was to blame. The report went only so far as to suggest that the Trust might have handled things better, but that it had not targeted Dr Holt. It did, tellingly, concede, however, that it disagreed with the lead clinician for the Trust; he had maintained that increased waiting times through excessive workload, lack of follow-up appointments and the unavailability of notes did not affect patient safety.[3] The report noted that Dr Holt was highly intelligent and committed.[4]

A social services example, in Wirral, involved a manager who raised whistleblowing concerns over a long period. He was finally vindicated when the council eventually and reluctantly commissioned an independent investigation which was made public (with significant details, including names of people and of organisations, omitted) – but only because he had been so persistent. Yet by 2008, when he approached the *Wirral Globe*, he claimed that he had been bullied out of his job and given a £40,000 payoff.

Financial and other abuse in supported living, and serious overcharging of vulnerable adults by the local authority. The scandal revolved around Supporting People services for people with learning disabilities. Concerns had included: (a) men with baseball bats turning up at a home run by an independent, unregistered 'service provider' and demanding money, involving an individual who had previously been investigated by the police for the laundering of drug money; (b) an allegation that a member of a 'service provider' staff had a conviction for assault with a deadly weapon;

1 Rose, D. 'Doctor who raised alarm at Baby P clinic sues Great Ormond St. to get her job back.' *The Times*, 20 September 2010.

2 Campbell, B. 'The persecution of NHS whistle blowers.' *The Guardian*, 11 December 2009.

3 Widdowson, D. and Persaud, N. *Report on an investigation into allegations made by Dr. Kim Holt, consultant community paediatrician.* London: NHS London, 2009, pp.5, 12, 44.

4 Rose, D. 'Doctor who raised alarm at Baby P clinic sues Great Ormond St. to get her job back.' *The Times*, 20 September 2010.

(c) an allegation of rape made by one of the vulnerable adults; (d) bank accounts being set up in the names of vulnerable adults and their benefits then removed from those accounts without permission.[1]

In addition, its chaotic approach to charging users of services meant that the local authority had eventually to repay 16 residents a total of £243,000 – which had been taken from them in improper charging practices. This was in fact the same amount of money the council paid for the independent review and report.[2] It transpired subsequently in 2012 that this repayment was an underestimate; a further £440,000 had to be repaid, making a total of some £700,000.[3]

WHISTLEBLOWING: RETALIATORY REFERRALS BY EMPLOYERS. One strategy adopted by employers is to refer a whistleblower to a professional regulator. And to link the concern raised with performance management issues about the whistleblower, which, of course, may or may not be justified – a complicating factor for the regulator in responding.[4] The General Medical Council accordingly felt impelled to commission a report from a retired judge. The latter confirmed the existence of the problem and made several recommendations to guard against it.[5] The following cases speak for themselves and do not require commentary on just how disturbing they are.

Hospital cardiologist raising patient safety concerns: 200 concerns referred to General Medical Council – awarded £1.2 million compensation. A cardiologist, Dr Raj Mattu, blew the whistle about overcrowding in 2001 after two patients died on a cardiac ward in Coventry. He claimed there was a dangerous 'five in four' practice at Walsgrave Hospital – meaning a

---

1   'Demand for sackings follows review that has shamed Wirral Council.' *Wirral Globe*, 12 January 2012.

2   'Whistleblower Martin Morton offered his job back by town hall chief.' *Wirral Globe*, 15 April 2011.

3   Murphy, L. 'Wirral Council to pay back an extra £440,000 to disabled people it overcharged.' *Liverpool Echo*, 22 August 2012.

4   Francis, R. *Freedom to Speak Up: an independent review into creating an open and honest reporting culture in the NHS*. London: Department of Health, 2015, p.63.

5   Hooper, A. *The handling by the General Medical Council of cases involving whistleblowers*. London: General Medical Council, 2015.

fifth bed in bays designed to take only four. He sounded the alarm along with five colleagues. They were concerned that the system was leaving vital services such as oxygen, suction and electricity harder to reach in the event of an emergency. Prior to this, a patient had suffered a heart attack and died after staff could not reach life-saving equipment in time.

He was sacked by University Hospitals Coventry and Warwickshire NHS Trust in 2010, but an Employment Tribunal later ruled he had been unfairly dismissed. The Trust spent millions of pounds pursuing around 200 allegations, over time, against him, which later proved to be false. The General Medical Council investigated these over many years (2002–2013) before rejecting the allegations. Management also spent thousands of pounds of public money hiring private investigators to look into his affairs and employed a public relations agency to deal with potentially damaging media fallout. He was eventually awarded £1.2 million by an Employment Tribunal.[1]

Nurse reported to police and Nursing and Midwifery Council for raising concerns at care home. A nurse matron raised concerns about care when interim managers were appointed at Warberries Nursing Home in Torquay. Despite having the overwhelming support of staff, she was referred to the police, the local authority, the health authority and the Nursing and Midwifery Council (NMC). She was cleared by the police of any wrongdoing and awarded £70,000 at an Employment Tribunal for wrongful dismissal. The NMC, however, found her guilty of misconduct and she faced being struck off – until a High Court judge found that the NMC's findings were perverse, contradicted by the records or based on evidence that was demonstrably unreliable or untruthful. Ultimately, the only finding that stood up was her trying to get test results directly from the laboratory instead of waiting for the doctor – simply to speed up the process, for the benefit of residents.[2]

---

1   Donnelly, L. 'NHS faces £20m bill for sacked doctor Raj Mattu.' *Daily Telegraph*, 4 May 2014. And: Martin, M. 'Vindicated: sacked whistleblower backed by the Mail wins £1.2m payout after NHS spent £10m trying to crush him after he exposed shocking failings in care.' *Daily Mail*, 4 February 2016.

2   'Whistleblowing: she's been framed.' *Private Eye*, May 2016, p.38. See also: *Suddock v Nursing and Midwifery Council* [2015] EWHC 3612 (Admin).

Hospital occupational therapist victimised for talking to a local authority Health Scrutiny Committee. An occupational therapist, Charlotte Monro, had worked for 26 years at Whipps Cross Hospital. In 2009, she had won an award for outstanding service. When cuts were proposed to reduce services for stroke patients, she opposed them. She was invited by the local council's Health Scrutiny Committee to give evidence. For this, she was subjected to disciplinary action, charged with bringing the Trust into disrepute by providing 'inaccurate information' and eventually dismissed for serious misconduct. The Trust recognised the flimsiness of this ground, so instead trawled back into her past and discovered a conviction for assaulting police and minor convictions dating back to protests back in the 1970s – dating back 35–44 years before. This became the ground for her dismissal. She was also referred to her regulatory body, but it found no grounds for action against her.

Eventually, she was reinstated following the resignations of the Trust's chief executive, chair, finance director and nursing director. The Trust had also been placed in special measures following a finding by the Care Quality Commission of a poor culture and of bullying.[1]

Care home employer victimising care worker by making unwarranted referral to have her barred. A Somerset care worker was employed at the Moorlands care home in 2008. The employer sacked the care worker. She went to an Employment Tribunal and won; he then referred her to the Independent Safeguarding Authority (ISA), to try to get her banned from working in the care sector. A further tribunal found 'that the giving of the anonymous information and then the formal referral were malicious and an attempt to get back at the claimant with the respondent believing that it would never come to light that it was him because of data protection'. The care worker succeeded in gaining further damages for this ill-founded disclosure to the ISA.[2]

NHS hospital doctor: discriminated against, victimised; referred to GMC by way of retaliation. This was not a whistleblowing case but illustrates the

---

1 Lintern, S. 'Barts reinstates whistleblower after claims about stroke care concerns.' *Nursing Times*, 1 April 2015. And: Norman, Z. 'Charlotte Monro says her treatment reflects growing climate of intimidation at Barts Trust.' *Epping Forest Guardian*, 8 January 2014.

2 'Somerset care home worker wins further damages.' *BBC News*, 30 May 2012. Accessed on 13 August 2012 at: www.bbc.co.uk/news/uk-england-somerset-18264272.

nature of retaliatory referrals. Ewa Michalak began employment as a doctor with the Mid Yorkshire Hospitals NHS Trust in April 2002. She remained in that employment until she was dismissed in July 2008. Following her dismissal, Dr Michalak brought an unfair dismissal claim against the Trust in the Employment Tribunal. The tribunal found that her dismissal had been unfair and contaminated by sex and race discrimination and victimisation – apparently on the basis of her being Polish in origin and having been the first consultant physician at the hospital to have taken maternity leave. Dr Michalak received a compensation award (£4.5 million) and a public apology from the Trust.

Before the Tribunal had issued its determination, the Trust had reported her to the General Medical Council (the GMC) in relation to her conduct, so that the question of whether she should continue to be registered as a medical practitioner could be considered. The Trust later accepted that there had not been proper grounds on which to refer her to the GMC. She remained registered as a medical practitioner. However, the GMC had begun fitness to practise proceedings. She claimed that the GMC, too, had discriminated against her and she sought to take an Employment Tribunal case against the GMC as well.[1]

Junior hospital: investigated by General Medical Council for speaking out. In 2000, a junior doctor, Dr Rita Pal, decided to raise issues with the GMC and the press about what she considered to be neglectful treatment of elderly patients on Ward 87 at the City General Hospital in Stoke-on-Trent, North Staffordshire. She had originally raised these matters within the hospital in 1998. Her concerns included lack of basic equipment such as drip sets, lack of support for junior doctors, lack of basic care for patients, inappropriate use of 'do not resuscitate' instructions and gross staffing shortages.[2]

Internal report backs up whistleblower's concerns. An internal report produced in 2001 for the NHS Trust found a substantial core of Dr Pal's concerns justified. Failings within the hospital identified by this investigation

1   *Michalak v General Medical Council* [2017] UKSC 71. See also: Booth, R. 'Doctor is awarded £4.5m compensation for workplace discrimination trauma.' *The Guardian*, 16 December 2011.

2   See Marsh, P. 'Doctor quit nightmare of the ward; people put their trust in hospitals and that trust is sometimes being abused.' *Birmingham Post*, 18 February 2000. Also: *North Staffordshire NHS Trust Ward 87: the evidence*. Accessed on 20 October 2010 at: http://sites.google.com/site/ward87whistleblower/home.

related to, for example, patient care, nursing, monitoring, care plans, adequate equipment, induction, supervision, staffing levels and allocation of patients to appropriate wards. There was also an inappropriate response to Dr Pal's concerns; the report noted that although other medical and nursing staff were worried, only Dr Pal spoke up. This seemed to be because either they had become accepting of what was happening or they felt unable to raise their concerns.[1]

Whistleblower's mental stability and fitness to practise question by General Medical Council. By 2003, she discovered that the General Medical Council was investigating her, rather than her allegations, and was questioning her mental stability and fitness to practise. She eventually took it to court, alleging breaches of data protection law, human rights breaches and defamation. The Council attempted to have the case dismissed early, by arguing that summary judgment should be given in its favour. The judge refused, holding that a defamation case could succeed. Before the case went to full hearing, the Council settled out of court.[2]

Court refers to the General Medical Council's approach as symptomatic of a totalitarian regime such as Stalin's Russia. During the course of this hearing, the judge likened the GMC's reaction to that of a totalitarian state:

> For myself I don't really see why somebody complaining about the behaviour of doctors or the GMC, if that is what they are doing, why that should raise a question about their mental stability, unless anybody who wishes to criticise 'the party' is automatically showing themselves to be mentally unstable because they don't agree with the point of view put forward on behalf of the GMC or the party...
> It is like a totalitarian regime: anybody who criticises it is said to be prima facie mentally ill – what used to happen in Russia.[3]

Care home employer victimising whistleblowing nurse with referral to Nursing and Midwifery Council. When a nurse alerted the police to the standard of care in a care home, an adult protection investigation was

---

1   North Staffordshire Hospital NHS Trust. *Report of the extended investigation into the allegations made by Dr R. Pal in November 1998. June 2001, 4th Draft*, 2010. Accessed on 20 October 2010 at: http://sites.google.com/site/ward87whistleblower/home.

2   Wells, T. 'Pay-out victory for doc.' *Sunday Mercury*, 2 October 2005. See also: *Dr Rita Pal v General Medical Council* [2004] EWHC 1485 (QB).

3   Transcript, day 2: *Dr Rita Pal v General Medical Council* [2004] EWHC 1485 (QB).

launched. The Commission for Social Care Inspection visited the home and produced a confidential report. The nurse used the Freedom of Information Act 2000 to bring about its publication. It noted, amongst other things, faeces on beds in empty rooms, unkempt residents, broken showers and toilets, pressure sores covered in faeces and emaciation – and the fact that the inspectors were shocked. The nurse was reported by the home to the Nursing and Midwifery Council for aggression towards a resident, but the hearing went in his favour.[1]

Undercover exposure of systemic poor hospital care: whistleblowing nurse struck off. A nurse called Margaret Haywood participated in a BBC Panorama programme about care at the Royal Sussex Hospital. Undercover filming took place. It revealed dreadful care for which Sussex University Hospitals NHS Trust apologised, admitting to serious lapses in the quality of care.[2]

Poor care and neglect. Patients were not helped to the toilet and nurses were filmed eating patients' food.[3] The programme showed a woman literally gasping with thirst, cancer patients not receiving their pain relief medication in time and crying out in pain, a patient waiting two hours to be helped to the toilet, a nurse speaking harshly to a patient who had called for help, people not getting help with food and drink (including a blind woman), fluid and food and weight charts not being kept, missing care plans, medication not being given, a low-grade albeit experienced nurse being left in charge of a ward, and people wearing split back gowns for ease of nursing and so losing dignity.[4]

Whistleblowing nurse struck off. The nurse received no thanks. The Nursing and Midwifery Council (NMC) struck her off the nursing register. This was for potential breach of patient confidentiality (though patient faces were 'pixelled' out) that occurred in the filming of the programme,

---

1   'Act used to show "shocking" care.' *Nursing Standard*, 13 April 2005.

2   Rose, D. '"Whistleblower" nurse Margaret Haywood struck off over Panorama film.' *The Times*, 17 April 2009.

3   'Whistle blower charges dropped.' *BBC News*, 27 November 2008. Accessed on 8 October 2018 at: http://news.bbc.co.uk/1/hi/programmes/panorama/7752691.stm.

4   'Margaret Haywood interview.' *BBC News*, 20 July 2005. Accessed on 8 October 2018 at: http://news.bbc.co.uk/1/hi/programmes/panorama/4701521.stm. Also: 'Interview with Peter Coles.' *BBC News*, 20 July 2005. Accessed on 8 October 2018 at: http://news.bbc.co.uk/1/hi/programmes/panorama/4701921.stm.

although no patients or relatives complained about this. In fact, they had been complaining, previously and without success, about something else: the poor care being provided. The Council stated that what she had done was a serious breach of the professional code and fundamentally incompatible with being a nurse. She had filmed elderly, vulnerable patients in the last stages of their lives who could not meaningfully give consent 'in circumstances where their dignity was most compromised'.[1]

Nurse wins 'nurse of the year' award, and NMC backs down in legal proceedings. Within a month, a petition in support of the nurse, launched by the Royal College of Nursing, attracted 40,000 signatures.[2] Later that year she won the Nursing Standard's 'nurse of the year' award.[3] In October 2009, the High Court overturned her striking off; she received a one-year caution instead.[4]

WHISTLEBLOWING: EMPLOYMENT TRIBUNAL EXAMPLES. Theoretical protection does not stop employers victimising whistleblowers in the real world. Workers who raise their concerns may have to resort to an Employment Tribunal in order to gain compensation for being sacked. However, even if they win the case, it might still be financially ruinous, so victories may be Pyrrhic. For example, one hospital consultant won his case to the tune of £17,500 in damages but faced legal costs of many tens of thousands of pounds.[5]

In the following Employment Tribunal case, wider disclosure in the form of a satirical letter was protected. It was about the atrocious standards of care suffered by elderly hospital patients at Christmas time. It concerned the following letter, published by *The Journal* newspaper in 2000, submitted by a highly qualified ward manager at Wansbeck Hospital.

---

1   Plunkett, J. 'Nurse who secretly filmed for Panorama is struck off the Register.' *The Guardian*, 16 April 2009.

2   Laurance, J. '40,000 names on petition for sacked NHS whistle blower.' *The Independent*, 11 May 2009.

3   'Whistleblowing nurse Margaret Haywood wins patient award.' *Nursingtimes.net*, 10 November 2009. Accessed on 8 October 2018 at: www.nursingtimes.net/news/whistleblowing/whistleblowing-nurse-margaret-haywood-wins-patient-award/5008374.article.

4   Smith, L. 'High Court reinstates nurse who exposed neglect.' *The Independent*, 13 October 2009.

5   Owens, N. 'Doctor suspended for warning against cuts faces £190k legal bill after clearing his name.' *Daily Mirror*, 10 October 2010.

A Christmas letter to the Prime Minister about poor, sickly old patients: protected disclosure.

So, Prime Minister, Mr Health Secretary and NHS Management Executive, as you return bleary-eyed from your Christmas break (no doubt well rested and well fed) spare a thought for the poor, sickly old patient lying hurting and exhausted on an NHS trolley...hang on a minute, we can't let patients lie around on trolleys, that would muck up the waiting time statistics. Quick, shove her into any bed you can find. What? We haven't got any beds. Well MAKE SOME. How about shoving those patients from the Elderly Ward into that old shed at the back – the one with the crib and baby in it? Yes, I know it's the Obs. and Gynae. Ward. They'll be fine there, even if they don't get any physiotherapy and the staff there haven't a clue about caring for elderly people. The old gerries won't complain; half of them are deaf and demented anyway. Tomorrow we can move them somewhere else – the laundry perhaps – with a bit of luck some of them might catch pneumonia there and create a few more beds. Happy New Year by the way. That new patient doesn't look too well, does she? No, poor old sod. Good job she's got the NHS to fall back on.[1]

His employer, Northumbria Healthcare NHS Trust, took both a dim view and disciplinary action; consequently, he went to an Employment Tribunal in 2001 and won.

Protected, wider disclosure. The manager had been disciplined and issued with a final written warning that he had acted in an unprofessional and totally unacceptable manner. The Employment Tribunal reached the conclusion that it was a protected disclosure; he had a reasonable belief that it was substantially true, it was not made for personal gain, and he had previously made a disclosure of substantially the same information to

---

1   *Kay v Northumbria Healthcare NHS Trust.* Employment Tribunal case no. 6405617/00, 29 November 2001 (Newcastle upon Tyne). From: Bowers, J. *et al. Whistleblowing: law and practice.* Oxford: Oxford University Press, 2007, pp.575–577.

his employer. He was not aware of any other route by which he could raise the matter. The Tribunal found in the ward manager's favour.[1]

The Trust commented that 'at all times, [it] had acted in the best interests of patients'. The Royal College of Nursing's regional officer's understanding was a little different, noting that staff were frightened to say anything, knowing that failure to toe the party line meant that they were finished.[2]

Other examples are:

NHS chief executive: victimised and sacked for insisting that the law be adhered to. The chief executive, John Watkinson, of Royal Cornwall Hospital NHS Trust, won an Employment Tribunal case. The tribunal ruled that he had been dismissed from his post by the Trust board because of pressure placed on the Trust from the strategic health authority. The chief executive and chairman of the SHA refused to give evidence at the Tribunal. But it appears that the SHA was irritated that he had insisted on a public consultation exercise – as, in fact, the law demanded – before local cancer services were removed. The Tribunal ruled that his dismissal flew in the face of fairness. The new Secretary of State for Health promptly ordered an inquiry.[3]

Hospital consultant, Queen Elizabeth Hospital, Woolwich: bullying and harassment. In 2010, a hospital consultant, Dr Ramon Niekrash, won damages in an Employment Tribunal case, for the bullying and harassment he suffered from his employer. He had criticised the Queen Elizabeth Hospital in Woolwich for reducing the number of specialist nurses and closing a specialist urology ward, both of which he argued were detrimental to patients. The hospital responded by excluding him from the hospital and suspending him.

---

1   *Kay v Northumbria Healthcare NHS Trust.* Employment Tribunal case no. 6405617/00, 29 November 2001 (Newcastle upon Tyne).

2   'Trust action to silence whistleblower nurse seen as sign of culture "uncomfortable with debate".' *Health Service Journal*, 6 December 2001.

3   Lakhani, N. 'Top-level review ordered into sacking of whistleblower.' *Independent on Sunday*, 16 May 2010.

The judge noted that there was a clear nexus between the consultant's actions and political and financial stipulations made by the Department of Health:

> What is immediately apparent is that there has been a tension between the professional desire of the claimant and his consultant colleagues to provide a good quality urology service for the patients and the requirement of management to reduce or limit costs and also comply with varying targets laid down by the Department of Health from time to time.[1]

Dr Antoinette Geoghegan: treated with contempt, impatience and vitriol. A consultant psychiatrist (who suffered with depression and, later, work-related stress) raised concerns in 2007 about management changes to working practices in her child and adolescent mental health department – at the Northumberland Tyne and Wear NHS Mental Health Trust. She referred to excessive workload, bullying and intimidation, inadequate staff numbers, poor communication and high use of agency workers (thereby putting patients at risk). The raising of these concerns led to subsequent discriminatory treatment.

In 2009, she had intervened after a young girl was, in the consultant's view, prematurely discharged. She was right; the girl was being sexually abused. The NHS Trust raised a 'serious untoward incident' report, not about the premature discharge but instead about the consultant's intervention. The Employment Tribunal later referred to this as 'malicious and capricious', and an example of 'oppressive and unjustified' criticism of her by the Trust.

The consultant then complained that her health was being jeopardised by the way the Trust was treating her. It banned her from patient contact. She became stressed and unfit for work. The Employment Tribunal found that at no time did the Trust show concern or compassion for her welfare; that there was a direct link between her complaints and the discriminatory treatment she suffered; and that she was treated with 'little more than contempt, impatience and vitriol'.[2]

---

1   Verkaik, R. 'Damages win for consultant who criticised cost-cutting.' *The Independent*, 3 February 2010.

2   'Tyne and Wear NHS: trust them.' *Private Eye*, 19 October 2012, p.31.

Sharmila Chowdhury: blew the whistle, subjected to false counter-allegation of fraud and marched off the premises. A radiology manager at a London district general hospital, at Ealing Hospital NHS Trust, alleged that medical colleagues were claiming, wrongly, thousands of pounds of public money every month for patient sessions they were not present at. The doctors and Trust denied this. Having made these allegations, she was subject to an unfounded counter-allegation of fraud, made by a junior colleague whom she had previously reported for breaching safety procedures. She was then marched off the premises.

The NHS Trust spent hundreds of thousands of pounds trying to get rid of her, leaving her depressed, unemployed and without income. She expected to lose her home. She won an Employment Tribunal case; the Tribunal ordered her reinstated – but she was then made redundant, with a severance package to be agreed. However, she had incurred legal costs of £100,000 in bringing the case. She had an unblemished work record of 20 years.[1]

Failures at children's home. When six employees spoke to the press about failures in a children's home, they were sacked – but subsequently were compensated by the council in advance of an Employment Tribunal. The settlement was reportedly in the region of £1 million.[2]

President of the Nepalese Nurses Association UK: sacked for whistleblowing. A nurse, president of the association, was sacked by the owners of a care home. She had raised concerns about abuse of elderly residents by colleagues and poor administration of medicines. For example, one care home resident was allegedly left outside in hot sunshine as a punishment and threatened with having water poured over his head when he refused medication. The nurse subsequently won an Employment Tribunal case, winning £15,000.

The Tribunal noted:

The respondent company had created an environment where there was an atmosphere that was not conducive to complaints being made by staff to the management about the care of residents. On

---

1   Lakhani, N. 'Hung out to dry: scandal of the abandoned NHS whistleblowers.' *The Independent*, 4 July 2012.

2   'Whistleblowers win payout.' *Community Care*, 23 August 2007, p.7.

the contrary...there was an atmosphere where it was difficult, if not impossible, for such allegations to be made without the complainant running some risk of their employment being jeopardised.[1]

Care worker forced out of her job by domiciliary care agency. A carer contacted the Care Quality Commission, concerned about practices by a domiciliary care agency for which she worked. She reported medication running out for a stroke victim, bed sheets unchanged for six weeks (including for an incontinent resident), inadequate diet for a diabetic patient, charges of £10 an hour being levied on patients for a free medication collection service, out-of-date care plans and risk assessments. She claimed she was forced out of her job, through constructive dismissal, went to an Employment Tribunal and won her case. She accused senior staff of lying when they denied that she had reported concerns to them. The Care Quality Commission had subsequently investigated and confirmed her concerns, producing a critical report.[2]

WHISTLEBLOWING: SUMMARY OF INCENTIVES NOT TO RAISE CONCERNS.

In reality, a number of practical reasons hinder the raising of concerns. These can include:

- timidity

- inexperience

- stress

- loyalty to colleagues/friends

- staff becoming so used to a culture of poor care that they no longer recognise it as a concern

- fear that, if the poor care is embedded in the system of work, they themselves may be implicated as well as other staff

- fear of victimisation by management – or by fellow workers

---

1   'Whistleblowing nurse wins £15,000 payout after unfair dismissal.' *Nursing Times*, 6 October 2011.

2   'Justice for Birmingham carer sacked by Care4U for reporting neglect.' *The Midlands Times*, 3 April 2012.

- lack of confidence in management

- fear of loss of job

- lack of confidentiality, anonymity

- belief that nothing will ever change

- explicit demand from managers to cover up or lie.

An example of victimisation by fellow employees was demonstrated in the following case, investigated by the Commission for Health Improvement (CHI).

Student nurses pilloried by colleagues for whistleblowing: North Lakelands. In the late 1990s, at North Lakeland NHS Trust, it took two sets of student whistleblowers – subsequently praised for their bravery – to raise the alarm about what they considered to be the shocking treatment of elderly patients. However, in contrast, the hospital consultant, in charge of the patients who had been abused, denied all knowledge, saying that he had felt he was a stranger on the ward. The CHI expressed itself greatly disturbed at his passive role, compounded by the fact that he was associate medical director of the Trust with joint responsibility for clinical governance.

Whistleblowing nurses intimidated and pilloried. The whistleblowers were subsequently intimidated and pilloried by other staff – and things had only got a little better when an external review, vindicating their concerns, was published. Even then they still experienced hostility.

Regulator not confident that abuse would be reported, or acted on, in future. The CHI referred to 'unprofessional, counter therapeutic and degrading, even cruel, practices' relating to elderly patients. It noted, however, that even during its investigation, following the external review, some staff still failed to recognise that abuse had taken place and that it represented unacceptable practice. The Commission had no confidence that further abuse would be reported or that the Trust would respond to it.[1]

---

1   Commission for Health Improvement. *Investigation into the North Lakeland NHS Trust, November*. London: CHI, 2000, p.1.

Collective whistleblowing – in effect, safety in numbers – would generally reduce the risk of victimisation either by the employer or by colleagues. Anonymous whistleblowing might also sometimes be effective.

Rowan Ward, Manchester: collective support for whistleblower. On Rowan Ward in Manchester, initial concerns, culminating in a Commission for Health Improvement report, relied on whistleblowing. Concerns had grown about the care and abuse of elderly patients suffering from dementia – including potential criminal offences. During a training event, staff had expressed their disquiet. One nurse agreed to use the whistleblowing procedure; other staff later supported the allegations the nurse had made.[1]

Stoke Mandeville, patient deaths: collective whistleblowing via the Royal College of Nursing (RCN) unsuccessful, followed by effective, anonymous whistleblowing to the press. At Stoke Mandeville Hospital, nurses were extremely worried and reported their concerns about infection control and avoidable deaths occurring from *Clostridium difficile*. These were not, however, acted on. The nurses then contacted (three times) the RCN, which took a grievance against the Trust – but even this led to no real or sustained improvement.

Likewise, clinical staff at the hospital, including doctors, were worried about patient movement between wards, failure to isolate patients, number of patients on inappropriate wards and the consequent degree of clinical risk. Many senior staff wrote to the executive team; the response was that nothing would change unless a disaster occurred – which it subsequently did, when nearly 40 patients died, avoidably. The nurses felt professionally compromised and helpless. In the end, Buckinghamshire Hospitals NHS Trust only took action when details of the infection outbreak and deaths were leaked, anonymously, to the national press.[2]

Mid Staffordshire NHS Foundation Trust: dearth of whistleblowing because nothing ever changed. The Mid Staffordshire Independent Inquiry recognised that, amidst the suffering and dying that took place in Stafford Hospital, the whistleblowing procedure was barely used: 'Many

---

1   Commission for Health Improvement. *Investigation into matters arising from care on Rowan Ward, Manchester Mental Health and Social Care Trust, September 2003*. London: CHI, 2003, p.8.

2   Healthcare Commission. *Investigation into outbreaks of* Clostridium difficile *at Stoke Mandeville Hospital, Buckinghamshire Hospitals NHS Trust, July 2006*. London: HC, 2006, p.28.

staff members did raise concerns, individually and collectively, but none experienced a satisfactory response. This discouraged persistent reporting of concerns. In the case of the medical staff, many appear to have been disengaged from the management process.'[1]

Mid Staffordshire NHS Foundation Trust: nurse ordered to lie. One nurse did raise concerns, to little effect, with senior managers in 2007. A woman with a bowel condition had been brought into accident and emergency (A&E) with acute abdominal pain. A junior doctor wished to examine her but was told to get on and discharge her. She waited seven hours for an ambulance to take her home; she died the next day of a perforated bowel. The nurse recounted also how she had been ordered to lie about how long people had waited in the A&E department and how:

> Patients were left for hours, unable to reach the buzzer, shouting for help, medication, soiling themselves because no one would assist them. It was completely horrific... I kept thinking what if that patient was my mother, or my grandmother? The way people were being treated was shocking.[2]

Mid Staffordshire NHS Foundation Trust: threats made against nurse who raised concerns. Helene Donnelly was a nurse who raised concerns about the care at Stafford Hospital. She explained that essentially it was bullying and intimidation and threats about having spoken out. Primarily, there was pressure about the fact that if anybody spoke out, that person's job could be in jeopardy and career restricted. In addition, personal threats were made, including from nurses. People said they knew where she lived and that she should watch her back when she was walking to her car.[3]

---

1 Francis, R. (Chair). *Independent Inquiry into care provided by Mid Staffordshire NHS Foundation Trust January 2005–March 2009*. London: The Stationery Office, pp.186, 281.

2 Donnelly, L. 'Nurse warned about Stafford scandal: a nurse warned managers about the abuse and neglect of patients at Stafford Hospital more than a year before one of the worst scandals in NHS history was publically exposed, it can be revealed.' *Daily Telegraph*, 16 May 2009.

3 'Stafford Hospital whistleblower speaks out about "terrible care".' *ITV News*, 5 February 2013. Accessed on 2 March 2018 at: www.itv.com/news/central/2013-02-05/stafford-hospital-whistleblower-speaks-out-about-terrible-care.

WHISTLEBLOWING: GAGGING CLAUSES. 'Gagging clauses' are sometimes used to suppress disclosures about poor, unsafe and neglectful care. These are imposed sometimes in contracts from the outset, sometimes in agreements made when a whistleblower reaches a settlement with his or her NHS employer. A gagging clause might, for example, state that the practitioner is never, until he or she dies, allowed to talk about the circumstances and reasons for their leaving the Trust's employment.

In some cases, the gagging clause also provides for a 'super gag' which prohibits not just disclosure of any issues of substance, but also disclosure that there is even a gag in place (i.e. it is a gag on a gag). However, in principle at least, no contractual gag would be effective if it seeks to prevent a public interest disclosure.

> **Manipulated NHS patient statistics and gagging clauses.** In 2001, the National Audit Office published a report about the manipulation of waiting list statistics and referred to the inappropriate use of gagging clauses on those managers who subsequently were suspended, retired or resigned, sometimes with compensation payments.[1]
>
> **Care Quality Commission: gagging clauses to silence its own staff.** Ironically, the Care Quality Commission (regulator of standards) has in the past itself been criticised by the House of Commons Public Accounts Committee:
>
> > The Commission has been criticised for being overly concerned with reputation management at the expense of transparency and accountability. Staff leaving the Commission have been made to sign compromise agreements containing confidentiality clauses, tantamount to gagging clauses. This Committee has expressed concern on previous occasions about the use of such clauses.
> >
> > The Department [of Health] confirmed that confidentiality clauses are not in themselves prohibited, but its guidance makes clear that clauses that seek to prevent the disclosure of information in the public interest should not be allowed. We are concerned,

---

1   National Audit Office. *Inappropriate adjustments to NHS waiting lists*. London: NAO, 2001, para 3.

however, that the use of confidentiality clauses makes people reluctant to speak out, even though their whistleblowing rights may be legally protected.[1]

In the following case, a gag and a super gag were imposed to silence an NHS Trust chief executive.

NHS chief executive: sacked for raising patient safety concerns in Lincolnshire and gagged. The chief executive of United Lincolnshire Hospitals NHS Trust, Gary Walker, had, in a two-year tenure, turned around performance, in terms of financial deficits and missed targets. However, by the winter of 2008, he was concerned – like his chairman, David Bowles – about patient safety because of increased accident and emergency admissions. His view was that adhering to targets, which included non-emergency care, would undermine the safety of patients in urgent and emergency need. He was told by the strategic health authority that he had to meet targets, come what may. The SHA then started publicly to cast doubts on governance at the Trust; and Gary Walker was told that if he did not leave, his career would be in ruins. He refused to resign after he had been offered £43,000 to sign a compromise agreement. So he was sacked, on the grounds that he had sworn (used bad language) nine times at meetings over a two-year period.[2]

He then claimed unfair dismissal but dropped this in favour of a severance deal. This involved payment to him of £500,000 but crucially, also, a compromise agreement, whereby he was now not allowed to talk about the reasons for his dismissal or patient safety: a gagging clause. Extraordinarily, other witnesses who would have appeared at the Employment Tribunal, including David Bowles (the former Trust chairman), also received gagging letters as part of the agreement. The Trust described the severance deal as amicable; Mr Walker's supporters said if he had not signed it, he might well have lost his house.[3]

---

1   House of Commons Public Accounts Committee. *The Care Quality Commission: regulating the quality and safety of health and adult social care.* London: The Stationery Office, 2012, p.8.

2   Hammond, P. and Bousfield, A. 'Shoot the messenger: how NHS whistleblowers are silenced and sacked.' *Private Eye*, 22 July 2011.

3   'Ex-NHS chief Gary Walker "being gagged".' *BBC News*, 29 June 2012. Accessed on 8 August 2012 at: www.bbc.co.uk/news/uk-18639088.

Department of Health guidance is clear that gagging clauses in NHS employment contracts and severance agreements, conflicting with the protection afforded by the Public Interest Disclosure Act, are void.[1] However, the guidance seeks to distinguish a (sometimes fine) line between a confidentiality clause and a gagging clause:

- **Gagging or confidentiality clause?** It is not contrary to the Department of Health's policy for confidentiality clauses to be contained in severance agreements. However, employers must consider with their legal advisers whether a confidentiality clause is necessary in the particular circumstances of each case. Further, if it is decided that a clause is appropriate, then its terms should go no further than is necessary to protect the NHS body's legitimate interests.[2]

It is contrary to professional conduct, as laid down by the General Medical Council, for any doctor to sign, or impose, a gagging clause, about patient safety:

- **Gagging: contrary to professional conduct.** 'You must not enter into contracts or agreements with your employing or contracting body that seek to prevent you from or restrict you in raising concerns about patient safety. Contracts or agreements are void if they intend to stop an employee from making a protected disclosure... If you have a management role or responsibility, you must make sure that...you do not try to prevent employees or former employees raising concerns about patient safety – for example, you must not propose or condone contracts or agreements that seek to restrict or remove the contractor's freedom to disclose information relevant to their concerns.'[3]

The National Audit Office has found that despite guidance – stating that payments rewarding failure, inappropriate behaviour or dishonesty should

---

1   HSC 1999/198. *Public Interest Disclosure Act 1998: whistleblowing in the NHS.* London: Department of Health, 1999. Also: HSC 2004/001. *Use of confidentiality and clawback clauses in connection with termination of a contract of employment.* London: Department of Health, 2004, para 10.

2   HSC 2004/001. *Use of confidentiality and clawback clauses in connection with termination of a contract of employment.* London: Department of Health, 2004, para 13.

3   General Medical Council. *Raising and acting on concerns about patient safety.* London: GMC, 2012, paras 8, 22.

not be approved – it nevertheless found cases involving elements of alleged gross misconduct or staff harassment.

> **Patient safety: manager prohibited in agreement from contacting Department of Health, Care Quality Commission, etc.** A manager in a hospital reported concerns about fraudulent behaviour and risks to patient safety arising from the behaviour of his/her colleagues. Another colleague then reported concerns about the manager's own behaviour. The hospital investigated both allegations and, following the hospital's investigation, the manager was dismissed.
>
> A month later, an interim Employment Tribunal ordered the hospital to restore the manager's contract of employment pending a full hearing. However, internal restructuring meant that the manager's post no longer existed. The hospital and the manager negotiated termination of the manager's employment with a settlement agreement, which included a confidentiality clause. The manager was forbidden from contacting the Information Commissioner, the Care Quality Commission, the Audit Commission, NHS London or the Department of Health.[1]

Wilful neglect or ill-treatment

Wilful neglect and ill-treatment constitute two key criminal offences relevant to safeguarding adults. Criminal in nature, they are distinct from the abuse or neglect referred to in the Care Act 2014, which is civil rather than criminal law. Essentially, neglect is an omission (something wasn't done which should have been); ill-treatment a commission (something was done which shouldn't have been).

Both offences require the 'criminal' mind, but this need not come in the form of deliberate intent; a reckless, 'couldn't care less' attitude would be enough. In addition, for the offence to be committed, the omission or commission is sufficient, insofar as it does not need to be proved that the neglect or ill-treatment caused harm.

---

1   National Audit Office. *Confidentiality clauses and special severance payments – follow up investigation.* London: NAO, 2013, Summary and para 2.3.

A bewildering and depressing range of cases and convictions illustrate the application of these two offences; a selection of these cases is summarised below. The offences occur in three different pieces of legislation in which the offences are essentially the same, but the context – in which the offences can be committed – differs. The maximum sentence is five years in prison. The following paragraphs are broken down as follows:

- Wilful neglect or ill-treatment: Mental Health Act 1983

- Wilful neglect or ill-treatment: Mental Capacity Act 2005

- Wilful neglect or ill-treatment: Criminal Justice and Courts Act 2015

- Wilful neglect or ill-treatment: separate offences

- Wilful neglect or ill-treatment: difficulty prosecuting wilful neglect

- Wilful neglect or ill-treatment: different rules in three pieces of legislation

- Wilful neglect or ill-treatment: mental capacity to refuse care

- Wilful neglect or ill-treatment: harm is not required

- Wilful neglect or ill-treatment: objective test, subjective test, recklessness, 'couldn't care less' attitude

- Wilful neglect or ill-treatment: seniority of perpetrator

- Wilful neglect or ill-treatment: informal care

- Wilful neglect or ill-treatment: Mental Health Act 1983 conviction examples

- Wilful neglect or ill-treatment: Mental Capacity Act 2005 conviction examples

- Wilful neglect or ill-treatment: Criminal Justice and Courts Act 2015 conviction examples.

WILFUL NEGLECT OR ILL-TREATMENT: MENTAL HEALTH ACT 1983.
Under section 127 of the Mental Health Act 1983, key points are:

- **Mental disorder.** The victim must have a mental disorder, as defined in section 1 of the Mental Health Act 1983: any disorder or disability of mind.

- **Offence: hospitals or care homes.** It is an offence for employees or managers of a hospital, independent hospital or care home to ill-treat or wilfully neglect a person receiving treatment for mental disorder as an inpatient in that hospital or home; likewise, ill-treatment or wilful neglect, on the premises of which the hospital or home forms a part, of a patient receiving such treatment as an outpatient.

- **Offence: any individual in any setting.** It is also an offence for any individual to ill-treat or to wilfully neglect a mentally disordered patient who is subject to his or her guardianship under the 1983 Act or otherwise in his or her custody or care.

In sum, it seems that the offence can be committed by anybody who (paid or otherwise), not just in a hospital or care home but *in any setting*, is caring for a person with a mental disorder (given the phrase 'or otherwise in his or her custody or care').

WILFUL NEGLECT OR ILL-TREATMENT: MENTAL CAPACITY ACT 2005.

Under section 44 of the Mental Capacity Act 2005, key points are:

- **Any individual in any setting.** It is an offence to wilfully neglect or ill-treat any person who has the care of another person who lacks, or who the first person reasonably believes to lack, capacity. (There is no restriction on the setting, and no requirement that the care be paid.)

- **Deputy or lasting power of attorney.** Similarly, it is an offence for any deputy or person with a lasting power of attorney appointed under the Mental Capacity Act 2005, or any person with an enduring power of attorney as created under previous legislation, to ill-treat or wilfully neglect a person lacking capacity, or reasonably believed by the attorney or deputy to lack capacity.

  In fact, the legislation does not explicitly include the requirement about lack of capacity (or reasonable belief in it), in relation to attorneys (deputies can only be appointed by the Court of Protection if the person lacks capacity). But the Court of Appeal has held that the legislation must be interpreted as including those conditions. Which means that one or the other has to be decided upon by the jury.[1]

---

1   *R v Kurtz (Emma-Jane)* [2018] EWCA Crim 2743, paras 54–59, 68–69.

WILFUL NEGLECT OR ILL-TREATMENT: CRIMINAL JUSTICE AND COURTS ACT 2015. Under sections 20–25 of the Criminal Justice and Courts Act 2015, key points, *in relation to adults* (people aged 18 or over – the Act applies to children as well), are, for care workers:

- **Care worker offences.** It is an offence for a care worker to wilfully neglect or ill-treat a person.

- **Care worker: paid.** A care worker is defined as an individual who, as paid work, provides: (a) health care for an adult or child, other than excluded health care (children's education and childcare settings), or (b) social care for an adult.

- **Supervisors, managers, directors, other senior officers.** The definition of care worker includes an individual who, as paid work, supervises or manages individuals providing such care or is a director or similar officer of an organisation which provides such care.

- **Paid work.** Does not include (a) payment for expenses, (b) a benefit under social security legislation, or (c) a payment made under arrangements under section 2 of the Employment and Training Act 1973 (arrangements to assist people to select, train for, obtain and retain employment).

- **Health care.** Health care is defined as including (a) all forms of health care provided for individuals, including health care relating to physical health or mental health and health care provided for or in connection with the protection or improvement of public health, and (b) procedures that are similar to forms of medical or surgical care but are not provided in connection with a medical condition.

- **Social care.** Is defined as including all forms of personal care and other practical assistance provided for individuals who need such care or assistance by reason of age, illness, disability, pregnancy, childbirth, dependence on alcohol or drugs or any other similar circumstances.

- **Incidental provision of health or social care.** A person providing health or social care does not include 'a person whose provision of such care is merely incidental to the carrying out of other activities by the person'.

In addition, there are separate offences for care providers – in other words, offences of corporate wilful neglect or corporate ill-treatment. Key points, as far as adults go, are:

- **Care providers: corporate offence.** A care provider commits an offence in the following circumstances:

  » an individual who has the care of another individual – by virtue of being part of the care provider's arrangements – ill-treats or wilfully neglects that individual

  » the care provider's activities are managed or organised in a way which amounts to a gross breach of duty of a relevant duty of care owed by the care provider, and

  » in the absence of the breach of the duty of care, the ill-treatment or wilful neglect would not have occurred or would have been less likely to occur.

- **Care provider.** A care provider is defined as a body corporate or unincorporated association which provides or arranges for the provision of (a) health care for an adult or child, other than excluded health care, or (b) social care for an adult.

  Alternatively, a care provider is an individual who provides such care and employs, or has otherwise made arrangements with, other persons to assist him or her in providing such care.

- **Being part of a care provider's arrangements.** An individual is 'part of a care provider's arrangements' where the individual (a) is not the care provider, but (b) provides health care or social care as part of health care or social care provided or arranged for by the care provider.

  This includes where the individual is not the care provider but supervises or manages individuals providing health care or social care – or is a director or similar officer of an organisation which provides health care or social care as described there.

- **Relevant duty of care.** A relevant duty of care means (a) a duty owed under the law of negligence, or (b) a duty that would be owed under the law of negligence but for a provision contained in legislation which provides for liability in place of negligence liability. But all this is limited to a duty owed in connection with providing, or arranging for the provision of, health care or social care.

- **Unlawful conduct or acceptance of risk of harm.** The following rule does not apply: any common law rule that has the effect of (a) preventing a duty of care from being owed by one person to another by reason of the fact that they are jointly engaged in unlawful conduct, or (b) preventing a duty of care being owed to a person by reason of that person's acceptance of a risk of harm.

- **Gross breach of duty of care.** A gross breach means breach of a duty of care by a care provider is 'gross' if the conduct alleged falls far below what can reasonably be expected of the care provider in the circumstances.

- **Direct payments.** Providing or arranging for the provision of health care or social care does not include making direct payments under the Care Act 2014 or the NHS Act 2006.

- **Care provider offence.** A guilty care provider is liable to a fine. In addition, the court may make a remedial order or a publicity order or both.

- **Remedial order.** This can require the provider to remedy (a) the breach, (b) anything the court thinks has resulted from the breach and is connected with the ill-treatment or neglect, or (c) any deficiency in the person's policies, systems or practices of which the relevant breach appears to the court to be an indication.

- **Publicity order.** This can require the provider to publicise, as specified, (a) the fact that the provider has been convicted of the offence, (b) specified particulars of the offence, (c) the amount of any fine imposed, and (d) the terms of any remedial order made.

WILFUL NEGLECT OR ILL-TREATMENT: SEPARATE OFFENCES. The courts have held that ill-treatment and wilful neglect are not the same and should be charged separately.[1] Neglect is essentially about omission (essentially, something that should have been done, but which wasn't), ill-treatment about commission (essentially, something that was done which shouldn't have been). The courts have contrasted the two offences, the one more about omission, the other more about a deliberate course of action.

---

1   *R v Newington* [1990] 91 Cr App R 247.

Distinction between omissions and courses of action. The case involved the owner of a residential home and allegations of assault and ill-treatment. Wilful neglect was a failure to act – typically an omission – when a moral duty demanded it, whereas ill-treatment was a deliberate course of action. The wider backdrop to the charges was described at trial by former members of staff. The owner referred to the older residents as 'babies', the home smelt of urine, there were insufficient staff, the food was inadequate, wet mattresses were never dried out, there were insufficient linen and blankets, residents' clothing was regarded as communal, residents were washed with a common flannel and soap, etc.[1]

The courts have stated about ill-treatment:

Ill-treatment: deliberate conduct, knowing or reckless ill-treatment. Ill-treatment must (a) be deliberate conduct which could be described as such, irrespective of whether it damages or threatens to damage the health of the victim, and (b) involve a guilty mind (*mens rea*), namely an appreciation by the perpetrator either that he or she was inexcusably ill-treating a patient or was reckless as to whether he or she was acting in that way.[2]

Ill-treatment and violence. Violence would not amount to ill-treatment if it was, for example, necessarily used for the reasonable control of a patient, and the accused genuinely believed that in using such conduct she was acting in the best interests of a patient; if the jury accepted that, she would not be guilty of the offence alleged.[3]

WILFUL NEGLECT OR ILL-TREATMENT: DIFFICULTY PROSECUTING WILFUL NEGLECT. It may be more difficult to prove neglect than ill-treatment: 'evidence of ill-treatment is generally less elusive than evidence purporting to establish wilful neglect'.[4]

---

1   *R v Newington* [1990] 91 Cr App R 247.

2   *R v Newington* [1990] 91 Cr App R 247.

3   *R v Newington* [1990] 91 Cr App R 247.

4   *R v Nursing* [2012] EWCA Crim 2521.

Large-scale investigation into wilful neglect results in little action. In 2013, it was revealed that the threshold for prosecution was not reached, for the most part, in a large-scale police operation (Operation Jasmine) about neglect in Welsh care homes. Spanning seven years, it considered over 60 deaths, involved 75 police officers and staff, 4000 statements, 10,500 exhibits – and 12.5 metric tonnes of documents stored in a Pontypool warehouse. It cost £11.6 million, including £500,000 for 11 experts to advise the police. The reasons given by the Crown Prosecution Service (CPS) for not proceeding were insufficient evidence (a) to identify failings or attribute them to individuals and (b) to prove wilfulness.[1] Amongst other things, the CPS referred to the difficulty of proving neglect – such as failure to provide sustenance, hydration and medical attention.[2]

Who is responsible for not doing something (neglect) may typically be more difficult to pinpoint than responsibility for doing something (ill-treatment), even if the neglect itself is clearly evident.

Lack of evidence and of specificity of charging by Crown Prosecution Service lead to collapse of prosecution against eight care home staff. Eight people were charged with wilful neglect at a Bradford care home. They included the manager, care staff and a cleaner. This was in respect of a resident, allegedly whose room was not fit for habitation, who had been left in abject squalor and filth, and who lived in urine-soaked clothes in a room containing a chair covered in dried faeces and a floor so dirty that visitors' feet stuck to it. The resident, who had suffered a stroke, had open sores on his groin and appeared to have lost weight when he was examined after leaving the home.

The trial collapsed, for reasons which included the following. The Crown Prosecution Service had not considered evidence from outside agencies, which they should have obtained but hadn't. Although the photograph showing the state of one of the resident's rooms was accurate, there was

---

1   Hansard. *Operation Jasmine (care home abuse)*. House of Commons, 13 March 2013, Columns 129WH–137WH. London: The Stationery Office. Also: British Broadcasting Corporation. *Transcript of 'File on 4' – 'Elderly care: neglected questions'*. Transmission on BBC Radio 4, Tuesday 4 June 2013. London: BBC.

2   Flynn, M. *In search of accountability: a review of the neglect of older people living in care homes investigated as Operation Jasmine*. Crown Copyright, 2015, p.11.

no evidence that six of the defendants were even on duty on the relevant day. The trial could have proceeded against two of the carers on a narrow issue of neglect on a particular date, but this had never been the basis of the prosecution's case, which instead had tried to prove neglect of the resident over a period of several months.[1]

Even a coroner's finding of neglect contributing to death is not the same as the Crown Prosecution Service attempting a prosecution, let alone securing a conviction.

Coroner finds neglect contributed to deaths of five care home residents: but no prosecution for wilful neglect or manslaughter. A coroner held that 19 residents suffered sub-optimal care and died of natural causes, but five died from natural causes which had been contributed to by neglect. Residents at Orchid View care home, run by Southern Cross, suffered from lack of respect and dignity and there were problems with medication and staffing levels. One resident had died after an overdose of the blood-thinning agent, warfarin, an overdose the manager had tried to cover up by ordering falsification of records. In relation to this death, five people were arrested but never charged on grounds of insufficient evidence. The care home was reported to have a five-star feel about it, but one member of staff referred to it as akin to a car: good from the outside, not so inside.[2]

WILFUL NEGLECT OR ILL-TREATMENT: DIFFERENT RULES IN THREE PIECES OF LEGISLATION. Three pieces of legislation now govern these criminal offences: Mental Health Act 1983 (MHA), Mental Capacity Act 2005 (MCA), Criminal Justice and Courts Act 2015 (CJCA). Whilst the core ingredients of the offences are common, their application in terms of victim and setting differ. Key distinctions are as follows:

---

1   Loweth, J. 'Bradford care home neglect trial collapses.' *Bradford Telegraph and Argus*, 6 May 2016. Also: Halliday, J. 'Care home "wilfully neglected" dementia patient, court hears.' *The Guardian*, 19 April 2016.

2   Press Association. 'Neglect contributes to deaths of five elderly people at care home.' *The Guardian*, 18 October 2013.

- **Mental disorder.** The MHA 1983 requires a person to have a mental disorder. If not, a prosecution under the CJCA 2015 is possible, assuming that the context is paid care, rather than informal.

- **Mental capacity.** The MCA 2005 requires the person to lack mental capacity in relation to the abusive or neglectful care or treatment in question.[1] This must be proved on the balance of probability only, not beyond reasonable doubt which is required for the proof of the criminal offence itself.[2]

  If capacity at the relevant time cannot be proved, then prosecution under the MHA 1983 might still be possible if the person has a condition amounting to a mental disorder (such as dementia or a learning disability). Or simply under the CJCA 2015, if the context is paid care.

  However, if, under the MCA 2005, a person did not in fact lack capacity, but the perpetrator reasonably believed that he or she did lack capacity, then a prosecution could be brought still under the MCA.

- **Setting.** Prosecution under the MHA 1983 or MCA 2005 can be brought irrespective of setting, whereas, under the CJCA 2015, the offence must be committed in relation to the provision of paid care.

WILFUL NEGLECT OR ILL-TREATMENT: MENTAL CAPACITY TO REFUSE CARE. A prosecution under the Mental Capacity Act 2005 requires a lack of capacity to be proved. However, more generally, under all three Acts, if a person has the mental capacity to refuse elements of care, and did so, then proving wilful neglect will not be possible.

> **Genuine belief in a woman's mental capacity to take decisions about care: could not be wilful neglect.** A woman with learning disabilities lived in a care home. When it closed, she went to live with the owners of the care home, occupying a rented annex at the top of the house. She needed care. Her brain functioned at the level of a child between five and nine years old. She did not understand the need to keep her clothes clean and needed encouragement to wash regularly. The prosecution centred on inattention to the woman's personal hygiene, failing to maintain her

---

1   *R v Dunn* [2010] EWCA Crim 2935.

2   *R v Hopkins, R v Priest* [2011] EWCA Crim 1513.

rooms in a clean condition and replace dirty bed linen, failing to administer medication correctly and at the right time, providing food and a balanced diet – ensuring that her personal habits did not create problems with food hygiene.

Wishes and autonomy of individual. The defence was that the woman would sometimes refuse help and that it would have been wrong to override her wishes. The court agreed with the view that it did not follow that a lack of capacity to make financial decisions meant, necessarily, that she lacked capacity to make decisions about her ordinary living arrangements and her personal hygiene. 'Therefore, actions or omissions, or a combination of both, which reflect or are believed to reflect the protected autonomy of the individual needing care do not constitute wilful neglect.'

Genuine belief in capacity and respect for autonomy: committal of offence not possible. This meant that if the defendant genuinely believed that the woman did not lack capacity in relation to care, then the former had no right to interfere. If the jury concluded that the defendant may have been motivated by the wish or sense of obligation to respect the woman's autonomy, then any apparent neglect would not be wilful.[1]

WILFUL NEGLECT OR ILL-TREATMENT: HARM IS NOT REQUIRED.

For the offences of wilful neglect and ill-treatment, the Court of Appeal has confirmed that harm does not have to be proved: 'We note that Section 44 does not require proof of any particular harm or proof of the risk of any particular harm.'[2]

Care worker slapping resident, putting vinegar and excess sugar in tea: no distress or injury but still an offence (ill-treatment). A care home worker was convicted and sentenced to six months in prison, under section 44 of the Mental Capacity Act, for ill-treating two elderly residents who suffered from Alzheimer's disease. She had slapped a wheelchair-bound resident on the back of the head. She had also put vinegar and excess sugar in the tea of another resident.

---

1   *R v Nursing* [2012] EWCA Crim 2521.

2   *R v Hopkins, R v Priest* [2011] EWCA Crim 1513. See also: *R v Patel* [2013] EWCA Crim 965.

> The court weighed up the effect on elderly residents of such treatment, against the implications of conviction and prison for a carer of previous good character:

> > Elderly people have a right to be treated with respect by everyone in the community. When they are ill and living in residential homes, they are entitled to expect, and we must demand, that they are properly cared for. What this appellant did was the opposite of that.

> > But the victims did not sustain distress or injury, the perpetrator was of good character and had two young daughters. However, we acknowledge that neither of the victims in fact sustained any distress or injury and they were very short incidents. The consequences for the appellant have been grave: she has lost her livelihood and has no realistic prospect of being able to work in her chosen field again and, if we may say so, rightly so. She has two young daughters at home. She is a woman in early middle age. The effect of a prison sentence upon someone like her, who was until now of previous good character, should not be underestimated.

> However, the conviction and sentence stood, even on appeal.[1]

WILFUL NEGLECT OR ILL-TREATMENT: OBJECTIVE TEST, SUBJECTIVE TEST, RECKLESSNESS, 'COULDN'T CARE LESS' ATTITUDE. There needs to be evidence of recklessness, but not necessarily deliberate intent. A 'couldn't care less' attitude can amount to recklessness, but there does need to be evidence of this. In the following example, this evidence was present in the case of a qualified staff nurse, but not in the case of the care manager of the care home.

> **Man with dementia left to die alone during the night: wilful neglect.** A 53-year-old man with frontal lobe dementia died during the night in a care home. For some period of time before his death he required one-to-one attention, for 24 hours a day from ten days before his death. He had also lost the power of speech. The crux of the prosecution (originally brought against seven other people) was that the one-to-one system of attendance

---

1   *R v Heaney* [2011] EWCA Crim 2682.

had broken down and that the patient had died unattended. The court started from the premise that for neglect to be proven, there needed to be not just an objective breach of a duty of care but also the element of subjective intention or recklessness.

Care manager on holiday: no evidence that she couldn't care less. The overall care manager was on holiday at the time but responsible for the one-to-one attention care plan, for which the care home had received additional funding. The court stated that it was not enough to show that the system of care drawn up was less than perfect. For the conviction to stand, evidence would be required that the manager had either intentionally fallen below a reasonable standard or simply could not have 'cared less' about what happened. There was no evidence of this.

Staff nurse: reckless disregard for attention required by man. It was different in the case of the staff nurse. In the court's view, there was not just an objective failure to meet standards but subjective recklessness on his part. First, he had not given any instruction or briefing at the outset of the session to ensure one-to-one attendance was maintained. Second, no one had been with the man when he died. Third, he maintained that he had carried out hourly checks but the evidence (including that relating to *rigor mortis*) suggested he was covering up his own failures, or those of other staff. All this was capable of showing reckless disregard in relation to care required. There were no grounds for overturning the jury's guilty verdict.[1]

Equally, there needs to be sufficient evidence of intent or recklessness.

Spraying deodorant into the mouth of a care home resident: insufficient evidence of criminal offence. A care home worker who sprayed deodorant around the head of a frail grandmother with severe dementia was cleared of ill-treating the 78-year-old care home resident. The latter had been taken from her bed and put into her chair. The carer then sprayed a body spray towards the lower part of the woman's body and then around her head. The resident had said 'stop' it and had moaned and groaned. The carer maintained she had just wanted the resident to smell nice. The court could not be satisfied that it was deliberate ill-treatment and accepted evidence

---

1   *R v Salisu* [2009] EWCA Crim 2702.

that the carer was trying to attend to the woman's care, albeit not following best practice.[1]

Recklessness is not legally the same as being careless.

Being clear about meaning of wilful neglect: not the same as gross carelessness. Three care home workers were convicted of wilful neglect of a resident. He suffered from Alzheimer's disease, osteoarthritis and hypertension. He was disorientated in time and place and at high risk of falling. One day he was agitated, and the staff were meant to put him to bed earlier, and to check on him during the night. The morning shift came on duty and found him in his room in a state of collapse. There was no evidence his bed had been slept in. He was on the floor, partially dressed, semi-conscious, partially hypothermic; he had soiled himself and was in pain. His condition suggested that he had never been put to bed. He was taken off to hospital but fortunately had suffered no significant or obvious injury.

The Court of Appeal overturned the convictions. This was on the ground that neglect was not enough to constitute a criminal offence, even of a vulnerable patient. The neglect had to be 'wilful' and that meant something more was required than a duty and what a reasonable person would regard as a reckless breach of that duty. The judge had, unfortunately, used a variety of expressions. He had used the word 'reckless' without defining it and without directing the jury that it was not simply an objective test. He had used the words 'careless' and 'carelessness' and 'grossly careless' as if they necessarily equated to a 'couldn't care less' attitude. They didn't; even 'gross carelessness' would not, of itself, have been sufficient to amount to wilful neglect.[2]

And recklessness would need to be distinguished from a genuine mistake, even if that mistake is made by an inexperienced practitioner, as opposed to a 'feckless' informal carer.

---

1   McCarthy, N. 'Care home worker Susan Draper cleared of ill-treating pensioner after appeal.' *Birmingham Mail*, 3 November 2017.

2   *R v Turbill* [2013] EWCA Crim 1422, paras 19–20.

Distinguishing deliberate intent, recklessness and genuine mistake. A registered nurse, the manager of a care home, was convicted of wilful neglect for failing to call for medical help after a care home resident fell and sustained significant bruising. She delayed at least two days in calling for medical help and an X-ray, and was convicted of wilful neglect, on the basis not of deliberate intent but of recklessness. She maintained it was a genuine mistake, not recklessness – and that she genuinely believed she had made the right decision at the time, although subsequently the X-ray showed he had broken ribs. Her conviction was overturned on appeal, because the judge had failed to direct the jury that if it concluded she had made a genuine mistake, she would have a defence.[1]

Equally, deliberate failure to do something which should have been done, even if linked to panic or stress, would still amount to wilful neglect.

Failure to administer CPR: not being able to face doing it: wilful neglect. A registered nurse was told that a resident was ill, his breathing was shallow and pulse faint. She phoned the resident's son in America. She then phoned for an ambulance. Five minutes later the ambulance service rang back asking whether the nurse was performing cardio-pulmonary resuscitation (CPR); the answer was no. A post-mortem suggested that CPR would have saved his life, but the question was whether, in the circumstances, CPR should have been attempted by the nurse and whether it was wilful neglect not to have done so, since, unlike manslaughter, wilful neglect does not need to have caused the harm but merely have taken place. She had not done so and claimed that this was because of stress and panic. She was convicted and appealed, unsuccessfully. For whatever reason, she could not face performing CPR even though she knew it was necessary, and this amounted to wilful neglect – even had this failure been due to stress or panic. The latter seemed to have been taken into account in the sentencing: a community order for 12 months with a requirement of 100 hours of unpaid work.[2]

---

1   *R v Morrell* [2002] EWCA Crim 2547, para 44.

2   *R v Patel* [2013] EWCA Crim 965.

WILFUL NEGLECT OR ILL-TREATMENT: SENIORITY OF PERPETRATOR.

The offences can be committed by managers with a hands-off role, not just frontline staff.

Deaths of residents from pressure sores: hands-off role of managers and closing of eyes. In a wilful neglect case involving deaths of residents from pressure sores in a care home, the court noted that the manager and owner of the home, who were prosecuted, both had a hands-off role. The court clearly accepted that they could be prosecuted but that proper consideration had to be given to whether they had fallen short in respect of that specific hands-off role:

> The jury needed to ask in respect of each one (1) are we sure lack of care is proved?; (2) if so, are we sure that it amounted to neglect?; (3) if so, are we sure either (i) that the defendant knew of the lack of care and deliberately or recklessly neglected to act, or (ii) that the defendant was unaware of the lack of care and deliberately or recklessly closed her mind to the obvious?
>
> We do not suggest that this is the form of question required in every case. But in this case the appellants were persons whose primary responsibility was supervision and management rather than hands-on care. The issue whether or not either or both of them was aware of the failing was a principal fact about which the jury required direction or, in the alternative, if unaware of that failing, whether the jury were sure that it was the consequence of a deliberate or reckless closing of the eyes to the obvious.[1]

The court went on to draw attention to the crucial distinction between wilful neglect and the honest, but overworked, efforts of a manager. The jury needed careful directions on the issue of delegation of tasks and upon the difference between wilful neglect of the welfare of residents on the one hand, and failure of honest efforts of an overworked but caring manager on the other.[2]

Suffering of 90-year-old woman with dementia. A 90-year-old woman was left unsupervised in a care home. She would tumble out of bed and crawl

---

1   *R v Hopkins, R v Priest* [2011] EWCA Crim 1513.

2   *R v Hopkins, R v Priest* [2011] EWCA Crim 1513.

naked along the floors of the Dalton unit of Stonedale Lodge, Croxteth, Liverpool. She was not kept clean by staff. She was often hungry and thirsty. She suffered for two months before being admitted to hospital where she died.

The prosecution lay against the manager. The resident had been largely funded by Liverpool City Council. The manager was given an eight-month prison sentence, suspended for two years – as well as 120 hours' unpaid work. She also had to pay £5000 costs. The judge criticised the company that ran the home, BUPA, which was not prosecuted. The manager had been ordered to cut costs, resulting in inadequate staffing levels. It transpired that unit managers had regularly told the manager of their concerns about staffing levels, but she did nothing about them; two managers had resigned over the issue. The judge put down the manager's inaction to her desire to please higher management at the expense of the care of the residents.[1]

Female resident left to die: endemic culture of neglect management failings. A female resident with dementia, in a Southern Cross care home, needed medical attention but was instead left to die. There was only one nurse looking after 29 residents on the night shift at the establishment in South Shields. The nurse pleaded guilty to wilful neglect, but in imposing a community sentence, the judge was in no doubt that there were wider issues in relation to a lack of training and management, and a regime that was not fit for purpose as a result of cost-cutting and the profit motive. The sentence was nine months in prison, suspended for 12 months, with supervision and 60 hours' unpaid work.[2]

Understaffed and underfunded care home leading to pressure sores: owner and manager convicted. A care home, Elm View in Halifax, had been understaffed and underfunded. The care home owner and the manager were both sentenced to 12 months in prison, guilty of wilful neglect. Some residents developed pressure sores due to bad care. The charges related to four residents in particular. The chronic understaffing meant that even the most basic care procedures were often neglected. Fundamental failures at the home included inadequate record-keeping, insufficient cleaning

1   Bunyan, N. 'Bupa put profit first at filthy and understaffed care home, says judge.' *Daily Telegraph*, 17 March 2012.

2   Kennedy, R. 'Nurse at Southern Cross home did not call doctor and Joyce Wordingham died, court hears.' *Evening Chronicle*, 3 March 2012.

materials, a lack of regular turning and toileting for at-risk residents and the provision of vital equipment such as pressure-relieving mattresses.

A police investigation had been launched in October 2011 after officers and a team of NHS nurses went into the home and found one elderly woman lying in a urine-soaked bed. The judge referred to the manager of the home as a liar and bully, who prioritised saving money over the welfare of elderly and vulnerable patients.[1]

Letting a highly needy and vulnerable patient die alone during night (wilful neglect: prosecution of staff, senior nurse and absent manager). An unnamed man died from natural causes in a nursing home on the night of 26 September 2004. The charge of wilful neglect, laid against a number of health care staff, was that he had died completely unattended, contrary to his care plan. He was 53 years old at the time and suffered from severe frontal lobe dementia sufficient to warrant detention under the Mental Health Act 1983. Having remained in a hospital bed for a year, he was then moved to a care home in which he lived for two years prior to his death.

Professional observers were unanimous that he had received a good standard of care over that period, and his family had wished for him to stay there. By the time of his death, he had lost the power of speech. He was not aggressive but lacked spatial awareness, bumped into things and people, and might manhandle the latter out of the way. He was therefore a risk both to himself and to others. About ten days before his death, his care plan had been amended to state that he required attention 24 hours a day; without this, the risks would have become intolerable. Following his death, eight defendants were prosecuted, the essence of the case being that 'the one-to-one system of attendance had broken down and that the poor patient had died unattended'.

Those prosecuted included four care assistants, the staff nurse on duty that night, the general manager of the home and the care manager of the home. Two were convicted, the staff nurse and care manager, although latter successfully appealed the conviction.[2]

1   Atkinson, N. 'Elm View care home pair Philip Bentley and Faheza Simpson jailed for neglect of elderly.' *Huddersfield Daily Examiner*, 24 December 2013.

2   *R v Salisu* [2009] EWCA Crim 2702.

WILFUL NEGLECT OR ILL-TREATMENT: INFORMAL CARE. Paid care is not a prerequisite under either the Mental Capacity Act 2005 or Mental Health Act 1983 (but is required under the Criminal Justice and Courts Act 2015).

Conviction of mother for wilful neglect. In 2012, a mother was convicted of neglect of her 18-year-old daughter. Despite her age, she looked about ten years old, because of the growth disorder, Russell Silver syndrome; she also had epilepsy, encephalitis and learning difficulties. She needed care and attention all the time, but her mother had gone to a public house and got drunk, leaving her daughter alone. The police attended. The mother was prosecuted and convicted of neglect. The report of the case does not mention the legislation under which she was convicted, but, given the daughter's age, it was, presumably, section 44 of the Mental Capacity Act.[1]

Some convictions have been secured against informal carers (see below for further case examples), although the numbers are very few compared to convictions of paid carers.

WILFUL NEGLECT OR ILL-TREATMENT: MENTAL HEALTH ACT 1983 CONVICTION EXAMPLES. The following is a selection of prosecutions and convictions brought under section 127 of the Mental Health Act 1983.

Hacking at the rotting flesh of pressure sores in filthy conditions (ill-treatment and wilful neglect). In a residential home near Oxford, relatives were encouraged to ring ahead of visiting, so that care workers could hide the stench of urine with air freshener and scrape faeces off the curtains. Upstairs, an 89-year-old man was lying with suppurating pressure sores, which had rotted his flesh down to the bones. He was in too much pain to move and too much confusion to cry out.

The owner attempted to clean the wounds by hacking at the skin around the sores with office scissors and ripping out pieces of rotting flesh – wearing gloves with which, moments before, he had scooped faeces from

---

1 Allen, E. 'Mother, 40, left her disabled daughter home alone while she went to the pub and got so drunk she ended up at hospital.' *Daily Mail*, 6 July 2012.

the sheets. The man was referred to by staff as the 'body in the attic'. The owner was charged with ill-treatment and wilful neglect under the 1983 Act and convicted; he served 12 weeks of a nine-month prison sentence.[1]

Kept in squalor (wilful neglect). When three mentally ill people were found living in squalor, a former mental health nurse and his wife admitted three counts of wilful neglect under the Mental Health Act 1983 and were sentenced to 200 hours of community service.[2]

Septicaemia, pneumonia, dehydration, death of resident (wilful neglect). A care home owner, originally charged with manslaughter, was convicted instead of wilful neglect. The resident concerned had mental health problems, as well as Alzheimer's disease and Parkinson's disease. He had been awarded the Sword of Honour during his career in the armed forces. He died from septicaemia and pneumonia, and had been found previously by his family lying in soiled clothing, sweating and unconscious. He was severely dehydrated at times and during a period of ten days he lost two stone.

The home was also in breach of many of the regulations applying to care homes. The judge stated that 'those who wilfully neglect, with serious consequences, should expect to go to prison. This is the message that should go out.' She was sentenced to six months' imprisonment under section 127 of the 1983 Act. She had been arrested after the coroner had informed the police, so concerned was he about the man's appearance.[3]

Not administering medication to resident (wilful neglect). An 84-year-old woman died within five weeks of entering a nursing home. A nurse working there pleaded guilty to wilful neglect under the 1983 Act for not administering the correct medication.[4]

Inciting residents racially to abuse and kick each other (wilful neglect and ill-treatment). When residents of a care home were incited racially to abuse each other and also to kick each other, the convictions of three

1   Hill, A. 'Tide of cruelty sweeps through our care homes.' *The Observer*, 18 February 2001.

2   'News.' *Community Care*, 25 June–1 July 1998.

3   Narain, J. 'Care home boss jailed after wilful neglect killed Alzheimer's patient.' *Daily Mail*, 21 May 2008.

4   'Neglect case "tragic" for nurse.' *BBC News*, 22 May 2008. Accessed on 8 October 2018 at: http://news.bbc.co.uk/1/hi/wales/south_east/7414850.stm.

carers and the manager of the care home followed – for wilful neglect and ill-treatment under the 1983 Act.[1]

Sedatives, rough handling, verbal abuse, bullying, slapping (ill-treatment); not taking person to hospital (wilful neglect): prosecution of two managers and a nurse. Two managers of a South Wales nursing home and another nurse were convicted under section 127, one for wilful neglect, the other two for ill-treatment. The ill-treatment included the administering of sedatives to keep patients quiet, rough handling, neglecting requests to be taken to the toilet, verbal abuse and bullying. The ill-treatment perpetrated by the nurse, not just at this nursing home but another – for which he had already been sentenced to 12 months in prison – included kicking footballs at residents, giving heavy doses of medication to residents so he could sleep undisturbed on his shift, throwing a 75-year-old man across a room, and leaving an elderly woman naked and exposed to the elements near open windows and doors. The wilful neglect included not taking a resident, who had suffered two broken ribs, to hospital for two days.[2]

Another care worker at the same home admitted ill-treatment and was sentenced to 150 hours' community service for slapping a resident.[3]

Pulling hair (ill-treatment) and excessive isolation (wilful neglect). A carer was convicted of ill-treatment, under the 1983 Act, for pulling the hair and nipping the nose of a care home resident aged 37, with a developmental age of two years, suffering from epilepsy and severe learning disabilities. In addition, she was convicted of wilful neglect for leaving another male resident in a sensory room by himself for too long; he was 54 years old but with a developmental age of 12 months. He was severely physically and mentally disabled, suffered from meningitis, was epileptic, communicated by grunting only, and was paralysed to some extent in all four limbs. She was sentenced to three months' imprisonment.[4]

---

1   Gadelrab, R. 'Patients abused at care home.' *Islington Tribune*, 22 December 2006.

2   'Care home bosses guilty of abuse.' *BBC News*, 28 June 2001. Accessed on 8 October 2018 at: http://news.bbc.co.uk/1/hi/wales/1412595.stm. And: 'Patient abuse: nurse struck off.' *BBC News*, 30 April 2003. Accessed on 8 October 2018 at: http://news.bbc.co.uk/1/hi/wales/2989241.stm.

3   'Care worker slapped patient.' *The Independent*, 3 January 2002.

4   *R v Lennon* [2005] EWCA Crim 3530.

Kicking, slapping, dragging hospital patients (ill-treatment). A four-month suspended sentence for ill-treatment, under the 1983 Act, was given to a hospital nurse who had kicked one patient, slapped another and dragged a third by his neck. She was subsequently struck off the nursing register.[1]

Placing a bag over the head of a resident (ill-treatment). A carer in a nursing home was convicted under section 127 of the 1983 Act for placing a bag over the head of an 88-year-old resident as he struggled to breathe. He told his horrified colleague not to worry, saying 'no bruise, no proof'. The convicted carer had almost completed his studies to become a doctor in his native Lithuania. He would be sentenced after an application for his deportation.[2]

Three-year regime of bullying, kicking, slapping, nipping, hair-tugging of residents (ill-treatment). In a Yorkshire care home, a regime of physical abuse had persisted for some three years. The eight victims with physical and learning disabilities had mental ages of less than two years old and could not speak for themselves. They suffered bullying, kicking, slapping, nipping, hair-tugging and other assaults. One resident was kicked five times in the groin by a female carer wearing high-heeled shoes; another had his face rubbed in urine as though he were a puppy; another resident was force-fed; another had incontinence pads changed roughly. One prevalent view was that these residents with learning disabilities did not feel pain in the normal way.

Of 33 charges, 23 were proven. Seven carers were sentenced to a total of 66 months in prison, mainly on grounds of ill-treatment and wilful neglect, under section 127 of the 1983 Act, variously; one who had shown genuine remorse and shame to ten months, another (mother of three children and five months pregnant) to 12 months, a third to 12 months, his sister (who was pregnant) to 12 months, a fifth (a supermarket worker with a previous conviction for wilful neglect of a child, but who had accepted her misbehaviour) to eight months, a sixth to nine months and a seventh to three months. Of the seven, six were women.[3]

---

1   'Nurse struck off.' *The Times*, 9 January 2002.

2   *R v Poderis* (2007) Chester Crown Court, 2007. See: McKeever, K. 'Cruel carer is guilty in landmark court case.' *Wilmslow Express*, 15 August 2007.

3   Wood, A. 'Cruel care home abusers are jailed.' *Yorkshire Post*, 22 March 2005.

Taking blood with a needle roughly and inappropriately (ill-treatment). Cleared of 15 charges of ill-treatment, a care home manager was convicted on the last charge under section 127 of the Mental Health Act 1983, concerning the taking of blood from the arm of a resident in her late eighties. He took the blood in a rough and inappropriate manner, such that the needle went right through the patient's arm, leaving her with bruises.[1]

WILFUL NEGLECT OR ILL-TREATMENT: MENTAL CAPACITY ACT 2005 CONVICTION EXAMPLES. The following is a selection of prosecutions and convictions brought under section 44 of the Mental Capacity Act 2005.

Care home owner convicted: pressure sores (wilful neglect). A care home owner was convicted of wilful neglect for allowing horrendous pressure sores to develop and then doing nothing about them. The resident was 97 years old, and was immobile and unable to communicate. A pressure sore developed, and the perpetrator told a carer to apply cream but no dressing. The sore got worse. Staff raised the issue but the care home owner did nothing and removed notes made by the staff about the sores. One of the sores was large enough to put a tennis ball in. After the resident was admitted to hospital following a fall, the sores were dressed. The care home owner took the resident home three hours later. A week later the dressings had not been changed. Finally, social services sent a doctor to the care home and the woman was admitted to hospital. However, she picked up an infection and died there. The care home owner was sentenced to six months in prison, suspended for two years.[2]

Care worker not attending to a nose bleed (wilful neglect). A care worker at a care home was convicted of wilful neglect. An elderly resident was found covered in dried blood in her room, following a nose bleed. She had done her best to clean herself up, but there was blood in her room and in the bathroom. She was found in a distressed and confused state. He admitted that he knew about the nose bleed but had been too busy to attend to the woman.

---

1   'Ex-care home boss cleared of 15 abuse charges.' *Cheshire Guardian*, 20 May 2004.

2   Adwent, C. 'Care home owner spared jail.' *East Anglian Daily Times*, 5 July 2012.

The carer was also convicted of ill-treatment, having pushed an elderly man, who had suffered a stroke and had dementia. He had been agitated. The carer said to him, 'What the f****** hell do you want now?' He then pushed him over. Falling on his back, he lay motionless for five minutes before being helped by another member of staff. It was Christmas Day.[1]

Care workers not attending to resident with dementia during the night (wilful neglect). Three care workers were convicted of wilful neglect, during the night, of an 85-year-old resident with dementia at a care home in Bromsgrove. He should, according to the care plan, have been checked every two hours. He was found in the morning wearing a pyjama jacket, daytime trousers, with one shoe and both socks on. He was very cold. The radiator was off.

The judge had directed the jury that they had to decide whether it was deliberate or reckless lack of care, or whether busy staff, with much to do, had forgotten the resident. It appeared that staff filled in the care plan book, without having seen the resident. For instance, one of the carers had stated that the man had slept well. Yet it appeared he had not been put to bed the previous evening and there were no impressions or creases on the bed.[2] They were given suspended jail sentences.[3]

Care home manager: unkempt residents, run-down environment (wilful neglect). A care home manager was convicted, under section 44 of the Mental Capacity Act, of wilful neglect of a number of mentally ill residents in her care in Colchester. She was given a suspended prison sentence. There was no heating, some patients were over-dressed, while others were not dressed properly, their bedding was damp and there was little food in the house. Some had what appeared to be long-standing scalp and foot infections.[4]

Nurse not resuscitating a patient (wilful neglect). A nurse working at a care home was given a community sentence of 100 hours for failing to perform

1   Hickey, A. 'Flintshire carer abused and neglected elderly at Prestatyn nursing home.' *Daily Post*, 10 July 2012.

2   'Trio convicted of neglect of 85-year-old at Bromsgrove care home.' *Bromsgrove Advertiser*, 19 July 2012.

3   'Bromsgrove care workers sentenced for neglect.' *Bromsgrove Advertiser*, 28 August 2012.

4   'Care home boss banned for neglect of mentally ill.' *Daily Gazette*, 9 July 2011.

cardio-pulmonary resuscitation on a 90-year-old resident. The man would have died in any case, but the nurse did not know this at the time. The nurse failed to act, even though she was fully trained in the procedure and knew that the home had a policy of giving resuscitation unless the resident was subject to a 'do not resuscitate' instruction.[1]

Care home manager locking people with learning disabilities in car on hot day (wilful neglect). A care home manager and an employee went to a betting shop and amusement arcade. For three hours during the visit, they locked three vulnerable people in a car on a hot and muggy day. The three had severe learning disabilities, autism and epilepsy. They were rescued when passers-by spotted them in distress and trying to get out. The police freed them and found them dehydrated and very hot.

The judge in the Crown Court sentenced the manager and employee to 300 hours and 250 hours of community service respectively for wilful neglect under section 44 of the Mental Capacity Act. They were in serious breach of their responsibilities, and the three men must have suffered very considerable stress and discomfort in the unventilated vehicle. They had been on the 'cusp' of going to prison but were previously model citizens. Both were sacked by their employer.[2]

Care worker leaving man with Down's syndrome in car for up to an hour (wilful neglect). A care worker was employed by a business called Out and About which provided temporary care cover for those who needed it. He was employed to support vulnerable adults, allowing them to undertake activities in the community for up to a few hours each day. He would support most of his clients either weekly or fortnightly. One of his regular clients had Down's syndrome, needed continuous stimulation and was not to be left on his own. He was accused of leaving the client for at least an hour on two occasions. The first charge was dismissed due to identification problems in the evidence. As to the second, he claimed he had left the person for no more than five or ten minutes. He was convicted, the judge preferring the evidence as to the longer period. He was sentenced to six

1   Hunt, K. '"Negligent" nurse Parulben Patel spared jail after leaving man to die.' *KentOnline*, 18 April 2012. Accessed on 28 August 2012 at: https://www.kentonline.co.uk/kent/news/negligent-nurse-parulben-patel-a65191.

2   'Vulnerable patients locked in car for three hours while carers went to the bookies.' *Daily Mail*, 21 January 2008.

months' imprisonment suspended for 24 months and ordered to pay a victim surcharge of £80 and £1200 towards prosecution costs.[1]

Leaving service user in minibus (wilful neglect). On the day in question, a care assistant and another worker had taken two service users out in a minibus. They, and one service user, went for a coffee somewhere, leaving the other service user in the minibus for about an hour. He was 42 years old, could become very agitated and anxious in vehicles, had to be put in a harness in vehicles, could not articulate for himself, and could not attend to his own personal care.

He could not see the others having coffee, and they could not see him. He became very distressed. The police were called. They arrested the care assistant and other worker. They were both convicted under section 44 of the 2005 Act and given a one-year community order and eight hours of unpaid work.[2]

Degrading photograph of 92-year-old semi-naked resident (wilful neglect). A nurse working in a care home took a photograph of a 92-year-old semi-naked resident and then circulated it. The woman was sentenced, for wilful neglect under section 44, to nine months' imprisonment suspended for a year, together with 200 hours of community service.[3]

Filming a semi-naked resident having an incontinence pad changed and encouraging a resident to swear: prison sentence (ill-treatment). A carer filmed a semi-naked elderly man having his incontinence pad changed. She encouraged another to swear. She was sent to prison for a year for ill-treatment under section 44 of the 2005 Act.

She was arrested after leaving her iPhone on a train. A member of the public handed it to police. There were three film clips of residents, at a Bupa-run care home, Elstree Court Nursing Home. The clips showed her asking a resident to open their eyes, clap their hands and give her a smile. In return for one of the requests she was heard saying she would give their glasses back to them. The second showed a semi-naked man having an

---

1   *R v Maghmoijj* [2016] EWCA Crim 1647.

2   *Newton v Secretary of State for Health* [2009] UKFTT 19 (HESC) (details of conviction recounted in this Care Standards Tribunal case).

3   Cambridgeshire County Council. 'UK nurse conviction makes legal history.' *News*, 24 August 2009.

incontinence pad changed, with more staff in the room than necessary. The last clip showed her encouraging a woman to swear.[1]

Care worker inflicting psychological and physical torment: throwing resident across the room, headlock, flicking orange juice, flicking ears, lying about a parcel the resident was expecting (ill-treatment). A care assistant working at a private hospital in Hexham, run by Castlebeck, was convicted of repeated ill-treatment of a 36-year-old man with learning difficulties, bipolar disorder and hyperactivity disorder. On one occasion, he was excitedly awaiting visitors and wouldn't move away from the door. The care assistant threw him across the room. On another occasion, after the resident had pressed his call bell, the care assistant put him in a headlock. Other instances included flicking orange juice into his hair, taunting him, flicking his ears – and pretending that a parcel, with a model kit in it, had been sent back because of his bad behaviour. The judge referred not just to the physical assaults but to the psychological torment that had been inflicted. The carer was sentenced to 16 months in prison.[2]

Care worker hitting a vulnerable resident's head (ill-treatment). A care worker at a care home run by Calderstones Partnership NHS Foundation Trust was seen hitting a vulnerable resident round the head, such as to cause his head to hit the wall three feet away. He was convicted of ill-treatment and given a community sentence, since it was a single incident and many letters of support from colleagues had been received.[3]

Support worker humiliating resident by dressing him up with a bra and speaking in a derogatory way (ill-treatment). A support worker at the Southview Independent Hospital was convicted of ill-treatment under section 44. She had humiliated a man, who had suffered a stroke, by putting a bra on him. She had also referred to a 'fucking tsunami', when an incontinent woman had wet herself. In addition, she had assaulted another woman, after the latter had tried to strangle the support worker's dog

1   'Eastbourne woman jailed after filming care home residents.' *Eastbourne Herald*, 22 July 2011.

2   Butcher, J. 'Hexham care assistant Michael Payne jailed for 16 months.' *The Journal*, 17 April 2012.

3   'Carer loses his job after passer-by sees him hit patient.' *Manchester Evening News*, 4 July 2012.

during a therapy visit. The worker was sentenced to a 12-month community order and 120 hours of unpaid work.[1]

Care worker hitting residents with dementia and flicking food at them (ill-treatment). A nursing home care worker worked on an 'intensive' ward at a nursing home, with responsibility for extremely vulnerable people who suffered from dementia. She banged the back of a 79-year-old man's head and ran away from him; pushed an 85-year-old woman; and hit an 84-year-old man's head as though she were knocking on a door. She flicked food at an 89-year-old woman's face, hit her in the face with a metal bib, thought it was funny and stood there laughing. She was given six months in prison, suspended for two years, under section 44 of the 2005 Act.[2]

NHS care home manager using the arms of one resident to hit another resident in a care home (ill-treatment). An NHS care home manager used the arms of other residents as 'weapons' to hit a woman with learning disabilities, in a home for people with severe learning disabilities. This was in retaliation for having her hair pulled. Under section 44, she was given a six-month prison sentence, suspended for 18 months.[3]

Care worker repeatedly assaulting woman with dementia, in her bed at a care home (ill-treatment). A nurse, concerned about the treatment of her 80-year-old mother in a care home, installed a secret camera in her room. A care worker was then caught on film when suddenly striking the resident, repeatedly slapping her arms and then hitting her in the abdomen four times. He was convicted of both assault and ill-treatment (under section 44 of the Mental Capacity Act) and given an 18-month prison sentence.

The woman's daughter pointed out that there were wider issues within the care home and that rules were regularly breached, such as that two care workers should have been present when a resident was put to bed, and bathing and cleaning to be carried out by a female care worker. Yet, in 2009, the care home had been judged excellent by the regulator.[4]

---

1 'Court orders Billingham carer to work in community.' *Northern Echo*, 26 May 2012.

2 'Carer who abused elderly suffering with Alzheimer's and dementia avoids jail at Liverpool court.' *Liverpool News*, 13 February 2010. Also: 'Tammy Knox trial: care worker tells Liverpool crown court how he learned of patient abuse.' *Liverpool Echo*, 15 January 2010.

3 Dudgeon, O. 'Care home boss spared prison in abuse case.' *Yorkshire Post*, 17 November 2009.

4 'Nurse filmed assaulting dementia patient, 80, on daughter's secret camera.' *Daily Mail*, 13 April 2012.

Care worker smothering care home residents with fleece and pillow (ill-treatment). A care home worker was helping a resident into bed. The resident cried out in pain, because of an injured hip. The care worker picked up a fleece and pulled it tightly over the old lady's face, telling her to 'shut up'. A second resident also cried out in pain when being moved, because of a dislocated shoulder. The care worker grabbed a pillow and held it with both hands over the resident's face. Both residents were elderly and had dementia. She was sentenced for ill-treatment, under section 44 of the Mental Capacity Act, to 12 months in prison.[1]

Senior care worker: rough handling, dragging residents, sitting on resident, screaming at residents, prising open their mouths (ill-treatment). A senior carer at a care home in Widnes was convicted under section 44 of the 2005 Act on a number of counts of ill-treatment of female residents with dementia. She dragged two elderly women along a corridor, kicking their heels from behind, to make them walk 'like a rag doll'. She grabbed another resident so roughly that she banged her head on a bedstead. She sat on another woman to get her to take eye drops. She screamed at residents, forcing them to take their medication by prising open their mouths.[2]

Two care workers: assault and verbal abuse of care home residents (ill-treatment). Two carers were convicted of ill-treatment at a care home in Farnworth, under section 44 of the Act. They were given prison sentences of 21 and 15 months respectively. The ill-treatment included assault and verbal abuse over a two-year period. The residents concerned had suffered several attacks, including being sprayed in the face with an air freshener and blocking bedroom doors with towels. On one occasion a resident had been restrained with a towel across his face. Another was dragged to her room and locked inside.[3]

---

1   'Jail warning for Cumbrian woman who ill-treated elderly women in care home.' *News & Star*, 12 November 2011. And: 'Care worker Kimberley Walker jailed for abusing women.' *BBC News*, 12 November 2011. Accessed on 9 October 2018 at: www.bbc.co.uk/news/uk-england-cumbria-16137039.

2   'Widnes mum Jeanette Judge found guilty on six charges of cruelty.' *Runcorn and Widnes World*, 1 February 2012. And: Jordan, B. '"Sentence is a damned insult", say families of abused victims.' *Runcorn and Widnes World*, 14 March 2012.

3   'Bolton women guilty of abusing care home patients.' *BBC News*, 6 July 2012. Accessed on 26 November 2018 at: https://www.bbc.co.uk/news/uk-england-manchester-18744102.

Care worker punching and slapping a resident with dementia (ill-treatment). A carer was convicted of ill-treatment under section 44 of the 2005 Act. She was given a suspended prison sentence of six months and ordered to do 140 hours' unpaid work. The resident, of the Chestnuts care home in Grimsby, suffered from vascular dementia and could become agitated and aggressive. At 2.30 in the morning, she had entered his room and punched and slapped him repeatedly around the head, as well as swearing at him. He suffered several bruises to his forearms where he had put them over his face while trying to protect himself. The carer was witnessed as being in a red-faced rage. The judge noted that she had showed no compassion towards the resident and that, by contesting a trial, she had shown no remorse.[1]

Nurse wrestling with and force-feeding patient (ill-treatment). A nurse working at Whitchurch Hospital, Cardiff, was convicted of ill-treatment of patients with dementia, under section 44 of the Mental Capacity Act. She was seen kneeling on top of one elderly man, force-feeding him medicine when he refused it. Another patient she was in charge of was spotted with a cut lip and skin tears on one arm after she had been at his bedside during an overnight shift. The nurse was given a six-month prison sentence, suspended for two years.[2]

Care worker hitting resident of care home (ill-treatment). A carer was convicted of ill-treating, under section 44 of the 2005 Act, a resident at Huntleigh Lodge Care Home, Cleethorpes. She was given a suspended prison sentence of six months and also 60 hours' unpaid work. The resident had severe dementia, was hard of hearing, had cataracts, was frail, had poor mobility and could not look after himself. Without warning, the carer had swung his legs towards her as he lay on his bed. His body became twisted. He kicked out into her stomach. She picked up a towel, twisted it and used it to hit him in the stomach. She also punched him on the shoulder and slapped him with force on the shoulder. The injuries were minor, but the judge considered the matter serious.[3]

1 'Is this justice for the elderly? Care worker who punched and slapped 87-year-old dementia sufferer walks free from court.' *Daily Mail*, 11 July 2011.

2 'Nurse sentenced for patient abuse.' *BBC News*, 23 November 2009. Accessed on 9 October 2018 at: http://news.bbc.co.uk/1/hi/wales/8375233.stm.

3 'Carer spared prison after hitting pensioner.' *Grimsby Telegraph*, 3 December 2011.

Manager of care home: incorrect hoisting, exposing a person, manhandling people by their clothing, abusive language, throwing walking aids (ill-treatment). The perpetrator was the manager of a care home in East London, whose residents were largely elderly people with dementia. She had provided good references, but a police investigation began when 14 members of the care home wrote a whistleblowing letter to the owner of the home. One resident in his eighties, utterly disorientated, was put in an incorrect position in a hoist and transported from the lounge into the conservatory with his genitals exposed. He was distressed by this and was incontinent of urine during the process. Afterwards he was taken to hospital by ambulance.

A second resident, in her nineties, was described as a pleasant lady with no behavioural problems. She was ill-treated when the perpetrator held her by her clothing so as to cause discomfort and pain. Her trousers were pulled up very high, in a degrading way. She was thus held and then allowed to slump to the floor. She also suffered osteoarthritis of the spine which meant that once she was on the floor she could not get up by herself.

A third resident, in his eighties, did have behavioural problems, including the molesting of female residents. The manager subjected him to abusive and offensive language and twice threw a walking frame at him.[1] Under section 44 of the 2005 Act, the manager was given a community sentence, consisting of 180 hours of unpaid work.[2]

Care worker: lifting resident and causing pain (ill-treatment). A care worker at a nursing home in Cannock was given a prison sentence of nine months under section 44 of the 2005 Act. He had taken a shortcut when changing the man, by lifting him and causing pain, instead of turning him. The resident's protests went unheeded. He then lashed out at the carer, who grabbed him by the wrists, leaving red marks.[3]

Care worker convicted of manhandling and swearing at a resident (ill-treatment). A care worker was convicted of ill-treatment under section 44 of the 2005 Act for pushing, manhandling and swearing at a mental health hospital. She was witnessed grabbing a patient (with early-onset dementia

1   *R v Dunn* [2010] EWCA Crim 2935.

2   'Appeal dismissed for care home manageress who neglected Romford dementia patients.' *Romford Recorder*, 26 November 2010.

3   'Prison term handed to care worker at Cannock nursing home.' *Express and Star*, 7 January 2012.

and schizophrenia) by the shoulder, shouting and swearing at her, pushing her and causing her to fall on to a mattress. The patient was screaming, although there were no physical or mental injuries caused. The care worker was sentenced to four months in prison, suspended for two years, and ordered to pay £1000 costs.[1]

Care worker tucking resident in so tight she was trapped under the covers and leaving her in the dark (ill-treatment). A care worker was convicted of ill-treatment for tucking a blanket so tightly around a 95-year-old resident with dementia that she was trapped under the covers. He then left her, switching off the light and leaving her in the dark, which she was afraid of, screaming in distress. On a separate occasion, he had tied her to a chair using a blanket. The care home, run by Prime Life, had already been rated 'poor' by the Care Quality Commission. He had also mistreated other residents.[2]

Care workers at Winterbourne View: range of abuse (ill-treatment). A BBC *Panorama* programme revealed extensive abuse of people with learning disabilities at a private hospital called Winterbourne View, run by Castlebeck Ltd. The abuse included, for example, staff poking residents' eyes, wrestling residents to the ground, slapping legs, bouncing on residents' laps, threatening to put residents' heads down the toilet, harsh hand-slapping, kicking, pinning people under chairs, threats with a cheese grater, the same resident being assaulted five times in one day, giving people showers fully clothed, tipping water from a flower vase over a resident's face. By August 2012, 11 members of staff had been convicted of ill-treatment. The prosecution argued that the ill-treatment amounted to disability hate crime.[3]

Staff: verbal abuse, dragging across bedroom floor and failing to give medicine in care home (ill-treatment and wilful neglect). Two staff at a

---

1 'Care home worker pushed patient.' *Evening Gazette*, 26 January 2010. And: 'Ex-care worker spared jail over treatment of vulnerable woman.' *Gazettelive*, 27 March 2010. Accessed on 9 October 2018 at: www.gazettelive.co.uk/news/teesside-news/2010/03/27/ex-care-worker-spared-jail-over-treatment-of-vulnerable-woman-84229-26118005.

2 Dolan, A. 'The cruelty of a "carer": judge jails worker who imprisoned Alzheimer's sufferers in bedrooms.' *Daily Mail*, 14 February 2012.

3 Ramesh, R. 'Winterbourne View abuse: last staff member pleads guilty.' *The Guardian*, 7 August 2012.

care home in Pontefract were found guilty of ill-treatment, one being given a prison sentence of four months, the other a community sentence. The family had left a camera in an alarm clock because of their fears about what was happening. The camera recorded five days of abuse, including her being threatened with violence, dragged across the floor and not receiving her medicine. She was struck and called a 'nasty old cow' and a 'horrible old lady'. The judge called the offences 'unforgivable and unacceptable'.[1]

Care workers: falsification of records, left during night, on floor, hypothermia, in faeces and urine (wilful neglect). Three care workers at a care home in Bromsgrove were convicted of wilful neglect of a resident during the night. In the documentation, the morning after, it was recorded that the resident had slept well. In fact, nobody had attended to him, and he had been found lying in the corner of his room, barely conscious, suffering from hypothermia. His clothes were soiled with urine and faeces. All three carers involved received suspended prison sentences and two were ordered to do community service.[2]

Senior care worker: slapping and kicking (ill-treatment). A senior care worker laughed while he abused two vulnerable adults with severe learning disabilities in a care home in Harwich. He received a prison sentence of eight months. He was accused of slapping a resident on the arm with a wooden spoon when he fell asleep, slamming a plastic beaker on to a man's hand and kicking someone under the table during a four-month period of abuse.[3]

Three care workers shoving, pushing, pulling, verbally abusing (ill-treatment). A woman's family placed a hidden camera in her room in a care home, the Granary Care Home, a specialist dementia centre. This was to find out why she had so many bruises. Three care workers were filmed pushing, shoving, pulling and verbally abusing her. The first was jailed for four months after admitting ill-treatment and also theft of the woman's food. The second was given a two-month sentence, suspended for

1   Peachey, P. 'Carer jailed after being caught on camera hitting and abusing a vulnerable 89-year-old woman.' *The Independent*, 29 August 2012.

2   Jackson, C. '"Neglectful" Bromsgrove care workers spared jail.' *Bromsgrove Standard*, 28 August 2012.

3   'Peter Crofts jailed for 8 months.' *Clacton Gazette*, 18 May 2018.

two years, and the third 180 hours of unpaid work. The three expressed remorse at what they had done. The woman's son noted that the wages were low and there were often staff shortages.[1]

Care worker sleeping, incontinence pads unchanged, bedside alarms disconnected (wilful neglect). A care worker was photographed sleeping while on duty at a Buckinghamshire care home. She was sentenced to prison for 18 months. Many of the 19 elderly residents had been left for hours with no change of incontinence pads. The judge described her conduct as cruel, lazy and unacceptable. She had been asleep for 20 minutes during her night shift on 17 August 2011. Curtains were drawn, a heater was on and a television was blaring in the room where she was found. Eleven bedside warning alarms had been disconnected, leaving vulnerable residents 'abandoned'.[2]

Nurse at NHS-run care home: poking and rough treatment of 92-year-old former nurse (ill-treatment). A nurse was secretly filmed as she poked an elderly dementia patient in the face, treated her roughly and told her to shut up. She was jailed for four months. The ill-treatment occurred in a care home run by Homerton University Hospital NHS Foundation Trust. The elderly woman, herself a nurse, had worked for four decades at the old Hackney Hospital.[3]

Faking blood test results by hospital nurses (wilful neglect). Two nurses were jailed for four and eight months respectively for their neglect of patients at the Princess of Wales Hospital in Bridgend in Wales. Another nurse was given a community order for the same offence. They failed on a number of occasions to check patients' blood glucose levels at least every two hours, faking the results in a 'deception' that could have been potentially harmful to some patients. The faked results came to light after

1   Perry, K. 'Shoved and sworn at: care workers abuse Alzheimer's patient.' *Daily Telegraph*, 23 June 2014.

2   'Buckinghamshire care home worker jailed for 18 months.' *BBC News*, 29 August 2013. Accessed on 21 June 2016 at: www.bbc.co.uk/news/uk-england-beds-bucks-herts-23886055.

3   Webb, S. 'Carer secretly filmed abusing 92-year-old dementia patient telling her to "shut your mouth" – and poking her in the face – but will be out of jail in just weeks.' *Daily Mail*, 11 July 2014.

discrepancies between blood glucose levels noted on patients' charts and readings on a glucose meter were noticed.[1]

Care worker snaps (ill-treatment). A care worker at the Chaseside Rest Home, St Annes, was sent to prison for four months. She snapped in a ground-floor bathroom while helping a woman with dementia. She slapped the pensioner across the hand, dug a ring into her hand, teased her by offering a walking stick but snatching it away, pinned her to a wall while trying to pull her underwear down – and pushed used toilet tissue into the woman's face. All this had been witnessed by another care worker.[2]

Care workers in person's own home: ramming object into mouth (ill-treatment). A man and wife, care workers in the community, were filmed abusing an elderly woman with dementia in her own home. He was convicted on the basis of twisting her fingers, ramming an object in her mouth to try to get her to take tablets, and slapping her across the head. He was sentenced to 28 months in prison; his wife to 38 weeks, suspended for two years.[3]

Pelted with bean bags, mocked, bullied, stamped on (ill-treatment). Three nursing home staff were jailed (eight, five and four months respectively) and a fourth given a community sentence (12 months) for tormenting and abusing elderly residents with dementia, actions described by the trial judge as 'gratuitous sport at the expense of vulnerable victims'. This was at Hillcroft nursing home, in Lancashire. Residents were pelted with bean bags, mocked and bullied on the assumption that their condition meant they would not remember the abuse. One man's foot was deliberately stamped on and another was nearly tipped out of his wheelchair. The judge referred to management failings: a lax regime which allowed the ill-treatment to carry on undetected and without proper and adequate control.[4]

Dragging a woman to bed and verbally abusing her (ill-treatment). A care home worker who physically and verbally abused a woman with learning

1   Bolton, D. 'Two nurses jailed for neglect after faking patients' blood glucose test results.' *The Independent*, 14 December 2015.

2   'Carer jailed after attack on gran, 89.' *Blackpool Gazette*, 24 May 2015.

3   'Carer Maurice Campbell jailed for abusing elderly woman.' *BBC News*, 22 November 2016.

4   Walker, P. 'Hillcroft nursing home care workers jailed for abusing elderly residents.' *The Guardian*, 10 January 2014.

difficulties was jailed for six months. He had become 'enraged' by the 30-year-old woman, who had refused to go to bed and had lain down in the hallway. He began by kicking a space hopper lightly against the woman to encourage her to go to bed. He then grabbed hold of her by the ankles and began dragging her towards the bedroom. He also subjected her to a tirade of abuse, picking on her, calling her names and making derogatory comments to her.[1]

Hospital health care assistant mocking patients and treating them roughly (ill-treatment). An abusive health care assistant who beat and taunted elderly dementia patients at Whipps Cross Hospital was sentenced to 12 months in prison. She held a bed sheet over an 87-year-old's head, telling her she was dead; put her hands on the resident's breast and mocked her; pushed a patient and shoved her into a chair when she refused to be washed; slapped a patient on the hip or bottom after she had soiled herself.[2]

Tying a woman's ankles together with cable in a care home (ill-treatment). Two carers at a specialist care home (High Noon in Pulborough) for people with learning disabilities were convicted of ill-treatment of a female resident. One of them had made a 31-second video on his mobile phone, showing him having tied the woman's ankles together using a cable. They then both laughed and shouted at her while she tried to walk, fell over and tried to crawl towards them. The video was later sent to another staff member, who alerted the management. They were later sentenced: one was given a 12-month community order (240 hours' unpaid work), the other a community order for 140 hours' unpaid work and 15 rehabilitation activity requirement (RAR) days.[3]

Locking resident out and giving him vile meals (ill-treatment). A care home worker, at the Dell home in Sudbury, locked a naked man outside in the cold and gave him disgusting meals of salted banana covered in ketchup. The 40-year-old resident suffered from cerebral palsy. The carer

1   'Wool care home worker jailed for six months after abuse.' *Dorset Echo*, 6 April 2013.

2   'Healthcare worker jailed for neglect of elderly patients at Whipps Cross Hospital.' *East London and West Essex Guardian*, 23 August 2013.

3   Wynn-Davies, S. 'Carers sentenced for filming and laughing at patient in their care.' *West Sussex County Times*, 21 March 2018.

was convicted of ill-treatment. The judge stated that the offences warranted a prison sentence but decided against this, so that the carer might be able to get another job in a care home. He had been working at the care home for five years when the two incidents occurred – for which there was no apparent motive.[1]

Not reporting alleged abuse to the Care Quality Commission: care home managers charged, but not convicted (wilful neglect). Two care home managers failed to report the alleged abuse of four elderly residents and were charged with wilful neglect. They had a duty to report this to the Care Quality Commission but failed to do so. However, the judge held that there was no evidence that this was deliberate. Instead, he accepted evidence that 'things got lost but not deliberately' amidst the 'turmoil of activity' at the home in 2012: disciplinary proceedings were ongoing at the time over allegations of bullying and misusing company property against four other junior carers, who were suspended. The judge ordered the jury to return not guilty verdicts.[2]

Foster carers: guilty of wilful neglect of woman with learning disabilities. A couple, husband and wife, fostered a person, first as a girl then as a woman, with learning disabilities. They were convicted of wilful neglect of her when she was aged 19 to 25 and were sentenced to three years in prison. The woman lacked capacity to make decisions in relation to her own personal upkeep – showering, washing, whether to use soap or shampoo, and other such matters.

Essentially, she was not allowed to eat or use the toilet or the shower when she wanted to. She was described by others as always hungry. She ate frozen food directly from the freezer. She was not allowed to sit with the family at mealtimes, not shown how to use sanitary products, and denied access to her own clothes. She was often dressed in soiled clothes that were inappropriate for the weather conditions. She was denied the use of a mobile telephone. She was forced to sleep in the loft without a bed or mattress and without a ladder to allow her to leave. On occasion she was

---

1   Corcoran, K. 'Care worker locked cerebral palsy sufferer out in the cold, fed him banana with tomato sauce…but is spared jail by judge who wants him to go back to working in care.' *Daily Mail*, 23 May 2014.

2   'Care home bosses not guilty of neglect in Cornwall.' *BBC News*, 20 January 2016. Accessed on 28 January 2016 at: www.bbc.co.uk/news/uk-england-cornwall-35362132.

forced to sleep in a tent in the garden. She would be locked out of the house. Evidence as to all this was given by step-siblings, by neighbours and others. Some had reported their concerns to social services.

They were convicted also of fraud, in relation to using the woman's state benefits for themselves; and the husband had also been convicted of sexual assault and rape offences.[1]

Son neglecting and defrauding 98-year-old mother. A man with power of attorney for his mother was convicted of fraud by abuse of position by taking tens of thousands of pounds – as well as trying to sell her home fraudulently (after Havering Council had gained control of her finances). He was also convicted of wilful neglect, since during this time he had left her living in a decrepit house in Havering with plants growing through the windows and no central heating. He was given a two-year suspended prison sentence, ordered to pay £20,000 compensation as well as £5000 in court costs – and was given a curfew to remain at his home address between 7pm and 6am for six months.[2]

Son neglecting, and obstructing help for, his father (wilful neglect). A 64-year-old man, informal carer for his father aged 91, was convicted of wilful neglect on eight counts – and sentenced to 18 months in prison. His father was finally admitted to hospital in December with severe pressure sores but died in January. His son had obstructed attempts by health and social care to help. The father was anyway a very independent man and as far back as 2005 had declined medical advice, ongoing medication and care. The son had subsequently done everything in his power to prevent access or treatment for his father and went to considerable trouble and expense to achieve this. He had disrupted safeguarding adults meetings, made repeated complaints against any official who challenged him about his father and eventually resorted to litigation, all in order to prevent access to assess or medically treat his father.[3]

---

1   *R v ESM* [2016] EWCA Crim 1496.

2   'Son who defrauded 98-year-old mother after leaving her in "squalid" conditions.' *Evening Standard*, 21 February 2015.

3   Doughty, S. 'William Hedley jailed: agencies tried to help tragic dad but were met with opposition from son.' *Newcastle Chronicle*, 10 March 2016. See also: Wood, T. *Case review overview report: the death of Adult D*. Newcastle: Newcastle Safeguarding Adults Board, 2016.

Court of Protection solicitor neglecting her own mother (wilful neglect by an attorney). A solicitor was convicted of wilful neglect of her mother – for whom she had power of attorney – under section 44 of the Mental Capacity Act 2005. She was sentenced to 30 months in prison.

Police had attended after ambulance staff had become concerned about the state of the mother's body after a report of her death had been received. The mother had been slumped over with her chin on her knees for five days. She had become incontinent and was covered from head to toe in faeces, had not changed her clothing for a decade and had urine burns. Her long hair had become matted into dreadlocks. The daughter had gone into the room three or four times a day. There had been many opportunities over months and years to help her and remove her from that situation. The daughter also looked after her father, who lived there as well.

The daughter was a member of the Court of Protection team setting up trusts for those with capacity and deputyships for those without, in respect of compensation awards for clients who have suffered clinical negligence or personal injury.

The judge said the daughter had metaphorically and literally closed the door on her mother. The case had involved weeks and months of the most severe neglect where a woman had been left to rot in her own faeces and urine: the state of the mother's body looked like a photographed scene from the end of the Second World War in one of the concentration camps.

In mitigation, it was stated that the daughter had weekly therapy after being diagnosed with mild autism and suffering from emotional deprivation and abuse due to her unusual upbringing caused by her mother's obsessive-compulsive disorder and rule over the family home that led to her father being banned from the kitchen. She had picked up from her mother traits of self-neglect and non-functional compulsions.[1] The conviction was subsequently overturned as unsafe by the Court of Appeal. This was owing to the failure, by the original judge, to give correct directions to the jury about the meaning of section 44 of the MCA in relation to a person with enduring power of attorney. The court suggested, however, that had that proper direction been given, the jury might well have still convicted.[2]

---

1   McFadyen, S. 'Lawyer specialising in the rights of the elderly is jailed after leaving her own 79-year-old mother to die in "horrifying" squalor covered in urine and faeces.' *Daily Mail*, 27 April 2018.

2   *R v Kurtz (Emma-Jane)* [2018] EWCA Crim 2743, paras 19, 74.

WILFUL NEGLECT OR ILL-TREATMENT: CRIMINAL JUSTICE AND COURTS ACT 2015 CONVICTION EXAMPLES. Examples include:

Mistreating therapeutic rag dolls for residents with dementia (ill-treatment). Two care home workers were referred to as bullies by a judge, for mistreating therapy dolls used by dementia patients, in Ashbourne House Care Home. One was sentenced to 13 months in youth detention, the other to 12 months in prison. This was believed to be the first conviction under the Criminal Justice and Courts Act 2015.[1]

Slamming a resident's head into a chair. A care worker was caught slamming the head of a 77-year-old woman with dementia into a chair on secret CCTV installed by her family. The woman's relatives put a camera in her room at Bupa's Perry Locks home in Birmingham after they found bruises on her, a court heard. The care worker was given a 12-month community order after admitting ill-treating and neglecting. (The conviction was probably under the 2015 Act.)[2]

Nurse threatening to kill resident (ill-treatment). A nurse was cautioned under section 20 of the CJCA after she admitted threatening to kill a resident at Cliff House Nursing and Residential Home in Chesterfield. A resident with dementia had lashed out, she took his arm and held it in an 'armpit' hold to take him to the sofa. She then sat him down and said, 'I'll kill you', to which he responded by threatening to kill the nurse. The resident's wife approached, and an argument ensued between her and the nurse. The latter shouted that if resident A went outside again, she would lock him out.[3]

Binding a woman in bed with a bath towel (wilful neglect and ill-treatment). A nursing home resident was trussed up like a mummy by a pair of carers looking to ensure they had a quiet shift. The 88-year-old, with dementia and mobility problems, was tightly bound in a large bath towel, leaving

1   Fitzgerald, T. 'Care home bullies exposed by the M.E.N. jailed for "comfort doll" cruelty to dementia patients.' *Manchester Evening News*, 21 November 2016.

2   Spillett, R. 'Bupa carer is caught on hidden camera manhandling dementia patient, 77, then slamming her head against chair at £1,000-a-month home.' *Daily Mail*, 2 February 2017.

3   Crowson, I. 'Nurse given police caution after threatening to KILL care home resident.' *Derbyshire Telegraph*, 8 March 2018.

her unable to move in bed at the Alistre Lodge Nursing Home in St Annes. She was discovered grey, sweating profusely and dehydrated. The home reported the incident to police immediately and sacked the two carers. They were later given 12-month suspended sentences. (It is unclear if the conviction was under the MCA or under the CJCA.)[1]

Wills

The relevance of wills to safeguarding and to local authorities is limited, in the sense that the detriment to the person would flow once the person had died. A local authority's duty to make enquiries is couched in the present tense: a dead person cannot sensibly experience or be at risk of abuse and neglect.

However, wills might involve forgery, fraud, undue influence, lack of mental capacity to make them – all of which generally take place whilst somebody is alive (although not necessarily – e.g. forgery after death). These also might be a part of wider financial abuse such as siphoning of assets during life. For examples of abuse – indeed, criminal offences – involving wills, see *Fraud*; *Forgery*. For examples of abuse, though not necessarily a criminal offence, see *Undue influence*.

WILLS: MENTAL CAPACITY. For wills, the common law test of capacity relates to an understanding of the nature of the act, the extent of the property, an appreciation of the claims of others, there being no disorder of mind poisoning the affections, and no 'insane delusions' influencing the disposal. This test is not generally displaced by capacity rules under the Mental Capacity Act 2005.

Common law test of capacity to make a will.

It is essential...that a testator shall understand the nature of the act and its effects; shall understand the extent of the property of which he is disposing; shall be able to comprehend and appreciate the claims to which he ought to give effect; and, with a view to the latter

---

1 'Carers could be jailed for trussing pensioner.' *Blackpool Gazette*, 25 May 2016.

> object, that no disorder of mind shall poison his affections, pervert
> his sense of right, or prevent the exercise of his natural faculties –
> that no insane delusion shall influence his will in disposing of his
> property and bring about a disposal of it which, if the mind had
> been sound, would not have been made.[1]

WILLS: LAWFULNESS. For a will to be lawful, the testator must have
capacity to make it, and also knowledge and approval of its contents.

- Due execution of an apparently rational and fair will would ordinarily satisfy
  the burden of proof on the propounder (the person acting under the will),
  unless there are circumstances which excite the suspicion of the court.

- In such a case, the propounder may be required affirmatively to prove
  knowledge and approval of the testator.

- This is an evidential rather than legal burden. The standard of proof is, as is
  in all civil proceedings, that of the balance of probabilities. Nonetheless the
  task of satisfying that standard will generally vary in proportion to the degree
  of suspicion engendered by the circumstances.[2]

A so-called 'golden rule' applies in that in the case of an older person, or
somebody who has suffered a serious illness, the will ought to be witnessed
or approved by a medical practitioner who confirms the capacity and
understanding of the testator, and records this.[3] If this does not happen, the
will is not necessarily invalid, but is more open to question and dispute.[4]

WILLS: STATUTORY. The Court of Protection has the power to make a
statutory will.[5] It must be in a person's best interests, so a person's past or
present wishes will not necessarily be decisive. In the following case, the court

---

1   *Banks v Goodfellow* [1870] LR 5 QB 549.

2   *Re Key* [2010] EWHC 408 (Ch).

3   *Re Simpson* (1977) 127 New LJ 487.

4   *Re Key deceased* [2010] EWHC 408 (Ch), [2010] WTLR 623, para 8.

5   Mental Capacity Act 2005, s.18.

authorised such a will, effectively to keep a woman's assets out of the hands of the person who had exploited her financially.

> **Making a statutory will overriding a previous valid one: in a person's best interests.** A woman had lived with a man and his family who cared for her. She had previously made a will leaving money to nine charities. She then revoked this will. The new one left her entire estate to the man, who also had power of attorney.
>
> She then lost capacity to take various decisions and, at the direction of the court, was now living in a care home. There was a question about whether she had had capacity when she changed her will, or, alternatively, whether she had been unduly influenced in changing it. Either way, the Court of Protection had no jurisdiction, under the Mental Capacity Act 2005, to rule on the validity of the will. But what it could do now was to authorise – in her best interests – the making of a statutory will, thus superseding the previous one, which harked back to her original intention of leaving her money to the charities.[1]

The court in this case – essentially a safeguarding case – also pointed out that the woman's best interests were relevant not only in life but also in death, in terms of funeral arrangements but also how she would be remembered. Nonetheless, this does not mean that the Court of Protection will simply step in, as a matter of course, to mollify matters and ensure that people without capacity are seen, after their death, to have done the right thing – if that would be entirely inconsistent with their behaviour throughout their life.[2]

Witness or juror intimidation

It is a criminal offence intentionally to intimidate a witness, victim or juror, with the intention to obstruct, pervert or interfere with the investigation or course of justice. It is also an offence intentionally to harm, or threaten to

---

1   *ITW v Z* [2009] EWHC 2525 (Fam).

2   *D v JC* [2012] MHLO 35 (COP).

harm, a person knowing that the person has been a victim, witness or juror in criminal proceedings.[1]

Witnesses

A number of 'special measures' are contained in the Youth Justice and Criminal Evidence Act 1999 to assist vulnerable and intimidated witnesses to give their 'best' evidence in court. In addition, the government has published guidance called *Achieving Best Evidence in Criminal Proceedings*. It is not legally binding, but a judge could raise a query as to why it has not been followed. Within the 1999 Act, vulnerable witnesses are defined as witnesses whose quality of evidence the court considers will be diminished because they, in summary:

- **mental disorder:** have a mental disorder as defined in the Mental Health Act 1983, or

- **impairment:** are significantly impaired in relation to intelligence and social functioning – that is, witnesses with learning disabilities – or

- **physical disability:** are physically disabled witnesses.[2]

A second category of witnesses are those who are intimidated. They are defined in section 17 of the 1999 Act as people suffering from fear or distress in relation to testifying in the case. Complainants in sexual offence cases automatically fall into this category, unless they wish to opt out. However, a witness displaying signs of distress in giving evidence would only exceptionally – because of that distress – be treated as vulnerable.[3]

WITNESSES: YOUTH JUSTICE AND CRIMINAL EVIDENCE ACT. Vulnerable and intimidated witnesses are eligible for special measures under the Youth Justice and Criminal Evidence Act 1999. These measures are, in summary:

---

1   Criminal Justice and Public Order Act 1994, s.51.

2   Youth Justice and Criminal Evidence Act 1999, s.16.

3   *R v SG* [2017] EWCA Crim 617, para 63.

- **screens:** in the court room shielding the witness from the defendant (section 23)

- **video link:** giving evidence via live video link from outside the court room (section 24)

- **evidence:** given in private (clearing the public gallery in sexual offence cases and those involving intimidation) (section 25)

- **removal:** of wigs and gowns (section 26)

- **evidence in chief:** video-recorded (section 27)

- **cross-examination or re-examination:** video-recorded (section 28, not yet in force)

- **intermediary:** examination of a witness through an intermediary (section 29)

- **communication:** aids to communication (section 30).

For instance, in the following case, evidence was given by live video link by two elderly women.

Giving live video link evidence. In a theft case, two elderly women gave evidence from a living room, by means of a mobile video-conferencing kit. They were giving evidence against a carer who had stolen money from them in their own homes. The carer was convicted and sentenced to prison for 18 months.[1]

Video evidence given by severely disabled women to convict a care home worker of sexual assaults against them. A care home worker was jailed for 12 years, after committing sexual assaults against four severely disabled women. Three had cerebral palsy and the fourth had brain injuries. One of the victims gave evidence by live video link, blinking her eyes in order to answer questions put to her. Another had, in a video-taped police interview, moved a pointer on a computer screen via the joystick on her wheelchair. A third could not communicate at all, and the fourth victim could no longer communicate by the time of the trial. Further evidence was provided by

---

1   *R v Atkins* (2004). Reported in: Humberside Crown Prosecution Services. *Humberside Annual Report 2003–04*, 2004, p.5.

> video link from Japan, by a former volunteer at the home, who had observed sexual touching of one of the victims by the man.[1]

The following case was about whether or not to admit video-recorded evidence, under section 27 of the Act.

> **Admitting or excluding video interview under section 27 of 1999 Act.** If it appeared that the witness was not competent at the time of the video interview, it would be a reason for declining to make a special measures direction under section 27 of the Act, and thus declining to admit the video interview.
>
> However, in this case, the question about the girl's competence had arisen only at time of trial. If it was clear that the witness was not competent immediately before the trial, then the video interview would normally not be admitted, because the witness would not be available for cross-examination. However, if the competence issue only arises after the video interview has been admitted, then it is open to the court to place little or no weight on it, precisely because it cannot be tested in cross-examination.[2]

In an unusual case, preceding the Youth Justice and Criminal Evidence Act 1999, it was one of the defendants who wanted the video evidence, given by a severely disabled man, admitted – whilst her co-defendant sought its exclusion.

> **Admissibility of transcript made by social worker.** An elderly man, living with his disabled son, had shown kindness to a female heroin addict. She went around to his flat with an acquaintance; they stole money, a television set and video-recorder. The elderly man was punched and kicked such that he died 16 days later. The woman was convicted of robbery and manslaughter. However, she denied this, arguing that she had not inflicted any injuries, that there had been no agreement about using violence, and that she had acted under duress from her companion.

---

1 de Bruxelles, S. 'Evidence by blinking helps convict James Watts of sexual assaults.' *The Times*, 6 November 2009.

2 *Director of Public Prosecutions v R* [2007] EWHC 1842 (Admin).

> Her version of events was supported by the elderly man's son (since deceased), whose interview had been video-taped. The son had been severely disabled, though with unimpaired mental faculties. He suffered from cerebral palsy, epilepsy, Parkinson's disease, severe speech difficulties and was confined to a wheelchair. He had acute difficulties in making himself understood, quite apart from a reluctance to speak to strangers.
>
> Only the social worker could understand what he was saying in what was supposed to have been a police interview; in fact, the man did not answer the police officers, so the social worker asked all the questions. The social worker then made a transcript record of what the man had been trying to say. The court concluded that the video and transcript could be admitted; the question would then be to decide at trial how much weight to place on them.[1]

WITNESSES: INTERMEDIARIES. An intermediary, under the Youth Justice and Criminal Evidence Act 1999, communicates questions to the witness and answers from the witness – and explains these so that the witness or person putting the question can understand them. An intermediary might come, for example, from the speech and language therapy or social work professions – and assist the witness to understand questions put to them and to be understood.[2]

Decisions on applications for special measures are for the court to determine – after taking into account the views of the witness.[3] The appointment of an intermediary is discretionary, and the fact that an intermediary would improve the trial process does not necessarily mean that one must be appointed. It is a question of what the judge feels the need to do, in order to achieve fairness.[4]

---

1   *R v Duffy* [1998] 3 WLR 1060 (Court of Appeal).

2   Ministry of Justice. *Achieving Best Evidence in Criminal Proceedings: guidance on interviewing victims and witnesses, and guidance on using special measures.* London: MoJ, 2011, para 2.117.

3   Youth Justice and Criminal Evidence Act 1999, s.16.

4   *R v Cox* [2012] EWCA Crim 549.

WITNESSES: ACHIEVING BEST EVIDENCE GUIDANCE. Guidance outlines the stages through which a witness will pass. It covers identification and definition of vulnerable witnesses, competence, compellability, oath taking, and how witnesses can be assisted. In summary:

- **Planning and conducting interviews with vulnerable adult witnesses:** including support, interpreters, intermediaries, therapeutic help.

- **Planning and conducting interviews with intimidated, reluctant and hostile witnesses.**

- **Witness support and preparation:** including supporters such as Victim Support volunteers, Witness Service volunteers, Witness Care officers, independent sexual violence advisers, independent domestic violence advisers, intermediaries, domestic violence officers, early special measures meeting, pre-trial therapy, risk assessment (e.g. in domestic violence) for managing a witness's safety during the pre-trial period.

- **Witnesses in court:** explanation of special measures including role of intermediary to communicate questions and answers to and from the witness.[1]

- **Therapy:** further specific guidance is available on therapy for vulnerable witnesses[2] – and on working with intimidated witnesses.[3] The guidance notes the importance of therapy for the welfare of the victim – but also of taking precautions so that it does not contaminate the evidence to be given by the vulnerable witness. The guidance does state that, ultimately, if there is a tension, priority should be given to the best interests of the witness.[4]

WITNESSES: COMPETENCE. Under section 53 of the Youth Justice and Criminal Evidence Act 1999, the general rule is that all people, whatever

---

1 Ministry of Justice. *Achieving Best Evidence in Criminal Proceedings: guidance on interviewing victims and witnesses, and guidance on using special measures.* London: MoJ, 2011.

2 Home Office, Crown Prosecution Service, Department of Health. *Provision of therapy for vulnerable adults or intimidated witnesses prior to a criminal trial: practice guidance,* 2002.

3 Office for Criminal Justice Reform. *Working with intimidated witnesses: a manual for police and practitioners responsible for identifying and supporting intimidated witnesses,* 2006.

4 Home Office, Crown Prosecution Service, Department of Health. *Provision of therapy for vulnerable adults or intimidated witnesses prior to a criminal trial: practice guidance,* 2002, para 2.117.

their age, are competent to act as witnesses in criminal proceedings – unless they cannot understand questions asked of them in court or cannot answer them in a way that can be understood (with, if necessary, the assistance of special measures).[1]

Admissibility of video evidence of elderly woman with Alzheimer's disease in rape trial. The defendant was accused of attempting to rape and of indecently assaulting an 81-year-old woman who had long-standing delusional problems associated with early Alzheimer's disease. He attempted to have video testimony given by the woman excluded from the trial – partly on the grounds that the woman lacked competence to give evidence under section 53 of the 1999 Act.

The Court of Appeal upheld the judge's decision to admit the video. Considering the video, the judge had applied the test of whether the woman had 'been able to understand the questions being put to her' and whether she was 'giving answers which could be understood'. The court stated that it agreed with the judge's view on this. But, further, she 'prima facie has a right to have her complaint placed before a jury and a right to have a jury assess whether they are sure that the complaint is established and the putting of the video before the jury is the only way in which that right can be upheld'. The defence would then be able to bring medical evidence and argue as to the reliability of the video at the time it was made.[2]

In a further case, the court emphasised the presumption at the outset, that everybody is competent to give evidence.

Giving of video evidence by another 81-year-old person with Alzheimer's disease. The victim, an 81-year-old woman suffering from Alzheimer's disease, was spotted one morning in someone's front garden, behaving strangely. The police were called. She made various rude comments suggestive of a sexual incident having taken place. She ultimately gave a video interview. At the time of the interview, and after it, she would not have been capable of giving evidence in court.

---

1   Youth Justice and Criminal Evidence Act 1999, s.53.

2   *R v D* [2002] EWCA Crim 990.

In respect of section 53 of the Act and her competence, the judge had taken the approach that she did not understand all the questions and not all her answers were understandable. But she understood, and was understood in part, sufficiently for a jury to evaluate her evidence. The Court of Appeal approved this approach, and the defendant's (a mini-cab driver) sentence for rape was upheld.[1]

WITNESSES: GIVING SWORN OR UNSWORN EVIDENCE. Section 55 of the Youth Justice and Criminal Evidence Act 1999 sets out how courts are to decide whether a witness should swear an oath (or affirm) before giving evidence.

An adult can give sworn evidence if he or she has a sufficient appreciation of the solemnity of the occasion and of the particular responsibility to tell the truth which is involved in taking an oath. This is presumed if he or she is able to give intelligible testimony; and intelligible testimony means that the witness can understand questions and give comprehensible answers.

If the witness cannot give intelligible testimony according to these rules then, under section 56 of the Act, unsworn evidence can still be given as long as the witness is still competent (under section 53).

---

1   *R v Ali Sed* [2004] EWCA Crim 1294.